Y0-CCS-819

ST/ESA/SER.A/292

Department of Economic and Social Affairs
Population Division

Child Adoption:
Trends and Policies

United Nations
New York, 2009

DESA

The Department of Economic and Social Affairs of the United Nations Secretariat is a vital interface between global policies in the economic, social and environmental spheres and national action. The Department works in three main interlinked areas: (i) it compiles, generates and analyses a wide range of economic, social and environmental data and information on which States Members of the United Nations draw to review common problems and take stock of policy options; (ii) it facilitates the negotiations of Member States in many intergovernmental bodies on joint courses of action to address ongoing or emerging global challenges; and (iii) it advises interested Governments on the ways and means of translating policy frameworks developed in United Nations conferences and summits into programmes at the country level and, through technical assistance, helps build national capacities.

Note

The designations employed and the presentation of the material in this publication do not imply the expression of any opinion whatsoever on the part of the Secretariat of the United Nations concerning the legal status of any country, city or area or of its authorities, or concerning the delimitation of its frontiers or boundaries.

The designations "developed" and "developing" countries and "more developed" and "less developed" regions are intended for statistical convenience and do not necessarily express a judgment about the stage reached by a particular country or area in the development process.

The term "country" as used in the text of this publication also refers, as appropriate, to territories or areas.

This publication has been issued without formal editing.

ST/ESA/SER.A/292

UNITED NATIONS PUBLICATION
Sales No. E.10.XIII.4
ISBN 978-92-1-151466-7

Copyright © United Nations, 2009
All rights reserved

PREFACE

The Population Division of the Department of Economic and Social Affairs of the United Nations Secretariat is in charge of monitoring population policies in all countries of the world. Since the United Nations convened its first intergovernmental conference on population in 1974, the Population Division has been responsible for reviewing and appraising the implementation of the plans or programmes of action adopted by the United Nations international conferences on population. As part of its work, the Population Division produces in-depth studies on specific issues related to population policy. This report, focusing on policies on child adoption and the resulting trends in 195 countries, aims to provide Governments with the evidence necessary to assess their policies in this area. One of its major conclusions is that available data on child adoptions have a number of limitations that prevent a thorough assessment of the determinants of the process and its consequences for the parties involved. The systematic collection and publication of more detailed data on adoption would provide useful insights about how the process of adoption functions and would validate measures that the authorities in charge could use to ensure the welfare of adopted children.

The World Population Plan of Action adopted in 1974 at the World Population Conference called for facilitating child adoption so that involuntarily sterile and sub-fecund couples could achieve their desired family size. Implicit in this recommendation was the idea that adoption is a means to approximate biological parenthood for couples who would otherwise be unable to have children. More than three decades later, the general view is that, in societies where marriage is being increasingly delayed, childbearing is postponed and levels of biological childlessness are on the rise, increasing numbers of persons are resorting to alternative means of experiencing parenthood, including through adoption. This report analyses adoption trends in light of changes in nuptiality and childbearing in order to assess the extent to which the generalized view presented above holds true.

This study, the first of its kind undertaken by the Population Division, presents comparable information for 195 countries. The information presented relates to: adoption policies and legislation; multilateral, regional and bilateral treaties on intercountry adoption; levels and trends of total, domestic and intercountry adoptions, and data on selected demographic characteristics of the individuals involved in an adoption, namely, the adopted person, the adoptive parents and the birth parents. The report surveys recent trends and policies on child adoption while providing the cultural and historical background necessary to understand differences in country practices.

Acknowledgement is due to Dr. Peter Selman, who contributed background material for several of the chapters of this study, and to Dr. Robert Gardner, who assisted in editing the publication. Responsibility for the design, execution and content of this study lies entirely with the Population Division.

This publication, as well as other population information, may be accessed on the Population Division's website, at www.unpopulation.org. For further information about this publication, please contact the office of Ms. Hania Zlotnik, Director, Population Division, Department of Economic and Social Affairs, United Nations, New York, N.Y. 10017; tel: (212) 963-3179; fax (212) 963-2147.

CONTENTS

ANNEXES

TEXT FIGURES

BOXES

Explanatory notes

Symbols of United Nations documents are composed of capital letters combined with figures.

The tables presented in this publication make use of the following symbols:

Two dots (..) indicates that the item is not applicable.
Three dots (…) indicate that data are not available or are not separately reported.
An em-dash (—) indicates that the amount is nil or negligible.
A minus sign (-) before a figure indicates a decrease.
A full stop (.) is used to indicate decimals.
Use of a hyphen (-) between years, for example 1995-2000, signifies the full period involved.

Percentages in tables and figures do not necessarily add to totals because of rounding.

EXECUTIVE SUMMARY

Adoption is one of the oldest social institutions. Nevertheless, adoption still raises highly emotive issues because of its fundamental implications for the meaning of familial ties. Questions on whether adoption serves the best interests of children, who should be allowed to adopt and the role of Governments in regulating such decisions are frequent subjects of debate. Yet, despite the heightened attention to these issues, much of the information on adoption remains anecdotal. Data on the number of children adopted domestically are rarely available and when they are, they tend to be out-of-date. Similarly, comparable information on trends in intercountry adoptions—that is, adoptions that involve a change of country of residence for the adopted person—is often lacking or is available for just a few countries.

Child Adoption: Trends and Policies is the first study focusing on adoption prepared by the Population Division of the Department of Economic and Social Affairs of the United Nations Secretariat. The study provides a solid foundation for furthering research on child adoption and, more specifically, on the demographic factors that shape the demand for and the availability of adoptable children. The focus of this report is on the nexus between adoption policies and trends at the national and global levels. Understanding adoption policies and their origins is all the more important today because, as adoption has become global, inconsistencies among the legal principles and traditions regarding adoption in different countries are increasingly coming to the fore. The major findings of this study are summarized below.

Key findings

1. **There are over a quarter of a million adoptions every year.** The United Nations Population Division estimates that some 260,000 children are adopted each year. This estimate implies that fewer than 12 children are adopted for every 100,000 persons under age 18 (figure I). Adoption remains, therefore, a relatively rare event.

2. **A few countries account for most adoptions** (figure II). The United States of America, with over 127,000 adoptions in 2001, accounts for nearly half of the total number of adoptions worldwide. Large numbers of adoptions also take place in China (almost 46,000 in 2001) and in the Russian Federation (more than 23,000 in 2001).

3. **The purpose of adoption has evolved over time**. Historically, adoption occurred primarily to preserve and transmit family lines or inheritance, to gain political power or to forge alliances between families. Adopted persons were usually adolescents or adults who could guarantee the continuation of the family line. The notion that adoption was a means for promoting children's welfare did not take hold until the mid-nineteenth century. Today, the principle of ensuring that the best interests of the child are served by adoption is the paramount consideration enshrined in most adoption laws.

4. **Over 160 countries recognize the legal institution of adoption but 20 countries do not have legal provisions allowing child adoption.** In most of the countries where adoption is not possible, alternative procedures, such as guardianship or the placement of children under the care of relatives are permitted. Religion often plays a key role in determining the conditions under which such alternative practices may be pursued.

5. **In some countries, informal adoption and fostering are perceived as preferable to formal adoption**. Informal or *de facto* adoption and fostering are practices that allow parents to put children in the care of others (usually relatives) without having to cut all ties with their children. These practices contrast markedly with the secrecy and finality that have come to characterize adoption in the western context.

Figure I. Number of adoptions of children under 18 per 100,000 children under 18, most recent data available, 1990-2005

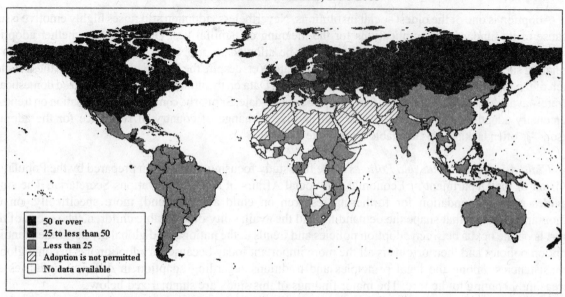

50 or over
25 to less than 50
Less than 25
Adoption is not permitted
No data available

Sources: For a complete list of country references, see annex II.

NOTES: The under-18 adoption rate is calculated by dividing the total number of adoptions of persons under age 18 by the number of persons under age 18. It is assumed that all persons adopted are under age 18 at the time of adoption. The boundaries shown on the present map do not imply official endorsement or acceptance by the United Nations.

6. **The consequences of an adoption for the rights of adopted children differ considerably among countries.** In some countries, adopted children acquire the same rights as birth children, including the right to inheritance, and adopted children sever all legal ties with their birth parents. In other countries, the termination of natural ties between birth parents and children is viewed as culturally unacceptable.

7. **Requirements for prospective adoptive parents vary considerably among countries**. In 81 countries, adoption laws establish a minimum age for prospective adoptive parents and in 15 countries, adoption laws also stipulate a maximum age. Single persons are allowed to adopt in 100 countries but in 15, only married couples can adopt. In many countries, laws have been amended to allow older persons or single persons to adopt. However, in some cases, the criteria that potential adoptive parents must meet have become more stringent. Adoption by step-parents, for instance, is currently discouraged in several countries because of the potentially detrimental effects that such adoptions are deemed to have on the child's relationship to his or her non-custodial biological parent. The requirements for intercountry adoptions have also been tightened in several countries of origin.

8. **Domestic adoptions far outnumber intercountry adoptions.** Almost 85 per cent of all adoptions involve citizens or residents of the same country. Domestic adoptions represent at least half of all adoptions in 57 of the 96 countries with data. Whereas the number of domestic adoptions has been declining in many developed countries, several developing countries have experienced an increase in the number of domestic adoptions, partly because of the implementation of policies to encourage local residents to adopt.

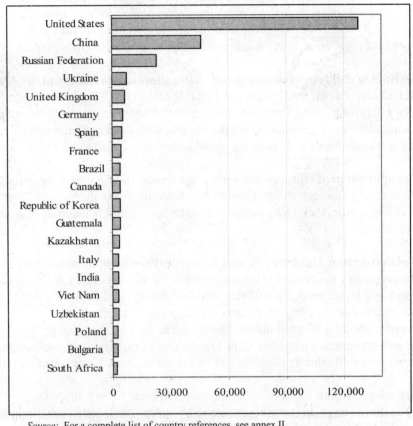

Figure II. Countries with the largest number of adoptions, most recent available data, 1999-2005

Source: For a complete list of country references, see annex II.
NOTES: Data for Canada and the Russian Federation are estimates. Data for Brazil refer to the state of São Paulo only. Data for Poland refer to adoption rulings by the courts.

9. **Adoptions by step-parents and other relatives account for more than half of all domestic adoptions.** Nevertheless, the number of adoptions by step-parents and other relatives has been declining in recent years. In some countries, the introduction of legislation discouraging adoptions by step-parents accounts partly for this trend. Declining re-marriage rates and an increasing prevalence of informal parenting arrangements are also contributing to that decline.

10. **The number of intercountry adoptions has been increasing.** Both the number of intercountry adoptions and their share among all adoptions have been increasing. In many European countries, intercountry adoptions now account for more than half of all adoptions.

11. **The United States, France and Spain, in order of importance, are the major countries of destination of children adopted internationally**. Other countries that experience large inflows of children adopted from abroad are Canada, Germany, Italy, the Netherlands and Sweden. Each of these countries has recorded over 1,000 foreign adoptions annually in recent years.

12. **Asian and East European countries are the major sources of children adopted through an intercountry procedure**. Relatively few children adopted internationally originate in Africa or Latin America and the Caribbean. The countries of origin accounting for most international adoptions are China, Guatemala, the Republic of Korea, the Russian Federation and Ukraine. More than half of the children adopted abroad originate in those five countries.

13. **The dwindling supply of children available for domestic adoption may partially explain the increase in the number of intercountry adoptions.** In developed countries, the widespread availability of reliable, safe and inexpensive contraception has meant that there are fewer children available for adoption. In addition, wider societal acceptance of single parenthood and the greater availability of welfare support have meant that fewer single mothers give up their children for adoption.

14. **The characteristics of children available for domestic adoption has also contributed to the increase in the number of intercountry adoptions.** Adoptable children within countries are often older than those desired by adoptive parents. The desire for younger children has probably prompted some parents to adopt children abroad. Intercountry adoptions are also favoured in contexts where adoption procedures are less demanding and faster for intercountry adoptions than for domestic adoption.

15. **Over 60 per cent of adopted children are under age five at the time of adoption.** Despite adoptive parents' preference for younger children, relatively few adoptions involve children under age one. Adoptions of children older than five years also tend to be rare and, when they occur, they frequently involve step-children.

16. **In countries of destination, children adopted domestically tend to be older than children adopted through an intercountry procedure.** This outcome results, at least in part, from the fact that domestic adoptions comprise a larger proportion of step-child adoptions, which usually involve older children. The preference of prospective adoptive parents for adopting younger children may also be a factor. In countries of origin, children adopted domestically tend to be younger than those adopted by foreign parents through an intercountry procedure. The principle of subsidiarity, whereby intercountry adoption is considered only after all other options have been exhausted, may be the reason for this difference.

17. **More girls are adopted than boys.** In both domestic and intercountry adoptions, the number of girls adopted exceeds that of boys. In some countries, this pattern is associated with imbalances in the sex distribution of children available for adoption. In other countries, the perception that girls are easier to raise or that female children are more likely to provide assistance with housework or care-giving activities may explain in part the higher percentage of adoptions involving girls.

18. **Most adoptive parents are in the 30-44 age group.** Adoptions by parents who are younger than 30 or older than 44 are less frequent, partly because of the maximum and minimum age limits imposed by the legislation of most countries. Female adoptive parents are generally younger, partly because they are less likely to adopt as step-parents.

19. **The numbers of male adoptive parents is roughly the same as that of female adoptive parents.** However, in countries with large numbers of adoptions by step-parents or where adoption by single persons is permitted, differences by sex are noticeable. Among adopting step-parents, men outnumber women, but women outnumber men among single persons who adopt.

20. **People who are unable to achieve their desired family size through childbearing often resort to adoption.** Country-level surveys and ethnographic studies indicate that persons who are involuntarily childless as a result of sterility, subfecundity or other factors often seek to adopt.

21. **Adoption is not simply a demographic response to achieve a desired family size for those suffering from involuntary sterility and sub-fecundity.** Whereas involuntary childlessness is often associated with adoption, in several countries a large percentage of persons seeking to adopt already have children of their own.

22. **Birth mothers who give up their children for the purpose of adoption tend to be young and unmarried.** However, having an extramarital birth, which in the past was a strong reason for placing a child for adoption is no longer strongly associated with the availability of adoptable children. In many societies, unmarried women are deciding to raise children born out of wedlock instead of placing them for adoption.

23. **Despite the perceived shortage of adoptable children domestically, the number of children in foster care or in institutions generally far exceeds the number of children who are being adopted.** This paradox arises because many children in foster care or in institutions are older or have health problems and are not, therefore, easy to place among prospective adoptive parents who prefer younger and healthy children. In addition, because many children in foster care or in institutions still have ties to their biological parents, they often are not formally adoptable.

24. **In countries highly affected by the AIDS epidemic, there are a large number of orphans who have lost both their parents to the disease and that could be adopted either domestically and internationally.** It is estimated that in Africa, the continent most affected by the epidemic, the current number of domestic adoptions would have to be multiplied by 2,000 to ensure that the estimated 7.7 million orphans in the continent would have an adoptive family. At a global level, the number of adoptions would have to increase by a factor of 60 to provide families to all AIDS orphans.

25. **Many countries have ratified multilateral, regional or bilateral agreements on intercountry adoption aimed at addressing conflicts of jurisdiction and protecting the welfare of children.** Seventy countries have ratified or acceded to the Convention on Protection of Children and Co-operation in Respect of Intercountry Adoption. As of January 2007, 117 countries had ratified the United Nations Optional Protocol to the Convention on the Rights of the Child on the Sale of Children, Child Prostitution and Child Pornography, which stipulates that coercive adoption should be a criminal offence. Nevertheless, child trafficking and selling of children for adoption are still a concern in several countries. Problems in making the various agreements operational have also emerged. Initiatives are under way to ensure that existing international legal mechanisms respond better to the evolving challenges raised by intercountry adoptions.

26. **Total lack of data on adoption or limitations in the data available represent a major obstacle to the understanding of the determinants of adoption, its changing patterns over space and time, and its major trends.** Out of the 195 countries considered in this study, only 118 publish data on the total number of adoptions and far fewer publish data on adoptions classified by type (domestic vs. intercountry) or on the characteristics of those involved in the adoption process (the adopted child, the biological parents and the adoptive parents). Variations in the concepts and definitions underlying the data available limit the usefulness of cross-country comparisons.

INTRODUCTION

In 1974, the World Population Plan of Action of the World Population Conference called on countries to facilitate child adoption so that all couples could achieve their desired number of children.[1] By doing so, the Plan of Action recognized that child adoption could play a role in approximating biological parenthood for couples who would otherwise be unable to have children. In the intervening years, many of the demographic trends associated with the demand for adoption have become more accentuated. Delayed marriage, the postponement of childbearing, rising levels of childlessness, high levels of divorce and the wider acceptance of new family forms are just some of the demographic trends associated with a larger pool of people having recourse to adoption.

At the same time, adoption as a legal institution has continued to evolve. Following the entry into force of the 1989 United Nations Convention on the Rights of the Child,[2] the principle of safeguarding the best interests of the child has been firmly established as the paramount consideration in all decisions relating to child adoption. Countries have modified existing legislation to recognize new forms of adoption and to allow adoptions by individuals who had been previously considered ineligible to adopt. A large number of countries have ratified multilateral and bilateral agreements relative to adoption in order to ensure clarity in matters of jurisdiction and applicable law where intercountry adoptions are concerned and to ensure that the welfare of the children involved is safeguarded.

Despite these developments, the broader demographic context in which adoptions take place remains generally unexplored.[3] The lack of comparable data on the number of children adopted each year and on the characteristics of the individuals involved, namely, the adopted person, the adoptive parents and the birth parents, has hindered such exploration. Important questions remain to be addressed. Will the postponement of childbearing result in an ever-increasing number of

persons seeking to adopt? How will fertility trends affect the availability of adoptable children? What role, if any, should adoption play in providing care for the nearly 8 million children who have lost both parents due to illness or conflict?

This study, the first on child adoption undertaken by the Population Division of the Department of Economic and Social Affairs of the United Nations Secretariat, focuses on the nexus between demography and policy to understand trends in child adoption. Clearly, Government policies on child adoption play a major role in shaping individual and social behaviour and are powerful determinants of overall trends. Decisions, such as lowering age requirements for prospective adoptive parents or extending the right to adoption to single persons, can contribute to increase the number of adoptions. Conversely, more stringent requirements regarding the age, marital status, health or income of prospective adoptive parents are likely to result in lower numbers of adoptions. This report assembles information for 195 countries on a number of aspects of adoption, including national legislation and ratification of multilateral treaties. Data on domestic adoptions, intercountry adoptions and the total number of adoptions as well as on selected characteristics of the individuals involved in the adoption process are also considered. The contents of each of the chapters of this report are described briefly below.

Chapter I examines the evolution of adoption laws and policies, starting with some of the earliest written legal codes. This chapter focuses mainly on the tradition of western legal jurisprudence, although adoption laws in other parts of the world are also considered. The chapter describes how adoption laws have changed from antiquity to the modern era, highlighting similarities and differences between past and present practices. Areas of current and future debate, including the role of intercountry adoption, adoption by step-parents and access to information on birth parents are also discussed.

Chapter II provides an overview of adoption practices in the context of religious law and traditional societies. In particular, it focuses on the different attitudes towards adoption in Canon law, *Sharia* law and *Halachic* law. The position on adoption in Hindu and Confucian legal traditions is also touched upon. The chapter then examines various alternatives to formal adoption, such as fostering and *de facto* adoption common in traditional societies in Africa, the Americas and Oceania. In doing so, the emphasis is on the different cultural and social functions that such practices have played in comparison with the role that formalised adoption plays today in the western legal context.

Chapter III discusses modern adoption laws and policies for 195 countries. It describes differences in adoption procedures among countries, focusing on the authorities responsible for overseeing, approving and granting adoptions. The chapter then examines the requirements that prospective adoptive parents and adopted children should meet, including those relative to age, sex, marital status, residency and citizenship. The different effects of adoption on the rights of the adopted child as outlined in the laws of various countries are also discussed, including the right to inheritance, the acquisition of the surname of the adoptive family and the right to acquire the citizenship of the adoptive parents when intercountry adoption is involved.

Chapter IV is devoted to a discussion of intercountry adoption, focusing on the role of multilateral, regional and bilateral agreements in regulating such flows. It describes the four major multilateral instruments relative to adoption: the 1961 United Nations Convention on the Reduction of Statelessness; the 1989 United Nations Convention on the Rights of the Child; the 1993 Convention on Protection of Children and Co-operation in Respect of Intercountry Adoption, and the 2000 United Nations Optional Protocol to the Convention on the Rights of the Child on the Sale of Children, Child Prostitution and Child Pornography. The chapter also considers two regional

instruments: the 1967 European Convention on the Adoption of Children and the 1984 Inter-American Convention on Conflict of Laws Concerning the Adoption of Minors. Child trafficking and selling children for the purpose of adoption are discussed as the two major concerns of Governments intent on combating international crime that affects minors. Lastly, the chapter discusses the problems faced in making the various multilateral, regional and bilateral agreements operational.

Chapter V offers on overview of levels and trends in the total number of adoptions and the number of domestic and intercountry adoptions. It provides a global estimate of the annual number of children adopted in the world and of the shares of intercountry and domestic adoptions. Various adoption rates and ratios are presented to provide an understanding of the relative magnitude of the phenomenon. Trends in domestic and intercountry adoption for selected countries are also discussed, as are changes in the major countries of origin and destination of intercountry adoptions.

Chapter VI examines the characteristics of the individuals involved in the adoption process (the adopted person, the adoptive parents and the birth parents). The age and sex of adopted persons at the time of adoption, their differences with respect to intercountry and domestic adoptions, the characteristics of adoptive parents (age, sex, marital status, relationship with adopted person) and the characteristics of birth mothers are analysed.

Chapter VII examines the relationships between demographic factors and the demand for, and the availability of, adoptable children. Adoption rates are compared with selected indicators of fertility and family formation, including desired family size, childlessness, presence of own children, mean age at marriage and total number of children per woman. To explore the determinants of the availability of adoptable children, adoption rates are compared with the percentage of children born outside of marriage, abortion rates and the prevalence of orphanhood.

Chapter VIII provides recommendations for the improvement of data on adoption. The chapter suggests a minimum set of data required to monitor the implementation of various multilateral instruments on intercountry adoption.

The comprehensive set of data compiled for this report is presented in annex tables.

NOTES

[1] See *Report of the United Nations World Population Conference, Bucharest, 19-30 August 1974* (United Nations publication, Sales No. E.75.XIII.3).

[2] United Nations (1990). *Treaty Series*, vol. 1577, No. 27531, p. 3.

[3] The Programme of Action of the 1994 International Conference on Population and Development called on countries to stem the practice of coercive adoption. See *Report of the International Conference on Population and Development, Cairo, 5-13 September 1994* (United Nations publication, Sales No. E.95.XIII.18), chap. I, resolution 1, annex.

I. HISTORY AND EVOLUTION OF MODERN ADOPTION LAWS

Literary and legal sources indicate that adoption was widely practised in many ancient societies (Brosnan, 1922; Huard, 1956). From the frequently cited example of the adoption of Moses to that of the Emperor Octavian Augustus, adoption played a "major part in the traditional law of many Eurasian societies" (Goody, 1969, p. 55). While adoption may be as old as human society itself (Benet, 1976), the motivations for adoption have changed markedly over time. Today, adoption is undertaken mainly to provide a home for children deprived of parental care and to satisfy the desire of individuals or couples to care for and rear a child (Goody, 1969; Tizard, 1977). In contrast, societies of the past regarded adoption as a means for preserving family lineage, enabling the continuation of ancestor worship, creating political alliances and ensuring care for adoptive parents in their old age (Derrett, 1957; Gardner, 1998, and Huard, 1956).

The norms regulating adoption have also shifted over time. In many early laws, for instance, persons with children of their own, individuals of reproductive age and women were not allowed to adopt. Further, ancient laws often did not permit the adoption of minors, clear evidence that the welfare and best interests of children were not the paramount consideration in the decisions related to adoption. Nevertheless, ancient legislation is the source of many of the key features of modern adoption laws, including the acquisition by the adopted person of the name of the adoptive parents, the right to inheritance from the adoptive family and the termination of the birth parents' guardianship rights. It is fitting therefore to begin this overview of adoption trends and policies by focusing briefly on the past, to uncover the roots of today's norms and practices.

This chapter focuses mainly on adoption laws in the western legal tradition, a choice made both to limit the scope of this overview and because modern adoption laws in many parts of the world have been profoundly influenced by western jurisprudence. The purpose of this chapter is threefold: to shed light on the genesis of modern adoption laws by providing a historical overview of past adoption customs and legislation, to offer an explanation for some of the differences that exist in current legal approaches towards adoption and to identify some of the areas where adoption laws are likely to continue evolving. Chapter II provides an overview of adoption practices in other cultural and societal contexts, looking at the role of norms in religion and in traditional societies.

A. ADOPTION LAWS IN ANTIQUITY

Adoption clearly played an important part in ancient life as attested by literary and legal sources dating back almost four millennia. Specific information on ancient adoption legislation remains, however, highly fragmented and it is difficult to reconstruct a comprehensive chronology of the history of such laws. Consequently, the following section provides only selected illustrations of adoption laws in antiquity.

1. Babylonia: The Code of Hammurabi

One of the earliest legal texts referring to adoption is the Code of Hammurabi (box I.1). This code, dating from the eighteenth century B.C., contains many features that are still relevant to modern adoption law (Cole and Donley, 1990). For example, the code established that adoption was a legal contract that could only be executed with the consent of the birth parents. As in many laws today, birth parents ceased to have any claim upon the child once the deed transferring the guardianship of an adopted child had been executed (Johns, 1910-1911). In addition, the Code of Hammurabi granted adopted children equal rights to those of birth children.

Nevertheless, the Code also contained many provisions that differ from modern practices. Adopted persons were severely punished for attempting to return to their birth families and the adoption contract could be annulled if the adopted child's filial duties were not properly fulfilled. These provisions had particularly severe consequences for individuals who had been slaves, because the termination of the adoption contract returned them into bondage. The adoption contract could also be dissolved by a court at the adopted

Box I.1. Selected articles of law related to adoption in the Code of Hammurabi, eighteenth century B.C.

185. If a man adopt a child and to his name as son, and rear him, this grown son cannot be demanded back again.

186. If a man adopt a son, and if after he has taken him he injure his foster father and mother, then this adopted son shall return to his father's house.

188. If an artisan has undertaken to rear a child and teaches him his craft, he cannot be demanded back.

189. If he has not taught him his craft, this adopted son may return to his father's house.

190. If a man does not maintain a child that he has adopted as a son and reared with his other children, then his adopted son may return to his father's house.

191. If a man, who had adopted a son and reared him, founded a household, and had children, wish to put this adopted son out, then this son shall not simply go his way. His adoptive father shall give him of his wealth one-third of a child's portion, and then he may go. He shall not give him of the field, garden, and house.

192. If a son of a paramour or a prostitute say to his adoptive father or mother: "You are not my father, or my mother," his tongue shall be cut off.

193. If the son of a paramour or a prostitute desire his father's house, and desert his adoptive father and adoptive mother, and goes to his father's house, then shall his eye be put out.

Source: L.W. King, 1910.

person's request if the adoptive parent failed to teach the adopted person a trade or if the adopted person had not been properly reared by the adoptive family. If an adoptive parent remarried and decided to dissolve the contract with the adopted child, the latter was entitled to inherit one-third of a child's share in goods but had no claim to the house or land of the adoptive family. Unlike most modern adoption laws, only the adoption of male children was permitted.

2. Greek laws on adoption

The laws of ancient Greece provide an additional illustration of some of the earliest adoption legislation. As with Hammurabi's Code, these laws often aimed at providing heirs for childless individuals. Persons who already had legitimate sons were not normally permitted to adopt. According to the laws of Solon (sixth century B.C.) and the Law Code of Gortyn (fifth century B.C.), for instance, only adult males who had no legitimate descendants and who were considered sound of mind were permitted to adopt (Rubenstein, 1993; Willetts, 1977). If, however, a male offspring was born after an adoption had

been completed, the adopted child and the birth child were entitled to equal shares of the inheritance (Goody, 1973; Willetts, 1977). Most modern adoption laws have preserved this concept by recognizing that birth descendants and adopted persons have equal rights to inheritance.

According to Solonic law, adoption could assume three distinct forms. Children could be adopted by a living person (*inter vivos:* between living persons); through testamentary adoption (that is, in the will of a deceased person), or posthumously by a relative in the name of a deceased family member (Rubenstein, 1993). Adoption *inter vivos* was a voluntary contractual relationship entered into by two individuals, whereas testamentary and posthumous adoptions were legal acts requiring confirmation by the People's Court. Adoption *inter vivos* was practised mainly to provide support for older adoptive parents, whereas testamentary adoption was undertaken for the purpose of ancestor worship. Adoption *inter vivos* was also used when a man with no male offspring adopted a son to prevent a kinsman from claiming his daughter as an heiress (Goody, 1969).

Regardless of the form, adoption in ancient Greece had the effect of terminating the ties between the adopted person and the birth father's relatives (Rubenstein, 1993). Adopted sons assumed the full filial status but were only able to perpetuate their new family line by direct male descent (Goody, 1969).

3. Roman laws on adoption

Roman law also recognized multiple forms of adoption. The *Institutes* of Gaius (circa 161 A.D.), for example, cites two forms: *adoptio* and *arrogatio* or *adrogatio* (from the Latin *rogare:* to ask) (Muirhead, 1880).[1] *Adoptio* consisted of a "ceremony by which a person who was in the power of his parent, whether child or grandchild, male or female, was transferred to the power of the person adopting him" (Long, 1878, p. 15). The adopted person was emancipated by his natural father and surrendered to the adoptive father. *Adoptio* was undertaken under the authority of a magistrate in the capital or by a governor in the provinces and could apply to children of any age and to daughters as well as sons.

Persons who were not under someone else's authority (*sui juris*), could be adopted by *arrogatio*, since in this case the adoptive parent, the adopted person and the people were all asked to agree to the adoption (Long, 1878). Arrogation was usually limited to sons above the age of puberty and was originally undertaken only in Rome, since it required a vote of the people (Muirhead, 1880). The need for such approval stemmed from the fact that, according to the laws of the Twelve Tables, the status of a Roman citizen could be modified only by a vote of the people in the assembly called *comitia curiata* (Long, 1878). After the third century A.D., arrogation could also be accomplished by an imperial rescript or edict (Gardner, 1998).

Some authors have observed that arrogation had more far-reaching effects than did *adoptio* (Gardner, 1998; Goody, 1969). Individuals who were arrogated renounced the worship of the gods of their birth family and passed into the worship of the new family (Goody, 1969). Through arrogation the adoptive parent acquired *potestas* (power, authority) not only over the arrogated son, but also

over his wife, his property and his children (Bechtel, 1896). Furthermore, the *familia* that the arrogated son had previously governed was terminated and its *sacra* (family cult) extinguished (Gardner, 1998). For these reasons a person could not legally be adopted by arrogation until he had made a satisfactory case in front of the relevant authorities. If the person to be adopted was the only male of his family group, the consent to *arrogatio* could be refused (Gardner, 1998). *Adoptio*, on the other hand, had a lesser impact. Although it conferred many of the same "rights, privileges and duties" as arrogation, including the relinquishing of the family name and the *sacra* of the old family, "the ties of blood relationship were not extinguished" and the rights acquired through *adoptio* were agnatic and not cognatic (Bechtel, 1896, p. 79).[2]

Under the Byzantine emperor Justinian (reigned 527 to 565 A.D.), the practice of *adoptio* was amended by limiting full adoption (*adoptio plena*) to natural ascendants, such as a grandfather, and by introducing simple adoption (*adoptio minus plena*) for adoptive parents who were not blood relatives (box I.2). Full adoption created an irrevocable bond equivalent to natural filiation and had the effect of permanently terminating pre-existing legal parent-child relationships. An adopted person acquired the same right as a birth child to inherit property from the adopted parents (Gardner, 1998). Furthermore the rights acquired through this type of adoption were extended to the adopted person's descendants. In contrast, simple adoption did not affect the rights of the birth father, although a son thus adopted did have the right of succession to the estate of his adoptive father if the adoptive father died without leaving a will. As later sections of this chapter will indicate, the modern adoption legislation of several countries, e.g., Argentina, France and Madagascar, preserves the distinction between full and simple adoption.

As other ancient laws did, Roman law established specific guidelines regarding who was allowed to adopt. For instance, a person could not adopt someone older, since adoption was supposed to imitate nature and it was seen as unnatural for a son to be older than his father. Anyone who wished to adopt or to arrogate a son had to be aged 60 or over and at least eighteen years older than the

---

BOX I.2. SELECTED ARTICLES OF LAW RELATED TO ADOPTION
IN THE INSTITUTES OF JUSTINIAN, 533 A.D.

1. Adoption takes place in two ways, either by imperial rescript or by the authority of the magistrate. The imperial rescript gives power to adopt persons of either sex who are *sui juris*; and this species of adoption is called *arrogation*. By the authority of the magistrate we adopt persons in the power of an ascendant, whether in the first degree, as sons and daughters, or in an inferior degree, as grandchildren or great grandchildren.

2. But now, by our constitution, when a *filius familias* is given in adoption by his natural father to a stranger, the power of the natural father is not dissolved; no right passes to the adoptive father, nor is the adopted son in his power, although we allow such son the right of succession to his adoptive father dying intestate. But if a natural father should give his son in adoption, not to a stranger, but to the son's maternal grandfather; or, supposing the natural father has been emancipated, if he gives the son in adoption to the son's paternal grandfather, or to the son's maternal great-grandfather, in this case, as the rights of nature and adoption concur in the same person, the power of the adoptive father, knit by natural ties and strengthened by the legal bond of adoption, is preserved undiminished, so that the adopted son is not only in the family, but in the power of his adoptive father.

4. A younger person cannot adopt an older; for adoption imitates nature; and it seems unnatural that a son should be older than his father. Any one, therefore, who wishes either to adopt or arrogate a son should be the elder by the term of complete puberty, that is, by eighteen years.

8. He who is either adopted or arrogated is assimilated, in many points, to a son born in lawful matrimony; and therefore, if any one adopts a person who is not a stranger by imperial rescript, or before the praetor, or the *praeses* of a province, he can afterwards give in adoption to another the person whom he has adopted.

9. It is a rule common to both kinds of adoption, that persons, although incapable of procreating, as, for instance, impotent persons, may, but those who are castrated cannot adopt.

10. Women, also, cannot adopt; for they have not even their own children in their power; but, by the indulgence of the emperor, as a comfort for the loss of their own children, they are allowed to adopt.

12. Cato, as we learn from the ancients, has with good reason written that slaves, when adopted by their masters, are thereby made free. In accordance with which opinion, we have decided by one of our constitutions that a slave to whom his master by a solemn deed gives the title of son is thereby made free, although he does not acquire thereby the rights of a son.

Source: O. J. Thatcher, 1907.

---

person he was seeking to adopt (Bechtel, 1896). Women were generally not allowed to adopt unless they had received the special authorization of the emperor, because women did not have *potestas* over other free persons (Sandars, 1905). In general, prospective adoptive parents were also required to be childless (Gardner, 1998; Long, 1878).

Roman law also contained guidelines relating to the adopted person. Arrogation of persons who had not yet become adults was allowed only under extraordinary circumstances. Initially, only sons could be arrogated although, under Justinian, arrogation was extended to daughters (Gardner, 1998). Marriage between the adopted person and those who had become related as ascendants and descendants through adoption was prohibited, as was marriage between adoptive siblings, unless one or the other had been emancipated from the adoption contract.

Although there are examples in Roman society of individuals adopting a child out of "kindness" (Boswell, 1988), several authors have noted that Roman adoption law paid little attention to the interests or welfare of the adopted person (Huard, 1956). Adoption was frequently undertaken to avoid the extinction of a family (Brosnan, 1922), to express political loyalty or affection (Boswell, 1988) or, in the case of emperors, as a means of being assured of a chosen successor (Altstein and Simon, 1991). Religious motivations, such as ancestor worship, also appear to have been fundamental (Huard, 1956).

The fact that child abandonment continued to be widespread into the second and third centuries A.D. (Pollack and others, 2004) illustrates how the modern concept of parental rights and responsibilities differs from that of the Romans. Roman law did not require that parents keep their birth children, and abandonment and even infanticide were not punishable because the authority of the father over his direct family members as well as his slaves was absolute (Boswell, 1988). Furthermore, until an edict by Constantine in 331 A.D., parents could reclaim a child that they had previously abandoned as long as they compensated the person who had reared the child in their absence. The fact that foundlings could be reclaimed by their birth parents may have been one of the reasons why they were rarely adopted.

B. ADOPTION LAWS FROM THE MIDDLE AGES TO THE MODERN ERA

1. Adoption laws during the Middle Ages

Although adoption was an essential and permanent reality throughout much of antiquity, by the early Middle Ages formal adoption had fallen into disuse in many of the provinces of the Roman Empire. There is nonetheless fragmentary evidence that adoption was practised sometimes. For instance, King Gunthchramn of Burgundy, being childless, adopted his nephew to inherit the throne in 577 A.D. (Jussen, 2000).

Several authors have noted that the medieval interpretation of adoption differed considerably from that of classic Roman law. Germanic and Frankish law, for example, recognized the custom of *adoptio in hereditate* or *affatomie* (from the Frankish *fathumjan:* to receive into the narrowest circle of the kindred) (Hübner and others, 1918). The *Pactus legis salicae*—the body of law established by Clovis I, King of the Franks between 507 and 511 A.D.—describes *affatomie* as a legal contractual form through which the adopted person acquired the same rights as a legitimate heir (Santinelli, 1999). The Markulf Collection—a compilation of legal practices from the second half of the seventh century or the first half of the eighth century A.D.—also contained an adoption formula whereby a man could bequeath

his property to a stranger on condition that the latter would take care of the adoptive father in his old age (Jussen, 2000). Such practices can be viewed as a sort of *inter vivos* donation, since "future rights to an inheritance were promised in exchange for filial care during the lifetime of the donor" (Gager, 1996, p. 40).

While adoption as a legal practice fell into disuse or in some cases, such as the English legal system, "remained absolutely unknown" (Hübner and others, 1918, p. 661), in some parts of Medieval Europe, the institution of adoption as outlined in Roman law was preserved (Boswell, 1988). In the Byzantine Empire (330 to 1453), for instance, the influence of ancient Roman law never waned. Nevertheless, adoption in Byzantine law gradually changed from the concepts set out in Justinian's *Institutes* to a form of adoption similar to the Roman simple adoption (Pitsakis, 1999). According to the *Epanagoge aucta*—a Byzantine legal code compiled during the tenth and eleventh centuries—adoptive parents could not take possession of the adopted person's patrimony and the adopted person's ties with his or her birth family were not extinguished through the act of adoption. Byzantine law also introduced several important changes to Roman law by, among other things, extending the right to adoption to all childless persons including women.

In the late Middle Ages (1300 to 1500), jurists in Western Europe began to rediscover ancient Roman law and to reconstruct the rules pertaining to adoptive filiation according to Justinian's *Institutes*, sometimes introducing fundamental changes (Roumy, 1999). For instance, in the thirteenth century, the *Partidas* of the Castilian King Alfonso X recognized the difference between *adoptio* and *arrogatio* as outlined in Roman law and established that only arrogated persons could be viewed as legitimate heirs (Garcia Marsilla, 1999). The Valencian code of James I (thirteenth century) permitted both women and men with no legitimate descendants to adopt a person at least twenty years their junior (Garcia Marsilla, 1999).[3]

Canonists during this period also approached adoption from the viewpoint of Roman law.

Tancred, a renowned canonist of the early thirteenth century, differentiated between arrogation and simple adoption (Pollack and others, 2004). As in Roman law, he contended that arrogation should be permitted only when the child was free from parental authority, while simple adoption could take place when the child was under someone else's power. However, in contrast with Roman law, the adoptive father was required to be capable of procreation and under the age of 70. Women were generally not permitted to adopt and only children under a certain age could be adopted. In the case of arrogation, adopted persons had the right to inherit from their adoptive parents, even if the latter died intestate.

The emphasis placed by medieval jurists on the view that adoptions should imitate nature led to the widespread perception that adoptive filiation was inferior to natural filiation (Roumy, 1999), and many authors agree that it was during the Middle Ages that adopted children began to be stigmatized. Customary French law of the eleventh and twelfth centuries discouraged the creation of fictive adoptive ties by "fixing the principle of devolution of family property firmly within the confines of consanguinity" (Gager, 1996, p. 69). In late medieval Florence, the preference given to blood ties contributed to making formal adoption extremely rare (Kuehn, 1999).

While legal adoption may have been infrequent during the Middle Ages, other means of providing for children deprived of parental care became widespread. For instance, oblation, a practice that consisted in "donating" a child to a convent or a monastery, was used during the Middle Ages (Boswell, 1988). The purpose of oblation was both practical and spiritual, since it unburdened the birth family of the obligation to provide for a child and at the same time was perceived as a highly pious gesture. Children were also placed in foundling homes, which were first created during the twelfth and thirteenth centuries with the purpose of providing a shelter for orphans and abandoned children (Kertzer, 2000). There is evidence that children placed in these institutions were sometimes adopted, although these adoptions were infrequent and often of an informal nature (Boswell, 1988).

2. Adoption laws in the early Modern Era

Information on adoption in the early Modern Era is highly fragmented and it is difficult to reconstruct an overall picture of the legal practices in effect during this period. Gager (1996), for instance, notes that in the sixteenth century, "French jurists herald[ed] their period as the critical turning point marking the 'disappearance' of adoption in French law" (p. 51). Early modern French jurists upheld the inheritance claims of birth children and collateral heirs above those of strangers. As a result, adopted children began to be perceived in French society as incomplete family members and were barred from inheriting in intestate successions.

During the same period, however, canonists continued expanding on the legal framework developed during the twelve and thirteenth centuries (Pollack and others, 2004). In *De Sancto Matrimonio,* one of the leading canonic treaties of its time, Tomás Sánchez asserted that there were two types of adoption: arrogation and simple adoption. Arrogation was viewed as "perfect adoption" in that "the one adopted was placed under his or her new father's paternal power and made his necessary heir." Under simple adoption, the person remained "subject to his or her natural father's paternal power and had the right to share in the natural father's estate, not that of the adoptive parents" (Pollack and others, 2004, p. 722). Later, Pope Benedict XIV (reigned 1740 to 1758) reiterated the distinction between arrogation and simple adoption and asserted that adoption was a legal Roman concept that the Church had made its own.

As formal adoption faded from legal frameworks, orphanages and institutions began to play an ever increasing role in the care of children deprived of parents. In 1764, for instance, Catherine the Great opened the Moscow Foundling Home with the purpose of rescuing abandoned or orphaned children and rearing them to become the so-called third estate or mercantile class (Ransel, 1988). In 1764, 523 children were admitted to the Moscow foundling home. By the 1860s, the number of children entering the home each year had climbed to over 11,000. Similarly in Florence and Paris, the number of admittances to foundling homes peaked during the first half of the nineteenth century, with annual admission of almost 5,000 children in Paris (Fuchs, 1984) and 2,500 children in Florence (Viazzo and others, 2000). The evidence suggests that children were not adopted from such institutions. According to Fuchs (1984), adoptions of abandoned children were rare in nineteenth century France because of the stigma associated with their presumed illegitimacy. Adoption of children in orphanages was also constrained because French authorities could refuse requests for adoption of abandoned children on the grounds that their "biological mothers should have the right to reclaim them at any time" (p. 30). Evidence from the Moscow Foundling Home also indicates that adoptions were infrequent. About 1,000 children were adopted from the Foundling Home between 1810 and 1838, a relatively small number given that over 140,000 children were placed there during the period and among these, 40,000 survived the high mortality rates prevalent in the institution (Ransel, 1988).[4]

3. The Napoleonic Code

Probably the most influential adoption law of the Modern Era is the French Civil Code of 1804, known also as the Napoleonic Code (box I.3). Based largely on Roman law, the Napoleonic Code limited adoption to persons who had already reached adulthood. Although adoptive parents conferred their name on the adopted person, the birth parents were required to give their consent, and adopted persons maintained the natural obligations towards their birth family. Adopted persons enjoyed the same rights to inherit from the adoptive parent as legitimate offspring but were not entitled to inherit from relations of the adoptive parents. If an adopted person died without leaving descendants, the property received from the adoptive parents was returned to the adoptive family or their descendants. The rights acquired through adoption were not considered transmissible even in the descending line.

The Napoleonic Code also laid out a series of requirements for prospective adoptive parents. Only persons over the age of 50 who had neither children nor legitimate descendants were permitted to adopt. The adoptive parent was also expected to be at least 15 years older than the adopted person.

Minors could be cared for only under the proviso of "benevolent guardianship". This type of arrangement involved the "obligation of supporting the ward, of bringing him up, and of putting him in a situation to gain his livelihood" (Spence, 1827, art. 364). Guardians were allowed to apply for the adoption of their charges once the latter had reached majority or after the death of the guardian, in a practice in many respects similar to Greek testamentary adoption. As the sections below indicate, the Napoleonic Code has influenced profoundly the modern adoption laws of many countries.

4. The first alternatives to institutional care

As economic and social conditions changed during the nineteenth century, orphanages and workhouses[5]—almshouses in the United States—began to be perceived as an unacceptable system for dealing with parentless children. Institutions were becoming overwhelmed by the number of destitute children needing care and education (Triseliotis and others, 1997). High mortality rates, the social stigma attached to institutionalization and the high costs of running such facilities also contributed to undermining the support for existing institutions.

In the middle of the nineteenth century, boarding out, a practice that consisted of placing a child with a family, became a popular alternative to institutionalization. This practice gained wide support because, besides offering a more suitable environment for raising children, it provided a source of income to the families that took in children. Other informal arrangements, such as "baby farms," where unwanted or illegitimate children were looked after for a fee, became common in Australia (Kociumbas, 1997), the United Kingdom (Shanley, 1989) and the United States (Carp, 2000; Riis, 1890).

During this period, large numbers of children were also forcibly relocated from workhouses in the United Kingdom to various British colonies, including Australia, Canada, New Zealand, South Africa and Zimbabwe (Bean and Melville, 1989). Such children were often removed without parental consent and were infrequently adopted (Eekelaar, 1994).[6] The social experiment of

---

BOX I.3. SELECTED ARTICLES OF LAW RELATED TO ADOPTION
IN THE FRENCH CIVIL CODE, 1804

343. Adoption is not permitted to persons of either sex, except to those above the age of fifty years, and who at the period of adoption shall have neither children nor legitimate descendants, and who shall be at the least fifteen years older than the individuals whom they propose to adopt.

344. No one can be adopted by more than one person, except by husband and wife. Except in the case in article 366, no married person can adopt without the consent of the other conjunct.

345. The faculty of adoption shall not be exercised except towards an individual, for whom, during minority, and for a period of at least six years, the party shall have supplied assistance, and employed uninterrupted care, or towards one who shall have saved the life of the party adopting, either in a fight, or in rescuing him from fire or water. It shall suffice, in this latter case, that the adopter have attained majority, be older than the adopted, without children, or lawful descendants, and if married, that his conjunct consent to the adoption.

346. Adoption shall not, in any case, take place before the majority of the adopted party. If the adopted having father and mother, or one of them, has not completed his twenty-fifth year, he shall be bound to produce the consent of his father and mother, or the survivor, to his adoption; and if he is more than twenty-five years of age, to require their counsel.

347. The adoption shall confer the name of the adopter on the adopted, in addition to the proper name of the latter.

348. The adopted shall continue in his own family, and shall there retain all his rights: nevertheless, marriage is prohibited,

Between the adopter, the adopted, and his descendants;

Between adopted children of the same individual;

Between the adopted, and the children who may be born to the adopter;

Between the adopted and the conjunct of the adopter, and reciprocally between the adopter and the conjunct of the adopted.

349. The natural obligation, which shall continue to exist between the adopted and his father and mother, to supply them with sustenance in cases determined by the law, shall be considered as common to the adopter and the adopted towards each other.

350. The adopted shall acquire no right of succession to the property of relations of the adopter; but he shall enjoy the same rights with regard to succession to the adopter as are possessed by a child born in wedlock, even though there should be other children of this latter description, born subsequently to the adoption.

351. If the adopted child die without lawful descendants, presents made by the adopter, or acquisitions by inheritance to him, and which shall actually exist at the decease of the adopted, shall return to the adopter or to his descendants, on condition of contributing to debts, without prejudice to third persons. The surplus of the property of the adopted shall belong to his own relations; and these shall exclude always, for the same objects specified in the present article, all the heirs of the adopter other than his descendants.

352. If during the life of the adopter, and after the decease of the adopted, children or descendants left by the latter, shall themselves die without issue, the adopter shall succeed to donations made by him, as is directed in the preceding article; but this right shall be inherent in the person of the adopter and not transmissible to his heirs, even in the descending line.

Source: G. Spence, 1827.

forcibly moving children from institutions was replicated within the United States with the so-called "orphan trains." Between 1854 and 1929, an estimated 200,000 children were relocated under the auspices of the Children's Aid Society of New York to families living in the mid-western states of Indiana, Iowa, Kansas, Michigan, Missouri and Ohio. Most of those moved were not even orphans and were never formally adopted (Holt, 1992; O'Connor, 2001).

C. MODERN ADOPTION LAWS

1. Modern adoption laws: 1850-1920

The first modern adoption laws were passed in the second half of the nineteenth century in response to the increasing belief that society should play a more proactive role in promoting the welfare of children. Under the influence of this new ideological framework, adoption began to be advocated not simply as a legal mechanism to establish heir status but as a means of promoting the best interests of children (Sokoloff, 1993).

The Massachusetts Adoption of Children Act (box I.4) is widely recognized as the first modern adoption law.[7] Enacted in 1851, this statute required the written consent of the birth parents, a joint application by the husband and wife and a complete severance of the child from its family of origin (Sokoloff, 1993). The bond created between the adopted child and the adoptive parent was regarded as equivalent to that of natural filiation, and all rights held by the birth parents were terminated upon the decree of adoption. One of the most striking features of the act was that it gave the judge the authority to assess whether the prospective adoptive parents had "sufficient ability to bring up the child, and furnish suitable nurture and education." This implied a "radical departure from the basic concept of the Roman law in that the primary concern was the welfare of the child rather than concern for the continuity of the adopter's family" (Huard, 1956, p. 749).

BOX I.4. THE MASSACHUSETTS ADOPTION OF CHILDREN ACT, 1851

Be it enacted by the Senate and House of Representatives, in General Court assembled, and by the authority of the same, as follows:

Sect. 1. Any inhabitant of this Commonwealth may petition the judge of probate, in the county wherein he or she may reside, for leave to adopt a child not his or her own by birth.

Sect. 2. If both or either of the parents of such child shall be living, they or the survivor of them, as the case may be, shall consent in writing to such adoption; if neither parent be living, such consent may be given by the legal guardian of such child; if there be no legal guardian, no father nor mother, the next of kin of such child within the State may give such consent; and if there be no such next of kin, the judge of probate may appoint some discreet and suitable person to act in the proceedings, as the next friend of such child, and give or withhold such consent.

Sect. 3. If the child be of the age of fourteen years or upwards, the adoption shall not be made without his or her consent.

Sect. 4. No petition by a person having a lawful wife shall be allowed unless such wife shall join therein, and no woman having a lawful husband shall be competent to present and prosecute such petition.

Sect. 5. If, upon such petition, so presented and consented to as aforesaid, the judge of probate shall be satisfied of the identity and relations of the persons, and that the petitioner, or, in case of husband and wife, the petitioners, are of sufficient ability to bring up the child, and furnish suitable nurture and education, having reference to the degree and condition of its parents, and that it is fit and proper that such adoption should take effect, he shall make a decree setting forth the said facts, and ordering that, from and after the date of the decree, such child should be deemed and taken, to all legal intents and purposes, the child of the petitioner or petitioners.

Sect. 6. A child so adopted, as aforesaid, shall be deemed, for the purposes of inheritance and succession by such child, custody of the person and right of obedience by such parent or parents by adoption, and all other legal consequences and incidents of the natural relation of parents and children, the same to all intents and purposes as if such child had been born in lawful wedlock of such parents or parent by adoption, saving only that such child shall not be deemed capable of taking property expressly limited to the heirs of the body or bodies of such petitioner or petitioners.

Sect. 7. The natural parent or parents of such child shall be deprived, by such decree of adoption, of all legal rights whatsoever as respects such child; and such child shall be freed from all legal obligations of maintenance and obedience, as respects such natural parent or parents.

Sect. 8. Any petitioner, or any child which is the subject of such a petition, by any next friend, may claim and prosecute an appeal to the Supreme Judicial Court from such decree of the judge of probate, in like manner and with the like effect as such appeals may now be claimed and prosecuted in cases of wills, saying only that in no case shall any bond be required of, nor any costs awarded against, such child or its next friend so appealing.

Source: W. H. Whitmore, 1876.

TABLE I.1. YEAR OF PROMULGATION OR ENACTMENT OF SELECTED ADOPTION LAWS, 1850-1956

Year	Country
1851	Massachusetts (United States)
1881	New Zealand
1896	Western Australia (Australia)
1900	Germany
1907	Switzerland
1914	Austria
1917	Sweden
1920	British Columbia (Canada)
1923	Denmark
1923	South Africa
1926	England and Wales (United Kingdom)
1926	U.S.S.R.
1936	Peru
1939	France[1]
1939	Poland
1940	Greece
1942	United Republic Tanganyika[2]
1945	Uruguay
1947	Guatemala
1948	Argentina
1952	Ireland
1956	India

Sources: P. Abel, 1960; J. F. Brosnan, 1922; K. Griffith, 1997; M. Kornitzer, 1952; K. Lilani, 1995; N. Lowe, 2000; K. O'Halloran, 2006; T. Rosenwald, 2004; B. A. Rwezaura and U. Wanitzek, 1988; United Nations, 1956 and W. J. Wadlington, 1966.

[1] Introduction of the concept of adoptive legitimation.

[2] On 26 April 1964, the United Republic of Tanganyika and Zanzibar ratified Articles of Union and on 1 November 1964, the United Republic of Tanzania was recognized by the United Nations.

A number of countries introduced new legislation between the second half of the nineteenth century and the first years of the twentieth century based on the Massachusetts Act of 1851 (table I.1). New Zealand, for instance, introduced the 1881 Adoption of Children Act, becoming the first country of the Commonwealth to pass an adoption law. The stated purpose of this Act was to benefit children who, being deprived of natural parents, would otherwise have been exposed to want and privation (Griffith, 1997). The Act also aimed at securing the rights of adoptive parents, who under the system of voluntary guardianship had been powerless to intervene in the case where birth parents wished to reclaim their child (New Zealand, Law Commission, 1999). Western Australia passed the Adoption of Children Act of 1896 in response to the "appalling conditions, high mortality rate and corruption in the

boarding houses of the nineteenth century" (Rosenwald, 2004, p. 2). As in the Massachusetts Act of 1851, prospective adoptive parents were required to prove their suitability and parental fitness in front of a judge.[8]

In many other countries, however, adoption legislation focused primarily on upholding the inheritance rights of legitimate descendants. Under the German Civil Code of 1900, for instance, an adoption order did not terminate the relationship with the birth relatives and adopted persons could be excluded from inheritance by their extended adoptive relatives. The code also included "provisions that one who has legitimate descendants living cannot adopt and that the adopting person must have completed the fiftieth year" (Brosnan, 1922, p. 334). Analogous restrictions existed in the Swiss Civil Code of 1907, which did not recognize the extinction of ties to the family of origin and allowed adopted persons to inherit from their birth families (Addis, 1953; United Nations, 1956). The Swiss code, like the Napoleonic Code, limited adoption to childless persons who were past childbearing age.

2. Modern adoption laws: 1920-1940

In the 1920s, the existence of many orphans and abandoned children in the aftermath of the First World War and the influenza epidemic of 1918, combined with concerns over the legal status of children permanently separated from their birth families, prompted many countries to enact new legislation or reintroduce or modify previously existing adoption laws. England and Wales, for instance, passed the first adoption law—the Adoption of Children Act—in 1926. Until that date, adoption had not been recognized as a formal legal concept in England and Wales, in part due to the emphasis given under common law to blood ties (Brosnan, 1922; Huard, 1956). As in the Massachusetts Act of 1851, the 1926 Adoption of Children Act required the consent of the birth parents as well as that of both adoptive parents. Although the Act recognized that adopted children benefited from the same rights, duties, obligations and liabilities as birth children, it did not ensure the child's full integration into the adoptive family, nor did it replace inheritance rights in the birth family (Bridge, 2001).[9]

In the Soviet Union, the Family Code of 1926 reinstated adoption, a legal practice that had been suspended in 1918 during the Russian Revolution of 1917-1919, to meet the needs of abandoned and orphaned children (Bernstein, 1997). In its initial formulation, the law did not attempt to equate adoptive relationships with biological ones, and as a result few restrictions were placed on who could adopt, as long as they were unlikely to "exploit, corrupt, or prejudice a budding Soviet citizen" (p. 209). In France, a legal decree of 29 July 1939 introduced the concept of adoptive legitimation (Wadlington, 1966), which recognized the termination of the ties between the adopted child and the birth parents for children under age five who had been declared abandoned by a court or were of unknown parentage.

3. Modern adoption laws: 1940-1980

A large number of countries enacted new adoption laws during or in the aftermath of the Second World War. For example, in Tanganyika (now the United Republic of Tanzania), the first adoption legislation—the Adoption of Infants Ordinance—was introduced in 1942, based on the English Adoption of Children Act of 1926 (Rwezaura and Wanitzek, 1988). This act was subsequently amended by the Adoption Ordinance of 1953. In Ireland, the first adoption law—the Adoption Act—was passed in 1952 (O'Halloran, 2006). It recognized that adopted children should enjoy the same rights and duties as legitimate offspring and established that adopted persons were entitled to inherit from their adoptive parents and relatives, even if the latter died intestate. Birth mothers lost all parental rights upon the adoption decree.[10] In India, the Hindu Adoptions and Maintenance Act was introduced in 1956 (Lilani, 1995). This Act recognized the equivalence between natural and adoptive filiation but also contained the proviso, as in the 1926 Adoption of Children Act of England and Wales, that "any property which vested in the adopted child before the adoption shall continue to vest in such person subject to the obligations, if any, attaching to the ownership of such property, including the obligation to maintain relatives in the family of his or her birth".[11] The Hindu Adoptions and Maintenance Act, which still governs adoption rulings in India, regulates adoptions by parents who are Hindus, Buddhists, Jains and Sikhs. Adoptions by Muslims, Christians, Parsis and Jews are governed by the Indian Guardians and Wards Act of 1890 (see also chapters II and III).[12] The Indian Guardians and Wards Act does not confer on the adopted person the same rights as a biological child in terms of the acquisition of the family name or property (Bhargava, 2005).

During 1940-1980, several countries also introduced amendments to earlier legislation. Many of these changes were aimed at broadening the effects of adoption and at better protecting the adopted person's welfare. In England and Wales, for instance, the Adoption of Children Act of 1949 guaranteed for the first time the full integration of adopted children into their adoptive families through the provision of inheritance rights (Lowe, 2000). Likewise in New Zealand, the Adoption Act of 1955 recognized adopted children as legitimate offspring of the adoptive family. Under this Act, the legal ties between adopted persons and their families of origin were terminated and courts were granted the possibility of dispensing with parental consent to an adoption in the case of abandonment or neglect (Armitage, 1995; Cameron, 1966). In Romania, Decree No. 131 of 1949 altered several provisions of the Civil Code of 1865, granting, among other things, people with children or legal descendents the right to adopt (Zugravescu and Iacovescu, 1995). In the Soviet Union, the revised Family Code of 1968 recognized that adopted persons and their descendants had the "same personal rights and obligations as any blood relatives in the adopters' family" (Bernstein, 1997, p. 216).

A number of countries also modified existing legislation to allow for new forms of adoption. In France, for example, adoptive legitimation was replaced in 1966 by the concept of full adoption, which equated the adopted child with a legitimate offspring of the adoptive family and terminated all ties between the adopted child and his or her birth family. The concept which had been known as adoption under the Napoleonic Code was renamed simple adoption (British Institute of International and Comparative Law, 1967). In Poland, as courts "became concerned with protecting the best interests of the child", a series of amendments were made, including the introduction of the concept of full adoption in the Family and Guardianship Code of 1965 (Holewinska-Lapinska, 1995, p. 74). In Germany, the concept of full adoption replaced that of simple adoption in 1976 (Hoffman-Riem, 1990). The German Civil Code was also amended to dispense with parental consent for the adoption of children who had been abused or neglected.[13]

4. Modern adoption laws: basic similarities and differences

As the discussion above suggests, current national legal frameworks are the product of historical processes. The French Civil Code of 1804, for instance, served as model for the civil codes of many former French colonies as well as those of many Latin American countries. Similarly, the laws of England and Wales shaped the legal framework of many former British colonies. Consequently, western precedents have influenced adoption laws in many regions of the world. While chapter III provides a more detailed overview of some of the similarities and differences between adoption laws, we focus here on a preliminary classification of the diverse set of national adoption legislation.

The first dimension of interest relates to whether legislation recognizes only one form of adoption or multiple forms of adoption (for example, full adoption and simple adoption). Countries that recognize only one modality of adoption include Albania, Togo and the United Kingdom. Countries that recognize multiple forms of adoption include Argentina, Benin, Japan, Madagascar and Uruguay.

A second dimension relates to how adoption laws affect the rights and responsibilities of adoptive parents, birth parents and adopted persons. Laws that embrace the concept of full adoption tend to interpret adoption as replacing the birth ties with adoptive ones and to view the rights and responsibilities acquired through adoption as equivalent to those gained through birth. In Brazil, for instance, the 1988 Constitution guarantees adopted children the same rights and duties as birth children, including the right to acquire the family name and inheritance.[14] Likewise in Turkey, the Civil Code establishes

that adopted children take the surname of their adoptive parents and become their legal heirs.[15] In the Russian Federation, the Family Code of 1995 grants adopted children and their progeny the same rights and responsibilities towards their adoptive parents and relatives as those of birth children.[16] In Albania, Law No. 7650 of 17 December 1992 recognizes that upon the act of adoption, the rights and obligations of the adopted child towards his or her family of origin cease.[17] A similar provision is part of the Individuals and Family Code of Togo of 1980.[18]

In contrast, laws using the concept of simple adoption usually do not equate adoption with a termination of the relationship between the adopted person and his or her birth family. As a result, children adopted through simple adoption frequently do not lose their original surname. Furthermore, they do not automatically acquire the right to inherit from their adoptive parents or other adoptive relatives. In Argentina, for instance, the rights and duties deriving from the adopted child's biological links are not extinguished by simple adoption.[19] Likewise, according to the French Civil Code, children who are adopted through simple adoption retain the right to succession from their birth family.[20] Under Bolivian law, children adopted through simple adoption keep the surname of their biological parents although the adoptive parents have parental authority.[21] In Rwanda, the Civil Code establishes that adoption does not break the ties between the natural family and the adoptive child. The latter retains all the rights and obligations towards his or her family of origin, including use of the surname and forenames acquired at birth. At the same time, the law recognizes that the adoptive parent is the sole person vested with parental authority over the adopted child and that the relationship arising out of adoption extends to the child's descendants.[22] Other examples of adoption practices that do not establish the termination of the rights of biological parents are presented in chapters II and III.

The third dimension of interest relates to whether the adoption contract is final or can be revoked under certain circumstances. According to the French Civil Code, full adoption is considered irrevocable,[23] while simple adoption can be revoked by a court under certain conditions.[20] Under Bolivian law, simple adoption can be revoked when the physical, moral or mental well-being or the patrimony of the adopted child or the adoptive parent is compromised.[21] In Denmark, the Danish Adoption (Consolidation) Act of 2004 recognizes that an adoption decree may be revoked by the Minister of Family and Consumer Affairs when the adopter and the adopted child so agree and when the revocation is in the best interests of the child (Denmark, Ministry of Family and Consumer Affairs, 2004). In contrast, the 1958 Adoption of Children Act of Jamaica makes no provision for the revocation of the adoption order, except where the adopted child is legitimated by the marriage of his or her parents, having been adopted by one of those parents (Jamaica, Supreme Court, 2003).

D. ADOPTION LAWS: PRESENT AND FUTURE CHALLENGES

A number of issues relating to adoption are being debated currently in courts and policy circles in many countries. They include: permanency planning and the right of children to live in a family setting; intercountry adoption; adoption by step-parents and other relatives; inter-racial adoption; the right to have access to information on the birth family, and the importance of protecting the anonymity of persons involved in the adoption procedure. This section provides a brief discussion of some of the more salient aspects of such debates.

1. Adoption as a response to the needs of children living in foster care or institutions

At the end of the nineteenth century, experts on child welfare began to focus on the family as the most appropriate setting for raising children deprived of the care of their birth parents. This concern arose in parallel with the rich body of research focusing on the detrimental effects of institutional care on children's emotional development (Hendrick, 2003; Shapiro and others, 2001). As a result of this research, many Governments have been actively encouraging the adoption of children living in foster or institutional care who cannot be reunited with their birth families. In the United States, for example, President Clinton called for doubling the number of adoptions of children placed in public care by the year 2002. The ensuing Adoption and Safe Families Act of 1997[24] introduced incentives to raise the number of adoptions and increased financial support to persons who adopted children (Pecora and others, 2000). Subsequently, President Bush committed his administration to encouraging adoption.

In the United Kingdom, Prime Minister Blair called for a concerted effort to overhaul and modernize the legal framework for adoption. A White Paper, "Adoption: A new approach,"[25] established the target of increasing the number of adoptions of looked-after children by 40 per cent by 2004-2005 (O'Halloran, 2006). In 2002, the Adoption and Children Act made the child's welfare the paramount consideration in any decision relating to adoption and established an adoption register to facilitate the matching of children waiting in care with potential adoptive families.[26]

Other countries have also begun to promote adoption as a key strategy to meet the needs of children living in care. For instance, since 1997 the Republic of Korea has provided tax incentives to adoptive families in order to promote domestic adoptions (Buck, 2005).[27] In the Russian Federation, the Family Code of 1995 recognizes adoption as the best form of care for children deprived of a family.[16] In Latvia, four legislative acts were amended in order to facilitate domestic adoptions.[28]

Not all countries, however, view adoption as the best approach for dealing with children in need of family care. In New Zealand, for instance, adoption is increasingly seen as only "one of several ways in which permanent care can be provided for a child" (New Zealand, Law Commission, 1999, p. 28; see also New Zealand Law Commission, 2000). As a result, the Care of Children Act of 2004 places more emphasis on maximizing the role of the extended family than on promoting adoption by strangers. Among other things, the act encourages the strengthening of links between children and wider family groups (New Zealand, Ministry of Justice, 2005).

2. Intercountry adoption

Intercountry adoption was a relatively uncommon phenomenon until the second half of the twentieth century. It became widespread in the aftermath of the Second World War, when orphaned children were sent from Germany, Greece and Japan to new homes in the United States (Altstein and Simon, 1991; Masson, 2001; Weil, 1984). Later, the Korean and Viet Nam wars resulted in a surge in intercountry adoptions, often involving children of mixed race, to Sweden, the United States and other countries. Because intercountry adoption had not been widely practised before, many countries did not have the necessary legal frameworks to protect the best interests of children adopted from abroad. In the United Kingdom, for instance, prior to the enactment of the Adoption of Children Act of 1949, courts did not have the power to issue an adoption order for a child who was not a British citizen or resident, as stipulated in the Adoption Act of 1926 (United Nations, 1953). In Ethiopia, the Civil Code of 1960 had no provisions regulating intercountry adoption (Bekstorm, 1972) and, consequently, when Dutch and Swedish couples attempted to adopt Ethiopian children in the 1960s, they often encountered difficulties.

As the number of intercountry adoptions rose during the 1960s and 1970s, new multilateral initiatives to regulate them arose. Increasing concern over child trafficking (Defence for Children International 1989 and 1991; Tolfree, 1995) led to the creation of a multilateral legal instrument to regulate intercountry adoptions, the Hague Convention on Protection of Children and Co-operation in Respect of Intercountry Adoption,[29] which entered into force on 1 May 1995. This convention was influenced by regional and multilateral legal instruments adopted earlier, including the 1967 European Convention on the Adoption of Children,[30] the 1984 Inter-American Convention on Conflict of Laws Concerning the Adoption of Minors,[31] the 1986 United Nations Declaration on Social and Legal Principles relating to the Protection and Welfare of Children, with Special Reference to Foster Placement and Adoption Nationally and Internationally[32] and the 1989 United Nations Convention on the Rights of the Child.[33]

More recently, some countries of origin have taken measures to limit the scope of intercountry adoption (Bartholet, 1993; Weil, 1984). The Republic of Korea, for instance, established a plan to phase out intercountry adoptions after adverse publicity at the time of the 1988 Seoul Olympics (Melosh, 2002). The Republic's current goal is to reduce the number of intercountry adoptions by 3 per cent to 5 per cent each year for the next two decades.[34] Similarly, after many failed attempts at moratoria, Romania passed legislation in 2004 that has effectively halted all intercountry adoptions by non-relatives (Buck, 2005). Other countries, including Benin, Poland, Viet Nam and Uruguay, apply the principle of subsidiarity whereby intercountry adoption is considered only after other options are exhausted.

A number of countries of destination of intercountry adoptions have also recently modified their laws to prevent abuse. The Government of New Zealand, for instance, passed the Citizens Amendment Act of 1992 to ensure that intercountry adoptions are not used to secure immigration status. As a result, individuals aged 14 years or over who are adopted by a New Zealand citizen do not acquire New Zealand citizenship automatically (Galvin, 2005). Other countries that limit the automatic acquisition of citizenship for foreign-born persons adopted internationally are Singapore[35] and the United Kingdom.[36] Chapters III and IV discuss further the problems arising from the lack of recognition of foreign adoption orders and conflicts between the laws of countries of origin and those of countries of destination of intercountry adoptions.

3. Adoption by step-parents and other relatives

Throughout history, children have been adopted by close relatives. In Justinian's *Institutes*, for instance, full adoption was limited to maternal grandfathers and great-grandfathers. Likewise, many of the anecdotal examples that have survived from the Middle Ages involved adoption by close relatives. In many countries, modern law continues to favour adoption by relatives. In Italy, for instance, the Law of 28 March 2001 awards relatives (up to the sixth degree) a special status in adopting a child who has been orphaned, waiving the requirement regarding marital status.[37] In the United States, a number of states specifically voice a preference for adoption by kin, because such adoptions are consider to provide greater continuity and permanency for the child (Brooks and others, 2005). In Thailand, close relatives or blood relations are exempted from the six-month probationary period required for other prospective adoptive parents.[38] Similarly, in China, the requirements for the adoption of a child by a "collateral relative by blood of the same generation and up to the third degree of kinship" are less demanding than those imposed on other prospective adoptive parents.[39] Similar distinctions are made in the 1989 Adoption Act of Sierra Leone (Lisk, 1992).

By contrast, some countries discourage adoption by relatives, the rationale being that such adoptions might distort biological family relationships. For instance, the New Zealand Law Commission (2000, p. 142) has recommended limiting adoptions by relatives on the grounds that "in the majority of cases of intra-family care, enduring guardianship or guardianship is preferable to adoption." Other countries that discourage adoptions by relatives are Australia (O'Halloran, 2006) and the Netherlands (Vonk, 2006).

Since 1950, as a result of increases in the number of divorces in many countries, there has been a rising trend in adoptions by step-parents. Because divorced people frequently remarry, there is a growing pool of people with the potential to adopt their partner's birth children. By the mid-1970s, adoptions by step-parents represented the most common form of domestic adoption in many developed countries (see chapter VI), and many countries had adopted explicit guidelines to regulate such adoptions. In France, Act No. 76-1179 of 22 December 1976 establishes that a step-parent adoption produces "the effects of an adoption by two spouses".[23] In El Salvador, the law recognizes that a spouse may adopt his or her partner's child.[40]

Some countries, however, have tried to limit the number of adoptions by step-parents arguing that it is not acceptable to deprive the divorced birth-parent who does not have primary custody

of a child of all his or her parental rights. Hence, in England and Wales, the Children Act of 1975 seeks to discourage such adoptions (Gibson, 1994; Selman, 2004). Likewise, the New Zealand Law Commission noted that adoptions by step-parents leave "a non-custodial parent without any legal rights of custody or access to the child" (1999, p. 51). In 2000, the Law Commission recommended that guardianship be granted as an alternative and sought to "impose a high threshold upon eligibility for step-parent adoption," arguing that the "court should not encourage the reshuffling and dealing out of a 'new' family. Rather, the emphasis should be upon people coming to terms with the reality of their family situation" (2000, p. 138). The Care of Children Act of 2004 recognizes this principle. In Western Australia, amendments were made in 2003 to the Adoption Act of 1994, effectively limiting adoption by step-parents and other relatives.[41] In Switzerland, the Civil Code was modified in 1998 so that step-parents could adopt a child of a spouse only if they had been married for at least five years instead of the previously required two years.[42]

4. The issue of race and ethnicity in adoption laws

Inter-racial adoption has been a contentious legal issue in some countries, especially Australia, New Zealand and the United States. The debate has focused on the importance of finding an adoptive family for children deprived of parental care, regardless of their racial and ethnic identity, and on the potential negative impact of placing children with adoptive parents who are not of the same background as the child. In the United States[43] this debate has centred around two landmark pieces of legislation: the Indian Child Welfare Act (ICWA) of 1978 and the Multi-ethnic Placement Act (MEPA) of 1994. The ICWA was adopted to reverse the highly discriminatory practice of removing Native American and Alaskan children from their families and communities and placing them in Caucasian adoptive families or foster homes (Silverman, 1993). The ICWA called for placing children of a given ethnic, racial and even religious background with a caregiver with similar characteristics, whenever possible. In 1994, however, the MEPA declared that states could not delay or deny an adoption on the basis of the race, colour or national origin of the adoptive or foster parent or of the child involved.

In Australia (Edwards and Read, 1989) and New Zealand (Rockell and Ryburn, 1988), the bitter history of inter-racial placements involving Aboriginal and Maori children, viewed by many as a form of cultural genocide, has led to the view that adoption is not the best strategy to secure permanent care for looked-after children and that care by relatives should be encouraged first (Love, 2000; O'Halloran, 2006) (see chapters II and III). Similar concerns have been raised in relation to the adoption of Roma children in Switzerland.

5. The right of adopted persons to have access to information on their birth family

In the past, adoption laws did not place emphasis on hiding the origins of the adopted persons, in part because adoption often involved consenting adults. During the first half of the twentieth century, however, "secrecy, anonymity, and the sealing of records became statutorily required and standard adoption practice" in the United States (Sokoloff, 1993, p. 21) and in many other countries. The need to protect adopted children from the stigma attached to their presumed illegitimacy was probably a major reason for Governments to order the concealment of the adopted child's origin. In Western Australia, for instance, the Adoption of Children Act of 1896 was amended in 1921 to restrict access to the records of adopted children. This measure was taken to protect the interests of the child, the birth mother and the adoptive parents.[41]

In the Soviet Union, adoption laws were tightened in the 1960s to protect the secrecy of adoption. The Family Code of 1968, for instance, authorized adoptive parents to modify the date of birth of their adopted child by six months in order to hide the "child's biological roots not only from the adoptee, but from friends and family" (Bernstein, 1997, p. 217). Disclosing information on the origins of an adopted child became a cause for criminal prosecution and penalties.

Until recently, only a few countries allowed adopted persons to gain access to information about their origins. In England and Wales, the Children Act of 1975 gave all adopted persons over 18 years of age the right of access to their original birth records (Haimes and Timms, 1985; Smith and Logan, 2003). The Adoption and Children Act of 2002 expanded on this legislation by giving birth parents limited rights to seek information about their adopted birth children, subject to the consent of those involved. Similarly, New Zealand recognizes the right of adopted persons to have access to their original birth certificate. The right of birth parents to ask for information about their children is also acknowledged, although both adopted persons and birth parents can veto the transmission of information (Goldson, 2003; Griffith, 1997). Other countries that grant access to adoption records to adopted persons after they reach a certain age are Canada, Finland and Israel.

In Portugal, Decree Law No. 185/93 asserts that knowledge of the family of origin can be detrimental to the development of the adopted persons "in view of the feelings of ambivalence and problems of identity such knowledge can give rise to, and of the feelings of concern of the adoptive parents and the negative consequences thereof on the tranquillity of the new adoptive family."[44] Despite these reservations, adopted children in Portugal may access information on their origins once they reach age 18.

Limitations on the access of an adopted person to information on his or her origins remain in several countries. The United States, for instance, has a long tradition of sealed records, and even today a majority of states require "a court order for adopted persons to gain access to their original birth certificates. . . . In many states, [however,] the laws are changing to allow easier access to these records" (United States, Child Welfare Information Gateway, 2004a, p. 3). The introduction of safe havens, which "allow mothers in crisis to safely relinquish their babies" while remaining anonymous (United States, Child Welfare Information Gateway, 2004b, p.1), could make it more difficult for adopted persons to access such information (Appell, 2002a, 2002b, and 2002c). In

France, article 341-1 of the Civil Code protects the anonymity of birth mothers. A law introduced in January 2002, however, encourages mothers to leave information regarding their identity in a sealed envelope so that adopted persons interested in obtaining information on their origins may do so.[45]

E. SUMMARY

As this chapter has documented, the welfare of the child as the primary concern of adoption is a relatively recent development. Throughout most of history, adoption has mainly occurred for religious purposes or to serve the needs of the adoptive parents, including their need to preserve and transmit family lines or inheritance, to gain political power or to forge alliances between families. Before 1850, arrangements to promote the welfare of children deprived of parental care included placement in foundling homes and orphanages, informal adoptions and apprenticeships. As societies became more sensitive towards the developmental needs of children, legislation was enacted that strengthened children's rights to have a family. A movement to deinstitutionalize children resulted and Governments began to promote adoption or the placement of children in foster families as better strategies to provide children with the care they need.

Laws also began to reflect more systematically concern about the welfare of children within adoptive families. State laws adopted in the United States at the beginning of the twentieth century, for instance, increasingly emphasized the need to assess the character and means of the adoptive parents and to monitor the quality of the adoptive relationship. Adoption thus became a process and not just the execution of a contract between two consenting parties, the adoptive parent and the birth parent. Nowadays, authorities in many countries reserve the right to terminate birth parents' rights and to make decisions regarding placement settings, including with adoptive families, in order to safeguard the best interests of the child.

As the purpose of adoption has changed over time, so have adoption laws. New issues and concerns are likely, therefore, to lead to further changes in adoption practices, especially in areas concerning permanency planning, intercountry adoption, adoption by step-parents and other relatives, inter-racial adoption and the right to have access to information on the birth family.

NOTES

[1] Testamentary adoption was also practiced, although its popularity steadily declined under Justinian thanks to reforms in the system of testamentary succession (Bechtel, 1896).

[2] An agnate is a blood relative or descendant on the father's or male side only; a cognate is a blood relative or descendant on the mother's side as well as the father's. According to Maine (1861, chapter 5), a "cognatic relationship is simply the inception of kinship familiar to modern ideas; it is the relationship arising through common descent from the same pair of married persons, whether the descent be traced through males or females. Agnatic relationship is something very different: it excludes a number of persons whom we in our day should certainly consider of kin to ourselves, and it includes many more whom we should never reckon among our kindred."

[3] Garcia Marsilla (1999) contends that Hispanic medieval society had already developed other strategies for acquiring descendants and consequently adoption did not have the popularity that the kings had expected.

[4] To increase the number of adoptions, the Tsar introduced a legislative amendment in 1837 that allowed parents to adopt a son even if they already had male offspring of their own (Ransel, 1988). As a result, the number of adoptions rose to 10,000 over the period 1838 to 1860, equivalent to one in seven of the children who survived placement in the Moscow institution during this period.

[5] An orphanage is a residential institution designed to host orphans and other children deprived of parental care. A workhouse was an institution in which the destitute of a parish received board and lodging in return for work.

[6] Various child migration schemes from the United Kingdom continued until the late 1960s (Gill, 1997).

[7] The states of Mississippi and Texas passed adoption laws in 1846 and 1850, respectively, but while these statutes did establish some procedures for adoption, they were not as comprehensive as the Massachusetts law (Carp, 1998).

[8] Western Australia, Department for Community Development, "Models of out of home placement". Available from http://www.signposts.communitydevelopment.wa.gov.au/type/view.aspx?TypeID=3#_ftn4 (accessed 28 September 2007).

[9] Article 5 (2) of the act stated that "an adoption order shall not deprive the adoptive child of any right to or interest in the property for which, but for the order, the child would have been entitled to".

[10] Ireland, Adoption Act, No. 25, 13 December 1952. Available from http://www.adoptionboard.ie/legislation/index.php (accessed 30 October 2006).

[11] India, The Hindu Adoptions and Maintenance Act, No. 78 of 21 December 1956. Available from http://nrcw.nic.in/shared/sublinkImages/67.htm (accessed 30 October 2006).

[12] See United Nations, "Second periodic reports of States parties due in 2000: India" (CRC/C/93/Add.5).

[13] Germany, Civil Code, book I, part II, title VII. Available from http://bundesrecht.juris.de/bgb/index.html (accessed 12 February 2006).

[14] See United Nations, "Initial reports of States parties due in 1992: Brazil" (CRC/C/3/Add.65).

[15] See United Nations, "Initial reports of States parties due in 1997: Turkey" (CRC/C/51/Add.4).

[16] See United Nations, "Periodic reports of States parties due in 1997: Russian Federation" (CRC/C/65/Add.5).

[17] See United Nations, "Initial periodic report of States parties due in 1994. Albania" (CRC/C/11/Add.27).

[18] See United Nations, "Second periodic reports of States parties due in 1997: Togo" (CRC/C/65/Add.27).

[19] See United Nations, "Periodic reports of States parties due in 1998: Argentina" (CRC/C/70/Add.10).

[20] France, Civil Code, book I, title VIII, chapter II, section II. Available http://195.83.177.9/code/liste.phtml?lang=uk&c=22&r=321 (accessed 29 October 2006).

[21] See United Nations, "Periodic reports of States parties due in 1997: Bolivia" (CRC/C/65/Add.1).

[22] See United Nations, "Second periodic reports of States parties due in 1998: Rwanda" (CRC/C/70/Add.22).

[23] France, Civil Code, book I, title VIII, chapter I, section III. Available from http://195.83.177.9/code/liste.phtml?lang=uk&c=22&r=318 (accessed 30 October 2006).

[24] United States, Adoption and Safe Families Act, Public Law 105-89 of 19 November 1997. Available from http://www.acf.dhhs.gov/programs/cb/laws_policies/cblaws/public_law/pl105_89/pl105_89.htm (accessed 27 October 2006).

[25] See United Kingdom, "Adoption: a new approach. A white paper". London: Department of Health. Available from http://www.dh.gov.uk/assetRoot/04/08/05/12/04080512.pdf (accessed 30 October 2006).

[26] United Kingdom, Adoption and Children Act 2002 Elizabeth II. Chapter 38. Available from http://www.opsi.gov.uk/acts/acts2002/20020038.htm (accessed 30 October 2006).

[27] See United Nations, "Periodic reports of States parties due in 1998: Republic of Korea" (CRC/C/70/Add.14).

[28] United Nations, "Second periodic reports of States parties due in 1999: Latvia" (CRC/C/83/Add.16), para. 209.

[29] Hague Conference on Private International Law, *Collection of Conventions (1951-1996)*, pp. 356-377.

[30] Council of Europe, *European Treaty Series*, No. 058.

[31] Organization of American States, General Secretariat, *Treaty Series*, No. 62.

[32] Resolution A/RES/41/85.

[33] United Nations (1990). *Treaty Series*, vol. 1577, No. 27531, p. 3.

[34] See Overseas Korean Foundation, "Guide to Korea for overseas adopted Koreans". Available from http://oaks.korean.net/download/pdf/guide-1.pdf (accessed 12 May 2006).

[35] See United Nations, "Initial reports of States parties due in 1997: Singapore" (CRC/C/51/Add.8).

[36] See United Nations, "Periodic reports of States parties due in 1998: United Kingdom of Great Britain and Northern Ireland" (CRC/C/83/Add.3).

[37] Italy, Law No. 149 of 28 March 2001. Available from http://www.giustizia.it/cassazione/leggi/l149_01.html (accessed 30 October 2006).

[38] See United Nations, "Initial reports of States parties due in 1994: Thailand" (CRC/C/11/Add.13).

[39] China, Adoption Law of the People's Republic of China of 29 December 1991, revised at the 5th Meeting of the Standing Committee of the 9th National People's Congress on 4 November 1998 and promulgated by Order No. 10 of the President of the People's Republic of China. Available from http://english.gov.cn/2005-08/31/content_26770.htm (accessed 12 May 2006).

[40] See United Nations, "Second periodic reports of States parties due in 1997: El Salvador" (CRC/C/65/Add.25).

[41] See Western Australia, Department for Community Development, "Policy for the adoption of children". Available from http://www.aph.gov.au/house/committee/fhs/adoption/subs/sub183attch1.pdf (accessed 30 October 2006).

[42] Switzerland, Civil Code, book II, part II, title VII, chapter IV, art. 264a. Available from http://www.admin.ch/ch/f/rs/210/a264a.html (accessed 12 February 2006).

[43] In the United States, inter-racial adoptions were relatively uncommon prior to the Second World War (Simon and Altstein, 2002). During the 1960s, however, they became more widespread, in part due to the growing number of adoptions involving children from abroad (Bartholet, 1991).

[44] United Nations, "Periodic reports due in 1997: Portugal" (CRC/C/65/Add.11), para. 196.

[45] France, Law No. 2002-93 of 22 January 2002. Available from http://www.legifrance.gouv.fr/WAspad/UnTexteDeJorf?numjo=MESX0205318L (accessed 29 October 2006).

II. ADOPTION IN RELIGIOUS LAW AND IN TRADITIONAL SOCIETIES

Chapter I has discussed how western jurisprudence has profoundly influenced adoption laws in many parts of the world. This chapter focuses on other traditions that have also shaped adoption practices and procedures, including religion and religious law. In countries that follow Islamic law, for instance, domestic or intercountry adoption is generally not allowed because the Koran, while explicitly acknowledging the importance of caring for orphaned children and encouraging guardianship and fostering, does not recognize the formal institution of adoption (Pollack and others, 2004). Confucianism and Hinduism, by emphasizing blood ties and inheritance passed through the male line have contributed to perpetuate customary adoptions, sometimes at the expense of other forms of adoption. These examples illustrate the relevance of religion for an understanding of adoption practices in the contemporary world.

Anthropologists have found that *de facto* adoption and fostering have played a central role in ensuring care for children in many traditional societies. Such practices have been followed for a variety of reasons, including expanding a child's social network, strengthening family ties and caring for children deprived of their birth parents by illness or death. Given the centrality of the community in the socialization of children, *de facto* adoption and fostering continue to be considered preferable to formal adoption in many traditional societies (Bowie, 2004). The openness and flexibility of such practices contrasts with modern adoption procedures in western culture, where secrecy and finality often characterize adoption laws, especially those enacted after 1950.

This chapter reviews the positions outlined in religious law with regard to the practice of adoption and then discusses *de facto* adoption and fostering in traditional societies. This review provides a sense of the complexity and richness of the topic and suggests some of the challenges faced in studying the practice of adoption globally given the different norms and practices prevalent in different countries. The review presented below is not comprehensive and does not fully reflect the diversity of views characterizing the various approaches to adoption.

A. ADOPTION AND RELIGIOUS LAW

1. Catholic Canon law[1]

As indicated in chapter I, the Catholic Church played a crucial role in preserving the institution of adoption as outlined in Roman law.[2] During the late Middle Ages and the early Modern Era, canonists elaborated on earlier legal concepts, laying the foundations for some of the features of modern legislation, including the termination of the birth parents' rights in the case of abandonment (Pollack and others, 2004). Since the eighteenth century, canon law has recognized that "most questions concerning the administration of adoption law should have as their starting point the civil law" (Pollack and others, 2004, p. 723). Two centuries later, the 1983 Code of Canon Law endorsed this view: "Children who have been adopted according to the norm of civil law are considered the children of the person or persons who have adopted them" (canon 110).[3]

The Code of Canon Law contains two other canons that deal with adoption. Canon 877 establishes that generally the names of both adoptive and birth parents should be entered into the baptismal register. Special regulations may, however, be issued to take into account concerns related to privacy and confidentiality. Canon 1094 prohibits marriage between the adopted person and those who have become related through adoption. Marriage to adoptive relatives in the direct line (that is, adoptive parents or grandparents) or up to the second degree in the collateral line (that is, adoptive siblings or cousins) is not permitted.[4] For the purpose of marriage, adoption does not sever the blood ties between the adopted person and his or her family of origin (Gibbons, 2004).

Canon law does not establish explicit requirements for prospective adoptive parents and children since it defers to the appropriate civil laws (Gibbons, 2004).[5] The Church, however, emphasizes the importance of ensuring that adoptions takes place in the best interests of the child and calls for adoption to be granted to "married couples who give real guarantees of stability, moral solidity, ability to accompany and exemplarity".[6] Many predominantly Catholic countries require prospective adoptive parents to be married (see chapter III).

In recent years, Catholic attitudes towards adoption have been influenced by the Church's "commitment to protecting innocent human life, especially against the evil of abortion" (Pollack and others, 2004, p. 722). The Church sees adoption as a natural remedy for infertility and highly preferable to the use of reproductive biotechnologies. The adoption of children whose birth families are unable to care for them is also considered part of the mission of a Christian family (Cahill, 2005, p. 148).

2. Confucian law

A number of authors have argued that Confucianism, with its emphasis on the importance of blood ties, has influenced attitudes and practices regarding adoption in several countries. In Korea during the early Chosŏn period (circa 1392-1598), for instance, women could be adopted and could inherit property (Peterson, 1996). However, with the onset of neo-Confucian family rites, agnatic adoption (a son adopted through the father's side) became the norm. Only an agnatic adopted son was entitled to become the heir for ritualistic purposes and could carry the family name. Agnatic adoption in Korean society was mainly practised for the purpose of ancestor worship (Roesch-Rhomberg, 2004), and adoption generally involved a younger brother giving one of his sons—preferably the oldest one—to an elder brother or an older brother giving one of his younger male offspring to a younger brother. Adoptions of sons-in-law and posthumous adoptions were also relatively common.

Historical sources indicate that adoption and, especially the adoption of related adult males, was also widespread in China and Japan.[7] As in other Confucian societies, adoption was primarily used as a means for childless couples to preserve family lineage, pass on inheritance and ensure the performance of the rituals of ancestor worship. The two countries, however, differed somewhat in the procedures used to regulate adoption. In China a more orthodox interpretation of Confucian legal

doctrine was applied and, consequently, penal codes during the Ming and Ch'ing dynasties (1368-1644 and 1644-1911) permitted adoption only within blood lines, preferably among agnates (Junjian, 1999; MacCormack, 1996).[8]

In Japan, because society placed more emphasis on the household (*ie*) than on blood ties, non-agnatic adoption was permitted (Goodman, 2000). Adoptions of adults, preferably with the same clan name (*honsei*), were widely practised during the Tokugawa period (circa 1603–1867) by members of the aristocracy and the warrior class (*samurai*) (Barr, 2002; Bryant, 1990; Goodman, 2000; Nakamura, 1964). Japanese Confucian scholars generally sanctioned such adoptions, although some attempted to prohibit non-agnatic adoption contending that it was detrimental to human relationships and the administration of the State (McMullen, 1975).[9]

Today, Confucian customs continue to influence adoption practices in a number of countries. In the Republic of Korea, for example, the emphasis placed by Confucianism on biological ties is believed to have hindered the contemporary development of domestic adoption, despite the fact that many traditional Confucian practices, including posthumous adoption and the adoption of sons-in-law were repealed after the amendments made to the Civil Code in 1990 (Roesch-Rhomberg, 2004). Johnson notes that, despite the Government's efforts, "the continuing grip of Confucianism, with its heavy emphasis on maintaining bloodlines, along with a strong preference for sons, has made it very difficult to promote domestic adoption in [the Republic of] Korea as a substitute for intercountry adoption" (2002, p. 380).

Similarly, in China and Japan, adoptions of sons-in-law or unrelated adults still occur in the context of agreements on inheritance and care for the elderly (Palmer, 1989; Goodman, 2000). As of the late 1980s, two-thirds of formal adoptions in Japan involved adults and the vast majority of persons adopted as minors were related to their adoptive parents (Bryant, 1990).

In recent years, some of the countries where customary adoption practices have been shaped by

Confucianism have enacted laws that focus on the best interests of the adopted child rather than on the preservation of the family or the household's lineage. In China, for example, the Adoption Law of 1991[10] specifies that adoption is permitted, irrespective of the relationship between the child and the perspective adoptive parent and that orphans, abandoned children and children whose parents are unable to rear them may be adopted (art. 4). Nevertheless, article 7 of the Act establishes that some restrictions on the prospective adoptive parents (minimum age, for instance) do not apply in the case of the "adoption of a child of a collateral relative by blood of the same generation and up to the third degree of kinship".[11]

In Japan, the practice of special adoption (*tokubetsu yōshi*) was introduced in 1988 to protect the interests of the child, especially in cases where the birth parents are considered unfit (Goodman, 1998). Special adoptions are limited to children under six years of age and have the effect of terminating the ties between the adopted child and his or her birth parents and relatives.[12] Some authors have noted that, since the introduction of special adoption, the total number of adoptions in Japan has declined markedly. Part of this decline has been attributed to improvements in the social security system, changes that have made the elderly less reliant on care provided by their children (Goodman, 2000). The stigma associated with the presumed illegitimacy of unrelated adoptive children and the fact that the system of family registration (*koseki*) makes anonymous adoption nearly impossible have been cited as other possible factors keeping the number of adoptions in Japan low.

3. Hindu law

Child adoption has been a common social practice in Hinduism since ancient times (Adamec and Pierce, 2002; Huard, 1956). As in other ancient societies (Huard, 1956), religious concerns, notably the continuation of the family lineage and ancestor worship, were fundamental motivations for adoption. According to the *Manu-smrti*, an authoritative book of Hindu code, which dates in its present form from the first century B.C., "he to whom nature has denied a son can adopt one, so that the funeral ceremonies may not cease" (Fustel

de Coulanges, 1901, p. 68). Other parental needs— namely, the perpetuation of the family name and lineage as well as care in old age—were also important motivations for adoption (Mehta, 2002). For these reasons, adoption under traditional Hindu laws was confined to sons who could, once adopted, become full legal heirs (Rwezaura and Wanitzek, 1988).

Hindu law recognized 12 different kinds of fictive sonship or filiation, the highest of which involved the adoption of a male grandchild by a man with no sons (*putrika putra*) (Mayne, 1892). In order for the adoption to be legally recognized, it had to be accompanied by a religious ritual called *datta homam* (Rocher, 1987). Given the importance placed on the perpetuation of lineage, adopted sons had the same privileges and obligations in their new family as birth sons but retained a minimal link to their birth family that extended to limitations regarding inter-marriage with blood relatives (Goody, 1969).

Hindu law also stipulated various requirements for adoptive parents and children to meet. The adoptive father was required to have no male offspring and had to belong to the same caste as the adopted person. The adopted child was required to receive the consent of a kinsman and to have male siblings to ensure the continuation of his own line of descent (Goody, 1969). It was also considered preferable for the adopted child to be a close relative of the adoptive parent. The adoption of orphaned children and females was not permitted (Diwan, 2000).

In India, traditional Hindu laws regulating adoption have been superseded by the Hindu Adoptions and Maintenance Act, which came into force in 1956 (Lilani, 1995). This Act requires adopted persons to be under 15 years of age at the time of adoption unless special circumstances apply (art. 10 (iv)).[13] Furthermore, orphaned children, both male and female, can be adopted outside of their family or caste group (Bhargava, 2005).

In other countries, customary Hindu practices have been incorporated into civil adoption law. In Nepal, for example, the Civil Code of 1963 (*Muluki Ain*) favours adoptions by close blood relatives or persons belonging to the same clan. Adoption is primarily viewed as an agreement involving inheritance or care for adoptive parents since an adoption can be revoked if the adopted person does not provide "food and clothing to the adoptive parents befitting their status, squanders the family cash and property . . . or misbehaves".[14] In Myanmar,[15] adoption is regulated by the Registration of Kittima Adoption Act of 1941. According to this act, adoption consists in a contractual agreement between two parties "sought for the express purpose of inheritance". The adoption of adults is permitted upon their consent.[16]

4. Islamic law (Sharia)

The custom of adopting children, especially sons, was common in pre-Islamic Arabia, but with the founding of Islam and the development of *Sharia* law, adoption as a legal institution was abolished (Boswell, 1988). A social obligation (*fard kifâya*) "to rescue abandoned children" remained (Pollack and others, 2004, p. 738), but the rescuer was not legally obliged to support the foundling from his own funds.

In the fifth verse of the thirty-third *Surah*, the Koran explicitly states that adopted sons shall be named after their birth father, not their adoptive father. That verse has been interpreted as prohibiting the conferment of inheritance rights and legitimacy to adopted persons. The prohibition results from two principles: first, that "a male adulterer has no rights on a child born of an illicit relationship," and second, that "a stranger . . . cannot, by mere social convention, accede to the legal rights and responsibilities of the child's legal father" (Pollack and others, 2004 p. 735). For this reason, countries that follow Islamic law do not recognize the institution of adoption. Among the 195 countries considered in this study, 20, all predominantly Muslim, do not recognize the institution of adoption (box II.1). Six of the 20 countries are in Africa and 14 in Asia, mostly in Western Asia. Nevertheless, some predominantly Muslim countries, such as Indonesia, Tunisia and Turkey, allow the practice of adoption.

Given the importance accorded in the Koran to blood and kinship ties, the preference is for orphaned or abandoned children to be placed with relatives. Many countries that follow Islamic law allow *kafalah* (from the Arabic *kafl*: to take care of) for children who have been declared abandoned by a judge. *Kafalah* does not give inheritance rights to the adopted person

---

BOX II.1. COUNTRIES THAT DO NOT RECOGNIZE THE INSTITUTION OF ADOPTION

Africa:
- Algeria
- Djibouti
- Egypt
- Libyan Arab Jamahiriya
- Mauritania
- Morocco

Asia:
- Afghanistan
- Bahrain
- Iran, Islamic Republic of
- Iraq
- Jordan
- Kuwait
- Maldives
- Oman
- Pakistan
- Qatar
- Saudi Arabia
- Syrian Arab Republic
- United Arab Emirates
- Yemen

Source: For a complete list of country references, see annex II.

(Bargach, 2002; Van Bueren, 1995a and 1995b) and in many cases, only Muslim couples who have been married for more than three years are allowed to practise *kafalah*. Children benefiting from *kafalah* preserve the name of their birth father. Although they are not automatically given rights of inheritance from the person who sponsors them, they may be appointed as legatees and inherit through a bequest.

Many of the countries that do not recognize the institution of adoption have developed laws outlining alternative strategies and procedures to meet the needs of children deprived of parental care. In Bahrain, for instance, the Cabinet has recently approved the Fosterage Act, which regulates the procedures needed to safeguard the rights of children in foster families and specifies their respective rights and obligations.[17] In the Syrian Arab Republic, Legislative Decree No. 107 of 4 May 1970 regulates the protection of the welfare of foundlings and the management of any property they owned as well as their placement with a family under the system of *kafalah*. The Act gives the Minister for Social Affairs and Labour the authority of placing such children. Placement has to be in the foundling's best interest and the caregivers, who can be either married couples or single women, must be able to provide for the care, upbringing, protection, education and maintenance of their charges.[18]

Because of the restrictions on adoption under Islam, some countries apply different laws depending on the religious affiliation of the child or parent. In Brunei Darussalam, for example, the Islamic Adoption of Children Order of 2001 regulates the care of Muslim children.[19] Under this law, children's rights to inherit from their natural parents are not prejudiced and the caregiver under *kafalah* may grant at most one-third of his property to his charge. Adoptions of non-Muslims by non-Muslims are governed by the Adoption of Children Order of 2001. In the Sudan, Muslim children deprived of a family environment can be cared for under *kafalah*, while non-Muslim children can be adopted in accordance to the Child Welfare Act of 1971.[20] A similar provision exists in the United Republic of Tanzania (Rwezaura and Wanitzek, 1988).

5. *Jewish law (Halacha)*

Despite a strong ethical mandate regarding the care of orphans, "adoption as a formal legal institution does not exist in Jewish law" (Pollack and others, 2004, p. 696). Jewish law does, however, encourage guardianship of orphaned children as an act of goodness and "as a social reality, adoption always existed in Jewish societies" (Pollack and others, 2004, p. 696). It is in this sense that adoption is discussed below.

In both the Bible and the Talmud there are numerous examples of individuals who take care of orphaned children. The most quoted instance is that of Michal, the wife of King David, who reared her sister's five children. According to the Talmud, "This teaches that whoever brings up an orphan in his home is regarded, according to Scripture, as though the child had been born to him" (Gold, 1994, p. 174).

Some authors have noted that adoption offers infertile Jewish couples a positive way of fulfilling the commandment (*mitzvah*) to "be fruitful and multiply" (Gold, 1994, p. 173). However, given the strong emphasis placed in Judaism on bloodlines, lineage and the obligation to procreate, formal adoption raises several halachic concerns (Broyde, 2005; Jaffe, 1991). One of these relates to marriage. Jewish law requires the adopted person to avoid inadvertently entering into an incestuous relationship with a biological sibling. A second concern stems from the prohibition under traditional Jewish law for males and females— other than spouses, mothers and sons, or fathers and daughters—to hug or kiss one another. A third issue relates to the conversion of non-Jewish children adopted by a Jewish family. Because children retain the right to renounce their conversion upon reaching the age of maturity (13 years for boys and 12 years for girls), a number of Talmudic experts have stressed the importance of informing adopted persons of their adoptive status (Pollack and others, 2004).

Countries have chosen different approaches to deal with halachic restrictions on adoption. In Israel, for example, adoption has been recognized as a legal institution since the 1960s. Prior to that time, there were no general procedures regulating adoption although adoptions did take place and were in some cases heard by rabbinical courts (Karayanni, 2005). Adoptions in Israel are currently governed by the 1981 Adoption of Children Law. According to that law, adoption creates ties between the adoptive parent and child equivalent to those of natural filiation. The law also requires the prospective adoptive parent to be of the same religion as the child (section 5).[21]

In India, halachic concerns among Jews are addressed through the Indian Guardians and Wards Act of 1890.[22] According to this act, adoptive parents become "the permanent, legal guardians of the child they adopt" although the "laws of inheritance, rights, and privileges are governed by the personal laws and customs of individual ethnic or religious groups" (Lilani, 1995, p. 25).

B. DE FACTO ADOPTION AND FOSTERING IN TRADITIONAL SOCIETIES

While adoption is now largely viewed as a "legal procedure through which a permanent family is created for a child whose birth parents are unable, unwilling or legally prohibited from caring for a child" (Triseliotis and others, 1997, p. 1), *de facto* adoptions—meaning the practice of caring for a child either temporarily or permanently without a legally recognized contract—have long been practised in many traditional societies. Cross-cultural studies of *de facto* adoptions reveal a wide variation in the nature of such arrangements and the social functions they perform (Selman, 2004). Unlike formal adoptions, many of these practices involve individuals who are not abandoned and who are sometimes adults. The ties between the birth parents and the child are usually maintained and informal adoptive practices in some societies are a means of strengthening the bond between different communities and clans. *De facto* adoptions also tend to place little emphasis on replicating the relationship of natural parenthood or do not entail the secrecy that often surrounds adoption in contemporary western cultures.

1. De facto adoption and fostering in Africa

De facto adoptions have been a common practice among various populations of sub-Saharan Africa. The Gallas and the Amharas of Ethiopia,

for instance, traditionally practised a form of adoption that required the consent of the child's parents or relatives and was sanctioned by a ritual ceremony. Only a person who had reached adulthood could become an adoptive parent, and adopted persons could not inherit from their birth families (Bekstorm, 1972). Other features of this practice, such as the acquisition of the adoptive parents' name and the right to succession from adoptive parents, were similar to those associated with formal adoption. The Kuria people of the United Republic of Tanzania also practised a form of informal adoption, whereby a wife who failed to have a male child in a later marriage was permitted to adopt one of her sons from a previous marriage (Rwezaura and Wanitzek, 1988). Similarly, among the Yakö of Nigeria, maternal relatives could adopt children after the divorce of the mother (Forde, 1939 and 1950), while among the Kikuyu in Kenya, clan members had the option of adopting an orphaned child or the child of an adulterous relationship who would otherwise have been put to death (Simmance, 1959).

Among East African pastoral peoples, it is still quite common for "infertile or childless women to adopt children from co-wives, sisters, sisters-in-law or other close female relatives" (Talle, 2004, p. 64). One of the prime motivations for such arrangements is to provide old-age support to childless couples. Among the pastoral Masai, for example, a childless household is viewed as a potential site of disorder that may endanger the prosperity of the community. Although adoption cannot remove the "sadness of the barren woman" (Talle, 2004, p. 76), it can bring order by ensuring that she has a child to nurture and that child is considered as hers.

In sub-Saharan Africa, child fostering is also a widespread and socially accepted practice. Parents send their children to live with another family—frequently that of a close relative, such as a maternal grandmother or a sibling—or take in children from another family. Goody (1973) observed that, unlike formal adoption, fostering by kin involves no permanent forfeiting of rights and duties, no change in the kinship terms used and no permanent change of status. Alber (2004) notes that among the Baatombu in Northern Benin, fostering is the norm and foster parents are often viewed as the real parents. Informal fostering is also common in Ghana (Goody, 1982) and Cameroon (Notermans, 2004). A recent study in Burkina Faso indicates that over one quarter of households had either sent or received a child between 1998 and 2000, and 10 per cent of children with ages ranging from 5 to 15 years had lived separated from their birth families for an average of two to three years (Akresh, 2004). During the late 1980s, an estimated 20 per cent to 40 per cent of children in Botswana, Ghana, Liberia and Western Nigeria were living with relatives (Hegar and Scannapieco, 1999).

There is evidence that traditional adoption and fostering practices are still widely preferred over formal adoption in some countries. In Madagascar, for instance, families frequently favour the informal system of godparents over other forms of adoption. By becoming a godparent, a family member with no dependents (usually an elder or a guarantor) may raise a young relative whose ties with his or her family of origin are maintained.[23] Formal adoptions are also uncommon in Liberia, where children are frequently entrusted to relatives or friends and are returned to their birth parents when either the birth parents or the child request so.[24]

African migrants living abroad have maintained the tradition of fostering and *de facto* adoption (Holman, 1973). The issue of placement with relatives, for instance, was recently raised by an inquiry into the death of a child from Côte d'Ivoire brought to England and entrusted to the care of a great aunt (Laming, 2003). This case has been cited as an illustration of the problems of cross-border kinship care, which typically involves "sending a child from a developing or a transition country to stay with relatives residing in an industrialised country" (ISS and UNICEF, 2004a, p. 6). Countries where the practice of intercountry fostering is common include Côte d'Ivoire, Ghana, Liberia, Nigeria and Sierra Leone.

In several countries of sub-Saharan Africa, the AIDS epidemic has killed many men and women in the prime of their lives and has led to a sharp decline in life expectancy (United Nations, 2005). Consequently, a large number of children have become orphans. In 2003, there were an estimated 8 million orphans in sub-Saharan Africa both of whose parents had died (UNAIDS, UNICEF and USAID, 2004). This situation has gravely strained the customary support system offered to children through extended family networks. It is estimated that, in countries such as Namibia, grandparents are caring for over half of all children orphaned by AIDS (UNICEF, 2003a).

The growing number of AIDS orphans is imposing a heavy burden on the ability of Governments to respond to the needs of these children (ISS and UNICEF, 2004b). As a result, alternative care arrangements are being explored in a number of countries (Subbarao and Coury, 2004). In South Africa, the Department of Welfare has proposed strategies to encourage foster care and adoption of AIDS orphans within the broader family and community.[25] Experts are studying the feasibility of promoting adoption for Ethiopian children orphaned because of AIDS (Varnis, 2001). So far, suggestions to promote intercountry adoption of AIDS orphans have generally come to nought. Restrictive practices and regulations regarding the adoption of HIV-positive children from abroad are common in receiving countries and constitute a major obstacle to such initiatives (Greene, 2002; Wooldridge, 2005).

2. *De facto adoption and fostering in the Americas*

Accounts of *de facto* adoption and fostering are also found in several traditional societies in the Americas. According to Silk (1987), for instance, informal adoptions were widespread among the indigenous peoples of the North American Artic regions and, in particular, the Inuit. Under these arrangements, birth parents often played an active role in the lives of their children and retained the right to reclaim them if they believed that their children were being mistreated by the adoptive parents.

Dunning (1962) studied the extent of *de facto* adoptions among Eskimo populations, finding that families with no offspring were more likely to adopt, while large families were more likely to give up their children for adoption. As in other populations, adoption among the Eskimo was primarily undertaken as a means of providing assistance to adoptive parents in their old age, to perform ritual ceremonies and to balance the sex ratio among offspring.

The Yukpa and other Carib-speaking indigenous populations of South America also developed a spectrum of parental concepts whereby the transfer of rights from the birth family to the adoptive family was a bi-directional process rather than a formal act of renunciation (Halbmayer, 2004).

3. De facto adoption and fostering in Oceania

De facto adoptions and fostering have been a common practice among the traditional populations of Oceania (Silk, 1980). Anthropological studies in Papua New Guinea indicate that children are often raised by persons, usually relatives, other than their biological parents during at least part of their childhood (Anderson, 2004; Demian, 2004). Such practices are so common that in some villages as many as half of the inhabitants are adopted (Anderson, 2004). Similarly, in New Zealand, the roots of adoption trace back to the Maori tradition of sharing the rearing of children among members of the wider family (Love, 2000). Customarily, such adoptions were not a means of disposing of unwanted children but were rather considered as a gift from the birth parents. Adopted children were often cared for in more than one home and had access to their birth family as they were growing up (Rockell and Ryburn, 1988).

As in other regions, informal adoptions in Oceania often assume multiple forms. In Hawaii,[26] for example, *de facto* adoption practices involved a wide range of arrangements, including cases where the adopted child became the adoptive parents' own child and lived with them and cases where adoptive parents did no more than provide food for the adopted child (Brosnan, 1922). Adoption was customarily transacted via an oral agreement and, unless explicitly stated, informally adopted children did not have the right to inherit from their adoptive parents.[27]

The inhabitants of Pingelap in Micronesia also practised various forms of adoption, distinguishing between adoption by grandparents, adoption by step-parents and adoption in general. Adoption among the inhabitants of Pingelap generally involved a change of residence, land transferral and the change of patrilineal affiliation (Damas, 1983).

The motivations for adoption also differ considerably among the peoples of Oceania (Benet, 1976; Brady, 1976; Carroll, 1970). Howard and Kirkpatrick (1989), for instance, noted that in Oceania, informal adoption often functioned as a mechanism to strengthen the relationships between families within the community and to create alliances among communities. Adopted children could help a family with domestic work and later become important economic contributors to the household. Adoption was also a powerful mechanism to achieve a more equitable distribution of resources, including land, without involving necessarily the termination of contact between the adopted person and his or her birth family.

In recent years, differences between such traditional practices and western-style adoption laws have caused some painful cultural misunderstandings. A study by Roby and Matsumura (2002), for instance, describes how women from the Marshall Islands in Micronesia allowed their children to be adopted by United States citizens under the belief that, having benefited from a better education in the United States, they would be returned to them as adults. Confronted with the irrevocability of those adoptions according to United States law and amid widespread reports of irregularities, the Parliament of the Marshall Islands imposed a moratorium from September 1999 to December 2000 on all international adoptions.[28]

While in many settings traditions allowing *de facto* adoptions are being eroded and substituted by formalized modern adoption laws, some countries are attempting to reconcile traditional practices with formal adoption and guardianship. In New Zealand, for instance, policy-makers have been exploring the legal recognition of Maori alternatives to adoption, such as additional guardianship (New Zealand, Law Commission, 1999 and 2000). Customary adoption and fostering have also contributed to a debate on open adoption—a practice that involves maintaining links between members of the birth family and the adopted child (Griffith, 1997;

Mullender, 1991). In Polynesia, the Government of Samoa, noting that intercountry adoptions were removing Samoan children from their "genealogical heritage and birthright in respect of their entitlement to customary lands and chiefly titles," imposed restrictions on adoptions by foreigners.[29] Adoptions by members of the child's extended family living abroad, however, have not been limited, since this practice provides greater opportunities for children without breaking their ties to the community of origin.

C. SUMMARY

In the past, religion played a crucial role in shaping adoption practices because of the emphasis it placed on ancestor worship, inheritance and the continuation of family lines. More recently, the importance accorded by some religions to blood ties has meant that alternative strategies to adoption are common in certain societies. Rules regarding who is adoptable and who can adopt, as well as guidelines for marriage, are also part of religious practices or laws. Many of these rules and guidelines are reflected in civil adoption laws.

Informal or *de facto* adoption and fostering are widespread in many traditional societies and the goals of such practices are diverse. Prominent among them are the goal of providing assistance and care for childless people in old age and the establishment of stronger ties between different groups and clans. *De facto* adoptions usually do not terminate the relationship between adopted children and their birth parents. Recently, mainly because of increasing numbers of intercountry adoptions, the inconsistencies between traditional practices and the tenets of formalized adoption law have gained prominence in certain contexts.

In sub-Saharan Africa, traditional care mechanisms are being pushed to the limit by the AIDS epidemic. The high mortality of young adults associated with the disease is undermining customary support networks provided by families and clans. The large number of orphans who have lost both parents is forcing the Governments of the most affected countries to find alternative strategies to provide adequate care for the AIDS orphans.

While traditional *de facto* adoption practices are being eroded in many contexts, in some countries they are being incorporated into formal adoption laws. The movement towards open adoption, which is being considered as a possible new standard in some countries, also draws on these traditions.

NOTES

[1] The Protestant and Orthodox Churches also support adoption as a solution for the care of children deprived of a family, and have traditionally promoted the placement of orphaned and abandoned children into adoptive families. In this chapter, however, these positions and views are not discussed.

[2] Some authors have argued that, with the establishment of Christianity, formal adoptions declined. This argument is based on the fact that Christians did not emphasize the worship of deceased ancestors, thereby removing what had previously been one of the prime motivations for adoption (Verdon, 1988).

[3] Code of Canon Law, book I, title VI, chapter I. Available from http://www.vatican.va/archive/ENG1104/__PC.HTM (accessed 1 October 2007).

[4] Code of Canon Law, book IV, part I, title VII, chapter III. Available from http://www.vatican.va/archive/ENG1104/__P3Y.HTM (accessed 1 October 2007).

[5] McIntyre (2000) has argued that by mentioning "person or persons", canon 110 leaves open the possibility for adoption by single individuals.

[6] López Trujillo, "Intervention made at the Special Session of the United Nations on Children on 9 May 2002". Available from http://www.vatican.va/roman_curia/secretariat_state/documents/rc_seg-st_doc_20020509_trujillo-onu_en.html (accessed 30 October 2006).

[7] In Japan, customary adoption practices were influenced by Confucian law as well as Buddhist and Taoist doctrines.

[8] There is nonetheless evidence that other types of adoption besides agnatic adoption did take place. Specifically, a traditional form of adoption (*minglingzi*) was widespread (Waltner, 1990). This practice, which emphasized the importance of likeness in the parent-child relationship and denied the impact of biological heredity, competed with the Confucian-based ideology and legal codes that limited adoption to blood relatives (Johnson, 2002). Another traditional practice that was widespread, *tongyangxi*, involved a couple "adopting" a female child who would eventually become the wife of their son (Johnson, 2002).

[9] According to McMullen (1975) the opposition by some orthodox Confucian scholars to non-agnatic adoption contributed to the development in Japan of *Kokugaku*, an anti-Confucian school of thought.

[10] See United Nations, "Initial reports of States parties due in 1994: China" (CRC/C/11/Add.7).

[11] China, Adoption Law of the People's Republic of China of 29 December 1991, revised at the 5th Meeting of the Standing Committee of the 9th National People's Congress on 4 November 1998 and promulgated by Order No. 10 of the President of the People's Republic of China. Available from http://english.gov.cn/2005-08/31/content_26770.htm (accessed 12 May 2006).

[12] See United Nations, "Second periodic reports of States parties due in 2001: Japan" (CRC/C/104/Add.2).

[13] India, The Hindu Adoptions and Maintenance Act, No. 78 of 21 December 1956. Available from http://nrcw.nic.in/shared/sublink images/67.htm (accessed 30 October 2006).

[14] United Nations, Initial reports of States parties due in 1992: Nepal" (CRC/C/3/Add.34), para. 194.

[15] In Myanmar, customary adoption practices were influenced by Hindu law (Buxbaum, 1968) as well as Buddhist doctrines.

[16] See United Nations, "Second periodic reports of States parties due in 1998: Myanmar" (CRC/C/70/Add.21).

[17] See United Nations, "Initial reports of States parties due in 1994: Bahrain" (CRC/C/11/Add.24).

[18] See United Nations, "Periodic reports of States parties due in 2000: Syrian Arab Republic" (CRC/C/93/Add.2).

[19] See United Nations, "Initial reports of States parties due in 1998: Brunei Darussalam" (CRC/C/61/Add.5).

[20] See United Nations, "Periodic reports of States parties due in 1997: Sudan" (CRC/C/65/Add.17).

[21] United Nations, "Periodic reports of States parties due in 1993: Israel" (CRC/C/8/Add.44), para. 558.

[22] See United Nations, "Second periodic reports of States parties due in 2000: India" (CRC/C/93/Add.5).

[23] See United Nations, "Second periodic reports of States parties due in 1998: Madagascar" (CRC/C/70/Add.18.).

[24] See United Nations, "Initial reports of States parties due in 1995: Liberia" (CRC/C/28/Add.21).

[25] See United Nations, "Initial reports of States parties due in 1997: South Africa" (CRC/C/51/Add.2).

[26] Hawaii is the one of the 50 states of the United States of America. However, geographically and historically, Hawaii is part of Polynesia. According to the geographical classification of the United Nations, Polynesia is a sub-region of Oceania. Consequently, the informal adoption practices of Hawaii are presented in the section on Oceania.

[27] While formal adoption legislation has widely eroded customary Hawaiian practices, children are still entrusted to grandparents, other relatives, or friends on an informal basis (Ito, 1999).

[28] See United Nations, "Second periodic reports of States parties due in 2000: Marshall Islands" (CRC/C/93/Add.8).

[29] United Nations, "Initial report of States parties: Samoa" (CRC/C/WSM/1), para. 159.

III. KEY FEATURES OF MODERN ADOPTION LAWS

Adoption laws have been evolving to meet the needs of their times. In recent years, pressure from would-be adoptive parents and public opinion has led to substantial changes in the procedures, requirements and effects of adoption laws. Consequently, the requirements that prospective adoptive parents have to meet have become less stringent in many contexts. As a result, countries have amended their laws to allow adoption by persons who are single and have eased their requirements for the age at which a person is eligible to adopt. The legal stipulations regarding the consent of birth parents have also become more lenient and some countries now permit competent authorities to dispense with parental consent when it is in the best interests of the child. The principles guiding adoption have also changed. As indicated in the United Nations Convention on the Rights of the Child,[1] safeguarding the best interests of the child has become the paramount consideration in all decisions relating to adoption (art. 21). Most countries have incorporated this principle into their adoption laws.

While many countries have amended their adoption laws, not all national statutory provisions and procedures affecting adoption have moved in the same direction. Despite attempts at standardization, adoption laws in different countries continue to reflect the specific historical processes that produced them as well as differences in societal norms. This chapter documents variations in adoption laws by focusing on three aspects: legal procedures regarding adoption, the requirements that prospective adoptive parents have to meet in order to adopt and those that persons have to fulfil in order to be declared adoptable, and the legal effects of adoption on the rights of the adopted person. This review draws extensively on the reports submitted to the Committee on the Rights of the Child[2] by States parties to the 1989 United Nations Convention on the Rights of the Child.

A. LEGAL PROCEDURES

Adoption procedures are complex and vary greatly among countries. In some countries, adoption is granted by a court order, while in others it is decided by an administrative authority. Adoptions may also be effected by a deed or exchange of consent between the parties concerned, which, in turn, may be ratified by a court order or by a competent authority. In some cases, countries that recognize multiple forms of adoption may apply different legal procedures for each form. Full adoption in Uruguay, for instance, is granted by the courts, while simple adoption is effected by a notarized deed accepted by the adopted person or his or her legal representatives.[3] In Madagascar, full adoption is granted by a competent court, while simple adoption is made by a declaration in front of a registrar.[4]

1. Adoption application

Most adoption procedures start with the prospective adoptive parents applying or petitioning for an adoption. This application may be lodged by an individual alone or by two persons jointly. Depending on the laws of the country, prospective adoptive parents may apply directly to the competent court or administrative authority or may avail themselves of an adoption agency, which may be private or State-run. In many countries, the suitability of prospective adoptive parents is vetted at this stage of the adoption process (see section III.B).

2. Declaration of adoptability

The second phase of the adoption procedure usually consists in identifying an adoptable child. One of the most common requirements for declaring a child adoptable is to obtain the consent of his or her birth parents or guardians. Almost all countries have statutory provisions regarding consent to the adoption by the birth parents or other guardians, especially when the adoption involves a minor. This is consistent with article 21 (a) of the United Nations Convention on the Rights of the Child, which states that, where appropriate, the persons concerned should give their informed consent to the adoption. In Liberia, parental consent is necessary for both formal and *de facto* adoption.[5] In Luxembourg, consent of the birth parents is required only if the person to be adopted is a minor.[6] Some countries dispense with parental consent when it is in the best interests of the child to do so. In Ethiopia, article 19 (1) of the revised Family Code states that, if both parents are alive and known, they must both consent to the adoption before it can take place. Yet, article 192 (2) of the same code adds that, if one of the parents is dead, absent, unknown or incapable, the consent of the other suffices.[7] In Belize, the court may dispense with parental consent if the birth parents have abandoned, deserted or persistently refused to support their child financially.[8] A similar proviso is included in the laws of Benin[9] and Dominica.[10]

Some countries make statutory provisions regarding the withdrawal of consent by a birth parent. In Hungary, a parent cannot revoke his or her consent to an open adoption. In closed adoptions, the statement showing consent to place a child for adoption, which can be presented prior to the birth of the baby, may be revoked until the child is two months of age.[11] In Saint Lucia, birth parents have the right to change their minds regarding the adoption of their infant, even after an Interim Care Order for temporary placement has been made.[12] Parents have six weeks following the placement to indicate that they would like to re-assume the responsibility for parenting their child.

3. Authority charged with overseeing, approving and granting the adoption

Once authorities have established that the adoption is in the best interests of the child, an adoption order or decision can be made. In most of the 164 countries for which data are available, the judiciary is responsible, either solely or in conjunction with another authority, for deciding whether an adoption can take place (table III.A.1). In Spain, for instance, adoption is granted by judicial order after taking into consideration the best interests of the child and the suitability of the prospective adoptive parents.[13] In the Russian Federation[14] and Turkey,[15] adoption decisions are also adjudicated by court order.

Depending on the country, different judicial authorities may be involved. In Germany[16] and

Poland,[17] adoptions are granted by the guardianship court. In Italy, applications for adoption must be submitted to the juvenile court, which pronounces upon the adoption after having ascertained that the child is adoptable and that the prospective adoptive parents are suitable.[18] In the United States, only state courts and, in some instances, Indian tribal courts are authorized to grant adoptions (Hollinger, 1993). In Chad, the N'Djaména High Court of Justice has jurisdiction over requests for intercountry adoption, while decisions on domestic adoptions are made by a magistrate in the place of residence of the adoptive parents.[19]

In a few countries, authorities other than the judiciary are involved in authorizing and granting adoptions. In the Democratic Republic of Korea, the local population administration organ is responsible.[20] In Hungary, adoptions are authorized by the city guardianship authorities who are also charged with carrying out in-depth home studies to ascertain the suitability of the prospective adoptive family.[11] In Ireland, adoption is regulated by the Adoption Board, an independent quasi-judicial statutory body appointed by the Government.[21] In other countries, government bodies that are frequently responsible, either in whole or in part, for the adoption process include Ministries of Social Welfare, Ministries of Health and Ministries of Labour.

In some countries, different authorities are involved in the various phases of the adoption process. In El Salvador, the Procurator-General of the Republic and the Salvadoran Institute for the Protection of Children are required, respectively, to authorize and collect relevant information regarding the parties involved in the adoption procedure, while judges in the place of habitual residence of the child have jurisdiction to decide on the adoption.[22] In France, adoption orders are made by the judiciary, after the President of the General Council responsible for child welfare services has authorized the adoption.[23]

In recent years, some countries have also set up or designated central adoption authorities to oversee the process of intercountry adoption, in accordance with article 6 (1) of the Convention on Protection of Children and Co-operation in Respect of Intercountry Adoption of 29 May 1993. The United States has designated the Department of State as its central authority.[24] In India, the Central Adoption Resource Agency (CARA) was set up in 1990 as an autonomous body under the Ministry of Welfare. CARA is charged with dealing with all matters concerning adoption in India.[25]

Chapter IV presents a more detailed discussion on the role of central adoption authorities.

4. Deeds or exchanges of consent

While contact between the adoptive parents and the birth parents is usually discouraged, a number of countries require a deed or exchange of consent between the parties involved in the adoption. In China, the Adoption Act of 1998 establishes that foreign adoptive parents must conclude a written agreement with the person or persons putting up the child for adoption.[26] In Hungary, open adoption requires a joint agreement by the birth parents and the adoptive parents authorizing the adoption, while for closed adoption this agreement is not required.[27] In the Republic of Korea, the process of domestic adoption requires an agreement between the child's guardians and the adoptive parents.[28] In Austria, adoption is based on a written agreement between the adopting persons, the birth parents or legal guardians and, if the prospective adopted person is 19 years of age or older, the adopted person as well.[29] The adoption agreement must be approved by the courts for it to enter into force.[30]

5. Probationary period

Some countries require children to live with their prospective adoptive parents for a certain period before an adoption can be completed. This procedure is meant to ensure that the adoption takes place in accordance with the child's best interests. In Germany, for instance, an adoption generally cannot be authorized until the child has been in the adoptive parents' care for an appropriate period. During that time, the child is generally under the guardianship of the youth welfare office.[31] In Italy, children are placed in the care of the prospective adoptive parents for a trial period of one year before the Juvenile Court can

pronounce upon their adoption.[32] In France, a period of six months must elapse after a child has been placed with a family before the adoption application is submitted.[23] This trial period is used by the welfare services or official adoption agencies to ascertain that the child is well integrated into the adoptive family. In Argentina, a similar procedure is outlined in Act No. 24.779 of 28 February 1997.[33] In Saint Lucia, the High Court must establish that the child has remained continuously under the care of the applicants for at least three consecutive months before the adoption order can proceed.[12]

Some jurisdictions have instituted specific probationary periods for children adopted through intercountry procedures. In the United Kingdom, local authorities or approved adoption agencies are required to monitor the progress of children brought to the United Kingdom for the purpose of intercountry adoption during at least one year prior to issuing the adoption order.[34,35] In the Philippines, foreign adoption agencies must submit bi-monthly reports to the Inter-Country Adoption Board (ICAB) during the six months immediately following a placement abroad. The reports should document the health status of the child and the prospective adoptive family, the financial situation of the family and the psychosocial adjustment and emotional readiness of the child. Based on these reports, the ICAB assesses whether the prospective foreign parents can petition for an adoption, whether a different foreign family should be identified or whether the Filipino child should be repatriated.[36]

6. Date of entry into force

National laws differ with respect to when an adoption takes effect. In Lithuania, individuals are considered the child's adoptive parents from the date of enforcement of the court decision.[37] In China, an adoption becomes effective from the date of its registration with the competent civil administrative authority.[26] In some countries, adoption can become effective retrospectively. In Senegal, for instance, the adoption enters into force from the date the adoption application is lodged with the competent court.[38] In Argentina, the adoption order takes effect from the date when custody is awarded and if a step-child is being adopted, the retroactive effect commences from the date of initiation of the proceedings.[33]

7. *Revocation or annulment of the adoption*

In many countries adoption is considered irrevocable. In Costa Rica, for instance, adoption is defined as a permanent, definitive alternative care option that excludes any return to the original family.[39] Some countries, however, recognize that an adoption may be annulled or revoked under certain circumstances. Thus, in Ethiopia, under Article 195 of the Family Code, a court may reverse an adoption decision in cases of abuse.[7] In Turkmenistan, an adoption may be invalidated or annulled if statutory provisions and procedures are breached or if the child's interests are prejudiced. Only the courts may annul or invalidate an adoption in such cases.[40]

Different rules are sometimes applied, based on the type of adoption. In France[23] and Senegal,[38] a full adoption is considered irrevocable, but a simple adoption may be revoked under certain circumstances. In Japan an ordinary adoption[41] may be dissolved by agreement, by judgment or by court decision on withdrawal of parental authority, but the dissolution of special adoptions[42] can be effected only by court decision and only when it is deemed to be in the best interests of the child to do so.[43]

8. *Post-adoption monitoring*

Some countries have put in place mechanisms to monitor the welfare of adopted persons. In Romania, competent authorities are required to monitor the wellbeing of adopted children for at least two years following the approval of the adoption order.[44] In Ukraine, the Cabinet of Ministers is responsible for monitoring the living conditions and the upbringing of children adopted domestically. The upbringing and wellbeing of children adopted by foreign nationals is supervised in accordance with the instructions issued by the Ministry of Foreign Affairs to Ukraine's consular offices, which keep records on such children until the age of 18.[45] Similarly, in the Russian Federation, government resolution No. 268 of 28 March 2003 establishes a framework for monitoring the welfare of Russian children adopted by foreign nationals or by Russian nationals permanently residing outside of the country.[46] Representatives of foreign organizations are required to send written reports, prepared by the competent authority of the State in which the child resides, on the living conditions of adopted children with their adoptive families. Such reports are submitted every six months during the first year following the adoption and annually during the second and third years.

B. LEGAL REQUIREMENTS FOR PROSPECTIVE ADOPTIVE PARENTS AND ADOPTED PERSONS

1. *The adoptive parents*

Many countries require prospective parents to meet specific criteria to be eligible to adopt. These criteria are generally established to ensure that the adoptive parents are able to satisfy the child's basic physical, emotional and financial needs. The sections below discuss some of the main requirements that adoptive parents should meet according to the laws of various countries. The most commonly stipulated requirements relate to the age, sex, marital status, citizenship and place of habitual residence of the prospective adoptive parents.

(a) Age

Most of the countries considered in this study establish explicit age limits for adoptive parents (table III.1).[47] Such constraints date back to Roman law, according to which adoption should imitate nature, implying that adoptive parents should be old enough to be the biological parents of the person being adopted (Wadlington, 1966).

There are essentially two ways in which countries regulate the age of prospective adoptive parents. The first consists in establishing absolute age limits, which may include a lower age limit, an upper age limit or both (table III.2). Eighty-one countries establish a lower age limit for adoptive parents, with 45 countries specifying 25 years as the minimum age. In comparison, only 15 countries stipulate maximum ages beyond which adoption is not permitted. Among these, seven establish 50 years as the maximum age for adoptive parents, while three require parents to be no older than 60.

TABLE III.1. NUMBER OF COUNTRIES REQUIRING THE PROSPECTIVE ADOPTIVE PARENT
TO BE OF A CERTAIN AGE BY TYPE OF AGE REQUIREMENT

| | Type of age requirement | | | | Number of countries, by type of age requirement |
| | Absolute | | Relative | | |
Type	Minimum	Maximum	Minimum age difference	Maximum age difference	
1	X	..	..	..	21
2	X	..	..	X	2
3	X	..	X	..	46
4	..	X	..	..	2
5	..	X	..	X	1
6	..	X	X	..	2
7	X	X	..	..	5
8	X	X	..	X	1
9	X	X	X	..	4
10	..	..	X	..	16
11	..	..	X	X	2
12	X	..	X	X	2
Total number of countries ..	81	15	72	8	104

Source: For a complete list of country references, see annex II.

NOTES: "X" indicates the type of age requirement. For the four countries that identified separate age requirements for persons adopting jointly, only the lowest of the two age requirements is reflected in this table.

Among the countries that establish absolute ages for prospective adoptive parents, 10 use age ranges. The Civil Code of Guinea-Bissau, for example, allows parents to adopt if they are between the ages of 25 and 60.[48] Other countries that establish both a lower and an upper age limit for adoptive parents are Croatia[49] and the Plurinational State of Bolivia.[50]

The European Convention on the Adoption of Children of 1967, whose purpose is to serve as a basis for the harmonization of adoption laws among Member States of the Council of Europe, requires prospective adoptive parents to be between 21 and 35 years of age (art. 7).[51] Nevertheless, none of the 18 ratifying State parties applies both the lower and the upper limits set forth by the Convention (see chapter IV).

The second approach used to regulate who may adopt focuses on the age difference between the adopted person and the prospective adoptive parents. Among the 104 countries with information available, 72 have established some form of minimum age difference and eight have a maximum age difference. Among the countries following the first approach, 25 require the adoptive parents to be at least 15 years older than the prospective adoptive child. Fourteen countries, including Israel[52] and San Marino,[53] establish a minimum age difference of 18 years, and 15 countries require the adoptive parents to be at least 21 years older than the person they are seeking to adopt. Countries that have established a maximum age difference between the prospective adoptive parents and the person they are intending to adopt include Finland[54] and Hungary.[11]

Fifty-eight countries combine the two approaches described above, requiring that prospective adoptive parents be older or younger than certain age limits and that their age difference with respect to the prospective adopted child be above a certain threshold. The Civil Code of Argentina, for example, requires adoptive parents to be at least 30 years of age and at least 18 years older than the child they are trying to adopt.[33] Persons under the age of 30 may adopt only if they have been married for more than three years. Likewise, in Cambodia, adoptive parents are required to be at least 25 years of age and 20 years older than the prospective adopted child.[55]

In cases where adoption is granted to a couple, four countries regulate the age of only one of the adopting adults. In Spain, for example, the Third

TABLE III.2. NUMBER OF COUNTRIES REQUIRING THE PROSPECTIVE ADOPTIVE PARENTS TO BE OF A CERTAIN AGE, BY AGE GROUP OF PROSPECTIVE ADOPTIVE PARENTS

Absolute age requirement[1]				Relative age requirement			
Minimum age		*Maximum age*		*Above a certain difference*		*Below a certain difference*	
Age	Number of countries	Age	Number of countries	Age difference (years)	Number of countries	Age difference (years)	Number of countries
15	1	30	1	12-14	4	40	3
18	3	35	1	15	25	45	4
20	1	40	1	16-17	6	50	1
21	8	46	1	18	14		
25	45	50	7	19-20	4		
26-28	5	59	1	21	15		
30	11	60	3	25	4		
35-40	7						
Total	81	Total	15	Total	72	Total	8

Source: For a complete list of country references, see annex II.

NOTE: For the four countries that identified separate age requirements for persons adopting jointly, only the lowest of the two age requirements was considered.

[1] Ten countries stipulate a range, i.e., both a minimum and a maximum.

Additional Provision to Act 21/1987 requires that one of the prospective parents be at least 25 years of age.[13] Some countries, however, regulate the age of both adoptive parents. In Luxembourg, for instance, one of the adoptive parents is required to be at least 25 years old, while the other must be at least 21 years old to be eligible for full adoption.[6] The law further requires each of the adoptive parents to be at least 15 years older than the prospective adoptive child. In Portugal, when a married couple adopts, both spouses must be at least 25 years of age.[56]

Some countries have eased their age requirements over time. In France, for instance, under the Civil Code of 1804, only persons aged 50 or over could adopt. The minimum age requirement for adoptive parents was later lowered to 35 years (Wadlington, 1966) and is currently 28 years.[57] Likewise, in Germany, the minimum age for adoptive parents was reduced from 50 in the Civil Code of 1900 to 35 years in the 1960s. Currently, the German Civil Code establishes 21 years as the minimum age for unmarried prospective adoptive parents.[58] In the case of adoption by a married couple, one of the spouses is required to be over age 25, while the other must be over age 21.

(b) Sex of adoptive parents

Very few countries have explicit statutory provisions regarding the sex of adoptive parents.

Those that do, frequently combine such requirement with other characteristics, such as marital status or whether the person is petitioning for an adoption jointly or alone. In India,[59] for instance, an unmarried or divorced woman may adopt on her own, while a married woman can only be a consenting party to an adoption. By contrast, men can adopt jointly or alone regardless of their marital status. In Kenya, Section 158 (3) of the Children's Act establishes that a sole foreign male is not allowed to adopt, while a sole foreign female may adopt under special circumstances.[60] There are also several countries where persons are precluded from adopting on their own a child of the opposite sex. In Zambia, for instance, men are not permitted to adopt girl children except under special circumstances.[61] A more detailed discussion of these eligibility criteria is presented in the section describing requirements related to the sex of the adopted person.

(c) Marital status

Among the nearly 120 countries that have established explicit requirements regarding the marital status of prospective adoptive parents, about 100 allow adoption by single persons (table III.3). In Europe, almost all countries recognize the right of unmarried people to adopt. In Oceania, the five countries with information available—

TABLE III.3.NUMBER OF COUNTRIES PERMITTING SINGLE PERSONS TO ADOPT
BY SEX OF THOSE PERSONS AND MAJOR AREA

Major area	Permitted	Not permitted	Not applicable	No information available	Total number of countries
			Male		
Africa	21[1]	6	6	20	53
Asia	18	3	14	12	47
Europe	29	7	..	8	44
Latin America and the Caribbean	26	2	..	5	33
Northern America	2[1]	..	..	..	2
Oceania	5	..	..	11	16
Total	101	18	20	56	195
			Female		
Africa	22[1]	4	6	21	53
Asia	17	3	14	13	47
Europe	29	7	..	8	44
Latin America and the Caribbean	27	1	..	5	33
Northern America	2[1]	..	..	..	2
Oceania	5	..	..	11	16
Total	102	15	20	58	195

Source: For a complete list of country references, see annex II.

NOTES: The category "Not applicable" refers to countries that do not recognize the institution of adoption. The category "Not permitted" refers to countries that do not allow adoption by a single person.

[1] In Nigeria and the United States the laws regarding adoption by single persons vary by state, and in Canada they vary by province.

Australia, the Federated States of Micronesia, the Marshall Islands, New Zealand and Samoa—permit adoption by single persons.

In Africa and Asia, relatively few countries—21 in Africa and 17 in Asia—allow unmarried individuals of either sex to adopt. However, information on the legality of adoption by single persons is not available for many countries in Africa and Asia. Some countries set more stringent age requirements for single persons. In Cameroon, for instance, single persons of either sex are legally permitted to adopt a child as long as they are at least 40 years of age.[62]

Some countries apply different requirements based on the citizenship or place of habitual residence of the prospective adoptive parents. The Children's Act of Ghana, for instance, allows unmarried Ghanaian citizens to adopt, but not single foreign persons.[63] In Chile, law No. 19620 extends the right to adopt to unmarried and widowed individuals, as long as they are permanent residents of Chile.[64]

While most countries allow single persons to adopt, 15 countries restrict adoption exclusively to married couples, in some cases even setting a minimal duration of marriage as a prerequisite (see box III.1). In Italy, for instance, only couples who have been married for at least three years are permitted to adopt.[18] However, this requirement is waived for adoptive parents who are close relatives of the prospective adopted person. In Guinea-Bissau, parents applying for an adoption are required to have been married for at least five years.[48] Other countries that allow adoption only by married or widowed persons are Mozambique[65] and Ireland.[66]

A number of countries not only limit the possibility of adopting jointly to married couples, as does the 1967 European Convention on the Adoption of Children, but require also that married couples adopt jointly.[51] This stipulation is made in article 10 of the Chinese Adoption Act.[67] Germany has a similar provision in its Civil Code.[58] In some of these countries, exceptions are made in cases where one of the married persons is adopting the biological child of his or her spouse. In that case, the step-parent is generally allowed to adopt alone.

A few countries allow *de facto* couples to adopt jointly. In Portugal, civil partners, but not same-sex couples, are allowed to adopt a child jointly.[68] In

---

BOX III.1. COUNTRIES THAT REQUIRE PROSPECTIVE ADOPTIVE PARENTS
TO BE MARRIED

Africa:	*Asia:*	*Europe:*	*Latin America and the Caribbean:*
Guinea-Bissau	Indonesia	Czech Republic[1]	Suriname
Mozambique	Israel[2,3]	Iceland[1]	
Niger	Thailand	Ireland[2,4]	
Tunisia[5]		Italy[2]	
		Liechtenstein	
		Lithuania[1]	
		Luxembourg[6]	

Source: For a complete list of country references, see annex II.

[1] Permission to adopt may be granted to single persons under special circumstances.
[2] Close relatives of the adopted person are permitted to adopt, regardless of their marital status.
[3] A sole person is permitted to adopt in cases where one spouse adopts the child of the other.
[4] Widowed persons are permitted to adopt.
[5] A judge may waive the marriage requirement for a widowed or divorced individual.
[6] Single persons aged 25 years or over may engage in simple adoptions.

Norway, individuals in a registered partnership have been able to adopt their partner's child since 1 January 2002. According to the Third Periodic Report submitted by Norway to the Committee on the Rights of the Child, "the purpose of the new provision is to give these children the same possibility for legal security and safeguards as children who live with a parent and his or her spouse."[69] In Sweden, adoption by *de facto* couples, including same-sex couples, is permitted.[70] A similar law entered into force in the Netherlands in 2001.[71] In Finland, cohabiting partners, including registered same-sex partners, are not permitted to adopt a child jointly.[54]

(d) Childlessness

In the past, countries such as Denmark, Guatemala, Italy, Peru and Switzerland, used to bar people who already had children of their own from adopting (United Nations, 1956; Wadlington, 1966). Today this restriction has largely been removed and most jurisdictions allow persons with biological children of their own to adopt. In China, the restriction limiting adoption to childless women has been lifted recently. Under the Chinese Adoption Act of 1998, adoptive parents who are not childless may adopt a child in cases where the adoption involves "orphans, disabled children or abandoned children of whom social welfare

institutions are unable to trace the natural parents".[72] In Myanmar, the Registration of Kittima Adoption Act of 1941 allows persons to adopt a child regardless of whether they already have offspring of their own.[73]

There are still some countries where having children of one's own makes adoption impossible. That is the case of Cameroon[62] and Gabon,[74] whose laws require that prospective adoptive parents be childless at the time of adoption. In Senegal, persons who already have children of their own or have legal descendants are permitted to adopt only if they have received the authorization of the President of the Republic.[38] In Madagascar, prospective adoptive parents are allowed to adopt only if they have fewer than three children.[4] In Switzerland, article 266 of the Civil Code stipulates that only persons with no descendants are permitted to adopt an adult.[75]

Some jurisdictions, while not limiting adoption solely to childless persons, require that the children and legal descendants of the prospective adoptive parents be consulted about the adoption. Such a provision is outlined in article 314 of the Civil Code of Argentina.[33] Likewise, in the Philippines, Section 9, article III of the Domestic Adoption Act of 1998 stipulates that all children of the adoptive family aged 10 years or over have to give their written consent before an adoption can take place.[36]

(e) Citizenship

Only five countries bar non-citizens from adopting their nationals (see box III.2). One such country is Namibia, where only citizens are allowed to adopt Namibian children, although exceptions are sometimes made in cases where one of the adoptive parents is a permanent resident who has applied and qualified for naturalization as a Namibian citizen.[76] A somewhat similar requirement is stipulated in the Children's Act of the Seychelles.[77]

Some countries, while not barring adoption by foreigners, establish additional conditions that non-citizens are required to meet in order to be eligible to adopt a child. In the former Yugoslav Republic of Macedonia, for instance, foreign nationals need special permission from the Ministry of Labour and Social Policy to adopt.[78] In Mozambique, adoptions are granted to foreign citizens only in exceptional cases, such as when all possibilities of identifying a Mozambican adoptive family have been exhausted or when the foreign adoptive family resides permanently in Mozambique.[65] Other countries impose residence requirements. In Ghana, for instance, an adoption order cannot be granted to a foreigner unless the foreign applicant and the child are both residents of Ghana.[63] A somewhat similar provision is set out in the Adoption Act of 1958 of Zambia.[61] In Eritrea, non-citizens are not permitted to adopt an Eritrean child unless they have resided in the country for at least six months.[79] In Uganda, the residence requirement for non-citizens is at least three years.[80]

(f) Residence

A number of countries establish residence requirements for prospective parents, regardless of whether they are citizens or not. In the United Republic of Tanzania, for example, adoption orders are restricted to applicants who are residents within the East African Territories.[81] Similarly, in Malawi, the Adoption of Children Act prohibits the adoption of Malawi children by non-residents.[82] In Antigua and Barbuda, Section 3 (5) of the Adoption of Children Act provides that an applicant who is not resident or domiciled in the country cannot adopt a citizen of the country. The reason for this provision is that the courts are reluctant to grant adoption orders that they may be unable to supervise.[83] In Argentina, non-residents are not permitted to adopt children residing in Argentinean territory.[33] These restrictions are motivated by concerns about trafficking in children and the limited number of children available for domestic adoption.

BOX III.2. COUNTRIES THAT IMPOSE RESTRICTIONS BASED ON THE CITIZENSHIP OR PLACE OF HABITUAL RESIDENCE OF THE ADOPTIVE PARENT

Based on citizenship	*Based on residence*
Bangladesh	Antigua and Barbuda
Federated States of Micronesia	Argentina[1]
Namibia[2]	Malawi
Nigeria	Solomon Islands[1]
Seychelles[2]	United Republic of Tanzania[3]

Source: For a complete list of country references, see annex II.

[1] Intercountry adoptions are granted only to prospective adoptive parents residing in the country who adopt children from abroad.

[2] Intercountry adoptions are granted only to nationals living abroad who are also related to the prospective adoptive child or to permanent residents who have applied and qualified for naturalization.

[3] Intercountry adoptions are granted only to prospective adoptive parents residing within the East African Territories.

Some countries allow persons who are not habitual residents to adopt under certain conditions. In Trinidad and Tobago, the Adoption of Children Act, No. 67 of 2000 indicates that an adoption order shall not be made in favour of any applicant who is not resident and domiciled in Trinidad and Tobago nor in respect of any child who is not a Commonwealth citizen and resident.[84] However, the Adoption of Children Act permits persons who are not nationals of Trinidad and Tobago and who live outside of Trinidad and Tobago to adopt, provided the Court is satisfied that all attempts to secure an adoption by applicants who are nationals of Trinidad and Tobago have failed and it is in the best interest of the child to grant the adoption. In Dominica, non-residents are generally not permitted to apply for an adoption.[10] The court, however, can decide to grant an adoption order in favour of such applicants when certain conditions are satisfied.

As indicated in previous sections, some jurisdictions specify a minimum residence requirement for prospective adoptive parents. In the United Kingdom, only persons who have been habitual residents in a part of the British Islands for a period of at least one year can apply.[85] In Malaysia, only persons who have resided in the country for at least two years are considered eligible.[86]

Yet, even countries that allow non-residents to adopt tend to follow the principle of subsidiarity whereby intercountry adoption is considered only after other options are exhausted. This principle is outlined in article 21 of the United Nations Convention on the Rights of the Child, which states that "inter-country adoption may be considered as an alternative means of child's care, if the child cannot be placed in a foster or an adoptive family or cannot in any suitable manner be cared for in the child's country of origin".[1] In the Plurinational State of Bolivia, international adoption is viewed as an exceptional measure to be contemplated only after all attempts at realizing a domestic adoption have been exhausted.[50] In Poland, the Public Adoption Care Centre has three months to identify a suitable adoptive parent in Poland, after which the child may be eligible for adoption abroad.[87] The Government of Romania also gives priority to adoptions by nationals over foreign citizens and

Romanians living abroad, in accordance with the principle of susbidiarity.[44] Since 2005, new legislation restricting intercountry adoptions exclusively to relatives of the child has entered into force.[88] Other countries that have incorporated the principle of subsidiarity into their legislation are Albania, Austria, Barbados, Benin, Chile, Croatia, El Salvador, Guyana, Lithuania, Serbia, Togo, Turkey, Viet Nam, Ukraine and Uruguay.

(g) Religious affiliation

Some countries require the prospective adoptive parents to be of a certain religion in order to qualify for adoption. In India, the Hindu Adoptions and Maintenance Act of 1956 regulates adoptions by parents who are Hindus, Buddhists, Jains and Sikhs. Adoptions by Muslims, Christians, Parsis and Jews are governed by the Indian Guardians and Wards Act of 1890, which permits affiliates of these religions to take a child in "guardianship".[59] In Brunei Darussalam, non-Muslims are not allowed to apply for the adoption of a child of unknown parentage or whose parents are Muslim.[89] Additional examples of such requirements are presented in the section focusing on the religious affiliation of the adopted person.

(h) Social and economic requirements

Many countries have instituted requirements regarding the physical, moral and mental health of prospective adoptive parents. Frequently, the competent authority carries out a formal investigation or requires the submission of affidavits attesting to the suitability of the prospective adoptive parents with respect to various characteristics. In Brazil, for example, prospective adoptive parents are assessed based on their motivation, way of life, personality and conjugal and family situation, as well as their place of residence.[90] In Samoa, under the Infants Ordinance of 1961, the Court must be satisfied that the prospective adoptive parents are of good repute and that the future environment of the adopted child is safe and secure.[91] In Kenya, an applicant who is of "unsound mind, has been charged or convicted of an offence by a court of competent jurisdiction, or is a homosexual" is barred from adoption.[92] In Ghana, the Department of Social Welfare is charged with investigating the financial and social status of the prospective adoptive parents before the court can grant an adoption order.[63] In Hungary, psychological aptitude tests are conducted with the aim of assessing the motivation, personality and views about child-rearing of prospective adoptive parents.[11] Health tests are also conducted to ensure that the adoptive parent is free from any disease or health impediment that might endanger the child's development.

Some countries have established more stringent requirements for foreign adoptive parents than for local applicants. In Ethiopia, for instance, non-citizens who wish to adopt an Ethiopian child are required to produce documentation proving that they have no incurable or contagious diseases, have no criminal record and have sufficient income to support the child.[7] Similar requirements are not explicitly outlined for Ethiopian citizens.[93] In China, article 21 of the Adoption Act of 1998[94] requires non-citizens wishing to adopt a Chinese child to provide, in addition to information on age, marital status and health status, which is also required for Chinese citizens,[67] proof of their profession, criminal record and ownership of property.[26] In the Plurinational State of Bolivia, besides the requirements set for nationals, foreign adoptive parents must demonstrate financial solvency.[50] El Salvador also imposes more stringent requirements for foreign adoptive parents than for Salvadorian citizens arguing that it is more difficult to monitor the wellbeing of Salvadorian children once they have left the country.[22]

2. The adopted person

A number of countries establish specific requirements that persons have to fulfil in order to be declared adoptable, including age, consent, sex, citizenship, residency status and religious affiliation. These requirements are discussed in the sections below.

(a) Age

Some laws set specific requirements for the age of the adopted person. In São Tomé and Principe, for instance, only persons aged 16 years or less, who have been abandoned or whose parents are unknown, may be adopted.[95] In Gabon a person aged 15 years or over cannot be adopted.[74] In Ireland, only children aged 18 years or less are eligible for adoption.[21] Similar provisions are in place in Israel[96] and the Plurinational State of Bolivia.[50] Some countries, however, impose no age limits for the adopted person. In Switzerland, for instance, the Civil Code outlines the procedure for adopting adults as well as children.[97] Likewise, in Guatemala, article 228 of the Civil Code establishes that adults may be adopted if they give their consent.[98]

(b) Consent

The notion that a child should be able to express an opinion relating to his or her adoption is reflected in the United Nations Convention on the Rights of the Child,[1] as well as in the legislation of many countries. Article 4 of the Convention on Protection of Children and Co-Operation in Respect of Intercountry Adoption requires Contracting States to ensure that a child "has been counselled and duly informed of the effects of the adoption and of his or her consent to the adoption, where such consent is required".[99]

In 90 countries there are specific age cut-offs above which the consent of the child is either required or sought (table III.4). Among these countries, the majority require the consent of children who are 10 years of age or older. In the Philippines, article III of the Domestic Adoption Act of 1998 stipulates that the adopted child as well as any children of the adoptive family aged 10 or over must give their written consent to the adoption.[36] Other countries that recognize age 10 as the cut-off point from which a child's consent is required for the adoption to be approved are: China,[26] the Russian Federation[14] and South Africa.[100] An additional 51 countries have established higher minimum ages. Twenty-six of these, including Brazil,[90] Mexico[101] and Spain,[13] require or seek the prospective adopted child's view starting at age 12. A further 10 countries require the child's consent if he or she is 14 years or older. They include Germany[58] and Guinea-Bissau.[48]

Relatively few countries require very young children to give their consent. Laws in Austria[30]

TABLE III.4. NUMBER OF COUNTRIES THAT REQUIRE OR
ALLOW THE CHILD TO CONSENT TO THE ADOPTION
BY THE AGE ABOVE WHICH THE CHILD'S
CONSENT IS SOUGHT

Minimum age[1]	Number of countries
5	2
7	4
9	2
10	31
12	26
13	2
14	10
15	8
16	5
Total	90

Source: For a complete list of country references see annex II.

[1] Minimum age at which consent of the child who is candidate for adoption is sought.

and Liechtenstein[102] indicate that children aged five or over have the right to a hearing, and four countries, including Mongolia[103] and São Tome and Principe[95] require or allow the child's opinion to be sought beginning at age seven.

In addition to the above-mentioned approaches, 16 countries require relevant authorities to appraise the child's maturity or capacity to understand before asking his or her consent with regard to the adoption. Under Slovak law, for instance, consent is required whenever the minor is able to assess the legal implications of the adoption. The court is charged with determining whether a child has this capacity.[104] In Zambia, the Adoption Act of 1958 provides that the court must seek the prospective adopted child's views when it is satisfied that the child is of an age to understand the effects of the adoption order.[61] Belize is another country that follows a similar approach.[105]

(c) Sex

Relatively few countries have legal requirements concerning the sex of the adopted person. One such country is Bangladesh, where Hindu personal law makes no provisions for the adoption of girls.[106] In Indonesia, the *Staatsblad* 1917 No. 129 allows for the adoption of male children only, but based on jurisprudence of 1963, the Supreme Court considers the adoption of

female children legal.[107] In India, the Hindu Adoptions and Maintenance Act of 1956 limits the adoption of children of a certain sex depending on the sex of any children or grandchildren that the adoptive parents might already have.[108] A number of countries also have requirements for the sex of the prospective adopted person based on the sex of the adoptive parent. In 12 countries, men are not allowed to adopt a girl on their own (see box III.3). A smaller number of countries do not permit boys to be adopted by single women.

(d) Citizenship

Very few countries impose limitations based on the citizenship of the prospective adopted persons. Even those that do, usually allow such persons to be adopted under special circumstances. In Mauritius, for instance, a Mauritian seeking to adopt a non-citizen needs the approval of the Prime Minister's Office.[109] In Kenya, any child who is a resident, regardless of whether he or she is a Kenyan citizen or was born in Kenya, may be adopted.[60]

(e) Residence

As indicated in previous sections, in some countries only residents are eligible to apply for an adoption. Relatively few countries, however, provide specific guidelines with regard to the residence of the adopted person. In Zambia, an adoption order cannot be made unless the prospective adopted child is a resident of the country and has been continuously in the care of the applicant for at least three consecutive months before the date of the adoption order.[61] Similarly, in Malawi, the Adoption of Children Act prohibits the adoption of non-resident children by Malawi residents.[82] Antigua and Barbuda,[83] Belize[8] and Dominica[10] also require the prospective adopted person to reside in the country.

Some countries of destination of intercountry adoption have introduced moratoria on the adoption of children originating in certain countries because of allegations concerning the sale of children or the trafficking in children for the purpose of adoption. For instance, France[23] and the United States[110] suspended temporarily adoptions

---

BOX III.3. COUNTRIES THAT RESTRICT ADOPTION OF CHILDREN
OF A CERTAIN SEX BASED ON THE SEX AND MARITAL STATUS
OF THE ADOPTIVE PARENT

Countries where a girl may not be adopted by an unmarried man

Antigua and Barbuda[1]
Bangladesh[3]
Brunei Darussalam[2]
Belize[1]
Dominica[1]
Guyana[1]
Jamaica[1]
Malawi
Panama
Saint Lucia[1]
Uganda[1]
Zambia[1]

Countries where a boy may not be adopted by an unmarried woman

Brunei Darussalam[2]
Malawi
Panama
Uganda[1]

Source: For a complete list of country references, see annex II.

[1] Only with special permission or under special circumstances.
[2] Not permitted unless the prospective adoptive parent is related by blood to the person he or she is seeking to adopt.
[3] Refers to Hindu men.

---

of children from Viet Nam, following allegations of irregularities. Likewise, Canada has suspended adoptions of children from a number of countries, including Cambodia, Guatemala and Viet Nam, because of concerns related to unethical or illegal practices.[111]

(f) Religious affiliation

Article 20 of the United Nations Convention on the Rights of the Child[112] calls on States parties to take into consideration the religious affiliation of prospective adoptive children when identifying suitable adoptive families. Only a small number of countries, however, have established requirements based on the religion of the child. In the Sudan, for example, Muslim children deprived of a family environment can only be cared for under *kafalah*, whereas Christian children enjoy the rights and duties stipulated in connection to their own religious laws.[113] A similar distinction is made in Lebanese law.[114]

C. EFFECTS OF ADOPTION

According to article 8 of the Declaration on Social and Legal Principles relating to the Protection and Welfare of Children, with Special Reference to Foster Placement and Adoption Nationally and Internationally, a "child should not, as a result of foster placement, adoption or any alternative regime, be deprived of his or her name, nationality or legal representative unless the child thereby acquires a new name, nationality or legal representative."[115] As indicated in chapter I, countries have opted for different strategies in this respect. In countries that recognize only full adoption, for instance, adoption creates an irrevocable bond equivalent to natural filiation and has the effect of permanently terminating pre-existing legal parent-child relationships. It also grants adopted persons the same rights and responsibilities as birth children, including the right to inherit from the adoptive parents and relatives. However, in countries that recognize simple adoption, adoption does not extinguish the ties to the adopted person's family of origin. Furthermore, simple adoption does not entail the automatic acquisition of the adoptive parents' name, nor does it ensure benefits equivalent to those of a birth child with regard to inheritance. The sections below examine some of the differences between country laws regarding the effect of adoption in terms of name, acquisition of citizenship, right to inheritance, the termination of ties between the adopted person and his or her birth parents or relatives, and limitations with regard to marriage.

1. Name

In most jurisdictions, adopted persons automatically acquire the surname of the adoptive parents. In Cape Verde, for instance, the adopted person loses his or her former surname and acquires the surname of his or her adoptive parents.[116] Other countries where the acquisition of the name of the adoptive family is automatic are Argentina[33] and Turkey.[15] Some countries, however, leave the decision of whether to change the name of the adopted person to the discretion of a judge or presiding authority. In Finland, for instance, the court has the authority to decide whether it is in the child's best interests to maintain his or her former family name.[54] Similarly, in São Tome and Principe, the adoption order states whether the adopted person should keep the name of his or her birth family or should take the name of the adoptive parents.[95]

A number of countries require the adopted person to give his or her consent to any change of name. In Lithuania, article 3.228 of the Civil Code provides that, while a child adopted through a court judgment is usually given the surname of the adoptive parents, upon request the adopted person may retain his or her original surname.[37] In France, adopted persons aged 13 or over must give their consent before any change is made to their family name or first name.[23]

In a number of countries, children retain their original name unless the judge, the presiding authority or the adoptive parent requires it to be changed. In the Democratic People's Republic of Korea, for example, the identity of a child is not changed by adoption unless it is deemed that maintaining the relation with the natural parents is detrimental to the child's best interests or the child requests it.[117] A similar position is taken by the Russian Federation, where an adoptive child keeps his or her given name, patronymic and family name unless the court decides otherwise following a request from the adoptive parents.[14]

A small number of countries permit the adopted person to carry either or both of the surnames of the adoptive parents and of the birth parents. In Mauritius, for instance, article 357 of the Civil Code provides that a judge can decide whether an adopted child will keep his or her name or whether the name of the child's family of origin be added to the name of the adoptive parents.[109]

2. Right to inheritance

Most of the countries that permit full adoption recognize that adopted persons have the same right to inherit from their adoptive parents and relatives as biological offspring. Examples of such countries are Brazil,[90] Myanmar[73] and Turkey.[15] In the Republic of Moldova, the law stipulates that adopted children who are incapable of work and who were supported by an adoptive parent prior to his or her death are entitled to inherit at least two-thirds of the share that would have been due to them in the case of legal succession, regardless of the content of their adoptive parent's will.[118]

The rights to inheritance tend to be more limited in the case of simple adoption. In France, for instance, simple adoption does not confer upon the adopted person or his descendants the status of compulsory heir with regard to the ascendants of the adoptive parent. Furthermore, if an adoptive parent dies intestate, the adopted person must return any property received through succession to the adoptive family.[57] Countries that recognize simple adoptions also tend not to preclude the adopted person's right to inherit from his or her birth parents and relatives. In Burkina Faso, for instance, simple adoption has the effect of making adopted children members of the adoptive family, while retaining their rights, including hereditary rights and the duty of sustenance, with respect to their birth family.[119] A number of countries also permit adopted persons to inherit from their birth parents if the latter die intestate. In Swaziland, for instance, section 6 (3) of the Adoption of Children Act of 1952 provides that an adopted child's right to inherit *ab intestato* from his or her birth parents or relatives is not affected by an adoption order.[120] Likewise, in the Philippines, article 189 of the

Family Code indicates that the adopted person remains an intestate heir of the biological parents and other blood relatives.[36]

3. Termination of relationship with the birth parents

In many countries, adoption terminates the birth parents' rights and responsibilities towards the adopted person. In Japan, for instance, the Civil Code acknowledges that special adoption ends existing relationships between the adopted child and his or her birth parents and blood relatives.[42] In Albania, Law No. 7650 of 17 December 1992 states that, upon adoption, the rights and obligations between the adopted child and his or her family of origin cease to exist.[121] In Paraguay, the adopted child's ties to his or her family of birth are terminated from the moment of adoption except under special circumstances.[122] In Ireland, the birth family loses all legal rights over the child and the responsibility for the adopted person's welfare passes over to the adoptive family. A similar provision is outlined in the 1980 Individuals and Family Code of Togo.[123]

In a number of countries, however, it is common to have arrangements that do not call for the termination of pre-existing legal relationships between the adopted person and the birth parents. Especially in countries that recognize simple adoption or where the extended family plays an important role in the socialization and upbringing of children, ties with the birth family may not be extinguished upon the act of adoption. In Argentina, for example, article 331 of the Civil Code establishes that the rights and duties deriving from the adopted child's biological link are not terminated by simple adoption.[33] Similar provisions are outlined in the Civil Codes of Belgium[124] and France.[57]

4. Citizenship

Countries that allow their citizens to adopt foreign children usually grant those children the right to citizenship. Under article 3 of the Turkish Citizenship Law of 1964, for instance, a foreign minor adopted by a Turkish family acquires Turkish citizenship in order to avoid statelessness.[15] Likewise, in Ireland, persons adopted by Irish citizens have an automatic right to Irish citizenship under the Adoption Act of 1952 and the Irish Nationality and Citizenship Act of 2004.[21] Similar provisions are laid out in article 19 of the Code on Nationality of Gabon,[74] section 4b of the Nationality Law of Israel[52] and in the 1995 Citizenship Act of Armenia.[125] However, Hungarian law stipulates that adoption does not automatically entail the acquisition of Hungarian citizenship, although it does lay the foundations for preferential naturalization.[11]

A number of countries establish age cut-offs after which the adopted person is not automatically eligible to acquire the citizenship of his or her adoptive parents. In New Zealand, the Citizens Amendment Act of 1992 establishes that children aged 14 years or over who are adopted by a New Zealand citizen do not automatically acquire New Zealand citizenship (Galvin, 2005). In Norway, children aged 12 years or over must give their consent before being granted Norwegian nationality.[126] In Botswana, children adopted under the age of three become citizens if the adoptive parent is a citizen at the time of adoption.[127] In the Republic of Moldova, adopted children must be younger than 16 to be granted citizenship.[118]

Some countries apply different regulations for the acquisition of citizenship to foreign-born children depending on where the adoption takes place. Under the British Nationality Act of 1981, a child adopted in the United Kingdom automatically becomes a British citizen if at least one of the adoptive parents was a British citizen at the time of the adoption order.[35] However, there are no similar provisions if the child is adopted by British citizens outside the United Kingdom. In that case, the decision to register a minor as a British citizen is left to the discretionary power of the Home Secretary. Likewise, children adopted by United States citizens residing overseas can file for naturalization during a legal, temporary visit to the United States so long as they are under 18 years of age and their adoptive parents or grandparents meet certain eligibility criteria.[128]

Countries that do not automatically award citizenship to foreign-born children adopted abroad often do so for fear that individuals might use

25

adoption as a loophole for obtaining citizenship. In the case of the United Kingdom, the British Nationality Act of 1981 explicitly aims to limit intercountry adoptions arranged by unscrupulous third parties with the sole purpose of circumventing immigration controls.[35] Likewise, Singapore reserves the right to refuse to issue a dependant's passport if there is sufficient evidence that an adoption is being carried out with the purpose of eluding an immigration restriction.[129]

Some countries require or allow their citizens adopted through an intercountry procedure to retain the citizenship of the country of origin. Based on the 1991 Act on Citizenship of Ukraine, for instance, children adopted by foreign nationals retain their Ukrainian citizenship.[45] A similar provision is outlined in the Armenian Citizenship Act of 1995[125] and in the Bolivian Code for Children and Adolescents of 1999.[50]

5. *Limitations on marriage*

A common feature of many adoption laws is the prohibition of marriage between the adopted person and his or her descendents and any close adoptive ascendants or descendents. In the case of full adoption, the Civil Code of Argentina, for instance, prohibits marriage between adopted persons and all adoptive ascendants, descendents and siblings.[130] Likewise, according to the French Civil Code, marriage is prohibited between the adoptive parent (or his or her spouse) and the adopted person (and his or her descendents). The adopted person is permitted to marry his or her adoptive siblings only by dispensation of the President of the Republic. In addition, adopted persons are prohibited from marrying close relatives of their birth family.[57] Somewhat similar provisions are laid out in the 1988 Family Code of Angola.[131]

D. SUMMARY

As indicated in this chapter, adoption laws differ greatly among countries. In some jurisdictions, for example, adoptions are overseen by a judge, while in others an administrative authority is charged with approving and granting adoptions. Countries also have different requirements for prospective adoptive parents and adopted children. In some jurisdictions, only persons of a certain age or marital status are permitted to adopt. In other cases, persons may be barred from adopting because they are unable to meet certain eligibility criteria for residency or citizenship. The effects of adoption also differ from country to country. Under some laws, adoptive children acquire the same rights as biological children with respect to their adoptive parents, including the right to inheritance. In some countries, adoption implies a termination of legal ties with birth parents, whereas in others such termination is culturally unacceptable. There are also differences with regard to the acquisition of citizenship. In some contexts, foreign-born children automatically acquire the citizenship of the adoptive parents, whereas in others, the acquisition of citizenship is not automatic and adoptive parents need to apply for the naturalization of their adopted children.

NOTES

[1] United Nations, *Treaty Series*, vol. 1577, No. 27531, p. 3.

[2] The Committee on the Rights of the Child is the body of independent experts that monitors the implementation of the United Nations Convention on the Rights of the Child by its State parties.

[3] See United Nations, "Initial reports of States parties due in 1992: Uruguay" (CRC/C/3/Add.37).

[4] See United Nations, "Second periodic reports of States parties due in 1998: Madagascar" (CRC/C/70/Add.18).

[5] See United Nations, "Initial reports of States parties due in 1995: Liberia" (CRC/C/28/Add.21).

[6] See United Nations, "Initial reports of States parties due in 1996: Luxembourg" (CRC/C/41/Add.2).

[7] See United Nations, "Third periodic report of States parties due in 2003: Ethiopia" (CRC/C/129/Add.8).

[8] See United Nations, "Initial reports of States parties due in 1992: Belize" (CRC/C/3/Add.46).

[9] See United Nations, "Second periodic reports of States parties due in 1997: Benin" (CRC/C/BEN/2).

[10] See United Nations, "Initial reports of States parties due in 1993: Dominica" (CRC/C/8/Add.48).

[11] See United Nations, "Second periodic reports of States parties due in 1998: Hungary" (CRC/C/70/Add.25).

[12] See United Nations, "Initial reports of States parties due in 1995: Saint Lucia" (CRC/C/28/Add.23).

[13] See United Nations, "Periodic reports of States parties due in 1999: Spain" (CRC/C/70/Add.9).

[14] See United Nations, "Periodic reports of States parties due in 1997: Russian Federation" (CRC/C/65/Add.5).

[15] See United Nations, "Initial reports of States parties due in 1997: Turkey" (CRC/C/51/Add.4).

[16] See United Nations, "Initial reports of States parties due in 1994: Germany" (CRC/C/11/Add.5).

[17] See United Nations, "Initial reports of States parties due in 1993: Poland" (CRC/C/8/Add.11).

[18] See United Nations, "Initial reports of States parties due in 1993: Italy" (CRC/C/8/Add.18).

[19] See United Nations, "Initial reports of States parties due in 1992: Chad" (CRC/C/3/Add.50).

[20] See United Nations, "Initial report of States parties due in 1992: Democratic People's Republic of Korea" (CRC/C/3/Add.41) and "Second periodic reports of States parties due in 1997: Democratic People's Republic of Korea" (CRC/C/65/Add.24).

[21] See United Nations, "Second periodic report of States parties due in 1999: Ireland" (CRC/C/IRL/2).

[22] See United Nations, "Second periodic reports of States parties due in 1997: El Salvador" (CRC/C/65/Add.25).

[23] See United Nations, "Second periodic reports of States due in 1997: France" (CRC/C/65/Add.26).

[24] See United States, Department of Homeland Security, Citizenship and Immigration Services, "Information sheet regarding the Intercountry Adoption Act of 2000". Available from http://www.uscis.gov/portal/site/uscis/menuitem.5af9bb95919f35e66f6 14176543f6d1a/?vgnextoid=009a98751de7d010VgnVCM10000048f3 d6a1RCRD&vgnextchannel=063807b03d92b010VgnVCM10000045f 3d6a1RCRD (accessed 12 May 2006).

[25] See India, Central Adoption Resource Agency, "Guidelines for adoption from India: 2006". Available from http://cara.nic.in/ adoptionfromindia.htm (accessed 12 May 2006).

[26] See United Nations, "Second periodic report of States parties due in 1997: China" (CRC/C/83/Add.9).

[27] In open adoption, the natural parent and the adoptive parent know each other and, essentially, file a joint request for the authorization of the adoption. In closed adoption, there is no personal contact between the birth parent and the adoptive parent. A child can be the subject of a closed adoption if the birth parent has consented to placing a child for adoption with an unknown person, if the court annuls the birth parent's parental rights or if the guardianship authorities rule in an absolute decree that a child raised in an institution or by foster parents can be adopted. United Nations, "Second periodic reports of States parties due in 1998: Hungary" (CRC/C/70/Add.25), para. 294.

[28] See United Nations, "Periodic reports of States parties due in 1998: Republic of Korea" (CRC/C/70/Add.14).

[29] See United States, Embassy to Austria, "Adopting a child in Austria". Available from http://vienna.usembassy.gov/en/embassy/ cons/adoption.htm (accessed 12 February 2006).

[30] See United Nations, "Second periodic report of States parties due in 1999: Austria" (CRC/C/83/Add.8).

[31] See United Nations, "Second periodic reports of States parties due in 1999: Germany" (CRC/C/83/Add.7).

[32] See United Nations, "Periodic reports of States parties due in 1998: Italy" (CRC/C/70/Add.13).

[33] See United Nations, "Periodic reports of States parties due in 1998: Argentina" (CRC/C/70/Add.10).

[34] Where a child has been adopted in a country whose adoption is automatically recognized by the United Kingdom, the adoption agency has no further involvement in the process once the child enters the United Kingdom.

[35] See United Nations, "Periodic reports of States parties due in 1998: United Kingdom of Great Britain and Northern Ireland" (CRC/C/83/Add.3).

[36] See United Nations, "Second periodic reports of States parties due in 1997: Philippines" (CRC/C/65/Add.31).

[37] See United Nations, "Second periodic reports of States parties due in 1999: Lithuania" (CRC/C/83/Add.14).

[38] See United Nations, "Initial reports of States parties due in 1992: Senegal" (CRC/C/3/Add.31).

[39] See United Nations, "Third periodic reports of States Parties due in 2002: Costa Rica" (CRC/C/125/Add.4).

[40] See United Nations, "Initial reports of States parties due in 1995: Turkmenistan" (CRC/C/TKM/1).

[41] An ordinary adoption creates a legal parental relation between the adopted person and the adoptive parents. The adoptive person acquires the status of a legitimate child. United Nations, "Initial reports of States parties due in 1996: Japan" (CRC/C/41/Add.1), paras. 143-144.

[42] Special adoption is effected if a child is, in principle, under six years of age at the time of request, by the Family Court. The judgment is made upon request from the person intending to become an adoptive parent, rather than by agreement between the adoptive parents and the adopted child. In special adoption, the family relation between the adopted child and his or her natural parents in addition to his or her blood relatives is terminated. Special adoption is undertaken only in extraordinary circumstances. United Nations, "Initial reports of States parties due in 1996: Japan" (CRC/C/41/Add.1), para. 145.

[43] See United Nations, "Second periodic reports of States parties due in 2001: Japan" (CRC/C/104/Add.2).

[44] See United Nations, "Periodic reports of States parties due in 1997: Romania" (CRC/C/65/Add.19).

[45] See United Nations, "Second periodic reports of States parties due in 1998: Ukraine" (CRC/C/70/Add.11).

[46] See United Nations, "Third periodic reports of States parties due in 2001: Russian Federation" (CRC/C/125/Add.5).

[47] In Canada the laws regarding age requirements for adoptive parents vary by province, while in Nigeria and the United States of America they vary by state.

[48] See United Nations, "Initial reports of States parties due in 1992: Guinea-Bissau" (CRC/C/3/Add.63).

[49] See United Nations, "Second periodic reports of States parties due in 1998: Croatia" (CRC/C/70/Add.23).

[50] See United Nations, "Third periodic reports of States parties due in 2002: Bolivia" (CRC/C/125/Add.2).

[51] Council of Europe, *European Treaty Series*, No. 058.

[52] See United Nations, "Periodic reports of States parties due in 1993: Israel" (CRC/C/8/Add.44).

[53] See United Nations, "Initial reports of States parties due in 1993: San Marino" (CRC/C/8/Add.46).

[54] See United Nations, "Third periodic reports of States parties due in 2003: Finland" CRC/C/129/Add.5.

[55] See United Nations, "Initial reports of States parties due in 1994: Cambodia" (CRC/C/11/Add.16).

[56] Portugal, Civil Code, book IV, title IV. Available from http://www.confap.pt/docs/codcivil.PDF (accessed 2 February 2007).

[57] France, Civil Code, book I, title VIII, chapter I. Available http://195.83.177.9/code/liste.phtml?lang=uk&c=22&r=315 (accessed 29 October 2006).

[58] Germany, Civil Code, book I, part II, title VII. Available from http://bundesrecht.juris.de/bgb/index.html (accessed 12 February 2006).

[59] See United Nations, "Second periodic reports of States parties due in 2000: India" (CRC/C/93/Add.5).

[60] See United Nations, "Second periodic report of States parties due in 1997: Kenya" (CRC/C/KEN/2).

[61] See United Nations, "Initial reports of States parties due in 1994: Zambia" (CRC/C/11/Add.25).

[62] See United Nations, "Initial reports of States parties due in 1995: Cameroon" (CRC/C/28/Add.16).

[63] See United Nations, "Second periodic reports of States parties due in 1997: Ghana" (CRC/C/65/Add.34).

[64] Chile, Act No. 19,620 of 1999. Available from http://www.sernam.gov.cl/admin/docdescargas/seccion/categorias/su bcategorias/subcat_164.doc (accessed 12 May 2006).

[65] See United Nations, "Initial report of States parties due in 1996: Mozambique" (CRC/C/41/Add.11).

[66] See Ireland, the Adoption Board, "Domestic adoption in Ireland: an introduction to domestic adoption in Ireland". Available from http://www.adoptionboard.ie/domestic/index.php (accessed 12 February 2006).

[67] China, Adoption Law of the People's Republic of China of 29 December 1991, revised at the 5th Meeting of the Standing Committee of the 9th National People's Congress on 4 November 1998 and promulgated by Order No. 10 of the President of the People's Republic of China. Available from http://english.gov.cn/2005-08/31/cont ent_26770.htm (accessed 12 May 2006).

[68] Portugal, Civil Code, book IV, title IV and Law No. 7 of 11 May 2001. Available from http://www.confap.pt/docs/codcivil.PDF

and http://www.dgci.min-financas.pt/NR/rdonlyres/6EAE2583-AE4D-4584-9783-8EF09A46B655/0/lei_7-2001_de_11_de_maio_i_serie_a.pdf (accessed 12 February 2006).

[69] United Nations, "Third periodic report of States parties due in 2003: Norway" (CRC/C/129/Add.1), para. 293.

[70] See United Nations, "Third periodic report of States parties due in 2002: Sweden" (CRC/C/125/Add.1).

[71] See United Nations, "Second periodic reports of States parties due in 2002: Netherlands" (CRC/C/117/Add.1).

[72] United Nations, "Second periodic report of States parties due in 1997: China" (CRC/C/83/Add.9), para. 154.

[73] See United Nations, "Second periodic reports of States parties due in 1998: Myanmar" (CRC/C/70/Add.21).

[74] See United Nations, "Initial reports of States parties due in 1996: Gabon" (CRC/C/41/Add.10).

[75] Switzerland, Civil Code, book II, part II, title VII, chapter IV, art. 266. Available from http://www.admin.ch/ch/f/rs/ 210/a266.html (accessed 12 February 2006).

[76] See United Nations, "Initial reports of States parties due in 1992: Namibia" (CRC/C/3/Add.12).

[77] See United Nations, "Initial reports of States parties due in 1995: Seychelles" (CRC/C/3/Add.64).

[78] See United Nations, "Initial report of States parties due in 1993: The former Yugoslav Republic of Macedonia" (CRC/C/8/Add.36).

[79] See United States, Bureau of Consular Affairs, "Intercountry adoption: Eritrea". Washington, D.C.: Department of State. Available from http://travel.state.gov/family/adoption/country/country_2975.html (accessed 20 February 2007).

[80] See United Nations, "Initial reports of States parties due in 1992: Uganda" (CRC/C/3/Add.40).

[81] See United Nations, "Second periodic reports of States parties due in 2004: United Republic of Tanzania" (CRC/C/70/Add.26).

[82] See United Nations, "Initial reports of States parties due in 1993: Malawi" (CRC/C/8/Add.43).

[83] See United Nations, "Initial reports of States parties due in 1995: Antigua and Barbuda" (CRC/C/28/Add.22).

[84] See United Nations, "Second periodic reports of States parties due in 1999: Trinidad and Tobago" (CRC/C/83/Add.12).

[85] United Kingdom, Adoption and Children Act 2002 Elizabeth II. Chapter 38. Available from http://www.opsi.gov.uk/acts/acts2002/20020038.htm (accessed 30 October 2006).

[86] See United Nations, "Initial report of States parties due in 1997: Malaysia" (CRC/C/MYS/1).

[87] See United Nations, "Periodic reports of States parties due in 1998: Poland" (CRC/C/70/Add.12).

[88] See Teodorescu, A.G., "The Functioning of the new legislation on adoptions and provisions on defining the procedures in the moratorium". Paper presented at the Joint Parliamentary Committee European Union, Brussels, 22-23 November, 2005. Available from http://www.cdep.ro/docs_comisii/IE/CPM19_tema6_EN.pdf (accessed 12 May 2006).

[89] See United Nations, "Initial reports of States parties due in 1998: Brunei Darussalam" (CRC/C/61/Add.5).

[90] See United Nations, "Initial reports of States parties due in 1992: Brazil" (CRC/C/3/Add.65).

[91] See United Nations, "Initial Report of States parties due in 1996: Samoa" (CRC/C/WSM/1).

[92] United Nations, "Second periodic reports of States parties due in 1997: Kenya" (CRC/C/KEN/2), para. 309.

[93] Ethiopia, The Revised Family Code of 2000, Proclamation No. 213/2000. Available from http://www.ethiopar.net/Archive/English /1stterm/5thyear/hopre/bills/1999_2000/pro213.html (accessed 12 May 2006).

[94] The Ministry of Civil Affairs has devised new guidelines regulating the adoption of Chinese children by foreigners. See China, "New criteria spelt out for adoption by foreigners". Available from http://english.gov.cn/2006-12/25/content_477509.htm (accessed 21 February 2007).

[95] See United Nations, "Initial reports of States parties due in 1993: São Tome and Principe" (CRC/C/8/Add.49).

[96] See United Nations, "Periodic reports of States parties due in 1993: Israel" (CRC/C/8/Add.44).

[97] Switzerland, Civil Code, book II, part II, title VII, chapter IV. Available http://www.admin.ch/ch/f/rs/210/index2.html#id-2-2-7-4 (accessed 12 February 2006).

[98] Guatemala, Civil Code, book I, title II, chapter VI. Available from http://www.mintrabajo.gob.gt/varios/compendio_leyes/codigo _civil (accessed 12 February 2006).

[99] Hague Conference on Private International Law, *Collection of Conventions (1951-1996)*, pp. 356-377.

[100] See United Nations, "Initial reports of States parties due in 1997: South Africa" (CRC/C/51/Add.2).

[101] Mexico, Civil Code, book I, title VII, chapter V. Available from http://www.diputados.gob.mx/LeyesBiblio/pdf/2.pdf (accessed 12 February 2006).

[102] See United Nations, "Initial report of States parties due in 1998: Liechtenstein" (CRC/C/61/Add.1).

[103] See United Nations, "Second periodic reports of States parties due in 1997: Mongolia" (CRC/C/65/Add.32).

[104] See United Nations, "Initial reports of States parties: Slovakia" (CRC/C/11/Add.17).

[105] See United Nations, "Second periodic report of States parties due in 1997: Belize" (CRC/C/65/Add.29).

[106] See United Nations, "Second periodic reports of States parties due in 1997: Bangladesh" (CRC/C/65/Add.22).

[107] See United Nations, "Second periodic reports of States parties due in 1997: Indonesia" (CRC/C/65/Add.23).

[108] India, The Hindu Adoptions and Maintenance Act, No. 78 of 21 December 1956. Available from http://nrcw.nic.in/shared/sublin kimages/67.htm (accessed 30 October 2006).

[109] See United Nations, "Second periodic reports of States parties due in 1997: Mauritius" (CRC/C/65/Add.35).

[110] See United States, Bureau of Consular Affairs, "Intercountry adoption: Viet Nam". Washington, D.C.: Department of State. Available from http://travel.state.gov/family/adoption/country/country _349.html (accessed 27 October 2006).

[111] See Canada, Adoption Council of Canada, "Survey of countries reveals closures, slowdowns in international adoption". Available from http://www.adoption.ca/news/040609cystatus.htm (accessed 5 May 2005).

[112] Article 20 (3) of the United Nations Convention on the Rights of the Child states that: "1. A child temporarily or permanently deprived of his or her family environment, or in whose own best interests cannot be allowed to remain in that environment, shall be entitled to special protection and assistance provided by the State. 2. States Parties shall in accordance with their national laws ensure alternative care for such a child. 3. Such care could include, inter alia, foster placement, *kafalah* of Islamic law, adoption or if necessary placement in suitable institutions for the care of children. When considering solutions, due regard shall be paid to the desirability of continuity in a child's upbringing and to the child's ethnic, religious, cultural and linguistic background."

[113] See United Nations, "Periodic reports of States parties due in 1997: Sudan" (CRC/C/65/Add.17).

[114] See United Nations, "Third periodic reports of States parties due in 2003: Lebanon" (CRC/C/129/Add.7).

[115] Resolution A/RES/41/85.

[116] See United Nations, "Periodic reports due in 1994: Cape Verde" (CRC/C/11/Add.23).

[117] See United Nations, "Second periodic reports of States parties due in 1997: Democratic People's Republic of Korea" (CRC/C/65/Add.24).

[118] See United Nations, "Initial reports of States parties due in 1995: Republic of Moldova" (CRC/C/28/Add.19).

[119] See United Nations, "Initial reports of States parties due in 1997: Burkina Faso" (CRC/C/65/Add.18).

[120] See United Nations, "First Periodic Report of States parties due in 1997: Swaziland" (CRC/C/SWZ/1).

[121] See United Nations, "Initial periodic report of States parties due in 1994: Albania" (CRC/C/11/Add.27).

[122] See United Nations, "Periodic reports of States parties due in 1997: Paraguay" (CRC/C/65/Add.12).

[123] See United Nations, "Initial reports of States Parties due in 1992: Togo" (CRC/C/3/Add.42).

[124] See Belgium, Ministry of Justice, "*L'Adoption*". Available from http://www.just.fgov.be/img_justice/publications/pdf/199.pdf (accessed 12 February 2006).

[125] See United Nations, "Second periodic reports of States parties due in 2000: Armenia" (CRC/C/93/Add.6).

[126] See United Nations, "Third periodic report of States parties due in 2003: Norway" (CRC/C/129/Add.1).

[127] See United Nations, "Initial reports of States parties due in 1997: Botswana" (CRC/C/51/Add.9).

[128] See United States, Department of Homeland Security, Citizenship and Immigration Services, "U.S. citizenship for a foreign-born adopted child". Available from http://www.uscis.gov/portal/site/uscis/menuitem.5af9bb95919f35e66f614176543f6d1a/?vgnextoid=28dc6138f898d010VgnVCM10000048f3d6a1RCRD&vgnextchannel=063807b03d92b010VgnVCM10000045f3d6a1RCRD (accessed 2 March 2007).

[129] See United Nations, "Initial reports of States parties due in 1997: Singapore" (CRC/C/51/Add.8).

[130] Argentina, Civil Code, book I, part II, title IV. Available from http://www.redetel.gov.ar/Normativa/Archivos%20de%20Normas/CodigoCivil.htm (accessed 12 February 2006).

[131] See United Nations, "Initial reports of States parties due in 1993: Angola" (CRC/C/3/Add.66).

IV. INTERNATIONAL, REGIONAL AND BILATERAL AGREEMENTS ON INTERCOUNTRY ADOPTION

Between the late 1940s and the late 1960s, intercountry adoption[1] was seen mainly as a humanitarian effort aimed at rescuing children orphaned as a result of the Second World War, the Korean War and, to a lesser extent, the Viet Nam War (Altstein and Simon, 1991; Masson, 2001). Children were predominantly adopted from a handful of countries—notably Germany, Japan, the Republic of Korea and Viet Nam—and the magnitude of intercountry adoption flows was relatively small. Since the 1970s, the number of children involved in intercountry adoptions has increased considerably (see chapter V) and children have originated from an ever growing number of countries (Kane, 1993; Weil, 1984). As intercountry adoption became more widespread, pressures on legal systems and problems arising from conflicting laws emerged. Because most modern adoption laws made no specific provisions for intercountry adoptions (see chapter I), persons adopted by foreigners could find themselves in situations where their interests were not protected and where they were at risk of becoming stateless. Furthermore, there were no internationally agreed mechanisms for recognizing adoption orders promulgated abroad or for translating those orders into comparable practices within the jurisdiction of the countries of destination of adopted persons. Also lacking were clear guidelines defining the jurisdiction of the various authorities involved in the intercountry adoption process.

The first initiatives to establish internationally recognized legal standards for intercountry adoptions were undertaken in the 1960s (Parra-Aranguren, 1996). Thus, the 1961 United Nations Convention on the Reduction of Statelessness[2] included provisions to prevent the statelessness of children adopted internationally. Other initiatives followed suit. The 1965 Convention on Jurisdiction, Applicable Law and Recognition of Decrees Relating to Adoptions[3], drafted by the Hague Conference on International Private Law, fostered common provisions on jurisdiction so as to facilitate the recognition of decrees relating to

adoption. The European Convention on the Adoption of Children[4] entered into force three years later with the purpose of harmonizing laws, regulations and practices among countries of the Council of Europe. These conventions were based on the European situation of the 1960s, when international adoptions spanned relatively short geographical distances and involved countries with comparable socio-economic, cultural and legal systems (Van Loon, 1995). By the time the Convention on Jurisdiction, Applicable Law and Recognition of Decrees Relating to Adoptions entered into force in 1978, "the social reality underlying intercountry adoption had already changed dramatically" (Van Loon, 1995, p. 463).

During the 1980s, the increasing scale of intercountry adoptions, combined with the realization that existing domestic and international legal instruments were insufficient, led to a new series of multilateral and bilateral initiatives aimed at defining questions of applicable law and jurisdiction. In 1989, the Permanent Bureau of the Hague Conference on International Private Law recommended the establishment of legally binding standards for intercountry adoptions and a system to supervise those standards (Parra-Aranguren, 1996). Incidents of trafficking in children and child selling (box IV.1), as well as allegations of irregularities involving intercountry adoptions, heightened the sense of urgency (Bartholet, 1993). In 1989, the United Nations Convention on the Rights of the Child[5] was drafted. One of its objectives was to ensure that the principle of safeguarding the best interests of the child became the paramount consideration in all decisions relating to child adoption. Four years later, the Convention on Protection of Children and Co-operation in Respect of Intercountry Adoption[6] was adopted by the Hague Conference on International Private Law with the aim of defining standards, safeguards and procedures for courts, administrative authorities and private intermediaries involved in intercountry adoption (Van Loon, 1995).

BOX IV.1. BABY SELLING AND HUMAN
TRAFFICKING FOR THE PURPOSE OF
ADOPTION

There is an important distinction between baby
selling and human trafficking for the purpose of
adoption. Baby selling involves coerced or
induced removal of a child, or a situation where
deception or undue compensation is used to
induce the relinquishment of a child. It is an
illegal practice which results in an individual or
set of individuals profiting from the sale of a
human being—in this case an adoptive child.
Trafficking, besides generating a financial gain,
also implies the exploitation of the child,
sexually or in terms of coerced labour.

Source: United States, Department of State, 2005, p. 21.

The international community has also
addressed concerns related to the sale of, and
traffic in, children through intercountry adoptions.
The Programme of Action of the 1994
International Conference on Population and
Development, for instance, called on countries of
origin of intercountry adoptions to stem the
practice of coercive adoption.[7] In 2000, the United
Nations Optional Protocol to the Convention on
the Rights of the Child on the Sale of Children,
Child Prostitution and Child Pornography,[8] was
adopted and opened for signature and ratification
by General Assembly resolution 54/263 of 25
May 2000.

This chapter provides an overview of selected
international, regional and bilateral instruments
that have dealt either in whole or in part with the
issue of intercountry adoption. It highlights key
features of these agreements and underscores
some of their similarities and differences.

A. INTERNATIONAL AGREEMENTS

Several international instruments have focused
either in whole or in part on the issue of
intercountry adoption. The purposes of these
instruments with respect to intercountry adoption
are diverse. The main aim of the United Nations
Convention on the Reduction of Statelessness of
1961, for instance, is to protect the interests of
minors and, in particular, to ensure that children
adopted through intercountry procedures do not

become stateless. The United Nations Optional
Protocol to the Convention on the Rights of the
Child on the Sale of Children, Child Prostitution
and Child Pornography,[8] aims at criminalizing the
improper inducement of consent, as an
intermediary, for the adoption of a child. The
section below reviews in chronological order
some of the multilateral instruments that have
dealt with the issue of intercountry adoption.

1. United Nations Convention on the Reduction of Statelessness (1961)[2]

The Convention on the Reduction of
Statelessness contains one paragraph that refers to
intercountry adoption. Paragraph 1 of article 5
states that if "the law of a contracting State entails
loss of nationality as a consequence of any change
in the personal status of a person such as
marriage, termination of marriage, legitimation,
recognition or adoption, such loss shall be
conditional upon possession or acquisition of
another nationality." The Convention entered into
force in December 1975 and, as of January 2007,
had been ratified by 33 countries (table A.IV.1).
Three additional countries were signatories but
had not yet ratified it. None of the countries that
have ratified the Convention has made any
declaration or reservations in relation to the
application of the paragraph relevant to
intercountry adoption.

2. Convention on Jurisdiction, Applicable Law and Recognition of Decrees Relating to Adoptions (1965)[3]

This Convention was one of the first
multilateral instruments seeking to establish
common provisions on jurisdiction, applicable law
and recognition of decrees relating to adoption. As
such, it is worthy of note, despite the fact that the
three Member States that ratified it—Austria,
Switzerland and the United Kingdom—later
denounced it, implying that the Convention no
longer has effect for them.

One of the essential features of the Convention
is that it provides guidelines as to the authority
responsible for various aspects of the adoption
procedure. The jurisdiction to grant an adoption is
vested in the authorities of the State in which the

adoptive parents either have their habitual residence or are nationals. These authorities may grant an adoption only when it is in the best interests of the child and only after having carried out a thorough inquiry relating to the prospective adoptive parents, child and birth family (art. 6). The authorities of the State in which the adopted person or the adoptive parents reside, as well as the State in which the adoption was granted, have jurisdiction to annul or revoke the adoption (art. 7). The Convention also stipulates in article 8 that contracting States must recognize, without further formality, every adoption governed by the Convention and granted by an authority having jurisdiction under the first paragraph of article 3.

The Convention does not establish specific requirements for the prospective adoptive parents, nor does it provide a detailed description of the legal ramifications of adoption. The Convention applies only to persons who are nationals and habitual residents of one of the contracting States. As in the European Convention on the Adoption of Children (section IV.B below), the prospective adopted persons must be minors and single.[9]

3. United Nations Declaration on Social and Legal Principles relating to the Protection and Welfare of Children, with Special Reference to Foster Placement and Adoption Nationally and Internationally (1986)[10]

This Declaration was adopted by General Assembly resolution 41/85 of 3 December 1986. The Declaration recognizes that a "child should not, as a result of foster placement, adoption or any alternative regime, be deprived of his or her name, nationality or legal representative unless the child thereby acquires a new name, nationality or legal representative" (art. 8). It also establishes the principle of subsidiarity, that is, that an intercountry adoption should only take place when suitable adoptive parents cannot be identified in the country of origin of the child (art. 17).

The Declaration calls upon the Governments of all Member States to "establish policy, legislation and effective supervision for the protection of children involved in intercountry adoption" (art. 18). The Declaration indicates that placements should be made through competent authorities or agencies with the same safeguards and standards as national adoptions and that in no case should an adoption result in improper financial gains for those involved (art. 20). The Declaration further states that intercountry adoption should not be considered before it has been established that the child is legally free for adoption and that all necessary documentation, such as the consent of the competent authorities, is available. The Declaration requires Member States to ascertain that the adopted child is able to migrate, to join the prospective adoptive parents and to obtain their nationality before authorizing an intercountry adoption (art. 22). The Declaration calls for giving all due weight to the laws of the States in which the child and the prospective adoptive parents are nationals. The Declaration also requires Member States to consider the child's cultural and religious background and interests (art. 24).

4. United Nations Convention on the Rights of the Child (1989)[5]

The Convention on the Rights of the Child dedicates several paragraphs to the issue of intercountry adoption. Under article 21 (c), for instance, States parties are required to ensure that children adopted through intercountry procedures enjoy the same safeguards and standards as children adopted domestically. The Convention also recognizes the principle of subsidiarity (art. 21 (b)) and indicates that States parties should take all appropriate measures to ensure that, in the case of intercountry adoptions, placement does not result in improper financial gains for those involved (art. 21 (d)). The Convention, similarly to the United Nations Declaration on Social and Legal Principles relating to the Protection and Welfare of Children, with Special Reference to Foster Placement and Adoption Nationally and Internationally, recognizes that the best interests of the child should be the paramount consideration.

The Convention entered into force in September 1990. As of January 2007, 193 countries were parties to the Convention (see table A.IV.1). Several of the ratifying States have entered reservations to the articles relevant to adoption. For instance, Egypt, Jordan, Kuwait, the

Syrian Arab Republic and the United Arab Emirates expressed reservations with respect to all clauses and provisions relating to adoption, because they do not include adoption among the ways and means of protecting and caring for children. Likewise, Argentina expressed reservations to subparagraphs (b), (c), (d) and (e) of article 21 of the Convention and declared that these subparagraphs do not apply within its jurisdiction, indicating that a stricter mechanism for the legal protection of children in matters of intercountry adoption was necessary in order to prevent trafficking in, and the sale of, children.

5. Convention on Protection of Children and Co-operation in Respect of Intercountry Adoption (1993)[6]

This Convention, frequently referred to as the Hague Convention, is probably the major multilateral instrument regulating intercountry adoptions. It has three main objectives. The first is to establish safeguards to ensure that intercountry adoptions take place in the best interests of the child. The second is to prevent the sale of, or traffic in, children through a system of cooperation among contracting States. The third objective is to secure the recognition among contracting States of adoptions made in accordance with the Convention (art. 1). The Convention applies only to children who are habitually residents in one contracting State—the State of origin—and are moved to another contracting State—the receiving State—either after their adoption or for the purpose of adoption (art. 2). Only adoptions that create permanent child-parent relationships fall under the jurisdiction of the Hague Convention.

The different responsibilities of States of origin and States of destination are outlined in chapter II of the Hague Convention. However, unlike many previous multilateral instruments, the Hague Convention does not simply delineate the rules of jurisdiction and applicable law but recognizes the need for coordination and direct cooperation between countries (Van Loon, 1995). Authorities in the State of origin are charged with establishing whether a child is adoptable and whether the placement is in the child's best interests (art. 4). The State of origin is also responsible for ascertaining that a permanent family cannot be found in the child's own country and that the persons, institutions and authorities whose consent is necessary for the adoption have given their consent freely and are duly informed of the effects of their consent. The competent authorities of the receiving States are responsible for determining that the prospective adoptive parents are "eligible and suited to adopt," that they have been appropriately counselled and that the child is or will be authorized to reside permanently in the receiving State (art. 5).

The Hague Convention calls upon contracting States to designate a central adoption authority and outlines the roles and responsibilities of this authority in chapter III. Specifically, the Convention calls on central authorities to cooperate with each other to protect children (art. 7). Central authorities are required to take measures to prevent improper financial or other gains in connection with an adoption and to deter all practices contrary to the objectives of the Convention (art. 8). Central authorities are charged with collecting and exchanging information regarding the child and the prospective adoptive parents, facilitating the adoption proceedings and promoting the development of adoption counselling (art. 9). The central authorities of both the State of origin and the receiving State must agree before an adoption can proceed (art. 17). Once an adoption has been authorized, the central authorities of both the receiving State and the State of origin are required to ensure the smooth transfer of the child (art. 19). In cases where the adoption takes place after the transfer of the child, the central authorities of the receiving State are responsible for taking the necessary measures to protect the child's best interests, including, if necessary, finding temporary care for the child, arranging a new placement or returning the child to his or her country of origin (art. 21).

Public authorities or other bodies duly accredited in a contracting State can also perform some of the responsibilities of central authorities outlined in article 9. These accredited bodies are required to pursue only non-profit objectives and must be directed and staffed by persons qualified to work in the field of intercountry adoption. Accredited bodies are subject to supervision by the competent authorities of their State as to their composition, operation and financial situation (art. 11). Paragraph 2 of article 22 of the Hague Convention, however, indicates that the functions of the central authority may also be performed by non-accredited bodies or persons as long as these "meet the requirements of integrity, professional competence, experience and accountability of that State and are qualified by their ethical standards and by training or experience to work in the field of intercountry adoption." Contracting States may refuse to allow such non-accredited agencies to arrange adoptions on their territory. The recognition of the role of accredited and non-accredited bodies stems from the "present reality that private organizations play an important role as intermediaries in the intercountry adoption process" (Van Loon, 1995, p. 466).

As did many previous instruments, the Hague Convention dedicates a chapter to the legal ramifications of adoption. According to article 26, adoption creates a legal child-parent relationship between the adopted person and his or her adoptive parents and terminates any pre-existing legal relationships between the adopted person and his or her birth parents. However, where an adoption granted in the State of origin does not have the effect of terminating pre-existing legal parent-child relationships, the receiving State can terminate those relationships, under the condition that the relevant persons, institutions and authorities—including, where appropriate, the birth parents and the child—freely consent and are duly informed of the effect of their consent (art. 27). With regards to the recognition of adoptions, contracting States are called upon to recognize all adoptions made in accordance with the Convention (art. 23). However, they may reserve the right not do so by applying article 39, paragraph 2 (art. 25).

Just as the United Nations Convention on the Rights of the Child, the Hague Convention also calls upon contracting parties to undertake all appropriate measures to ensure that placements do not result in improper financial gains. Specifically, paragraphs 1 and 2 of article 32 establish that "no one shall derive improper financial or other gain from an activity related to an intercountry adoption. Only costs and expenses, including reasonable professional fees of persons involved

in the adoption, may be charged or paid." The remuneration of directors, administrators and employees of bodies involved, furthermore, should not be unreasonable given the services rendered (art. 32 (3)). The Convention specifies that direct contact between the adoptive parents and birth parents is generally prohibited (art. 29) and that adoptive parents are responsible for the cost of translation of any documents required by the authorities of the State of destination (art. 34). The Convention entered into force in May 1995. As of January 2007, 70 States had ratified or acceded to the Hague Convention, and three States—Ireland, the Russian Federation and the United States—were signatories to the Convention but had not yet ratified it (table A.IV.1).

6. United Nations Optional Protocol to the Convention on the Rights of the Child on the Sale of Children, Child Prostitution and Child Pornography (2000)[8]

The Optional Protocol to the Convention on the Rights of the Child was adopted at the fifty-fourth session of the General Assembly of the United Nations on 25 May 2000 (Resolution 54/263). Paragraph 1 (a) (ii) of article 3 of the Optional Protocol calls on States parties to ensure that coercive adoption is fully covered under their criminal or penal law, regardless of whether such an offence is committed domestically or transnationally and whether it is committed on an individual or organized basis. Specifically, the article criminalizes the act of "improperly inducing consent, as an intermediary, for the adoption of a child" (art. 3, para. 1 (c) (ii)). Paragraph 5 of article 3 of the Optional Protocol further calls on States parties to take all appropriate legal and administrative measures to ensure that all persons involved in the adoption act do so in conformity with applicable international legal instruments.

The Optional Protocol entered into force in January 2002 and by January 2007, it had been ratified by 117 States (table A.IV.1). Some countries have advanced reservations to some of the paragraphs of article 3 relevant to adoption. Argentina, for instance, stated that it "has not signed international instruments on the international adoption of minors . . . and does not permit international adoption of children domiciled or resident in its jurisdiction". The Government of the Republic of Korea specified that it understands article 3 (1) (a) (ii) to be applicable only to States that are parties to the Convention on Protection of Children and Co-operation in Respect of Intercountry Adoption. The Syrian Arab Republic entered a reservation to the provisions set forth in article 3, paragraph 5, and article 3, paragraph 1 (a) (ii) of the Optional Protocol because it does not recognize the institution of adoption.

B. REGIONAL AGREEMENTS

Regional agreements have been seen as a means of harmonizing laws, of identifying common principles and practices and as a way of minimizing the conflicts of jurisdiction that can occur in intercountry adoptions. Two major regional agreements are examined in this chapter: the European Convention on the Adoption of Children of 1967 and the Inter-American Convention on Conflict of Laws Concerning the Adoption of Minors of 1984.

1. European Convention on the Adoption of Children (1967)[4]

The European Convention on the Adoption of Children was developed with the purpose of harmonizing adoption laws among Member States of the Council of Europe. The Convention calls for common principles and practices to promote the welfare of adopted children and aims to harmonize some of the principles governing adoption, the procedures affecting it, and its legal consequences. The Convention only applies to legal adoptions involving unmarried minors[9] (art. 3).

The Convention contains a core of essential provisions which each State party undertakes to incorporate into its legislation, as well as a list of supplementary provisions which States parties are free to adopt or not. Among its essential provisions, the Convention stipulates that adoption must be granted by a competent judicial or administrative authority (art. 4), that birth parents must freely consent to the adoption (art. 5) and that the adoption must be in the best interests of the child (art. 8). Article 15 requires States parties to make

provisions to prohibit any improper financial advantages arising from the adoption of a child. The Convention requires prospective adoptive parents to be between 21 and 35 years of age (art. 7) and limits joint adoption to married couples (art. 6). Some procedural rules are also outlined among the essential provisions of the Convention. One such requirement is that competent authorities conduct a series of enquiries to ensure the suitability of the prospective adoptive parents (articles 8 and 9). The Convention also addresses the procedures for revoking or annulling an adoption (art. 13) and for sharing the information collected through the enquiries (art. 14).

With respect to the legal ramifications of adoption, article 10 of the Convention recognizes that adoption terminates all rights and obligations between the adopted person and his or her birth parents and that adopted persons have the same rights and obligations as legitimate offspring, including the right to inheritance. With regard to the acquisition of the adoptive parents' name, the Convention stipulates that, as a general rule, the adopted child should acquire the surname of the adoptive parents either in substitution for, or in addition to, his or her own name. Article 11 recognizes that, where the adopted person does not have the same nationality as the adoptive parents, the acquisition of nationality of the adoptive parents should be facilitated and any eventual loss of nationality resulting from an adoption should be conditional upon the possession or acquisition of another nationality.

Among the supplementary provisions, the Convention calls on Member States to ensure that adoptions are completed without disclosing the identity of the adoptive parents to the child's birth family and to enable adoption proceedings to take place in camera (art. 20).

The Convention entered into force in April 1968 and, as of January 2007, had been ratified by 18 of the 46 Member States of the Council of Europe, while three Member States were signatories but had not yet ratified it (table IV.1). Some of the countries that ratified the Convention made reservations to specific articles or paragraphs. Countries such as Romania and the former Yugoslav Republic of Macedonia, for instance, declared that instead of the age requirements set out in article 7, paragraph 1 of the Convention, they would apply the age requirements established in their own legislation.

2. Inter-American Convention on Conflict of Laws Concerning the Adoption of Minors (1984)[11]

This Convention was developed with the purpose of harmonizing national laws, regulations and procedures regarding the adoption of minors, addressing conflicting stipulations within these laws and regulations, and identifying clear guidelines as to the authority responsible for various aspects of the adoption procedure. The Convention applies only when the prospective adoptive parents are domiciled in one State party

and the adopted person is domiciled in another State party.

Instead of establishing specific statutory requirements, the Convention defines the jurisdiction of the various authorities involved in the adoption procedure. The authorities of the State of habitual residence of the child at the time of adoption are, for instance, considered competent to grant the adoption (art. 15) and to decide on its eventual annulment or revocation (art. 16). The laws of the country of habitual residence of the prospective adopted child also govern the "capacity, consent, and other requirements for adoption, as well as those procedures and formalities that are necessary for creating the relationship" (art. 3). The laws of the country of domicile of the adoptive parents govern the

TABLE IV.1. COUNTRIES THAT HAVE RATIFIED THE EUROPEAN
CONVENTION ON THE ADOPTION OF CHILDREN, 1967

Country	Year of ratification
Austria	1980
Czech Republic	2000
Denmark	1978
France	..
Germany	1980
Greece	1980
Iceland	..
Ireland	1968
Italy	1976
Latvia	2000
Liechtenstein	1981
Luxembourg	..
Malta	1967
Norway	1972
Poland	1996
Portugal	1990
Romania	1993
Sweden	1968
Switzerland	1972
The former Yugoslav Republic of Macedonia	2003
United Kingdom[1]	1967
Total number of ratifications	18

Source: Council of Europe, 1967.

NOTES: As of January 2007. Ratification includes acceptance, approval, accession or succession. Two dots (..) indicate that the treaty has been signed but not ratified.

[1] In 2005 the United Kingdom denounced the Convention except for the Bailiwicks of Jersey and Guernsey.

TABLE IV.2. COUNTRIES THAT HAVE RATIFIED
THE INTER-AMERICAN CONVENTION ON CONFLICT OF LAWS
CONCERNING THE ADOPTION OF MINORS, 1984

Country	Year of ratification
Belize..	1997
Bolivia (Plurinational State of).................	..
Brazil	1997
Chile	2001
Colombia	1988
Dominican Republic	..
Ecuador..	..
Haiti	..
Mexico..	1987
Panama	1999
Paraguay	..
Uruguay	..
Venezuela (Bolivarian Republic of)	..
Total number of ratifications	6

Source: Organization of American States, General Secretariat, 1984.

NOTES: As of January 2007. Ratification includes acceptance, approval, accession or succession. Two dots (..) indicate that the treaty has been signed but not ratified.

requirements relating to the age and marital status of the prospective adoptive parents, as well as the consent of any eventual spouse of the adoptive parent (art. 4). The Convention recognizes that the conversion of a simple adoption into a full adoption[12] can be governed either by the laws of the country of habitual residence of the adopted person at the time of the adoption or by the laws of the country in which the adoptive parents have their domicile (art. 13).

In describing the effects of adoption, the Convention distinguishes between full adoption and simple adoption. In relation to full adoption, the Convention recognizes that the relations between the adoptive parents and the adopted child are equivalent to those between biological offspring and their parents (art. 9). The termination of ties with the family of origin and the right to succession are also recognized (articles 9 and 11). In the case of simple adoption, the effects of the adoption are determined by the laws of the country of habitual residence of the adoptive parents (art. 10). The potential loss of nationality of an adopted child is not addressed in the Convention. As of January 2007, six Member

States had ratified the Convention, while an additional seven Member States were signatories (table IV.2).

C. BILATERAL AGREEMENTS

As indicated in the United Nations Convention on the Rights of the Child, bilateral agreements offer an important tool for ensuring that intercountry adoptions take place in accordance with established rules and under conditions that protect the interests of minors.[13] One of the most common objectives of bilateral agreements has been to streamline the adoption process. In Ireland, for instance, the Adoption Board has concluded bilateral or working agreements on intercountry adoption with Belarus, China, the Philippines and Thailand.[14] The effect of these agreements has been to simplify the adoption procedure by eliminating the need for the involvement of third parties. Ireland has also entered into a Government-to-Government agreement with Romania, which allows prospective adoptive parents who wish to adopt a Romanian child to avail themselves directly of accredited Romanian adoption agencies.[14] Similarly, Spain has concluded bilateral agreements on civil and commercial matters with Bulgaria and China that have facilitated intercountry adoptions by exempting certain documents from authentication.[15] Australia also concluded a bilateral agreement with China— the Australia-China Adoption Agreement— ensuring that intercountry adoptions undertaken by Australian nationals in China are automatically recognized under Australian law.[16]

In addition to bilateral agreements aimed at facilitating intercountry adoption procedures, a growing number of countries have sought to prevent and criminalize the abduction and sale of or trafficking in children in connection with intercountry adoptions. Australia, for instance, has entered into bilateral agreements with a number of countries in Africa, Asia, Europe and South America with the stated objective of ensuring that children "are protected from being bought or sold and to provide protection for families who wish to adopt a child from overseas."[16] Similarly, Costa Rica reported that it was in the process of drafting and signing bilateral agreements on intercountry adoptions with Canada, France, Italy, the Netherlands and the United Kingdom. The purpose of these agreements is to ensure that "all measures relating to intercountry adoption are duly implemented" and to prevent the abduction of and trafficking in children and adolescents.[17] Viet Nam has required countries to enter into bilateral agreements with its Government following allegations of irregularities. In response to this requirement, the United States signed a bilateral agreement on adoptions with Viet Nam, which entered into force on 1 September 2005.[18] Canada[19] and Ireland[20] have also concluded bilateral agreements with Viet Nam.

While many countries have availed themselves of bilateral agreements to facilitate intercountry adoption procedures and protect the interests of adopted persons, some countries have indicated that they view multilateral approaches as preferable. The Netherlands, for instance, stated in a recent report to the Committee on the Rights of the Child that it is "not in favour of bilateral agreements on adoption and child abduction," preferring instead to use existing multilateral agreements. The Netherlands further indicated that it did not support bilateral treaty negotiations

with States that are not parties to such multilateral Conventions because this might dissuade them from ratifying.[21] Likewise, the Government of the United States prefers to enter into multilateral treaties on private international law rather than into bilateral agreements because a multilateral instrument "offers substantially all the mutual benefits that could be expected from a bilateral treaty, and at the same time, facilitates the development of a single, unified legal regime among the countries party to it."[22] Another reason cited is that "negotiating, concluding and obtaining senate consent to ratifying bilateral treaties has proven to be a long, uncertain, and resource intensive process."[22]

D. RECENT INITIATIVES AND FUTURE CHALLENGES RELATED TO INTERCOUNTRY ADOPTIONS

In recent years, the growing willingness of Governments to enter into multilateral, regional and bilateral agreements on adoption has resulted in significant progress in improving procedures and adding safeguards to the intercountry adoption process. Thus, after ratifying the Hague Convention in 1998, Lithuania established a public adoption authority—the Adoption Agency—that receives information regularly from contracting foreign authorities on the well-being of Lithuanian children adopted abroad.[23] In Nicaragua, a central adoption authority was established to oversee and report on international adoptions originating in the country in accordance with the Hague Convention.[24]

Progress has also been made in enacting laws to criminalize the act of obtaining improper gains from intercountry adoptions. Brazil[25] and Germany,[26] for instance, have modified their civil and criminal laws to criminalize the sale of children and trafficking in children for the purpose of adoption. In Romania, parents, legal guardians, custodians or third parties facilitating an adoption are subject to imprisonment for demanding or receiving money or any other benefits in exchange for the adoption.[27]

A number of countries have developed mechanisms for recognizing adoption orders promulgated abroad or for translating those orders into practices consistent with the jurisdiction of the receiving country. In France, Act No. 2001-111 of 6 February 2001 stipulates that an adoption order lawfully issued abroad has the effect of a full adoption in France, if a full and irrevocable break is made with the previous filiation.[28] Otherwise, the order has the effect of a simple adoption. According to that Act, a simple adoption ordered abroad can be converted into a full adoption if the concerned persons give their express consent after being informed of the implications of the conversion.[28] In the United Kingdom, the Adoption and Children Act of 2002 requires birth parents to be duly informed of the effects of adoption and requires their consent to a full adoption prior to granting an adoption order.[29] Many of these changes were introduced to comply with international agreements.

Recent events, however, have indicated that, especially during emergency situations, children are still particularly vulnerable to being the victims of trafficking or sale for the purpose of adoption. Following the 2004 tsunami in South-eastern Asia, for example, several countries temporarily suspended both domestic and intercountry adoptions in order to prevent abuses. Similar issues have arisen in conflict situations. Thus, some children who were evacuated to Europe during the conflict in Rwanda were adopted without following appropriate legal procedures. A recent report submitted by Rwanda to the Committee on the Rights of the Child cites the case of 41 Rwandan children who were adopted irregularly by parents in Italy.[30]

Instances of trafficking in and sale of children continue to take place in conjunction with intercountry adoptions in many parts of the world (box IV.2). In Thailand, for instance, the Centre for the Protection of Children's Rights has documented instances of trafficking.[31] About 100 children, many very young, are believed to have been trafficked into Malaysia for the purpose of adoption between 1986 and 1995. In Guatemala, a study by the Association "Casa Alianza" and the Office of the National Procurator-General showed that the trafficking in children and the sale of children for the purpose of intercountry adoption were widespread. The existence of networks of child traffickers and irregularities in the procedures followed by some judicial bodies all contributed to make those criminal activities possible. Guatemala has responded by creating the "Consejo Nacional de Adopciones", a body charged with overseeing and monitoring domestic and intercountry adoptions.[32] Several receiving countries have suspended intercountry adoptions from Guatemala or require DNA samples as evidence of the authenticity of the birth mother's consent.[33]

BOX IV.2. COUNTRIES THAT HAVE RAISED CONCERNS ABOUT THE SALE OF CHILDREN OR TRAFFIC IN CHILDREN IN RELATION TO INTERCOUNTRY ADOPTION

Africa:	*Asia:*
Central African Republic	Azerbaijan
Equatorial Guinea	Cambodia
Madagascar	Indonesia[1]
Mauritius	Sri Lanka[1]
Rwanda	Thailand[1]
	Viet Nam

Latin America and the Caribbean:	*Oceania:*
Argentina	Fiji
Guatemala	Marshal Islands
Paraguay	

Source: For a complete list of country references, see annex II.
[1]Concerns voiced in the wake of the South-eastern Asian tsunami of December 2004.

A number of States parties have also voiced concerns about practical issues related to the implementation of various aspects of multilateral instruments on intercountry adoption. At the meeting of the Permanent Bureau of the Hague Conference on Private International Law, held from 28 November to 1 December 2000, several Latin American delegations described the difficulties they were experiencing in shifting to a system in which central authorities instead of the courts monitored intercountry adoptions. Similarly, EurAdopt and the Nordic Adoption Council, representing 26 adoption organizations and 13 European countries, voiced concern about the role of accredited bodies and called for better guidelines in this respect. The United Kingdom, on behalf of the informal Working Conference of European Contracting States, echoed many of the same concerns and its representative emphasized the need for States parties to uphold the same standards for intercountry adoptions.

Some scholars and experts have also pointed to areas where multilateral initiatives focusing on intercountry adoption could be strengthened. For instance, Bartholet, writing just before the Hague Convention was adopted, recognized the significance of the Declaration on Social and Legal Principles Relating to Adoption and Foster Placement of Children Nationally and Internationally and of the Convention on the Rights of the Child but noted that "these documents do not establish standards for the processing of international adoptions" (Bartholet, 1993, p. 94). Seven years after the adoption of the Hague Convention and five years after its entrance into force, a similar observation was made by Lovelock (2000).

Another common criticism has been that the multilateral instruments developed thus far place too much emphasis on "the political will of the implementing countries" (Lovelock, 2000, p. 941). Thus, Masson noted that the Hague Convention "only works against abuses indirectly; it is not an international criminal code. The enactment and enforcement of laws regulating adoption is a matter for the competent authorities in each contracting State" (Masson, 2001, p. 151). The vagueness of the terminology used in these instruments has also been criticized. Lovelock (2000) noted that important terms, such as "reasonable compensation," "non-profit objectives" and "adoptability" are left undefined in the Hague Convention, leaving room for the possibility of misunderstanding and abuse. The fact that the Hague Convention does not apply to children from non-contracting States and that contracting States are permitted to receive children from non-contracting countries has also been noted with concern by some authors (Lovelock, 2000; Masson, 2001).

Fears of excessive bureaucratisation of the adoption process have also been raised. Bartholet, for instance, remarked on the risk that the Hague Convention "will simply establish additional barriers to the placement of children" and "will do little to establish the kind of new legal framework needed to make the international adoption process work effectively" (Bartholet, 1993, p. 95).

These challenges were discussed by the Special Commission on the Practical Operation of the Hague Convention when it met from 17 to 23 September 2005. The Special Commission recommended that the Permanent Bureau should continue to gather information from different contracting States with the view of developing clearer standards for dealing with the issue of accreditation (Hague Conference on Private International Law, 2005). The Special Commission also recommended that the Permanent Bureau, in consultation with contracting States and non-governmental organizations, develop a model form for the consent of the child (art. 4 (d) (3)), as well as model forms or protocols regarding the operation of articles 15 and 16 of the Convention. The Special Commission further recommended that States actively discourage direct contact between prospective adoptive parents and authorities in the State of origin until authorized to do so. With regard to nationality, the Special Commission recommended that children be automatically accorded the nationality of one of the adoptive parents or of the receiving State, without the need to rely on any action by the adoptive parents. Receiving States that do not automatically recognize the acquisition of citizenship were encouraged to provide the necessary assistance to ensure that an adopted child does not become stateless.

E. SUMMARY

International, regional and bilateral instruments on adoption are necessary because intercountry adoption, by its very nature, involves the interaction of at least two countries whose legal principles might differ. Over the past decades, countries have responded to the increasing magnitude and complexity of intercountry adoption flows by calling for greater international co-operation and by emphasizing the need for improved mechanisms to protect the wellbeing of adopted persons (Lovelock, 2000). The principle of safeguarding the best interests of the child, as outlined in the United Nations Convention on the Rights of the Child, has become the paramount consideration guiding the provisions included in recent multilateral and bilateral instruments.

Since 1990, States have made substantial progress in laying the legal framework to prevent the use of adoption as a means of child exploitation. Thus, several Governments have passed laws to punish the sale of and traffic in children for the purpose of adoption. Countries have also developed multilateral and bilateral mechanisms to address conflicts of jurisdiction and applicable law that would eliminate loopholes exploited by traffickers. Despite such progress, several challenges remain. Instances of child trafficking and selling continue to occur. A major challenge is to make the various agreements operational. It has been argued that existing multilateral instruments may be unenforceable and may rely too much on Governments' political will to comply. The fact that key terms used in international instruments remain ill defined and open to interpretation undermine efforts to achieve greater harmonization. Aware of these challenges, Governments continue to engage in international initiatives to ensure that existing international legal mechanisms respond better to the evolving reality of intercountry adoptions.

NOTES

[1] Some experts have made a distinction between intercountry adoptions, which entail a change of the child's habitual country of residence but not necessarily of the child's citizenship, and international adoptions, which involve parents and children of a different citizenship regardless of their place of residence (UNICEF, 1998). This distinction is not made in this chapter. A more detailed discussion of these concepts is given in chapter VIII.

[2] United Nations, *Treaty Series*, vol. 989, No. 14458, p. 175.

[3] Hague Conference on Private International Law, *Collection of Conventions (1951-1996)*, pp. 64-75.

[4] Council of Europe, *European Treaty Series*, No. 058.

[5] United Nations, *Treaty Series*, vol. 1577, No. 27531, p. 3.

[6] Hague Conference on Private International Law, *Collection of Conventions (1951-1996)*, pp. 356-377.

[7] Paragraph 10.18 states that "Governments of both receiving countries and countries of origin should adopt effective sanctions against those who organize undocumented migration, exploit undocumented migrants or engage in trafficking in undocumented migrants, especially those who engage in any form of international traffic in women, youth and children. Governments of countries of origin, where the activities of agents or other intermediaries in the migration process are legal, should regulate such activities in order to prevent abuses, especially exploitation, prostitution and coercive adoption." *Report of the International Conference on Population and Development, Cairo, 5-13 September 1994* (United Nations publication, Sales No. E.95.XIII.18), chap. I, resolution 1, annex.

[8] United Nations, *Treaty Series*, vol. 2171, No. 27531, p. 227.

[9] A minor is defined in the Convention as a person who has not attained the age of 18 at the time when the adoptive parent applies for the adoption.

[10] Resolution A/RES/41/85.

[11] Organization of American States, General Secretariat, *Treaty Series*, No. 62.

[12] The treaty also refers to adoptive legitimation as having similar effects to full adoption. Descriptions of adoptive legitimation and of simple and full adoption are given in chapter I.

[13] According to article 21 of the Convention on the Rights of the Child, "States Parties that recognize and/or permit the system of adoption shall ensure that the best interests of the child shall be the paramount consideration and they shall: . . . (e) Promote, where appropriate, the objectives of the present article by concluding bilateral or multilateral arrangements or agreements, and endeavour, within this framework, to ensure that the placement of the child in another country is carried out by competent authorities or organs."

[14] See Ireland, International Adoption Association, "Bilateral agreements". Available from http://www.iaaireland.org/guide/bilateral agreements.htm (accessed 12 February 2006).

[15] See United Nations, "Periodic reports of States parties due in 1999: Spain" (CRC/C/70/Add.9). Spain has also signed administrative protocols coordinating procedures on intercountry adoptions with Colombia, Ecuador, Peru, the Plurinational State of Bolivia and Romania.

[16] See Australia, Department of Immigration and Citizenship, "Child migration". Available from http://www.immi.gov.au/allforms/booklets/1128.pdf (accessed 12 February 2006).

[17] See United Nations, "Third periodic reports of States parties due in 2002: Costa Rica" (CRC/C/125/Add.4).

[18] See United States, Government Accountability Office, "Foreign affairs: agencies have improved the intercountry adoption process, but further enhancements are needed" (Report No. GAO-06-133). Available from http://www.gao.gov/htext/d06133.html (accessed 21 February 2006).

[19] See Canada, Adoption Council, "Country survey reveals status of international adoption". Available from http://www.adoption.ca/news/050730cystatus.htm (accessed 21 February 2006).

[20] See Ireland, Department of Health and Children, "Minister Lenihan announces a bilateral adoption agreement between Ireland and Vietnam". Available from http://www.dohc.ie/press/releases/2003/20030716a.html (accessed 21 February 2006).

[21] See United Nations, "Second periodic reports of States parties due in 2002: Netherlands" (CRC/C/117/Add.1).

[22] See United States, Bureau of Consular Affairs, "What is the Office of Children's Issues?" Washington, D.C.: Department of State.

Available from http://travel.state.gov/family/about/faq/faq_602.html (accessed 21 February 2006).

[23] See United Nations, "Second periodic reports of States parties due in 1999: Lithuania" (CRC/C/83/Add.14).

[24] See United Nations, "Third periodic reports of States parties due in 2002: Nicaragua" (CRC/C/125/Add.3).

[25] See United Nations, "Initial reports of States parties due in 1992: Brazil" (CRC/C/3/Add.65).

[26] See United Nations, "Second periodic reports of States parties due in 1999: Germany" (CRC/C/83/Add.7).

[27] See United Nations, "Periodic reports of States parties due in 1997: Romania" (CRC/C/65/Add.19).

[28] See United Nations, "Second periodic reports of States parties due in 1997: France" (CRC/C/65/Add.26).

[29] United Kingdom, Adoption and Children Act 2002 Elizabeth II. Chapter 38. Available from http://www.opsi.gov.uk/acts/acts 2002/20020038.htm (accessed 30 October 2006).

[30] See United Nations, "Second periodic reports of States parties due in 1998: Rwanda" (CRC/C/70/Add.22).

[31] See United Nations, "Initial reports of States parties due in 1994: Thailand" (CRC/C/11/Add.13).

[32] See United Nations, "Second periodic reports of States parties due in 1997: Guatemala" (CRC/C/65/Add.10).

[33] See United States, Bureau of Consular Affairs, "Intercountry adoption: Guatemala". Washington, D.C.: Department of State. Available from http://travel.state.gov/family/adoption/country/country_ 389.html (accessed 21 February 2006).

V. LEVELS AND TRENDS IN CHILD ADOPTIONS

There is a generalized view that the number of adoptions is high and increasing worldwide. Yet, data on the number of adoptions are fragmentary, lack wide dissemination or, in some countries, are not routinely compiled or published. This chapter uses the data available to derive estimates of the total number of adoptions worldwide,[1] the share of all adoptions that involve intercountry procedures, and the number and characteristics of domestic adoptions.

Intercountry adoptions are those that involve a change in the country of residence of the adopted child. Because such a change of residence is an essential part of an intercountry adoption, both the country of origin and the country of destination require procedures allowing the migration of the adopted child from one to the other. The country of destination, in particular, must have in place laws or regulations for the admission of foreign children for the purpose of adoption. Usually, those laws or regulations establish the conditions under which citizens of the country in question may secure the admission of a foreign child coming from abroad for the purpose of adoption. In some countries, long-term residents who are not citizens may also have the possibility of engaging in intercountry adoptions.

Data on intercountry adoptions are obtained both from countries of origin of the children involved and from countries of destination. The data produced by countries of origin usually reflect the number of adoptions processed via an intercountry procedure. Data produced by countries of destination often reflect the number of foreign children admitted for the purpose of adoption and indicate the country of origin of the children involved. Data disseminated by countries of origin are less likely to show the country of destination of the children being adopted. None of the two sources of data provide enough inform- ation on the citizenship or country of residence of adoptive parents. Hence, it is not straightforward to disentangle how these characteristics of adoptive parents condition intercountry adoptions.

There is no universally accepted definition of a domestic adoption. For the purposes of this chapter, domestic adoptions are characterized as all those adoptions that do not involve an intercountry procedure. In domestic adoptions there is, therefore, no expectation that the adopted child will have to change country of residence because of the adoption. In countries where adoption is allowed, citizens are able to adopt. Whether long-term residents who are not citizens also have the possibility of adopting depends on the laws and regulations of each State. Some States may also impose restrictions on adoptions by their citizens residing abroad. Data on domestic adoptions are usually derived from the documentation produced by the administrative or judicial procedures leading to the adoption.

Among the 195 countries in the world, adoption is allowed in 173 and some data on the number of adoptions are available for all but 47 of them. In addition, for the 22 countries where children can be placed through *kafalah*, two have information on the number of children involved. Hence, there are 128 countries with some data available and among them 88 have information on both domestic and intercountry adoptions. An additional 23 countries have data only on the overall number of adoptions and a further eight have data only on domestic adoptions, seven of which do not allow intercountry adoptions. In addition, nine countries have data only on intercountry adoptions.

On the basis of these data, this chapter presents a comprehensive overview of levels and trends in child adoption. It corroborates that the number of intercountry adoptions has been increasing in several developed countries and that their share of all adoptions in the major receiving countries is high. Nevertheless, at the world level, 85 per cent of all adoptions are still domestic and the intensity of adoption in most countries is low. Furthermore, most adoptions are concentrated in relatively few countries. These and other findings are presented in detail below.

A. LEVELS AND TRENDS IN THE TOTAL NUMBER OF ADOPTIONS

1. How many children are adopted annually?

The United Nations Population Division estimates that, at the global level, at least 260,000 children[2] were adopted annually around 2005. Most of these adoptions occur in a few countries. The United States, with over 127,000 adoptions in 2001, accounts for nearly half of all adoptions (table V.1). Large numbers of adoptions also take place in China (almost 46,000 in 2001) and the Russian Federation (more than 23,000 in 2001).[3] Other countries with sizeable numbers of adoptions are Germany, Ukraine and the United Kingdom, each with over 5,000 adoptions annually. Brazil,[4] Canada, France and Spain also record significant numbers, ranging from 4,000 to 5,000 adoptions per year.

The remaining adoptions are distributed among a large number of countries. In 48 of the 118 countries having data on the total number of adoptions, between 100 and 1,000 adoptions occur annually. In another 40 countries, fewer than 100 adoptions take place each year. These countries include Mozambique and Sudan, both of which have large child populations, with at least ten million children each (United Nations, 2005).

2. How common is adoption?

One way of addressing this question is to compare the number of adoptions to the pool of potentially adoptable children worldwide. To do so, one must determine first who is adoptable. Minors who have lost both parents are one possible group. A comparison of the number of adoptions to the number of children under age 18 who have lost both parents indicates that adoption is not very common. The estimated number of children who had lost both parents by 2003 was more than 60 times the number of children adopted globally on an annual basis (UNAIDS, UNICEF and USAID, 2004).

Another way of assessing the magnitude of adoption is to compare the number of adoptions to the number of children living in institutions. However, data on the number of children in

institutions are not available for most countries. Considering the data for just three countries—China (China, Ministry of Civil Affairs, 2005), the Russian Federation[5] and the United States (Barber and Delfabbro, 2004)—the global number of adoptions is small compared to the number of children in institutions or in foster care.

A third approach to measuring the intensity of adoption is to relate the annual number of adoptions (flow data) to the overall number of children at a given point in time (stock data). While this approach has the advantage that the denominators required for such calculation are readily available (United Nations, 2005), the overall number of children in a population does not represent the number of potentially adoptable children. Furthermore, the share of the latter among all children is likely to vary from one country to another depending on factors such as: levels of adult mortality, maternal mortality and fertility; the incidence of unwanted births; levels of divorce and remarriage, and the prevalence of poverty. Nevertheless, consideration of the "adoption rate" sheds some light on the relative importance of adoption in each country. For purposes of comparison two rates are used in this report and presented in table V.1.

According to Article 1 of the Convention on the Rights of the Child, children are persons under 18 years of age. Therefore, the total number of adoptions can be related to the number of persons under 18 to produce the "under-18 adoption rate". Based on this measure, the adoption rate at the global level is quite low, with fewer than 12 children adopted each year for every 100,000 persons under age 18.

At the country level, Palau[6] and Samoa have the highest under-18 adoption rate among the 118 countries with data available: in those islands over 500 adoptions occurred for every 100,000 children under 18. Mongolia, with 187 children adopted in 2004 for every 100,000 persons under 18 and the United States, with a rate of 173, display the third and fourth highest rates respectively. Bulgaria, Cyprus, Denmark and Monaco[6] also show relatively high under-18 adoption rates, with values ranging from 101 to 144 adoptions per 100,000 persons under 18 (table A.V.1). In contrast, Asian

TABLE V.1. COUNTRIES WITH THE LARGEST TOTAL NUMBER OF ADOPTIONS AND DIFFERENT ADOPTION RATES

Rank	Country	Year	Total adoptions	Adoption rate (per 100,000 persons)		Adoptions per 100,000 births
				Under age 5	Under age 18	
1	United States of America......	2001	127 407	385.3	172.6	3 156.4
2	China	2001	45 844	29.5	12.2	252.0
3	Russian Federation[1]	2001	23 108	209.6	69.6	1656.0
4	Ukraine	2001	7 593	225.0	71.2	1 921.8
5	United Kingdom	2002	6 239	108.0	46.8	923.6
6	Germany	2002	5 668	89.9	36.9	797.4
7	Spain	2003	4 847	139.0	65.8	1 107.4
8	France	2003	4 445	71.9	33.4	596.5
9	Brazil[2]	2003	4 150	14.0	6.7	111.4
10	Canada[1]	2000-2001[3]	4 118	142.5	58.2	1 233.8
11	Republic of Korea	2004	3 899	92.8	35.3	834.2
12	Guatemala.....................	2004	3 834	115.7	62.1	885.8
13	Kazakhstan	2002	3 600	196.6	75.7	1 500.9
14	Italy	1999	3 197	72.0	31.6	601.9
15	India	2003	3 047	1.5	0.7	11.7
16	Viet Nam	2001	2 881	22.4	9.2	178.0
17	Uzbekistan	2005	2 836	59.9	26.4	461.1
18	Poland[4]	1997	2 441	64.1	23.7	584.9
19	Bulgaria	1999	2 288	410.3	140.4	3 460.7
20	South Africa..................	2001	2 218	25.3	12.1	199.2
21	Venezuela (Bolivarian Republic of).....................	1995	1 992	43.5	21.3	352.2
22	Japan.........................	1995	1 931	19.3	7.7	159.6
23	Philippines	2003	1 902	11.6	5.6	93.5
24	Mongolia......................	2004	1 890	422.4	187.3	3 247.6
25	Kyrgyzstan[5]	1999	1 683	184.7	82.3	1 468.8
26	Romania......................	2004	1 673	94.4	37.3	786.2
27	Sweden	2004	1 669	208.9	85.6	1 755.3
28	Colombia	2004	1 409	17.9	8.4	145.2
29	Netherlands[6]...................	2004	1 368	83.9	38.5	721.6
30	Denmark	2003	1 249	225.8	104.7	1 956.7
Median...............................		..	261	42.8	17.9	354.2

Sources: For a complete list of country references see annex II. For the population under age five and under age 18 and the number of births, see United Nations, 2005.

NOTES: The total number of adoptions is the sum of the number of domestic and intercountry adoptions as reported by each country. For countries that are primarily destinations for intercountry adoptions (listed in annex I), data include foreign-born children adopted from abroad. For countries of origin of intercountry adoptions, data include nationals adopted by non-citizens abroad. Because intercountry adoptions are included in both the data of the country of origin and the country of destination, the total number of adoptions in the world cannot be computed by summing the number of total adoptions for each country as shown in this table. For a description of the estimation procedure used to obtain the total number of adoptions worldwide see annex I. The under-five adoption rate is calculated by dividing the total number of adoptions of children under age five by the number of children under age five. It is assumed that 60 per cent of children are under age five at the time of adoption. The under-18 adoption rate is calculated by dividing the total number of adoptions of persons under age 18 by the number of persons under age 18. It is assumed that all persons are under age 18 at the time of adoption. The adoption ratio is calculated by dividing the total number of adoptions by the number of live births. The median is calculated for all 118 countries for which data are available on the total number of adoptions. For a complete list of countries for which data are available see table A.V.1.

[1] Estimate.
[2] Data refer only to the state of São Paulo.
[3] Data refer to the fiscal year.
[4] Data refer to adoption rulings by the courts.
[5] Data include children who have been adopted as well as placed with guardians.
[6] Data refer to adoptions granted by Dutch courts.

countries such as Bangladesh, Indonesia and Myanmar have some of the lowest under-18 adoption rates in the world, with fewer than six adoptions for every ten million persons under age 18. Many countries in Africa also record low rates of formal adoptions. In Benin, Mozambique, Niger and the United Republic of Tanzania, for example, there is only about one adoption for every million persons under age 18.

Table V.1 also presents the "under-five adoption rate", which relates the number of adoptions of children under five years of age to the population under age five. Because the majority of the children adopted are under age five, the under-five adoption rate provides an important indication of the intensity of adoption among younger children. However, few countries publish information on the age of children at the time of adoption. Since the data available suggest that approximately 60 per cent of all children adopted annually are under the age of five at the time of adoption, that proportion is used to estimate the necessary numerators for the calculation of the under-five adoption rate for countries lacking data on the age of children at the time of adoption. The denominators are derived from the official population estimates and projections prepared by the United Nations (United Nations, 2005). The resulting under-five adoption rates show that, once more, Palau[6] and Samoa display the highest levels: 1,211 and 964 adoptions of children under five per 100,000 persons under five, respectively. Mongolia and Bulgaria have the third and fourth highest rates, with 422 and 410 children under five adopted per 100,000 persons under five, respectively (table A.V.1). The United States exhibits the fifth highest rate, at 385 adoptions per 100,000 children under five in 2001. Six other countries—Cyprus, Denmark, Monaco,[6] the Russian Federation, Sweden and Ukraine—have under-five adoption rates higher than 200. As in the case of the under-18 adoption rate, countries in Africa and Asia have the lowest under-five adoption rates, with Bangladesh, Indonesia, Myanmar, Niger and the United Republic of Tanzania reporting fewer than two adoptions of children under five for every million children in the same age group.

An alternative indicator used to illustrate the intensity of adoption is the "adoption ratio" calculated as the number of adoptions per 100,000

live births. This measure, which relates flow data on two events, adoptions and live births, is a weak and possibly misleading indicator of the intensity of adoption because adoptions involve children of all ages whereas the number of births is indicative only of the number of infants (children under age one) present over a given year. Available data on the age of adopted children at the time of adoption indicate that only a small proportion is adopted before the age of one (see chapter VI). In relative terms, the adoption ratio yields results similar to those obtained when considering adoption rates. Once more, Palau[6] and Samoa have the highest adoption ratios, with over 11,000 and 8,000 adoptions per 100,000 births, respectively. Bulgaria, Mongolia and the United States also display high adoption ratios, with over 3,000 adoptions per 100,000 births in each. The countries with the lowest number of adoptions relative to births are Bangladesh, Indonesia, Myanmar, Niger and the United Republic of Tanzania, which experience just about one adoption per 100,000 births.

Other measures to assess the relative intensity of adoption, such as indicators that relate the number of adoptions to the number of individuals or couples seeking to adopt or the number of adopted persons to the total population, would likely yield similar results. However, the denominators necessary to calculate some of these indicators are not readily available. Consequently, they are not examined here.

B. LEVELS AND TRENDS IN DOMESTIC ADOPTION

While information on the total number of adoptions provides useful insights into how widespread adoption is at the global and national levels, for analytical purposes it is best to focus separately on the two components of all adoptions, namely, domestic and intercountry adoptions as characterized in the introduction to this chapter.

1. Global estimate of the number of domestic adoptions

The majority of adoptions worldwide are domestic, that is they do not involve a change of country of residence for the adopted child. About 220,000 children are adopted domestically each year, accounting for almost 85 per cent of all adoptions occurring annually. The United States records the highest number of domestic adoptions, with nearly 110,000 children adopted domestically in 2001 (table V.2). China and the Russian Federation also record large numbers of domestic adoptions, with more than 37,000 and 17,000 children adopted, respectively, in 2001. Three additional countries—Brazil,[4] Ukraine and the United Kingdom—reported more than 4,000 domestic adoptions in the most recent year for which data are available.

As with the total number of adoptions, domestic adoptions are highly concentrated in a few countries.

TABLE V.2. COUNTRIES WITH THE LARGEST NUMBER OF DOMESTIC ADOPTIONS

| Rank | Country | Year | Domestic adoptions | | Domestic adoption rate under age 5 (per 100,000 persons) |
			Number	As a percentage of total adoptions	
1	United States of America	2001	108 351	85	327.6
2	China	2001	37 200	81	23.9
3	Russian Federation[1]	2001	17 331	75	157.2
4	United Kingdom[1]	2002	5 910	95	102.3
5	Ukraine	2001	4 921	65	145.9
6	Brazil[2]	2003	4 030	97	13.6
7	Germany	2002	3 749	66	59.5
8	Uzbekistan	2005	2 828	100	59.7
9	Kazakhstan	2002	2 652	74	144.8
10	Canada[1]	2000-2001[3]	2 243	54	77.6
11	Poland[4]	1997	2 236	92	58.7
12	India	2003	1 949	64	1.0
13	South Africa	2001	1 906	86	21.7
14	Mongolia	2004	1 861	98	415.9
15	Republic of Korea	2004	1 641	42	39.1
16	Japan[5]	1995	1 632	85	16.3
17	Viet Nam	2001	1 462	51	11.4
18	Romania	2004	1 422	85	80.2
19	Bulgaria	1999	1 278	56	229.2
20	Italy	1999	1 020	32	23.0
21	Spain	2003	896	18	25.7
22	Sri Lanka	2001	881	95	32.3
23	Mexico	2004	873	90	4.8
24	Azerbaijan[1]	2004	715	93	70.3
25	Malawi[6]	2001	714	100	19.1
26	Hungary	2004	656	87	81.9
27	Sweden	2004	576	35	72.1
28	Colombia	2004	563	40	7.1
29	Denmark	2003	561	45	101.4
30	Ghana	2004	529	99	10.3
Median		..	137	63	19.3

Source: For a complete list of country references, see annex II.

NOTES: The percentage of domestic adoptions is calculated using the total number of adoptions as shown in table A.V.2. For countries of destination, the remaining adoptions are primarily foreign-born children adopted from abroad. For countries of origin, the remaining adoptions are primarily nationals adopted by non-citizens abroad. The median is calculated for all 96 countries for which data on domestic adoptions are available. For the complete list of countries for which data are available see table A.V.2.

[1] Estimate.
[2] Data refer only to the state of São Paulo.
[3] Data refer to the fiscal year.
[4] Data refer to adoption rulings by the courts.
[5] Data include regular and special adoptions.
[6] Intercountry adoptions are not permitted.

Over 86 per cent of domestic adoptions take place in just ten countries. The remaining 14 per cent, equivalent to about 31,000 adoptions, are distributed among 86 countries, 42 of which record fewer than 100 domestic adoptions per year.

The countries with the highest numbers of domestic adoptions also tend to have the highest under-five domestic adoption rates. Thus, Kazakhstan, the Russian Federation, Ukraine, the United Kingdom and the United States have relatively high domestic adoption rates, with values ranging from over 100 to nearly 330 domestic adoptions of children under five per 100,000 persons under five. Exceptions occur, however. China, with the second largest number of domestic adoptions worldwide, has a relatively low under-five domestic adoption rate, with fewer than 24 children under five adopted domestically for every 100,000 persons under five. Similarly, India has an under-five domestic adoption rate of one, although it recorded nearly 2,000 domestic adoptions in 2003. Some

countries have high domestic adoption rates despite recording relatively low numbers of domestic adoptions. That is the case of Belize, Bulgaria, Denmark, and Mongolia, where domestic adoptions are more common relative to the size of the population under five than in the most populous countries of the world.

2. Domestic adoptions as a percentage of the total number of adoptions

A high proportion of domestic adoptions among all adoptions indicates that the local demand for adoption is mainly being met by the local supply of adoptable children. In 57 of the 96 countries with data available, domestic adoptions represent at least half of all adoptions (table A.V.2) and in seven of them—Argentina, Bangladesh, Malawi, Namibia, Seychelles, Solomon Islands and the United Republic of Tanzania—domestic adoptions constitute the totality of adoptions because intercountry adoptions are not permitted. As box V.1

BOX V.1. COUNTRIES WITH THE HIGHEST PERCENTAGE OF DOMESTIC ADOPTIONS

70 to 79 per cent	*80 to 89 per cent*	*90 per cent or more*
Benin[1]	Chile	Azerbaijan
Indonesia	China	Belize
Kazakhstan	Estonia	Brazil[3]
Russian Federation[2]	Fiji[2]	Croatia
	Hungary	Czech Republic[2]
	Jamaica	Democratic Peoples Republic of Korea
	Japan[4]	Ghana
	Mauritius[5]	Mongolia
	Mexico	Panama[1]
	Nicaragua[2]	Poland[6]
	Romania	Portugal
	South Africa	Slovenia
	United States of America	Sri Lanka
		Turkey
		United Kingdom[2]
		Uzbekistan

Source: For a complete list of country references, see annex II.

NOTES: The percentage of domestic adoptions is calculated using as denominator the total number of adoptions as shown in table A.V.2. The box does not include the seven countries for which data are available on domestic adoptions but where intercountry adoptions are not permitted.

[1] Because the number of adoptions is very small in many of the countries considered, some of the percentages and rates may not be very reliable.

[2] Estimate.

[3] Data refer only to the state of São Paulo.

[4] Data include regular and special adoptions.

[5] Data include both simple and full adoptions.

[6] Data refer to adoption rulings by the courts.

indicates, there are 16 countries where domestic adoptions account for at least 90 per cent of all adoptions. They include Brazil,[4] Mongolia, Turkey and the United Kingdom. In an additional 13 countries, between 80 per cent and 89 per cent of all adoptions are domestic. They include China, Japan, Mexico and the United States.

While domestic adoptions represent the majority of adoptions worldwide, there are important regional differences in the relative importance of domestic adoptions. In most West European countries,[7] for instance, fewer than half of all adoptions are domestic, though Germany, Malta,[6] Portugal and the United Kingdom are exceptions.

In contrast, domestic adoptions represent 50 per cent or more of all adoptions in 13 of the 19 countries in Latin America and the Caribbean for which data are available, including Chile, Ecuador and Peru. Likewise, the majority of countries in Africa, Asia and East Europe[8] having the required data register high percentages of domestic adoptions. In Africa, domestic adoptions represent more than 50 per cent of all adoptions in 10 of the 16 countries[9] with data available, while in Asia the same holds for 14 of the 20 countries with data. Among East European countries, 12 out of the 15

with data available have more domestic adoptions than intercountry adoptions.

3. Trends in the number of domestic adoptions

The scarcity of time series information on adoption precludes a thorough assessment of long-term trends in the number of domestic adoptions. According to the data available, it would appear that the number of domestic adoptions has followed an inverted U-shaped curve since the Second World War, rising to reach a peak between the 1960s and the early 1980s and declining thereafter. Adoptions in New Zealand offer an example of this trend. In 1955, there were about 1,400 domestic adoptions in that country (New Zealand, Law Commission, 2000) and by 1969, that figure had more than doubled, reaching 3,500 (figure V.1). Since then, the reported number of domestic adoptions in New Zealand has declined steadily, falling to 295 in 2003 (New Zealand, Department of Child, Youth and Family Services, 2005). Similarly, the number of domestic adoptions in Ireland rose sharply from 1960 to 1967, reached a plateau and began a rapid decline in 1985. In 2003, the number of domestic adoptions in Ireland stood at 263 children, a figure that is barely one-sixth of the high numbers recorded in 1967 and 1975 (Ireland, The Adoption Board, 2004).

Figure V.1. Number of domestic adoptions in Ireland and New Zealand, 1955-2003

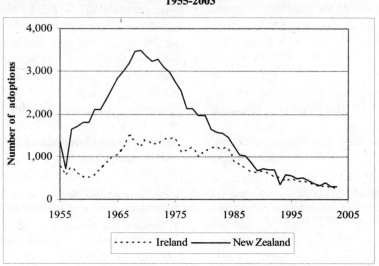

Sources: Ireland, The Adoption Board, 2004; New Zealand, Law Commission, 2000, and Department of Child, Youth and Family Services, 2005.

In the United Kingdom and the United States, the number of domestic adoptions also rose throughout the 1950s and 1960s, reaching maxima of 27,000 adoptions in the late 1960s in the United Kingdom and 175,000 in the early 1970s in the United States (Mather, 2001; Stolley, 1993). In the United Kingdom, the number of domestic adoptions fell to an estimated 4,700 in 1999 and has been increasing since then (United Kingdom, Office for National Statistics, 2004 and Department for Education and Skills, 2005). In the United States, the number of domestic adoptions declined to 104,000 in 1986 and has remained relatively stable since then (Stolley, 1993).

While information on long-term trends is limited, statistics on domestic adoptions are available for a large number of countries starting in the late 1980s. According to these data, the number of domestic adoptions has declined in many developed countries. In Australia, for instance, the number of domestic adoptions fell from 1,107 in 1989 to 132 in 2004 so that, as a percentage of all adoptions, domestic adoptions dropped from 74 per cent in 1989 to 26 per cent in 2004 (Australia, Australian Institute of Health and Welfare, 2004). In Germany, the reported number of domestic adoptions declined from 6,326 in 1995 to 3,749 in 2002, passing from 79 per cent to 66 per cent of all adoptions (Germany, Federal Statistics Office, 2004). France, Norway and Switzerland have also experienced downward trends in the number of domestic adoptions since the 1990s.

Why have these declines taken place? One reason is the increasing shortage of adoptable children domestically. In developed countries, the widespread availability of reliable, safe and low cost contraception, as well as of legal abortion, has meant that fewer children are born who might be put up for adoption (UNICEF, 1998). In addition, the increased acceptance of single parenthood and the greater availability of welfare support have meant that fewer single mothers relinquish their children for adoption (Akerlof and others, 1996; Donnelly and Voydanoff, 1991; Knitzer, 2001; United States, Child Welfare Information Gateway, 2005). Furthermore, children available for adoption domestically do not necessarily have the characteristics sought by prospective adoptive parents (Steltzner, 2003). The desire for younger or healthier children has likely prompted increasing numbers of adoptive parents in developed countries to adopt foreign-born children instead of those eligible for domestic adoption.

The decline in the number of adoptions by step-parents and other relatives, which in many countries constitute the majority of domestic adoptions, has also contributed to the declining number of domestic adoptions (see chapter VI). The enactment of more restrictive legislation regarding adoptions by step-parents together with declining rates of remarriage and an increasing tendency for step-parents not to adopt step-children formally have all resulted in fewer children being adopted domestically (Stolley, 1993). In Australia, for instance, the decline in the number of domestic adoptions closely mirrors that of adoptions by step-parents and other relatives (figure V.2). In 1989, 500 children, equivalent to 45 per cent of all domestic adoptions, were adopted by a relative or a step-parent; by 2004 that figure had fallen to 34 children, equivalent to 26 per cent of domestic adoptions.

Domestic adoptions have also declined in many East European countries, despite a widespread increase in the number of children left in public care (UNICEF, 2003b). This decline has been associated with a variety of factors, including the rising incidence of poverty during the 1990s, the negative financial repercussions of the transition to a market economy on child protection services and the sharp increase in the number of adoptions of children from East European countries by foreigners (UNICEF, 2003b). In Poland, for instance, the number of children adopted domestically fell from 2,837 in 1991[10] to 2,236 in 1997. According to the Government, factors contributing to this reduction include declining fertility, the country's deteriorating socio-economic situation, a preference for young and healthy children on the part of adoptive parents and the significant increase in financial support to families with foster children.[11] Other countries that have experienced a decline in the number of domestic adoptions since the 1990s are Albania, Belarus,

**Figure V.2. Number of domestic adoptions and adoptions by
step-parents and other relatives, Australia, 1990-2004**

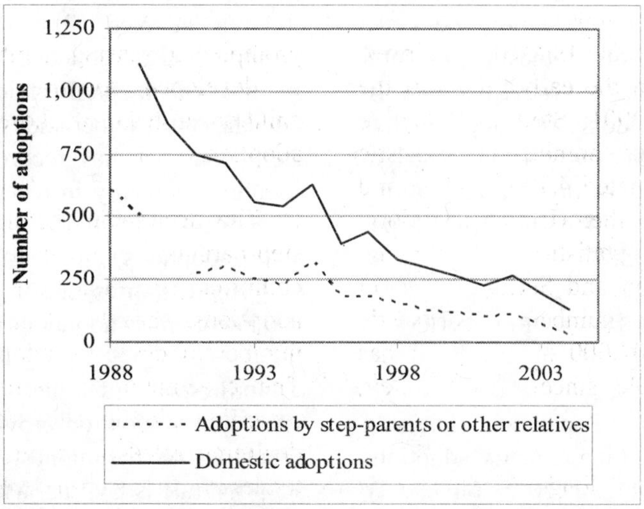

Source: Australia, Australian Institute of Health and Welfare, 2004.

Bulgaria, Estonia, Hungary, Latvia and Ukraine. A number of Governments of East European countries have responded to this decline with incentives to promote domestic adoption and with measures to lower the number of adoptions by foreign parents (see box V.2).

There are exceptions to the downward trend in the number of domestic adoptions experienced by developed countries. In the United Kingdom, for example, the number of domestic adoptions increased from around 4,700 in 1998 to over 5,900 in 2002 (United Kingdom, Office for National Statistics, 2004 and Department for Education and Skills, 2005). This increase is believed to have been the result of the Government's efforts to raise by 40 per cent the number of adoptions of children waiting in care (O'Halloran, 2006; Parkinson, 2003). Italy and Spain have also experienced an increase in the number of domestic adoptions since the early 1990s. In Italy, the number of domestic adoptions rose from 800 in 1993 to 1,020 in 1999, while in Spain, the number of domestic adoptions increased from 531 in 1990[12] to 896 in 2003 (Italy, Ministry of Justice, 2003; Spain, Ministry of Labour and Social Affairs, 2005). In Italy the percentage of domestic adoptions among total adoptions rose from 28 per cent in 1993 to 32 per cent in 1999 but in Spain that percentage declined from 61 per cent in 1990 to 18 per cent in 2003.

Several developing countries have also experienced an increase in the number of domestic adoptions. In the Republic of Korea, for instance, the number of domestic adoptions rose from 1,190 in 1992 to 1,641 in 2004 (Republic of Korea, Ministry of Health and Welfare, 2005). This increase may stem from the commitment of the Government to promote domestic adoptions through tax incentives and medical allowances for disabled adopted children.[13] In India, both the number of domestic and that of total adoptions have been rising since the late 1980s. In 1989,

---

BOX V.2. GOVERNMENT EFFORTS TO PROMOTE
DOMESTIC ADOPTIONS IN LATVIA

In Latvia, the number of domestic adoptions fell from 383 in 1993 to 27 by 2003 and, as a percentage of the total number of adoptions, domestic adoptions dropped from nearly 82 per cent to 25 per cent. The Government reacted to this situation by instituting a temporary moratorium on intercountry adoptions in 2000. It also enacted the Law on the Protection of Children's Rights, which restricted intercountry adoptions exclusively to adoptive parents who were citizens of countries that had concluded bilateral agreements with Latvia and guaranteed children's rights (Vaskis, 2000 and 2001). Recently, in an attempt to promote domestic adoption, the Minister for Special Assignments for Children and Family Affairs drafted amendments to four legislative acts, providing childcare leave and a monthly allowance of 1,495 Euros to adoptive parents.[14]

---

about 700 children were adopted by Indian citizens (Selman, 2002) and by 2003 that number had nearly trebled to 1,949.[15] During the same period, the percentage of domestic to total adoptions rose from 36 per cent to 64 per cent. In Sri Lanka, the number of domestic adoptions has also increased, rising from 549 in 1994 to 881 in 2001, while the percentage of domestic adoptions among the total rose from 74 per cent to 95 per cent during the same period.[16]

C. LEVELS AND TRENDS IN INTERCOUNTRY ADOPTION

The United Nations Population Division estimates that about 40,000 intercountry adoptions took place each year around 2005 (annex I). According to that estimate, intercountry adoptions account for 15 per cent of the total number of adoptions. As with domestic adoptions, the majority of intercountry adoptions involve relatively few countries.

The data available do not permit to distinguish intercountry adoptions, which entail a change of the adopted child's habitual country of residence but not necessarily of the child's citizenship, from international adoptions, which involve adoptive parents and adopted children with different citizenships regardless of their place of residence. Hence, to the extent that countries include international adoptions in their statistics on adoptions carried out through intercountry procedures, that type of adoption is included below in the totals for intercountry adoption.

1. Receiving countries

Data relative to receiving countries indicate that the United States is the major destination of foreign adopted children, with 19,056 intercountry adoptions in 2001 (United States, Child Welfare Information Gateway, 2004c). Citizens of the United States adopt more foreign children than the citizens of the next 13 major receiving countries combined (table V.3). France is the second largest recipient of children adopted from abroad, with 3,995 intercountry adoptions in 2003, followed by Spain with 3,951 intercountry adoptions in 2003.

Large numbers of intercountry adoptions also take place in Germany and Italy, with around 2,000 children adopted abroad by citizens of each country. Other countries that experience large inflows of adopted children from abroad are Canada, the Netherlands and Sweden. Each of these countries has recorded over 1,000 foreign adoptions annually in recent years. The remaining 13 per cent of intercountry adoptions, equivalent to 5,300 adoptions, are distributed among 19 major receiving countries, six of which record fewer than 100 intercountry adoptions per year.

Indicators of the relative intensity of intercountry adoption provide another picture. The country with the highest under-five intercountry adoption rate is Cyprus, with over 192 intercountry adoptions of children under age five per 100,000 children under five. Denmark, Luxembourg,[6] Norway, Singapore, Spain and Sweden are other countries with high under-five intercountry adoption rates, whose values range from 107 to 140 intercountry adoptions of children under age five for every 100,000 children under five. In contrast, countries such as Canada, France and the United States, which are among the main countries of destination of intercountry adoptions, display much lower under-five intercountry adoption rates. The countries with the lowest rates are Japan, Portugal and the United Kingdom, with fewer than six intercountry adoptions of children under age five per 100,000 persons under five.

With the availability of domestic adoptable children declining as the demand for adoptions remains high, prospective parents, especially in developed countries, have increasingly resorted to adopting children abroad (Masson, 2001). In consequence, intercountry adoptions constitute more than half of all adoptions in 20 of the 27 major receiving countries. In some of these countries, intercountry adoptions are a very high percentage of all adoptions (box V.3). In Belgium,[17] France and Luxembourg, for instance, intercountry adoptions account for 90 per cent or more of all adoptions. In six other countries—Cyprus, Liechtenstein,[6] the Netherlands, Norway, Spain and Switzerland—intercountry adoptions constitute at least 75 per cent of all adoptions.

TABLE V.3. COUNTRIES OF DESTINATION WITH THE LARGEST NUMBER OF
INTERCOUNTRY ADOPTIONS AND MAIN COUNTRY OF ORIGIN

| Rank | Receiving country | Year | Intercountry adoptions | | Intercountry adoption rate under age 5 (per 100,000 persons) | Main country of origin |
			Number	As a percentage of total adoptions		
1	United States of America [1]	2001	19 056	15	57.6	China
2	France	2003	3 995	90	64.6	Haiti
3	Spain	2003	3 951	82	113.3	Russian Federation
4	Italy	1999	2 177	68	49.0	Russian Federation
5	Germany	2002	1 919	34	30.5	Russian Federation
6	Canada	2000-2001 [2]	1 875	46	64.9	China
7	Sweden	2004	1 093	65	136.8	China
8	Netherlands [3,4]	2004	1 069	78	65.6	China
9	Denmark	2003	688	55	124.4	China
10	Norway	2003	664	76	137.6	China
11	Switzerland	2002	558	79	88.4	Colombia
12	Singapore	2002	448	63	107.1	Malaysia
13	Belgium [5]	2003	430	95	45.6	China [6]
14	Australia	2003-2004 [2]	370	74	17.5	China
15	Ireland [7]	2003	358	58	74.7	Russian Federation
16	New Zealand	2002-2003 [2]	336	53	72.7	…
17	United Kingdom [8]	2002	329	5	5.7	China
18	Japan	1995	299	15	3.0	…
19	Finland	2004	289	58	61.7	China
20	Israel	2003	256	67	23.5	Ukraine
21	Cyprus	2001	165	76	192.4	…
22	Luxembourg [9]	2003	51	94	106.9	Republic of Korea
23	Iceland [10]	2003	23	52	66.1	China
24	Portugal [10,11]	2003	6	1	0.6	…
25	Malta [10]	1996	5	42	11.7	Romania
26	Liechtenstein [3,10]	2004	3	83	78.9	…
27	Andorra [3,10]	2002	2	64	38.8	Romania
Median		..	370	64	64.9	..

Source: For a complete list of country references, see annex II.

NOTES: The percentage of intercountry adoptions is calculated using as denominator the total number of adoptions, as shown in table A.V.2. The median relates to the 27 major receiving countries of intercountry adoptions listed in this table.

[1] Data refer to children who entered under an orphan visa for purposes of adoption. These include children with an IR-3 visa status who were adopted abroad and children with an IR-4 status who were to be adopted in the United States.

[2] Data refer to the fiscal year.

[3] Estimate.

[4] Data refer to adoptions granted by Dutch courts.

[5] Data refer to intercountry adoptions in the regions of Flanders and Wallonia.

[6] Main country of origin for the region of Flanders only.

[7] Data refer to number of adoptions overseas.

[8] Data refer to the number of applications for intercountry adoptions received by the Department of Health during the year ending 31 March.

[9] Data refer to children in the process of undergoing adoption.

[10] Because the number of adoptions is very small in many of the countries considered, some of the percentages and rates may not be subject to large year-to-year variations.

[11] Data include 1 foreign child adopted by Portuguese citizens as well as 5 Portuguese children adopted abroad.

BOX V.3. COUNTRIES WITH THE HIGHEST PERCENTAGE OF INTERCOUNTRY ADOPTIONS

	60 to 74 per cent	*75 to 89 per cent*	*90 per cent or more*
Receiving countries	Andorra[1]	Cyprus	Belgium[2]
	Australia	Liechtenstein[1]	France
	Israel	Netherlands[3]	Luxembourg[4]
	Italy	Norway	
	Singapore	Spain	
	Sweden	Switzerland	

	60 to 74 per cent	*75 to 89 per cent*	*90 per cent or more*
Countries of origin	Colombia	Georgia	Ethiopia
	Latvia	Haiti	Guatemala
	Grenada[1]		Mali
	Honduras		Thailand
	Niger[5]		
	Togo[1]		

Source: For a complete list of country references, see annex II.
NOTE: The percentage of intercountry adoptions is calculated by using as denominator the total number of adoptions, as shown in table A.V.2.
[1] Because the number of adoptions is very small in many of the countries considered, some of the percentages and rates may be subject to large year to year fluctuations.
[2] Data refer to intercountry adoptions in the regions of Flanders and Wallonia.
[3] Data refer to adoptions granted by Dutch courts.
[4] Data refer to children in the process of undergoing adoption.
[5] Data refer to adoptions of abandoned children.

2. *Countries of origin*

Data produced by the countries of origin indicate that China and the Russian Federation are the two major sources of children adopted through intercountry procedures (table V.4). In 2001, 8,600 Chinese and 5,800 Russian children were adopted by foreign parents. Together, the two countries are the origin of 35 per cent of all intercountry adoptions worldwide. Other major countries of origin are Bulgaria, Guatemala, India, the Republic of Korea, Ukraine and Viet Nam. In recent years, each of these countries has been the origin of more than 1,000 children adopted annually through an intercountry procedure.

In most of the other countries of origin, the reported numbers of intercountry adoptions have been lower. Fewer than 1,000 intercountry adoptions were reported each year by 62 countries and in 46 of them the annual number of intercountry adoptions did not surpass 100, as in Burkina Faso, Chile, Nicaragua and Indonesia.

Most of the countries of origin with the highest numbers of intercountry adoptions also exhibit high rates of intercountry adoptions among children under five. That is the case of Bulgaria, Guatemala, Kazakhstan, the Republic of Korea, the Russian Federation and Ukraine, whose intercountry adoption rates range from 52 to 181 intercountry adoptions of children under five for every 100,000 persons under five. The major exception is China, which ranks first as country of origin of intercountry adoptions but where the intercountry adoption rate is just six intercountry adoptions of children under five per 100,000 persons under five. India and Viet Nam, each of which has been the origin of over 1,000 children adopted annually through an intercountry procedure in recent years, also exhibit relatively low intercountry adoption rates for children under five: less than one per 100,000 in India and 11 per 100,000 in Viet Nam.

According to the data available, intercountry adoptions account for a small proportion of all adoptions in countries of origin. Out of the 70 countries with the required information, only in 18 do intercountry adoptions represent more than half of all adoptions. In four of them—Ethiopia, Guatemala, Mali and Thailand—intercountry

TABLE V.4. COUNTRIES OF ORIGIN WITH THE LARGEST NUMBER OF INTERCOUNTRY ADOPTIONS
AND MAIN COUNTRY OF DESTINATION

| Rank | Country of origin | Year | Intercountry adoptions | | Intercountry adoption rate under age 5 (per 100,000 persons) | Main receiving country |
			Number	As a percentage of total number of adoptions		
1	China	2001	8 644	19	5.6	United States[1]
2	Russian Federation	2001	5 777	25	52.4	United States[1]
3	Guatemala	2004	3 726	97	112.4	United States
4	Ukraine	2001	2 672	35	79.2	United States[1]
5	Republic of Korea	2004	2 258	58	53.7	United States[1]
6	Viet Nam	2001	1 419	49	11.0	United States[1]
7	India	2003	1 098	36	0.5	United States
8	Bulgaria	1999	1 010	44	181.1	Italy[1]
9	Kazakhstan	2002	948	26	51.8	United States[1]
10	Colombia	2004	846	60	10.7	France
11	Ethiopia	2002-2003[2]	810	93	3.8	France[1]
12	Belarus	2001	447	51	61.9	Italy[1]
13	Madagascar	2002	373	...	7.5	...
14	Haiti[3]	1996	350	86	19.5	...
15	South Africa	2001	312	14	3.6	Sweden
16	Romania[4]	2004	251	15	14.2	Italy[1]
17	Poland[5]	1997	205	8	5.4	...
18	Bolivia (Plurinational State of)	2003	203	58	10.0	Spain[1]
19	Mali	2003	134	99	3.3	France[1]
20	Brazil[6]	2003	120	3	0.4	Italy[1]
21	Georgia	2002	119	77	28.3	United States[1]
22	El Salvador	2003	117	46	8.7	...
23	Lithuania	2004	103	53	40.0	Italy
24	Mexico[7]	2004	100	10	0.5	...
25	Peru	2004	92	49	1.8	Spain
26	Chile	2003	91	17	4.3	Italy
27	Hungary[8]	2004	94	13	11.7	Italy
28	Republic of Moldova	2004	82	37	23.3	United States
29	Latvia	2003	79	75	49.0	France
30	Nepal	2000	78	...	1.3	Spain[1]
31	Armenia[3]	2002	57	34	19.3	...
32	Azerbaijan[3]	2004	57	7	5.6	...
33	Congo[3,9]	2000	52	50	4.8	...
34	Sri Lanka	2001	51	5	1.9	Germany
35	Burundi[3]	1998	50	...	2.6	...
Median		..	50	34	4.4	..

Source: For a complete list of country references, see annex II.

NOTES: The percentage of intercountry adoptions is calculated using as denominator the total number of adoptions as shown in table A.V.2. The median is calculated for all 70 countries for which data are available on intercountry adoption and that are not major destinations of intercountry adoption. For the complete list of countries for which data are available see table A.V.2.

[1] Estimate based on data from selected receiving countries.

[2] Data refer to fiscal year

[3] Estimate.

[4] Data refer to children previously protected in public or private placement centres or in substitute families.

[5] Data refer to adoption rulings by the courts.

[6] Data refer only to the state of São Paulo.

[7] Data refer to intercountry adoptions by citizens of States that are parties to the Convention on Protection of Children and Co-operation in Respect of Intercountry Adoption.

[8] Data include 14 foreign children adopted by Hungarian citizens as well as 80 Hungarian children adopted abroad.

[9] Data refer to adoptions heard in the Brazzaville District Court.

adoptions exceed 90 per cent of all adoptions, and in Georgia and Haiti they account for more than 75 per cent of all adoptions (box V.3).

3. Inter-regional flows of adopted children

There are clear regional patterns in the flows of children adopted via intercountry procedures. Asia[18] and the region constituted by all East European countries[19] are the main regions of origin of children adopted by citizens of Northern American countries[20] (figure V.3). Thus, half of all the foreign children admitted for purposes of adoption in Northern America originate in Asia and a third in East European countries.

Children originating in Asia and East European countries also account for the majority of the foreign children adopted in West European countries,[21] with each of those regions of origin accounting for about a third of the foreign children adopted in West European countries. Latin America and the Caribbean[22] and Africa[23] are, respectively, the third and fourth major regions of origin of foreign children adopted in West European countries in recent years.

In 2001, about 2,500 children originating in Latin America and the Caribbean were admitted for purposes of adoption by West European countries, a figure comparable to the 3,000 from the same region admitted by countries in Northern America. However, children from Latin America and the Caribbean account for a higher proportion of all those adopted through intercountry procedures in West European countries than they do in Northern America. In 2001, about 1,600 children originating in Africa were adopted in West European countries compared to just about 300 in Northern America.

4. Inter-country flows of adopted children

At the country level, China and the Russian Federation are the major countries of origin of intercountry adoptions for both West European countries as a group and Northern America (figure V.4). In West European countries, more than a quarter of foreign children admitted for the purpose of adoption in 2001 originated in either China or the Russian Federation. In Northern America, children from those two countries accounted for about half of the foreign children admitted for the

Figure V.3. Number of intercountry adoptions in Northern America[1] and in West European countries as a group,[2] by region of origin, 2001

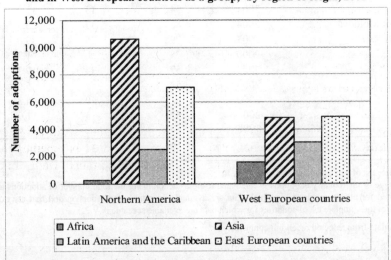

Source: For a complete list of country references see annex II.

[1] Data for Northern America refer to Canada and the United States. Data for Canada refer to 2002.

[2] Data for West European countries refer to the following countries: Belgium, Denmark, Finland, France, Germany, Iceland, Ireland, Italy, Luxembourg, Malta, Norway, Spain, Sweden and Switzerland. Data for Belgium refer to intercountry adoptions in the regions of Flanders and Wallonia in 2002. Data for France refer to 2004.

**Figure V.4. Number of intercountry adoptions in Northern America[1]
and in West European countries as a group,[2] by country of origin, 2001**

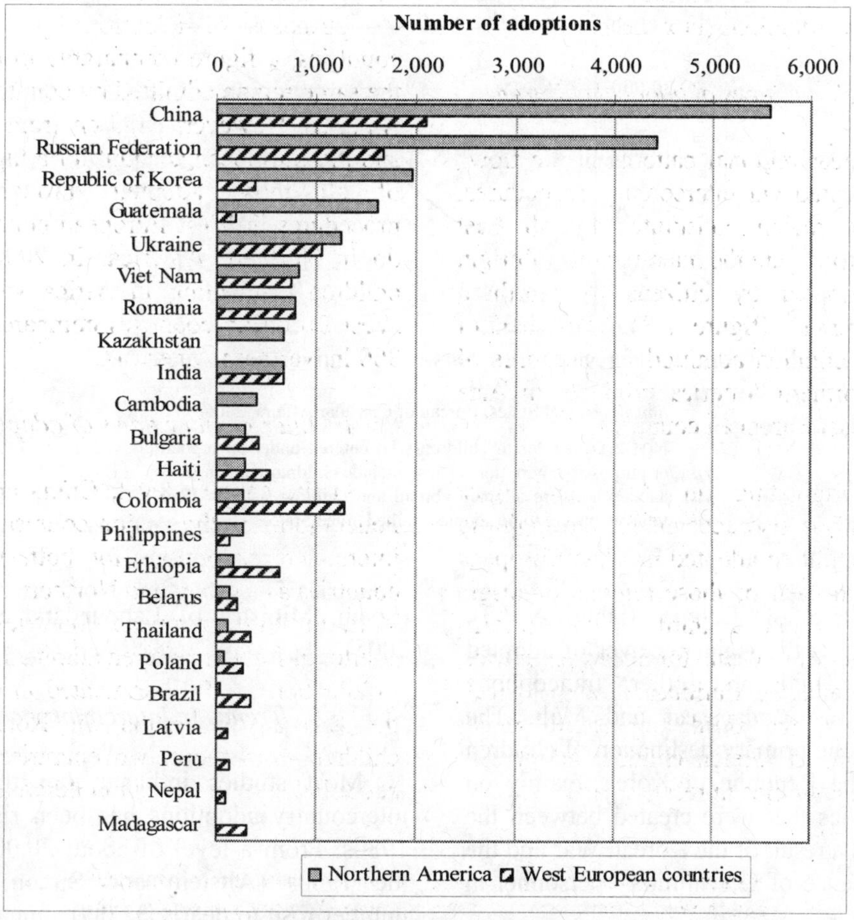

Number of adoptions

	Northern America	West European countries

Source: For a complete list of country references see annex II.

[1] Data for Northern America refer to Canada and the United States. Data for Canada refer to 2002.

[2] Data for West European countries refer to the following countries: Belgium, Denmark, Finland, France, Germany, Iceland, Ireland, Italy, Luxembourg, Malta, Norway, Spain, Sweden and Switzerland. Data for Belgium refer to intercountry adoptions in the regions of Flanders and Wallonia in 2002. Data for France refer to 2004.

purpose of adoption in 2001. West European countries and countries in Northern America also admitted large numbers of children adopted from India, Romania, Ukraine and Viet Nam.

Some regions have established preferential ties with certain countries of origin. Parents in Northern America, for instance, adopt nine times more children from Guatemala than do parents in West European countries. Northern America also received 24 times more foreign adopted children from Kazakhstan and five times more adopted children from the Republic of Korea than West

European countries did around 2001. In contrast, adopted children originating in Brazil, Bulgaria, Colombia, Ethiopia, Haiti, Latvia and Thailand were more numerous in flows to West European countries than in those directed to Northern America.

As with other types of migration, cultural, political and historical ties shape the flows of children adopted through intercountry procedures. Thus, Spain is the major country of destination for adopted children originating in Latin American countries, such as Costa Rica, Peru and the

**Figure V.5. Number of intercountry adoptions
in the United States, 1990-2005**

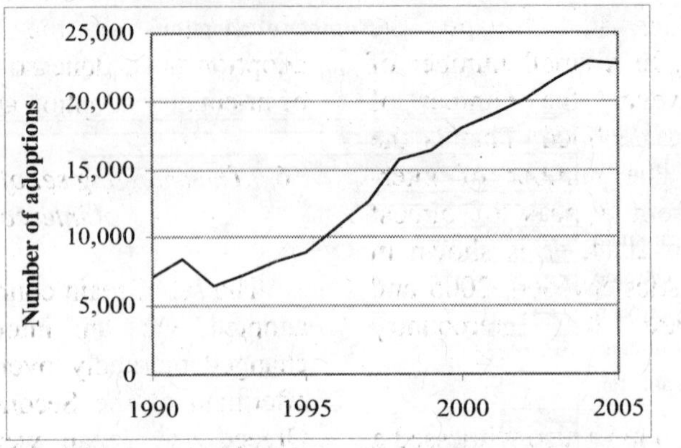

Source: United States, Bureau of Consular Affairs, 2006.

NOTE: Data refer to children who entered under an orphan visa for purposes of adoption. These include children with an IR-3 visa status who were adopted abroad and children with an IR-4 visa status who were to be adopted in the United States.

Plurinational State of Bolivia (table A.V.3). Likewise, France is the major receiver of adopted children from Haiti and other francophone countries, such as Madagascar and Mali. The United States is the primary destination of children adopted from the Republic of Korea, mainly on account of the ties that were created between the two countries as a result of the Korean War and the subsequent presence of U.S. military personnel in the country.

Bilateral and multilateral agreements also play a role in shaping flows. The German Federal Ministry for Family Affairs, Senior Citizens, Women and Youth, for example, concluded an agreement with the Romanian Adoption Committee in 1998.[24] In that agreement, terms of reference for cooperation in the adoption of Romanian children by prospective German parents were set out. As a result, Romania ranked fourth among the countries of origin of foreign adopted children in Germany in 2002 (Germany, Federal Statistics Office, 2004). Similarly, an agreement between Spain and China on civil and commercial matters may have facilitated intercountry adoption procedures for Chinese children by exempting certain documents from the need for authentication.[25] As of 2003, China was the second major country of origin of foreign children adopted by Spanish parents, after the Russian Federation

(Spain, Ministry of Labour and Social Affairs, 2005).

5. Trends in intercountry adoption

Most studies indicate that the number of intercountry adoptions has been rising since the 1980s. From a level of about 20,000 annually in the 1980s (Altstein and Simon, 1991), their number rose to nearly 32,000 annually by the end of the 1990s (Selman, 2002) and is estimated at 40,000 annually around 2005 according to data presented in this report. In the United States, the number of intercountry adoptions more than tripled, rising from 7,093 in 1990 to 22,728 in 2005, as is shown in figure V.5 (United States, Bureau of Consular Affairs, 2006).

Several West European countries have also experienced a sharp increase in the number of intercountry adoptions. Notable in this respect are France, Italy and Spain. In France, intercountry adoptions climbed from below 1,000 in 1980[26] to more than 4,000 in 2005 (France, Ministry of Foreign Affairs, 2006). In Italy, the number increased from 2,015 in 1993 to 2,840 in 2005 (Italy, Ministry of Justice, 2003; Office of the Prime Minister, 2006), whereas in Spain, the number of intercountry adoptions rose from around 300 in the early 1990s[13] to over 3,900 in

2003 (Spain, Ministry of Labour and Social Affairs, 2005). Intercountry adoptions have also increased in Finland, Germany, Ireland, the Netherlands and Norway. In a small number of European countries, however, the number of intercountry adoptions has declined. That is the case of Sweden, where the number of inter-country adoptions fell from a peak of almost 1,900 in 1977 to 1,093 in 2004, as is shown in figure V.6 (Sweden, Statistics Sweden, 2005 and Swedish National Board for Intercountry adoptions, 2005).

Some countries of origin have also witnessed a decline in the number of their citizens adopted through an intercountry procedure. In Chile, for example, the number of intercountry adoptions involving Chilean children fell from 1,020 in 1989[27] to 91 in 2003.[28] Likewise, the number of Romanian children adopted by foreign parents dropped from 3,035 in 2000 to 1,521 the following year[29] and to 251 by 2004 (Romania, Ministry of Labour, Social Solidarity and Family, 2005). In the case of Romania, this decline can be attributed to a moratorium on intercountry adoptions imposed for the second time by the Government of Romania in 2001 (figure V.7). A first moratorium had been imposed in 1991, following widespread allegations of child trafficking (UNICEF, 1998).[30] Many of the countries that have sought to reduce the outflow of children for the purpose of intercountry adoption have done so through the development of in-country adoption and fostering.

6. The changing set of main countries of origin of intercountry adoptions

The set of main countries of origin of children adopted via an intercountry procedure has changed markedly over time. In the immediate aftermath of the Second World War, Germany, Greece and Japan were the main sources of children adopted by foreigners (Altstein and Simon, 1991). In the early 1950s, with the onset of the Korean War, the Republic of Korea emerged as a major country of origin. During the 1980s, as intercountry adoptions shifted from being mainly a humanitarian response to protect children victimized by war to being a means of helping children deprived of parental care because of extreme poverty (Lovelock, 2000), countries such as India, the Philippines and Sri Lanka in Asia or Brazil, Chile and Colombia in South America gained prominence as countries of origin of children adopted by foreigners (Kane, 1993). During that period, the number of countries of origin increased from 22 to 63 (Kane, 1993).

**Figure V.6. Number of intercountry adoptions
in France and Sweden, 1975-2005**

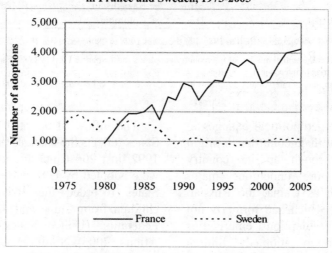

Sources: France, Ministry of Foreign Affairs, 2006; Sweden, Statistics Sweden, 2005 and Swedish National Board for Intercountry Adoptions, 2005.

**Figure V.7. Number of domestic and intercountry adoptions
in Romania, 1994-2004**

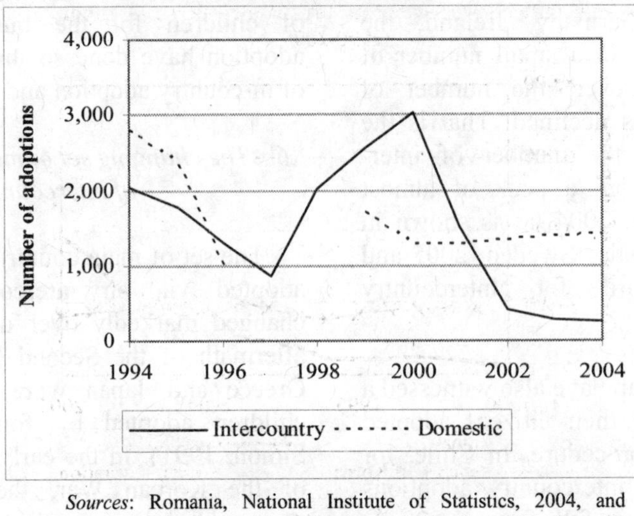

Sources: Romania, National Institute of Statistics, 2004, and Ministry of Labour, Social Solidarity and Family, 2005. For the complete list of references for Romania, see annex II.

TABLE V.5. NUMBER OF INTERCOUNTRY ADOPTIONS BY MAIN COUNTRY OF ORIGIN,
1980-1989 AND 1998-2005

	1980-1989		1998-2006	
Rank	Country	Number[1]	Country	Number[2]
1	Republic of Korea................	6 123	China...........................	8 644
2	India.......................................	1 532	Russian Federation..................	5 777
3	Colombia	1 484	Guatemala	3 726
4	Brazil	753	Ukraine	2 672
5	Sri Lanka	682	Republic of Korea....................	2 258
6	Chile	524	Viet Nam.................................	1 419
7	Philippines	517	India..	1 098
8	Guatemala	224	Bulgaria..................................	1 010
9	Peru	221	Kazakhstan	948
10	El Salvador	218	Colombia................................	846

Sources: S. Kane, 1993, for the series 1980 to 1989. For the series 1998 to 2006, see annex II.

[1] Data refer to the average annual number of intercountry adoptions for the period 1980 to 1989. Estimate based on data from 21 receiving countries of intercountry adoptions.

[2] Data refer to the number of intercountry adoptions for the most recent year between 1998 and 2006.

As a result of major geo-political changes in the early 1990s, the set of main countries of origin of children adopted through an intercountry procedure has once more undergone major changes. Countries such as China, the Russian Federation and Ukraine, which had formerly not been open to intercountry adoptions, emerged as major sources of foreign adopted children worldwide (table V.5).

The inflow of adopted children to the United States reflects the changes taking place. Whereas in 1992, just 206 Chinese and 324 Russian children were adopted by U.S. citizens, in 2005 the United States recorded the arrival of 7,906 adopted children from China and 4,639 from the Russian Federation (United States, Bureau of Consular Affairs, 2006). Similarly, the number of children adopted from Guatemala rose from 257 in 1990 to

**Figure V.8. Number of intercountry adoptions received by
the United States from the four main countries of origin,
1990-2005**

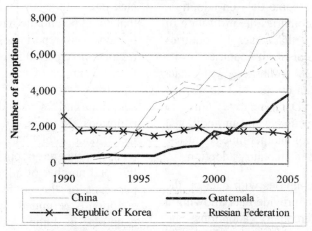

Source: United States, Bureau of Consular Affairs, 2006.
NOTE: Data refer to children who entered under an orphan visa for
purposes of adoption. These include children with an IR-3 visa status
who were adopted abroad and children with an IR-4 visa status who
were to be adopted in the United States.

3,783 in 2005 (figure V.8). In contrast, during the same period, the number of children from the Republic of Korea adopted by U.S. citizens declined from 2,620 to 1,630. As of 2005, four countries—China, the Russian Federation, Guatemala and the Republic of Korea, in order of importance—were the major sources of foreign-born children adopted by citizens of the United States (table A.V.4).

The ranking of major countries of origin for foreign adopted children has also changed considerably in other receiving countries. In France, for example, the number of adoptions from Asia fell sharply between 1999 and 2001, partly as a result of the suspension of adoptions from Viet Nam, which had been one of the main countries of origin of foreign children adopted by French citizens.[26] At the same time, the number of adoptions from Latin America and the Caribbean increased, especially those of children adopted by French citizens in Haiti.

Italy has witnessed a pronounced increase in both the number and the percentage of children adopted in East European countries. Between 2001 and 2005, the number of Russian children brought to Italy for purposes of adoption increased from 92 to 623, and their share of all foreign children

arriving in Italy as a result of an intercountry adoption procedure rose form 5 per cent to 22 per cent (Italy, Office of the Prime Minister, 2006). The number of children adopted by Italian citizens in Belarus and Poland also rose sharply during the same period.

In Spain, bilateral agreements with Bulgaria and China concluded in the late 1990s contributed to a shift in the major countries of origin of children adopted through an intercountry procedure.[25] Until 1999, Latin America had been the primary source of foreign-born children adopted by Spanish parents. In 1997, only 33 per cent of the foreign children adopted in Spain originated in Asia or East European countries, but by 2004, those regions accounted for 85 per cent of all intercountry adoptions recorded in Spain (Spain, Ministry of Labour and Social Affairs, 2005).

D. DATA LIMITATIONS AND STEPS TO HARMONIZE
THE COLLECTION OF DATA ON CHILD ADOPTIONS

1. Data gaps

This chapter has provided an overview of levels and trends in adoption by focusing on the total number of adoptions reported by countries and on those relative to domestic and intercountry adoptions taking place each year. The analysis presented is constrained by the limitations of data available. Out of the 195 countries considered in this study, only 128 have some data on adoption. Given that in at least 20 countries the institution of adoption is not recognized, that leaves 47 countries without data or 24 per cent of all countries in the world. Among the 128 countries with data available, 118 provide data on the total number of adoptions (table V.6). Data relative only to domestic adoptions are available for an additional country (Swaziland) and for another nine countries, data are available only on intercountry adoptions.

Only 88 of the 118 countries with data on the total number of adoptions provide data allowing a distinction between intercountry adoptions and the rest, denominated here "domestic adoptions". In a further seven countries—Argentina, Bangladesh, Malawi, Namibia, Seychelles, Solomon Islands and the United Republic of Tanzania—the data available refer only to domestic adoptions because intercountry adoptions are not allowed. Consequently, the study of domestic adoptions is based on data for 96 countries and data on intercountry adoptions are available for 97 countries. For an additional 23 countries, data are available only on the total number of adoptions.

2. Differences in regional coverage

Data coverage is particularly deficient in the developing regions. In Oceania, data are lacking for half of the countries in the region and only 44 per cent have data on the total number of adoptions. In Africa, 32 per cent of the countries in the region lack data altogether and just 47 per cent of those that could potentially have data on the total number of adoptions report those data. Africa is also the region where partial information is available for the largest number of countries. Thus, seven African countries provide data only on intercountry adoptions and Swaziland does so only for domestic adoptions. In Asia, one of every five countries lacks data altogether but, disregarding the 14 countries where adoption is not possible, data on the total number of adoptions are available for 70 per cent of the countries in the region where adoption is permitted. Similarly, 73 per cent of the countries in Latin America and the Caribbean provide data on the total number of adoptions, leaving slightly more than a quarter with no data whatsoever. Even in Europe, about a tenth of all countries lack data on adoptions. Northern America, where Canada and the United States publish data on adoptions with some regularity, is the only region where all countries have at least minimal information on adoption.

Coverage is even weaker when the focus is on separate reporting of data on intercountry and domestic adoptions. Among the countries that could potentially produce those data, coverage in Oceania amounts to 20 per cent and in Africa to 28 per cent. In Asia and Latin America and the

TABLE V.6. COUNTRIES PUBLISHING DATA ON ADOPTION BY TYPE OF ADOPTION AND BY MAJOR AREA

Major area	Total number of countries	Number providing data on				Not applicable	No data on adoption available
		Total number of adoptions	Only on domestic adoptions	Only on intercountry adoptions	Both domestic and intercountry adoptions[1]		
Africa	53	22	5	7	12	6[2]	17
Asia	47	23	1	1	19	14	9
Europe	44	40	—	—	34	..	4
Latin America and the Caribbean	33	24	1	—	18	..	9
Northern America	2	2	—	—	2	..	—
Oceania	16	7	1	1	3	..	8
Total	195	118	8	9	88	20	47

Source: For a complete list of country references see annex II.

NOTE: The category "total number of adoptions" includes the seven countries that have data only on domestic adoptions but do not allow intercountry adoptions. The category "Not applicable" refers to countries that do not recognize the institution of adoption.

[1] Data do not include the seven countries for which data are available on domestic adoptions, but where intercountry adoptions are not permitted.

[2] For two countries, Algeria and Mauritania, data are available on children placed through *kafalah*.

Caribbean, coverage is 59 per cent and 56 per cent, respectively. Even in Europe, just 77 per cent of all countries report data separately on intercountry and domestic adoptions.

The overall number of adoptions reported by countries in Africa (5,500 annually) and those of Oceania (2,000 annually) is biased downward because of the lack of data for significant numbers of countries in those regions. It may be, however, that lack of reporting is related to the low numbers of adoptions occurring in the countries involved.

3. Lack of common concepts and definitions

Aside from the lack of data, the study of adoption is also hampered by other limitations in the data available. One of them is the lack of standard practices, concepts and definitions underpinning the production of adoption statistics in different countries. For instance, practices differ with regard to the types of events covered, with some countries publishing data on the number of adoption orders granted during a certain period, others reporting data on applications processed and yet others reporting data on adoption applications received. In addition, some countries consider all adoptions undertaken by residents as "domestic" regardless of differences in citizenship between the adoptive parents and the child involved, whereas others do not.

The approaches used by countries to record intercountry adoptions also vary considerably. In countries of origin, data on children adopted by non-residents often do not indicate the country of destination of the children involved. Similarly, countries of destination do not report consistently the country of origin of adopted children. Lack of such information hampers the estimation of the number of children involved in intercountry adoptions because it is not always possible to avoid double-counting when data produced by both countries of origin and countries of destination are used as the basis for estimation. Furthermore, when both countries of origin and destination of adopted children produce data specifying the origin and destination of the children involved, inconsistencies

often arise and it is not uncommon for the reported number of adopted children moving from country A to country Z to be different from the reported number of children received by country Z from country A. In those cases, more information is needed to ascertain whether the discrepancies detected are caused by lags in the timing of registration in the receiving country with respect to that in the country of origin or by differences in the type of events being recorded at origin and destination. More information on how the data are generated would go a long way in allowing an understanding of why the differences detected arise and permitting the development of methods to adjust for them. Furthermore, were the differences be found to be real and not just an artefact of the data reporting processes, they might be an important indicator of illegal activity relating to the international transfer of children for the purposes of adoption.

Without timely, complete, reliable and well documented statistics on the number of children moving from one country to another because of intercountry adoptions, it is not possible to ensure that the provisions of bilateral, regional or multilateral instruments aimed at safeguarding children's best interests are being properly implemented. Reliable and timely data are necessary to monitor that "intercountry adoptions take place in the best interests of the child and with respect for his or her fundamental rights as recognized in international law", as is stated in the 1993 Convention on Protection of Children and Co-operation in Respect of Intercountry Adoption.[31]

4. International standards for the production of adoption statistics

The *Principles and Recommendations for a Vital Statistics System, Revision 2* defines adoption as the "legal and voluntary taking and treating of the child of other parents as one's own, in so far as provided by the laws of each country" (United Nations, 2001, p. 11). The *Principles and Recommendations* do not, however, provide specific guidelines on how to collect and disseminate data on adoptions.

The Committee on the Rights of the Child, which oversees the implementation of the United Nations Convention on the Rights of the Child, requests the 193 State parties to the Convention to provide periodically data on the number of domestic and intercountry adoptions, classified by age, sex, ethnic or national background of the child, and rural or urban residence. However, the reporting guidelines provided by the Committee on the Rights of the Child do not include specific definitions for the terms used nor do they present a set of suggested tabulations. Consequently, the data provided by State parties show considerable variability in terms of the events covered, with some State parties reporting the annual number of adoptions (flow data) and others presenting data on the total number of persons adopted up to a certain point in time (stock data). Furthermore, data on the number of adoptions reported to the Committee on the Rights of the Child frequently do not match the official data published by national sources.

In order to monitor the implementation of the Convention on Protection of Children and Co-operation in Respect of Intercountry Adoption (the Hague Convention), EurAdopt and the Nordic Adoption Council have recently developed a questionnaire for the compilation of national data on adoption. This instrument for data collection requests that statistics on the number of intercountry adoptions be provided by age, sex and country of origin of the adopted child. It also requests information on the number of domestic adoptions. Consistent use of this instrument to compile data from the State parties to the Hague Convention is expected to promote standardization of reporting procedures. However, this initiative does not go far enough in providing guidance regarding methods of data collection at the country level or in discussing the variety of definitions that underlie the data available.

It would appear, therefore, that in order to promote harmonization in the gathering and reporting of statistical information on adoption, a discussion of the data required for the demographic analysis of adoption levels and trends and of the definitions or concepts underlying available data is needed. Chapter VIII of this report focuses on these issues. For the time being, it bears noting that countries ought to give equal attention to the collection and dissemination of data on domestic adoptions as to intercountry adoptions. Many countries provide more detailed and timely statistics on the adoption of children through intercountry procedures than they do on domestic adoptions. Without the latter, it is not possible to carry out the effective monitoring of the work of child-welfare agencies in charge of placing children in adoptive families.

Lastly, it bears underscoring that, in disseminating adoption data, it is important to provide information on the demographic and social characteristics of the adopted child, the adoptive parents and the birth parents. Availability of data on those characteristics is very limited. Fewer than one in seven countries publish data on the age of the child at the time of adoption, and only 39 of the 195 countries considered in this report produce data on adoptions classified by sex of the child. Just six of the 195 countries considered reported data classified by the age of the adoptive parents at the time of adoption and even fewer produced data classified by the sex of the adoptive parents. Data on the characteristics of birth parents are even scarcer. These lacunae on the availability of data prevent an adequate understanding of the demographic dynamics underlying the adoption process and hinder the production of evidence to guide the implementation or development of policies to ensure the wellbeing of adoptable children.

E. SUMMARY

According to the United Nations Population Division, the number of adoptions has been increasing since 1995 and over 260,000 adoptions took place globally in 2005. The majority of adoptions are domestic: 85 per cent of all adoptions do not involve an immediate change of country of residence for the adopted child. However, the number of domestic adoptions has been declining in many countries, both because of the dwindling supply of adoptable children and the decline in the number of adoptions by step-parents and other relatives. At the same time, the number of intercountry adoptions has been rising both in absolute terms and as a percentage of all adoptions. In 2005, there were an estimated 40,000 intercountry adoptions globally.

The majority of adoptions are concentrated in a few countries. The United States accounts for nearly half of all the adoptions worldwide. Other countries with large numbers of children adopted annually are China, the Russian Federation, Ukraine and the United Kingdom. Countries where the number of adoptions is high as a proportion of the population under age five include Bulgaria, Mongolia, Palau,[6] Samoa and the United States.

In the majority of countries (57 of the 96 countries with data available), domestic adoptions constitute at least half of all adoptions and in 16 of them, domestic adoptions account for at least 90 per cent of all adoptions. In an additional 13 countries, including China and the United States, between 80 per cent and 89 per cent of all adoptions are domestic.

Several developed countries have data on the number of domestic adoptions since the 1980s and in many of them their number has been declining. A similar trend has been prevalent more recently in several East European countries where the number of children left in public care has increased. Exceptions to this trend include Italy, Spain and the United Kingdom, where the number of domestic adoptions has increased over the past decade or so.

In many developed countries, the availability of domestic adoptable children has been declining but the demand for adoption has remained high. Consequently, prospective adoptive parents have increasingly resorted to adopting children abroad. Therefore, especially since 1995, the number of intercountry adoptions has risen sharply, particularly in developed countries. Today, in 20 of the 27 major receiving countries, intercountry adoptions constitute more than half of all adoptions.

The major countries of origin and destination of intercountry adoptions have changed over time. Recently, China and the Russian Federation have become the main countries of origin of children adopted by persons living in Northern America or in West European countries. The United States remains the major destination of foreign adopted children but France, Italy and Spain have emerged as important destinations of children moving as a result of intercountry adoption.

The data available to assess levels and trends in adoption are deficient in several respects. Not all countries publish the necessary information. Those that do, present data according to their own practices and definitions. There is a need for a minimal standardization of the concepts and definitions underlying adoption data. Also necessary, is greater harmonization in the types of tabulations published, both with regard to domestic and to intercountry adoptions, so as to improve comparability in the data produced by different countries.

NOTES

[1] This review is based primarily on the reports submitted to the Committee on the Rights of the Child by States parties to the 1989 United Nations Convention on the Rights of the Child. Also used as sources of information were the country replies to the questionnaire on the implementation of the Convention on Protection of Children and Co-operation in Respect of Intercountry Adoption as well as other official national sources.

[2] This figure probably underestimates the global number of children adopted annually. An estimate of the missing values yields an additional 10,000 adoptions per year. For a detailed discussion of how the estimate of 260,000 adoptions was computed see annex I. For information on how many countries provide data on the total number of adoptions, and on the numbers of domestic and intercountry adoptions separately, see table V.6.

[3] The total number of adoptions is the sum of domestic and intercountry adoptions as reported by a country. For countries that are primarily destinations for intercountry adoptions, such as the United States (listed in annex I), data include foreign-born children adopted from abroad. For countries of origin of intercountry adoptions, such as China and the Russian Federation, the data include nationals adopted abroad by persons who are not Chinese or Russian citizens, respectively.

[4] Data refer only to the state of São Paulo.

[5] See United Nations, "Written replies by the Government of the Russian Federation (CRC/C/RESP/92) concerning the list of issues received by the Committee on the Rights of the Child (CRC/C/Q/RUS/3) relating to the consideration of the third periodic report of the Russian Federation".

[6] Because the number of adoptions is very small in many of the countries considered, some of the percentages and rates are subject to large year on year fluctuations and should be interpreted with caution.

[7] Data for West European countries refer to the following countries: Andorra, Belgium, Denmark, Finland, France, Germany, Iceland, Ireland, Italy, Liechtenstein, Luxembourg, Malta, the Netherlands, Norway, Portugal, Spain, Sweden, Switzerland and the United Kingdom. This classification is used for ease of presentation and does not represent a standard geographical classification used by the United Nations.

[8] Data for East European countries refer to the following countries: Albania, Belarus, Bulgaria, Croatia, Czech Republic, Estonia, Hungary, Latvia, Lithuania, Poland, the Republic of Moldova, Romania, the Russian Federation, Slovenia and Ukraine. This classification is used for ease of presentation and does not represent a standard geographical classification used by the United Nations.

[9] For Swaziland, data are available on domestic adoptions but not on the total number of adoptions for the year 2005.

[10] See United Nations, "Initial reports of States parties due in 1993: Poland" (CRC/C/8/Add.11).

[11] See United Nations, "Periodic reports of States parties due in 1998: Poland" (CRC/C/70/Add.12).

[12] See United Nations, "Initial reports of States parties due in 1993: Spain" (CRC/C/8/Add.6).

[13] See United Nations, "Periodic reports of States parties due in 1998: Republic of Korea" (CRC/C/70/Add.14).

[14] See United Nations, "Second periodic reports of States parties due in 1999: Latvia" (CRC/C/83/Add.16).

[15] See India, "Response to the 2005 questionnaire on the practical operation of the Hague Convention of 29 May 1993 on Protection of Children and Co-operation in Respect of Intercountry Adoption".

[16] See United Nations, "Second periodic reports of States parties due in 1998: Sri Lanka" (CRC/C/70/Add.17) and "Written replies by the Government of Sri Lanka (CRC/C/RESP/35) concerning the list of issues received by the Committee on the Rights of Child (CRC/C/Q/LKA/2) relating to the consideration of the second periodic report of Sri Lanka".

[17] Data refer to intercountry adoptions in the regions of Flanders and Wallonia.

[18] Data for Asia refer to the following countries: Cambodia, China, India, Kazakhstan, the Philippines, the Republic of Korea, Thailand and Viet Nam.

[19] Data for East European countries refer to the following countries: Belarus, Bulgaria, Latvia, Poland, Romania, the Russian Federation and Ukraine.

[20] Data for Northern America refer to Canada and the United States.

[21] Data for West European countries refer to the following countries: Belgium, Denmark, Finland, France, Germany, Iceland, Ireland, Italy, Luxembourg, Malta, Norway, Spain, Sweden and Switzerland.

[22] Data for Latin America and the Caribbean refer to the following countries: Brazil, Chile, Colombia, Guatemala, Haiti, Jamaica, Mexico, Peru and the Plurinational State of Bolivia.

[23] Data for Africa refer to the following countries: Burkina Faso, Cameroon, Ethiopia, Liberia, Mali, Madagascar and South Africa.

[24] See United Nations, "Second periodic reports of States parties due in 1999: Germany" (CRC/C/83/Add.7).

[25] See United Nations, "Periodic reports of States parties due in 1999: Spain" (CRC/C/70/Add.9).

[26] See United Nations, "Second periodic reports of States parties due in 1997: France" (CRC/C/65/Add.26).

[27] See United Nations, "Periodic reports of States parties due in 1997: Chile" (CRC/C/65/Add.13).

[28] See Chile, National Service for Minors, "Response to the 2005 questionnaire on the practical operation of the Hague Convention of 29 May 1993 on Protection of Children and Co-operation in Respect of Intercountry Adoption".

[29] See United Nations, "Written replies by the Government of Romania (CRC/C/RESP/ROM/1) concerning the list of issues received by the Committee on the Rights of the Child (CRC/C/Q/ROM/2) relating to the consideration of the second periodic report of Romania".

[30] In 2004, Romanian President Iliescu signed into law a draft adoption bill that limits international adoption to a child's grandparents. The law entered into force on 1 January 2005. See Teodorescu, A.G., "The Functioning of the new legislation on adoptions and provisions on defining the procedures in the moratorium". Paper presented at the Joint Parliamentary Committee European Union, Brussels, 22-23 November, 2005.

[31] Hague Conference on Private International Law, *Collection of Conventions (1951-1996)*, pp. 356-377.

VI. THE CHARACTERISTICS OF ADOPTIVE CHILDREN, ADOPTIVE PARENTS AND BIRTH PARENTS

Two hypotheses have been proposed to explain observed changes in the number of domestic and intercountry adoptions over time. According to the first, the decline in the number of domestic adoptions in developed countries is mainly the result of a falling supply of domestically adoptable children. In those countries, the widespread availability of safe and reliable contraception combined with the pervasive postponement of childbearing as well as with legal access to abortion in most of them has resulted in a sharp reduction of unwanted births and, consequently, in a reduction of the number of adoptable children (UNICEF, 1998). Furthermore, single motherhood is no longer stigmatized as it once was and single mothers can count on State support to help them keep and raise their children (Akerlof and others, 1996; Donnelly and Voydanoff, 1991; Knitzer, 2001). As a consequence, there are not enough adoptable children in developed countries for the residents of those countries wishing to adopt and prospective adoptive parents have increasingly resorted to adopting children abroad.

The second hypothesis contends that shifts in the numbers of domestic and intercountry adoptions have been brought about mainly by changes in demand. Accordingly, it is not the reduced domestic supply of adoptable children but rather the preferences of adoptive parents for children with characteristics other than those available locally that has led to a decline in the number of domestic adoptions and a rise in the number of intercountry adoptions (Steltzner, 2003).

This chapter presents an analysis of the evidence available to understand the dynamics of adoption in ways that may shed light on possible reasons for changing adoption trends. It focuses on selected demographic characteristics of the adopted children, the adoptive parents and the birth parents. Thus, it analyses the data available on the age and sex of adopted children as well as on the age, sex and marital status of adoptive parents at the time of adoption and their relationship to the adopted child. Chapter VII examines how developments in

selected demographic processes are associated with the demand for and availability of adoptable children.

A. SELECTED CHARACTERISTICS OF ADOPTED CHILDREN

1. Age of children at the time of adoption[1]

Of the 195 countries considered in this report, fewer than one in seven publish data on the age of children at the time of adoption. Furthermore, such data are not readily available for two of the countries that report the largest number of adoptions—China and the Russian Federation. Based on available information, however, some patterns are discernible.

(a) Total number of adoptions

Information on the age of children at the time of adoption is available for 26 countries. For these countries, the mean age of children at the time of adoption varies considerably, ranging from less than two years in Belgium[2] to over 11 years in the Gambia[3] (table A.VI.1). However, for about half of the countries with data, the mean age of children at the time of adoption falls between four and six years.

In none of the countries with data are a majority of children adopted as infants, that is, before age one. Marked differences exist, however, among countries. In Australia and Belgium,[2] for instance, 43 per cent of the children adopted are adopted before age one. In Chile, France and Norway, about 30 per cent of the persons adopted are adopted as infants. In contrast, in 12 countries, at most 20 per cent of adopted children were under age one at the time of adoption. In Ecuador, Germany, Switzerland and the United Kingdom, at most 5 per cent of those adopted were infants.

According to the data for 17 countries, over 60 per cent of adopted children are under age five at the time of adoption. Andorra,[3] Australia and Belgium[2] have the highest percentage of adopted children who were under age five at the time of adoption: 100 per cent in Andorra, 94 per cent in Belgium and 84 per cent in Australia. Other countries with high percentages of adopted persons who were under five at the time of adoption are Armenia, Chile, Colombia, Croatia, Ecuador and Ireland.

Older children account for the majority of all adoptions in only seven of the countries with data available. In the Gambia,[3] Germany, New Zealand, the Philippines, Samoa, Switzerland and the United Kingdom, at least half of all adoptions involve children aged five or over. The Gambia[3] and Samoa have the highest percentage of children aged six or over (over 80 per cent), followed by Germany (59 per cent) and the Philippines (54 per cent). In some countries, particularly those where many adults are adopted (see box VI.1), the mean age of adopted persons at the time of adoption is quite high (over eight years).

(b) Domestic adoptions

Data on the age of children adopted domestically provide a similar picture as that yielded by data on all adoptions, although generalizations are compromised by the paucity of data.

For domestic adoptions, the mean age at the time of adoption ranges between less than two years in Andorra[3] and nearly 16 years in Denmark (table A.VI.2). The median mean age for the 21 countries with data is 5.4 years, a figure higher than the median mean age among the 26 countries with data on the total number of adoptions (4.8 years). Among the 16 countries with data on both total and domestic adoptions, the median mean ages are, respectively, 4.8 and 5.7 years.

In three countries—Andorra,[3] France and the Netherlands[3]—children under age one constitute at least half of all children adopted domestically (table A.VI.2). Australia, where 48 per cent of the children adopted domestically were under age one at the time of adoption and Chile where 39 per cent were in that age group also register high percentages of infants among the children adopted domestically. In contrast, in Ecuador, Norway, Switzerland and the United States, infants account for less than 10 per cent of domestic adoptions.

In 11 of the countries with the requisite data, the majority of domestic adoptions involve children under age five. Andorra,[3] Chile, Costa Rica,[3] Ecuador and the Netherlands[3] have the highest percentages of adopted children under five at the time of adoption, with values exceeding 70 per cent. At the other end of the spectrum there are six countries in which at least half of domestic adoptions involve children over age five. In Switzerland, children aged five years or over constitute 85 per cent of all those adopted domestically, while in Ireland they constitute 68 per cent. In Denmark and the Gambia,[3] at least 80 per cent of children adopted domestically were aged six or over at the time of adoption. In nine countries, the mean age of children at the time of adoption is higher than six years and in three of them—Denmark, the Gambia[3] and Norway—it exceeds 12 years.

(c) Intercountry adoptions

Information on the age of children adopted through an intercountry procedure is available for

---

BOX VI.1. THE ADOPTION OF ADULTS

Data for a few countries indicate that a relatively large number of people are adopted as adults. In Denmark, nearly 300 persons out of the 1,249 who were adopted in 2003 were aged 20 years or over at the time of adoption. Almost all such adoptions (91 per cent) involved step-parents (Denmark, Statistics Denmark, 2004). In Samoa, 25 persons out of the 438 adopted in 2002 were aged 19 or over at the time of adoption, constituting nearly 6 per cent of all adoptions.[4] In Switzerland, nearly 7 per cent of the 702 adoptions taking place in 2002 involved persons aged 20 or over at the time of adoption (Switzerland, Swiss Federal Statistical Office, 2004).

In most adoption cases involving adults, the adopted person and the adoptive parents already know each other, as is the case of adoptions by step-parents. Such adoptions may be prompted, as in historical times, by considerations relative to inheritance or taxation. They may also occur after the adopted person reaches the age of legal majority because of problems in securing the agreement of birth parents or legal guardians when the person was a child.

27 countries. Children adopted through an intercountry procedure in the Gambia[3] exhibit the highest mean age at the time of adoption, nine years, whereas those in Ireland have the lowest, at two years. The median mean age among the 27 countries is 4.4 years, that is, about a year lower than that for domestic adoptions. Among the 16 countries with data on both domestic and intercountry adoptions, the median mean age for domestic adoptions is 5.7 years, higher than the median mean age for intercountry adoptions, 5.3 years (table VI.1).

In none of the countries with data are at least half of the children adopted through an intercountry procedure younger than one year at the time of adoption (table A.VI.3). The highest proportions under age one were recorded in Australia, Ireland and the United States, where at least 40 per cent of children adopted through an intercountry procedure are infants. In 12 of the 27 countries with data available, infants account for at most 10 per cent of all children adopted through an intercountry procedure.

As in the case of children adopted domestically, most of those adopted through an intercountry procedure are under age five at the time of adoption. Only in seven countries do at least half of all intercountry adoptions involve children over age five. Costa Rica[3] recorded the highest percentage of children aged five or over among those adopted through an intercountry procedure (89 per cent). It is followed by Chile (80 per cent), New Zealand (68 per cent) and Switzerland (54 per cent). The countries with the highest percentage of intercountry adoptions involving children aged six years or over are Costa Rica,[3] the Gambia[3] and Germany.

(d) Age differences at the time of adoption between children adopted domestically and those adopted through an intercountry procedure

In the main countries of destination of children adopted through an intercountry procedure, those children tend to be, on average, younger than children adopted domestically. This conclusion stems from data for the 16 countries that publish, for the same year, information on both, children adopted domestically and those adopted through an intercountry procedure, classified by age, thus permitting to estimate the difference between the mean ages of each group. When the difference is positive, children adopted through an intercountry procedure are, on average, younger than children adopted domestically, and the reverse holds when the difference is negative. The difference is positive in most countries that are major destinations of intercountry adoptions, whereas it is negative in several countries of origin of intercountry adoptions (table VI.1).

In Norway in 2003, the difference was 10 years, with the mean age of children adopted domestically being 12.2 years and that of children adopted through an intercountry procedure 2.2 years. Out of the 206 children adopted domestically, over 67 per cent were aged 12 years or over at the time of adoption (Norway, Statistics Norway, 2004a). In contrast, just 2 per cent of the 664 foreign-born children adopted in 2003 by Norwegian citizens were aged 12 years or over and 87 per cent were under age three (figure VI.1).

In Australia, the difference between the mean ages amounted to 3.6 years in 2004, with 45 per cent of the 132 children adopted domestically being five years of age or over at the time of adoption but fewer than 7 per cent of the 370 children adopted from abroad during the same period being in that age group (Australia, Australian Institute of Health and Welfare, 2004).

Denmark, Ireland and Switzerland are other countries of destination exhibiting a positive difference in the mean ages at which domestic and intercountry adoptions occur. The evidence suggests that the high mean ages of children adopted domestically are caused, in large part, by the high proportion of adoptions by step-parents or other relatives. In Denmark, for instance, 87 per cent of the 561 domestic adoptions recorded in 2003 involved step-parents or other relatives and nearly half of those adoptions involved adopted persons aged 20 years or over (Denmark, Statistics Denmark, 2004). Other countries of destination with high percentages of domestic adoptions by step-parents or other relatives are Iceland,[3] Ireland and Norway (table VI.6).

TABLE VI.1. MEAN AGE OF CHILDREN AT THE TIME OF ADOPTION BY TYPE OF ADOPTION

| Country | Year | Total number of adoptions | Mean age of children at the time of adoption[1] | | | Statistical significance |
			Domestic (1)	Intercountry (2)	Difference (1) – (2) (years)	
Andorra	2001-2003	11	1.5	2.5	-1.0	..
Australia	2003-2004[2]	502	5.9	2.3	3.6	***
Chile	2003	536	2.6	7.5	-4.9	***
Colombia	2004	1 409	5.2	3.9	1.3	***
Costa Rica	2003	64	2.6	7.9	-5.3	..
Denmark	2003	1 249	15.8	4.0	11.8	***
Ecuador	2004	118	5.4	4.4	1.0	
France	2003	4 445	2.7	3.4	-0.7	***
Gambia[3]	1998-2000	18	14.3	9.0	5.3	..
Germany	2002	5 668	7.9	8.3	-0.4	***
Ireland	2003	621	8.2	1.8	6.4	***
Lithuania	2004	196	3.2	6.2	-3.0	***
New Zealand	2002-2003[2]	631	6.7	8.6	-1.9	***
Norway	2003	870	12.2	2.2	10.0	***
Republic of Moldova	2004	219	4.8	6.5	-1.7	
Switzerland	2002	702	11.9	6.8	5.1	***
Median	..	..	5.7	5.3	0.3	..

Source: For a complete list of country references, see annex II.

NOTES: Based on the Chi-square test, comparing the age of children at the time of adoption for domestic and intercountry procedures. Two dots (..) indicate that the there are not enough observations to conduct the Chi-square test. Two stars (**) indicate that the Chi-square test is significant at a level of p< 0.01. Three stars (***) indicate that the Chi-square test is significant at a level of p< 0.001.

[1] Estimate.

[2] Data refer to the fiscal year.

[3] All domestic adoptions between 1998 and 2000 involved children over age six.

In countries of destination where the mean age of children adopted through intercoutry procedures is lower than that of children adopted domestically, this difference may owe much to the inability of citizens to adopt young and healthy children domestically because of long waiting lists for young adoptable children (Bartholet, 1991; Lovelock, 2000). Surveys among applicants for adoption indicate that prospective parents often have strong preferences regarding the age of prospective adoptive children. In the United States, for instance, almost 60 per cent of women interviewed in the 1995 National Survey of Family Growth indicated that they would prefer to adopt a child under the age of two (Chandra and others, 1999). Similarly, data collected by the Ministry of Social Affairs and Health of Finland indicated that 59 per cent of Finnish parents applying for an intercountry adoption in 2003 expressed a preference for adopting a child under the age of three (Finland, Finnish Adoption Board, 2004).

Factors determining the supply of adoptable children in countries of origin also play a role in the differences detected. According to a report by the United States Agency for International Development (USAID), in Romania, young children were adopted mostly by foreign citizens, whereas children over the age of three, who were harder to place abroad, were slated for domestic adoption (Ambrose and Coburn, 2001). There is some concern that the income generated by intercountry adoption may weaken the implementation of the principle of subsidiarity, whereby intercountry adoption should be considered only after all other options have been exhausted, and may delay the development of or weaken domestic adoption services (Dickens, 2002).

In contrast to other countries of destination, in France, Germany and New Zealand, children adopted domestically are, on average, younger than children adopted from abroad. In France, measures facilitating the adoption of newborns

**Figure VI.1. Age distribution of children adopted domestically
or through an intercountry procedure, Norway, 2003**

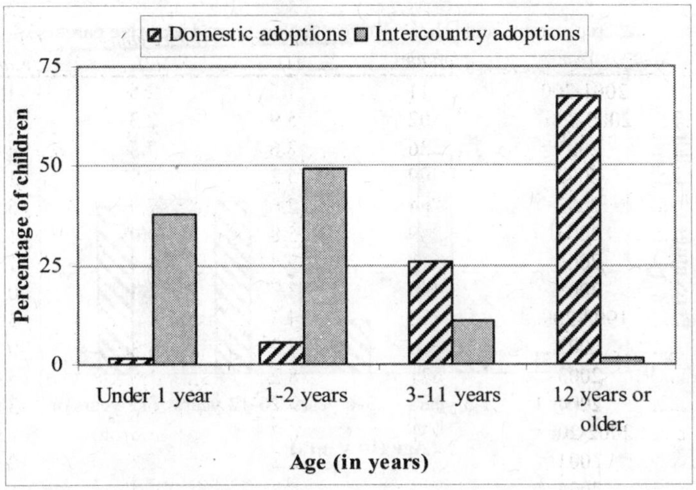

Source: Norway, Statistics Norway, 2004a.

may have contributed to this outcome: in 2003, 57 per cent of the 450 children adopted domestically were infants, while only 31 per cent of the nearly 4,000 children adopted through an intercountry procedure were under age one (Halifax and Villeneuve-Gokalp, 2005).

In Germany and New Zealand, the prevalence of adoptions of foreign-born children by step-parents or other relatives contributes to increase the mean age of children adopted through intercountry procedures. In Germany, where the average age difference between children adopted domestically and those adopted through an intercountry procedure is small, adoptions by step-parents account for more than half of all intercountry adoptions and children adopted by step-parents tend to be older (Germany, Federal Statistics Office, 2004). In 2002, almost 84 per cent of the 3,489 children adopted in Germany by a step-parent or another relative were at least six years of age, compared to just 19 per cent of the 2,179 children adopted by a person or persons not related to them (figure VI.2).

In New Zealand, data for fiscal year 2000 show a high percentage of adoptions by step-parents or other relatives among intercountry adoptions (New Zealand Law Commission, 2000). More recent data indicate that over 60 per cent of

foreign-born children adopted by step-parents in New Zealand were aged 10 years or over at the time of the adoption, a figure more than 20 percentage points higher than the equivalent for domestic adoptions.[5]

Turning now to the countries of origin of intercountry adoptions, in Colombia, Ecuador[3] and the Gambia,[3] the mean age of children adopted domestically is higher than that of children adopted through intercountry procedures. Once more, differences in the prevalence of adoptions by step-parents between domestic and intercountry adoptions contribute to that outcome as does the extent of local demand for formal adoptions.

In contrast to the situation in Colombia, Ecuador and the Gambia, the mean age of children adopted domestically is lower than the mean age of children adopted through an intercountry procedure in Chile, Costa Rica,[3] Lithuania and the Republic of Moldova. In Chile in 2003, the average age of children adopted domestically was 2.6 years, compared to 7.5 years for Chilean children adopted from abroad.[6] In Lithuania, children adopted domestically in 2004 were, on average, three years younger than children adopted through an intercountry procedure.[7]

**Figure VI.2. Age distribution of children adopted
by step-parents and by non-related adoptive parents, Germany, 2002**

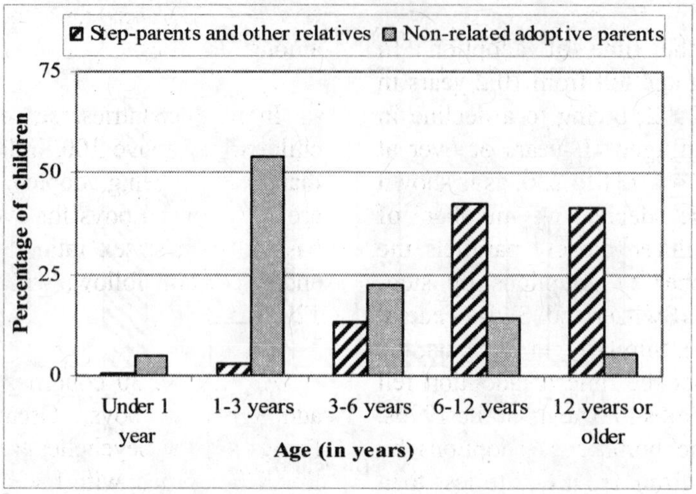

Source: Germany, Federal Statistics Office, 2004.

In the Republic of Moldova, the mean age of children adopted domestically in 2004 was 4.8 years, whereas that of Moldovan children adopted from abroad was 6.5 years. Furthermore, 35 per cent of the domestic adoptions taking place in 2004 involved children under age one, compared to less than 3 per cent of Moldovan children adopted from abroad.[8] Almost half of the 82 intercountry adoptions that originated in the Republic of Moldova involved children between the ages of one and five.

Full application of the principle of subsidiarity probably contributes to facilitate the domestic adoption of young children in the four countries where the mean age of children adopted domestically is lower than that of those adopted from abroad.

In countries of destination, the mean ages of children adopted through intercountry procedures vary significantly by countries of origin. In Italy, children adopted from Belarus had a mean age of 11 years, those adopted from Chile were, on average, 9 years old and those adopted from Lithuania had a mean age of 7 years (Italy, Office of the Prime Minister, 2004). In contrast, children adopted from Burkina Faso, Cambodia, Mexico, the Plurinational State of Bolivia and Viet Nam had mean ages below three years.

In Ireland, children adopted from Guatemala, Kazakhstan and Viet Nam were, on average, younger than children adopted from Belarus or the Russian Federation (Ireland, The Adoption Board, 2004). In France, the mean age of children adopted from Brazil in 2003 was 7 years, whereas children adopted from the Republic of Korea were, on average, six months of age (Halifax and Villeneuve-Gokalp, 2005).

(e) Trends in the age of children at the time of adoption

In most countries with data available, the age of children at the time of adoption has been decreasing. In England and Wales, for instance, children are being adopted at increasingly younger ages: the mean age at the time of adoption declined from 6.8 years in 1991 to 5.8 years in 2005 owing to a rising proportion of children adopted between the ages of one and four (from 29 per cent in 1991 to 52 per cent in 2005). In addition, over the same period, the proportion of children adopted at ages 10 to 14 dropped from 19 per cent to 12 per cent (United Kingdom, Office for National Statistics, 2002 and 2007).

In countries of destination, an increasing percentage of adoptions involving foreign-born children, who tend to be younger, and a declining percentage of adoptions by step-parents and other relatives, which frequently involve older children, are some of the reasons for the declining mean age of children at the time of adoption. In Switzerland, that mean age fell from 10.2 years in 1980 to 8.5 years in 2002, owing to a decline in the number of children aged 10 years or over at the time of adoption (from 731 to 230, as is shown in figure VI.3). The decreasing number of adoptions of older children closely parallels the reduction in the number of adoptions by step-parents over the period (Switzerland, Swiss Federal Statistical Office, 2004). Similarly, in Slovenia, the mean age of children at the time of adoption fell from 6.8 years in the 1960s to 6 years in the 1990s. During that period, the number of adoptions by step-parents decreased from about 640 to less than 300 (Banovec, 2001).

2. Sex of the adopted child

Data on the sex of adopted children are available only for 39 of the 195 countries considered in this study.

(a) Sex ratios among the total number of adoptions

According to the data available, more girls are being adopted than boys, with the median sex ratio of adopted children being 87 boys for every 100

girls among the 39 countries considered and most countries exhibiting sex ratios below 100 (table A.VI.4). However, there are marked differences among countries.

In nine countries, sex ratios among adopted children are above 100, indicating that more boys than girls are being adopted. Thailand, where there are 148 adopted boys for every 100 adopted girls, has the highest sex ratio. Sudan,[9] Togo,[3] Turkey and Viet Nam follow, with sex ratios surpassing 120.

Among the 30 countries where more girls are adopted than boys, Grenada, India, Norway, Paraguay,[3] the Seychelles[3] and Sweden display the lowest sex ratios, with fewer than 60 boys adopted for every 100 girls.

(b) Sex ratios among domestic adoptions

Among the 30 countries with data on the sex of children adopted domestically, the number of adopted girls surpasses that of adopted boys in 18 (table A.VI.5). In the Myanmar, the Republic of Moldova and Togo,[3] over 60 per cent of domestic adoptions involve girls. Other countries where the number of girls adopted domestically exceeds that of boys are India, Lithuania, Norway and Sri Lanka. Three additional countries—Andorra,[3]

**Figure VI.3. Adoptions by step-parents and adoptions of children aged 10
or over, Switzerland, 1980-2001**

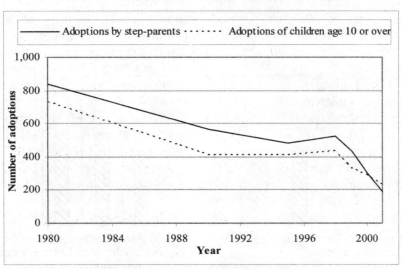

Source: Switzerland, Swiss Federal Statistical Office, 2004.

Costa Rica[3] and the Gambia[3]—report the same number of boys as that of girls adopted domestically.

In nine countries, including Australia, Germany and Singapore, more boys than girls are adopted domestically. The highest sex ratios among children adopted domestically are reported by Ethiopia, at 226 boys per 100 girls, and Viet Nam, at 164 boys per 100 girls.

(c) Sex ratios of intercountry adoptions

Data on the sex of children adopted through an intercountry procedure indicate that more girls are adopted than boys. In 25 of the 36 countries with data, girls outnumber boys among children adopted internationally (table A.VI.6). In Ireland, 208 girls were adopted from abroad in 2003 but just 150 boys (Ireland, The Adoption Board, 2004). In Singapore, there were 263 girls and 185 boys adopted internationally in 2002 (figure VI.4).[10] In 2003, Norwegian parents adopted almost twice as many girls as boys from abroad (Norway, Statistics Norway, 2004a), while in Denmark, intercountry adoptions involved 397 girls and 291 boys (Denmark, Statistics Denmark, 2004).

In eleven countries, boys exceed girls among children adopted through an intercountry procedure. In Colombia, Ecuador, Slovakia,

Thailand and Togo[3], all countries of origin, over 120 boys are adopted from abroad for every 100 girls. Among countries of destination, intercountry adoptions in Italy involve 133 boys for every 100 girls, while in Germany the equivalent sex ratio is 104.

(d) Comparing the sex distribution of domestic and intercountry adoptions

As already noted, in the majority of countries with the required data, more girls than boys are adopted either domestically or through an intercountry procedure. For the 30 countries with data on the sex of children adopted domestically, the median sex ratio is 87 boys per 100 girls. Similarly, among the 36 countries with data on the sex of children adopted through an intercountry procedure, the median sex ratio is 89 boys per 100 girls.

However, comparing the proportion of boys among children adopted domestically with that among children adopted through an intercountry procedure for the 24 countries with data relative to both types of adoption for the same year reveals a more complex picture (table VI.2).

In 17 countries, the percentage of boys among domestic adoptions is higher than that among intercountry adoptions. Seven are countries of

Figure VI.4. Number of domestic and intercountry adoptions by sex of the adoptive child, Singapore,[10] 2000-2002

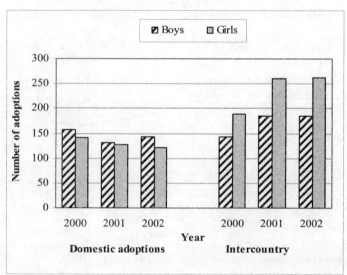

TABLE VI.2. SEX RATIO AND PERCENTAGE OF BOYS AMONG ADOPTED CHILDREN
AT THE TIME OF ADOPTION BY TYPE OF ADOPTION

Country	Year	Sex ratio of adopted children (boys per 100 girls)		Boys as a percentage of adopted children			
		Domestic	Intercountry	Domestic (1)	Intercountry (2)	Difference (2) – (1) (percentage points)	Statistical significance
Andorra	2001-2003	100.0	75.0	50.0	42.9	-7.1	..
Australia..........................	2003-2004[2]	134.0	68.9	57.3	40.8	-16.5	**
Chile	2003	84.6	97.8	45.8	49.5	3.7	
Colombia.........................	2004	76.5	121.5	43.3	54.8	11.5	***
Costa Rica	2003	100.0	60.0	50.0	37.5	-12.5	..
Denmark	2003	82.1	73.3	45.1	42.3	-2.8	
Ecuador	2004	82.9	126.3	45.3	55.8	10.5	
Ethiopia...........................	2002-2003[2]	226.3	86.6	69.4	46.4	-23.0	***
France	2003	116.3	97.0	53.8	49.2	-4.6	
Gambia............................	1998-2000	100.0	66.7	50.0	40.0	-10.0	..
Georgia............................	2002	94.4	83.1	48.6	45.4	-3.2	
Germany	2002	104.4	104.1	51.1	51.0	-0.1	
India	2003	67.7	44.3	40.4	30.7	-9.7	***
Ireland	2003	115.6	72.1	53.6	41.9	-11.7	**
Jamaica...........................	2002	75.2	111.8	42.9	52.8	9.9	
New Zealand	2002-2003[2]	85.5	86.8	46.1	46.5	0.4	
Norway............................	2003	67.5	50.9	40.3	33.7	-6.6	
Republic of Moldova	2004	63.1	90.7	38.7	47.6	8.9	
Singapore	2002	119.0	70.3	54.3	41.3	-13.0	***
Sweden............................	2004	77.8	49.5	43.8	33.1	-10.7	***
Switzerland	2002	97.3	96.5	49.3	49.1	-0.2	
Thailand	2002-2005	150.0	147.8	60.0	59.6	-0.4	..
Togo................................	2003	50.0	212.5	33.3	68.0	34.7	..
Viet Nam.........................	2001	163.9	103.0	62.1	50.7	-11.4	**
Median............................	..	95.9	86.7	49.0	46.5	-3.9	..

Source: For a complete list of country references, see annex II.

NOTES: Based on the Chi-square test, comparing the sex distribution of children adopted domestically and through an intercountry procedure. Two dots (..) indicate that the there are not enough observations to conduct the Chi-square test. Two stars (**) indicate that the Chi-square test is significant at a level of $p< 0.01$. Three stars (***) indicate that the Chi-square test is significant at a level of $p< 0.001$.

[1] Estimate.

[2] Data refer to the fiscal year.

origin of intercountry adoptions, namely, Costa Rica,[3] Ethiopia, the Gambia,[3] Georgia, India, Thailand[3] and Viet Nam. The other ten are major receivers of intercountry adoptions. In Australia, for instance, 57 per cent of the 132 children adopted domestically in 2004 were boys, compared to 41 per cent of the foreign-born children adopted by Australian parents (Australia Australian Institute of Health and Welfare, 2004). A similar difference is found in Norway, where 40 per cent of the 206 children adopted domestically in 2003 were boys, compared to 34 per cent of the 664 children adopted through an intercountry procedure (Norway, Statistics

Norway, 2004a). Other countries of destination where the percentage of boys among children adopted domestically exceeds the percentage of boys among children adopted abroad are Andorra,[3] Denmark, France, Germany, Ireland, Singapore, Sweden and Switzerland.

In another seven countries, most of which are countries of origin of intercountry adoptions, boys constitute a lower proportion of domestic adoptions than of those involving an intercountry procedure. These countries are: Colombia, Chile, Ecuador, Jamaica, New Zealand, the Republic of Moldova and Togo.[3] In all of them, the sex ratio of domestic adoptions is below 100, indicating that more girls are adopted domestically than boys but that is not always the case regarding intercountry adoptions. Thus, in Colombia in 2004, boys accounted for 43 per cent of the 563 children adopted domestically but for 55 per cent of the 846 Colombian children adopted through an intercountry procedure.[11] In the Republic of Moldova, girls outnumber boys in both domestic and intercountry adoptions but, whereas 39 per cent of the 137 children adopted domestically in 2004 were boys, boys constituted 48 per cent of the 82 Moldovan children adopted by foreign parents.

As in the case of age, the children's country of origin plays a role in determining sex ratios. Thus, in 2003, adoptive parents residing in Denmark, Ireland and Norway adopted more boys than girls from Belarus, Colombia, the Republic of Korea and Thailand, but more girls than boys from China, Ethiopia, India and Viet Nam (table VI.3). Parents' preference for boys in some Asian societies and the greater probability that birth parents abandon girls has resulted in more

adoptable girls than boys in countries such as China, India and Viet Nam (Johnson and others, 1998). In addition, the preference of adoptive parents in those countries for adopting boys also contributes to leave an excess of adoptable girls available for intercountry adoptions.

B. SELECTED CHARACTERISTICS OF ADOPTIVE PARENTS

1. *Age of parents at the time of adoption*[1]

Data on the age of parents at the time of adoption are available for only six countries and for five of those the data are incomplete. In Finland and Italy, for instance, data refer to the age of prospective adoptive parents at the time of application for an intercountry adoption. In Ireland, only information on the age of parents who adopted through a domestic procedure is available, while in Denmark data do not include adoptions by step-parents. Despite these limitations, some patterns can be gleaned from the available data (table VI.4).

TABLE VI.3. OVERALL NUMBER OF INTERCOUNTRY ADOPTIONS BY COUNTRY OF ORIGIN AND SEX OF THE CHILD FOR DENMARK, IRELAND AND NORWAY COMBINED, 2003

Country of origin	Number of adoptions	Sex ratio of adopted children (boys per 100 girls)	Percentage distribution of adopted children		Difference (1)-(2) (Percentage points)
			Boys (1)	Girls (2)	
Belarus	57	159.1	61.4	38.6	22.8
Brazil	27	170.0	63.0	37.0	26.0
China	502	3.3	3.2	96.8	-93.6
Colombia	174	145.1	59.2	40.8	18.4
Ethiopia	76	85.4	46.1	53.9	-7.8
India	113	39.5	28.3	71.7	-43.4
Philippines	29	163.6	62.1	37.9	24.2
Republic of Korea	123	232.4	69.9	30.1	39.8
Russian Federation	174	132.0	56.9	43.1	13.8
Thailand	74	221.7	68.9	31.1	37.8
Viet Nam	73	35.2	26.0	74.0	-48.0
Other	288	114.9	53.5	46.5	7.0
Total	1 710	63.6	38.9	61.1	-22.2

Sources: Denmark, Statistics Denmark, 2004; Ireland, The Adoption Board, 2004; and Norway, Norway, Statistics Norway, 2004a.
NOTE: Data refer to children received through intercountry adoption in Denmark, Ireland and Norway in 2003.

TABLE VI.4. AGE OF PARENTS AT THE TIME OF ADOPTION, VARIOUS INDICATORS

Country	Year	Number of adoptive parents	Percentage distribution of parents by age at the time of adoption					Mean age[2]	Median age[2]
			Under 30	30-39	40 or older	45 or older	50 or older		
Australia[1] ...	2003-2004	874	1.8	44.2	54.0	21.2	...	40.4	40.6
Denmark[3] ...	2003	1 340[4]	2.3	53.2	44.5	13.5	4.3	39.6	39.3
Croatia[5]	2001-2003	437	27.0[6]	43.5[7]	29.5	...	...	38.8	37.6
Finland[8]	2003	637	5.0	57.3	37.7	9.9	1.3	38.3	38.2
Ireland[9]	2003	523	16.6	57.9	25.4	9.9	...	35.5	35.3
Italy[8]	2000-2004	17 642	1.7	51.0	47.3	18.9	6.5	40.1	39.6
Median.........	..	..	3.7	52.1	41.1	13.5	4.3	39.2	38.8

Source: For a complete list of country references, see annex II.
NOTE: Data include both male and female adoptive parents.

[1] Data refer to the total number of placement adoptions and do not include 'known' child adoptions, that is, adoptions by step-parents, other relatives or caregivers. Data refer to the fiscal year.
[2] Estimate.
[3] Data do not include step-parent adoptions.
[4] Of these, 69 are of unknown age.
[5] Data refer to adoptions by step-parents and other relatives.
[6] Data refer to adoptive parents and relatives under age 35.
[7] Data refer to adoptive parents and relatives ageg 35 to 40 years.
[8] Data refer to applicants for intercountry adoptions.
[9] Data refer to domestic adoptions.

In four of the six countries, at least half of adoptive parents are aged 30 to 39. Parents in Australia and Italy have the highest mean age at the time of adoption (around 40 years), while parents in Ireland have the lowest mean age (35.5 years).

Adoption by parents under age 30 is not frequent. In Australia, Denmark and Italy less than 3 per cent of parents were under age 30 at the time of adoption. Only Croatia and Ireland register relatively high percentages of younger adoptive parents. In Croatia,[12] 27 per cent of parents who adopted a child in 2001-2003 were under age 35, while in Ireland, nearly 17 per cent of parents who undertook an adoption in 2003 were under age 30 (Ireland, The Adoption Board, 2004).

Adoptions by persons aged 45 or over are also relatively rare. Among the six countries considered, Australia has the highest percentage: in 2004, 19 per cent of adoptive Australian mothers were 45 or over, while 23 per cent of adoptive fathers were in that age group (Australia, Australian Institute of Health and Welfare, 2004). In Italy, nearly 20 per cent of persons applying for an intercountry adoption between 2000 and 2004 were aged 45 or over (Italy, Office of the Prime Minister, 2004). In Denmark, Finland and Ireland, less than 15 per

cent of adoptive parents were in that age group at the time of the adoption.

Laws and regulations establishing who can adopt condition the ages of adoptive parents. As indicated in chapter III, upper and lower age limits for adoptive parents are established following the principle that adoption should imitate nature. Thus, the Finnish Adoption Act (153/1985) and the supplementary decree (508/1997) require adoptive parents to be at least 25 years of age.[13] In addition, the Act requires adoptive parents to be at most 45 years older than the adopted child. In Croatia, the Family Act establishes that persons seeking to adopt should be between the ages of 21 and 35,[12] although it permits older persons to adopt if it is in the child's best interest and if the age difference between adoptive parents and the adopted child does not exceed 40 years.

(a) Age difference between adoptive mothers and fathers

In all six countries having the required data, adoptive fathers are, on average, older than adoptive mothers at the time of adoption. In Australia, the average age of men who adopted a child in 2004 was 40.9 years, while that of women was 39.9 years, as is shown in figure VI.5 (Australia, Australian Institute of Health and Welfare, 2004). In Italy, the mean age of Italian parents applying for an intercountry adoption in 2000-2004 was 41 years for men and 39 years for women (Italy, Office of the Prime Minister, 2004), while in Finland, the mean age of male applicants in 2003 was 38.7 years, compared to 37.8 years for female applicants (Finland, Finnish Adoption Board, 2004).

Such differences reflect mostly the typical age differences between spouses (United Nations, 2004b) as well as men's greater likelihood of re-marrying and adopting step-children.

(b) Trends in the age of adoptive parents

There is some evidence that the mean age of adoptive parents has been increasing over time. In Denmark, for example, the mean age of women at the time of adopting a child increased from 33.7 years in 1959 to over 37 years in 2000. In Finland, the mean age of women applying for an intercountry adoption rose from 35.8 years in 1985 to over 37.8 years in 2003 (Finland, Finnish Adoption Board, 2004). This increase was mainly driven by a major increase in the number of applications by women aged 40 to 44, from five in 1985 to almost 100 in 2003. Among Finnish men, the mean age at the time of application for an intercountry adoption also increased: from 37.1 years in 1985 to 38.7 years in 2003.

In European countries, the increasing age of adoptive parents at the time of adoption owes much to a broader trend toward the postponement of marriage and the increasing age of parents at first birth.

2. Sex of the adoptive parents

Data on the sex of adoptive parents are available for three countries and suggest that the number of male adoptive parents nearly matches that of female adoptive parents, as would be expected when married or cohabiting heterosexual couples constitute the majority of adoptive parents (see VI.B.3 below). Nevertheless, in countries where a high percentage of adoptions are by step-parents or single individuals, significant differences may arise.

Figure VI.5. Number of adoptions by age and sex of the adoptive parent, Australia, 2003-2004

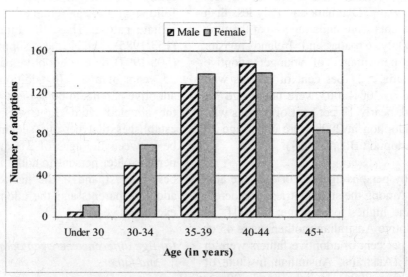

Source: Australia, Australian Institute of Health and Welfare, 2004.
NOTES: Data refer to the total number of placement adoptions. Data do not include adoptions of children already known by the adoptive parents (i.e., adoptions by a step-parent, another relative or a caregiver). Data refer to the fiscal year.

In the countries with data available, female adoptive parents outnumber males slightly. In Finland, for instance, 47 more women than men applied to adopt a child in 2003 (Finland, Finnish Adoption Board, 2004). Likewise, in Australia, 10 more women than men became adoptive parents in 2004—443 women compared to 433 men—and adoptions by single women accounted for the difference (Australia, Australian Institute of Health and Welfare, 2004).

Data for the United States suggest that similar differences exist. According to a sample of the 2000 population census of the United States, there were nearly three and a half as many adopted children under age 18 living in households headed by single women as there were adopted children living in households headed by single men (United States, Bureau of the Census, 2003).

3. *Marital status of the adoptive parents*

As noted in chapter III, 15 countries restrict adoption exclusively to married couples and the data available show that, even in countries where single persons are permitted to adopt, married couples constitute the majority of all adoptive parents. In Australia, almost 96 per cent of the adoptions concluded in 2004 were by married adoptive parents (Australia, Australian Institute of Health and Welfare, 2004).

In Slovakia, among the 465 children adopted in 1999 through a decision of the court, only 18 (4 per cent) were adopted by single persons, while 302 were adopted by couples (145 were adopted by step-parents).[14] In the United States, data from the 2000 census indicate that 78 per cent of all adopted children under age 18 lived with a married couple (United States, Bureau of the Census, 2003).

(a) *Adoptions by single persons*

Among the six countries that publish data on adoptions by single parents (table VI.5), Australia, Slovakia and Switzerland record fewer than 4 per cent of all adoptions involving single adoptive parents.

Finland has the highest percentage of adoptions by single parents: 14 per cent of applicants for intercountry adoption in 2003 were single and, among those single applicants, females outnumbered males by 48 to 1 (Finland, Finnish Adoption Board, 2004). In addition, the number of single persons applying for an intercountry adoption increased from 4 in 1985 to 49 in 2003 (Finland, Finnish Adoption Board, 2004).

Denmark also records a relatively high number of adoptions by single persons. In 2004, 71 intercountry adoptions, equivalent to 10 per cent of all such adoptions, were undertaken by single

TABLE VI.5. NUMBER AND PERCENTAGE OF ADOPTIONS
BY SINGLE PARENTS

| Country | Year | Adoptions by single parents | |
		Number	As percentage of the total number of adoptions
Australia[1]	2003-2004	10	2.3
Denmark[2]	2004	71	10.3
Finland[3]	2003	49	14.3
France[4]	2001-2002	126[5]	6.8
Slovakia	1999	18	3.9
Switzerland	2002	16	2.3
Median	..	34	5.4

Source: For a complete list of country references, see annex II.

[1] Data refer to the total number of placement adoptions by single persons. Data do not include adoptions of children already known by the adoptive parents (i.e., adoptions by a step-parent, another relative or a caregiver). Data refer to the fiscal year.

[2] Data refer to intercountry adoptions.

[3] Data refer to applicants for intercountry adoptions.

[4] Data refer to adoption applications.

[5] Estimate.

persons. Furthermore, the number of single persons approved to become adoptive parents rose from 25 in 1997 to 71 in 2004 (Denmark, Danish National Board of Adoption, 2005).

Studies in the United States also indicate that the percentage of adoptions undertaken by single persons has increased considerably, at least since 1970 when they involved only one per cent of all adoptions (Feigelman and Silverman, 1993; Stolley, 1993).

Switzerland presents a case where the number and percentage of adoptions by single persons have declined. In 1980, 57 adoptions involved single adoptive parents or almost 4 per cent of the total. By 2002, adoptions by single persons in Switzerland numbered 16 and represented just 2 per cent of the total (Switzerland, Swiss Federal Statistical Office, 2004).

(b) Adoptions by persons living in a consensual union

Data on adoptions by persons living in consensual unions are available for only two countries. In Australia, data for 2004 indicate that seven adoptions involved couples in consensual unions, equivalent to less than 2 per cent of all placement adoptions (Australia, Australian Institute of Health and Welfare, 2004).

In the United States, according to the 2000 census, nearly 4 per cent of adopted children were living in households headed by an adoptive parent cohabiting with a partner. There were approximately equal numbers of male and female adoptive parents living in consensual unions (United States, Bureau of the Census, 2003).

4. Adoptions by step-parents and other relatives

Since the mid-1970s, adoptions by step-parents and other relatives have become increasingly common in Canada, the United States and many European countries. This trend is associated with the increasing number of divorces and re-marriages occurring since the 1970s (United Nations, 2004a).

(a) All adoptions

Among the 12 countries with data on the total number of adoptions classified by relationship with adoptive parents, Germany has by far the largest number of adoptions by step-parents or other relatives: 3,489 in 2002 (table VI.6). Canada, Denmark and New Zealand also register sizable numbers of adoptions by step-parents or other relatives, ranging between 300 and 600 annually. The Gambia,[3] Lithuania and Slovenia report fewer than 100 such adoptions in the most recent year for which data are available.

In four of the 12 countries with the relevant data, step-parents and other relatives account for 50 per cent or more of the total number of adoptions. New Zealand has the highest percentage (75 per cent), followed by the Gambia[3] (67 per cent) and Germany (62 per cent). Denmark and Lithuania also register high percentages of such adoptions, with step-parents and other relatives accounting for 46 per cent of all adoptions in Denmark and 38 per cent in Lithuania.

(b) Domestic adoptions

Data on domestic adoptions by step-parents and other relatives are available for 17 countries. Once more, Germany has the highest number of such adoptions: 2,454 in 2002. Denmark, Ghana, Italy, the Netherlands and New Zealand each report over 200 domestic adoptions by step-parents and other relatives.

Adoptions by step-parents and other relatives account for at least half of domestic adoptions in 14 of the 17 countries with relevant data. Croatia, Denmark, the Gambia[3] and Haiti have the highest proportions, each with over 87 per cent of domestic adoptions involving a relative or a step-parent. In Iceland[3] and the Netherlands, at least 75 per cent of domestic adoptions are by a step-parent or another relative. In contrast, in Colombia and Italy, just 32 per cent and 35 per cent, respectively, of domestic adoptions involve a step-parent or another relative.

TABLE VI.6. NUMBER AND PERCENTAGE OF ADOPTIONS BY STEP-PARENTS AND OTHER RELATIVES

| Country | Year | Total | | Adoptions by step-parents and other relatives — Of which | | | |
| | | | | Domestic | | Intercountry | |
		Number	As percentage of the total number of adoptions	Number	As percentage of domestic adoptions	Number	As percentage of intercountry adoptions
Australia	2003-2004[1]	...	...	34	25.7	...	...
Canada[2,3]	2000-2001[1]	527	12.8	...	...	...	...
Colombia[4]	2004	...	...	178	31.6	...	...
Croatia[4]	2003	...	...	130	87.8	...	...
Denmark[5]	2003	579	46.4	490	87.3	89	12.9
Estonia[5]	2003	...	...	63	54.8	...	...
Gambia[3,4]	1999	4	66.7	2	87.5	2	50.0
Germany	2002	3 489	61.6	2 454	65.5	1 035	53.9
Ghana[4]	2004	...	...	277	52.4	...	...
Haiti[4]	1996	...	...	56[3]	100.0	...	...
Iceland[5]	2003	...	...	17	80.9	...	...
Ireland	2003	...	...	171	65.0	...	...
Italy	1999	...	...	356	34.9	...	...
Kazakhstan	2002	65[6]	1.8	...	...	...	...
Lithuania[5]	2002	87	37.8	84	52.8	3	4.2
Netherlands[5,7]	2004	252	18.4	225[3]	75.0[3]	27[3]	2.5[3]
New Zealand	1999-2000[1]	327	74.7	237	71.4	90	84.9
Norway[5]	2003	158	18.2	150	72.8	8	1.2
Slovakia[5]	1999	145	31.2	...	...	...	...
Slovenia[5]	2002	23	50.0	...	...	...	...
Sweden[5]	2003	...	...	112[8]	70.4[8]	...	...
Switzerland[5]	2002	180	25.6	...	...	...	...
Median	..	169	34.5	150	70.4	27	12.9

Source: For a complete list of country references, see annex II.

[1] Data refer to fiscal year.
[2] Data refer to the provinces of Alberta, Newfoundland and Labrador, Nova Scotia, Prince Edward Island and Saskatchewan.
[3] Estimate.
[4] Data refer to adoptions by relatives.
[5] Data refer to adoptions by step-parents only.
[6] Data refer to children adopted by relatives outside of Kazakhstan.
[7] Data refer to adoptions granted by Dutch courts.
[8] Data refer to adoptions recorded in the Population Register.

(c) Intercountry adoptions

While the majority of adoptions by step-parents and other relatives involve nationals of the same country, a significant number of step-parents are adopting children from abroad. Thus, data for Germany indicate that over 1,000 children were adopted abroad by German step-parents in 2002, accounting for 54 per cent of all intercountry adoptions (Germany, Federal Statistics Office, 2004). Almost half of the foreign-born step-children originated in Eastern European countries, with 69 coming from Poland, 78 from Romania, 177 from the Russian Federation and 75 from Ukraine.

In Denmark, 89 foreign children were adopted by Danish step-parents in 2003, accounting for 13 per cent of all intercountry adoptions (Denmark, Statistics Denmark, 2004). Of these, 31 children were from other European countries, including Germany, Poland and the Russian Federation, and 15 were from Asian countries (the Republic of Korea, Thailand and Viet Nam).

In New Zealand, almost 85 per cent of the 90 intercountry adoptions that took place in 2000 were by step-parents or other relatives (New Zealand Law Commission, 2000). In contrast, very low percentages of recent intercountry adoptions involved step-parents or other relatives in Lithuania,[3] the Netherlands[3] and Norway.[3]

(d) Sex of the step-parent

The scant data available indicate that men are more likely to adopt a spouse's child than women, a tendency that owes much to custodial arrangements of divorced parents and the fact that children tend to remain with their mothers (Hetherington and Jodl, 1994). In Denmark, for example, the ratio of male to female step-parents among persons adopting is twelve to one, with 487 adoptions by step-fathers in 2003 to only 41 adoptions by step-mothers (Denmark, Statistics Denmark, 2004).

In Switzerland, there were 12 to 25 times more adoptions by step-fathers than by step-mothers over the period 1980-2002, and in Slovakia recently, adoptions by step-fathers have outnumbered adoptions by step-mothers by up to 70 to 1.[14]

(e) Trends in adoptions by step-parents

Over the last few decades, the number of adoptions by step-parents and other relatives has declined in most countries. Part of this decline can be ascribed to legislative changes. In England and Wales, for example, the number of adoptions by step-parents peaked in 1975, when over 9,200 such adoptions were reported (Lowe, 2000). By 1982, that number had declined to 3,560 (Selman, 1988), partly because the 1975 Children Act discouraged adoptions by step-parents. Since the 1980s, the number of adoptions by step-parents has continued to fall, passing from 1,614 in 1999 to 866 in 2005 (Selman, 2006).

In Australia, the number of domestic adoptions by step-parents and other relatives has dropped from 500 in 1989 to 34 in 2004 and their share of all domestic adoptions has fallen from 45 per cent to 26 per cent (Australia, Australian Institute of Health and Welfare, 2004). In Australia, adoptions by step-parents and other relatives are currently discouraged because of their potentially detrimental effects on the child's relationship to his or her biological parents (Australia, Australian Institute of Health and Welfare, 2004).

In Switzerland, the number of adoptions by step-parents fell from 842 in 1980 to 180 in 2002 (figure VI.3). This decline was especially pronounced for step-fathers (Switzerland, Swiss Federal Statistical Office, 2004).

In Estonia, the number of adoptions by step-parents declined from 188 in 1995 to 53 in 2003, while their share of all domestic adoptions fell from 77 per cent to 55 per cent (Estonia, Ministry of Social Affairs, 2004).

The number of adoptions by step-parents also decreased in the United States during the 1980s, but may have stabilized since then. After reaching a peak of over 90,000 in 1982, the number of adoptions by step-parents and other relatives fell to about 53,000 in 1986 (Stolley, 1993). Some authors have attributed this reduction to an increase in informal care arrangements among parents and to decreasing remarriage rates (Stolley, 1993). In 1992, adoptions by step-parents totalled over 54,000 and accounted for about 42 per cent of all adoptions in the United States (United States, Child Welfare Information Gateway, 2004c).

C. SELECTED CHARACTERISTICS OF THE BIRTH MOTHER

1. Age of the birth mother[1]

Very few countries systematically collect and disseminate data on birth mothers, partly because of regulations protecting their anonymity. Data on birth fathers are even scarcer. As a result, the characteristics of birth parents are the least known part of the adoption triad.

In Ireland, many of the women who relinquish children for adoption are quite young. In 2003, almost 40 per cent of the 92 women who gave a child up for adoption were under 21 years of age at the time of the birth of the child (Ireland, The

Adoption Board, 2004). This finding is consistent with research undertaken in the United States, which indicates that younger women are more likely to give a child up for adoption, especially if they lack support from a partner or other family members (United States, Child Welfare Information Gateway, 2005).

In contrast, data for Australia indicate that only 26 per cent of children adopted through local placements had mothers under age 20 (table VI.7). Most of the children—59 per cent—had birth mothers aged 20 to 39. Furthermore, a quarter of the adopted children had mothers aged 30 or over (Australia, Australian Institute of Health and Welfare, 2004).

2. Marital status of the birth mother

The scant data available suggest that the majority of women who give a child up for adoption are unmarried. Data for Australia indicate that, out of the 73 children who were placed through local adoptions in 2004, 65 children, equivalent to 92 per cent, were born to unmarried mothers (table VI.7). More than a quarter of those unmarried women were under age 20.

In England and Wales, 76 per cent of children adopted in 2005 were born out of wedlock (United Kingdom, Office for National Statistics, 2007). Similarly, in the Republic of Korea, about 98 per cent of all children who were given up for adoption in 1998 were born to unmarried mothers. Poverty and divorce are some of the major factors cited by the Korean Government as influencing a woman's decision to place a child for adoption.[15]

In some countries, the percentage of adopted children born to unmarried mothers has increased in recent years. Data for England and Wales, for instance, show a fairly steady increase, with 76 per cent of children adopted in 2005 born outside of marriage compared to 58 per cent in 1991 (United Kingdom, Office for National Statistics, 2002 and 2007). Likewise, in Australia the percentage of adopted children born to unmarried mothers rose from 89 per cent in 1988 to 92 per cent in 2004 (Australia, Australian Institute of Health and Welfare, 2004).

D. SUMMARY

This chapter has reviewed what is known about key characteristics of the individuals involved in adoptions on the basis of the few data sets having the relevant information. Paucity of data is a major limitation. Thus, data on the age of adopted children are available for just 26 countries and information on their sex could be obtained for only 39 countries. That is, just 22 per cent and 33 per cent of countries releasing some data on adoption also disseminate information on the age or sex of adopted children, respectively. Data on key characteristics of adoptive parents or birth parents are even scarcer. Therefore, no firm conclusions can be reached on several aspects of adoption that are basic to understanding the dynamics of the process. Clearly, it is necessary to work towards a more systematic production and dissemination of detailed information on the demographic characteristics of the persons involved in the adoption triad.

TABLE VI.7. ADOPTIONS BY AGE AND MARITAL STATUS OF THE BIRTH MOTHER, AUSTRALIA, 2003-2004

	Married		Not married		Total	
	Number	Percentage	Number	Percentage	Number	Percentage
Under age 20	...	...	18	27.7	19[1]	26.0
20-24	1	16.7	17	26.2	19[1]	26.0
25-29	...	...	11	16.9	11	15.1
30-34	...	...	6	9.2	6	8.2
35-39	4	66.7	3	4.6	7	9.6
40 years or older	1	16.7	4	6.2	5	6.8
Unknown	...	...	6	9.2	6	8.2
Total	6	100.0	65	100.0	73	100.0

Source: Australia, Australian Institute of Health and Welfare, 2004.
NOTE: Data refer to the fiscal year.
[1]Of these, one is of unknown marital status.

The data available suggest that over 60 per cent of adopted children are under five years of age at the time of adoption, although that percentage varies widely from country to country. Despite the preference of parents for younger children, relatively few adoptions involve children under age one. Adoptions of children over age five also tend to be rare and frequently involve step-children. The data indicate that in several countries of origin of intercountry adoptions, children adopted domestically tend to be younger than those adopted through an intercountry procedure, whereas in most countries of destination, the opposite tends to be true.

In recent years, the mean age of children at the time of adoption has declined, partly because of the increasing number of intercountry adoptions, which involve younger children, and because of the drop in the number of adoptions by step-parents, which generally involve older children.

Data on the sex of adopted children indicate that, overall, fewer boys are adopted than girls in most countries with data available, with the median sex ratio among those with data being 87 boys adopted for every 100 girls. Girls tend to outnumber boys in both domestic and intercountry adoptions. However, in a number of countries, many of which are countries of origin, the percentage of boys among children adopted domestically is higher than that among children adopted through an intercountry procedure. Such sex imbalances are partly the result of local preference for adopting boys.

The age of most parents at the time of adoption ranges from 30 to 44 years. Adoptive parents are less likely to be under age 30 or over age 44. This distribution is shaped both by the legal requirements on the minimum or maximum ages of potential adoptive parents and by trends in marital formation and childbearing.

Female adoptive parents are generally younger than male adoptive parents, mainly because women marry younger than men and are less likely to become step-parents. In many countries, especially developed countries, the mean age of adoptive parents is rising, largely echoing the overall postponement of marriage and childbearing.

Although the number of male and female adoptive parents tends to be roughly equivalent, women slightly outnumber men as adoptive parents in the countries with data available. Furthermore, men tend to outnumber women as step-parents and women tend to outnumber men among single adoptive parents.

Countries having data on the number of adoptions by step-parents and other relatives show that these adoptions often constitute very high proportions of all domestic adoptions. The number of adoptions by step-parents, however, has been declining in a number of countries, partly as a result of legislation discouraging the severance of legal ties between birth parents and children as a result of divorce. Declining re-marriage rates and an increasing tendency to opt for informal care arrangements are other factors that may be contributing to this trend.

Information on the characteristics of birth parents is very scarce. In the few countries with data available, birth mothers who relinquish their children for adoption tend to be young and unmarried.

NOTES

[1] The mean ages of children, adoptive and birth parents at the time of adoption are estimated by the United Nations Population Division based on available data.

[2] Data refer to domestic adoptions in the region of Flanders.

[3] Because the number of adoptions is very small in many of the countries considered, some of the percentages and rates are subject to large year on year fluctuations and should be interpreted with caution.

[4] See United Nations, "Initial report of States parties due in 1996: Samoa" (CRC/C/WSM/1).

[5] See New Zealand, Department of Child, Youth and Family Services, "Response to the 2005 questionnaire on the practical operation of the Hague Convention of 29 May 1993 on Protection of Children and Co-operation in Respect of Intercountry adoption". Data on intercountry adoptions by step-parents and other relatives are incomplete.

[6] See Chile, National Service for Minors, "Response to the 2005 questionnaire on the practical operation of the Hague Convention of 29 May 1993 on Protection of Children and Co-operation in Respect of Intercountry adoption".

[7] See Lithuania, Ministry of Social Security and Labour, "Response to the 2005 questionnaire on the practical operation of the Hague Convention of 29 May 1993 on Protection of Children and Co-operation in Respect of Intercountry adoption".

[8] See Republic of Moldova, "Response to the 2005 questionnaire on the practical operation of the Hague Convention of 29 May 1993 on Protection of Children and Co-operation in Respect of Intercountry adoption".

[9] Data refer only to the State of Khartoum.

[10] See United Nations, "Initial reports of States parties due in 1997: Singapore" (CRC/C/51/Add.8); and "Written replies by the Government of Singapore (CRC/C/RESP/43) concerning the list of issues received by the Committee on the Rights of the Child (CRC/C/Q/SGP/1) relating to the consideration of the initial report of Singapore".

[11] See Colombia, Colombian Family Welfare Institute, "Response to the 2005 questionnaire on the practical operation of the Hague Convention of 29 May 1993 on Protection of Children and Co-operation in Respect of Intercountry adoption".

[12] See United Nations, "Second periodic reports of States parties due in 1998: Croatia" (CRC/C/70/Add.23).

[13] See United Nations, "Third periodic reports of States parties due in 2003: Finland" (CRC/C/129/Add.5).

[14] See United Nations, "Initial reports of States parties: Slovakia" (CRC/C/11/Add.17); and "Written replies by the Government of Slovakia (CRC/C/RESP/SLO/1) concerning the list of issues received by the Committee on the Rights of the Child (CRC/C/Q/SLO/1) relating to the consideration of the initial report of Slovakia".

[15] See United Nations, "Periodic reports of States parties due in 1998: Republic of Korea" (CRC/C/70/Add.14).

VII. THE DEMAND FOR AND AVAILABILITY OF ADOPTABLE CHILDREN

In 1974, the World Population Plan of Action of the World Population Conference[1] recommended that all Governments facilitate child adoption so as to assist involuntarily sterile and subfecund couples in achieving their desired family size (United Nations, 1975b). This recommendation implied that couples could use adoption to approximate biological parenthood when they were otherwise unable to have children of their own. Changes occurring since the 1970s in many countries, including delaying marriage, the postponement of childbearing, higher levels of childlessness and the wider acceptance of new family forms suggest that there may be a growing demand for adoptable children.

Yet the evidence suggests that the number of children available for adoption is declining, especially in developed countries. Women's increased capacity to control their fertility and societal changes that have made it both acceptable and possible for unmarried women to raise children on their own are partly responsible for such a decline. In countries where the availability of adoptable children—especially of healthy infants—has decreased, prospective adoptive parents have sought to adopt children abroad (Sokoloff, 1993; Steltzner, 2003). As a result, intercountry adoptions have become the means of satisfying part of the demand for adoptable children in many developed countries.

This chapter examines the relationship between various demographic factors and the demand for and availability of adoptable children. In terms of demand, it focuses on the relationship between adoption and age at marriage, age at first birth and various indicators of fertility, including the number of children per woman. With respect to the availability of adoptable children, it examines the relationship between the number of adoptions, unwanted fertility and extra-marital births. The impacts of orphanhood and the HIV/AIDS epidemic on the supply of adoptable children are also discussed. As in previous chapters, the analysis is limited by the paucity of relevant data.

A. THE DEMAND FOR ADOPTION FROM THE PERSPECTIVE OF ADOPTIVE PARENTS

Since at least the 1970s, many countries have witnessed a widening gap between the number of families wishing to adopt and the number of children available for adoption domestically. In Italy, for instance, an estimated 15 couples wish to adopt for every local child eligible for adoption.[2] In the United States, only one out of every three women who seek to adopt actually succeeds in doing so (Bachrach and others, 1991; Chandra and others, 1999).[3] In France[4] and Singapore,[5] the demand for adoptable children also exceeds the local supply.

Information on the number and characteristics of persons seeking to adopt is scarce. Very few countries publish data on the number of adoption applications and adoption orders granted. While such information throws some light on the demand for adoption, it has at least three drawbacks. First, adoption applications and orders refer to events and not persons and therefore do not provide direct information on the number of persons seeking to adopt, since a person may apply to adopt alone or as part of a couple.[6] Second, such data do not reflect the "adoption attrition", that is, they do not provide information on the number of persons who, having failed to adopt a child within a certain period, give up. In the United States, one estimate indicated that 62 per cent of women who have ever sought to adopt ended renouncing their plan[7] (Bachrach and others, 1991). Adoption applications may therefore underestimate the actual demand for adoption. Third, in most cases, countries disseminate information on the number of adoption applications recorded during a specified period, usually a year. However, to study the demand for adoption, information is required on the overall number of pending applications at one point in time, a measure of stock. Since it often takes more than one year to process an adoption order,[8] focusing only on the applications filed over a year underestimates the unfulfilled demand for adoption. A discussion of the data required to monitor the demand for adoption can be found in chapter VIII.

1. *Adoption applications and orders granted*

Despite the limitations of the information available, a few inferences can be made from data on adoption applications and orders granted. In all countries with the required data, the demand for adoption exceeds the supply of adoptable children. The gap between adoption applications and adoption orders granted is particularly large in the developing countries having the required data (table VII.1). In the Gambia, for instance, only 18 of the 95 applications submitted between 1998 and 2000 were approved or just 19 per cent of such applications.[9] In Fiji, 89 placements were made in 1994 whereas 509 adoption applications were submitted that year.[10] In Guyana, the Adoption Board approved just 25 per cent of the more than 1,500 applications received between 1999 and 2002.[11] Compared to developed countries, developing countries receive fewer adoption applications and approve lower proportions of them, a difference that is statistically significant at the p<0.01 level according to a Pearson correlation test.

These differences may arise because developed countries tend to have more efficient procedures for screening applicants, allowing only persons who meet the required eligibility criteria to apply. However, because the data available for developed countries refer primarily to applications for intercountry adoptions, it has been suggested that applicants may appear to be more successful because countries of origin may not be upholding the principle of subsidiarity, whereby intercountry adoption is considered only after all other options have been exhausted. The data available do not support this explanation. Countries of origin do not appear to give preferential treatment to applications by persons residing abroad over those filed by local residents. In Jamaica, for instance, persons residing overseas and local residents have virtually the same likelihood of being granted an adoption.[12] Similarly, in the Gambia, slightly more applications for domestic adoption were granted between 1998 and 2000 than intercountry adoptions filed during the same period.[9] Moreover, in the Gambia, half of the cases of intercountry adoption involved children adopted by a relative residing abroad.

A second finding is that certain groups of people, such as married couples or relatives of the child involved, are sometimes favoured in the adoption process. In Denmark, nearly 91 per cent of the 5,560 decisions on intercountry adoptions submitted by couples during 1997-2004 were granted, compared to 75 per cent of the 367 decisions on adoptions by single persons issued during the same period (Denmark, Danish National Board of Adoption, 2005).[13] In Ireland, a slightly higher proportion of applications submitted by step-fathers and other relatives were approved than of those submitted by persons unrelated to the child (Ireland, The Adoption Board, 2004).

TABLE VII.1. NUMBER OF ADOPTION APPLICATIONS AND APPROVALS

Country	Year	Number of applications	Of which approved	
			Number	Percentage
Denmark[1]	1997-2004	5 927	5 330	89.9
Fiji	1991-1994	1 449	384	26.5
Finland[1]	2003	343	339	98.5
Gambia	1998-2000	95	18	18.9
Guyana	1999-2002	1 505	382	25.4
Ireland[2]	1994-2003	3 852	3 583	93.0
Jamaica	2000-2002	1 148	720	62.7

Source: For a complete list of country references see annex II.

[1] Data refer only to applications and approvals for intercountry adoptions.
[2] Data refer only to applications and approvals for domestic adoption.

2. The preferences of prospective adoptive parents

While adoption applications offer an indication of the number of persons seeking to adopt, other factors, such as the preferences of prospective adoptive parents regarding the number and characteristics of children they wish to adopt, also need to be considered in determining whether the supply of adoptable children is adequate to meet the demand. Preferences with respect to the age and sex of the adopted child explain why prospective parents, especially those in developed countries, often have recourse to intercountry adoption (Lovelock, 2000; Steltzner, 2003).

(a) The number of children that prospective parents wish to adopt

A few countries provide information on the number of children that prospective adoptive parents wish to adopt. The data confirm that the vast majority of applicants seek to adopt and are granted one child at a time.

In Italy, the majority of couples who sought to adopt through an intercountry procedure between 2001 and 2005 requested only one child (figure VII.1) but 16 per cent of couples applied for two children and just under 3 per cent applied for three

children or more (Italy, Office of the Prime Minister, 2006).[14]

In the United States, 65 per cent of women interviewed in the 1995 National Survey of Family Growth (NSFG) expressed a preference for adopting a single child, while 26 per cent indicated that they would prefer to adopt two or more siblings and the remaining 9 per cent replied that they had no preference. In addition, respondents indicated flexibility in agreeing to adopt more than one child if that was their only option (Chandra and others, 1999).

In Finland, the majority of applicants for intercountry adoption expressed no preference as to the number of children they wanted but 15 per cent said they wished to adopt two children or more (Finland, Finnish Adoption Board, 2004).

These examples suggest that the overall demand for adoptable children may be higher than indicated by the number of adoption applications, which are usually constrained to a single child.

(b) Sex of prospective adopted children

Preferences regarding family composition shape the demand for adoption.[15] Thus, persons may adopt a child of a certain sex to achieve a

Figure VII.1. Applications for intercountry adoption according to the number of persons that prospective parents were seeking to adopt, Italy, 2001-2005

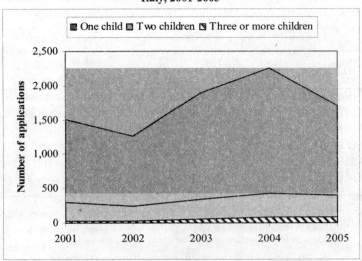

Source: Italy, Office of the Prime Minister, 2006.

more balanced sex ratio among their offspring or for reasons related to inheritance of land or titles (Carroll 1970; Damas, 1972). In China, data relative to the period 1950-1987 indicate that childless women who adopted did not show a preference for the sex of the child, whereas women who already had children used adoption to achieve a better sex balance among their offspring (Liu, Larsen and Wyshak, 2004). Johnson and others (1998) validated this conclusion on the basis of a sample of 392 adoptions by Chinese families carried out between the late 1940s and the mid-1990s. In this study, 130 of the 134 families with sons but no daughters adopted a girl and families that already had daughters were more likely to adopt a son. These preferences matched the views expressed by adoptive families regarding the ideal family: it should include both a daughter and a son (Johnson and others, 1998).

The limited data available suggest that the preferences of prospective adoptive parents often mirror broader societal preferences regarding the sex composition of families. In Jamaica, where there is a slight preference for daughters (Sargent and Harris, 1992), 282 applications were made for adopting a girl in 2002 compared to 160 applications for adopting a boy.[12] Adoption orders were granted for 142 girls and 113 boys, implying that only half of the adoption applications concerning girls were satisfied, whereas 70 per cent of adoption applications for boys could be satisfied, a difference significant at the $p < 0.05$ level.

In countries where there is no overwhelming preference regarding the sex of offspring or where there is a preference for a balanced sex distribution of children within a family, prospective parents often seek to adopt equal numbers of boys and girls (Hank and Kohler, 2000; Pebley and Westoff, 1982).

In Italy, over 70 per cent of couples seeking to adopt reported that they had no preference regarding the sex of the prospective adopted child. Among those who did express a preference, the majority of couples preferred to adopt a girl (Italy, National Statistical Institute, 2005). Similarly, in the United States, respondents to the 1997 National Survey of Family Growth signalled that they would accept to adopt a child of either sex, although a

slightly higher percentage of women said that they would prefer to adopt a girl (Chandra and others, 1999).[16] In the Gambia, more applications were submitted for adopting boys than girls over the period 1998-2000,[9] indicating a slight son preference consistent with that common in other countries of sub-Saharan Africa (Arnold, 1992).

(c) Age of prospective adopted children

As indicated in chapter VI, prospective adoptive parents often prefer adopting younger children. In Finland, the average preferred age of children adopted through an intercountry procedure, as reported by prospective parents, has declined from nearly two years in 1996 to less than one year and a half in 2003. The mean age of children adopted from abroad in 2003, however, was nearly three years, indicating that, despite the preference of parents for adopting infants, they had to settle for older children (Finland, Finnish Adoption Board, 2004).[17]

In the United States, women also appear to prefer adopting young children. Thus, the majority of ever married women aged 18 to 44 interviewed in various rounds of the National Survey of Family Growth declared that they would prefer to adopt a child under the age of two (Chandra and others, 1999).

In Italy, 35 per cent of couples interviewed responded that they would like to adopt an infant (that is, a child under age one) and nearly 50 per cent said they would prefer to adopt a child aged two to four years (Italy, National Statistical Institute, 2005).

In Belgium, the majority of persons who had children of their own and were seeking to adopt, wanted children younger than the children they already had (Belgium, Kind en Gezin, 2003).[18]

B. THE DEMOGRAPHIC FACTORS ASSOCIATED WITH THE DEMAND FOR ADOPTION

This section explores the demographic factors that are likely to play a role in determining the demand for adoption. One such factor is the extent of childlessness, especially that caused by biological impediments to conceive or bring a pregnancy to term. Individuals who have no children because of sterility, subfecundity or other factors can have recourse to adoption to build a family.

It is also useful to consider trends in certain determinants of total fertility, [19] such as the mean age at first birth or the mean age at marriage since, the longer a woman waits to have children, the less likely she is to achieve her target family size if it is not zero or one.

In considering adoption as the main strategy that persons who are involuntarily childless have in order to achieve their desired family size, one must bear in mind that those who actually resort to adoption include many people who already have children or are able to have them biologically but for whom adoption is a choice based on other considerations, including providing orphans with a family, adopting step-children[20] or realizing preferences in terms of family composition (Feigelman and Silverman, 1997).

The sections below focus on some of the demographic factors commonly associated with the unfulfilled desire for children or, described demographically, factors preventing the realized family size from reaching a large desired family size (Bongaarts, 1997 and 2001; Livi Bacci, 2001). Comparisons made on the basis of national data are used to suggest hypotheses about how the demand for adoption is shaped, which are then validated, to the extent possible, with evidence derived from individual-level data gathered through ethnographic studies, sample surveys or censuses.

1. Desired number of children

Individuals or couples decide to adopt because they wish to have more children than they are able or willing to bear. In the United States, a study based on the 1988 National Survey of Family Growth showed that ever married women aged 15 to 44 who wanted more children than they expected to bear were substantially more likely to have sought to adopt a child than women who desired fewer children, although this relationship was not statistically significant (Bachrach and others, 1991). Furthermore "the odds of having

sought to adopt increase[d] as the discrepancy between the desired and expected number of children widen[ed]" (Bachrach and others, 1991, p. 712). Women who wanted one child more than they expected to bear were three times more likely to seek adoption than women who did not desire more children than they expected to have. The odds of seeking adoption increased to nearly five times for women who desired two more children than they expected to bear and to over eight times for those desiring three or more children than they expected to bear.

Some insight into the relationship between the desired family size and adoption can also be gleaned from information on the parity[21] of prospective adoptive parents. In general, the more children a person already has, the less likely he or she is to want to have another child. A number of studies, most of which relate to the United States, have confirmed this relationship. According to the 1973 National Survey of Family Growth, 42 per cent of currently married women aged 15 to 44 who wanted more children but already had one biological child expressed the intention to adopt. For women with two children, the proportion was 30 per cent and for those with three or more children it was 22 per cent (Bonham, 1977). Chandra and others (1999), using data from later rounds of the same survey, found that the proportion of ever married women aged 18 to 44 who had considered adoption declined steadily with increasing parity, being 28 per cent for those with one child, 24 per cent for those with two children and 22 per cent for those with three or more.

Data on applications for intercountry adoptions among persons who already have children, whether biological or adoptive, also support the conclusion that the demand for adoption decreases with the number of children a person or couple already has.[22] In Finland, couples applying for intercountry adoptions were more likely to have smaller than larger families: in 2003, 47 families with one biological child, 13 families with two biological children, eight families with three children, and two families with four children or more applied for an intercountry adoption, implying a difference between families with at most two children and larger families that was significant at a p< 0.001 level using a Chi-square test (figure VII.2). A similar distribution was found among families with adopted children, significant at the same level.

In Italy, the more children prospective adoptive couples already have, the less likely they are to seek to adopt more children. Furthermore, adoption applications are consistent with an ideal family size of two children. Thus, a larger than expected number of couples with no children sought to adopt two children and a larger than expected number of couples who already had one child applied to adopt another child. Yet, a smaller than expected number of couples with only one child sought to adopt two children (Italy, Office of the Prime Minister, 2006).

Aggregate population data confirm some of these relations. Among countries that are major receivers of intercountry adoptions,[23] those where respondents to a recent Population Policy Acceptance Study (PPAS) reported large numbers of desired children also tended to have higher total under-five adoption rates (table VII.2) and the relationship between the average desired number of children and the under-five intercountry adoption rate was positive and statistically significant at the p< 0.05 level, an indication that families in developed countries may be turning to

intercountry adoption as a way to reach their desired family size.

Countries where relatively high proportions of men and women reported that they wanted three children or more also recorded higher intercountry under-five adoption rates (significant at a level of p< 0.05 according to a non-parametric correlation test). These findings are consistent with those of Bachrach and others (1991) and suggest that, when the desired number of children is large, couples are more likely to resort to adoption to get the number of children they desire.

A different picture emerges for countries that are not major receivers of intercountry adoptions.[24] A non-parametric correlation test shows a negative and statistically significant relationship at the p< 0.05 level between the domestic under-five adoption rate and desired family size as reported in recent Demographic and Health Surveys (DHS) (Zlidar and others, 2003). Countries with the highest number of desired children among married women aged 15 to 49, such as the Central African Republic, Chad, Mozambique and Niger, have some of the lowest under-five domestic adoption rates in the world. Not all countries, however, conform to this pattern. Among countries with relatively low levels of desired fertility (three children or less),

Figure VII.2. Applications for intercountry adoption by number of biological and adopted children, Finland, 2003

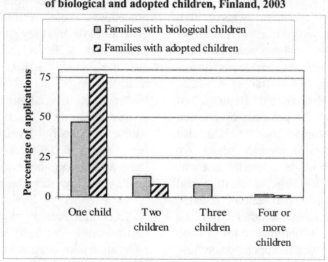

Source: Finland, Finnish Adoption Board, 2004.

TABLE VII.2. AVERAGE DESIRED NUMBER OF CHILDREN AND DISTRIBUTION OF PERSONS BY NUMBER OF CHILDREN DESIRED FOR
SELECTED COUNTRIES OF DESTINATION OF INTERCOUNTRY ADOPTIONS

| | Under-five adoption rate (per 100,000 children under five) | | Average desired number of children | | Percentage distribution by number of children desired | | | | | | | |
| | | | | | 0 | | 1 | | 2 | | 3+ | |
Country	Total	Intercountry	Women	Men	Women	Men	Women	Men	Women	Men	Women	Men
Austria...........	123.4	...	1.84	1.78	8.2	11.1	32.7	33.5	35.1	34.4	24.0	21.1
Belgium.........	47.8	45.6	1.86	1.81	10.4	15.3	22.7	19.6	45.3	43.3	21.5	21.8
Cyprus...........	251.9	192.4	2.36	2.42	0.9	1.6	23.5	27.0	33.6	25.1	42.0	46.2
Finland	105.9	61.7	2.18	2.14	7.5	10.7	14.0	14.4	44.5	41.3	34.0	33.6
Germany........	89.9	30.5	1.75	1.59	15.4	22.8	18.3	19.1	49.3	41.1	17.0	16.9
Italy	72.0	49.0	1.92	1.86	7.1	9.1	18.9	16.9	53.4	56.9	20.6	17.1
Netherlands ...	83.9	65.6	2.13	1.98	12.9	17.5	7.3	5.3	49.2	52.7	30.7	24.4
Median	89.9	55.4	1.92	1.86	8.2	11.1	18.9	19.1	45.3	41.3	24.0	21.8

Sources: For a complete list of country references, see annex II. The data on the desired number of children were obtained from Germany, Federal Institute for Population Research and the Robert Bosch Foundation, 2005.

there is considerable variability in terms of the domestic under-five adoption rates, with countries such as Armenia, Brazil, Kazakhstan and Uzbekistan having relatively high domestic adoption rates. In contrast, countries with similar average numbers of desired children, such as Colombia or Peru in Latin America or India and Indonesia in Asia, have much lower under-five domestic adoption rates (table A.VII.1).

Among countries that are not major receivers of intercountry adoptions, there is also a negative correlation between the proportion of women who want more children than they already have and the under-five domestic adoption rate, which is significant at the p< 0.01 level according to a non-parametric test. Thus, countries where high proportions of married women aged 15 to 49 reported that they wanted to have another child, either within two years or later, had lower under-five domestic adoption rates (table A.VII.2). Benin, Ethiopia and the United Republic of Tanzania, where at least 20 per cent of married women aged 15 to 49 wanted another child, also displayed some of the lowest domestic under-five adoption rates. Conversely, in countries such as Azerbaijan, the Czech Republic, Mauritius and Ukraine, where at most 14 per cent of married women aged 15 to 49 wanted another child, the domestic under-five adoption rates were considerably higher. It would appear, therefore, that in countries that are not major destinations of children adopted through an intercountry procedure, the desire for children is fulfilled

predominantly through childbearing. However, in some countries, institutions other than formal adoption may also provide a means to achieve the desired family size. In sub-Saharan Africa, for instance, *de facto* adoption and fostering are often alternative practices to meet family building goals.

Exploring the relationship between adoption rates and total fertility[25] (obtained from United Nations, 2005) can provide further evidence about the use of adoption to achieve a desired family size, since the desired number of children is highly correlated with total fertility.[26]

Among developed countries that are also major receivers of children adopted through intercountry procedures, total fertility levels are already generally low and they show a low correlation with adoption rates. In Ireland, New Zealand, Norway and the United States, where total fertility is relatively high, at 1.8 children per woman or higher, under-five adoption rates are also high, but so are those in Canada, Singapore and Spain, whose total fertility levels are at most 1.6 children per woman. A few countries, including Greece, Italy and Japan, have both low levels of total fertility and low adoption rates.

In contrast, among countries that are not major destinations of children adopted through intercountry procedures, there is a strong negative relationship between total fertility and adoption rates, significant at the p< 0.01 level according to a non-parametric test. That is, among this group of countries, high total fertility goes hand in hand with low domestic adoption rates and vice versa (figure VII.3). Benin, Ethiopia, Mali, Mozambique, Niger and Togo, all of which have total fertility levels above five children per woman, report under-five domestic adoption rates under one per 100,000. Furthermore, countries with low total fertility levels, such as Bulgaria, Estonia, the Russian Federation and Ukraine, report some of the highest domestic adoption rates.

These observations are consistent with the expectation that adoption would be more common in countries where expressed fertility preferences are likely to exceed completed cohort fertility, which is related to period total fertility[27] (Bongaarts, 2001). Furthermore, the data also corroborate that in populations where observed fertility exceeds desired family size, there is less demand for adoption.

2. Sterility and childlessness

People who are biologically unable to bear children must resort to adoption or allied practices if they wish to become legal parents. Therefore, one of the determinants of the potential demand for adoption is the number of couples where at least one partner is sterile or subfecund.[28] Data on the prevalence of sterility and subfecundity can be derived from surveys inquiring about the desire for children and the ability to have them.[29] However, the responses to those surveys are often deficient because women affected by subfecundity may be unaware of their condition.

Another indicator of the possible demand for adoption is the level of childlessness in a population. However, women may remain childless out of choice or because, if they remain single, it might be difficult for them to rear children on their own. Moreover, because couples

Figure VII.3. Domestic under-five adoption rate and total fertility per women in countries that are not major destinations of intercountry adoptions

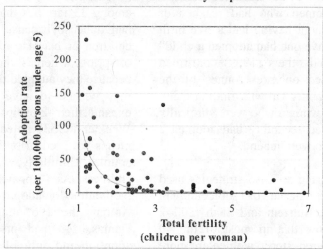

Sources: See table A.VII.4. For a complete list of country references, see annex II. The population under age five and total fertility estimates were obtained from United Nations, 2005.

NOTES: The domestic under-five adoption rate is calculated by dividing the number of domestic adoptions of children under five by the number of children under five. If data on domestic adoptions are not classified by age, it is assumed that 60 per cent of adopted children were under age five at the time of adoption. The data on total fertility represent children per woman and refer to 2005; the data on total fertility and on adoptions do not necessarily refer to the same year.

that already have or are able to have biological children also opt for adoption, the level of childlessness by itself may not be indicative of the potential demand for adoption. Nevertheless, levels of childlessness are compared with adoption rates for the sake of completeness.

(a) Sterility

A number of studies focusing on the United States have concluded that sterility is often associated with a higher propensity to adopt. Using survey data, Bonham (1977) found that sterile and subfecund women in the United States were more likely to have adopted a child than fecund women. Data from the National Survey of Family Growth indicate that nearly 5 per cent of married women who are sterile and slightly over 7 per cent of those who are subfecund had adopted a child, whereas less than 1 per cent of fecund married women had done so. Similarly, Bachrach (1983) concluded that adoptions in the United States were disproportionately concentrated among couples who had difficulties bearing children: "nearly half of the estimated 274,000 currently married women who had reached or surpassed age 30 without having had a live birth and were unable to have one had adopted a child" (p. 862). Chandra and others (1999) confirmed this relationship based on later rounds of the National Survey of Family Growth, finding that a greater proportion of women who were surgically sterile or had impaired fecundity had adopted a child than women who were fecund. [30]

Adoption or fostering are also strategies used by women who are sterile or subfecund in developing countries. Rutstein and Shah (2004), using DHS data, show that in most of the 40 countries they considered, sterile women are more likely to adopt or foster a child than fertile women. [31] The highest percentages of women who, suffering from primary sterility, lived with at least one adoptive or foster child were found in Benin (61 per cent) and Guinea (58 per cent).

Given these findings and considering that in most developing countries few women wish to remain childless (Germany, Federal Institute for Population Research and the Robert Bosch Foundation, 2005; Rutstein and Shah, 2004),

countries with higher levels of sterility would be expected to have, on average, higher adoption rates. Yet the relationship between domestic under-five adoption rates and the prevalence of primary sterility measured by DHS surveys (Rutstein and Shah, 2004) is not statistically significant. This weak relationship is at least partly the result of the continued practice of *de facto* adoption and child fostering in many developing countries, practices that are not reflected by the adoption data used in this report.

(b) Childlessness

Data on childlessness[32] are widely available, since the population censuses and surveys of most developing countries collect information on the number of children women have ever borne. Because few women in developing wish to remain childless, levels of childlessness are expected to be associated positively with adoption rates. [33]

Adoption is a strategy to avoid childlessness, as ethnographic studies corroborate. Dunning (1962), studying Eskimo populations, found that among 33 families that had adopted children, 16 had done so because they were unable to have children or because of the death of one of their offspring, whereas the other 17 did so mainly because they adopted the children of deceased kin, they wished to have a son or they wanted to expand their kinship bonds. In Micronesia, as Weckler (1953) noted, adoption was used as a means of redistributing children to childless couples. Similarly, Damas (1983) found that childlessness ("apparent sterility") was a prime motivation for adoption in the atoll of Pingelap. Among the 196 adoptive families studied by Damas, 113 had no children at the time of adoption and only 14 had two children or more. Damas also observed a positive relationship between childlessness and adoption over four generations of women. Despite confirming this association, Damas found that childless women in the cohorts born after 1944 were less likely to adopt than childless women born in 1870-1894 or 1895-1919. He attributed this decline to weakening kinship ties and demographic factors. [34]

Data on the number of children present in families before adoption can provide insights about the relationship between childlessness and adoption (table VII.3). In Finland, for example, the majority of adoptive parents are childless (80 per cent in 2003): among the 343 persons who applied for an intercountry adoption in 2003, 273 had no biological children of their own. Among the 70 applicants who had biological children, almost 70 per cent had only one child (Finland, Finnish Adoption Board, 2004). Similarly, in Italy, almost 91 per cent of the couples who applied for an intercountry adoption in 2000-2006 had no children (Italy, Office of the Prime Minister, 2004).[35]

In Australia, 59 per cent of children adopted during 2003-2004 were adopted by parents with no biological children, whereas 15 per cent of children were adopted by parents who had biological children, 22 per cent by parents who had another adopted child and 4 per cent by parents who had both biological and other adopted children (Australia, Australian Institute of Health and Welfare, 2004).

While in many countries a high proportion of adoptive parents are childless, there are exceptions. In Ireland in 2003, 157 of the 263 families who adopted a child domestically, representing 64 per cent, already had a child (Ireland, The Adoption Board, 2004). The proportion of families who already had one or more biological children was particularly high for adoptions that involve relatives or step-parents, where factors other than the desired number of children play a key role in the decision to adopt. Among those adoptions, 80 per cent of adoptive families had a biological child and 5 per cent had both a biological and an adopted child. As already noted in previous chapters, children adopted by relatives or step-parents are older on average than those adopted by persons unrelated to them, suggesting that the motivations for adopting differ between the two groups.

Belgium[18] and Israel[36] also record high proportions of adoptions involving parents who already had children. In Belgium, 52 per cent of the

TABLE VII.3. NUMBER OF ADOPTIONS BY PERSONS WITH AND WITHOUT CHILDREN
AT THE TIME OF ADOPTION

| | | | Percentage of adoptions by parents | | |
| | | | without children (1) | with children (2) | Difference (1)-(2) |
Country	Year	Number			
Australia	2003-2004[1]	353[2]	59.0	41.0[3]	18.0
Belgium[4]	2003	186	47.9	52.1	-4.2
Finland[5]	1996-2003	1 870	84.2	15.8	68.4
Ireland[6]	2003	263	36.1	63.9[7]	-27.8
Israel[8]	1985-1995	343	46.6	53.4	-6.8
Italy[5]	2000-2006[9]	12 161	90.6	9.4	81.2
United States[10]	2000	1 687 108	48.4	51.6	-3.2
Median	..	..	48.4	51.6	-3.2

Source: For a complete list of country references, see annex II.
NOTE: Children include biological children, adopted children and step-children.

[1] Data refer to the fiscal year.
[2] Of these, the family composition is unknown for two adoptions.
[3] Of these, 3.7 per cent have both adopted and biological children.
[4] Data refer only to the region of Flanders.
[5] Data refer to applicants for intercountry adoption.
[6] Data refer to domestic adoptions.
[7] Of these, 4.2 per cent have both adopted and biological children.
[8] Data refer only to older children.
[9] Data for 2006 refer only to the first six months.
[10] Data refer to the number of households containing an adopted person as reported in the sample of the 2000 U.S. population census. Among those households, 1.8 per cent had adopted children and step-children, and 1.9 per cent had adopted children, step-children and biological children.

186 children adopted in 2003 went to parents who already had children of their own. Similarly in Israel, 53 per cent of the 343 persons who applied for an adoption between 1985 and 1995, amounting to 183 cases, already had children.

In the United States, the 2000 population census sample indicates that almost 4 per cent of households with children had at least one adopted child. Among those 1.7 million households, almost 50 per cent had both biological and adopted children. Less than 4 per cent of those households, had either a combination of adopted and step-children or a combination of birth, adopted and step-children (United States Census Bureau, 2003).

There is no clear relationship between the proportion childless among women aged 40 to 44 and adoption rates.[37] Some countries with high percentages of childless women have high adoption rates (table A.VII.3). The United States, for instance, has one of the highest under-five adoption rates and a high proportion of childless women (21.5 per cent of women aged 40-44) and so does Canada, but countries such as France, Italy and Portugal have intermediate levels of childlessness—ranging from 10 per cent to 14 per cent of women aged 40-44—and relatively low under-five adoption rates (below 80 adoptions per 100,000). In Australia, the under-five adoption rate is low compared to that of other major receiving countries of intercountry adoptions but the percentage of childless women is also low. None of the countries of destination of intercountry adoptions registers both high levels of childlessness and low under-five adoption rates. However, some countries, including Ireland, Norway and Singapore, have low levels of childlessness and high under-five adoption rates.

Among countries that are not major destinations of intercountry adoptions, the relationship between childlessness and adoption is even weaker (table A.VII.4). Thus, Mongolia, a country with one of the lowest levels of childlessness in the world, has an under-five domestic adoption rate just above 415 per 100,000. Countries such as Argentina, the Central African Republic and Thailand, all of which record relatively high proportions childless among women aged 40-44 (over 10 per cent), exhibit extremely low under-five domestic adoption rates.

That is, at the population level, childlessness does not appear to be the major determinant of formal adoption in most societies.

3. Factors influencing the timing of fertility

A late start of childbearing[38] is an important determinant of the number of children a woman has and, hence, of whether desired family size is achieved. A woman's ability to conceive and bear children declines with age and women who postpone childbearing too long may be unable to have as many children as they would like, especially if the desired number of children is large.

Few studies have considered how the proximate determinants of fertility, such as the mean age at marriage or the mean age at first birth, relate to adoption. Attention has focused mostly on the age of prospective adoptive parents (see chapter VI). Thus, Bachrach and others (1991) as well as Chandra and others (1999) have found that the proportion of ever married women who had ever sought to adopt increases with age, a finding consistent with the increasing likelihood of subfecundity or sterility as age increases.

Age at first marriage has been rising in most countries and so has the mean age of women at the birth of their first child (United Nations, 2004b). In the absence of changes in other factors,[39] these trends could result in a rising demand for adoption (Bachrach, 1983; Bitler and Zavodny, 2002; Sobol and Daly, 1994). The mean ages at first marriage and at first birth have reached particularly high levels in developed countries (United Nations, 2004b). This section explores the relationship between the mean age at marriage and the mean age of women at the birth of their first child, on the one hand, and adoption rates on the other, using estimates at the national level derived from the United Nations (2004a).

(a) Age at marriage

At the population level, the female singulate mean age at marriage[40] (SMAM) is an indicator of the average length of single life for women who marry before age 50 and is commonly used as an indicator of the mean age at marriage.

Among countries that are major destinations of intercountry adoptions, several exhibit both high singulate mean ages at marriage and high under-five adoption rates or vice-versa (table A.VII.3). Thus, Denmark, Iceland, Ireland and Norway have some of the highest female singulate mean ages at marriage in the world as well as some of the highest under-five adoption rates, and countries such as Greece, Israel, Malta and Portugal, have both relatively low female singulate mean ages at marriage and low under-five adoption rates. Overall, however, the relationship between the two indicators is not statistically significant partly because, for a number of countries, relatively high under-five adoption rates are paired with moderate singulate mean ages at marriage (e.g., Singapore, Spain and the United States) or low under-five adoption rates are paired with comparatively high female singulate mean ages at marriage (e.g., Australia, Belgium and France).

Among the countries that are not major destinations of intercountry adoptions, there is a positive and significant association at the $p < 0.01$ level between the singulate mean age at marriage and the under-five domestic adoption rate (table A.VII.4). Several countries, including Benin, Mozambique and Togo in sub-Saharan Africa, and Bangladesh and India in South-central Asia, have both low female singulate mean ages at marriage and low under-five domestic adoption rates. Several countries in Eastern Europe, including Bulgaria, the Russian Federation and Ukraine, have low singulate mean ages at marriage (ranging from 21 to 23 years) and high under-five domestic adoption rates. Lastly, yet other countries exhibit relatively high singulate mean ages at marriage (above 27 years) and low under-five domestic adoption rates (e.g., Bahamas, Slovenia and South Africa). Consequently, despite the statistically significant relationship between the indicators considered, high singulate mean ages at marriage do not translate necessarily into high adoption rates.

(b) Age at first birth

Generally, the age at first marriage is highly correlated with the age at first birth. For purposes of assessing the impact of delayed childbearing on the demand for adoption, the mean age at first birth is a better indicator than the age at first marriage because, in some countries, there is a substantial interval between marriage and first birth and, in others, particularly those in Europe and Northern America, the proportion of births outside marriage is high (United Nations, 2004b). In both cases, the reproductive period is different from that implied by the age at first marriage.

The mean age at first birth is expected to be positively associated with the adoption rate because, the more women delay the birth of their first child, the shorter their effective reproductive life becomes and the less likely that they will bear their desired number of children if it is higher than one.

Among countries that are major destinations of intercountry adoptions, many where the mean age at first birth is above 28 years also have high total under-five adoption rates, as is case for Cyprus, Ireland, Singapore and Spain (table A.VII.3). In addition, some countries have both a low total under-five adoption rate and a low mean age at first birth (e.g. Belgium and Israel). However, the relationship between those two measures is not statistically significant because in several countries a relatively low mean age at first birth (under 27 years of age) coexists with a high total under-five adoption rate (e.g., Canada and Iceland). Similarly, Norway and the United States display some of the highest total under-five adoption rates but have mean ages at first birth lower than other major receiving countries, including New Zealand, Spain and the United Kingdom.

A stronger relationship between the mean age at first birth and the adoption rate is found among the countries that are not major destinations of intercountry adoptions (figure VII.4, table A.VII.4), where a non-parametric correlation test indicates that the relationship between the two is positive and statistically significant at the $p < 0.01$ level. Thus, Bangladesh, the Central African Republic, Niger, Togo and the United Republic of Tanzania display low mean ages at first birth (at around 19 years) and very low under-five adoption rates. Nevertheless, there are some exceptions. In Bulgaria and the Russian Federation, the mean age at first birth is relatively low and the domestic

**Figure VII.4. Domestic under-five adoption rate
versus the mean age at first birth in countries that are not major
destinations of intercountry adoptions**

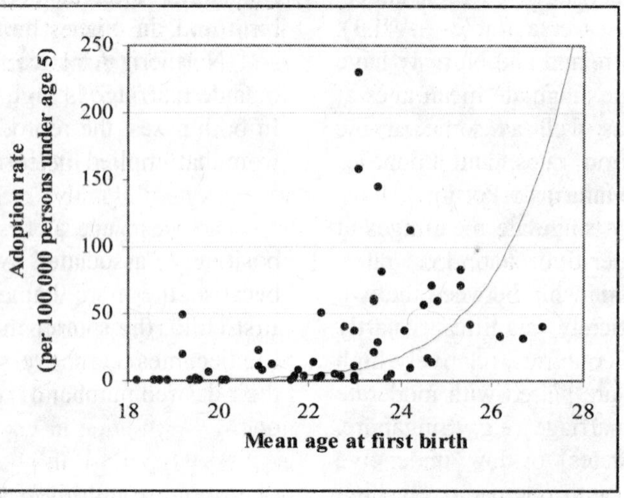

Sources: See table A.VII.4. For a complete list of country references see annex II. The population under five was obtained from United Nations, 2005, and the mean age at first birth was obtained from United Nations, 2004a.

NOTE: The domestic under-five adoption rate is calculated by dividing the number of domestic adoptions of children under age five by the number of children under five. If data are not classified by age, it is assumed that 60 per cent of adopted children were under age five at the time of adoption. The estimated mean age at first birth was derived from survey data referring to some year within the period 1985-2002; the estimated mean age at first birth and the adoption rate do not necessarily refer to the same year.

under-five adoption rate is higher than would be expected on the basis of the timing of first births.

C. THE AVAILABILITY OF ADOPTABLE CHILDREN

An assessment of the potential availability of adoptable children is not straightforward. As this report has shown, children may be adopted in different ways. Some children are adopted from institutions and other care facilities where they have been placed because they lack the support and protection of their biological parents. Although not all children in care are adoptable, in most countries at least some of the children in institutional care may be adopted. In some countries, children can also be adopted directly from their parents, that is, they pass from the care of their biological parents (generally the mother) to the care of adoptive parents. In such cases, the biological parents opt for adoption because they cannot care or support the children involved or because they find themselves in situations where it is not socially acceptable to have children (for

instance, women having children out of wedlock). Lastly, as this report has shown, many children are adopted by their step-parents and, therefore, do not cease being under the care of at least one of their biological parents. Thus, in order to assess the availability of children for adoption, these different paths to becoming adoptable need to be considered.

Another indicator of the potential availability of children for adoption is provided by estimates of the number of orphaned children who have lost both of their parents. Usually, minors who have no living parents must be under the guardianship of some adult, normally a relative, but may not need to be adopted formally. Furthermore, some may end up in institutional care and, therefore, be included in the statistics relative to children in care. Nevertheless, a discussion of orphanhood and adoption is appropriate mainly because it will show that adoption is not the main mechanism through which care for orphaned children is ensured.

This section presents the data available on the number of children in care and their characteristics; an analysis of the processes that may cause parents to have more children than those they feel able to support or care for; data on trends in out-of-wedlock fertility and remarriage, and estimates of the number of orphaned children in relation to adoption rates. Although the data presented do not yield an estimate of the number of children potentially available for adoption, they provide useful insights about key processes that help determine the number of adoptable children.

1. Children in care

Children in foster care or in other types of institutions for children who are orphaned or whose parents cannot care for them are of interest because, under certain circumstances, they may be or become adoptable. Data on the number of children in care are scarce. Few countries publish them on a regular basis and the data published are often not comparable among countries. The Russian Federation, the United Kingdom and the United States, for instance, publish data on both the number of children entering care each year (flow data) and the number of children in care at a particular point in time (stock data). Other countries, such as the Czech Republic, publish data only on children who enter care each year. Countries in yet a third group release data but do not make clear whether those data refer to stocks of children in care or flows of children admitted into care.[41] Generally, the stock of children in care is expected to be larger than the inflow of children into care. However, when only one number is published, errors of interpretation may arise. This possibility must be borne in mind in considering the evidence presented below.

Among countries publishing the relevant data, there is considerable variability in the proportion of children placed in foster care or in institutions (table VII.4). In Cyprus, the Czech Republic, Latvia, Malawi, Nicaragua and Swaziland more than 80 per 100,000 children under age 18 enter care each year. In Benin, China and the Philippines the equivalent rate of entry is lower than 40 per 100,000 children under age 18.

Among countries that publish stock data, Hungary, the Russian Federation and the United States have the highest proportions of children in care, while Sri Lanka and Venezuela have the lowest (table VII.4).

The differences detected depend on both the prevalence of family problems leading to the enforced separation of parents and children for the protection of the latter and the type of settings providing care to the children who need it. Countries differ in terms of the type of placement that is most common. In Cyprus, Estonia, Slovenia, the United Kingdom and the United States, the vast majority of children in care are placed with foster families. In contrast, in Nicaragua, the Philippines, Swaziland and Venezuela, children in need of care are more likely to be placed in institutions.

A comparison of the number of children in care to the number of children who exit care via adoption shows that, in most countries, the proportion of children adopted from care is very low. Among the nine countries that disseminate information on the stock of children in care, in all but two—the Russian Federation and Venezuela— at most 15 per cent of children in care are adopted annually.

Among countries that publish data on annual inflows of children into care, in Benin, Nicaragua and Swaziland, annual adoptions of children from care are equivalent to less than 3 per cent of the children entering care over the same year. In China, the Philippines and Singapore, annual adoptions of children from care are equivalent to at least 40 per cent of children entering care over the year.

These comparisons are less than ideal because the children in care are not always adoptable. Often, the number of children in care who have been declared adoptable is considerably smaller than the overall number of children in care. In the United States, just 114,000 of the 513,000 children in care in 2005 were available for adoption[42] (United States, Administration for Children and Families, 2006), implying that the number of children adopted from care in 2005 amounted to nearly 45 per cent of the adoptable children in care.

TABLE VII.4. NUMBER OF CHILDREN IN CARE AND ADOPTIONS OF CHILDREN IN CARE

Country	Year	Total children in care				Total adoptions of children in care		
			Of which		Per 100,000 children under age 18		Of which	As a percentage of children in care
		Number	In institutions	In family foster care		Number	Domestic	
Flow data[1]								
Benin	2005	468[2]	15	17	10.9	4	3	0.9
China	2005	113 000	62 000	...	31.5	51 000	38 000	45.1
Cyprus	2001	184	34	150	86.1	216	51	27.7[3]
Czech Republic...	2004	1 871	...	...	97.6	542[4]	...	28.9
Latvia................	2003	1 004	983	21	208.1	86	15	8.6
Malawi...............	2001	5 507	3 435[5]	2 072	88.1	714	714	13.0
Nicaragua...........	2004	3 416	3 059	357	136.0	40	...	1.2
Philippines.........	2003	3 956	2 686	1 270	11.6	1 893	...	47.9
Seychelles[6].........	2000	18	17	1	69.8	8	...	44.4
Singapore...........	2002	510[7]	417[8]	93	49.1	713	265	52.0[3]
Swaziland	2005	828	780[9]	48	161.2	...	24	2.9[3]
Median.................	..	1 004	882	93	86.1	379	51	27.7
Stock data[10]								
Estonia...............	2003	1 575	37[11]	1 538	558.7	130	115	8.3
Hungary.............	2004	17 051	8 225	8 826	855.6	750[12]	656	4.4
Russian Federation...........	2004	200 600[13]	188 800[14]	11 800[15]	673.3	8 808[16]	2 831[16]	44.1[16]
Serbia[17]	2001	6 198	3 929[18]	2 269	243.2	247	...	4.0
Slovenia.............	2002	1 657	218	1 439	449.0	46	45	2.8
Sri Lanka	2001	9 288	...	...	147.4	932	881	10.0
United Kingdom[4]	2005[19]	64 653[20]	10 690	50 119	492.9	4 280	...	6.6
United States of America.........	2005[21]	513 000	51 210	360 928	684.7	51 000[22]	...	9.9
Venezuela..........	2000	6 207	4 630	1 577	63.7	990[23]	...	15.9
Median.................	..	9 288	6 428	5 548	492.9	932	656	8.3

Source: For a complete list of country references, see annex II.

[1]   Data refer to the number of children entering and exiting care during the specified year.
[2]   Data include orphans, abandoned children and children in other vulnerable groups.
[3]   Data refer only to domestic adoptions.
[4]   Estimate.
[5]   Data refer to children in orphanages.
[6]   Because the number of adoptions is very small, the percentages and rates presented here are subject to considerable variability.
[7]   Data refer to the period July 2002-June 2003.
[8]   Data refer to children admitted to voluntary children homes.
[9]   Data refer to children in registered homes only.
[10]   Data refer to the number of children in care at a certain point in time and exiting care during a specific year.
[11]   Data refer to children in welfare institutions as of 31 December 2003.
[12]   Data include 14 foreign children adopted by Hungarian citizens.
[13]   Data do not include children in guardianship care.
[14]   Data refer to children in institutions, children homes-cum-schools, boarding schools for orphans, ordinary boarding schools at residential homes and boarding schools for children with developmental abnormalities.
[15]   Data refer to orphans in foster families and family-type children's homes.
[16]   Data refer to children exiting children's institutions. Data do not include children exiting from: children homes-cum-schools, boarding schools for orphans, ordinary boarding schools at residential homes, boarding schools for children with developmental abnormalities, foster families and family-type children's homes.
[17]   Data refer to Serbia and Montenegro. Data refer to interventions or cases and not persons.
[18]   Data refer to children placed in social welfare institutions.
[19]   Data on child placements for England refer to 2006, for Northern Ireland, Scotland and Wales data on child placements refer to 2005. Data on adoptions for England refer to 2006, data for Northern Ireland refer to 2000, data on adoptions for Scotland refer to 2004 and data on adoptions for Wales refer to 2005.
[20]   Data do not include children placed for adoption or children living with their families.
[21]   Data refer to children in care as of 30 September 2005.
[22]   Data refer to the number of children exiting care through adoption.
[23]   Data refer to children in the process of being adopted.

As discussed in section VII.A, prospective adoptive parents often have specific preferences regarding the age and sex of the children they are willing to adopt. Hence, it is of interest to document the characteristics of children in care.

(a) The sex distribution of children in care

The sex distribution of children in care varies considerably from one country to another. In Hungary, a report by the Hungarian Government to the Committee on the Rights of the Child noted that, in 2004, there were 126 boys for every 100 girls among children in children's homes and 106 boys per 100 girls among those in foster care.[43] In the Seychelles, the United Kingdom and the United States, boys also outnumbered girls among children in care. In contrast, in Benin, 261 girls but just 175 boys were placed in care centres during 2005.[44] Girls also outnumbered boys among children in care in Malawi, Sri Lanka and Swaziland.

In the Philippines in 2003, girls outnumbered boys among children entering family foster care (715 girls and 555 boys), but the reverse held among children entering children's homes (boys constituted 62 per cent of the 2,600 children admitted by children's homes).[45] In Nicaragua, more boys than girls were placed in family foster care, but more girls than boys were placed in institutions.[46]

The sex selectivity of adoption does not seem to depend on the sex selectivity of children in care. In six of the nine countries with the required data, more girls than boys were adopted from care although more boys than girls were being placed in care (table VII.5). In the Philippines, for instance, fewer boys than girls were adopted from care in all age groups, including among children aged 13 years or over, although more boys entered care than girls.[45] The role of girls in providing assistance with domestic chores and caregiving[47] probably accounts in part for the excess of girls over boys among adopted children. In view of the shortage of girls available for adoption, the Intercountry Adoption Board of the Philippines has revised the application procedures for prospective adoptive parents who wish to adopt female children.[48]

In Malawi in 2001, 387 girls were adopted from among the 3,462 in care, whereas 327 boys were adopted from among the 2,035 boys in care, suggesting that girls outnumber boys among adopted children partly because of the higher availability of girls than boys for adoption.[49]

In Singapore in 2002, 144 boys and 121 girls were adopted domestically, whereas among children in care, half were girls.[5] Among children adopted through an intercountry procedure by foreign parents, girls strongly outnumbered boys.

(b) The age distribution of children in care

As discussed in previous chapters, adoptive parents often prefer to adopt younger children and may not be willing to adopt a child unless he or she is under a certain age. Only five countries provide data on children in care classified by age: the Russian Federation, the United Kingdom and the United States publish such data relative to the stock of children in care, whereas the Philippines and Singapore publish data by age of children entering care annually.

The age distribution of children in care varies considerably from one country to another. In the Russian Federation, children under one year of age accounted for 32 per cent of the 19,962 children living in institutions in 2004 and children between the ages of one and three accounted for an additional 48 per cent. In the Philippines, children under the age of six years constituted 71 per cent of those placed in foster care in 2003.

Children in care in the other three countries considered tended to be older. In Singapore, the mean age of children admitted into "voluntary homes" during 2003 was about 12 years, whereas that of children entering foster care was 5 years.[5] In Sri Lanka, children in voluntary children's homes were, on average, 10.4 years old, whereas the mean age of children in "state receiving homes" was 4.5 years.[50] In the United States in 2005, children in care had a mean age of 10 years,

TABLE VII.5. SEX RATIO OF CHILDREN IN CARE AND OF THOSE ADOPTED FROM CARE

Country	Year	Sex ratio of children (boys per 100 girls)		Boys as a percentage of children			
		In care	Adopted from care	In care (1)	Adopted from care (2)	Difference (2) – (1) (percentage points)	Statistical significance
Latvia[1]	2003	116.5[2]	65.4	53.8[2]	39.5	-14.3	**
Malawi[1]	2001	58.8[3]	84.5	37.0[3]	45.8	8.8	***
Nicaragua	2004	85.2[3]	81.8	46.0[3]	45.0	-1.0	
Philippines[1]	2003	126.6[3]	71.5	55.9[3]	41.7	-14.2	***
Seychelles[1,4]	2000	157.1	60.0	61.1	37.5	-23.6	..
Singapore[1]	2003[5]	100.0[3]	119.0[6]	50.0[3]	54.3[6]	4.3	
Sri Lanka[7]	2001	86.8	69.7[6]	46.5	41.1[6]	-5.4	**
United Kingdom[7,8]	2005[9]	123.2	105.3[10]	55.2	51.3[10]	-3.9	***
United States[7]	2005[11]	110.3	103.7	52.4	50.9	-1.5	***
Median	..	110.3	81.8	52.4	45.0	-3.9	..

Source: For a complete list of country references, see annex II.

NOTE: Statistical significance is based on the Chi-square test, comparing the sex distribution of children in care and adopted from care. Two dots (..) indicate that there are not enough observations to conduct the Chi-square test. Two stars (**) indicate that the Chi-square test is significant at a level of p< 0.01. Three stars (***) indicate that the Chi-square test is significant at a level of p< 0.001.

[1] Data refer to the number of children entering and exiting care during the specified year.
[2] Data refer only to children in institutions.
[3] Data refer to children in foster families and in institutions.
[4] Because the number of adoptions is very small, some of the percentages and rates may not be reliable.
[5] Data refer to the period July 2002-June 2003.
[6] Data refer only to domestic adoptions.
[7] Data refer to the number of children in care at a certain point in time and exiting care during a specific year.
[8] Estimate.
[9] Data on child placements for England refer to 2006. For Northern Ireland, Scotland and Wales data on child placements refer to 2005. Data on adoptions for England and Wales refer to 2005.
[10] Data refer only to England and Wales.
[11] Data refer to children in care as of 30 September 2005.

whereas children declared adoptable had a mean age of 8.6 years (United States, Administration for Children and Families, 2006).

Four countries have data classified by age on both children in care and children adopted from care. In three of those countries, adopted children were younger than children in care (table VII.6). In the United States, for instance, the mean age of children adopted from care was 6.7 years, whereas that of adoptable children in care was 8.6 years (United States, Administration for Children and Families, 2006). In Singapore, 535 of the 713 adoptions undertaken in 2002 (75 per cent) involved children under 3 years of age[5] and the mean age of adopted children was 3.2 years, considerably lower than the mean age of 11 years for all children in care. Such a large difference owes much to the high proportion of children adopted from abroad (60 per cent) who tend to be younger than children adopted domestically (see chapter VI).

In the United Kingdom, children in care had a mean age of 10.2 years whereas the majority of children adopted from care were between the ages of one and four (United Kingdom, British Association for Adoption and Fostering, 2006a and 2006b).

A different pattern is found in the Philippines: in 2003, children entering foster care were, on average, several years younger than children being adopted, but the data on children entering care refer to flows and not to stocks as in previous comparisons.[45]

(c) The health and disability status of children in care

The health status of adoptable children is another determinant of adoption. However, data on the health status of children in care are generally not available. Data on three countries indicate that a large number of children in care suffer from some

TABLE VII.6. MEAN AGES OF CHILDREN IN CARE AND OF ADOPTED CHILDREN
AT THE TIME OF ADOPTION FROM CARE

		Mean age of children			
Country	Year	In care (1)	At the time of adoption from care (2)	Difference (2) – (1) (percentage points)	Statistical significance
Philippines[1]	2003	5.2[2]	7.7	2.5	***
Singapore[1]	2003[3]	11.0[4]	3.2[5]	-7.8	***
United Kingdom[6,7]	2005[8]	10.2	4.2[9]	-6.0	***
United States of America[6] ...	2005[10]	8.6[11]	6.7	-1.9	***

Source: For a complete list of country references, see annex II.
NOTE: Statistical significance is based on the Chi-square test, comparing the age distribution of children in care and that of those adopted from care. Three stars (***) indicate that the Chi-square test is significant at a level of $p < 0.001$.
[1] Data refer to the number of children entering and exiting care during the specified year.
[2] Data refer only to children in foster families.
[3] Data refer to the period July 2002-June 2003.
[4] Data refer to children in foster families as well as institutions.
[5] Data refer to total adoptions.
[6] Data refer to the number of children in care at a certain point in time and exiting care during a specific year.
[7] Estimate.
[8] Data on child placements for England refer to 2006. For Northern Ireland, Scotland and Wales data on child placements refer to 2005. Data on adoptions for England refer to 2006 and data on adoptions for Wales refer to 2005.
[9] Data refer to England and Wales only.
[10] Data refer to children in care as of 30 September 2005.
[11] Data refer to children available for adoption.

form of mental disability or other health problems. In Cyprus, for instance, 41 per cent of the 34 children admitted into care institutions in 2001 had a disability.[51] In the Russian Federation, about half the children in institutional care in 2004 had been diagnosed as having some form of retardation to their physical development and 76 per cent had problems affecting their mental developmental. In addition, 24 per cent suffered from nutritional disorders, 22 per cent from anaemia and 13 per cent from rickets.[52]

In the Czech Republic, over 32 per cent of the 1,800 children admitted into care in 2004 had health problems and an additional 22 per cent had health and social problems (Bruthansová and others, 2005). A moderate proportion of those children were also diagnosed as having mental handicaps.

In Estonia, just 31 of the 1,538 children who entered foster care during 2003 (2 per cent) were diagnosed as being disabled, a very small proportion compared to the other countries considered here (Estonia, Ministry of Social Affairs, 2004).

Generally, children with health problems are less likely to be adopted. In Serbia,[53] 213 of the

6,198 children who received care in 2001 were classified as "socially or emotionally maladjusted", 1,163 children were considered "mentally handicapped" and 371 children "physically handicapped" (Serbia and Montenegro, Statistical Office, 2004). In relation to the number of children in care with a diagnosed disability, fewer children with mental or physical handicaps were adopted, a difference significant at the $p < 0.01$ level according to a Chi-square test.

In some cases, disabled children may have better than average chances of being adopted because of other factors. Thus, Chinese boys with a diagnosed health problem or disability were more likely than the average adoptable child to be adopted because of their sex (Johnson and others, 1998).

2. Fertility trends and their determinants in relation to adoption

(a) Children born out of wedlock

In many societies, especially in past centuries, unmarried women who became pregnant faced social disapproval and economic difficulties in raising a child on their own. Consequently, they often opted to give up their children. Thus, between 1815 and 1835, nearly half of all children born out of wedlock in Paris and the Department of the Seine were abandoned (Fuchs, 1984). In Moscow, between 1900 and 1914, illegitimate children constituted the majority of those admitted to the foundling home (Ransel, 1988).

In developed countries, especially since the 1950s, the stigma attached to extramarital fertility has been decreasing at the same time that increasing work opportunities for women and better welfare support for unmarried mothers has reduced the economic barriers to raising a child on one's own. Consequently, the proportion of women who opt to keep the children born out of wedlock has been rising and those births have become a diminishing source of adoptable children (Bitler and Zavodny, 2002). Thus, in Canada, the percentage of single mothers who decided to raise their own children increased from 46 per cent in 1981 to almost 60 per cent in 1989 (Sobol and Daly, 1994). In the United States, the proportion of children born to never married women who were given up for adoption declined from an average of 9 per cent before 1973 to 2 per cent in 1982-1988 and to less than 1 per cent in 1989-1995 (Chandra and others, 1999). This decline was particularly pronounced among white women (Bachrach, 1986; Bachrach and others, 1992).

In England and Wales in the 1960s, about 20 per cent of children born out of wedlock were put up for adoption. By the 1970s, that percentage had fallen considerably, despite the increasing number of children born to single women (Selman, 1976, 1988 and 2006). In Ireland until the mid-1960s, most children born outside marriage were given up for adoption (Ireland, The Adoption Board, 2004). Since the early 1970s, however, out-of-wedlock births have increased while the number of adoptions has fallen (figure VII.5).

At a population level, there is a positive and statistically significant relationship at the p< 0.05 level between the percentage of extramarital births in countries that are major receivers of intercountry adoptions and the domestic under-five adoption rate (table A.VII.5). In Canada, Denmark, Iceland, the United Kingdom and the

United States, high percentages of extramarital births coexist with high domestic adoption rates. Conversely, in countries with relatively low percentages of extramarital births, such as Japan, Israel or Italy, domestic adoption rates tend to be low. This finding suggests that a higher prevalence of out-of-wedlock births does lead to a higher number of adoptable children, since in many developed countries the majority of children given up for adoption are born to single mothers (see chapter VI). There are also important differences among countries in attitudes towards non-traditional forms of family formation, including both adoption and single-motherhood.

Among countries that are not major receivers of intercountry adoptions, a non-parametric correlation test shows that there is a negative but not statistically significant relationship between the proportion of extramarital births and domestic under-five adoption rates (table A.VII.6), suggesting that factors other than legitimacy status are at play in determining the supply of children available for adoption. This result is consistent with findings regarding child abandonment, which indicate that, under certain circumstances, poverty may be a more important reason than illegitimacy for giving a child up for adoption.[54]

(b) Unwanted fertility

If a woman becomes pregnant when she is not ready to become a mother or when she already has the number of children she wants, she may decide to give up the child for adoption (Nock, 1994; Stolley and Hall, 1994). The evidence available suggests that relatively few of those "unwanted" children are given up for adoption. Strong and DeVault (1994) estimate that among the unmarried women who became pregnant without desiring it, 47 per cent decided to bring the pregnancy to term and the majority decided to keep their children (97 per cent), while just 3 per cent resorted to giving the child up for adoption. Bachrach (1986) found that less than 4 per cent of women aged 15 to 44 who experienced a pre-marital first pregnancy in 1982 opted for adoption. Nearly 65 per cent of women raised the child themselves, either alone or with their partner, while 32 per cent lost the pregnancy through

**Figure VII.5. Out-of-wedlock births and adoptions
in Ireland, 1955-2003**

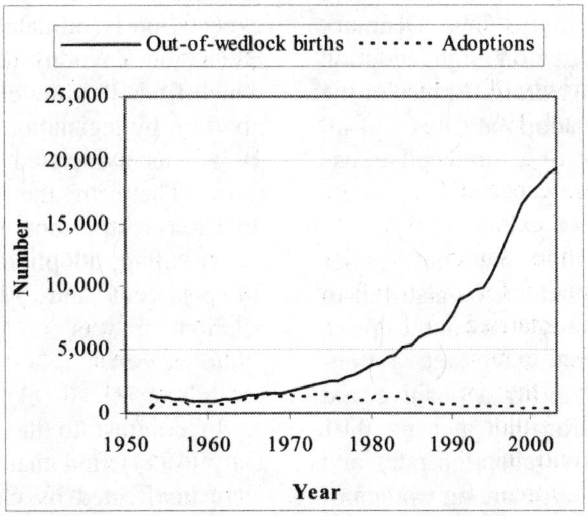

Source: Ireland, The Adoption Board, 2004.

miscarriage or induced abortion or had a pregnancy that resulted in a stillbirth.

There is no conclusive evidence as to whether the propensity of birth parents to relinquish children for adoption is related primarily to their desired family size or other factors, such as the child's birth order and sex. In China, Johnson and others (1998) found that, among the parents of a sample of 240 abandoned Chinese children, those most likely to give up a girl for adoption already had more than one girl and had parity three or higher. In the United States, Bachrach and others (1992) found that unmarried white women aged 15 to 44 were twice as likely to give up girls for adoption than boys. These findings are context specific. Historical and ethnographic studies show considerable variability in the sex ratio of abandoned children.[55]

At an aggregate level, a non-parametric correlation test indicates that there is a positive and statistically significant relationship with a probability level of p< 0.01 between the total under-five adoption rate[56] and different indicators of unwanted fertility as captured in recent DHS surveys[57] (Zlidar and others, 2003). Specifically, for countries that are not major receivers of intercountry adoptions, the higher the percentage of married women aged 15 to 49 who want no more children or want to end childbearing, the

higher the total under-five adoption rate. However, the relationship is not linear. In Azerbaijan, the Czech Republic and Ukraine, for example, there are high proportions of married women wanting no more children (60 per cent and more) as well as high total under-five adoption rates. In contrast, in many sub-Saharan African countries, including the Central African Republic, Eritrea, Mozambique and Niger, married women who do not want another child constitute less than 20 per cent of the total and total under-five adoption rates are also low (under one per 100,000 children under-five).

(c) Contraceptive prevalence

Women who do not have access to contraception are more likely to have unplanned pregnancies if they are sexually active and therefore to consider the option of giving up a child for adoption. Consequently, at an aggregate level, higher levels of contraceptive use[58] are expected to be associated with lower adoption rates. As with the demand for adoptive children, desired family size would mediate the relationship between contraceptive use and the availability of adoptable children.

Despite these expectations, adoption rates in countries that are major destinations of intercountry adoptions are not significantly related to contraceptive prevalence because, whereas most of them have already reached very high levels of contraceptive use, their domestic under-five adoption rates vary considerably. Thus, Denmark and the United Kingdom exhibit high adoption rates while others, such as Australia, France or the Netherlands, exhibit lower adoption rates, but all have similarly high levels of contraceptive use (table A.VII.7).

Data for countries that are not major destinations of intercountry adoptions also fail to show a negative correlation between contraceptive prevalence and adoption rates. In fact, a non-parametric correlation test shows a positive and statistically significant relationship at a $p < 0.01$ level between total under-five adoption rates and overall contraceptive prevalence among women of reproductive age who are married or in union as well as between the same adoption rates and use of modern contraception among those women (table A.VII.8). Thus, several countries in Africa, such as Eritrea, Guinea-Bissau, Mali or Sudan, exhibit very low levels of contraceptive use (below 10 per cent) and also record very low total under-five adoption rates, whereas countries with high levels of contraceptive use, such as Kazakhstan, Mongolia, the Republic of Korea or Ukraine, register higher total under-five adoption rates. Moreover, desired family size tends to be higher in countries with low contraceptive prevalence and in societies where contraceptive levels are high, unwanted fertility tends to be higher among lower-income groups that face greater barriers in accessing and using modern contraception as well as among single women. As discussed earlier, for women in those groups adoption may be an option when unwanted pregnancies occur (Stolley and Hall, 1994).

In sum, the findings in this section suggest that both adoption and contraceptive use are means of addressing unwanted fertility. In societies where desired family size is low, contraception is used to prevent unwanted pregnancies but, when these occur, adoption is an option.

(d) Induced abortion

In many countries, women resort to abortion when an unwanted pregnancy occurs. The incidence of induced abortion would be expected,

therefore, to be negatively correlated with the availability of adoptable children. This expectation is validated by studies such as that by Bitler and Zavodny (2002) in the United States, which finds that the elimination of restrictions on abortion by legislation adopted between 1961 and 1975 was associated with declines in adoption rates. Thus, in the states that repealed their abortion restrictions before the 1973 Supreme Court ruling, adoption rates dropped by between 34 per cent and 37 per cent. The negative relationship was statistically significant only for white women.

In contrast to the above finding, Sobol and Daly (1994) find that, in Canada, adoption rates were unaffected by changes in the abortion rate and, instead, the decline in the supply of adoptable children was associated with the increasing tendency of never married women who became pregnant to raise their children by themselves.

Our analysis of the relationship between abortion rates (measured as the annual number of abortions per 1,000 women aged 15 to 44) and adoption rates shows that, contrary to expectation, there is a positive correlation between the two.

Thus, among countries that are major destinations of intercountry adoptions, a non-parametric test confirms that there is a positive and statistically significant relationship at a probability level of $p < 0.05$ between the abortion rate and the domestic under-five adoption rate. In countries with relatively high abortion rates (17 abortions per 1,000 women aged 15 to 44 or higher), such as New Zealand, Sweden or the United States, under-five domestic adoption rates also tend to be high (above 60 adoptions per 100,000 children under age five), as shown in table A.VII.7. In addition, many of the countries with lower abortion rates, such as Belgium,[18] Spain or Switzerland, also have low domestic under-five adoption rates (below 30 adoptions per 100,000 children under-five).

The association is also positive among countries that are not major receivers of intercountry adoptions: a non-parametric test shows a statistically significant correlation at the $p < 0.01$ level between abortion rates and total under-five adoption rates (table A.VII.8). Countries having some of the highest abortion rates in the world, such as Belarus, Estonia, Kazakhstan or the Russian Federation, also have some of the highest total under-five adoption rates. Conversely, countries with lower abortion rates, such as India, Mexico or South Africa, also record lower total under-five adoption rates.

For Estonia and Latvia, where there is a time series of data on both the number of abortions and that of adoptions, there is also a strong positive and statistically significant correlation at a probability level of p< 0.01 between the two over the period 1995-2003 (Estonia, Ministry of Social Affairs, 2004; United Nations, 2006b; UNICEF, 2003c).

These findings suggest that abortion and relinquishing children for adoption are both symptomatic of the same underlying cause: the inability of women or couples to cope with births resulting from unwanted pregnancies. In societies where the number of unwanted pregnancies is high, both the number of abortions and the availability of adoptable children is likely to be high and the reverse holds when the number of unwanted pregnancies is low. The incidence of unwanted pregnancies is, in turn, determined by other factors, including desired family size, access to contraception, socio-economic status, societal attitudes towards single mothers and the type of support available to them.

3. Orphaned children

Historically, a large proportion of the children available for adoption were orphans[59] (Fuchs, 1984; Hunecke, 1987). Today, orphanhood is a rare event in developed countries but many developing countries, especially those with high HIV/AIDS prevalence, have large numbers of orphans (table A.VII.9). In many sub-Saharan African countries, including the Central African Republic, Kenya, Malawi, Rwanda, Swaziland and the United Republic of Tanzania, children who have lost both parents (double orphans) constitute 3 per cent or more of the population under age 18. In Bangladesh, India, Haiti and Myanmar, the proportion of double orphans surpasses 1 per cent.

Because of the major impact that deaths caused by AIDS are having on families and communities in the most affected countries, strategies to care for the large and increasing numbers of orphans are not relying mainly on formal adoption. Instead, orphans are being cared for by relatives and both Governments and non-governmental organizations are devising strategies to encourage families to care for orphans (Matshalaga and Powell, 2002). The Governments in Botswana, Malawi, Rwanda, South Africa and Uganda, for example, are providing material support and monthly allowances to promote formal fostering and, where appropriate, adoption (Subbarao and Coury, 2004). Intercountry adoptions are also being promoted but some receiving countries forbid the adoption of HIV-positive children.

Currently, among countries that are not major receivers of intercountry adoptions, those with the highest proportions of orphans also tend to have low total under-five adoption rates (table A.VII.9). A non-parametric correlation test shows that the relationship between the two is negative and significant at the p< 0.01 level. Thus, whereas many of the countries with the highest proportions of double orphans among the population under 18, such as the Central African Republic, Kenya, Mozambique or the United Republic of Tanzania, exhibit very low total under-five adoption rates, those with lower proportions of orphans, such as Belize, Jamaica or the Republic of Korea, exhibit relatively high total under-five adoption rates.

These findings confirm that in the countries most affected by the HIV/AIDS epidemic, formal adoption is not being the main vehicle to ensure the care of AIDS orphans. Partly because many of those countries have a strong tradition of child fostering within extended families and partly because the legal processes involved in formal adoption represent a barrier for families coping with the effects of HIV/AIDS, adoption remains rare compared to potential needs. In Africa alone, the current number of domestic adoptions would need to be multiplied by 2,000 to cover the estimated 7.7 million double orphans living in the region (UNAIDS, UNICEF and USAID, 2004). Globally, the number of adoptions would have to increase by a factor of 60 to cover the estimated number of double orphans.

4. Children affected by marital dissolution and remarriage

When a divorced or widowed person with children remarries, the new spouse may wish to adopt his or her partner's children. As discussed in chapter VI, this type of adoption is common and adoptions by step-parents constitute a large proportion of domestic adoptions in many developed countries.

There is a positive but not statistically significant relationship between indicators of marital dissolution and rates of domestic under-five adoptions by step-parents (table VII.7). Countries with relatively high divorce rates or large proportions of divorced persons among the

ever married population, such as Denmark, Estonia or Iceland, record high rates of domestic adoptions by step-parents. However, other countries with similar proportions of divorced persons, such as the Netherlands or Sweden, register relatively low rates of domestic adoptions by step-parents.

Other indicators of marital instability, such as the proportion of marriages in which at least one of the partners was previously divorced or widowed, are also positively correlated with the domestic rate of under-five adoptions by step-parents, although once more the relationship is not statistically significant. Estonia and New Zealand, for instance, record both high proportions of marriages where at least one of the partners is widowed or divorced and relatively high rates of domestic under-five adoptions by step-parents. Italy registers both low proportions of marriages

TABLE VII.7. DOMESTIC RATE OF UNDER-FIVE ADOPTIONS BY STEP-PARENTS AND
SELECTED INDICATORS OF MARITAL DISSOLUTION

	Domestic adoptions by step-parents			Percentage			
Country	Number	Under-five adoption rate (per 100,000 children under five)	Divorce rate (per woman)	Divorced among the ever married population	Marriages in which at least one partner was previously divorced	Marriages in which at least one partner was previously widowed	Divorces involving at least one child
Australia	31	1.5	0.33	10.8	32.0	3.9	49.8
Denmark	490	88.6	0.28	7.8	31.5	3.6	...
Estonia	63	61.3	0.50	11.0	41.8	6.2	57.5
Germany	2 337	37.1	0.26	8.3	33.3	3.2	50.1
Iceland[1]	17	48.9	0.40	...	24.6	2.1	62.0
Ireland	165	34.4	...	2.0	0.0	1.2	...
Italy	332	7.5	0.05	2.0	7.2	1.6	36.9
Lithuania	84	30.0	0.34	12.0	24.4	4.1	64.8
Netherlands[2]	225	13.8	0.25	10.4	24.5	2.4	58.1
New Zealand	77	16.7	0.30	5.5	34.0	4.9	44.0
Norway	150	31.1	0.27	8.1	26.9	1.7	58.0
Sweden	112	14.4	0.29	18.6	30.0	1.8	59.2
Median	..	30.6	0.29	8.3	28.5	2.8	57.8

Sources: For a complete list of country references see annex II. The population under five was obtained from United Nations, 2005; the divorce rate per woman was obtained from United Nations, 2004a, the percentage divorced among the ever married population was obtained from United Nations, 2006c.

NOTES: The rate of domestic under-five adoptions by step-parents is calculated by dividing the total number of domestic adoptions of children under age five by step-parents by the number of children under five and is expressed per 100,000 children. If data on the age distribution of adopted children is not available, it is assumed that 60 per cent of adopted children are under age five at the time of adoption. The data used are those for the most recent date available; the data on divorces and adoptions by step-parents do not necessarily refer to the same year.

[1] Because the number of adoptions is very small, some of the percentages and rates presented here are affected by high random variability and should be interpreted with caution.
[2] Estimated.

**Figure VII.6. Adoptions by step-parents and marriages involving
at least one partner who was previously married,
Norway, 1986-2003**

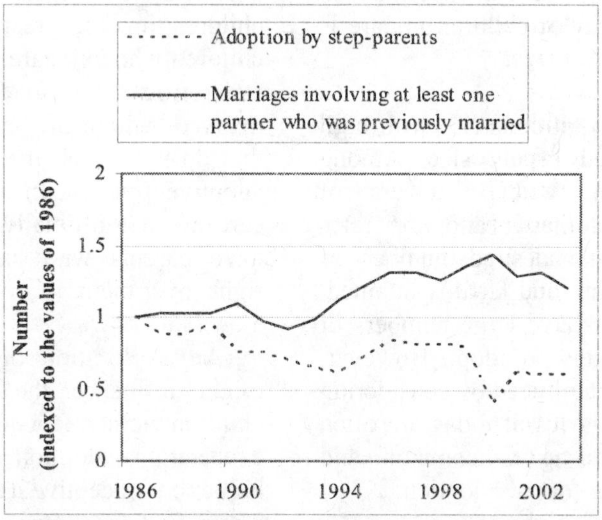

Source: Statistics Norway, 2004a and 2004b.

involving at least one partner who had been previously married and a low rate of domestic adoptions by step-parents. Denmark or Iceland have high rates of domestic adoptions by step-parents relative to the proportion of marriages involving at least one partner who was divorced or widowed, but Australia and Sweden have low rates of adoptions by step-parents relative to the proportion of marriages involving divorced or widowed persons. The relationship between the rate of domestic adoptions by step-parents and the proportion of divorces where the couple had at least one child is similarly inconclusive.

Cross-country comparisons fail to provide a clear cut picture because other factors are at play, including variations in legislation and social customs. A better indication of the relationship between adoptions by step-parents and marital dissolution can be obtained from time series data. In Norway, for instance, there is a close relationship between the number of step-parent adoptions and the number of marriages involving at least one previously married partner (Norway, Statistics Norway, 2004a and 2004b). However, the ratio of the two has declined since the mid-1990s, implying that fewer adoptions by step-parents are taking place compared to the number of persons who are remarrying (figure VII.6). In England and Wales, the number of step-parent

adoptions has declined from over 9,000 in 1975 to around to 866 in 2005, while the proportion of divorced persons who remarry has increased (Selman, 1976, 1988 and 2006; United Nations, 2006c). A similar trend is found in relation to adoptions by step-parents and marriages of men to previously married women in New Zealand between the early 1970s and the mid-1990s (New Zealand Law Commission, 2000; United Nations, 2006c). The divergence between the two series is likely the result of the previously documented trend towards facilitating the maintenance of ties between biological parents and their children even after divorce (see chapter I and VI). Nevertheless, divorce and remarriage remain important factors shaping overall adoption trends.[60]

D. SUMMARY

This chapter has explored some of the demographic trends and factors shaping adoption levels. Although it has uncovered few strong relationships between demographic indicators and adoption levels, a number of interesting patterns have emerged. A marked difference between adoption applications and adoption orders granted was found in many countries, especially those in the developing world. Inefficiencies in case processing and a shortage of adoptable children are likely at the root of such differences. Proactive government policies can contribute to reduce processing time and may be able to improve the availability of adoptable children, especially in societies where the number of children in care is significant.

Adoption is less likely in countries with high fertility and high desired family size. Among countries that are not major receivers of intercountry adoptions, domestic adoption rates are lower the higher the desired number of children and the higher the total fertility attained. Thus, when most couples have large numbers of children they are less likely to adopt. However, this conclusion should be tempered by considering that the high-fertility countries of today are often those where child fostering is common and fostering is a substitute for formal adoption.

Domestic adoption rates tend to be higher in countries with very low fertility levels, most of which have well established procedures and systems to allow formal adoption. In particular, among countries that are major destinations of intercountry adoption, there is a positive and statistically significant relationship between the average desired number of children and the under-five intercountry adoption rate.

Domestic adoptions are more likely the higher the mean age at marriage or the mean age at first birth in countries that are not major receivers of intercountry adoptions. This finding suggests that couples who are unable to achieve their desired family size through childbearing often resort to adoption. However, in a number of countries, adoptive families are not predominantly childless. According to the evidence available, people who are subfecund, sterile or otherwise unable to have children on their own are not the only ones or even the majority of those adopting children in most countries. Societal norms, socio-economic status, personal values and desires also shape the decisions of couples and individuals to adopt, even when they already have children of their own.

An assessment of factors shaping the availability of children for adoption reveals that the proportion of children placed in care varies considerably among countries as does the proportion of children who exit care through adoption. Despite deficiencies in the data available, they indicate that the number of children in care greatly exceeds the number of children who exit care via adoption. This outcome stems from the characteristics of children in care, many of whom are older or disabled, categories that do not match the preferences of prospective adoptive parents. In addition, many children in care are not officially "adoptable" because they have parents who have not relinquished their rights over them.

An exploration of demographic trends that might influence the availability of adoptable children yielded few definitive results. Contrary to expectation, adoption rates tend to increase with higher contraceptive use and higher abortion rates. These findings suggest that all three variables are associated with the prevalence of unwanted pregnancies, which is driven, in turn, by other factors, including desired family size, ease of access to effective methods of contraception, societal norms regarding motherhood among unmarried women and the degree of support single mothers can expect. Thus, in societies where the stigma against births occurring out-or-wedlock has diminished and where there is greater support for single mothers, the number of extramarital births is no longer, as it once was, an adequate predictor of the number of children available for adoption.

Because adoptions by step-parents constitute a large proportion of domestic adoptions in many developed countries, some relationship was expected between indicators of marriage dissolution and adoption. However, the data show only a weak correlation between the two, largely because rules aimed at maintaining relations between children of divorced parents and both of their biological parents after divorce have resulted in fewer children being adopted by step-parents.

In countries where mortality remains high, particularly those affected by the HIV/AIDS epidemic, the number of orphaned children has been growing. Nevertheless, in most of those countries adoption has not been the main means of ensuring care for orphans. Instead, Governments have been promoting care within the extended family and, in some cases, providing support through monthly allowances. Data on adoption shows that countries with high proportions of orphans tend to have low adoption rates and this relationship is statistically significant.

This chapter has explored systematically the interrelations between demographic processes and the incidence of adoption. The analysis presented here has two major limitations. The first is the paucity of detailed data on adoption that would permit the estimation of better indicators. The second is the reliance on cross-country comparisons of bivariate relationships. A more thorough analysis would involve a multivariate approach with more appropriate dependent variables. However, even this exploratory analysis has yielded important insights, the main one being that societal norms and legislative traditions affect the propensity to resort to adoption and that such factors can be powerful determinants of adoption levels and trends. To understand better the drivers of adoption it is necessary both to improve the data on adoption and to devise measures to reflect the underlying drivers of the availability of children for adoption and of the demand for those children. The next chapter focuses on ways of improving the data on adoption.

NOTES

[1] Paragraph 29 (c) states that "Consistent with the Proclamation of the International Conference on Human Rights, the Declaration on Social Progress and Development, the relevant targets of the Second United Nations Development Decade and the other international instruments on the subject, it is recommended that all countries: . . . (c) Ensure that family planning, medical and related social services aim not only at the prevention of unwanted pregnancies but also at the elimination of involuntary sterility and subfecundity in order that all couples may be permitted to achieve their desired number of children, and that child adoption may be facilitated." *Report of the United Nations World Population Conference, Bucharest, 19-30 August 1974* (United Nations publication, Sales No. E.75.XIII.3), chapter I.

[2] See United Nations, "Periodic reports of States parties due in 1998: Italy" (CRC/C/70/Add.13).

[3] Based on weighted data for women aged 15 to 44 who replied to various waves of the U.S. National Survey of Family Growth. A woman was considered to have ever sought to adopt if she indicated that she had ever contacted a lawyer or an adoption agency about adopting a child.

[4] See United Nations, "Second periodic reports of States due in 1997: France" (CRC/C/65/Add.26).

[5] See United Nations, "Initial reports of States parties due in 1997: Singapore" (CRC/C/51/Add.8); and "Written replies by the Government of Singapore (CRC/C/RESP/43) concerning the list of issues received by the Committee on the Rights of the Child

(CRC/C/Q/SGP/1) relating to the consideration of the initial report of Singapore".

[6] Application and adoption orders are also not suitable for approximating the number of persons adopted since an application or an adoption order may involve more than one person, as is in the case of the adoption of siblings.

[7] Having had a biological child, changes in lifestyle, barriers to adoption and lack of success in identifying an adoptable child were among the factors cited as contributing to this decision.

[8] While in some countries, the waiting time for an adoption is relatively short—in Finland, for instance, 99 per cent of the 343 applications for an intercountry adoption submitted in 2003 were either approved or refused within three months of application (Finland, Finnish Adoption Board, 2004)—in many countries waiting times are much longer. In Ireland, for example, in 2003 the average time for processing an adoption application surpassed 15 months (Ireland, The Adoption Board, 2004).

[9] See United Nations, "Written replies by the Government of Gambia (CRC/C/RESP/GAM/1) concerning the list of issues received by the Committee on the Rights of the Child (CRC/C/Q/GAM/1) relating to the consideration of the initial report of Gambia".

[10] See United Nations, "Initial reports of States parties due in 1995: Fiji" (CRC/C/28/Add.7).

[11] See United Nations, "Initial reports of States parties due in 1993: Guyana" (CRC/C/8/Add.47).

[12] See United Nations, "Periodic reports of States parties due in 1998: Jamaica" (CRC/C/70/Add.15).

[13] In recent years, the gap between the two groups has narrowed and in 2004 there was no significant difference between the percentage of applications approved for single and joint applicants.

[14] In Italy, the number and proportion of persons applying for more than one child has increased slightly in recent years.

[15] Such findings are consistent with much of the literature on desired family size. Arnold (1992), for example, found that the sex composition of living children influences fertility attitudes and behaviours, resulting, in some cases, in higher fertility. Parents who have specific preferences regarding the sex of their offspring are more likely to continue to have children in order to achieve the desired sex composition (Sheps, 1963; Stash, 1996). Adoption may serve similar purposes in families that already have children.

[16] In both Italy and the United States, a moderate preference for adopting girls may stem from the perception that girls are easier to raise (Adamec and Pierce, 2000).

[17] The mean ages of adopted children are estimated by the United Nations Population Division based on available data.

[18] Data refer only to the region of Flanders.

[19] According to Bongaarts (2001), factors that contribute to reduce fertility relative to desired family size include increasing age at the start of childbearing, involuntary infertility and competing preferences.

[20] From a demographic perspective, this could be viewed as the equivalent of the "new union commitment effect" (Vikat and others, 1999). Adoption by step-parents is examined in reference to the availability of adoptable children (see section VII.C).

[21] Parity is the number of live births a woman has had by the time of observation.

[22] While individual-level data show that fewer children are adopted by parents who already have large numbers of children, there is some evidence that adopted children tend to live in larger families than biological children. In France, Halifax (2001) found that adopted children were more likely to live in a family with other children than biological children.

[23] For countries that are major destinations of intercountry adoption, the total adoption rate is used as an indicator of the demand for adoption. For countries that are not major destinations of intercountry adoption, the domestic under-five adoption rate is used instead.

[24] The term "countries that are not major destinations of intercountry adoption" refers to all countries that are not net receivers of children adopted internationally.

[25] Total fertility is a synthetic measure of the level of fertility over a period. It represents the average number of children a woman would have were she subject during all her reproductive life to the age-specific fertility rates observed during the period in question.

[26] In developing countries, desired family size and total fertility are positively correlated (Bongaarts, 1990 and 2001). In countries undergoing the transition to low fertility, total fertility tends to be higher than the desired family size. The countries where the transition has been completed, total fertility tends to be lower than desired family size.

[27] In countries where the mean age at first birth has been rising, current total fertility underestimates the actual number of children that some cohorts of women will eventually have.

[28] *Fertility* refers to proven ability to conceive and give birth. Thus, a fertile woman is a woman who has given birth. *Fecundity* refers to the physiological ability to conceive and give birth. Thus, a fecund woman may not yet have given birth. *Subfecundity* refers to a situation where "it would be difficult but not impossible to have a child due to physical or medical reasons" (Bonham, 1977, p. 303). *Infecundity* refers to the inability to conceive and give birth after being exposed to the risk of pregnancy for a number of years. "[P]rimary infertility (also called *primary sterility*) is defined as the inability to bear any children, either due to the inability to conceive or the inability to carry a pregnancy to a live birth. . . *Secondary infertility*, which has been shown to have a high geographical correlation with primary infertility . . . is the inability to bear a child after having an earlier birth" (Rutstein and Shah, 2004, p. 3).

[29] Typically, "[w]omen are classified as sterile if they or their husbands [have] had a sterilizing operation, if they [have] reached menopause, or if they or their husbands [are] sterile due to accident, illness, or other reason" (Bonham, 1977, p. 303).

[30] The proportion of ever married women with impaired fecundity or who have undergone sterilization and who have ever adopted has been declining since the early 1980s.

[31] On the basis of data gathered in the DHS, Rutstein and Shah (2004, p. 7) have identified women with primary infertility as "women who have been married for the past five years, who have ever had sexual intercourse, who have not used contraception during the past five years, and who have not had any births." Women with secondary infertility were identified as "women with no births in the past five years but who have had a birth at some time, among women who have been married for the past five years and did not use contraception during that period."

[32] A childless woman is defined here as a woman who has never had a live birth.

[33] As documented in chapters I and III, childlessness used to be one of the requirements to be granted an adoption. Today many countries have removed this requirement. In China, for example, the 1992 Adoption Law required adoptive parents to be childless, and they could adopt only one child, with the exception of orphans or disabled children. In 1998, the law was amended to allow exemptions from the one-child policy for the adoption of children living in social welfare institutions or abandoned infants (Liu, Larsen and Wyshak, 2004).

[34] Damas (1983, p. 340) argues that "there are places in Oceania, such as Pingelap and Romonum, where the rise and fall of adoption rates are highly sensitive to demographic changes, such as those caused by fluctuating fertility rates, and where systems of adoption are drastically modified by altered demographic conditions".

[35] Time series for a few countries indicate that the proportion of childless persons seeking to adopt has not varied by much. In Finland, for example, the proportion of applications by childless families rose from around 80 per cent in the late 1980 to around 90 per cent in the late 1990s. As of 2003, it had fallen again to levels around 80 per cent (Finland, Finnish Adoption Board, 2004). In Italy, the proportion childless among persons seeking to adopt fluctuated between 90 and 94 per cent over the period 2003-2006 (Government of Italy, Office of the Prime Minister, 2004, 2005 and 2006).

[36] See United Nations, "Periodic reports of States parties due in 1993: Israel" (CRC/C/8/Add.44).

[37] Because the majority of women who adopt children are aged between 30 and 40 years, it is more appropriate to examine the relationship between adoption and childlessness among women aged 35 to 39. However, a non-parametric correlation test applied to the percentage of childless among women aged 35 to 39 indicates that there is no statistically significant relationship between that percentage and the under-five adoption rate.

[38] The notion that overall fertility is affected by timing is well established. Malthus, in his famous *Essay on Population* published in 1798, noted that a delay in marriage was a key means for reducing fertility. Historical data show a strong association between age at first marriage (or the start of cohabitation) and ability to control marital fertility (Coale, 1992; Finnas and Hoem, 1980; Leasure, 1963), both of which are related to other factors, such as a women's decision-making capacity and education (Bumpass, 1969; Bumpass and others, 1978; Rodriguez and others, 1984). However, it is well known that during the period in which the age at marriage increases, period indicators of fertility will overstate the fertility reduction actually taking place among cohorts of women.

[39] This chapter does not focus specifically on the effects of other factors, such as desired family size, which are likely to be important in shaping adoption levels.

[40] In populations with accurate vital registration statistics, the female mean age at marriage can be calculated from data on registered marriages by age of brides. If such information is not available or is unreliable, the singulate mean age at marriage (SMAM) can be calculated from the proportions of single women classified by age derived from census or survey data. The SMAM represents the average length of single life among those who marry before age 50. In this report, SMAM is used as the indicator of age at marriage.

[41] In cases where it was not obvious from the published tabulation whether data refer to stocks or flows, the following convention was used: data in tabulations referring to children placed in care during a certain year were considered flows, whereas data referring to the provision of services to children in care were considered stocks.

[42] Children are usually considered adoptable when the rights of their legal guardians have been terminated.

[43] See United Nations, "Written replies by the Government of Hungary (CRC/C/HUN/Q/2/Add.1) concerning the list of issues received by the Committee on the Rights of the Child (CRC/C/HUN/Q/2) relating to the consideration of the second periodic report of Hungary".

[44] See United Nations, "Written replies by the Government of Benin concerning the list of issues received by the Committee on the Rights of the Child (CRC/C/BEN/Q/2) relating to the consideration of the second periodic report of Benin".

[45] See United Nations, "Written replies by the Government of Philippines (CRC/C/RESP/84) concerning the list of issues received by the Committee on the Rights of the Child (CRC/C/Q/PHL/2) relating to the consideration of the second periodic report of Philippines".

[46] See United Nations, "Written replies by the Government of Nicaragua (CRC/C/RESP/83) concerning the list of issues received by the Committee on the Rights of the Child (CRC/C/Q/NIC/3) relating to the consideration of the third periodic report of Nicaragua".

[47] Child domestic workers are common in the Philippines (Flores-Oebanda, 2006).

[48] See United Kingdom, Department for Children, Schools and Families. "Intercountry adoption". Available from http://www.dfes.gov.uk/intercountryadoption/ (accessed 28 November 2006).

[49] See United Nations, "Written replies by the Government of Malawi (CRC/C/8/Add.43) concerning the list of issues received by the Committee on the Rights of the Child (CRC/C/Q/MALA/1) relating to the consideration of the initial report of Malawi".

[50] See United Nations, "Written replies by the Government of Sri Lanka concerning (CRC/C/RESP/35) the list of issues received by the Committee on the Rights of Child (CRC/C/Q/LKA/2) relating to the consideration of the second periodic report of Sri Lanka".

[51] See United Nations, "Written replies by the Government of Cyprus (CRC/C/RESP/CYP/2) concerning the list of issues received by the Committee on the Rights of the Child (CRC/C/Q/CYP/2) relating to the consideration of the second periodic report of Cyprus".

[52] See United Nations, "Written replies by the Government of the Russian Federation (CRC/C/RESP/92) concerning the list of issues received by the Committee on the Rights of the Child (CRC/C/Q/RUS/3) relating to the consideration of the third periodic report of the Russian Federation".

[53] Data refer to Serbia and Montenegro.

[54] The literature indicates that legitimate children are more likely to be abandoned by poor families during periods of economic crisis (Fuchs, 1984; Hunecke, 1987) or in response to food shortages (Food and Agriculture Organization of the United Nations, 1996; Fuchs, 1987; Guemple, 1979).

[55] Damas (1983), for example, concluded that while there was a strong preference for adopting boys among families in Pingelap, "not only did more than one-third of the donor families give up their first-born, but in nearly half of the 187 cases for which there is information, the first-born of each sex was given in adoption" (p. 333). Fuchs (1987), focusing on nineteenth century France, concluded that the sex of children was not a significant factor in explaining why women decided to give up their children. In contrast, Kerzter (1991) found that in fifteenth century Italy, girls were twice as likely as boys to be abandoned, though by the nineteenth century there was near gender parity in the number of abandoned boys and girls.

[56] For countries that are major destinations of intercountry adoption, the total under-five adoption rate is used as an indicator of the availability of adoptable children. For countries that are not major destinations of intercountry adoption, the domestic under-five adoption rate is used instead.

[57] Estimating unwanted fertility can only be done indirectly (Bongaarts, 1990; Casterline and others, 2003). One way of assessing the level of unwanted fertility is by comparing the desired number of children with the number of living children a person has.

[58] Contraceptive prevalence is measured as the percentage of women aged 15 to 49 who are married or in union and who are using, or whose partner is using, any method of contraception.

[59] In this discussion, the term "orphans" means double orphans, that is, children with no living parents.

[60] Adoptions by step-parents are different from other types of adoption because the children adopted often continue to be under the guardianship of their biological parents and are only "available" for adoption to the spouse of one of their biological parents. Therefore, the supply of children available for adoption by step-parents is not directly comparable to the supply of other adoptable children.

VIII. A FRAMEWORK FOR FURTHERING THE STUDY OF ADOPTION

This report has posed and tried to answer key questions about the factors that determine levels and trends in adoption. The answers provided have often fallen short of the mark because of the paucity of data available on adoptions. As documented in this report, only about half of the countries in the world report some data on adoptions. Furthermore, there is great variability in the data available in terms of completeness, coverage and meaning. Only 88 countries publish information on both intercountry and domestic adoptions and information on the characteristics of adoptive parents, adopted persons and birth parents is severely limited. The absence of harmonization in the ways countries collect, compile and disseminate information on adoption is a major obstacle in understanding how adoption is changing and the factors leading to those changes. It also limits the possibility of answering policy-relevant questions and investigating the overall effects of adoption on children.

This chapter offers guidelines about the type of information required to improve the evidence for the study of adoption. Although the guidelines presented here are developed specifically for countries that recognize the institution of adoption, they can also be useful for countries wishing to improve their information on alternative forms of child guardianship, such as *kafalah.*

The presentation of guidelines starts with the simplest case, namely, adoptions that take place within the jurisdiction of a single country. It then proceeds to consider the more complex situation in which adoptions involve the jurisdiction of two or more countries.

Two attributes of adoptable children and adoptive parents must be taken into account to determine whether the jurisdiction of more than one country is involved: their countries of citizenship and their respective countries of residence. If the adoptable child and the prospective adoptive parent or parents are all citizens and residents of the same country, only one jurisdiction is involved. At the other extreme, if the three actors involved in an adoption all have different countries of citizenship and of residence, there could be up to six jurisdictions involved.

According to the concepts used in this report (chapter V), a domestic adoption involves persons who are habitual residents of the same country, regardless of whether they are citizens of that country or not.[1] Domestic adoption is not defined explicitly in international instruments. In contrast, intercountry adoption is normally defined as an adoption that involves a change in the country of habitual residence of the adopted person, a definition consistent with the principles contained in the Hague Convention on Protection of Children and Co-operation in Respect of Intercountry Adoption[2] (UNICEF, 1998). Consequently, an intercountry adoption always involves the jurisdiction of at least two countries.

Usually, the actors in domestic adoptions are both habitual residents and citizens of the country in which the adoption takes place. However, in rare cases, the adoption may involve persons who are habitual residents of the country where the adoption takes place but citizens of different countries. There are also cases in which the adoptive parents and the adopted person are citizens of the same country, but habitual residents of different countries. In those two cases, whether the adoption procedure is considered domestic or intercountry depends on the laws and regulations of the country of residence of the persons involved. Because those cases tend to be rare, the discussion in this chapter assumes that domestic adoptions fall under the jurisdiction of a single country, namely, the country of residence of the adoptable person.

Section VIII.A describes the proposed framework for the collection, compilation and dissemination of statistics on domestic adoption. Section VIII.B expands the framework for use in cases of intercountry adoption.

A. FRAMEWORK FOR THE GENERATION AND COLLECTION OF STATISTICS ON DOMESTIC ADOPTION

In order to determine the data required for the demographic study of adoption, we focus on the "adoption triangle", consisting of the adoptive parents, the adopted person and the person or persons giving up guardianship (usually the birth mother or the birth parents). The number of persons involved in that triangle varies depending on the circumstances of each adoption and on the laws and regulations establishing who can adopt. If single persons are allowed to adopt and the birth parents of the adoptable child are unknown, the adoption may involve only two persons and, perhaps, the State as the entity relinquishing guardianship. If a couple adopts a child having two known and engaged biological parents, five persons would be involved: the two birth parents, the two adoptive parents and the adopted person. The number of persons for which data needs to be recorded ranges, therefore, from a minimum of two to a maximum of five.

Form 1, as presented below, is recommended as the instrument to record the basic information needed on the persons involved in an adoption. The Form records information on: the type of adoption involved, the dates of several key steps in the adoption procedure and the place where the adoption takes place (in terms of locality and state or province). It also records the date of birth, the sex, the place of habitual residence and the country of citizenship of each person involved in the adoption triangle. Other information recorded includes the current marital status of each of the adoptive parents and of each of the persons relinquishing guardianship as well as their relationship to the adopted child (to distinguish adoptions by step-parents or other relatives from other adoptions and to ascertain whether birth parents were the persons relinquishing guardianship of the adopted person).

Form 1 requires that information be recorded on both persons and events, a crucial distinction that is usually not made explicitly in adoption statistics. Because information on the type of data being reported is generally lacking, this report has treated data on events and persons as equivalent, a

less than ideal approach because there are cases in which multiple children are covered by a single legal decree or "event". To prevent confusion, Form 1 should be filled for *each* child being adopted, irrespective of whether only one decree is issued for multiple children or a decree is issued for each. Copies of the form could then be submitted by the appropriate administrative or judicial authority to the National Statistical Office of the country concerned for processing and the eventual dissemination of adoption statistics.

Note that the names of the persons involved are not recorded in Form 1. Therefore, the National Statistical Office would receive anonymized records, a procedure that would ensure the privacy of the persons concerned. National Statistical Offices have considerable experience in protecting the privacy of individuals and most of them comply with the privacy provisions contained in the Fundamental Principles of Official Statistics.[3]

We describe below the type of information that ought to be recorded in each of the entries in Form 1.

1. Characteristics of the adoption event

Type of adoption: As discussed in chapter I, the laws or regulations of some countries differentiate between different types of adoption, the most common being simple and full adoption. Whatever the categories in existence in a country, it is important that the type of each adoption be recorded explicitly. The legal provisions of each country will determine the relevant categorization. Availability of such data will permit analysts to ensure that the comparisons made are appropriate. It will also permit a better understanding of the differences existing within and between countries.

Date when the adoption request was received: This entry and the two following in Form 1 relate to the timing of different stages in the adoption process. It is important to record them separately because a major source of data heterogeneity in existing adoption statistics stems from the practices of different countries with respect to the dates used for statistical reporting. Note that all

FORM 1. MINIMUM DATA NEEDED TO MONITOR DOMESTIC ADOPTION

COUNTRY: _____

DATE WHEN THE FORM IS FILLED (DD/MM/YEAR): _____

CHARACTERISTICS OF THE EVENT

Type of adoption (e.g. simple or full):					
Date when the adoption request was received:					
Date when the adoption request was granted:					
Date when the adoption came into effect:					
Authority granting the adoption:					
Place of the adoption:					
Locality (town or city)					
State/Province					

CHARACTERISTICS OF THE PERSONS INVOLVED IN THE EVENT

	Persons relinquishing guardianship		Adopted person	Persons adopting	
	Person 1	Person 2	Person 0	Person 3	Person 4
Sex					
Date of birth					
Place of habitual residence:					
Locality (town or city)					
State/Province					
Country of citizenship					
Number of children before adoption comes into effect			Not applicable		
Of which, biological children			Not applicable		
Marital status			Not applicable		
Relationship to adopted person			Not applicable		

dates should be recorded in terms of day, month and year. The date considered here should be the date when the official adoption process starts. The terminology used may vary among countries but the concept is straightforward. Some terms used to refer to this date include: date of deposit of the adoption application with the competent court; date of filing of the adoption application; date of application, or date received. It is implicit in Form 1 that information on an adoption should be transmitted for statistical processing only when the adoption has come into effect. At that point, having a record of the starting date of the process allows useful analysis of the length of the process in relation to other characteristics. Available statistics indicate that some countries carry out statistical reporting as soon as an adoption petition is filed, while others do so only when the adoption is approved and yet others wait until the adoption comes into effect. Standard use of Form 1 for statistical reporting will make it easier to reach

comparability by fostering statistical reporting at the end of the process.

Date when the adoption request was granted: This is the date, recorded in terms of day, month and year, when the appropriate authority adjudicates in favour of the adoption request. Usually, there is some delay between the granting of an adoption and the time when the adopted person is put in the custody of the adoptive parents, that is, when the adoption actually comes into effect. Form 1 allows authorities to reflect these two different stages of the adoption separately. In cases where the two dates coincide, they should be repeated in Form 1.

Date when the adoption came into effect: This is the date, recorded in terms of day, month and year, when the adopted person is actually relinquished to the adoptive parents. As noted above, if it coincides with the date when the adoption request is granted, the same date should be recorded for the two items. In some countries, the adoption becomes effective when the adopted person is registered and obtains a new birth certificate. The registration date would therefore be the date recorded under this item. Since the nomenclature used by different countries for the different stages of the adoption process varies, it is recommended that each country adds to Form 1 the particular term used to describe the event whose date is being recorded.

Authority granting the adoption: The type of authority granting the adoption should be recorded since, as previous chapters have noted, the type of authority involved varies among countries. Distinguishing between civil and judicial authorities is important.

Place of the adoption: The place of the adoption should be recorded in terms of the locality and state or province where the authority granting the adoption is located. The locality may be a town, city or other form of administrative territorial unit. Availability of this information allows authorities to compare workload as well as the characteristics of events and their outcomes among different geographical locations. In countries with a federal organization, the practices of different states or provinces may vary and such differences should be reflected in Form 1 (for instance, differences in the terminology used for the different stages of the adoption procedure).

2. Characteristics of the persons affected by the adoption

Sex: The sex of each and every person involved in the adoption triangle—adoptive parents, adopted person, and the persons relinquishing guardianship (generally, the birth parent or parents)—should always be recorded explicitly. Such information should not be deduced from the name of a person or from other indirect evidence.

Date of birth: The date of birth in terms of day, month and year should be recorded for each and every person involved in the adoption triangle. Statisticians can then derive relevant measures of age in relation to the dates in which different stages of the adoption process took

place. It is important to record date of birth for every person involved, irrespective of whether laws or regulations impose restrictions on the ages that adoptive parents may have or on that of the person being adopted.

Place of habitual residence: The place of habitual residence, defined in terms of locality and state or province, should be recorded for each person involved in the adoption triangle. Because Form 1 is intended for use in recording information about domestic adoptions only, it is not expected that any of the persons involved would have a habitual residence outside the country where the adoption is being processed. However, if the regulations of a country allow persons residing abroad to be part of a domestic adoption, their country of habitual residence should also be recorded.

Country of citizenship: The country of citizenship of each and every person involved in the adoption triangle should be recorded. It is preferable to record country of citizenship than citizenship by itself to avoid confusion between citizenship and ethnic group. If a person has multiple citizenships, including that of his or her country of habitual residence, the citizenship corresponding to the country of habitual residence should be the one recorded.

Number of children before the adoption comes into effect: Recording the number of children that the person or persons relinquishing guardianship have (including the person put up for adoption) and the number of children that the adoptive parents already have (excluding the person being adopted) is important in order to study how the presence of other children affects the decision to put a child up for adoption in the case of the persons relinquishing guardianship or the decision to adopt in the case of the adoptive parents. Note that the number of children should be recorded separately for each of the adults involved in the adoption triangle, even if the two members of a couple report the same number. That number should be repeated for each member of the couple.

Number of biological children: It is also useful to record the number of biological children that the persons relinquishing guardianship and the adoptive parents had before the adoption came into effect. Once more, although the number of biological children may be the same for both partners in a couple, the item should be recorded separately for each.

Marital status: Information on current marital status should be recorded for each of the adoptive parents and each of the persons relinquishing guardianship (usually, the birth parents). Marital status should be recorded using at least the following categories: (*1*) never-married; (*2*) married; (*3*) in consensual union; (*4*) separated; (*5*) divorced, and (*6*) widowed.

Relationship to the adopted person: The relationship to the adopted person of each person relinquishing guardianship should be recorded. It is also important to record the relationship, if any, between the adopted person and the adoptive parents, particularly when one of the latter is a step-parent. Information about the relationship to the adopted person should include, at a minimum, the following categories: (*1*) birth mother; (*2*) birth father; (*3*) step-mother; (*4*) step-father; (*5*) grandmother; (*6*) grandfather; (*7*) aunt; (*8*) uncle; (*9*) sister; (*10*) brother; (*11*) other relative and (*12*) not related.

3. Dissemination of data on domestic adoption

Once the data on each adopted person has been recorded by the appropriate administrative or judicial authority, the set of Forms 1, properly filled, should be transmitted for statistical processing to the National Statistical Office or some other centralized governmental entity. The information gathered can then be disseminated in a variety of ways, including via databases accessible on the internet, special releases of data on the cases completed over a certain period or through routine tabulations.

Box VIII.1 provides a suggested list of tabulations useful for monitoring trends in domestic adoptions and their characteristics. The tabulations suggested should be made for all adoptions completed during a year, be it a calendar year or a fiscal year. The tabulations highlighted in bold should be given priority.

In presenting statistics on adoption, countries should make an effort to standardize the way certain characteristics are tabulated to improve the international comparability of data on adoption. Specifically, it is recommended that information on the age of persons relinquishing guardianship and adoptive parents be tabulated by five-year age group starting with 10 to 14 and ending with 65 years or over as the open-ended interval.

For the adopted persons a more detailed age distribution would be useful, either by single years of age or at least having the following age groups: under one year of age; 1 to 3; 3 to 5; 5 to 9; 10 to 14; 15 to 17, and 18 or over. Given that countries often limit adoption to children under a certain age, that age will generally be the upper age limit for tabulations regarding adopted persons by age.

With respect to country of citizenship or country of habitual residence, it is recommended that the standard classification of countries or areas presented in the *Standard Country or Area Codes for Statistical Use, Revision 4* (United Nations, 1998a) be used in tabulating data by country of citizenship. Combining countries into *ad hoc* groups should be avoided. However, aggregates for the major regional groups may be presented, provided data are also tabulated by individual country of citizenship or country of habitual residence, as the case may be.

Several tabulations call for data to be classified according to the number of children ("by number of adopted children", "by number of children" or "by number of biological children"). In setting the categories for reporting the number of children it is recommended that individual numbers be presented separately, even if they are very high. The practice of using an open-ended category, such as 10 children or more, limits the usefulness of the data. If an open-ended category has to be used, its lower limit should be 10 or higher.

As the list of tabulations contained in Box VIII.1 indicates, it is important to tabulate the characteristics of adopted persons in relation to those of the adoptive parents or those of the persons relinquishing guardianship. In depth

---

BOX VIII.1. RECOMMENDED TABULATIONS ON DOMESTIC ADOPTION

The following tabulations should be made for all persons adopted over a given year, be it a calendar year or a fiscal year. Tabulations in bold should be accorded priority.

Tabulations on adopted persons by characteristics of the adoption

1. **Number of persons adopted domestically by sex, age group and type of adoption**
2. Number of persons adopted domestically by sex, age group and place of adoption
3. Number of persons adopted domestically by sex and month in which the adoption came into effect

Tabulations on persons adopted domestically by characteristics of adoptive parents

4. **Number of adopted persons by sex and by marital status and age group of adoptive mother**
5. **Number of adopted persons by sex and by marital status and age group of adoptive father**
6. **Number of adopted persons by sex, age group and relationship to adoptive mother**
7. **Number of adopted persons by sex, age group and relationship to adoptive father**
8. Number of adopted persons by sex, age group and country of citizenship of adoptive mother
9. Number of adopted persons by sex, age group and country of citizenship of adoptive father

Tabulations on persons adopted domestically by characteristics of persons relinquishing guardianship

10. **Number of adopted persons by sex, age group and relationship to female persons relinquishing guardianship**

11. **Number of adopted persons by sex, age group and relationship with male persons relinquishing guardianship**
12. **Number of adopted persons by sex and by the marital status and age group of the birth mother**
13. **Number of adopted persons by sex and by the marital status and age group of the birth father**

Tabulations on the adoptive parents of persons adopted domestically

14. **Number of adoptive parents by sex, age group and country of citizenship**
15. **Number of adoptive mothers by marital status, age group and number of biological children**
16. **Number of adoptive fathers by marital status, age group and number of biological children**
17. Number of adoptive mothers by marital status, age group and number of children before the adoption
18. Number of adoptive fathers by marital status, age group and number of children before the adoption

Tabulations on the persons relinquishing guardianship of persons adopted domestically

19. **Number of birth mothers by marital status, age group and number of biological children**
20. Number of female persons relinquishing guardianship by marital status, age group and number of children before the adoption
21. Number of male persons relinquishing guardianship by marital status, age group and number of children before the adoption

---

analysis of the interrelations among the characteristics of all three requires access to data for individual adoption cases so that appropriate multivariate analysis can be carried out. Barring that possibility, tabulations that relate the characteristics of adopted persons to adoptive parents of each sex separately or of persons relinquishing guardianship for each sex separately would go a long way in providing useful insights about the adoption process.

B. FRAMEWORK FOR THE COLLECTION OF STATISTICS ON INTERCOUNTRY ADOPTION

When an adoption involves the jurisdiction of more than one country, more information needs to be gathered on the event than that recorded in Form 1. Form 2 presents the minimum set of items of information needed to monitor trends in and the characteristics of adoptions that involve the jurisdiction of two countries. Note that Form 2

FORM 2. MINIMUM DATA NEEDED TO MONITOR INTERCOUNTRY ADOPTION

CHARACTERISTICS OF THE INTERCOUNTRY EVENT	
FORM ID:	
PART TO BE FILLED BY AUTHORITIES IN COUNTRY OF ORIGIN	**PART TO BE FILLED BY AUTHORITIES IN COUNTRY OF DESTINATION**
Country of origin:	Country of destination:
Country of destination:	Country of origin:
Current date:	Current date:
Type of adoption (simple or full):	Type of adoption (simple or full):
Date when adoption request was received:	Date when adoption abroad was recognized:
Date when adoption request was granted:	Date when adoption request was granted:
Date when the adoption came into effect:	Date when the adoption came into effect:
Place of the adoption:	Place where the adoption was recognized or granted:
Locality (town or city)	Locality (town or city)
State/Province	State/Province
Date of departure:	Date of arrival:
Type of exit permit (if required):	Type of visa:
	Type of residence permit (if appropriate):

CHARACTERISTICS OF THE PERSONS INVOLVED IN THE EVENT					
	Persons relinquishing guardianship		**Adopted person**	**Persons adopting**	
	Persons 1	Person 2	Person 0	Person 3	Person 4
Sex					
Date of birth					
Country of habitual residence					
Locality (town or city)					
State/Province					
Country of citizenship					
Number of children before adoption comes into effect			Not applicable		
Of which, biological children			Not applicable		
Marital status			Not applicable		
Relationship to child			Not applicable		

differs from Form 1 mainly in that the adoption may involve two events: one in the country of residence of the persons being adopted (hereafter called "country of origin") and another in the country of destination. Depending on the laws and regulations of each, the event may be registered at different times in the two jurisdictions involved. In addition, because the adopted person is expected to migrate from one country to another, information about the type of visa granted is also of relevance. Otherwise, the items of information gathered on the persons involved in the adoption are the same as in Form 1 and will not be discussed again below (see subsection VIII.A.2 above for a detailed discussion of those items).

1. Recording the characteristics of the adoption in two countries

As noted earlier, countries normally have jurisdiction to authorize the adoption of individuals legally residing within their own territory. When the adoptive parents also reside in the country's territory, the adoption need not involve another jurisdiction. However, when the adopted person and the adoptive parents reside in two different countries, conflicts of jurisdiction and applicable law may arise between the two countries concerned. To avoid such complications, countries often recognize adoption orders promulgated abroad or, if the country of destination does not recognize an adoption order issued abroad, a second adoption order may be issued when the child is brought into the country.

To record the relevant characteristics of the adoption event or events involved, it is recommended that authorities in both, the country of origin and the country of destination, record the relevant characteristics of the event occurring in their respective jurisdictions. In Form 2, the left part of the upper panel is meant to be filled by the authorities of the country of origin, whereas the right part would be filled by the authorities of the country of destination. Ideally, authorities in the country of origin would use Form 2 to record information on the adoption and the persons involved in it before the adopted person leaves the country. Then, they could keep a copy of Form 2, duly filled, and transmit another copy to the country of destination, preferably as part of the set of documents that adoptive parents have to present to authorities in the country of destination. Authorities in the country of destination can then use the same Form 2 to complete the information on the adoption process according to the procedures in their country. Following that procedure, the statistical unit of the country of destination could then carry out the statistical processing of the full set of information gathered using Form 2.

Furthermore, by adding a unique identifier to Form 2, the country of destination could transmit a copy of the completed Form 2 to the country of origin so that it might be matched with the copy left behind to ensure that all children who left a country of origin for a given destination actually arrived there. Ideally, the country of origin would process the first set of information it collected using Form 2 as soon possible so that computer-assisted matching might be carried out when the duplicate and fully completed Form 2 was received from the country of destination.

Matching forms would have the added value of permitting countries where an adopted child lives with the adoptive parents during a probationary period before an intercountry adoption is granted, to have better control on the fate of the children involved in intercountry adoptions.

(a) Characteristics of the adoption event recorded in the country of origin

These characteristics are to be recorded on the left side of the upper panel of Form 2. The items in Form 2 that are different from those in Form 1 are described in detail below.

Country of origin: The name of the country of origin should appear explicitly in Form 2 because a copy of it will be shared with several countries of destination.

Country of destination: Recording the name of the country of destination on the left side of Form 2 is necessary for the country of origin to keep track of the number of adopted children going to each destination.

Current date: This is the date when the form is filled in the country of origin (left side). It should be recorded in terms day, month and year.

The type of adoption: The type of adoption (for instance, simple or full adoption) should be recorded according to the country origin. Note that Form 2 makes allowance for recording the type of adoption also from the perspective of the country of destination, in order to make explicit when the type may differ from one jurisdiction to another.

Date when the adoption request was received by authorities in the country of origin: As in Form 1, this entry and the two following on the left side of Form 2 relate to the timing of different stages in the adoption process in the country of origin. It is important to record those dates separately because a major source of data heterogeneity in existing adoption statistics stems from different national practices regarding the dates used for statistical reporting. Note that all dates should be recorded in terms of day, month and year. The date considered here should be the date when the official adoption process started in the country of origin. The terminology used for this event may vary among countries but the concept is straightforward. Some terms used to refer to the date of this event include: date of deposit of the adoption application with the competent court; date of filing of the adoption application; date of application, or date received. It is implicit in Form 2 that information on an adoption should be transmitted for statistical processing in the country of origin only when the adoption process has been completed according to its jurisdiction. As mentioned earlier, the information in Form 2 may be processed as soon as the part of Form 2 referring to procedures in the country of origin and to the characteristics of the persons involved are filled so that if, at a later stage, the duplicate is received back from the country of destination, computer-assisted matching can be carried out. The early processing of the country-of-origin information would permit the timely reporting of statistics on intercountry adoption from the country of origin's perspective.

Date when the adoption request was granted by authorities in the country of origin: This is the date, recorded in terms of day, month and year, when the appropriate authority in the country of origin adjudicates in favour of the adoption request. Usually, there is some delay between the granting of an adoption and the time when the adopted person is put in the custody of the adoptive parents, that is, when the adoption actually comes into effect. Form 2 allows the authorities of the country of origin to reflect separately those two different dates in the adoption process. In cases where the two dates coincide, they should be repeated in the appropriate entries on the left side of Form 2.

Date when the adoption came into effect in the country of origin: This is the date, recorded in terms of day, month and year, when the adopted person is actually relinquished to the adoptive parents by the authorities in the country of origin. As noted above, if it coincides with the date when the adoption request is granted, the same date should be recorded for the two items on the left side of Form 2. In some countries, the adoption only becomes effective when the adopted person is registered with the authorities of the country of destination. In those cases, the date in which the adoption becomes effective may be left blank on the left side of Form 2. Since the nomenclature used by different countries for the different stages of the adoption process varies, it is recommended

that each country adds to Form 2 the particular terminology used to describe the event whose date is being recorded.

Authority granting the adoption in the country of origin: The type of authority granting the adoption in the country of origin should be recorded on the left side of Form 2. Distinguishing between civil and judicial authorities is important.

Place of the adoption in the country of origin: The place of the adoption should be recorded in terms of the locality and state or province where the authority granting the adoption is located. The locality may be a town, city or other form of administrative territorial unit. Availability of this information can allow authorities to compare workload as well as the characteristics of events and their outcomes among different geographical locations. In countries with a federal organization, the practices of different states or provinces may vary and such differences should be reflected in Form 2 (as, for instance, differences in the terminology used for the different stages of the adoption procedure).

Date of departure from the country of origin: The authorities of the country of origin should record, as accurately as possible, the date of departure of the child from the country of origin. When feasible, the date reported should be corroborated by appropriate documentation (airplane ticket or reservation in other means of transport). Such information is relevant to monitor adoption cases, especially in terms of the timing of departure from the country of origin and arrival in the country of destination (see below).

Type of exit permit: If the country of origin requires a special permit to allow the child to leave the country, the type of permit should be recorded.

(b) Characteristics of the event recorded in the country of destination

These characteristics are to be recorded on the right side of the upper panel in Form 2.

Country of destination: Because a copy of Form 2 will be transmitted to the country of destination, it is important to record explicitly the country that received it and whose authorities filled the information requested on the right side of the Form.

Country of origin: By filling in this entry, authorities in the country of destination corroborate that the country of origin where the left side of the form was filled is indeed that from which the adopted person originates.

Current date: This is the date when the form is filled in the country of destination (right side). It should be recorded in terms day, month and year.

The type of adoption: The type of adoption (for instance, simple or full adoption) should be recorded according to the regulations and procedures of the country of destination (right side) in order to allow for the possibility that the type of adoption in the country of destination may differ from that in the country of origin.

Date when the adoption abroad was recognized: In countries that recognize adoptions granted abroad, the authorities filling the right side of Form 2 should record the date, in terms of day, month and year, when the adoption abroad was recognized by the country of destination. Generally, that date will be the only one relevant to the adoption procedure in the country of destination and the two entries following may be marked as "not applicable".

Date when the adoption request was granted by authorities in the country of destination: In cases where the adoption abroad is not recognized automatically by the country of destination, a procedure to reconfirm the adoption according to the rules and regulations of the country of destination will have to be undertaken. In that case, the date when the adoption was granted by authorities in the country of destination should be recorded on the right side of Form 2 in terms of day, month and year. Note that in this case the date in which the procedure starts is not recorded because it is contingent on the timing of the procedure in the country of origin.

Date when the adoption comes into effect in the country of destination: There is usually some delay between the time when the adoption is granted and the time when it comes into effect. Form 2 allows the authorities of the country of destination to reflect separately those two dates in the adoption process when applicable. In cases where the two dates coincide, they should be repeated in the appropriate items on the right side of Form 2.

Place where the adoption was recognized or granted: Authorities in the country of destination should record the place where the adoption was either recognized or granted. Place should be recorded in terms of locality, town or city at a first level and in terms of province or state at a second level of geographical aggregation.

Date of arrival: Authorities in the country of destination should record the date of arrival of the adopted person in its territory. The date should be recorded in terms of day, month and year.

Type of visa issued: Some countries of destination allow children to enter their territory on a temporary visa when the purpose of their entry is to be adopted. Countries of destination should record the type of visa under which the child entered the country.

Type of residence permit (if appropriate): The country of destination may provide a special type of residence permit to a foreign child that is a candidate for adoption while the adoption is being processed. In that case, the type of permit granted should be recorded on the right side of Form 2.

(c) Characteristics of the persons involved in the adoption

The characteristics of the persons involved in the adoption should be recorded in Form 2 by authorities in the country of origin. Most entries are the same as those included in Form 1 and a description of each can be found in subsection VIII.A.2. Note that, for intercountry adoptions, the country of habitual residence of the adopted person is expected to be different from that of the adoptive parents. Since a copy of Form 2 would be submitted to the authorities in the country of destination, they would have the opportunity, if they so wished, of checking the accuracy of the information relative to the adoptive parents.

2. Tabulations on intercountry adoption

Box VIII.2 presents two lists of suggested tabulations on intercountry adoptions and the persons involved in them to guide countries of origin and countries of destination, respectively, on the type of statistics that it would be useful to disseminate in regard to intercountry adoptions. Bold face is used to indicate which tabulations should have priority.

Countries of origin should focus on disseminating information on the adoptions of their residents adopted abroad, while countries of destination should provide data on adoptions involving residents of other countries by their own residents. All tabulations should refer to events occurring during a year, be it a calendar or a fiscal year. The recommendations made in subsection VIII.A.3 about the categories to be used in tabulating age of children, age of adults, relationships between persons or the marital status of adults should be followed. Similarly, in tabulating data by country (of destination, origin, citizenship or habitual residence), it is important to list each country separately and to avoid reporting data in terms of ad hoc country groupings.

C. CONCLUSION

The systematic study of adoption trends and characteristics worldwide is severely hampered by both the scarcity of data and their lack of comparability, which is in turn exacerbated by the paucity of information on the concepts and definitions that underlie the statistics available. Although perfect comparability might not be possible because of differences in the legal principles and national regulations governing adoption, much could be done to improve the transparency of existing data by providing better documentation on their meaning and scope. In addition, as this chapter has suggested, a

concerted effort to collect systematically, for every person being adopted, the same information regarding the event and the characteristics of the persons involved in it, would go a long way to provide the evidence required to understand better the social and demographic dimensions of adoption.

With regard to intercountry adoption, timely and detailed statistics are necessary to monitor the implementation of relevant multilateral, regional and bilateral instruments. The evidence suggests that countries that are parties to such instruments are making an effort to produce the relevant statistics. However, much remains to be done to improve dissemination of the available data and to provide the detail necessary for assessing important aspects of the adoption process.

This chapter has provided guidelines on the type of information that could be collected on domestic and intercountry adoptions and has suggested a list of tabulations that would provide the information necessary to improve the assessment of trends in adoption and the characteristics of the persons involved in the event.

Yet, preparation of such guidelines is only the first step on the path to improving adoption statistics. The authorities in charge of monitoring adoptions, both nationally and internationally, need to consider the guidelines proposed and be willing to embark on a process of change.

NOTES

[1]The definition of domestic adoption used in this publication is broader than the one employed by UNICEF (1998), according to which a domestic adoption involves citizens and habitual residents of the same country.

[2]From a legal perspective, the Hague Convention is unambiguous: it applies only to children who are habitual residents in one contracting State—the State of origin—and are moved to another contracting State—the receiving State—either after their adoption or for the purpose of adoption (art. 2).

[3]See United Nations, "Fundamental Principles of Official Statistics" (ST/ESA/STAT/OFFICIALSTATISTICS/WWW). Available from http://unstats.un.org/unsd/methods/statorg/FP-English.htm (accessed 24 March 2007).

BOX VIII.2. RECOMMENDED TABULATIONS ON INTERCOUNTRY ADOPTION

The following tabulations should be made for all persons adopted over a given year, be it a calendar year or a fiscal year. Tabulations in bold should be accorded priority. Different tabulations should be made about resident persons adopted from abroad (for whom the reporting country is origin) and about non-residents adopted by residents (for whom the reporting country is the country of destination).

Country of origin

Tabulations on persons adopted via an intercountry procedure by characteristics of the adoption

1. **Number of resident persons adopted via an intercountry procedure by sex, age group and type of adoption**
2. **Number of resident persons adopted via an intercountry procedure by sex, age group and country of destination**
3. Number of resident persons adopted via an intercountry procedure by sex, age group and place of adoption
4. Number of resident persons adopted via an intercountry procedure by sex and by month in which the adoption came into effect
5. Number of resident persons adopted via an intercountry procedure by sex and by month of departure for the country of destination

Tabulations on persons adopted via an intercountry procedure by characteristics of the adoptive parents

6. **Number of resident persons adopted via an intercountry procedure by sex and by marital status and age group of adoptive mother**
7. **Number of resident persons adopted via an intercountry procedure by sex and by marital status and age group of adoptive father**
8. **Number of resident persons adopted via an intercountry procedure by sex, age group and relationship to adoptive mother**
9. **Number of resident persons adopted via an intercountry procedure by sex, age group and relationship to adoptive father**
10. Number of resident persons adopted via an intercountry procedure by sex, age group and country of citizenship of adoptive mother
11. Number of resident persons adopted via an intercountry procedure by sex, age group and country of citizenship of adoptive father

Country of destination

Tabulations on persons adopted abroad by characteristics of the adoption

1. **Number of persons adopted via an intercountry procedure by sex, age group and type of adoption**
2. **Number of persons adopted via an intercountry procedure by sex, age group and country of origin**
3. Number of persons adopted via an intercountry procedure by sex, age group and place of adoption
4. Number of persons adopted via an intercountry procedure by sex and by month in which the adoption was recognized or came into effect
5. Number of persons adopted via an intercountry procedure by sex and by month of arrival

Tabulations on persons adopted abroad by characteristics of the adoptive parents

6. **Number of persons adopted via an intercountry procedure by sex and by marital status and age group of adoptive mother**
7. **Number of persons adopted via an intercountry procedure by sex and by marital status and age group of adoptive father**
8. **Number of persons adopted via an intercountry procedure by sex, age group, country of origin and relationship to adoptive mother**
9. **Number of persons adopted via an intercountry procedure by sex, age group, country of origin and relationship to adoptive father**
10. Number of persons adopted via an intercountry procedure by sex, age group and country of citizenship of adoptive mother
11. Number of persons adopted via an intercountry procedure by sex, age group and country of citizenship of adoptive father

Box VIII.2. (*continued*)

Country of origin	Country of destination

Tabulations on persons adopted via an intercountry procedure by characteristics of persons relinquishing guardianship

12. **Number of resident persons adopted via an intercountry procedure by sex, age group and relationship to female persons relinquishing guardianship**
13. **Number of resident persons adopted via an intercountry procedure by sex, age group and relationship to male persons relinquishing guardianship**
14. **Number of resident persons adopted via an intercountry procedure by sex and by marital status and age group of birth mother**
15. Number of resident persons adopted via an intercountry procedure by sex and by marital status and age group of birth father

Tabulations on persons adopted abroad by characteristics of persons relinquishing guardianship

12. **Number of persons adopted via an intercountry procedure by sex, age group and relationship to female persons relinquishing guardianship**
13. **Number of persons adopted via an intercountry procedure by sex, age group and relationship to male persons relinquishing guardianship**
14. **Number of persons adopted via an intercountry procedure by sex and by marital status and age group of birth mother**
15. Number of persons adopted via an intercountry procedure by sex and by marital status and age group of birth father

Tabulations on the characteristics of adoptive parents of persons adopted via an intercountry procedure

16. **Number of adoptive mothers by marital status, age group and country of citizenship**
17. **Number of adoptive fathers by marital status, age group and country of citizenship**
18. Number of adoptive parents by sex, age group and country of citizenship
19. **Number of adoptive mothers by marital status, age group and number of biological children**
20. **Number of adoptive fathers by marital status, age group and number of biological children**
21. Number of adoptive mothers by marital status, age group and number of children before the adoption
22. Number of adoptive fathers by marital status, age group and number of children before the adoption

Tabulations on the characteristics of adoptive parents of persons adopted abroad

16. **Number of adoptive mothers by marital status, age group and country of citizenship**
17. **Number of adoptive fathers by marital status, age group and country of citizenship**
18. Number of adoptive parents by sex, age group and country of citizenship
19. **Number of adoptive mothers by marital status, age group and number of biological children**
20. **Number of adoptive fathers by marital status, age group and number of biological children**
21. Number of adoptive mothers by marital status, age group and number of children before the adoption
22. Number of adoptive fathers by marital status, age group and number of children before the adoption

Tabulations on the persons relinquishing guardianship of persons adopted via an intercountry procedure

23. **Number of birth mothers by marital status, age group and number of biological children**
24. Number of female persons relinquishing guardianship by marital status, age group and number of children before the adoption
25. Number of male persons relinquishing guardianship by marital status, age group and number of children before the adoption

Tabulations on the persons relinquishing guardianship of persons adopted abroad

23. **Number of birth mothers by marital status, age group and number of biological children**
24. **Number of birth mothers by marital status, age group, number of biological children and country of citizenship**
25. Number of female persons relinquishing guardianship by marital status, age group and number of children before the adoption
26. Number of male persons relinquishing guardianship by marital status, age group and number of children before the adoption

GLOSSARY

Abortion rate:	The number of abortions per 1,000 women aged 15-44 years, unless otherwise indicated.
Adoption:	A legal institution that creates ties equivalent to natural filiation between an adopted person and one or two adoptive parents, so far as provided by the laws of the country. In some countries, especially those within the French legal tradition, there is more than one type of adoption.
Adopted person:	An individual who has been legally adopted by means of a judicial or administrative process.
Adoptive parent:	An individual who has legally assumed the parental rights over, and responsibilities for, another person through adoption.
Adoption rate (also total adoption rate):	The number of adopted persons in a certain age group divided by the number of persons in that same age group. The under-five adoption rate used in this report is calculated by dividing the total number of adoptions of children under age five by the number of children under age five, expressed per 100,000. It is assumed that 60 per cent of adopted children are under age five at the time of adoption. (See also domestic adoption rate, intercountry adoption rate.)
Adoption ratio:	The number of adoptions during a certain time period divided by the number of live births during the same time period.
Age of consent (to adoption):	The youngest age at which an individual is required or permitted to give his or her consent to adoption.
Birth parent:	The biological parent of an individual.
Childless woman:	A woman who has never had a live birth.
Closed adoption:	A type of adoption where there is no personal contact between the prospective adoptive parent and the birth parent.
Committee on the Rights of the Child:	A body composed of 18 independent experts that monitors the implementation of the Convention on the Rights of the Child by States parties.
Country of destination:	A country that is primarily a recipient of children adopted through intercountry procedures.
Country of origin:	A country that is primarily a source of children adopted through intercountry procedures.

De facto adoption:	An informal arrangement through which one or more individuals assume parental rights over, and responsibilities for, another person. Such adoptions do not have legal validity.
Domestic adoption:	An adoption where both the adoptive parents and the adopted person are citizens and habitual residents of the same country.
Domestic adoption rate:	Total number of domestic adoptions of children in a certain age group divided by the number of children in that same age group, expressed per 100,000.
Double orphan:	An individual that has lost both parents due to death.
Fecundity:	The physiological ability to conceive and give birth.
Fertility:	The proven ability to conceive and give birth.
Foster care:	A system enabling a child who lacks parental support and protection to be placed in the care of a person or family, usually by court order.
Full adoption:	A type of adoption that permanently terminates the legal ties between the adopted person and his or her birth parents and replaces those ties with equivalent ones between the adopted person and his or her adoptive parents. In the French legal tradition, full adoption is contrasted with simple adoption.
Infecundity:	The inability to conceive and give birth after being exposed to the risk of pregnancy for a number of years.
Intercountry adoption:	An adoption that involves a change in the adopted person's country of habitual residence. For any given country, this includes both adoptions by citizens of that country of children who were resident elsewhere (i.e., the children become immigrants) and adoptions by citizens of other countries of children born in that country (i.e., the children become emigrants).
Intercountry adoption rate:	Total number of intercountry adoptions of children in a certain age group divided by the number of children in that same age group, expressed per 100,000.
International adoption:	An adoption where the adoptive parents and the adopted person are citizens, but not necessarily residents, of different countries.
Inter-racial adoption:	An adoption where at least one of the adoptive parents and the adopted person are identified as belonging to different racial groups.
Kafalah:	A practice similar to guardianship, recognised under *Sharia* law. *Kafalah* does not terminate the legal ties between the person under guardianship and his or her birth parents nor does it grant automatic inheritance rights with respect to the guardian's property.

Mean age at first birth (MAFB):	The mean age of mothers at the birth of the first child. It is computed from age-specific fertility rates derived from information on first births only. Data on first births by age of mother are normally obtained from a civil registration system, but can also be obtained from retrospective questions included in censuses and surveys.
Mean age at (first) marriage (MAM):	The mean age at (first) marriage of men or women in a population. It is calculated from age-specific (first) marriage rates derived from a civil registration system and a census. When data from civil registration is not available, the mean age at marriage can be calculated from data obtained using retrospective questions included in censuses and surveys. A commonly used proxy is the singulate mean age at marriage (SMAM), which is estimated from the proportions never married by age reported by censuses or surveys. In this report, SMAM is used as the indicator of mean age at first marriage even if it is referred to as "the mean age at marriage".
Open adoption:	A type of adoption where the birth parent and the adoptive parent file a joint request for the authorization of the adoption.
Ordinary adoption:	A type of adoption recognized in Japan, which creates a legal parental relation between the adoptive parents and the adopted person, who acquires the status of a legitimate child. If the child to be adopted is a minor, permission of the family court is needed.
Parity:	The total number of live births that a woman has had during her life, usually reported for women in different age groups.
Percentage of childless women by age group:	The percentage of women in a particular age group who have never experienced a live birth. It is usually derived from census or survey data on women classified by the number of children ever born.
Percentage ever married by age group:	The percentage of persons in each age group who are not single. These percentages are derived from census data on the population classified by current marital status, sex and age group. The ever married population includes all those who are currently married or living in a consensual union or are divorced or widowed.
Percentage of extramarital births among all births:	The percentage of live births occurring to parents who, according to national law, were not married at the time of the birth.
Percentage using a modern contraceptive method:	The percentage of women of reproductive age (usually 15 to 49) who are currently married or in union and are using a modern method of contraception. Modern contraceptive methods include sterilization (female or male), the pill, injectables, intra-uterine devices (IUDs), condoms, vaginal barrier methods and implants. Data on use of modern contraceptives are usually derived from surveys.

Percentage using any contraceptive method: — The percentage of women of reproductive age (usually 15 to 49) who are currently married or in union and are using either a traditional or a modern contraceptive method. Traditional contraceptive methods include rhythm (also called periodic abstinence or calendar method), withdrawal, breastfeeding, douching and various folk methods. Modern contraceptive methods include sterilization (female or male), the pill, injectables, intra-uterine devices (IUDs), condoms, vaginal barrier methods and implants.

Primary infertility (also primary sterility): — The inability to bear any children, either due to the inability to conceive or the inability to carry a pregnancy to a live birth.

Secondary infertility: — The inability to bear a child after having an earlier birth.

Simple adoption: — A type of adoption where the adopted person maintains some legal and financial ties with his or her birth family, including inheritance rights. Simple adoption is common in countries with a French legal heritage.

Singulate mean age at marriage (SMAM): — The average age of single life for those under age 5, which is considered equivalent to the mean age at first marriage. It is calculated from the proportions single reported by censuses or surveys.

Step-parent adoption: — An adoption where the adoptive parent is married to one of the birth parents of the adopted person.

Subfecundity: — A situation where, due to physical or medical reasons, it is difficult but not impossible for a person to have a child.

Total fertility per woman: — The average number of live births a woman would have by age 50 if she were subject, throughout her life, to the age-specific fertility rates observed in a given year or period. Its calculation assumes that there is no mortality before age 50. Total fertility is expressed as the number of children per woman.

Total divorce rate: — The number of divorces that a person would have gone through by age 50 if the age-specific divorce rates observed in a given year were applied throughout his or her life. This measure is expressed as number of divorces per person.

REFERENCES

Abel, P. (1960). Reform of the Austrian adoption legislation. *The International and Comparative Law Quarterly*, vol. 9. No. 3, pp. 481-486.

Adamec, C., and W. Pierce (2000). *The Encyclopaedia of Adoption,* 2nd ed. New York: Facts on File.

Addis, R. S. (1953). Some points of English and foreign adoption law. *The International and Comparative Law Quarterly*, vol. 2, No. 3, pp. 387-390.

Akerlof, G. A. and others (1996). An analysis of out-of-wedlock childbearing in the United States. *The Quarterly Journal of Economics*, vol. 111, No. 2 (May), pp. 277-317.

Akresh, R. (2004). Adjusting household structure: school enrollment impacts of child fostering in Burkina Faso. IZA Discussion Papers 1379. Bonn: Institute for the Study of Labor. Available from ftp://repec.iza.org/RePEc/Discussionpaper/dp1379 .pdf (accessed 30 October 2006).

Alber, E. (2004). 'The real parents are the foster parents': social parenthood among the Baatombu in Northern Benin. In *Cross-Cultural Approaches to Adoption*, F. Bowie, ed. London; New York: Routledge, pp. 33-47.

Altstein, H. and R. Simon, eds. (1991). *Intercountry Adoption: a Multinational Perspective*. New York: Praeger.

Ambrose, M., and A. M. Coburn (2001). Report on intercountry adoption in Romania. Washington, D.C.: United States Agency for International Development. Available from http://www.laprimo genita.it/Documenti/romanadopt.pdf (accessed 30 October 2006).

Anderson, A. (2004). Adoption and belonging in Wogeo, Papua New Guinea. In *Cross-Cultural Approaches to Adoption*, F. Bowie, ed. London; New York: Routledge, pp. 111-126.

Appell, R. A. (2002a). Safe havens to abandon babies: Part 1: the law. *Adoption Quarterly*, vol. 5, No. 4, pp. 59-69.

_____ (2002b). Safe havens to abandon babies: Part 2: the fit. *Adoption Quarterly*, vol. 6, No. 1, pp. 61-69.

_____ (2002c). Safe havens to abandon babies: Part 3: the effects. *Adoption Quarterly*, vol. 6, No. 2, pp. 67-75.

Armitage, A. (1995). *Comparing the Policy of Aboriginal Assimilation: Australia, Canada, and New Zealand*. Vancouver: UBC Press.

Arnold, F. (1992). Sex preference and its demographic and health implications. *International Family Planning Perspectives*, vol. 18, No. 3 (September), pp. 93-101.

Australia, Australian Institute of Health and Welfare (2004). *Adoptions Australia 2003-2004*. Child Welfare Series No. 35. Canberra. Available from http://www.aihw.gov.au/publications/cws/aa03-04/aa03-04.pdf (accessed 30 October 2006).

Australia, Department of Immigration and Citizenship (2007). *Child Migration*. Available from http://www.immi.gov.au/allforms/booklets/books2. htm (accessed 07 December 2007).

Bachrach, C. (1983). Adoption as a means of family formation: data from the National Surveys of Family Growth. *Journal of Marriage and the Family*, vol. 45, No. 4 (November), pp. 859-865.

_____ (1986). Adoption plans, adopted children, and adoptive mothers. *Journal of Marriage and the Family*, vol. 48, No. 2 (May), pp. 243-253.

_____ and others (1991). On the path to adoption: adoption seeking in the United States, 1988. *Journal of Marriage and the Family*, vol. 53, No. 3 (August), pp. 705-718

Bachrach, C. and others (1992). Relinquishment of Premarital births: evidence from national survey data. *Family Planning Perspectives*, vol. 24, No. 1 (January), pp. 27-48.

Banovec, T. (2001). Trends and indicators on child and family well-being in Slovenia, 1989-1999. Background paper prepared for *A Decade of Transition. Regional Monitoring Report*, No. 8. Florence, Italy: UNICEF Innocenti Research Centre. Available from http://www.unicef-icdc.org/research/ESP/CountryReports2000_01/Sl ovenia00.pdf (accessed 30 October 2006).

Barber, J. G. and P.H. Delfabbro (2004). *Children in Foster Care*. London: Routledge.

Bargach, J. (2002). *Orphans of Islam: Family, Abandonment, and Secret Adoption in Morocco*. Lanham, Maryland: Rowman and Littlefield Publishers.

Barr, M. D. (2002). *Cultural Politics and Asian Values: The Tepid War*. London: Routledge.

Bartholet, E. (1991). Where do black children belong? The politics of race matching in adoption. *University of Pennsylvania Law Review*, vol. 139, No. 5, pp. 1163-1256.

_____ (1993). International adoption: current status and future prospects. *The Future of Children*, vol. 3, No. 1, pp. 89-103. Available from http://www.futureofchildren.org/usr_doc/vol3no1en tire_journal.PDF (accessed 30 October 2006).

Bean, P., and J. Melville (1989). *Lost Children of the Empire*. London: Unwin Hyman.

Bechtel, E. A. (1896). A study of the Roman law of adoption. *The Northwestern Law Review*, vol. 4, pp. 73-82.

Bekstorm, J. H. (1972). Adoption in Ethiopia ten years after the Civil Code. *Journal of African Law*, vol. 16, No. 2, pp. 145-168.

Belgium, Kind en Gezin, Flemish Minister of Welfare (2003). *The Child in Flanders 2003*. Available from http://www.kindengezin.be/Images/Child_in_Flanders_2003_tcm149-37000.pdf (accessed 10 October 2007).

Benet, M. K. (1976). *The Character of Adoption*. London: Jonathan Cape.

Bernstein, L. (1997). The evolution of Soviet adoption law. *Journal of Family History*, vol. 22, No. 2, pp. 204-226.

Bhargava, V. (2005). *Adoption in India: Policies and Experiences*. New Delhi: Sage Publications.

Bitler, M., and M. Zavodny (2002). Did abortion legalization reduce the number of unwanted children? Evidence from adoptions. *Perspectives on Sexual and Reproductive Health*, vol. 34, No. 1 (Jan.-Feb.), pp. 25-33.

Black, V. (1994). GATT for kids: new rules for intercountry adoption of children. *Canadian Family Law Quarterly*, vol. 11, pp. 253-315.

Bongaarts, J. (1990). The measurement of wanted fertility. *Population and Development Review*, vol. 16, No. 3 (September), pp. 487-506

_____ (1997). Trends in unwanted childbearing in the developing world. *Studies in Family Planning*, vol. 28, No. 4, pp. 267-277.

_____ (2001). Fertility and reproductive preferences in post-transitional societies. *Population and Development Review*, vol. 27, Supplement: Global Fertility Transition, pp. 260-281.

Bonham, G. (1977). Who adopts: the relationship of adoption and social-demographic characteristics of women. *Journal of Marriage and the Family*, vol. 39, No. 2 (May), pp. 295-306.

Boswell, J. (1988). *The Kindness of Strangers: the Abandonment of Children in Western Europe from Late Antiquity to the Renaissance*. London; New York: Penguin.

Bowie F., ed. (2004). *Cross-Cultural Approaches to Adoption*. London; New York: Routledge.

Brady, I., ed. (1976). *Transactions in Kinship: Adoption and Fostering in Oceania*. Honolulu, Hawaii: University of Hawaii Press.

Bridge, C. (2001). Adoption law: a balance of interests. In *Family Law: Issues, Debates, Policy*, J. Herring, ed. Cullompton, United Kingdom: Willan Publishing, pp. 198-234.

British Institute of International and Comparative Law (1967). France. *The International and Comparative Law Quarterly*, vol. 16, No. 2 (April), pp. 551-552.

Brooks, D. and others (2005). Contemporary adoption in the United States: implications for the next wave of adoption theory research and practice. In *Psychological Issues in Adoption: Research and Practice*, D.M. Brodzinsky and J. Palacios, eds. Westport, Connecticut: Praeger Publishers, pp. 1-26.

Brosnan, J. F. (1922). The law of adoption. *Columbia Law Review*, vol. 22, No. 4 (April), pp. 332-342.

Broyde, M. J. (2005). Adoption, personal status, and Jewish law. In *The Morality of Adoption: Social-Psychological, Theological, and Legal Perspectives*, T. P. Jackson, ed. Grand Rapids, Michigan: W.B. Eerdmans, pp. 128-147.

Bruthansová, D. and others (2005). Institutional health and social care aiming to children under three. Prague, RILSA - Research Centre Brno. Available from http://www.vupsv.cz/Fulltext/vz_177.pdf (accessed 6 July 2006).

Bryant, T. L. (1990). Sons and lovers: adoption in Japan. *The American Journal of Comparative Law*, vol. 38, No. 2. (Spring), pp. 299-336.

Buck, T. (2005). *International Child Law*. London: Cavendish Publishing.

Bumpass, L. L. (1969). Age at marriage as a variable in socio-economic differentials in fertility. *Demography*, vol. 6, No. 1, pp. 45-54.

_____ and others (1978). Age and marital status at first birth and the pace of subsequent fertility. *Demography*, vol. 15, No. 1, pp. 75-86.

Buxbaum, D. C. (1968*). Family Law and Customary Law in Asia: A Contemporary Legal Perspective*. The Hague: Martinus Nijhoff Publishers.

Cahill, L. S. (2005). Adoption: a Roman Catholic perspective. In *The Morality of Adoption: Social-Psychological, Theological, and Legal Perspectives*, T.P. Jackson, ed. Grand Rapids, Michigan: W.B. Eerdmans, pp. 148-171.

Cameron, B. J. (1966). Adoption. In *An Encyclopaedia of New Zealand*, A.H. McLintock, ed. Wellington: Government Printer.

Canada, Adoption Council (2005). China leads adoption statistics for 2004. Ottawa: Adoption Council of Canada. Available from http://www.adoption.ca/news/050527stats04.htm (accessed 27 October 2006).

Canada, Citizenship and Immigration Canada (2003). International adoptions. *The Monitor* (Fall). Available from http://www.cic.gc.ca/english/monitor/issue03/index.html and http://www.cic.gc.ca/francais/ressources/statistiques/observateur/issue03/06-de_fonds.asp (accessed 27 October 2006).

Canada, Human Resources and Social Development (2004). *Child and Family Services Statistical Report*

1998-1999 to 2000-2001. Available from http://ww w.sdc.gc.ca/en/cs/sp/sdc/socpol/publications/statistics /2004-002599/page02.shtml (accessed 04 December 2007).

Carp, E.W. (1998). *Family Matters: Secrecy and Disclosure in the History of Adoption.* Cambridge, Massachusetts: Harvard University Press.

_____ (2000). *Adoption in America: Historical Perspectives.* Ann Arbor: University of Michigan.

Carroll, V., ed. (1970). *Adoption in Eastern Oceania.* Honolulu: University of Hawaii Press.

Casterline, J. B. and others (2003). Unmet need and unintended fertility: longitudinal evidence from Upper Egypt. International *Family Planning Perspectives,* vol. 29, No. 4.

Chandra, A. and others (1999). Adoption, adoption seeking, and relinquishment for adoption in the United States. *Advance Data,* No. 306. Hyattsville, Maryland: National Center for Health Statistics, U.S. Department of Health and Human Services.

China, Ministry of Civil Affairs (2005). *Statistical Yearbook 2005.* Beijing: China Statistics Press.

China, National Bureau of Statistics of the People's Republic of China (2002). *China Statistical Yearbook 2002.* Beijing: China Statistics Press.

Coale, A.J. (1992). Age of entry into marriage and the date of the initiation of voluntary birth control. *Demography,* vol. 29, No. 3, pp. 333-341.

Cole, E., and K. Donley (1990). History, values and placement policy issues in adoption. In *The Psychology of Adoption,* D. Brodzinsky and M. Schechter, eds. New York: Oxford University Press, pp. 273-294.

Council of Europe (1967). European Convention on the Adoption of Children. *European Treaty Series,* No. 058.

Cretney, S. M. and others (2003). The Adoption and Children Act 2002. Supplement to *Principles of Family Law.*

Czech Republic, Institute of Health Information and Statistics (2005). *Czech Health Statistics Yearbook 2004.* Prague.

Damas, D. (1972). The copper Eskimo. In *Hunters and Gatherers Today,* M.G. Bicchieri, ed. pp. 3-50. New York: Holt, Rinehart, and Winston.

_____ (1983). Demography and kinship as variables of adoption in the Carolines. *American Ethnologist,* vol. 10, No. 2, pp. 328-344.

Defence for Children International (1989). Protecting Children's Rights in International Adoption: Selected Documents on the Problem of Trafficking and Sale of Children. Geneva.

_____ (1991). Romania: The Adoption of Romanian Children by Foreigners: Report of a Group of Experts on the Rights of the Child in Intercountry Adoption. Geneva.

Demian, M. (2004). Transactions in rights, transactions in children: a view of adoption from Papua New Guinea. In *Cross-Cultural Approaches to Adoption,* F. Bowie, ed. London; New York: Routledge, pp. 97-110.

Denmark, Danish National Board of Adoption (2005). Statistical information–some figures on foreign adoptions in Denmark. Available from http://www.adoptionsnaevnet.dk/info_english/defa ult.htm (accessed 30 October 2006).

Denmark, Ministry of Family and Consumer Affairs (2004). The Danish Adoption (Consolidation) Act. Available from http://www.fam iliestyrelsen.dk/ adoption/lovgivning/love/the-danish-adoption-consolidation-act/ (accessed 28 October 2006).

Denmark, Statistics Denmark (2004). *Statistical News. Population and Elections,* No. 5, Copenhagen, Denmark.

_____ (2005). The age of the female adoptant at adoption. *Statistical News.* Available from http://statistik.adoption.dk/generelt/adoptivmodres alder.htm (accessed 29 October 2006).

Derrett, J. D. (1957). Private international law. Adoption. *The Modern Law Review,* vol. 20, No. 1, pp. 65-70.

Dickens, J. (2002). The paradox of inter-country adoption: analysing Romania's experience as a sending country. *International Journal of Social Welfare,* No. 11, pp. 76-83.

Diwan, P. (2000). *Law of Adoption Minority Guardianship and Custody, Third Edition.* Delhi: Universal Law. Publishing Co.

Donnelly, B. W., and P. Voydanoff (1991). Factors associated with releasing for adoption among adolescent mothers. *Family Relations,* vol. 40, No. 4 (October), pp. 404-410.

Dunning, R. W. (1962). A note on adoption among the Southampton Island Eskimo. *Man,* vol. 62 (November), pp. 163-167.

Edwards, C., and P. Read (1989). *The Lost Children: Thirteen Australians taken from their Aboriginal Families tell of their Struggle to find their Natural Parents.* Sydney: Doubleday.

Eekelaar, J. (1994). 'The Chief Glory': the export of children from the United Kingdom. *Journal of Law and Society,* vol. 21, No. 4 (December), pp. 487-504.

Estonia, Ministry of Social Affairs (2004). Social Sector in Figures 2004. Tallinn. Available from http://www.sm.ee/eng/HtmlPages/social_sector_20 04/$file/social_sector_2004.pdf (accessed 27 October 2006).

_____ (2005). Response to the 2005 questionnaire on the practical operation of the Hague Convention of 29 May 1993 on Protection of Children and Co-operation in Respect of Intercountry Adoption.

Available from http://www.hcch.net/upload/adop 2005_ee.pdf (accessed 6 July 2006).

European Commission (2002). Maternity leave: prior to and after confinement. Available from http://europa.eu.int/comm/employment_social/mis soc/2002/missoc_87_en.htm (accessed 26 October 2006).

Fauve-Chamaux, A. (1996). Beyond adoption: orphans and family strategies in pre-industrial France. *The History of the Family*, vol. 1, No. 1, pp. 1-13.

Feigelman, W., and A.R. Silverman (1997). Single parent adoption. In *The Handbook for Single Adoptive Parents*. H. Marindin Chevy Chase, Maryland: National Council for Single Adoptive Parents, pp. 123-129.

Finland, Finnish Adoption Board (2004). *Annual Report 2003*. Helsinki: Ministry of Social Affairs and Health. Available from http//stm.fi/Resource. hx/publishing/store/2004/06/mk1087197406074/ passthru.pdf (accessed 30 October 2006).

Finnas, F., and J. M. Hoem (1980). Starting age and subsequent birth intervals in cohabitational unions in current Danish cohorts, 1975. *Demography*, vol. 17, No. 3, pp. 275-295.

Flores-Oebanda, C. (2006). Addressing vulnerability and exploitation of child domestic workers: an open challenge to end a hidden shame. Paper presented at the Expert Group Meeting "Elimination of all forms of discrimination and violence against the girl child", UNICEF Innocenti Research Centre, Florence, Italy, 25-28 September 2006. Available from http://www.un.org/womenwatch/ daw/egm/elim-disc-viol-girlchild/ExpertPapers/EP. 10%20%20 Flores%20Oebanda.pdf (accessed 12 November 2006).

Folsom, R. H., and J. H. Minan (1989). *Law in the People's Republic of China: Commentary, Readings, and Materials*. Dordrecht; Boston: Martinus Nijhoff Publishers.

Food and Agriculture Organization of the United Nations (FAO) (1996). Study on the impact of armed conflicts on the nutritional situation of children. Rome. Available from http://www.fao. org/docrep/005/w2357e/W2357E00.htm (accessed 12 November 2006).

Forde, D. (1939). Kinship in Umor—Double unilateral organization in a semi-Bantu society. *American Anthropologist*, New Series, vol. 41, No. 4, pp. 523-553.

_____ (1950). Double descent among the Yakö. In *African Systems of Kinship and Marriage*, A. R. Radcliffe-Brown and D. Forde, eds. London: Oxford University Press, pp. 285-332.

France, Ministry of Foreign Affairs (2006). *Adoption Internationale: Statistiques 2005*. Available from http://www.diplomatie.gouv.fr/fr/IMG/pdf/stat_ adoption_2005.pdf (accessed 30 October 2006).

Fuchs, R. G. (1984). *Abandoned Children: Foundlings and Child Welfare in Nineteenth-century France*. Albany: State University of New York Press.

_____ (1987). Legislation, poverty, and child-abandonment in nineteenth-century Paris. *Journal of Interdisciplinary History*, vol. 18, No. 1 (Summer), pp. 55-80.

Fustel de Coulanges, N. D. (1901). *The Ancient City: a Study on the Religion, Laws, and Institutions of Greece and Rome*, 10th ed. W. Small, trans. Boston: Lee and Shepherd.

Gaber, I., and J. Aldridge (1994). *In the Best Interests of the Child: Culture, Identity, and Transracial Adoption*. London: Free Association Books.

Gager, K. E. (1996). *Blood Ties and Fictive Ties: Adoption and Family Life in Early Modern France*. Princeton: Princeton University Press.

Galvin, W. (2005). International adoption—the good, the bad and the ugly: a South Pacific perspective. Paper presented at the International Bar Association 2005 Conference, Prague, Czech Republic, 24-30 September. Available from http://www.galvinmcgowan.co.nz/ article_goodbadugly.html (accessed 30 October 2006).

Garcia Marsilla, J. V. (1999). Adoption in Spanish legal texts of the thirteenth century. *Revues Médiévales*, No. 35, pp. 61-68.

Gardner, J. F. (1998). *Family and Familia in Roman Law and Life*. New York: Oxford University Press.

Geen, R. (2000). In the interest of children: rethinking federal and state policies affecting kinship care. *Policy and Practice of Public Human Services*, vol. 58, No. 1, pp. 19-27.

Germany, Federal Institute for Population Research, and the Robert Bosch Foundation (2005). *The Demographic Future of Europe—Facts, Figures, policies. Results of the Population Policy Acceptance Study (PPAS)*. Available from http://www.bosch-stiftung.de/content/language1/downloads/PPAS_en. pdf (accessed 30 October 2006).

Germany, Federal Statistics Office (2004). *Statistical Yearbook 2004 for the Federal Republic of Germany*. Wiesbaden, Germany.

Gibbons, R. C. (2004). Adoption. In *The Modern Catholic Encyclopedia*, M. Glazier and M.K. Hellwig, eds. Collegeville: Liturgical Press, p. 12.

Gibson, C. S. (1994). *Dissolving Wedlock*. London; New York: Routledge.

Gill, A. (1997). *Orphans of the Empire: The Shocking Story of Child Migration to Australia*. Alexandria: Millennium Books.

Global Legal Information Network (2006). *Kafala*. In Subject term index. Available from http://www.glin. gov/lookup.do (accessed 30 October 2006).

Gold, M. (1994). Adoption as a Jewish option. In *The Jewish Family and Jewish Continuity*, S. Bayme and G. Rosen, eds. Hoboken: KTAV Publishing House, pp. 173-180.

Goldson, J. (2003). Adoption in New Zealand: an international perspective. In *Adoption: Changing Families, Changing Times*, A. Douglas and T. Philpot, eds. London: Routledge, pp. 246-250.

Goodenough, R. G. (1970). Adoption on Romonum, Truk. In *Adoption in Eastern Oceania*. ASAO Monograph No. 1, V. Carroll, ed. Honolulu, Hawaii: University of Hawaii Press, pp. 314-340.

Goodman, R. (1998). A child in time: changing adoption and fostering in Japan. In *Interpreting Japanese Society: Anthropological Approaches*, J. Hendry, ed. London: Routledge, pp. 145-166.

_____ (2000). *Children of the Japanese State: The Changing Role of Child Protection Institutions in Contemporary Japan*. Oxford: Oxford University Press.

Goody, E. (1973). *Contexts of Kinship: an Essay in the Family Sociology of the Gonja of Northern Ghana*. Cambridge, United Kingdom: Cambridge University Press.

_____ (1982). *Parenthood and Social Reproduction: Fostering and Occupational Roles in West Africa*. Cambridge; New York: Cambridge University Press.

Goody, J. (1969). Adoption in cross-cultural perspective. *Comparative Studies in Society and History*, vol. 11, No. 1 (January), pp. 55-78.

Greene, M. F. (2002). What will become of Africa's AIDS orphans? *New York Times Magazine*.

Griffith, K. (1997). *New Zealand Adoption: History and Practice, Social and Legal, 1840-1996*. Wellington: K.C. Griffith.

Guemple, L. (1979). Inuit Adoption. *Canadian Ethnology Service*, No. 47. Ottawa: National, Museums of Canada.

Hague Conference on Private International Law (1996). *Collection of Conventions (1951-1996)*, pp. 356-377.

_____ (2005). Conclusions and recommendations of the second meeting of the Special Commission on the practical operation of the Hague Convention of 29 May 1993 on Protection of Children and Co-operation in Respect of Intercountry Adoption. Meeting of the Permanent Bureau, 17-23 September 2005. Available from http://www.hcch.net/upload/wop/concl33sc05_e.pdf (accessed 30 October 2006).

Haimes, E., and N. Timms (1985). *Adoption, Identity and Social Policy: the Search for Distant Relatives*. London: Gower.

Halbmayer, E. (2004). 'The one who feeds has rights': adoption and fostering of kin, affines and enemies among the Yukpa and other Carib-speaking Indians of Lowland South America. In *Cross-Cultural Approaches to Adoption,* F. Bowie, ed. London; New York: Routledge, pp. 145-164.

Halifax, J. (2001). *L'insertion Sociale des Enfants Adoptes. Résultats de l'Enquête "Adoption Internationale et Insertion Sociale", 2000.* Available from http://www.ined.fr/fichier/t_publication/1069/ publi_pdfl_98.pdf (accessed 04 December 2007).

_____ and C. Villeneuve-Gokalp (2005). L'adoption en France: qui sont les adoptés, qui sont les adoptants? *Population et Sociétés*, No. 417, pp. 1-4.

Hank, K., and H.-P. Kohler (2000). Gender preferences for children in Europe: empirical results from 17 FFS Countries. *Demographic Research*, vol. 2. Available from http://www.demographic-research.org/Volumes/Vol2/1/2-1.pdf (accessed 30 October 2006).

Hegar, R. L., and M. Scannapieco, eds. (1999). *Kinship Foster Care: Policy, Practice and Research*. New York: Oxford University Press.

Hendrick, H. (2003). *Child Welfare: Historical Dimensions, Contemporary Debates*. Bristol: The Policy Press.

Herman, E. (2002). The paradoxical rationalization of modern adoption. *Journal of Social History*, vol. 36, No. 6, pp. 339-385.

Hetherington, E. M., and K. M. Jodl, (1994). Stepfamilies as settings for child development. In *Stepfamilies: Who Benefits? Who Does Not?* A. Booth and J. Dunn, eds. Hillsdale, New Jersey: Lawrence Erlbaum Associates, pp. 55-80.

Hoffman-Riem, C. (1990). *The Adopted Child: Family Life with Double Parenthood*. M. Brookman, trans. New Brunswick; London: Transaction Publishers.

Holewinska-Lapinska, E. (1995). The legal procedures for adopting children in Poland by local citizens and foreign nationals. In *Intercountry Adoptions: Laws and Perspectives of "Sending" Countries*, E. D. Jaffe, ed. Dordrecht; Boston; London: Martinus Nijhoff Publishers, pp. 73-94.

Hollinger, J. H. (1993). Adoption law. *The Future of Children*, vol. 3, No. 1, pp. 43-61. Available from http://www.futureofchildren.org/usr_doc/vol3no1ent ire_journal.PDF (accessed 30 October 2006).

Holman, R. (1973). *Trading in Children: a Study of Private Fostering*. London; Boston: Routledge and Kegan Paul.

Holt, M. I. (1992). *The Orphan Trains: Placing Out in America*. Lincoln: University of Nebraska Press.

Howard, A., and J. Kirkpatrick (1989). Social organization. In *Developments in Polynesian Ethnology*, A. Howard and R. Borofsky, eds. Honolulu: University of Hawaii Press, pp. 47-94.

Huard, L. A. (1956). The law of adoption: ancient and modern. *The Vanderbilt Law Review,* vol. 9, pp. 743-763.

Hübner, R. (1918). *A History of Germanic Private Law.* F. S. Philbrick, trans. Boston: Little, Brown, and Company.

Hunecke, V. (1987). *Die Findelkinder von Mailand: Kindsaussetzung und Aussetzende Eltern vom 17. bis zum 19 Jh.* Stuttgart: Klett-Cotta.

International Social Service (ISS) and United Nations Children's Fund (UNICEF) (2004a). Improving protection for children without parental care. Kinship care: an issue for international standards. Geneva; New York. Available from http://www.unicef.org/videoaudio/PDFs/kinship_note.pdf (accessed 30 October 2006).

_____ (2004b). Care for children affected by HIV/AIDS: the urgent need for international standards. Geneva; New York. Available from http://www.unicef.org/protection/files/HIV_NOTE_FINAL.pdf (accessed 30 October 2006).

Ireland, The Adoption Board (2004). *Report of An Bord Uchtála 2003.* Dublin: The Stationery Office. Available from http://www.adoptionboard.ie/booklets/adoption_report_nov_25.pdf (accessed 27 October 2006).

Italy, Ministry of Justice (2003). *Disciplina dell'Adozione e dell'Affidamento dei Minori negli Anni 1993-1999,* Analisi Statistica. Rome. Available from http://www.giustizia.it/statistiche/statistiche_dgm/analisi_statistiche/adoz1993_99.htm (accessed 27 October 2006).

Italy, Ministry of Labour and Social Policies (2003). Legge 24 novembre 2003, n. 326, "Conversione in legge, con modificazioni, del decreto-legge 30 settembre 2003, n. 269, recante disposizioni urgenti per favorire lo sviluppo e per la correzione dell'andamento dei conti pubblici". Available from https://sistemats.sanita.finanze.it/simossDocumentation/normativa/Legge_24_novembre_2003.pdf (accessed 29 October 2006).

Italy, National Statistical Institute (2005). Le coppie che chiedono l'adozione di un bambino. Anno 2003. Available from http://www.istat.it/salastampa/comunicati/non_calendario/20050201_01/testo integrale.pdf (accessed 26 October 2006).

Italy, Office of the Prime Minister, Commission for Intercountry Adoption (2004). Coppie e bambini nelle adozioni internazionali. Florence: UNICEF Innocenti Research Centre. Available from http://www.commissioneadozioni.it/FileServices/Download.aspx?id=83 (accessed 27 October 2006).

_____ (2005). Coppie e bambini nelle adozioni internazionali. Florence: UNICEF Innocenti Research Centre.

_____ (2006). Coppie e bambini nelle adozioni internazionali. Florence: UNICEF Innocenti Research Centre. Available from http://www.commissioneadozioni.it/FileServices/Download.aspx?ID=244 (accessed 02 October 2007).

Ito, K.L. (1999). *Lady Friends: Hawaiian Ways and the Ties that Define.* Ithaca, New York: Cornell University Press.

Jaffe, E.D. (1991). Foreign adoptions in Israel: private paths to parenthood. In *Intercountry Adoption: a Multinational Perspective*, H. Altstein and R. Simon, eds. New York: Praeger, pp. 161-182.

Jamaica, Supreme Court (2003). Claim No. HCV 0343/2003. Available from http://www.sc.gov.jm/Judgments/sc/HCV0343_2003.pdf (accessed 30 October 2006).

Johns, C.H.W. (1910-1911). Babylonian law—The Code of Hammurabi. In *Encyclopedia Britannica*, 11th ed. Cambridge, United Kingdom: Cambridge University Press.

Johnson, K. (2002). Politics of international and domestic adoption in China. *Law and Society Review*, vol. 36, No. 2, pp. 379-396.

_____ and others (1998). Infant abandonment and adoption in China. *Population and Development Review*, vol. 24, No. 3, pp. 469-510.

Joint United Nations Programme on HIV/AIDS (UNAIDS), United Nations Children's Fund (UNICEF) and US Agency for International Development (USAID) (2004). *Children on the Brink 2004. A Joint Report of New Orphan Estimates and a Framework for Action.* New York: UNICEF. Available from http://www.unicef.org/publications/files/cob_layout6-013.pdf (accessed 30 October 2006).

Junjian, J. (1999). Legislation related to the civil economy in the Qing dynasty. In *Civil Law in Qing and Republican China*, K. Bernhardt and P. Huang, eds. Stanford: Stanford University Press, pp. 42-84.

Jussen, B. (2000). *Spiritual Kinship as Social Practice: Godparenthood and Adoption in the Early Middle Ages.* P. Selwyn, trans. Cranbury; London: Associated University Presses.

Kane, S. (1993). The movement of children for international adoption: an epidemiological perspective. *The Social Science Journal*, vol. 30, No. 4, pp. 323-339.

Karayanni, M. (2005). The religious matching requirement under Israeli adoption law: a historical ontology. Paper presented at "Multiculturalism and the Antidiscrimination Principle" Conference of Ramat-Gan College Law, Ramat-Gan, on December 10-12. Available from http://rg-law.ac.il/workshops/2005/articles/micael.pdf (accessed 30 October 2006).

Kertzer, D. I. (1991). Gender ideology and infant abandonment in nineteenth-century Italy. *Journal of Interdisciplinary History*, vol. 22, No. 1 (Summer), pp. 1-25.

_____ (2000). The lives of foundlings in nineteenth-century Italy. In *Abandoned Children*, C. Panter-Brick and M.T. Smith, eds. Cambridge; New York: Cambridge University Press, pp. 41-56.

King, L. W., trans. (1910). *The Code of Hammurabi*. Available from http://www.yale.edu/lawweb/avalon/medieval/hamframe.htm (accessed 30 October 2006).

Knitzer, J. (2001). Federal and State efforts to improve care for infants and toddlers. *The Future of Children*, vol. 11, No. 1, Caring for Infants and Toddlers. (Spring - Summer), pp. 79-97.

Kociumbas, J. (1997). *Australian Childhood: a History*. St. Leonards: Allen and Unwin.

Kornitzer, M. (1952). *Child Adoption in the Modern World*. New York, Philosophical Library.

Kuehn, T. (1999). Adoption in late medieval Florence. *Revues Médiévales*, No. 35, pp. 69-81.

Laming, L. (2003). *The Victoria Climbié Inquiry*. London: Stationery Office.

Latvia, Ministry for Children and Family Affairs (2007). *Adoption to Foreign Countries on 1st November, 2006*. Available from http://www.bm.gov.lv/eng/adoption/statistics/?doc=4998 (accessed 07 December 2007).

Leasure, J. W. (1963). Malthus, marriage and multiplication. *The Milbank Memorial Fund Quarterly*, vol. 41, No. 4, Part 1, pp. 419-435.

Lilani, K. (1995). Adoption of children from India. In *Intercountry Adoptions: Laws and Perspectives of "Sending" Countries*, E. D. Jaffe, ed. Dordrecht; Boston; London: Martinus Nijhoff Publishers, pp. 23-38.

Lisk, I. E. (1992). The Adoption Act of Sierra Leone. *Journal of African Law*, vol. 36, No. 1 (Spring), pp. 28-42.

Liu, J., U. Larsen and G. Wyshak (2004). Factors affecting adoption in China, 1950-1987. *Population Studies,* vol. 58, No. 1, pp. 21-36.

Livi Bacci, M. (2001). Comment: desired family size and the future course of fertility. *Population and Development Review*, vol. 27, Supplement: Global Fertility Transition, pp. 282-289.

Long, G. (1878). Adoptio. In *A dictionary of Greek and Roman Antiquities*, W. Smith, ed. London: John Murray, pp. 14-16.

Love, C. (2000). Cultural origins, sharing, and appropriation: a Maori reflection. In *Family Group Conferencing: New Directions in Community-Centered Child and Family Practice*, G. Burford and J. Hudson, eds. New York: Aldine de Gruyter, pp. 15-30.

Lovelock, K. (2000). Intercountry adoption as a migratory practice: a comparative analysis of intercountry adoption and immigration policy and practice in the United States, Canada and New Zealand in the post W.W. II period. *International Migration Review,* vol. 34, No. 3, pp. 907-949.

Lowe, N. (2000). English adoption law: past, present, and future. In *Cross Currents: Family Law and Policy in the United States and England*, S.N. Katz and others, eds. Oxford; New York: Oxford University Press, pp. 307-340.

Luxembourg, Central Service of Statistics and Economic Studies. (2006). *Statistiques des Adoptions 1997-2006*. Available from http://www.statistiques.public.lu/stat/TableViewer/tableView.aspx?ReportId=1162 (accessed 04 December 2007).

MacCormack, G. (1996). *The Spirit of Traditional Chinese Law*. Athens, Georgia: University of Georgia Press.

Maine, H. S. (1861). *Ancient Law: Its Connection with the Early History of Society, and Its Relation to Modern Ideas*. London: John Murray.

Maluccio, A. (1986). *Permanency Planning for Children*. London: Tavistock.

Mannes, M. (1995). Factors and events leading to the passage of the Indian Child Welfare Act. *Child Welfare*, vol. 74, No. 1, pp. 264-282.

Marshall, A., and M. McDonald (2001). *The Many-sided Triangle: Adoption in Australia*. Carlton South, Victoria, Australia: Melbourne University Press.

Masson, J. (2001). Intercountry adoption: a global problem or a global solution? *Journal of International Affairs*, vol. 55, No. 1, pp. 141-166.

Mather, M. (2001). Adoption. *British Medical Journal*, vol. 322, No. 7302 (30 June), pp. 1556-1557.

Matshalaga, N. R. and G. Powell (2002). Mass orphanhood in the era of HIV/AIDS. Bold support for alleviation of poverty and education may avert a social disaster. *British Medical Journal,* vol. 324, No. 7331 (26 January), pp. 185-186.

Maurice, P. (1999). The adoption and donation of children in Gévaudan in the late Middle Ages. *Revues Médiévales*, No. 35.

Mayne, J. D. (1892). *A treatise on Hindu Law and Usage*. Madras: Higginbotham.

McIntyre, J. P. (2000). The Canonical condition of physical persons. In *New Commentary on the Code of Canon Law*, J.A. Beal and others, eds. New York: Paulist Press, pp. 140-153.

McMullen, I. J. (1975). Non-agnatic adoption: a Confucian controversy in seventeenth- and eighteenth-century Japan. *Harvard Journal of Asiatic Studies*, vol. 35, pp. 133-189.

Mehta, N. (2002). An overview of child adoption in India: background, current scenario and future challenges. Paper presented at the Fourth International Conference on Adoption, New Delhi, October.

Melosh, B. (2002). *Strangers and Kin: The American Way of Adoption*. Cambridge, Massachusetts: Harvard University Press.

Muirhead, J., ed./trans. (1880). *The Institutes of Gaius and Rules of Ulpian: the Former Studemund's Apograph of the Verona Code*. Edinburgh: T. and T. Clark.

Mullender, A., ed. (1991). *Open Adoption: The Philosophy and Practice*. London: British Association for Adoption and Fostering.

Nakamura, H. (1964). *Ways of Thinking of Eastern Peoples: India, China, Tibet, Japan*. P.P. Wiener, ed. Honolulu, Hawaii: East-West Center Press.

Netherlands, Statistics Netherlands (2005). Adoptions from China continue to rise. Web Magazine. Available from http://www.cbs.nl/en-GB/menu/themas/bevolking/publicaties/artikelen/archief/200 5/2005-1722-wm.htm (accessed 30 October 2006).

New Zealand, Department of Child, Youth and Family Services (2005). Response to the 2005 questionnaire on the practical operation of the Hague Convention of 29 May 1993 on Protection of ' Children and Co-operation in Respect of Intercountry adoption.

New Zealand, Law Commission (1999). Adoption: options for reform. *Preliminary Paper*, No. 38. Wellington. Available from http://www.lawcom. govt.nz/UploadFiles/Publications/Publication_72_ 143_PP38.pdf (accessed 23 October 2006).

_____ (2000). Adoption and its alternatives: a different approach and a new framework. *New Zealand Law Commission Report*, No. 65. Wellington. Available from http://www.lawcom. govt.nz/UploadFiles/Publications/Publication_72_ 144_R65.pdf?ProjectID=72 (accessed 23 October 2006).

_____ (2006). Access to court records–terms of reference. *New Zealand Law Commission Report*, No. 93. Wellington. Available from http://www.law com.govt.nz/UploadFiles/Publications/Publication_ 119_330_R93.pdf (accessed 04 December 2007).

New Zealand, Ministry of Justice (2005). Introduction to the Care of Children Act. Wellington. Available from http://www.justice.govt.nz/family/what-family court-does/children/introduction.asp (accessed 30 October 2006).

Nock, S. L. (1994). Abortion, adoption, and marriage: alternative resolutions of an unwanted pregnancy. *Family Relations*, vol. 43, No. 3, pp. 277-279.

Norway, Statistics Norway (2004a). Adoptions, 2004. Available from http://www.ssb.no/vis/english/ subjects/02/02/10/adopsjon_en/art-2005-06-16-01-en.html (accessed 18 January 2006).

_____ (2004b). Population statistics. Marriages and divorces. Available from http://www.ssb.no/ skilsmisse_en/arkiv/tab-2005-09-01-03-en.html (accessed 30 October 2006).

Notermans, C. (2004). Fosterage and the politics of marriage and kinship in East Cameroon. In *Cross-Cultural Approaches to Adoption*, F. Bowie, ed. London; New York: Routledge, pp. 48-63.

O'Connor, S. (2001). *Orphan Trains: The Story of Charles Loring Brace and the Children he Saved and Failed*. Boston: Houghton Mifflin.

O'Halloran, K. (2006). *The Politics of Adoption: International Perspectives on Law, Policy and Practice*. Dordrecht, The Netherlands: Springer.

Organization of American States, General Secretariat, (1984). Inter-American Convention on Conflict of Laws Concerning the Adoption of Minors, *Treaty Series*, No. 62.

Palmer, M. J. E. (1989). Civil adoption in contemporary Chinese law: a contract to care. *Modern Asian Studies*, vol. 23, No. 2, pp. 373-410.

Parkinson, P. (2003). Child protection, permanency planning and children's right to family life. *International Journal of Law, Policy and the Family*, vol. 17, No. 2, pp. 147-172.

Parra-Aranguren, G. (1996). History, philosophy and general structure of the Hague adoption convention. In *Children on the Move: How to Implement Their Right to Family Life*, J.E. Doek and others, eds. The Hague; Boston: Martinus Nijhoff, pp. 63-74.

Pebley, A. R., and C.F. Westoff (1982). Women's sex preferences in the United States: 1970 to 1975. *Demography*, vol. 19, No. 2 (May), pp. 177-189.

Pecora, P. J. and others (2000). *The Child Welfare Challenge: Policy, Practice, and Research, Second Edition*. New York: Aldine de Gruyter.

Peterson, M. A. (1996). *Korean Adoption and Inheritance: Case Studies in the Creation of a Classic Confucian Society*. Ithaca, New York: East Asia Program, Cornell University.

Pitsakis, C. G. (1999). Adoption in Byzantine law. In *Revues Médiévales*, No. 35, pp. 19-32.

Pollack, D. and others (2004). Classical religious perspectives of adoption law. *Notre Dame Law Review*, vol. 79, No. 2, pp. 693-753.

Ransel, D. L. (1988). *Mothers of Misery: Child Abandonment in Russia*. Princeton, New Jersey: Princeton University Press.

Republic of Korea, Ministry of Health and Welfare (2005). Domestic adoption of children increases 5% in 2004.

Republic of Korea, National Statistical Office (2004). *Yearbook of Health and Welfare Statistics*. Seoul: Ministry of Health and Welfare.

Riis, J. A. (1890). *How the Other Half Lives: Studies Among the Tenements of New York*. New York: Charles Scribner's Sons.

Roby, J., and S. Matsumara (2002). If I give you my child, aren't we family? A study of birthmothers participating in Marshall Islands-U.S. adoptions. *Adoption Quarterly,* vol. 5, No. 4, pp. 7-31.

Rocher, L. (1987). Can a murderer inherit his victim's estate? British responses to troublesome questions in Hindu law. *Journal of the American Oriental Society*, vol. 107, No. 1, pp. 1-10.

Rockell, J., and M. Ryburn (1988). *Adoption Today: Change and Choice in New Zealand*. Auckland: Heinemann Reed.

Rodriguez, G., and J. Cleland. (1981). The effects of socioeconomic characteristics on fertility in 20 countries. *International Family Planning Perspectives*, vol. 7, No. 3, pp. 93-101.

Roesch-Rhomberg, I. (2004). Korean institutionalised adoption. In *Cross-cultural Approaches to Adoption*, F. Bowie, ed. London; New York: Routledge, pp. 81-96.

Romania, Ministry of Labour, Social Solidarity and Family (2005). *Statistical Bulletin in the Field of Labour, Social Solidarity and Family*, No. 1 (49). Bucharest. Available from http://www.insse.ro/cms/files/pdf/ro/cap6.pdf (accessed 2 October 2007).

Romania, National Institute of Statistics (2004). *Romanian Statistical Yearbook 2004*. Bucharest.

Rosenwald, T. (2004). From the trenches of the war on adoption in Australia. Paper presented at "Knowledge into Action" Conference of the Association of Children's Welfare Agencies, Sydney, Australia, 2-4 August. Available from http://www.acwa.asn.au/Conf2004/acwa2004papers/15_McCullagh_War.pdf (accessed 30 October 2006).

Roumy, F. (1999). Adoptio naturam imitatur: the scope and consequences of an Aristotelian maxim in medieval juridical thought (twelfth-fifteenth centuries). In *Revues Médiévales*, No. 35, pp. 51-60.

Rubenstein, L. (1993). *Adoption in IV Century Athens*. Copenhagen: Museum Tusculanum Press.

Rutstein, S. O., and I. H. Shah (2004). *Infecundity, Infertility, and Childlessness in Developing Countries*. DHS Comparative Reports No. 9. Calverton, Maryland: ORC Macro and the World Health Organization. Available from http://www.measuredhs.com/pubs/pdf/CR9/CR9.pdf (accessed 10 October 2006).

Rwezaura, B. A., and U. Wanitzek (1988). The law and practices relating to the adoption of children in Tanzania. *Journal of African Law*, vol. 32, No. 2, pp. 124-163.

Sandars, T.C. (1905). *The Institutes of Justinian: With English Introduction, Translation and Notes*. London: Longmans, Green.

Santinelli, E. (1999). Continuity or fracture? Adoption in Merovingian law. *Revues Médiévales*, No. 35, pp. 9-18.

Sargent, C. and M. Harris (1992). Gender ideology, childrearing, and child health in Jamaica. *American Ethnologist*, vol. 19, No. 3 (August), pp. 523-537.

Save Abandoned Babies Foundation (2006). *Legislative summary of Illinois' Abandoned Newborn Infant Protection Act*. Available from http://www.saveabandonedbabies.org/summary.html (accessed 30 October 2006).

Selman, P. (1976). Patterns of Adoption in England and Wales since 1959. *Social Work Today*, vol. 7, No. 7, pp. 194-197.

_____ (1988). Family Planning. *Reviews of UK Statistical Sources Series*, vol. XXV, Royal Statistical Society and the Economic and Social Research Council, London: Chapman and Hall.

_____ (1998). Intercountry adoption in Europe after the Hague Convention. In *Developments in European Social Policy: Convergence and Diversity*, R. Sykes and P. Alcock, eds. Bristol, United Kingdom: Policy Press, pp. 147-170.

_____, ed. (2000). *Intercountry adoption: Developments, Trends and Perspectives*. London: Skyline House/British Association for Adoption and Fostering.

_____ (2002). Intercountry adoption in the new millennium; the "quiet" migration revisited. *Population Research and Policy Review*, vol. 21, No. 3, pp. 205-225.

_____ (2004). Adoption: a cure for (too) many ills? In *Cross-Cultural Approaches to Adoption,* F. Bowie, ed. London; New York: Routledge, pp. 257-273.

_____ (2006). Towards demography of adoption: making sense of official statistics on child adoption and the search for origins. Paper presented at the Second International Conference on Adoption Research, University of East Anglia, 17-21 July.

Serbia and Montenegro, Statistical Office (2004). *Statistical Yearbook of Serbia and Montenegro*. Belgrade.

Shanley, M. L. (1989). *Feminism, Marriage, and the Law in Victorian England, 1850–1895*. Princeton, New Jersey: Princeton University Press.

Shapiro, V. B. and others (2001). *Complex Adoption and Assisted Reproductive Technology: A Developmental Approach to Clinical Practice*. New York: The Guilford Press.

Sheps, M. C. (1963). Effects on family size and sex ratio of preferences regarding the sex of children. *Population Studies*, vol. 17, No. 1 (July), pp. 66-72.

Silk, J. B. (1980). Adoption and kinship in Oceania. *American Anthropologist*, vol. 82, No. 4, pp. 799-820.

_____ (1987). Adoption among the Inuit. *Ethos*, vol. 15, No. 3. (September), pp. 320-330.

Silverman, A. R. (1993). Outcomes of transracial adoption. *The Future of Children*, vol. 3, No. 1, pp. 104-118. Available from http://www.futureof children.org/usr_doc/vol3no1entire_journal.PDF (accessed 30 October 2006).

Simmance, A. J. F. (1959). The adoption of children among the Kikuyu of Kiambu District. *Journal of African Law*, vol. 3, No. 1, pp. 33-38.

Simon, R., and H. Altstein (2002). *Adoption, Race, and Identity: From Infancy to Young Adulthood*. New Brunswick, New Jersey: Transaction Publishers.

Smith, C. R., and J. Logan (2003). *After Adoption: Direct Contact and Relationships*. London: Routledge.

Sobol, M., and K. Daly (1994). Canadian adoption statistics: 1981-1990. *Journal of Marriage and the Family*, vol. 56, No. 2 (May), pp. 493-499.

Sokoloff, B. Z. (1993). Antecedents of American adoption. *The Future of Children*, vol. 3, No. 1, pp. 17-25. Available from http://www.futureof children.org/usr_doc/vol3no1entire_journal.PDF (accessed 30 October 2006).

Spain, Ministry of Labour and Social Affairs (2001). *Estadísticas sobre Adopción Internacional*. Madrid. Available from http://www.mtas.es/SGAS/ FamiliaInfanc/infancia/Adopcion/EstadisAdopcion Intern.htm (accessed 30 October 2006).

_____ (2005). *Estadísticas sobre Adopción Internacional*. Madrid. Available from http://www. mtas.es/SGAS/FamiliaInfanc/infancia/Adopcion/ Adopcion.pdf (accessed 30 October 2006).

_____ (2007). *Adopción Internacional*. Available from http://www.mae.es/es/MenuPpal/Consulares/ Servicios+Consulares/Espa%C3%B1oles+en+el +extranjero/Adopcion+Internacional/ (accessed 07 November 2007).

Spence, G., trans. (1827). *The French Civil Code*. London: William Benning.

Stash, S. (1996). Ideal-family-size and sex-composition preferences among wives and husbands in Nepal. *Studies in Family Planning*, vol. 27, No. 2 (March), pp. 107-118.

Steltzner, D. M. (2003). Intercountry adoption: toward a regime that recognizes the "best interests" of adoptive parents. *Case Western Reserve Journal of International Law*, vol. 35, No. 1, pp. 113-152.

Stolley, K. S. (1993). Statistics on adoption in the United States. *The Future of Children*, vol. 3, No. 1, pp. 26-42. Available from http://www.futureof children.org/usr_doc/vol3no1entire_journal.PDF (accessed 30 October 2006).

_____ and E.J. Hall (1994). The presentation of abortion and adoption in marriage and family textbooks. *Family Relations*, vol. 43, No. 3, pp. 267-273.

Strong, B., and C. DeVault (1994). Response to Stolley and Hall. *Family Relations*, vol. 43, No. 3 (July), pp. 274-276.

Subbarao, K., and D. Coury. (2004). *Reaching Out to Africa's Orphans: A Framework for Public Action*. Washington, D.C.: World Bank. Available from http://siteresources.worldbank.org/INTHIVAIDS/ Resources/375798-1103037153392/ReachingOutto AfricasOrphans.pdf (accessed 3 October 2007).

Sweden, National Board for Intercountry Adoption (2005). Survey of the number of foreign adoptive children placed into Swedish families over the years 1969-2003 by countries of origin.

Sweden, Statistics Sweden (2005). *Statistical Yearbook of Sweden 2006*. Edita Norstedts Tryckeri AB: Stockholm. Available from http://www.scb.se/ templates/Standard____155777.asp (accessed 26 October 2006).

Switzerland, Swiss Federal Statistical Office (2004). *Statistical Yearbook of Switzerland 2004*. Neuchâtel: Editions Verlag Neue Zürcher Zeitung.

Talle, A. (2004). Adoption practices among the pastoral Masai of East Africa: enacting fertility. In *Cross-Cultural Approaches to Adoption,* F. Bowie, ed. London; New York: Routledge, pp. 64-78.

Teodorescu, A. G. (2005) The Functioning of the new legislation on adoptions and provisions on defining the procedures in the moratorium. Paper presented at the Joint Parliamentary Committee European Union, Brussels, 22-23 November. Available from http://www.cdep.ro/docs_comisii/IE/CPM19_tema 6_EN.pdf (accessed 26 October 2006).

Tessler, R., and Y. Ning (2001). How Chinese people feel about Americans adopting Chinese children. Paper presented at the Annual Meeting of the Eastern Sociological Society, March. Available from http://www.fccny.org/newsletter/default.asp?30 (accessed 30 October 2006).

Thatcher, O. J., ed./trans. (1907). Adoption. In *The Library of Original Sources,* vol. 3. London; New York: University Research Extension, pp. 109-111.

Tizard, B. (1977). *Adoption: A Second Chance*. London: Open Books.

Tolfree, D. (1995). *Roofs and Roots: The Care of Separated Children in the Developing World*. Aldershot: Arena.

Triseliotis, J. and others (1997). *Adoption: Theory, Policy and Practice*. London: Cassell.

United Kingdom, British Association for Adoption and Fostering (2006a). *Summary Statistics on Children in Care and Children Adopted from Care, and Searching for Birth Relatives in England.* Available from http://www.baaf.org.uk/info/stats/england.shtml (accessed 8 December 2006).

_____ (2006b). *Summary Statistics on Children in Care and Children Adopted from Care, and Searching for Birth Relatives in Wales.* Available from http://www.baaf.org.uk/info/stats/wales.shtml (accessed 8 December 2006).

United Kingdom, Department for Education and Skills (2005). *Adoption Statistics: Intercountry Adoptions in the United Kingdom.* London. Available from http://www.dfes.gov.uk/adoption/adoptionreforms/statistics.shtml (accessed 10 October 2005).

United Kingdom, Office for National Statistics (2002). *Marriage, Divorce and Adoption Statistics.* Review of the Registrar General on marriages, divorces and adoptions in England and Wales, 2000. Series FM2 No. 28. London: The Stationery Office. Available from http://www.statistics.gov.uk/downloads/theme_population/FM2_2000/FM2_28_v2.pdf (accessed 3 October 2007).

_____ (2004). *Annual Abstract of Statistics, 2004 Edition.* London: The Stationery Office. Available from http://www.statistics.gov.uk/downloads/theme_compendia/Aa2004/AA2004.pdf (accessed 30 October 2006).

_____ (2007). *Marriage, Divorce and Adoption Statistics.* Review of the Registrar General on marriages and divorces in 2004, and adoptions in 2005, in England and Wales. Series FM2 No. 32. London: The Stationery Office. Available from http://www.statistics.gov.uk/downloads/theme_population/FM2no32/FM2_32.pdf (accessed 3 October 2007).

United Nations (1953). *Biennial Report on Family, Child and Youth Welfare 1949-1950, United Kingdom of Great Britain and Northern Ireland,* p. 7. United Nations publication ST/SOA/SER.D/2.

_____ (1956). *Comparative Analysis of Adoption Laws.* United Nations publication, Sales No. 1956.IV.5.

_____ (1975a). *Treaty Series,* vol. 989, No. 14458, p. 175,

_____ (1975b). *Report of the United Nations World Population Conference, Bucharest, 19-30 August 1974.* United Nations publication, Sales No.: E.75.XIII.3.

_____ (1990). *Treaty Series,* vol. 1577, No. 27531, p. 3.

_____ (1995). *Report of the International Conference on Population and Development, Cairo, 5-13 September 1994.* United Nations publication, Sales No. E.95.XIII.18, chap. I, resolution 1, annex.

_____ (1998a). *Standard Country or Area Codes for Statistical Use, Revision 4.* United Nations publication, Sales No. 98.XVII.9.

_____ (1998b). *Recommendations on Statistics of International Migration, Revision 1.* United Nations publication, Series M, No.58/Rev.1, Sales No. 98.XVII.14.

_____ (1999). *Demographic Yearbook Historical Supplement 1948-1997.* United Nations publication, Sales No. E/F.99.XIII.12.

_____ (2001). *Principles and Recommendations for a Vital Statistics System, Revision 2.* United Nations publication, Sales No. 01.XVII.10.

_____ (2002). *Treaty Series,* vol. 2171, No. 27531, p. 227.

_____ (2003). *Manual for the Development of a System of Criminal Justice Statistics.* United Nations publication, Series F, No. 89, Sales No. 03.XVII.6. Available from http://unstats.un.org/unsd/publication/SeriesF/SeriesF_89E.pdf (accessed 30 October 2006).

_____ (2004a). *World Fertility Report 2003.* United Nations publication, Sales No. E.04.XIII.10. Available from http://www.un.org/esa/population/publications/worldfertility/World_Fertility_Report.htm (accessed 30 October 2006).

_____ (2004b). *World Population Monitoring 2002. Reproductive Rights and Reproductive Health.* United Nations publication, Sales No. E.02.XIII.14. Available from http://www.un.org/esa/population/publications/2003monitoring/WorldPopMonitoring_2002.pdf (accessed 27 October 2006).

_____ (2005). *World Population Prospects: The 2004 Revision.* Population database Available from http://esa.un.org/unpp/ (accessed 30 October 2006).

_____ (2006a). *World Contraceptive Use 2006.* (database).

_____ (2006b). *Demographic Yearbook 2003* United Nations publication, Sales No. E/F.06.XIII.1. Available from http://unstats.un.org/unsd/demographic/products/dyb/dyb2003.htm (accessed 27 October 2006).

_____ (2006c). *Demographic Yearbook.* (database).

_____ (2007). *World Abortion Policies 2006.* United Nations publication, Sales No. E.07.XIII.6. Available from http://www.un.org/esa/population/publications/2007_Abortion_Policies_Chart/2007_WallChart.pdf (accessed 3 October 2007).

_____ (Forthcoming). *Childlessness Worldwide: Fate or Choice?*

United Nations Children's Fund (UNICEF) (1998). Intercountry Adoption. *Innocenti Digest* (Florence), No. 4. Available from http://www.unicef-icdc.org/publications/pdf/digest4e.pdf (accessed 29 October 2006).

_____ (2001). *A Decade of Transition. Regional Monitoring Report*, No. 8. Florence: UNICEF Innocenti Research Centre. Available from http://www.unicef-irc.org/publications/pdf/monee8/eng/cover_monee8.pdf (accessed 29 October 2006).

_____ (2003a). *Africa's Orphaned Generations.* New York. Available from http://www.unicef.org/media/files/orphans.pdf (accessed 24 October 2006).

_____ (2003b). Intercountry adoption: trends and consequences. In *Innocenti Social Monitor 2003*. Florence: UNICEF Innocenti Research Centre. Available from http://www.unicef-irc.org/publications/pdf/monitor03/monitor2003.pdf (accessed 24 October 2006).

_____ (2003c). Situation analysis of children and women in Latvia 2003. Republic of Latvia National Committee for UNICEF. Riga: Republic of Latvia National Committee for UNICEF.

United States, Administration for Children and Families (2005). How many children were in foster care on September 30, 2003? 520,000. *AFCARS Report*, No. 10. Washington, D.C.: Department of Health and Human Services. Available from http://www.acf.hhs.gov/programs/cb/stats_research/afcars/tar/report10.htm (accessed 27 October 2006).

_____ (2006). How many children were in foster care on September 30, 2005? 513,000. *AFCARS Report*, No. 13. Washington, D.C.: Department of Health and Human Services. Available from http://www.acf.hhs.gov/programs/cb/stats_research/afcars/tar/report13.pdf (accessed 27 October 2006).

United States, Bureau of the Census (2003). Adopted Children and Stepchildren: 2000. *Census 2000 Special Reports*. Available from http://www.census.gov/prod/2003pubs/censr-6.pdf (accessed 30 October 2006).

United States, Bureau of Consular Affairs (2006). Immigrant visas issued to orphans coming to the U.S. Washington, D.C.: Department of State. Available from http://travel.state.gov/family/adoption/stats/stats_451.html (accessed 27 October 2006).

United States, Child Welfare Information Gateway (2004a). *Access to Family Information by Adopted Persons: Summary of State Laws*. Washington, D.C.: Department of Health and Human Services. Available from http://www.childwelfare.gov/systemwide/laws_policies/statutes/infoaccessapall.pdf (accessed 23 October 2006).

_____ (2004b). *Infant Safe Haven Laws: Summary of State Laws*. Washington, D.C.: Department of Health and Human Services. Available from http://www.childwelfare.gov/systemwide/laws_policies/statutes/safehaven.pdf (accessed 23 October 2006).

_____ (2004c). *How Many Children were Adopted in 2000 and 2001?* Washington, D.C.: Department of Health and Human Services. Available from http://www.childwelfare.gov/pubs/s_adopted/index.cfm (accessed 23 October 2006).

_____ (2005). *Voluntary Relinquishment for Adoption: Numbers and Trends*. Washington, D.C.: Department of Health and Human Services. Available from http://www.childwelfare.gov/pubs/s_place.pdf (accessed 23 October 2006).

United States, Department of State (2005). *Trafficking in Persons Report*. Washington, D.C.: Department of State. Available from http://www.state.gov/g/tip/rls/tiprpt/2005/ (accessed 27 October 2006).

Van Bueren, G. (1995a). Children's access to adoption records: state discretion or an enforceable international right? *The Modern Law Review*, vol. 58, No. 1, pp. 37-53.

_____ (1995b). *The International Law on the Rights of the Child*. Dordrecht; Boston; London: Martinus Nijhoff Publishers.

Van Loon, J. H. A. (1990). Report on Intercountry Adoption. The Hague, Netherlands: Hague Conference on Private International Law, Proceedings of the Seventeenth Session, Vol. II, pp. 37-39.

_____ (1995). Hague Convention of 29 May 1993 on Protection of Children and Co-operation in Respect of Intercountry Adoption. *International Journal of Children's Rights*, vol. 3, pp. 463-468.

Varnis, S. L. (2001). Promoting child protection through community resources: care arrangements for Ethiopian AIDS orphans. *Northeast African Studies*, vol. 8, No. 1, pp. 143-158.

Vaskis, E., co-ordinator (2000). Trends and indicators on child and family well-being in Latvia. Background paper prepared for *A Decade of Transition. Regional Monitoring Report*, No. 8. Riga, Latvia: Central Statistical Bureau of Latvia; and Florence, Italy: UNICEF Innocenti Research Centre.

_____ (2001). Poverty and welfare trends in Latvia over the 1990s. Background paper prepared for the *Innocenti Social Monitor, 2002*. Riga, Latvia: Central Statistical Bureau of Latvia and Florence, Italy: UNICEF Innocenti Research Centre.

Verdon, M. (1988). Virgins and widows: European kinship and early Christianity. *Man,* vol. 23, No. 3, pp. 488-505.

Viazzo, P. P. and others. (2000). Five centuries of foundling history in Florence: changing patterns of abandonment, care and mortality. In *Abandoned Children*, C. Panter-Brick and M. T. Smith, eds. Cambridge, United Kingdom: Cambridge University Press.

Vikat, A. and others (1999). Stepfamily fertility in contemporary Sweden: the impact of childbearing before the Current Union. *Population Studies*, vol. 53, No. 2 (July), pp. 211-225.

Vonk, M. J. (2006). Tensions between legal, biological and social conceptions of parentage. In *Netherlands Reports to the seventeenth International Congress ofComparative Law*, J. H. M. Van Erp, and L. P. W. Van Vliet, eds. Antwerpen; Oxford: Intersentia, pp. 83-108.

Wadlington, W. J. (1966). Minimum age difference as a requisite for adoption. *Duke Law Journal*, vol. 1966, No. 2 (Spring), pp. 392-414.

Waltner, A. (1990). *Getting an Heir: Adoption and the Construction of Kinship in Late Imperial China*. Honolulu, Hawaii: University of Hawaii Press.

Weckler, J. E. (1953). Adoption on Mokil. *American Anthropologist*, vol. 55, No. 4. (October), pp. 555-568.

Weil, R. H. (1984). International adoptions: the quiet migration. *International Migration Review*, vol. 18, No. 2, pp. 276-293.

Weinstein, E. (1968). Adoption. In *International Encyclopaedia of the Social Sciences*. New York: MacMillan.

Western Australia, Law Reform Commission (2002). Succession rights of adopted children. In *Thirtieth Anniversary Reform Implementation Report*, p. 78.

Western Australia, Department for Community Development (2003). Policy for the adoption of children. Available from http://www.aph.gov.au/house/committee/fhs/adoption/subs/sub183attch1.pdf (accessed 30 October 2006).

Whitmore, W. H. (1876). *The Law of Adoption in the United States, and Especially in Massachusetts*. Albany: J. Munsell.

Willetts, R. F. (1977). *The Civilization of Ancient Crete*. London: Batsford.

Wooldridge, M. (2005). *Adopting Ethiopia's AIDS Orphans*. BBC News, Belgium.

Zlidar, V. M., and others (2003). New survey findings: the reproductive revolution continues. *Population Reports*, Series M, No. 17. Baltimore, Johns Hopkins Bloomberg School of Public Health. Available from http://www.infoforhealth.org/pr/m17/m17.pdf (accessed 30 October 2006).

Zugravescu, A., and A. Iacovescu (1995). The adoption of children in Romania. In *Intercountry Adoptions: Laws and Perspectives of "Sending" Countries*, E. D. Jaffe, ed. Dordrecht; Boston; London: Martinus Nijhoff Publishers, pp. 39-52.

COUNTRY PROFILES

Government policies

Type of adoption permitted
    Domestic adoption .... No
    Intercountry adoption... No

Single male permitted to adopt .... Not applicable

Single female permitted to adopt .... Not applicable

Age requirements for adopting parents .... Not applicable

Child's age of consent for adoption .... Not applicable

Year of ratification of legal instruments on child adoption
    Convention on the Rights of the Child...................... 1994
    Hague Convention on Intercountry Adoption .... Not ratified

National legislation governing adoption .... Not applicable

Government body responsible for adoption approval ...... Not applicable

Adoption indicators	Year	Number	Percentage
Total children adopted	...	..	..
Of which:			
Domestic adoptions...	...	..	..
Intercountry adoptions	...	..	..
Of which:			
Adoptions by step-parents or other relatives.............	...	..	..
Adoptions per 100,000 births..	...	..	
Adoptions per 100,000 children under age 18	...	..	
Adoptions per 100,000 children under age 5	...	..	

Demographic indicators	Year	Value
Female singulate mean age at marriage (years)	1979	17.8
Mean age at first birth (years)...	...	...
Total fertility (children per woman).................................	2000-2005	7.5
Percentage of childless women, aged 40 - 44	...	...
Divorce rate (per woman)	...	...

Government policies

Type of adoption permitted
  Domestic adoption .... Yes
  Intercountry adoption.. Yes

Single male permitted to adopt .... Yes

Single female permitted to adopt .... Yes

Age requirements for adopting parents .... At least 18 years older than the child

Child's age of consent for adoption .... Aged 10 years or older

Year of ratification of legal instruments on child adoption
  Convention on the Rights of the Child....................... 1992
  Hague Convention on Intercountry Adoption 2000

National legislation governing adoption .... Family Code; Law No. 7650 of 17 December 1992; Law No. 8624 of 15 June 2000

Government body responsible for adoption approval ...... Judiciary; Albanian Committee for Adoption

Adoption indicators	Year	Number	Percentage
Total children adopted	2003	82	100
Of which:			
Domestic adoptions..	2003	56	68
Intercountry adoptions[1]	2003	26	32
Of which:			
Adoptions by step-parents or other relatives..............	...	...	...
Adoptions per 100,000 births..	2003	154.6	
Adoptions per 100,000 children under age 18	2003	7.7	
Adoptions per 100,000 children under age 5[2]................	2003	18.8	

Demographic indicators	Year	Value
Female singulate mean age at marriage (years)	1989	22.9
Mean age at first birth (years).......................................	1989	24.7
Total fertility (children per woman)..............................	2000-2005	2.3
Percentage of childless women, aged 40 - 44	2002	6.6
Divorce rate (per woman)...	...	...

[1] Based on data from selected receiving countries, the main receiving country: United States of America.
[2] It was assumed that 60 per cent of adoptive children are under age five.

Government policies

Type of adoption permitted
    Domestic adoption .... No
    Intercountry adoption .... No

Single male permitted to adopt .... Not applicable

Single female permitted to adopt .... Not applicable

Age requirements for adopting parents .... Not applicable

Child's age of consent for adoption .... Not applicable

Year of ratification of legal instruments on child adoption
    Convention on the Rights of the Child 1993
    Hague Convention on Intercountry Adoption .... Not ratified

National legislation governing adoption .... Not applicable

Government body responsible for adoption approval ...... Not applicable

Adoption indicators	*Year*	*Number*	*Percentage*
Total children adopted[1]	2004	1 275	100
Of which:			
Domestic adoptions[1]	2004	1 030	81
Intercountry adoptions[1]	2004	245	19
Of which:			
Adoptions by step-parents or other relatives	...	...	...
Adoptions per 100,000 births[1]	2004	189.9	
Adoptions per 100,000 children under age 18[1]	2004	10.5	
Adoptions per 100,000 children under age 5[2]	2004	24.7	

Demographic indicators	*Year*	*Value*
Female singulate mean age at marriage (years)	1992	25.9
Mean age at first birth (years)[3]	1992	24.9
Total fertility (children per woman)	2000-2005	2.5
Percentage of childless women, aged 40 - 44	1992	8.7
Divorce rate (per woman)	...	...

[1] Data refer to children placed through kafalah.
[2] Data refer to children placed through kafalah. It was assumed that 60 per cent of adoptive children are under age five.
[3] Median age at first birth among women aged 25 to 29 years at the date of the survey.

Government policies

Type of adoption permitted[1]	
Domestic adoption	Yes
Intercountry adoption	Yes
Single male permitted to adopt	Yes
Single female permitted to adopt	Yes
Age requirements for adopting parents	...
Child's age of consent for adoption[2]	Aged 12 years or older
Year of ratification of legal instruments on child adoption	
Convention on the Rights of the Child	1996
Hague Convention on Intercountry Adoption	1997
National legislation governing adoption	Qualified Law on Adoption of 21 March 1996; Regulations for Adoption of 10 June 1998
Government body responsible for adoption approval	Judiciary; Adoption Service; Ministry of Foreign Affairs

Adoption indicators	Year	Number	Percentage
Total children adopted	2001-2003	11	100
Of which:			
Domestic adoptions	2001-2003	4	36
Intercountry adoptions[3]	2001-2003	7	64
Of which:			
Adoptions by step-parents or other relatives	...	...	...
Adoptions per 100,000 births	2001-2003	508.6	
Adoptions per 100,000 children under age 18	2001-2003	29.6	
Adoptions per 100,000 children under age 5[4]	2001-2003	60.9	

Demographic indicators	Year	Value
Female singulate mean age at marriage (years)	...	...
Mean age at first birth (years)	...	...
Total fertility (children per woman)	2000-2005	1.3
Percentage of childless women, aged 40 - 44	...	...
Divorce rate (per woman)	...	...

[1] Adopted children must be under 18 years of age.
[2] The views of the adoptive child may be sought from 10 years of age.
[3] Main country of origin: Romania.
[4] It was assumed that 60 per cent of adoptive children are under age five.

Government policies

Type of adoption permitted
    Domestic adoption .... Yes
    Intercountry adoption.. Yes

Single male permitted to adopt ....

Single female permitted to adopt ....

Age requirements for adopting parents ....

Child's age of consent for adoption .... Aged 10 years or older

Year of ratification of legal instruments on child adoption
    Convention on the Rights of the Child...................... 1990
    Hague Convention on Intercountry Adoption .... Not ratified

National legislation governing adoption .... Angolan Adoption Act of 27 August 1980 (Act No. 7/80); Family Code

Government body responsible for adoption approval ...... Judiciary; National Assembly

Adoption indicators	Year	Number	Percentage
Total children adopted	...	...	...
Of which:			
Domestic adoptions...	...	...	...
Intercountry adoptions	...	...	...
Of which:			
Adoptions by step-parents or other relatives..............	...		...
Adoptions per 100,000 births......................................	...	...	
Adoptions per 100,000 children under age 18	...	...	
Adoptions per 100,000 children under age 5	...	...	

Demographic indicators	Year	Value
Female singulate mean age at marriage (years)	1970	19.4
Mean age at first birth (years)..	...	...
Total fertility (children per woman)...............................	2000-2005	6.8
Percentage of childless women, aged 40 - 44	...	...
Divorce rate (per woman)	...	...

Government policies

Type of adoption permitted
    Domestic adoption .... Yes
    Intercountry adoption.. No
Single male permitted to adopt[1] .... Yes
Single female permitted to adopt .... Yes
Age requirements for adopting parents .... Aged 25 years or older and at least 21 years older than the child
Child's age of consent for adoption .... Maturity of child considered
Year of ratification of legal instruments on child adoption
    Convention on the Rights of the Child...................... 1993
    Hague Convention on Intercountry Adoption .... Not ratified
National legislation governing adoption .... Adoption of Children Act
Government body responsible for adoption approval ...... Judiciary

Adoption indicators	Year	Number	Percentage
Total children adopted	...	...	...
Of which:			
Domestic adoptions...	...	...	...
Intercountry adoptions	...	..	..
Of which:			
Adoptions by step-parents or other relatives..............	...	...	...
Adoptions per 100,000 births...	...	...	
Adoptions per 100,000 children under age 18	...	...	
Adoptions per 100,000 children under age 5	...	...	

Demographic indicators	Year	Value
Female singulate mean age at marriage (years)	...	...
Mean age at first birth (years)	...	...
Total fertility (children per woman)..............................	2000-2005	2.2
Percentage of childless women, aged 40 - 44	...	...
Divorce rate (per woman)	...	...

[1] A sole male applicant is not permitted to adopt a girl, except under special circumstances.

Government policies

Type of adoption permitted[1]
  Domestic adoption[2] .... Yes
  Intercountry adoption[3] .... No

Single male permitted to adopt .... Yes

Single female permitted to adopt .... Yes

Age requirements for adopting parents[4] .... Aged 30 years or older and at least 18 years older than the child

Child's age of consent for adoption ....

Year of ratification of legal instruments on child adoption
  Convention on the Rights of the Child 1990
  Hague Convention on Intercountry Adoption .... Not ratified

National legislation governing adoption .... Civil Code; Act No. 24.779 of 28 February 1997

Government body responsible for adoption approval ...... Judiciary; Ministry of Health and Social Welfare

Adoption indicators

	Year	Number	Percentage
Total children adopted	1998	80	100
Of which:			
Domestic adoptions	1998	80	100
Intercountry adoptions	...	..	..
Of which:			
Adoptions by step-parents or other relatives	...	...	...
Adoptions per 100,000 births	1998	11.4	
Adoptions per 100,000 children under age 18	1998	0.7	
Adoptions per 100,000 children under age 5[5]	1998	1.4	

Demographic indicators

	Year	Value
Female singulate mean age at marriage (years)	1991	23.3
Mean age at first birth (years)	1987	23.7
Total fertility (children per woman)	2000-2005	2.4
Percentage of childless women, aged 40 - 44	1980	12.9
Divorce rate (per woman)	...	...

[1] Prospective adoptive parents must have had the child in their care and custody for at least six months prior to the date of the adoption order.
[2] Prospective adoptive parents must have resided in the country for at least five years.
[3] Argentina's legislation does not pronounce against intercountry adoptions granted under the law of another country.
[4] Prospective adoptive parents under age 30 are permitted to adopt if they have been married for at least three years.
[5] It was assumed that 60 per cent of adoptive children are under age five.

Government policies

Type of adoption permitted
    Domestic adoption ....   Yes
    Intercountry adoption...   Yes

Single male permitted to adopt ....   Yes

Single female permitted to adopt ....   Yes

Age requirements for adopting parents ....

Child's age of consent for adoption ....   Aged 10 years or older

Year of ratification of legal instruments on child adoption
    Convention on the Rights of the Child......................   1993
    Hague Convention on Intercountry Adoption ....   Not ratified

National legislation governing adoption ....   Marriage and Family Code; Civil Code

Government body responsible for adoption approval ......   Judiciary; Commission on Adoption Issues; Ministry of Social Welfare

Adoption indicators	Year	Number	Percentage
Total children adopted[1]	2001-2003	415	100
Of which:			
Domestic adoptions[1]	2001-2003	272	66
Intercountry adoptions[1]	2001-2003	143	34
Of which:			
Adoptions by step-parents or other relatives..............	...	...	...
Adoptions per 100,000 births[1]	2001-2003	482.8	
Adoptions per 100,000 children under age 18[1]	2001-2003	17.9	
Adoptions per 100,000 children under age 5[2]	2001-2003	55.9	

Demographic indicators	Year	Value
Female singulate mean age at marriage (years)	2000	23.0
Mean age at first birth (years).......................................	2000	23.0
Total fertility (children per woman)...............................	2000-2005	1.3
Percentage of childless women, aged 40 - 44	2000	10.5
Divorce rate (per woman)	1996	0.08

[1] Data for 2003 refer to the first six months only.
[2] Data for 2003 refer to the first six months only. It was assumed that 60 per cent of adoptive children are under age five.

Government policies

Type of adoption permitted
    Domestic adoption .... Yes
    Intercountry adoption....................................... Yes

Single male permitted to adopt .... Yes

Single female permitted to adopt .... Yes

Age requirements for adopting parents ....

Child's age of consent for adoption .... Maturity of child considered

Year of ratification of legal instruments on child adoption
    Convention on the Rights of the Child....................... 1990
    Hague Convention on Intercountry Adoption 1998

National legislation governing adoption .... Varies by state

Government body responsible for adoption approval ...... Varies by state

Adoption indicators	Year	Number	Percentage
Total children adopted[1]	2003-2004	502	100
Of which:			
Domestic adoptions[1]	2003-2004	132	26
Intercountry adoptions[2]	2003-2004	370	74
Of which:			
Adoptions by step-parents or other relatives[3]	2003-2004	34	25.7
Adoptions per 100,000 births[1]	2003-2004	201.8	
Adoptions per 100,000 children under age 18[1]	2003-2004	10.4	
Adoptions per 100,000 children under age 5[4]	2003-2004	23.8	

Demographic indicators	Year	Value
Female singulate mean age at marriage (years)	2000	28.7
Mean age at first birth (years)...	1996	27.7
Total fertility (children per woman)................................	2000-2005	1.7
Percentage of childless women, aged 40 - 44	1986	9.7
Divorce rate (per woman)	1996	0.33

[1] Data refer to the fiscal year.
[2] Data refer to the fiscal year. Main country of origin: China.
[3] Data refer to domestic adoptions only. The percentage is calculated based on the total number of domestic adoptions. Data refer to the fiscal year.
[4] Data refer to the fiscal year. It was assumed that 60 per cent of adoptive children are under age five.

Government policies

Type of adoption permitted	
Domestic adoption	Yes
Intercountry adoption..	Yes
Single male permitted to adopt	...
Single female permitted to adopt	...
Age requirements for adopting parents	The male adoptive parent must be aged 30 years or older and the female adoptive parent must be aged 28 years or older
Child's age of consent for adoption	Aged 5 years or older
Year of ratification of legal instruments on child adoption	
Convention on the Rights of the Child......................	1992
Hague Convention on Intercountry Adoption	1999
National legislation governing adoption	Civil Code
Government body responsible for adoption approval	Varies by state

Adoption indicators	Year	Number	Percentage
Total children adopted	1999	862	100
Of which:			
Domestic adoptions..	...	...	...
Intercountry adoptions	...	...	...
Of which:			
Adoptions by step-parents or other relatives..............	...	...	...
Adoptions per 100,000 births...	1999	1 075.7	
Adoptions per 100,000 children under age 18	1999	52.3	
Adoptions per 100,000 children under age 5[1]	1999	123.4	

Demographic indicators	Year	Value
Female singulate mean age at marriage (years)	1991	26.1
Mean age at first birth (years).......................................	2001	23.0
Total fertility (children per woman)..............................	2000-2005	1.4
Percentage of childless women, aged 40 - 44	1995-1996	10.1
Divorce rate (per woman)	1997	0.27

[1] It was assumed that 60 per cent of adoptive children are under age five.

Government policies

Type of adoption permitted
    Domestic adoption .... Yes
    Intercountry adoption .... Yes

Single male permitted to adopt[1] .... Yes

Single female permitted to adopt[1] .... Yes

Age requirements for adopting parents ....

Child's age of consent for adoption .... Aged 10 years or older

Year of ratification of legal instruments on child adoption
    Convention on the Rights of the Child...................... 1992
    Hague Convention on Intercountry Adoption 2004

National legislation governing adoption .... Family Code of 28 December 1999

Government body responsible for adoption approval ...... Judiciary; Commission on Adoption Affairs of the Cabinet of Ministers

Adoption indicators	Year	Number	Percentage
Total children adopted[2]	2003-2005	1 930	100
Of which:			
Domestic adoptions[2]	2003-2005	1 787	93
Intercountry adoptions[2]	2003-2005	143	7
Of which:			
Adoptions by step-parents or other relatives..............	...	...	...
Adoptions per 100,000 births[2]	2003-2005	583.8	
Adoptions per 100,000 children under age 18[2]	2003-2005	27.4	
Adoptions per 100,000 children under age 5[3]	2003-2005	76.0	

Demographic indicators	Year	Value
Female singulate mean age at marriage (years)	1999	23.9
Mean age at first birth (years)...	2001	24.7
Total fertility (children per woman).................................	2000-2005	.1.9
Percentage of childless women, aged 40 - 44	2001	13.5
Divorce rate (per woman)..	1996	0.09

[1] Prospective adoptive parents must be at least 16 years older than the child.
[2] Data for 2005 refer to the first six months only.
[3] Data for 2005 refer to the first six months only. It was assumed that 60 per cent of adoptive children are under age five.

Government policies

Type of adoption permitted
    Domestic adoption .... Yes
    Intercountry adoption.. Yes

Single male permitted to adopt .... Yes

Single female permitted to adopt .... Yes

Age requirements for adopting parents[1]........................... Aged 25 years or older and at least 21 years older than the child

Child's age of consent for adoption ....

Year of ratification of legal instruments on child adoption
    Convention on the Rights of the Child...................... 1991
    Hague Convention on Intercountry Adoption .... Not ratified

National legislation governing adoption .... Adoption of Children Act of 1954

Government body responsible for adoption approval ...... Judiciary; Department of Social Services

Adoption indicators	Year	Number	Percentage
Total children adopted	2001	22	100
Of which:			
Domestic adoptions..	2001	14	64
Intercountry adoptions	2001	8	36
Of which:			
Adoptions by step-parents or other relatives..............	...	...	...
Adoptions per 100,000 births.......................................	2001	356.1	
Adoptions per 100,000 children under age 18	2001	20.5	
Adoptions per 100,000 children under age 5[2]..............	2001	43.4	

Demographic indicators	Year	Value
Female singulate mean age at marriage (years)	1990	27.2
Mean age at first birth (years).......................................	1996	23.5
Total fertility (children per woman)...............................	2000-2005	2.3
Percentage of childless women, aged 40 - 44	1990	8.3
Divorce rate (per woman)	1996	0.17

[1] Prospective adoptive parents must be aged 18 years or older to adopt a relative.
[2] It was assumed that 60 per cent of adoptive children are under age five.

Government policies

Type of adoption permitted	
Domestic adoption	No
Intercountry adoption...	No
Single male permitted to adopt	Not applicable
Single female permitted to adopt	Not applicable
Age requirements for adopting parents	Not applicable
Child's age of consent for adoption	Not applicable
Year of ratification of legal instruments on child adoption	
Convention on the Rights of the Child.....................	1992
Hague Convention on Intercountry Adoption	Not ratified
National legislation governing adoption	Not applicable
Government body responsible for adoption approval	Not applicable

Adoption indicators	Year	Number	Percentage
Total children adopted	...	..	..
Of which:			
Domestic adoptions...	...	..	..
Intercountry adoptions	...	..	..
Of which:			
Adoptions by step-parents or other relatives..............	...	..	..
Adoptions per 100,000 births..	...	..	
Adoptions per 100,000 children under age 18	...	..	
Adoptions per 100,000 children under age 5	...	..	

Demographic indicators	Year	Value
Female singulate mean age at marriage (years)	1991	25.6
Mean age at first birth (years)..	1997	25.3
Total fertility (children per woman).................................	2000-2005	2.5
Percentage of childless women, aged 40 - 44	1995	11.3
Divorce rate (per woman)	1995	0.15

Government policies

Type of adoption permitted[1]	
Domestic adoption	Yes
Intercountry adoption[2]	No
Single male permitted to adopt[3]	Yes
Single female permitted to adopt	...
Age requirements for adopting parents	Aged 15 years or older
Child's age of consent for adoption	...
Year of ratification of legal instruments on child adoption	
Convention on the Rights of the Child........................	1990
Hague Convention on Intercountry Adoption	Not ratified
National legislation governing adoption[4]	Varies depending on the religion of the adoptive child or parent
Government body responsible for adoption approval	Judiciary

Adoption indicators

	Year	Number	Percentage
Total children adopted[5]	2001-2003	100	100
Of which:			
Domestic adoptions[5]	2001-2003	100	100
Intercountry adoptions	...	..	..
Of which:			
Adoptions by step-parents or other relatives	...	...	...
Adoptions per 100,000 births[5]	2001-2003	0.9	
Adoptions per 100,000 children under age 18[5]	2001-2003	0.1	
Adoptions per 100,000 children under age 5[6]	2001-2003	0.1	

Demographic indicators

	Year	Value
Female singulate mean age at marriage (years)	2000	18.7
Mean age at first birth (years)[7]	1999-2000	18.2
Total fertility (children per woman)...............................	2000-2005	3.2
Percentage of childless women, aged 40 - 44	2004	4.7
Divorce rate (per woman)	...	...

[1] Procedures differ according to the religion of the adoptive child or parent.

[2] Non-citizens are not permitted to adopt.

[3] Unmarried Hindu men are not permitted to adopt a girl.

[4] The country does not have civil laws governing adoption, but under the Hindu, Christian and Buddhist personal laws, adoption is permitted.

[5] Estimate. Data refer to children placed in families.

[6] Estimate. Data refer to children placed in families. It was assumed that 60 per cent of adoptive children are under age five.

[7] Median age at first birth among women aged 25 to 29 years at the date of the survey.

Government policies

Type of adoption permitted
    Domestic adoption ....   Yes
    Intercountry adoption..   Yes

Single male permitted to adopt ....

Single female permitted to adopt ....

Age requirements for adopting parents ....

Child's age of consent for adoption[1] ....   Aged 16 years or older

Year of ratification of legal instruments on child adoption
    Convention on the Rights of the Child......................   1990
    Hague Convention on Intercountry Adoption ....   Not ratified

National legislation governing adoption ....   Adoption Act of 1955; Child Care Board Act of 1981; Adoption (Amendment) Act of 1981; Adoption Regulations of 1986

Government body responsible for adoption approval ......   Judiciary; Child Care Board

Adoption indicators	Year	Number	Percentage
Total children adopted	...	...	...
Of which:			
Domestic adoptions..	...	...	...
Intercountry adoptions	...	...	...
Of which:			
Adoptions by step-parents or other relatives..............	...	...	...
Adoptions per 100,000 births....................................	...	...	
Adoptions per 100,000 children under age 18	...	...	
Adoptions per 100,000 children under age 5	...	...	

Demographic indicators	Year	Value
Female singulate mean age at marriage (years)	1990	31.8
Mean age at first birth (years)...	...	...
Total fertility (children per woman)................................	2000-2005	1.5
Percentage of childless women, aged 40 - 44	1980	10.7
Divorce rate (per woman)	1991	0.18

---

[1] The maturity of the child is also considered.

Government policies

Type of adoption permitted
    Domestic adoption .... Yes
    Intercountry adoption... Yes

Single male permitted to adopt .... Yes

Single female permitted to adopt .... Yes

Age requirements for adopting parents .... At least 16 years older than the child

Child's age of consent for adoption .... Aged 10 years or older

Year of ratification of legal instruments on child adoption
    Convention on the Rights of the Child...................... 1990
    Hague Convention on Intercountry Adoption 2003

National legislation governing adoption .... Marriage and Family Code

Government body responsible for adoption approval ...... Judiciary; National Adoption Center; Ministry of Education

Adoption indicators	*Year*	*Number*	*Percentage*
Total children adopted	2001	868	100
Of which:			
Domestic adoptions..	2001	421	49
Intercountry adoptions[1]	2001	447	51
Of which:			
Adoptions by step-parents or other relatives..............	...	...	...
Adoptions per 100,000 births.......................................	2001	974.3	
Adoptions per 100,000 children under age 18	2001	37.7	
Adoptions per 100,000 children under age 5[2]	2001	120.2	

Demographic indicators	*Year*	*Value*
Female singulate mean age at marriage (years)	1999	22.8
Mean age at first birth (years)	2001	23.4
Total fertility (children per woman)..............................	2000-2005	1.2
Percentage of childless women, aged 40 - 44	1999	6.0
Divorce rate (per woman)	...	...

[1] Based on data from selected receiving countries, the main receiving country: Italy.
[2] It was assumed that 60 per cent of adoptive children are under age five.

Government policies

Type of adoption permitted
    Domestic adoption .... Yes
    Intercountry adoption.. Yes

Single male permitted to adopt .... Yes

Single female permitted to adopt .... Yes

Age requirements for adopting parents .... Aged 25 years or older and at least 15 years older than the child

Child's age of consent for adoption .... Aged 12 years or older

Year of ratification of legal instruments on child adoption
    Convention on the Rights of the Child...................... 1991
    Hague Convention on Intercountry Adoption 2005

National legislation governing adoption .... Civil Code; Law of 24 April 2003

Government body responsible for adoption approval ...... Varies by community

Adoption indicators	Year	Number	Percentage
Total children adopted	2003	451	100
Of which:			
Domestic adoptions[1]	2003	21	5
Intercountry adoptions[2]...	2003	430	95
Of which:			
Adoptions by step-parents or other relatives.............	...	...	...
Adoptions per 100,000 births..	2003	402.7	
Adoptions per 100,000 children under age 18	2003	21.1	
Adoptions per 100,000 children under age 5[3]	2003	47.8	

Demographic indicators	Year	Value
Female singulate mean age at marriage (years)	2000	27.9
Mean age at first birth (years).......................................	1990	26.4
Total fertility (children per woman)................................	2000-2005	1.7
Percentage of childless women, aged 40 - 44[4]	1970	10.2
Divorce rate (per woman)	1995	0.42

[1] Data refer to domestic adoptions in the region of Flanders.
[2] Data refer to intercountry adoptions in the regions of Flanders and Wallonia. Main country of origin for the region of Flanders: China.
[3] It was assumed that 60 per cent of adoptive children are under age five.
[4] Data refer only to the Dutch-speaking community of the Flemish Region of Belgium.

Government policies

Type of adoption permitted	
Domestic adoption	Yes
Intercountry adoption...	Yes
Single male permitted to adopt[1]	Yes
Single female permitted to adopt	Yes
Age requirements for adopting parents	Aged 25 years or older and at least 12 years older than the child
Child's age of consent for adoption	Maturity of child considered
Year of ratification of legal instruments on child adoption	
Convention on the Rights of the Child.......................	1990
Hague Convention on Intercountry Adoption	2005
National legislation governing adoption	Families and Children Act (Revised 31 December 2000)
Government body responsible for adoption approval	Judiciary; Department of Human Development

---

Adoption indicators	Year	Number	Percentage
Total children adopted	2003	79	100
Of which:			
Domestic adoptions...	2003	74	94
Intercountry adoptions	2003	5	6
Of which:			
Adoptions by step-parents or other relatives..............	...	...	...
Adoptions per 100,000 births..	2003	1 128.7	
Adoptions per 100,000 children under age 18	2003	68.5	
Adoptions per 100,000 children under age 5[2]	2003	141.0	

Demographic indicators	Year	Value
Female singulate mean age at marriage (years)	1991	26.2
Mean age at first birth (years)	...	...
Total fertility (children per woman)...............................	2000-2005	3.2
Percentage of childless women, aged 40 - 44	2000	6.0
Divorce rate (per woman)	...	...

---

[1] A sole male applicant is not permitted to adopt a girl, except under special circumstances.
[2] It was assumed that 60 per cent of adoptive children are under age five.

Government policies

Type of adoption permitted
    Domestic adoption .... Yes
    Intercountry adoption .... Yes

Single male permitted to adopt ....

Single female permitted to adopt ....

Age requirements for adopting parents ....

Child's age of consent for adoption ....

Year of ratification of legal instruments on child adoption
    Convention on the Rights of the Child 1990
    Hague Convention on Intercountry Adoption .... Not ratified

National legislation governing adoption .... French Civil Code (1958 version); Dahomy Code of Customary Law

Government body responsible for adoption approval ...... Judiciary

Adoption indicators	Year	Number	Percentage
Total children adopted	2005	4	100
Of which:			
Domestic adoptions	2005	3	75
Intercountry adoptions	2005	1	25
Of which:			
Adoptions by step-parents or other relatives	...	...	...
Adoptions per 100,000 births	2005	1.1	
Adoptions per 100,000 children under age 18	2005	0.1	
Adoptions per 100,000 children under age 5[1]	2005	0.2	

Demographic indicators	Year	Value
Female singulate mean age at marriage (years)	1996	19.9
Mean age at first birth (years)[2]	2001	20.2
Total fertility (children per woman)	2000-2005	5.9
Percentage of childless women, aged 40 - 44	2001	3.3
Divorce rate (per woman)	...	...

[1] It was assumed that 60 per cent of adoptive children are under age five.
[2] Median age at first birth among women aged 25 to 29 years at the date of the survey.

Government policies

Type of adoption permitted
Domestic adoption .... Yes
Intercountry adoption....................................... Yes

Single male permitted to adopt ....

Single female permitted to adopt ....

Age requirements for adopting parents ....

Child's age of consent for adoption ....

Year of ratification of legal instruments on child adoption
Convention on the Rights of the Child...................... 1990
Hague Convention on Intercountry Adoption .... Not ratified

National legislation governing adoption .... Resolution 4 of the sixty-seventh session of the National Assembly of 1988

Government body responsible for adoption approval ...... Judiciary

Adoption indicators	Year	Number	Percentage
Total children adopted	...	...	...
Of which:			
Domestic adoptions..	...	...	...
Intercountry adoptions	...	...	...
Of which:			
Adoptions by step-parents or other relatives..............	...	...	...
Adoptions per 100,000 births...........................	...	...	
Adoptions per 100,000 children under age 18	...	...	
Adoptions per 100,000 children under age 5	...	...	

Demographic indicators	Year	Value
Female singulate mean age at marriage (years)	1990	20.5
Mean age at first birth (years)	...	...
Total fertility (children per woman)...............................	2000-2005	4.4
Percentage of childless women, aged 40 - 44	...	...
Divorce rate (per woman)	...	...

Government policies

Type of adoption permitted[1]
    Domestic adoption .... Yes
    Intercountry adoption.. Yes

Single male permitted to adopt .... Yes

Single female permitted to adopt .... Yes

Age requirements for adopting parents .... Aged 25 to 50 years and at least 15 years older than the child

Child's age of consent for adoption ....

Year of ratification of legal instruments on child adoption
    Convention on the Rights of the Child..................... 1990
    Hague Convention on Intercountry Adoption 2002

National legislation governing adoption .... Family Code; Code for Children and Adolescents

Government body responsible for adoption approval ...... Juvenile Court; Vice-Ministry of Gender, Generational and Family Affairs

Adoption indicators	Year	Number	Percentage
Total children adopted	2003	348	100
Of which:			
Domestic adoptions...	2003	145	42
Intercountry adoptions[2]...	2003	203	58
Of which:			
Adoptions by step-parents or other relatives.............	...	...	...
Adoptions per 100,000 births..	2003	131.6	
Adoptions per 100,000 children under age 18	2003	8.7	
Adoptions per 100,000 children under age 5[3].................	2003	17.1	

Demographic indicators	Year	Value
Female singulate mean age at marriage (years)	1998	22.8
Mean age at first birth (years)[4]..	1998	21.0
Total fertility (children per woman).................................	2000-2005	4.0
Percentage of childless women, aged 40 - 44	2003	6.5
Divorce rate (per woman)	...	...

---

[1] Adopted children must be under 18 years of age.

[2] Based on data from selected receiving countries, the main receiving country: Spain.

[3] It was assumed that 60 per cent of adoptive children are under age five.

[4] Median age at first birth among women aged 25 to 29 years at the date of the survey.

Government policies

Type of adoption permitted
    Domestic adoption .... Yes
    Intercountry adoption... Yes

Single male permitted to adopt ....

Single female permitted to adopt ....

Age requirements for adopting parents ....

Child's age of consent for adoption .... Aged 10 years or older

Year of ratification of legal instruments on child adoption
    Convention on the Rights of the Child....................... 1993
    Hague Convention on Intercountry Adoption .... Not ratified

National legislation governing adoption .... Family Law

Government body responsible for adoption approval[1] ..... Judiciary; Ministry of Social Welfare; Ministry of the Interior

Adoption indicators	Year	Number	Percentage
Total children adopted	2002	71	100
Of which:			
Domestic adoptions...	...	...	...
Intercountry adoptions	...	...	...
Of which:			
Adoptions by step-parents or other relatives..............	...	...	...
Adoptions per 100,000 births.....................................	2002	186.7	
Adoptions per 100,000 children under age 18	2002	8.2	
Adoptions per 100,000 children under age 5[2]	2002	19.9	

Demographic indicators	Year	Value
Female singulate mean age at marriage (years)	...	...
Mean age at first birth (years)......................................	1990	23.6
Total fertility (children per woman).............................	2000-2005	1.3
Percentage of childless women, aged 40 - 44	...	...
Divorce rate (per woman)	1991	0.04

---

[1] Varies by municipality.
[2] It was assumed that 60 per cent of adoptive children are under age five.

Government policies

Type of adoption permitted
    Domestic adoption .... Yes
    Intercountry adoption[1] .... Yes

Single male permitted to adopt .... Yes

Single female permitted to adopt .... Yes

Age requirements for adopting parents[2] .... Aged 25 years or older

Child's age of consent for adoption .... Aged 10 years or older

Year of ratification of legal instruments on child adoption
    Convention on the Rights of the Child...................... 1995
    Hague Convention on Intercountry Adoption .... Not ratified

National legislation governing adoption .... Adoption of Children Act

Government body responsible for adoption approval ...... Judiciary

Adoption indicators	Year	Number	Percentage
Total children adopted	…	…	…
Of which:			
Domestic adoptions..	…	…	…
Intercountry adoptions	…	…	…
Of which:			
Adoptions by step-parents or other relatives..............	…	…	…
Adoptions per 100,000 births..	…	…	
Adoptions per 100,000 children under age 18	…	…	
Adoptions per 100,000 children under age 5	…	…	

Demographic indicators	Year	Value	
Female singulate mean age at marriage (years)	1991	26.9	
Mean age at first birth (years)...	…	…	
Total fertility (children per woman)..............................	2000-2005	3.2	
Percentage of childless women, aged 40 - 44	1991	4.0	
Divorce rate (per woman)...	…	…	

[1] The adopted person must remain in the country for at least 12 months following the adoption decree.
[2] Prospective adoptive parents must be at least 25 years older than the child if the child is aged 16 years or older.

Government policies

Type of adoption permitted
 Domestic adoption .... Yes
 Intercountry adoption[1] .... Yes

Single male permitted to adopt .... Yes

Single female permitted to adopt .... Yes

Age requirements for adopting parents .... Aged 21 years or older and at least 16 years older than the child

Child's age of consent for adoption .... Aged 12 years or older

Year of ratification of legal instruments on child adoption
 Convention on the Rights of the Child........................ 1990
 Hague Convention on Intercountry Adoption 1999

National legislation governing adoption .... Statute of the Child and Adolescent, Law No. 8.069 of 13 July 1990; Decree 2,427 of 17 December 1997; Decree 3,087 of 21 June 1999

Government body responsible for adoption approval ...... State Judiciary Commission on Adoption; Department for the Child and Adolescent, Secretary of State for Human Rights of the Ministry of Justice

Adoption indicators	Year	Number	Percentage
Total children adopted[2]	2003	4 150	100
Of which:			
Domestic adoptions[2]	2003	4 030	97
Intercountry adoptions[3]..	2003	120	3
Of which:			
Adoptions by step-parents or other relatives..............	...	...	...
Adoptions per 100,000 births[2]	2003	111.4	
Adoptions per 100,000 children under age 18[2]	2003	6.7	
Adoptions per 100,000 children under age 5[4]	2003	14.0	

Demographic indicators	Year	Value
Female singulate mean age at marriage (years)	1996	23.4
Mean age at first birth (years)[5]......................................	1996	22.1
Total fertility (children per woman)..............................	2000-2005	2.3
Percentage of childless women, aged 40 - 44	1996	11.1
Divorce rate (per woman)	...	...

[1] Prospective adoptive parents must remain in the country up to one month (and no less than 15 days) before the completion of the adoption procedure.
[2] Data refer only to the state of São Paulo.
[3] Data refer only to the state of São Paulo. Based on data from selected receiving countries, the main receiving country: Italy.
[4] Data refer only to the state of São Paulo. It was assumed that 60 per cent of adoptive children are under age five.
[5] Median age at first birth among women aged 25 to 29 years at the date of the survey.

Government policies	
Type of adoption permitted	
Domestic adoption	Yes
Intercountry adoption...	Yes
Single male permitted to adopt[1]	Yes
Single female permitted to adopt[2]	Yes
Age requirements for adopting parents	...
Child's age of consent for adoption	Maturity of child considered
Year of ratification of legal instruments on child adoption	
Convention on the Rights of the Child......................	1995
Hague Convention on Intercountry Adoption	Not ratified
National legislation governing adoption[3]	Varies depending on the religion of the adoptive child or parent
Government body responsible for adoption approval[4]	Sharia Court; High Court; Social Affairs Services Unit

Adoption indicators	Year	Number	Percentage
Total children adopted	...	...	...
Of which:			
Domestic adoptions...	...	...	
Intercountry adoptions	...	...	
Of which:			
Adoptions by step-parents or other relatives..............	...	...	...
Adoptions per 100,000 births..	...	...	
Adoptions per 100,000 children under age 18	...	...	
Adoptions per 100,000 children under age 5	...	...	

Demographic indicators	Year	Value
Female singulate mean age at marriage (years)	1991	25.1
Mean age at first birth (years)..	1988	24.8
Total fertility (children per woman)................................	2000-2005	2.5
Percentage of childless women, aged 40 - 44	1960	6.6
Divorce rate (per woman)	...	...

[1] A sole male applicant is not permitted to adopt a girl, unless they are related by blood.
[2] A sole female applicant is not permitted to adopt a boy, unless they are related by blood.
[3] The Islamic Adoption of Children Order 2001 applies to Muslims, and the Adoption of Children Order 2001 applies to non-Muslims.
[4] Adoptions made under the Islamic Adoption of Children Order 2001 must be approved by the Sharia Courts, and adoptions made under the Adoption of Children Order 2001 must be approved by the High Court.

Government policies

Type of adoption permitted	
Domestic adoption	Yes
Intercountry adoption..	Yes
Single male permitted to adopt	Yes
Single female permitted to adopt	Yes
Age requirements for adopting parents...........................	Aged 18 years or older and at least 15 years older than the child
Child's age of consent for adoption	Aged 14 years or older
Year of ratification of legal instruments on child adoption	
Convention on the Rights of the Child.......................	1991
Hague Convention on Intercountry Adoption	2002
National legislation governing adoption	Family Code No. 41/28.05.1985 Amended SG No. 11 &15/1992; Regulation of the Ministry of Justice on the Manner and Procedure for Adoption of 1992
Government body responsible for adoption approval	Judiciary

Adoption indicators

	Year	Number	Percentage
Total children adopted	1999	2 288	100
Of which:			
Domestic adoptions...	1999	1 278	56
Intercountry adoptions[1]...	1999	1 010	44
Of which:			
Adoptions by step-parents or other relatives..............	…	…	…
Adoptions per 100,000 births...	1999	3 460.7	
Adoptions per 100,000 children under age 18	1999	140.4	
Adoptions per 100,000 children under age 5[2]	1999	410.3	

Demographic indicators

	Year	Value
Female singulate mean age at marriage (years)	1985	21.1
Mean age at first birth (years).......................................	2001	23.1
Total fertility (children per woman)..............................	2000-2005	1.2
Percentage of childless women, aged 40 - 44	1997	10.7
Divorce rate (per woman)	1997	0.15

[1] Based on data from selected receiving countries, the main receiving country: Italy.

[2] It was assumed that 60 per cent of adoptive children are under age five.

Government policies

Type of adoption permitted
    Domestic adoption .... Yes
    Intercountry adoption... Yes

Single male permitted to adopt ....

Single female permitted to adopt ....

Age requirements for adopting parents ....

Child's age of consent for adoption .... Aged 15 years or older

Year of ratification of legal instruments on child adoption
    Convention on the Rights of the Child....................... 1990
    Hague Convention on Intercountry Adoption 1996

National legislation governing adoption .... Code on the Individual and the Family

Government body responsible for adoption approval ...... Judiciary; Ministry of Social Action and the Family

Adoption indicators	Year	Number	Percentage
Total children adopted	...	...	...
Of which:			
Domestic adoptions..	...	...	...
Intercountry adoptions	1996	48	...
Of which:			
Adoptions by step-parents or other relatives..............	...	...	...
Adoptions per 100,000 births...	...	...	
Adoptions per 100,000 children under age 18	...	...	
Adoptions per 100,000 children under age 5	...	...	

Demographic indicators	Year	Value
Female singulate mean age at marriage (years)	1999	18.9
Mean age at first birth (years)[1]	1999	19.0
Total fertility (children per woman)................................	2000-2005	6.7
Percentage of childless women, aged 40 - 44	2003	4.1
Divorce rate (per woman)	...	...

[1] Median age at first birth among women aged 25 to 29 years at the date of the survey.

Government policies

Type of adoption permitted
    Domestic adoption .... Yes
    Intercountry adoption.. Yes

Single male permitted to adopt .... Yes

Single female permitted to adopt .... Yes

Age requirements for adopting parents[1].......................... Under age 30 and at least 15 years older than the child

Child's age of consent for adoption .... Aged 16 years or older

Year of ratification of legal instruments on child adoption
    Convention on the Rights of the Child....................... 1990
    Hague Convention on Intercountry Adoption 1998

National legislation governing adoption .... Code of Personal and Family Affairs

Government body responsible for adoption approval ...... Judiciary; Ministry for the Advancement of Women and Social Action

Adoption indicators	Year	Number	Percentage
Total children adopted	...	...	...
Of which:			
Domestic adoptions..	...	...	...
Intercountry adoptions[2]...	1998	50	...
Of which:			
Adoptions by step-parents or other relatives..............	...	...	...
Adoptions per 100,000 births...	...	...	
Adoptions per 100,000 children under age 18	...	...	
Adoptions per 100,000 children under age 5	...	...	

Demographic indicators	Year	Value
Female singulate mean age at marriage (years)	1990	22.5
Mean age at first birth (years)[3].......................................	1987	20.9
Total fertility (children per woman).............................	2000-2005	6.8
Percentage of childless women, aged 40 - 44	1990	5.7
Divorce rate (per woman)	...	...

[1] Different age requirements apply to adoptions by step-parents.
[2] Estimate.
[3] Median age at first birth among women aged 25 to 29 years at the date of the survey.

Government policies

Type of adoption permitted
    Domestic adoption .... Yes
    Intercountry adoption.. Yes

Single male permitted to adopt ....

Single female permitted to adopt ....

Age requirements for adopting parents .... Aged 25 years or older and at least 20 years older than the child

Child's age of consent for adoption ....

Year of ratification of legal instruments on child adoption
    Convention on the Rights of the Child...................... 1992
    Hague Convention on Intercountry Adoption .... Not ratified

National legislation governing adoption .... Marriage and Family Act; Council of Ministers Letter No.549 of 25 March 1991; Council of Ministers Decision of 23 June 1991

Government body responsible for adoption approval ...... Communal authorities

Adoption indicators	Year	Number	Percentage
Total children adopted	...	...	...
Of which:			
Domestic adoptions..	...	...	...
Intercountry adoptions	...	...	...
Of which:			
Adoptions by step-parents or other relatives	...	...	...
Adoptions per 100,000 births..	...	...	
Adoptions per 100,000 children under age 18	...	...	
Adoptions per 100,000 children under age 5	...	...	

Demographic indicators	Year	Value
Female singulate mean age at marriage (years)	1998	22.5
Mean age at first birth (years)[1]..	2000	21.5
Total fertility (children per woman).................................	2000-2005	4.1
Percentage of childless women, aged 40 - 44	2000	9.3
Divorce rate (per woman)	...	...

[1] Median age at first birth among women aged 25 to 29 years at the date of the survey.

Government policies

Type of adoption permitted
    Domestic adoption ....   Yes
    Intercountry adoption[1] ....   Yes

Single male permitted to adopt[2] ....   Yes

Single female permitted to adopt[2] ....   Yes

Age requirements for adopting parents[3] ....   One adoptive parent must be aged 35 years or older and at least 15 years older than the child

Child's age of consent for adoption ....   Aged 16 years or older

Year of ratification of legal instruments on child adoption
    Convention on the Rights of the Child......................   1993
    Hague Convention on Intercountry Adoption ....   Not ratified

National legislation governing adoption ....   Civil Code

Government body responsible for adoption approval ......   Judiciary; Ministry of Social Affairs

Adoption indicators	Year	Number	Percentage
Total children adopted	...	...	...
Of which:			
Domestic adoptions...	...	...	...
Intercountry adoptions[4]	1996-1997	12	...
Of which:			
Adoptions by step-parents or other relatives	...	...	...
Adoptions per 100,000 births......................................	...	...	
Adoptions per 100,000 children under age 18	...	...	
Adoptions per 100,000 children under age 5	...	...	

Demographic indicators	Year	Value
Female singulate mean age at marriage (years)	1998	20.2
Mean age at first birth (years)[5]	1998	20.3
Total fertility (children per woman)...............................	2000-2005	4.6
Percentage of childless women, aged 40 - 44	2004	6.1
Divorce rate (per woman)	...	...

[1] Prospective adoptive parents must have resided in the country and had the child in their care and custody for at least three consecutive months prior to the date of the adoption application.
[2] Prospective adoptive parents must be aged 40 years or older.
[3] Age requirements apply to prospective adoptive parents who have been married at least ten years. Different age requirements apply to single adoptive parents.
[4] Data refer to intercountry adoption requests. Main requesting countries: France and Switzerland.
[5] Median age at first birth among women aged 25 to 29 years at the date of the survey.

Government policies

Type of adoption permitted
    Domestic adoption .... Yes
    Intercountry adoption.................................... Yes

Single male permitted to adopt .... Varies by province

Single female permitted to adopt .... Varies by province

Age requirements for adopting parents .... Varies by province

Child's age of consent for adoption ....

Year of ratification of legal instruments on child adoption
    Convention on the Rights of the Child...................... 1991
    Hague Convention on Intercountry Adoption 1996

National legislation governing adoption .... Varies by province or territory

Government body responsible for adoption approval[1] ..... National Adoption Desk

Adoption indicators	Year	Number	Percentage
Total children adopted[2]	2000-2001	4 118	100
Of which:			
Domestic adoptions[2]	2000-2001	2 243	54
Intercountry adoptions[3]	2000-2001	1 875	46
Of which:			
Adoptions by step-parents or other relatives[4]	2000-2001	527	12.8
Adoptions per 100,000 births[2]	2000-2001	1 233.8	
Adoptions per 100,000 children under age 18[2]	2000-2001	58.2	
Adoptions per 100,000 children under age 5[5]	2000-2001	142.5	

Demographic indicators	Year	Value
Female singulate mean age at marriage (years)	2002	26.8
Mean age at first birth (years)...................................	1997	26.7
Total fertility (children per woman).............................	2000-2005	1.5
Percentage of childless women, aged 40 - 44	1991	15.9
Divorce rate (per woman)	1995	0.29

[1] The National Adoption Desk coordinates intercountry adoptions for all provinces, with the exception of Quebec.
[2] Estimate. Data refer to the fiscal year.
[3] Data refer to the fiscal year. Main country of origin: China.
[4] Estimate. Data refer to adoptions by step-parents and other relatives in the provinces of Alberta, Newfoundland and Labrador, Nova Scotia, Prince Edward Island and Saskatchewan. Data refer to the fiscal year.
[5] Estimate. Data refer to the fiscal year. It was assumed that 60 per cent of adoptive children are under age five.

Government policies

Type of adoption permitted
    Domestic adoption .... Yes
    Intercountry adoption.. Yes

Single male permitted to adopt ....

Single female permitted to adopt ....

Age requirements for adopting parents ....

Child's age of consent for adoption .... Aged 12 years or older

Year of ratification of legal instruments on child adoption
    Convention on the Rights of the Child...................... 1992
    Hague Convention on Intercountry Adoption .... Not ratified

National legislation governing adoption .... Civil Code

Government body responsible for adoption approval ...... Judiciary

Adoption indicators	Year	Number	Percentage
Total children adopted	...	...	...
Of which:			
Domestic adoptions..	...	...	...
Intercountry adoptions	...	...	...
Of which:			
Adoptions by step-parents or other relatives..............	...	...	...
Adoptions per 100,000 births..	...	...	
Adoptions per 100,000 children under age 18	...	...	
Adoptions per 100,000 children under age 5	...	...	

Demographic indicators	Year	Value
Female singulate mean age at marriage (years)	1990	25.7
Mean age at first birth (years)...	...	...
Total fertility (children per woman)................................	2000-2005	3.8
Percentage of childless women, aged 40 - 44	1998	8.4
Divorce rate (per woman)..	...	...

Government policies

Type of adoption permitted
    Domestic adoption .... Yes
    Intercountry adoption... Yes

Single male permitted to adopt ....

Single female permitted to adopt ....

Age requirements for adopting parents ....

Child's age of consent for adoption ....

Year of ratification of legal instruments on child adoption
    Convention on the Rights of the Child...................... 1992
    Hague Convention on Intercountry Adoption .... Not ratified

National legislation governing adoption .... French Civil Code

Government body responsible for adoption approval[1] ..... Judiciary; Adoption Committee

Adoption indicators	Year	Number	Percentage
Total children adopted	1995-1998	24	100
Of which:			
Domestic adoptions...	1995-1998	11	46
Intercountry adoptions	1995-1998	13	54
Of which:			
Adoptions by step-parents or other relatives..............	...	...	...
Adoptions per 100,000 births.......................................	1995-1998	4.2	
Adoptions per 100,000 children under age 18	1995-1998	0.3	
Adoptions per 100,000 children under age 5[2]	1995-1998	0.6	

Demographic indicators	Year	Value
Female singulate mean age at marriage (years)	1995	19.7
Mean age at first birth (years)[3].......................................	1994-1995	19.4
Total fertility (children per woman)...............................	2000-2005	5.0
Percentage of childless women, aged 40 - 44	1994-1995	10.2
Divorce rate (per woman)	...	...

[1] The Adoption Committee was established by Decree No. 95/06 of 21 April 1995.
[2] It was assumed that 60 per cent of adoptive children are under age five.
[3] Median age at first birth among women aged 25 to 29 years at the date of the survey.

Government policies

Type of adoption permitted
    Domestic adoption .... Yes
    Intercountry adoption...................................... Yes

Single male permitted to adopt ....

Single female permitted to adopt ....

Age requirements for adopting parents ....

Child's age of consent for adoption ....

Year of ratification of legal instruments on child adoption
    Convention on the Rights of the Child...................... 1990
    Hague Convention on Intercountry Adoption............ Not ratified

National legislation governing adoption .... Civil Code

Government body responsible for adoption approval ...... Judiciary; Child Protection Office

Adoption indicators	Year	Number	Percentage
Total children adopted	...	...	...
Of which:			
Domestic adoptions................................	...	...	...
Intercountry adoptions[1].........................	1993-1996	4	...
Of which:			
Adoptions by step-parents or other relatives.............	...	...	...
Adoptions per 100,000 births.......................	...	...	
Adoptions per 100,000 children under age 18	...	...	
Adoptions per 100,000 children under age 5	...	...	

Demographic indicators	Year	Value
Female singulate mean age at marriage (years)	1996	18.1
Mean age at first birth (years)[2].......................	1996-1997	18.2
Total fertility (children per woman)..............................	2000-2005	6.7
Percentage of childless women, aged 40 - 44	1996-1997	6.3
Divorce rate (per woman)	...	...

[1] Estimate.
[2] Median age at first birth among women aged 25 to 29 years at the date of the survey.

Government policies

Type of adoption permitted	
Domestic adoption	Yes
Intercountry adoption..	Yes
Single male permitted to adopt[1]	Yes
Single female permitted to adopt[1]	Yes
Age requirements for adopting parents	Aged 26 to 59 years and at least 20 years older than the child
Child's age of consent for adoption[2]...............................	Aged 14 years or older
Year of ratification of legal instruments on child adoption	
Convention on the Rights of the Child......................	1990
Hague Convention on Intercountry Adoption	1999
National legislation governing adoption	Act No. 7613 of 1943; Act No. 18,703 of 1988; Act No. 19,620 of 1999; Act No. 19,670 of 2000; Act No. 19,910 of 2003
Government body responsible for adoption approval	Judiciary; National Service for Minors

Adoption indicators	Year	Number	Percentage
Total children adopted	2003	536	100
Of which:			
Domestic adoptions..	2003	445	83
Intercountry adoptions[3]...	2003	91	17
Of which:			
Adoptions by step-parents or other relatives..............	...	...	...
Adoptions per 100,000 births..	2003	215.0	
Adoptions per 100,000 children under age 18	2003	10.7	
Adoptions per 100,000 children under age 5[4].................	2003	25.5	

Demographic indicators	Year	Value
Female singulate mean age at marriage (years)	1992	23.4
Mean age at first birth (years)...	1998	23.4
Total fertility (children per woman).................................	2000-2005	2.0
Percentage of childless women, aged 40 - 44	1992	7.9
Divorce rate (per woman)...	1997	0.05

[1] Prospective adoptive parents must be permanent residents in the country.
[2] A female child above the age of 12 must be heard.
[3] Main receiving country: Italy.
[4] It was assumed that 60 per cent of adoptive children are under age five.

Government policies

Type of adoption permitted	
Domestic adoption	Yes
Intercountry adoption..	Yes
Single male permitted to adopt[1]	Yes
Single female permitted to adopt[1]	Yes
Age requirements for adopting parents[2].........................	Aged 30 years or older
Child's age of consent for adoption	Aged 10 years or older
Year of ratification of legal instruments on child adoption	
Convention on the Rights of the Child.......................	1992
Hague Convention on Intercountry Adoption	2005
National legislation governing adoption	Adoption Act; Marriage Act
Government body responsible for adoption approval	Chinese Center for Adoption Affairs, Ministry of Civil Administration

Adoption indicators

	Year	Number	Percentage
Total children adopted	2001	45 844	100
Of which:			
Domestic adoptions..	2001	37 200	81
Intercountry adoptions[3]..	2001	8 644	19
Of which:			
Adoptions by step-parents or other relatives..............	...	...	...
Adoptions per 100,000 births..	2001	252.0	
Adoptions per 100,000 children under age 18	2001	12.2	
Adoptions per 100,000 children under age 5[4]...............	2001	29.5	

Demographic indicators

	Year	Value
Female singulate mean age at marriage (years)	1999	23.1
Mean age at first birth (years)......................................	...	...
Total fertility (children per woman)...............................	2000-2005	1.7
Percentage of childless women, aged 40 - 44	1990	1.1
Divorce rate (per woman)	...	...

---

[1] The Ministry of Civil Affairs has devised new guidelines that require foreign prospective adoptive parents to have been married at least two years.

[2] The Ministry of Civil Affairs has devised new guidelines that require foreign prospective adoptive parents to be aged 30 to 50 years.

[3] Based on data from selected receiving countries, the main receiving country: United States of America.

[4] It was assumed that 60 per cent of adoptive children are under age five.

Government policies

Type of adoption permitted	
Domestic adoption	Yes
Intercountry adoption...	Yes
Single male permitted to adopt	Yes
Single female permitted to adopt	Yes
Age requirements for adopting parents	Aged 25 years or older and at least 15 years older than the child
Child's age of consent for adoption	...
Year of ratification of legal instruments on child adoption	
Convention on the Rights of the Child......................	1991
Hague Convention on Intercountry Adoption	1998
National legislation governing adoption	Juvenile Code, Decree No. 2737 of 27 November 1989; Resolution No. 1267 of 1994
Government body responsible for adoption approval	Judiciary; Adoption Division, Colombian Family Welfare Institute

Adoption indicators

Adoption indicators	Year	Number	Percentage
Total children adopted	2004	1 409	100
Of which:			
Domestic adoptions..	2004	563	40
Intercountry adoptions[1]	2004	846	60
Of which:			
Adoptions by step-parents or other relatives[2]............	2004	178	31.6
Adoptions per 100,000 births..	2004	145.2	
Adoptions per 100,000 children under age 18	2004	8.4	
Adoptions per 100,000 children under age 5[3]	2004	17.9	

Demographic indicators

Demographic indicators	Year	Value
Female singulate mean age at marriage (years)	2000	23.1
Mean age at first birth (years)[4].......................................	2000	21.8
Total fertility (children per woman).................................	2000-2005	2.6
Percentage of childless women, aged 40 - 44	2000	11.0
Divorce rate (per woman)	...	...

---

[1] Main receiving country: France.

[2] Data refer to domestic adoptions by relatives only. The percentage is calculated based on the total number of domestic adoptions.

[3] It was assumed that 60 per cent of adoptive children are under age five.

[4] Median age at first birth among women aged 25 to 29 years at the date of the survey.

Government policies

Type of adoption permitted	
Domestic adoption	Yes
Intercountry adoption...	...
Single male permitted to adopt	...
Single female permitted to adopt	...
Age requirements for adopting parents	...
Child's age of consent for adoption	...
Year of ratification of legal instruments on child adoption	
Convention on the Rights of the Child......................	1993
Hague Convention on Intercountry Adoption	Not ratified
National legislation governing adoption[1]	French Civil Code
Government body responsible for adoption approval	Judiciary

Adoption indicators

	Year	Number	Percentage
Total children adopted	...	...	...
Of which:			
Domestic adoptions..	...	...	...
Intercountry adoptions	...	...	...
Of which:			
Adoptions by step-parents or other relatives..............	...	...	...
Adoptions per 100,000 births..	...	...	
Adoptions per 100,000 children under age 18	...	...	
Adoptions per 100,000 children under age 5	...	...	

Demographic indicators

	Year	Value
Female singulate mean age at marriage (years)	1996	23.6
Mean age at first birth (years)[2]	1996	22.4
Total fertility (children per woman)...............................	2000-2005	4.9
Percentage of childless women, aged 40 - 44	1996	7.0
Divorce rate (per woman)	...	...

[1] Adoption is not permitted under Sharia law, but it is legitimised, if necessary, by resorting to French Civil Law.
[2] Median age at first birth among women aged 25 to 29 years at the date of the survey.

Government policies

Type of adoption permitted
    Domestic adoption .... Yes
    Intercountry adoption.. Yes

Single male permitted to adopt ....

Single female permitted to adopt ....

Age requirements for adopting parents ....

Child's age of consent for adoption .... Aged 15 years or older

Year of ratification of legal instruments on child adoption
    Convention on the Rights of the Child....................... 1993
    Hague Convention on Intercountry Adoption .... Not ratified

National legislation governing adoption .... Family Code

Government body responsible for adoption approval ...... Judiciary

Adoption indicators	Year	Number	Percentage
Total children adopted[1]	2000	103	100
Of which:			
Domestic adoptions[1]	2000	51	50
Intercountry adoptions[1]..	2000	52	50
Of which:			
Adoptions by step-parents or other relatives..............	...	...	...
Adoptions per 100,000 births[1]	2000	67.9	
Adoptions per 100,000 children under age 18[1]	2000	5.6	
Adoptions per 100,000 children under age 5[2]	2000	9.6	

Demographic indicators	Year	Value
Female singulate mean age at marriage (years)	1984	22.6
Mean age at first birth (years)..	...	...
Total fertility (children per woman)................................	2000-2005	6.3
Percentage of childless women, aged 40 - 44	...	...
Divorce rate (per woman)...	...	...

[1] Estimate. Data refer to adoptions heard by the Brazzaville District Court.
[2] Estimate. Data refer to adoptions heard by the Brazzaville District Court. It was assumed that 60 per cent of adoptive children are under age five.

Government policies

Type of adoption permitted	
Domestic adoption	...
Intercountry adoption..	...
Single male permitted to adopt	...
Single female permitted to adopt	...
Age requirements for adopting parents	...
Child's age of consent for adoption	...
Year of ratification of legal instruments on child adoption	
Convention on the Rights of the Child......................	1997
Hague Convention on Intercountry Adoption	Not ratified
National legislation governing adoption	...
Government body responsible for adoption approval	...

Adoption indicators

	Year	Number	Percentage
Total children adopted	...	...	...
Of which:			
Domestic adoptions...	...	...	...
Intercountry adoptions	...	...	...
Of which:			
Adoptions by step-parents or other relatives	...	...	...
Adoptions per 100,000 births..	...	...	
Adoptions per 100,000 children under age 18	...	...	
Adoptions per 100,000 children under age 5	...	...	

Demographic indicators

	Year	Value
Female singulate mean age at marriage (years)	...	...
Mean age at first birth (years)	...	...
Total fertility (children per woman)..............................	2000-2005	2.7
Percentage of childless women, aged 40 - 44	...	...
Divorce rate (per woman)	...	...

Government policies

Type of adoption permitted
    Domestic adoption .... Yes
    Intercountry adoption[1] .... Yes

Single male permitted to adopt .... Yes

Single female permitted to adopt .... Yes

Age requirements for adopting parents ....

Child's age of consent for adoption ....

Year of ratification of legal instruments on child adoption
    Convention on the Rights of the Child...................... 1990
    Hague Convention on Intercountry Adoption 1995

National legislation governing adoption .... Adoptions Act; Family Code Law No. 7538 of 22 August 1995; Law No. 7517 of 1995

Government body responsible for adoption approval ...... Judiciary; National Adoption Council; National Children's Trust

Adoption indicators	*Year*	*Number*	*Percentage*
Total children adopted	2003	64	100
Of which:			
Domestic adoptions[2]	2003	32	50
Intercountry adoptions[3]	2003	32	50
Of which:			
Adoptions by step-parents or other relatives.............	...	...	...
Adoptions per 100,000 births..........................	2003	80.9	
Adoptions per 100,000 children under age 18	2003	4.3	
Adoptions per 100,000 children under age 5[4]	2003	9.8	

Demographic indicators	*Year*	*Value*
Female singulate mean age at marriage (years)	1986	20.9
Mean age at first birth (years)......................................	1997	22.6
Total fertility (children per woman)...............................	2000-2005	2.3
Percentage of childless women, aged 40 - 44	1984	8.9
Divorce rate (per woman)	1981	0.12

[1] Intercountry adoptions to countries that have not implemented the Convention on Protection of Children and Co-operation in Respect of Intercountry Adoption were suspended.
[2] Data refer to adoptions arranged by the National Children's Trust.
[3] Data refer to both adoptions arranged by the National Children's Trust and by direct contact between the parties concerned in the metropolitan area. Main receiving country: Spain.
[4] It was assumed that 60 per cent of adoptive children are under age five.

Government policies

Type of adoption permitted	
Domestic adoption	Yes
Intercountry adoption	Yes
Single male permitted to adopt	...
Single female permitted to adopt	...
Age requirements for adopting parents	Aged 30 years or older and at least 15 years older than the child
Child's age of consent for adoption	Aged 16 years or older
Year of ratification of legal instruments on child adoption	
Convention on the Rights of the Child......................	1991
Hague Convention on Intercountry Adoption	Not ratified
National legislation governing adoption	Law No.83-802 of 2 August 1983 modifying Law No. 64-378 of 7 October 1964 on Adoption; Code de la nationalité ivoirienne
Government body responsible for adoption approval	Judiciary; Ministry of Health and Social Welfare

Adoption indicators	*Year*	*Number*	*Percentage*
Total children adopted	...	...	...
Of which:			
Domestic adoptions..	...	...	...
Intercountry adoptions	...	...	...
Of which:			
Adoptions by step-parents or other relatives..............	...	...	...
Adoptions per 100,000 births...	...	...	
Adoptions per 100,000 children under age 18	...	...	
Adoptions per 100,000 children under age 5	...	...	

Demographic indicators	*Year*	*Value*
Female singulate mean age at marriage (years)	1999	22.0
Mean age at first birth (years)[1]	1998-1999	19.5
Total fertility (children per woman)..............................	2000-2005	5.1
Percentage of childless women, aged 40 - 44	1998-1999	4.8
Divorce rate (per woman)	...	...

[1] Median age at first birth among women aged 25 to 29 years at the date of the survey.

Government policies

Type of adoption permitted	
Domestic adoption	Yes
Intercountry adoption..	Yes
Single male permitted to adopt	Yes
Single female permitted to adopt	Yes
Age requirements for adopting parents[1]	Aged 21 to 35 years and less than 40 years older than the child
Child's age of consent for adoption	Aged 12 years or older
Year of ratification of legal instruments on child adoption	
Convention on the Rights of the Child......................	1992
Hague Convention on Intercountry Adoption	Not ratified
National legislation governing adoption	Family Act of 1998
Government body responsible for adoption approval	Judiciary; Ministry of Labor and Social Policy

Adoption indicators

	Year	Number	Percentage
Total children adopted	2003	151	100
Of which:			
Domestic adoptions...	2003	148	98
Intercountry adoptions	2003	3	2
Of which:			
Adoptions by step-parents or other relatives[2].............	2003	130	87.8
Adoptions per 100,000 births...	2003	365.2	
Adoptions per 100,000 children under age 18	2003	16.8	
Adoptions per 100,000 children under age 5[3]	2003	42.1	

Demographic indicators

	Year	Value
Female singulate mean age at marriage (years)	2001	26.2
Mean age at first birth (years)..	2000	25.5
Total fertility (children per woman)...............................	2000-2005	1.3
Percentage of childless women, aged 40 - 44	1991	9.3
Divorce rate (per woman)..	1997	0.11

[1] Prospective adoptive parents aged 35 years or older are permitted to adopt under special circumstances.
[2] Data refer to domestic adoptions by relatives only. The percentage is calculated based on the total number of domestic adoptions.
[3] It was assumed that 60 per cent of adoptive children are under age five.

Government policies

Type of adoption permitted
    Domestic adoption ....
    Intercountry adoption...   ...

Single male permitted to adopt ....

Single female permitted to adopt ....

Age requirements for adopting parents ....

Child's age of consent for adoption ....

Year of ratification of legal instruments on child adoption
    Convention on the Rights of the Child......................   1991
    Hague Convention on Intercountry Adoption ....   Not ratified

National legislation governing adoption ....

Government body responsible for adoption approval ....

Adoption indicators

	Year	Number	Percentage
Total children adopted	...	...	...
Of which:			
Domestic adoptions...	...	...	...
Intercountry adoptions	...	...	...
Of which:			
Adoptions by step-parents or other relatives..............	...	...	...
Adoptions per 100,000 births...	...	...	
Adoptions per 100,000 children under age 18	...	...	
Adoptions per 100,000 children under age 5	...	...	

Demographic indicators

	Year	Value
Female singulate mean age at marriage (years)	1970	19.5
Mean age at first birth (years).......................................	1996	23.1
Total fertility (children per woman)...............................	2000-2005	1.6
Percentage of childless women, aged 40 - 44	1981	7.6
Divorce rate (per woman)	1996	0.39

Government policies

Type of adoption permitted
    Domestic adoption .... Yes
    Intercountry adoption.. Yes

Single male permitted to adopt ....

Single female permitted to adopt ....

Age requirements for adopting parents ....

Child's age of consent for adoption ....

Year of ratification of legal instruments on child adoption
    Convention on the Rights of the Child...................... 1991
    Hague Convention on Intercountry Adoption 1995

National legislation governing adoption .... Adoption Law No. 19(I) of 1995

Government body responsible for adoption approval ...... Judiciary; Ministry of Labour and Social Insurance

Adoption indicators	Year	Number	Percentage
Total children adopted	2001	216	100
Of which:			
Domestic adoptions..	2001	51	24
Intercountry adoptions	2001	165	76
Of which:			
Adoptions by step-parents or other relatives..............	...	...	...
Adoptions per 100,000 births..	2001	2 173.7	
Adoptions per 100,000 children under age 18	2001	101.0	
Adoptions per 100,000 children under age 5[1]	2001	251.9	

Demographic indicators	Year	Value
Female singulate mean age at marriage (years)	1992	23.1
Mean age at first birth (years)...	2001	28.6
Total fertility (children per woman).................................	2000-2005	1.6
Percentage of childless women, aged 40 - 44[2]	1992	11.5
Divorce rate (per woman)	2000	0.21

---

[1] It was assumed that 60 per cent of adoptive children are under age five.
[2] Never married added.

Government policies

Type of adoption permitted
　　Domestic adoption .... Yes
　　Intercountry adoption.. Yes

Single male permitted to adopt[1] .... No

Single female permitted to adopt[1] .... No

Age requirements for adopting parents ....

Child's age of consent for adoption .... Maturity of child considered

Year of ratification of legal instruments on child adoption
　　Convention on the Rights of the Child....................... 1993
　　Hague Convention on Intercountry Adoption 2000

National legislation governing adoption .... Act on the Family (Act No. 94/1963 Coll., as amended by Act No. 91/1998 Coll.)

Government body responsible for adoption approval ...... Judiciary; Ministry of Labour and Social Affairs; Office for International Legal Protection of Children

Adoption indicators	Year	Number	Percentage
Total children adopted[2]	2001	545	100
Of which:			
Domestic adoptions[3]	2001	519	95
Intercountry adoptions[4]...	2001	26	5
Of which:			
Adoptions by step-parents or other relatives..............	...	...	...
Adoptions per 100,000 births[2]	2001	614.4	
Adoptions per 100,000 children under age 18[2]	2001	26.8	
Adoptions per 100,000 children under age 5[5]	2001	74.3	

Demographic indicators	Year	Value
Female singulate mean age at marriage (years)	2000	25.3
Mean age at first birth (years)......................................	2001	25.3
Total fertility (children per woman)..............................	2000-2005	1.2
Percentage of childless women, aged 40 - 44	1991	5.5
Divorce rate (per woman)	1997	0.41

[1] Permission for adoption may be granted to a single person under special circumstances.
[2] Data refer to children placed in pre-adoption care.
[3] Estimate. Data refer to children placed in pre-adoption care.
[4] Data refer to children placed in pre-adoption care. Main receiving country: Denmark.
[5] Data refer to children placed in pre-adoption care. It was assumed that 60 per cent of adoptive children are under age five.

Government policies

Type of adoption permitted
    Domestic adoption ....   Yes
    Intercountry adoption..   Yes

Single male permitted to adopt ....

Single female permitted to adopt ....

Age requirements for adopting parents ....

Child's age of consent for adoption ....   Maturity of child considered

Year of ratification of legal instruments on child adoption
    Convention on the Rights of the Child......................   1990
    Hague Convention on Intercountry Adoption ....   Not ratified

National legislation governing adoption ....   Family Law of October 1990

Government body responsible for adoption approval ......   Local population administration authorities

Adoption indicators	Year	Number	Percentage
Total children adopted	2003	267	100
Of which:			
Domestic adoptions.............................	2003	267	100
Intercountry adoptions	2003	0	0
Of which:			
Adoptions by step-parents or other relatives..............	...	...	...
Adoptions per 100,000 births..	2003	74.6	
Adoptions per 100,000 children under age 18	2003	3.9	
Adoptions per 100,000 children under age 5[1]	2003	8.9	

Demographic indicators	Year	Value
Female singulate mean age at marriage (years)	...	...
Mean age at first birth (years)...	...	...
Total fertility (children per woman)...............................	2000-2005	2.0
Percentage of childless women, aged 40 - 44	1970	1.8
Divorce rate (per woman)	...	...

[1] It was assumed that 60 per cent of adoptive children are under age five.

Government policies

Type of adoption permitted
    Domestic adoption ....   Yes
    Intercountry adoption...   Yes

Single male permitted to adopt ....

Single female permitted to adopt ....

Age requirements for adopting parents ....

Child's age of consent for adoption ....

Year of ratification of legal instruments on child adoption
    Convention on the Rights of the Child......................   1990
    Hague Convention on Intercountry Adoption ....   Not ratified

National legislation governing adoption ....   Family Code

Government body responsible for adoption approval ......   Ministry of Justice; the Tribunal de Paix

Adoption indicators

	Year	Number	Percentage
Total children adopted	...	...	...
Of which:			
Domestic adoptions..	...	...	...
Intercountry adoptions...	...	...	...
Of which:			
Adoptions by step-parents or other relatives..............	...	..	..
Adoptions per 100,000 births.......................................	...	..	
Adoptions per 100,000 children under age 18	...	...	
Adoptions per 100,000 children under age 5	...	...	

Demographic indicators

	Year	Value
Female singulate mean age at marriage (years)	1984	20.0
Mean age at first birth (years)......................................	...	...
Total fertility (children per woman)..............................	2000-2005	6.7
Percentage of childless women, aged 40 - 44	...	...
Divorce rate (per woman)...	...	...

Government policies

Type of adoption permitted
　Domestic adoption ....　Yes
　Intercountry adoption ....　Yes

Single male permitted to adopt ....　Yes

Single female permitted to adopt ....　Yes

Age requirements for adopting parents ....　Aged 25 years or older

Child's age of consent for adoption ....　Aged 12 years or older

Year of ratification of legal instruments on child adoption
　Convention on the Rights of the Child ....　1991
　Hague Convention on Intercountry Adoption ....　1997

National legislation governing adoption ....　Danish Adoption Act, cf. Consolidated Act No. 1040 of 16 December 1999; Adoption (Consolidation) Act , Act. No. 928 of 14 September 2004

Government body responsible for adoption approval ......　Judiciary; Ministry of Family and Consumer Affairs; Regional Government Department; Central Adoption Board

Adoption indicators	Year	Number	Percentage
Total children adopted	2003	1 249	100
Of which:			
Domestic adoptions..	2003	561	45
Intercountry adoptions[1]	2003	688	55
Of which:			
Adoptions by step-parents or other relatives[2]	2003	579	46.4
Adoptions per 100,000 births..	2003	1 956.7	
Adoptions per 100,000 children under age 18	2003	104.7	
Adoptions per 100,000 children under age 5[3]	2003	225.8	

Demographic indicators	Year	Value
Female singulate mean age at marriage (years)	2001	30.7
Mean age at first birth (years)..	1995	27.4
Total fertility (children per woman)................................	2000-2005	1.8
Percentage of childless women, aged 40 - 44	…	…
Divorce rate (per woman)..	1997	0.28

[1]　Main country of origin: China.

[2]　Data refer to adoptions by step-parents only.

[3]　It was assumed that 60 per cent of adoptive children are under age five.

Government policies

Type of adoption permitted
    Domestic adoption .... No
    Intercountry adoption.. No

Single male permitted to adopt .... Not applicable

Single female permitted to adopt .... Not applicable

Age requirements for adopting parents .... Not applicable

Child's age of consent for adoption .... Not applicable

Year of ratification of legal instruments on child adoption
    Convention on the Rights of the Child...................... 1990
    Hague Convention on Intercountry Adoption .... Not ratified

National legislation governing adoption .... Not applicable

Government body responsible for adoption approval ...... Not applicable

Adoption indicators

	Year	Number	Percentage
Total children adopted	...	..	..
Of which:			
Domestic adoptions	...	..	..
Intercountry adoptions	...	..	..
Of which:			
Adoptions by step-parents or other relatives	...	..	..
Adoptions per 100,000 births	...	..	
Adoptions per 100,000 children under age 18	...	..	
Adoptions per 100,000 children under age 5	...	..	

Demographic indicators

	Year	Value
Female singulate mean age at marriage (years)	...	...
Mean age at first birth (years)	...	...
Total fertility (children per woman)	2000-2005	5.1
Percentage of childless women, aged 40 - 44	...	...
Divorce rate (per woman)	...	...

Government policies

Type of adoption permitted	
Domestic adoption	Yes
Intercountry adoption[1]	Yes
Single male permitted to adopt[2]	Yes
Single female permitted to adopt	Yes
Age requirements for adopting parents	Aged 25 years or older and at least 21 years older than the child
Child's age of consent for adoption	Maturity of child considered
Year of ratification of legal instruments on child adoption	
Convention on the Rights of the Child......................	1991
Hague Convention on Intercountry Adoption	Not ratified
National legislation governing adoption	Adoption of Infants Act; Guardianship of Infant Act
Government body responsible for adoption approval	Judiciary; Welfare Division Foster Care Program

Adoption indicators	Year	Number	Percentage
Total children adopted[3]	2003	15	100
Of which:			
Domestic adoptions....................................	...	...	...
Intercountry adoptions	...	...	...
Of which:			
Adoptions by step-parents or other relatives..............	...	...	...
Adoptions per 100,000 births[3]	2003	1 168.2	
Adoptions per 100,000 children under age 18[3]	2003	65.8	
Adoptions per 100,000 children under age 5[4]	2003	143.4	

Demographic indicators	Year	Value
Female singulate mean age at marriage (years)	...	...
Mean age at first birth (years)........................	...	...
Total fertility (children per woman).............................	2000-2005	2.0
Percentage of childless women, aged 40 - 44	...	...
Divorce rate (per woman)	...	...

---

[1] Intercountry adoptions are granted only in exceptional cases.

[2] A sole male applicant is not permitted to adopt a girl, except under special circumstances.

[3] Estimate.

[4] Estimate. It was assumed that 60 per cent of adoptive children are under age five.

Government policies

Type of adoption permitted
  Domestic adoption .... Yes
  Intercountry adoption... Yes

Single male permitted to adopt .... Yes

Single female permitted to adopt .... Yes

Age requirements for adopting parents .... Aged 30 to 60 years

Child's age of consent for adoption .... Aged 12 years or older

Year of ratification of legal instruments on child adoption
  Convention on the Rights of the Child...................... 1991
  Hague Convention on Intercountry Adoption 2006

National legislation governing adoption .... Act No. 14-94; Act No. 24-97; Code for the Protection and Fundamental Rights of Children and Adolescents, Law No. 136-03

Government body responsible for adoption approval ...... Executive Technical Department of the Governing Body of the System for the Protection of Children and Adolescents

Adoption indicators	Year	Number	Percentage
Total children adopted	...	...	...
Of which:			
Domestic adoptions...	...	...	...
Intercountry adoptions	...	...	...
Of which:			
Adoptions by step-parents or other relatives	...	...	...
Adoptions per 100,000 births.....................................	...	...	
Adoptions per 100,000 children under age 18	...	...	
Adoptions per 100,000 children under age 5	...	...	

Demographic indicators	Year	Value
Female singulate mean age at marriage (years)	1996	21.3
Mean age at first birth (years)[1]	1999	21.1
Total fertility (children per woman)...............................	2000-2005	2.7
Percentage of childless women, aged 40 - 44	2002	7.5
Divorce rate (per woman)	1984	0.06

[1] Median age at first birth among women aged 25 to 29 years at the date of the survey.

Government policies

Type of adoption permitted
    Domestic adoption .... Yes
    Intercountry adoption .... Yes

Single male permitted to adopt .... Yes

Single female permitted to adopt .... Yes

Age requirements for adopting parents[1] .... Aged 25 years or older and 14 to 45 years older than the child

Child's age of consent for adoption ....

Year of ratification of legal instruments on child adoption
    Convention on the Rights of the Child 1990
    Hague Convention on Intercountry Adoption 1995

National legislation governing adoption .... Children's and Youth Code, Codification No. 2002-100. R.O. 737 of 3 January 2003

Government body responsible for adoption approval ...... Judiciary; Ministry of Social Welfare

Adoption indicators	Year	Number	Percentage
Total children adopted	2004	118	100
Of which:			
Domestic adoptions..	2004	75	64
Intercountry adoptions[2]	2004	43	36
Of which:			
Adoptions by step-parents or other relatives	...	...	...
Adoptions per 100,000 births..	2004	39.9	
Adoptions per 100,000 children under age 18	2004	2.3	
Adoptions per 100,000 children under age 5[3]	2004	4.9	

Demographic indicators	Year	Value
Female singulate mean age at marriage (years)	2001	21.5
Mean age at first birth (years)...	1998	23.0
Total fertility (children per woman).................................	2000-2005	2.8
Percentage of childless women, aged 40 - 44	2001	7.9
Divorce rate (per woman)...	1997	0.10

---

[1] Step-parents must be at least 10 years older than the child.
[2] Main receiving country: United States of America.
[3] It was assumed that 60 per cent of adoptive children are under age five.

Government policies

Type of adoption permitted
    Domestic adoption .... No
    Intercountry adoption .... No

Single male permitted to adopt .... Not applicable

Single female permitted to adopt .... Not applicable

Age requirements for adopting parents .... Not applicable

Child's age of consent for adoption .... Not applicable

Year of ratification of legal instruments on child adoption
    Convention on the Rights of the Child....................... 1990
    Hague Convention on Intercountry Adoption .... Not ratified

National legislation governing adoption .... Not applicable

Government body responsible for adoption approval ...... Not applicable

Adoption indicators	Year	Number	Percentage
Total children adopted	...	..	..
Of which:			
Domestic adoptions..	...	..	..
Intercountry adoptions	...	..	..
Of which:			
Adoptions by step-parents or other relatives..............	...	..	..
Adoptions per 100,000 births.............................	...	..	
Adoptions per 100,000 children under age 18	...	..	
Adoptions per 100,000 children under age 5	...	..	

Demographic indicators	Year	Value
Female singulate mean age at marriage (years)	1996	22.3
Mean age at first birth (years)..	1995	27.1
Total fertility (children per woman)...............................	2000-2005	3.3
Percentage of childless women, aged 40 - 44	2003	8.4
Divorce rate (per woman)	1996	0.14

Government policies

Type of adoption permitted
    Domestic adoption .... Yes
    Intercountry adoption.. Yes

Single male permitted to adopt[1] .... Yes

Single female permitted to adopt[1] .... Yes

Age requirements for adopting parents .... Aged 25 years or older and at least 15 years older than the child

Child's age of consent for adoption .... Aged 12 years or older

Year of ratification of legal instruments on child adoption
    Convention on the Rights of the Child....................... 1990
    Hague Convention on Intercountry Adoption 1998

National legislation governing adoption .... Family Code, D.L. No. 677 of 11 October 1993; Family Court Procedure Act, D.L. No. 133 of 14 September 1994

Government body responsible for adoption approval ...... Office of the Procurator-General of the Republic; Salvadoran Institute for the Protection of Children

Adoption indicators	Year	Number	Percentage
Total children adopted	2003	253	100
Of which:			
Domestic adoptions..	2003	136	54
Intercountry adoptions	2003	117	46
Of which:			
Adoptions by step-parents or other relatives..............	...	...	...
Adoptions per 100,000 births...	2003	152.1	
Adoptions per 100,000 children under age 18	2003	9.4	
Adoptions per 100,000 children under age 5[2]	2003	18.9	

Demographic indicators	Year	Value
Female singulate mean age at marriage (years)	2000	22.3
Mean age at first birth (years)...	1998	23.0
Total fertility (children per woman)................................	2000-2005	2.9
Percentage of childless women, aged 40 - 44	2002-2003	7.2
Divorce rate (per woman)	1997	0.06

[1] Unmarried foreign citizens residing outside of the country are not permitted to adopt.
[2] It was assumed that 60 per cent of adoptive children are under age five.

Government policies

Type of adoption permitted
    Domestic adoption .... Yes
    Intercountry adoption... ...

Single male permitted to adopt ....

Single female permitted to adopt ....

Age requirements for adopting parents .... Aged 25 years or older and at least 14 years older than the child

Child's age of consent for adoption .... Aged 12 years or older

Year of ratification of legal instruments on child adoption
    Convention on the Rights of the Child....................... 1992
    Hague Convention on Intercountry Adoption .... Not ratified

National legislation governing adoption .... Spanish Civil Code

Government body responsible for adoption approval ...... Government Procurator's Office

Adoption indicators	Year	Number	Percentage
Total children adopted	...	...	...
Of which:			
Domestic adoptions...	...	...	...
Intercountry adoptions	...	...	...
Of which:			
Adoptions by step-parents or other relatives..............	...	...	...
Adoptions per 100,000 births......................................	...	...	
Adoptions per 100,000 children under age 18	...	...	
Adoptions per 100,000 children under age 5	...	...	

Demographic indicators	Year	Value
Female singulate mean age at marriage (years)	1983	21.7
Mean age at first birth (years)......................................	...	...
Total fertility (children per woman)..............................	2000-2005	5.9
Percentage of childless women, aged 40 - 44	...	...
Divorce rate (per woman)	...	...

Government policies

Type of adoption permitted
    Domestic adoption ....   Yes
    Intercountry adoption[1] ....   Yes

Single male permitted to adopt ....

Single female permitted to adopt ....

Age requirements for adopting parents ....

Child's age of consent for adoption ....   Aged 10 years or older

Year of ratification of legal instruments on child adoption
    Convention on the Rights of the Child   1994
    Hague Convention on Intercountry Adoption ....   Not ratified

National legislation governing adoption ....   Transitional Civil Code of Eritrea

Government body responsible for adoption approval ......   Judiciary; Ministry of Labour and Human Welfare

Adoption indicators	Year	Number	Percentage
Total children adopted[2]	1993-2002	50	100
Of which:			
Domestic adoptions	...	...	...
Intercountry adoptions	...	...	...
Of which:			
Adoptions by step-parents or other relatives	...	...	...
Adoptions per 100,000 births[2]	1993-2002	3.6	
Adoptions per 100,000 children under age 18[2]	1993-2002	0.3	
Adoptions per 100,000 children under age 5[3]	1993-2002	0.5	

Demographic indicators	Year	Value
Female singulate mean age at marriage (years)	1995	19.6
Mean age at first birth (years)[4]	2002	20.6
Total fertility (children per woman)	2000-2005	5.5
Percentage of childless women, aged 40 - 44	2002	5.4
Divorce rate (per woman)	...	...

[1] Prospective adoptive parents who are not citizens must have resided in the country for at least six months prior to the date of the adoption application.
[2] Estimate.
[3] Estimate. It was assumed that 60 per cent of adoptive children are under age five.
[4] Median age at first birth among women aged 25 to 29 years at the date of the survey.

Government policies

Type of adoption permitted
    Domestic adoption .... Yes
    Intercountry adoption................................... Yes

Single male permitted to adopt .... Yes

Single female permitted to adopt .... Yes

Age requirements for adopting parents .... Aged 25 years or older

Child's age of consent for adoption[1] .... Aged 10 years or older

Year of ratification of legal instruments on child adoption
    Convention on the Rights of the Child...................... 1991
    Hague Convention on Intercountry Adoption 2002

National legislation governing adoption .... Family Law Act; Child Protection Act; Social Welfare Act

Government body responsible for adoption approval ...... Judiciary; Ministry of Social Affairs

Adoption indicators	Year	Number	Percentage
Total children adopted	2003	130	100
Of which:			
Domestic adoptions.....................................	2003	115	88
Intercountry adoptions[2]...............................	2003	15	12
Of which:			
Adoptions by step-parents or other relatives[3]............	2003	63	54.8
Adoptions per 100,000 births........................	2003	999.3	
Adoptions per 100,000 children under age 18	2003	46.1	
Adoptions per 100,000 children under age 5[4]	2003	126.5	

Demographic indicators	Year	Value
Female singulate mean age at marriage (years)	1989	22.1
Mean age at first birth (years).......................	2001	24.2
Total fertility (children per woman)..............................	2000-2005	1.4
Percentage of childless women, aged 40 - 44[5]	1994	9.1
Divorce rate (per woman)	1996	0.50

[1] The maturity of the child is also considered.
[2] Main receiving country: United States of America.
[3] Data refer to domestic adoptions by step-parents only. The percentage is calculated based on the total number of domestic adoptions.
[4] It was assumed that 60 per cent of adoptive children are under age five.
[5] Native and foreign born.

Government policies

Type of adoption permitted
    Domestic adoption .... Yes
    Intercountry adoption.. Yes

Single male permitted to adopt .... Yes

Single female permitted to adopt .... Yes

Age requirements for adopting parents .... Aged 25 years or older

Child's age of consent for adoption ....

Year of ratification of legal instruments on child adoption
    Convention on the Rights of the Child....................... 1991
    Hague Convention on Intercountry Adoption .... Not ratified

National legislation governing adoption .... Civil Code; Family Code

Government body responsible for adoption approval ...... Judiciary; Ministry of Labor and Social Affairs

Adoption indicators

	Year	Number	Percentage
Total children adopted[1]	2002-2003	872	100
Of which:			
Domestic adoptions[1]	2002-2003	62	7
Intercountry adoptions[2]...	2002-2003	810	93
Of which:			
Adoptions by step-parents or other relatives..............	...	...	...
Adoptions per 100,000 births[1]	2002-2003	28.8	
Adoptions per 100,000 children under age 18[1]	2002-2003	2.3	
Adoptions per 100,000 children under age 5[3]	2002-2003	4.1	

Demographic indicators

	Year	Value
Female singulate mean age at marriage (years)	2000	20.5
Mean age at first birth (years)[4]..	2000	20.1
Total fertility (children per woman).................................	2000-2005	5.9
Percentage of childless women, aged 40 - 44	2000	4.1
Divorce rate (per woman)	...	...

---

[1] Data refer to the fiscal year.

[2] Data refer to the fiscal year. Based on data from selected receiving countries, the main receiving country: France.

[3] Data refer to the fiscal year. It was assumed that 60 per cent of adoptive children are under age five.

[4] Median age at first birth among women aged 25 to 29 years at the date of the survey.

Government policies

Type of adoption permitted	
Domestic adoption	Yes
Intercountry adoption	Yes
Single male permitted to adopt	...
Single female permitted to adopt	...
Age requirements for adopting parents	...
Child's age of consent for adoption	...
Year of ratification of legal instruments on child adoption	
Convention on the Rights of the Child	1993
Hague Convention on Intercountry Adoption	Not ratified
National legislation governing adoption	Juveniles Act; Adoption of Infants Act
Government body responsible for adoption approval	Department of Social Welfare, Ministry of Heath and Social Welfare; Adoption Court

Adoption indicators	Year	Number	Percentage
Total children adopted	1994	89	100
Of which:			
Domestic adoptions[1]	1994	79	89
Intercountry adoptions[1]	1994	10	11
Of which:			
Adoptions by step-parents or other relatives	...	...	...
Adoptions per 100,000 births	1994	434.0	
Adoptions per 100,000 children under age 18	1994	27.4	
Adoptions per 100,000 children under age 5[2]	1994	56.3	

Demographic indicators	Year	Value
Female singulate mean age at marriage (years)	1996	22.9
Mean age at first birth (years)	1987	22.3
Total fertility (children per woman)	2000-2005	2.9
Percentage of childless women, aged 40 - 44	1986	7.2
Divorce rate (per woman)	...	...

[1] Estimate.
[2] It was assumed that 60 per cent of adoptive children are under age five.

Government policies

Type of adoption permitted	
Domestic adoption	Yes
Intercountry adoption...	Yes
Single male permitted to adopt	Yes
Single female permitted to adopt	Yes
Age requirements for adopting parents	Aged 25 years or older and less than 45 years older than the child
Child's age of consent for adoption	Aged 12 years or older
Year of ratification of legal instruments on child adoption	
Convention on the Rights of the Child.......................	1991
Hague Convention on Intercountry Adoption	1997
National legislation governing adoption	Adoption Act (153/1985); Decree on the Finnish Board of Inter-Country Adoption Affairs (508/1997)
Government body responsible for adoption approval	Judiciary; The Finnish Adoption Board, Ministry of Social Affairs and Health

Adoption indicators

	Year	Number	Percentage
Total children adopted	2004	496	100
Of which:			
Domestic adoptions..	2004	207	42
Intercountry adoptions[1]	2004	289	58
Of which:			
Adoptions by step-parents or other relatives..............	...	...	...
Adoptions per 100,000 births..	2004	895.6	
Adoptions per 100,000 children under age 18	2004	44.8	
Adoptions per 100,000 children under age 5[2]	2004	105.9	

Demographic indicators

	Year	Value
Female singulate mean age at marriage (years)	2000	30.2
Mean age at first birth (years)...	2001	27.5
Total fertility (children per woman).................................	2000-2005	1.7
Percentage of childless women, aged 40 - 44	2000	16.8
Divorce rate (per woman)	1997	0.32

[1] Main country of origin: China.

[2] It was assumed that 60 per cent of adoptive children are under age five.

Government policies

Type of adoption permitted	
Domestic adoption[1]	Yes
Intercountry adoption	Yes
Single male permitted to adopt	Yes
Single female permitted to adopt	Yes
Age requirements for adopting parents[2]	Aged 28 years or older and at least 15 years older than the child
Child's age of consent for adoption	Aged 13 years or older
Year of ratification of legal instruments on child adoption	
Convention on the Rights of the Child	1990
Hague Convention on Intercountry Adoption	1998
National legislation governing adoption	Civil Code; Family and Social Welfare Code of 1985; Adoption Act No. 96-604 of 5 July 1996; Act No. 2001-111 of 6 February 2001
Government body responsible for adoption approval	Judiciary; Family Council of Children in Care; Higher Council for Adoption; Intercountry Adoption Office, Minister of Foreign Affairs

Adoption indicators	Year	Number	Percentage
Total children adopted	2003	4 445	100
Of which:			
Domestic adoptions	2003	450	10
Intercountry adoptions[3]	2003	3 995	90
Of which:			
Adoptions by step-parents or other relatives	...	...	...
Adoptions per 100,000 births	2003	596.5	
Adoptions per 100,000 children under age 18	2003	33.4	
Adoptions per 100,000 children under age 5[4]	2003	71.9	

Demographic indicators	Year	Value
Female singulate mean age at marriage (years)	2000	30.2
Mean age at first birth (years)[5]	1999	28.7
Total fertility (children per woman)	2000-2005	1.9
Percentage of childless women, aged 40 - 44	1994	10.2
Divorce rate (per woman)	1993	0.24

[1] Prospective adoptive parents must have had the child in their care and custody for at least six months to engage in a full adoption.
[2] Step-parents must be at least 10 years older than the child.
[3] Main country of origin: Haiti.
[4] It was assumed that 60 per cent of adoptive children are under age five.
[5] Mean age at first birth within current marriage.

Government policies

Type of adoption permitted[1]
    Domestic adoption .... Yes
    Intercountry adoption... ...

Single male permitted to adopt .... Yes

Single female permitted to adopt .... Yes

Age requirements for adopting parents .... Aged 35 years or older and at least 15 years older than the child

Child's age of consent for adoption ....

Year of ratification of legal instruments on child adoption
    Convention on the Rights of the Child...................... 1994
    Hague Convention on Intercountry Adoption .... Not ratified

National legislation governing adoption .... Civil Code

Government body responsible for adoption approval ...... Judiciary; Department of Social Affairs

Adoption indicators	Year	Number	Percentage
Total children adopted	1980-1998	40	100
Of which:			
Domestic adoptions...	...	...	...
Intercountry adoptions	...	...	...
Of which:			
Adoptions by step-parents or other relatives..............	...	...	...
Adoptions per 100,000 births..	1980-1998	5.9	
Adoptions per 100,000 children under age 18	1980-1998	0.5	
Adoptions per 100,000 children under age 5[2]	1980-1998	0.8	

Demographic indicators	Year	Value
Female singulate mean age at marriage (years)	2001	22.1
Mean age at first birth (years)[3]	2000	18.7
Total fertility (children per woman)................................	2000-2005	4.0
Percentage of childless women, aged 40 - 44	2000	5.4
Divorce rate (per woman)...	...	...

[1] Adoptive children must be under 15 years of age.
[2] It was assumed that 60 per cent of adoptive children are under age five.
[3] Median age at first birth among women aged 25 to 29 years at the date of the survey.

Government policies

Type of adoption permitted
    Domestic adoption .... Yes
    Intercountry adoption[1] .... Yes

Single male permitted to adopt ....

Single female permitted to adopt ....

Age requirements for adopting parents ....

Child's age of consent for adoption ....

Year of ratification of legal instruments on child adoption
    Convention on the Rights of the Child...................... 1990
    Hague Convention on Intercountry Adoption .... Not ratified

National legislation governing adoption .... Adoption Act (Act No. 15 of 1992)

Government body responsible for adoption approval ...... Judiciary; Department of Social Welfare

Adoption indicators

	Year	Number	Percentage
Total children adopted	1998-2000	18	100
Of which:			
Domestic adoptions......................................	1998-2000	8	44
Intercountry adoptions	1998-2000	10	56
Of which:			
Adoptions by step-parents or other relatives[2]............	1998-2000	12	66.7
Adoptions per 100,000 births..	1998-2000	12.4	
Adoptions per 100,000 children under age 18	1998-2000	1.0	
Adoptions per 100,000 children under age 5[3]	1998-2000	1.8	

Demographic indicators

	Year	Value
Female singulate mean age at marriage (years)	1993	19.6
Mean age at first birth (years).....................................	...	...
Total fertility (children per woman)..............................	2000-2005	4.7
Percentage of childless women, aged 40 - 44	1973	12.0
Divorce rate (per woman)	...	...

---

[1] Prospective adoptive parents who are not citizens must have resided in the country for at least six months prior to the date of the adoption.
[2] Data refer to adoptions by relatives only.
[3] It was assumed that 60 per cent of adoptive children are under age five.

Government policies

Type of adoption permitted
    Domestic adoption .... Yes
    Intercountry adoption.. Yes

Single male permitted to adopt .... Yes

Single female permitted to adopt .... Yes

Age requirements for adopting parents ....

Child's age of consent for adoption .... Aged 10 years or older

Year of ratification of legal instruments on child adoption
    Convention on the Rights of the Child...................... 1994
    Hague Convention on Intercountry Adoption 1999

National legislation governing adoption .... Law on Adoption Regulations of 17 November 1997; Orphaned and Neglected Children (Adoption Procedure) Act of 1999

Government body responsible for adoption approval ...... Judiciary; Ministry of Education

Adoption indicators	Year	Number	Percentage
Total children adopted	2002	154	100
Of which:			
Domestic adoptions...	2002	35	23
Intercountry adoptions[1]...	2002	119	77
Of which:			
Adoptions by step-parents or other relatives..............	...	...	...
Adoptions per 100,000 births...	2002	301.2	
Adoptions per 100,000 children under age 18	2002	13.0	
Adoptions per 100,000 children under age 5[2]	2002	36.6	

Demographic indicators	Year	Value
Female singulate mean age at marriage (years)	1999	24.3
Mean age at first birth (years)	2000	24.2
Total fertility (children per woman).................................	2000-2005	1.5
Percentage of childless women, aged 40 - 44	1999-2000	13.1
Divorce rate (per woman)	1996	0.05

[1] Based on data from selected receiving countries, the main receiving country: United States of America.
[2] It was assumed that 60 per cent of adoptive children are under age five.

Government policies

Type of adoption permitted
  Domestic adoption .... Yes
  Intercountry adoption.. Yes

Single male permitted to adopt .... Yes

Single female permitted to adopt .... Yes

Age requirements for adopting parents[1]........................... Aged 21 years or older

Child's age of consent for adoption .... Aged 14 years or older

Year of ratification of legal instruments on child adoption
  Convention on the Rights of the Child....................... 1992
  Hague Convention on Intercountry Adoption 2001

National legislation governing adoption .... Civil Code; Adoption on the Protection of Children and the Co-operation in the Field of International Adoption; Act on the Effects of the Adoption According to Foreign Law; Act on the Adoption Placement and the Ban on the Arrangement of Surrogate Mothers; Act on the Implementation of the Hague Convention of 29 May 1993

Government body responsible for adoption approval[2] ..... Guardianship Court; Federal Central Office for Intercountry Adoption

Adoption indicators	Year	Number	Percentage
Total children adopted	2002	5 668	100
Of which:			
Domestic adoptions...	2002	3 749	66
Intercountry adoptions[3]	2002	1 919	34
Of which:			
Adoptions by step-parents or other relatives..............	2002	3 489	61.6
Adoptions per 100,000 births.......................................	2002	797.4	
Adoptions per 100,000 children under age 18	2002	36.9	
Adoptions per 100,000 children under age 5[4]...............	2002	89.9	

Demographic indicators	Year	Value
Female singulate mean age at marriage (years)	...	...
Mean age at first birth (years)	2000	28.2
Total fertility (children per woman)...............................	2000-2005	1.3
Percentage of childless women, aged 40 - 44	...	...
Divorce rate (per woman)	1996	0.26

[1] In the case of adoption by a couple, one adoptive parent must be aged 25 years or older and the other must be aged 21 years or older.
[2] Varies by state.
[3] Main country of origin: Russian Federation.
[4] It was assumed that 60 per cent of adoptive children are under age five.

Government policies

Type of adoption permitted
    Domestic adoption .... Yes
    Intercountry adoption[1] .... Yes

Single male permitted to adopt[2] .... Yes

Single female permitted to adopt[2] .... Yes

Age requirements for adopting parents ....

Child's age of consent for adoption ....

Year of ratification of legal instruments on child adoption
    Convention on the Rights of the Child...................... 1990
    Hague Convention on Intercountry Adoption .... Not ratified

National legislation governing adoption .... Adoption Act of 1962 (Act 104); Children's Act of 1998

Government body responsible for adoption approval ...... Judiciary; Department of Social Welfare

Adoption indicators

	Year	Number	Percentage
Total children adopted	2004	534	100
Of which:			
Domestic adoptions..	2004	529	99
Intercountry adoptions	2004	5	1
Of which:			
Adoptions by step-parents or other relatives[3].............	2004	277	52.4
Adoptions per 100,000 births..	2004	78.6	
Adoptions per 100,000 children under age 18	2004	5.3	
Adoptions per 100,000 children under age 5[4]	2004	10.4	

Demographic indicators

	Year	Value
Female singulate mean age at marriage (years)	1998	21.2
Mean age at first birth (years)[5]......................................	1998	20.9
Total fertility (children per woman)...............................	2000-2005	4.4
Percentage of childless women, aged 40 - 44	2003	5.1
Divorce rate (per woman)	...	...

---

[1] Prospective adoptive parents who are not citizens must have resided in the country for at least six months prior to the date of the adoption.

[2] Unmarried foreign citizens are not permitted to adopt.

[3] Data refer to domestic adoptions by relatives only. The percentage is calculated based on the total number of domestic adoptions.

[4] It was assumed that 60 per cent of adoptive children are under age five.

[5] Median age at first birth among women aged 25 to 29 years at the date of the survey.

Government policies

Type of adoption permitted
    Domestic adoption .... Yes
    Intercountry adoption... Yes

Single male permitted to adopt .... Yes

Single female permitted to adopt .... Yes

Age requirements for adopting parents[1] .... Aged 18 to 50 years older than the child

Child's age of consent for adoption .... Aged 12 years or older

Year of ratification of legal instruments on child adoption
    Convention on the Rights of the Child........................ 1993
    Hague Convention on Intercountry Adoption .... Not ratified

National legislation governing adoption .... Civil Code; Adoption Code (Law 2447/1996); Law 1049/1980; Presidential Decree 193/1973

Government body responsible for adoption approval ...... Judiciary; Ministry of Health and Welfare

Adoption indicators	Year	Number	Percentage
Total children adopted[2]	2001	600	100
Of which:			
Domestic adoptions...	…	…	…
Intercountry adoptions	…	…	…
Of which:			
Adoptions by step-parents or other relatives..............	…	…	…
Adoptions per 100,000 births[2]	2001	580.7	
Adoptions per 100,000 children under age 18[2]	2001	29.1	
Adoptions per 100,000 children under age 5[3]	2001	68.8	

Demographic indicators	Year	Value
Female singulate mean age at marriage (years)	1991	24.5
Mean age at first birth (years).....................................	1999	27.3
Total fertility (children per woman)..............................	2000-2005	1.3
Percentage of childless women, aged 40 - 44	…	…
Divorce rate (per woman)	1997	0.09

[1] Different age requirements apply to adoptions by step-parents.
[2] Estimate.
[3] Estimate. It was assumed that 60 per cent of adoptive children are under age five.

Government policies

Type of adoption permitted[1]	
Domestic adoption	Yes
Intercountry adoption..	Yes
Single male permitted to adopt	...
Single female permitted to adopt	...
Age requirements for adopting parents	Aged 25 years or older and at least 21 years older than the child
Child's age of consent for adoption	...
Year of ratification of legal instruments on child adoption	
Convention on the Rights of the Child......................	1990
Hague Convention on Intercountry Adoption	Not ratified
National legislation governing adoption	Adoption (Amendment) Act No. 17 of 1994
Government body responsible for adoption approval	Judiciary; Department of Social Security, Grenada Adoption Board

Adoption indicators	Year	Number	Percentage
Total children adopted	1995	15	100
Of which:			
Domestic adoptions...	1995	4	27
Intercountry adoptions	1995	11	73
Of which:			
Adoptions by step-parents or other relatives..............	...	...	...
Adoptions per 100,000 births..	1995	601.4	
Adoptions per 100,000 children under age 18	1995	32.5	
Adoptions per 100,000 children under age 5[2]	1995	73.2	

Demographic indicators	Year	Value
Female singulate mean age at marriage (years)	...	...
Mean age at first birth (years)...	...	...
Total fertility (children per woman)................................	2000-2005	2.4
Percentage of childless women, aged 40 - 44	...	...
Divorce rate (per woman)	...	...

[1] Prospective adoptive parents must have had the child in their care and custody for at least three months prior to the date of the adoption order.
[2] It was assumed that 60 per cent of adoptive children are under age five.

Government policies

Type of adoption permitted
Domestic adoption .... Yes
Intercountry adoption.. Yes

Single male permitted to adopt ....

Single female permitted to adopt ....

Age requirements for adopting parents ....

Child's age of consent for adoption ....

Year of ratification of legal instruments on child adoption
Convention on the Rights of the Child...................... 1990
Hague Convention on Intercountry Adoption 2002

National legislation governing adoption .... Civil Code; Children and Adolescents Code of 1996

Government body responsible for adoption approval ...... Office of the National Procurator-General; Office of Child and Family Welfare

Adoption indicators	Year	Number	Percentage
Total children adopted	2004	3 834	100
Of which:			
Domestic adoptions..	2004	108	3
Intercountry adoptions[1]...	2004	3 726	97
Of which:			
Adoptions by step-parents or other relatives..............	...	...	...
Adoptions per 100,000 births..	2004	885.8	
Adoptions per 100,000 children under age 18	2004	62.1	
Adoptions per 100,000 children under age 5[2]...............	2004	115.7	

Demographic indicators	Year	Value
Female singulate mean age at marriage (years)	1999	20.5
Mean age at first birth (years)[3].......................................	1998-1999	22.7
Total fertility (children per woman)...............................	2000-2005	4.6
Percentage of childless women, aged 40 - 44	1998-1999	8.7
Divorce rate (per woman)	1993	0.02

[1] Main receiving country: United States of America.
[2] It was assumed that 60 per cent of adoptive children are under age five.
[3] Median age at first birth among women aged 25 to 29 years at the date of the survey.

Government policies

Type of adoption permitted	
Domestic adoption	Yes
Intercountry adoption	Yes
Single male permitted to adopt	...
Single female permitted to adopt	...
Age requirements for adopting parents	Aged 35 years or older and at least 15 years older than the child
Child's age of consent for adoption	Aged 16 years or older
Year of ratification of legal instruments on child adoption	
Convention on the Rights of the Child	1990
Hague Convention on Intercountry Adoption	2003
National legislation governing adoption	Civil Code
Government body responsible for adoption approval	Judiciary; Ministry for the Promotion of Women and Children

Adoption indicators	Year	Number	Percentage
Total children adopted	...	...	...
Of which:			
Domestic adoptions	...	...	...
Intercountry adoptions	...	...	...
Of which:			
Adoptions by step-parents or other relatives	...	...	...
Adoptions per 100,000 births	...	...	
Adoptions per 100,000 children under age 18	...	...	
Adoptions per 100,000 children under age 5	...	...	

Demographic indicators	Year	Value
Female singulate mean age at marriage (years)	1999	18.7
Mean age at first birth (years)[1]	1999	18.6
Total fertility (children per woman)	2000-2005	5.9
Percentage of childless women, aged 40 - 44	1999	4.7
Divorce rate (per woman)	...	...

[1] Median age at first birth among women aged 25 to 29 years at the date of the survey.

Government policies

Type of adoption permitted	
Domestic adoption	Yes
Intercountry adoption..	…
Single male permitted to adopt[1]	No
Single female permitted to adopt[1]	No
Age requirements for adopting parents	Aged 25 to 60 years
Child's age of consent for adoption	Aged 14 years or older
Year of ratification of legal instruments on child adoption	
Convention on the Rights of the Child......................	1990
Hague Convention on Intercountry Adoption	Not ratified
National legislation governing adoption	Civil Code
Government body responsible for adoption approval	Judiciary; Ministry of Child Protection

Adoption indicators	Year	Number	Percentage
Total children adopted	1998-2000	13	100
Of which:			
Domestic adoptions..	…	…	…
Intercountry adoptions	…	…	…
Of which:			
Adoptions by step-parents or other relatives	…	…	…
Adoptions per 100,000 births..	1998-2000	6.5	
Adoptions per 100,000 children under age 18	1998-2000	0.6	
Adoptions per 100,000 children under age 5[2]	1998-2000	1.0	

Demographic indicators	Year	Value
Female singulate mean age at marriage (years)	…	…
Mean age at first birth (years)......................................	…	…
Total fertility (children per woman)...............................	2000-2005	7.1
Percentage of childless women, aged 40 - 44	…	…
Divorce rate (per woman)	…	…

[1] Prospective adoptive parents must have been married at least five years.

[2] It was assumed that 60 per cent of adoptive children are under age five.

Government policies

Type of adoption permitted	
Domestic adoption	Yes
Intercountry adoption...	Yes
Single male permitted to adopt[1]	Yes
Single female permitted to adopt	Yes
Age requirements for adopting parents	Aged 25 years or older and at least 21 years older than the child
Child's age of consent for adoption	Maturity of child considered
Year of ratification of legal instruments on child adoption	
Convention on the Rights of the Child.......................	1991
Hague Convention on Intercountry Adoption	Not ratified
National legislation governing adoption	Adoption of Children Act; Adoption (Amendment) Act of 1997
Government body responsible for adoption approval	Judiciary; Adoption Board

Adoption indicators

	Year	Number	Percentage
Total children adopted	2002	123	100
Of which:			
Domestic adoptions...	...	...	...
Intercountry adoptions	...	...	...
Of which:			
Adoptions by step-parents or other relatives..............	...	...	...
Adoptions per 100,000 births..	2002	745.1	
Adoptions per 100,000 children under age 18	2002	45.5	
Adoptions per 100,000 children under age 5[2].................	2002	93.7	

Demographic indicators

	Year	Value
Female singulate mean age at marriage (years)	1991	27.8
Mean age at first birth (years)[3]	1975	20.4
Total fertility (children per woman)................................	2000-2005	2.3
Percentage of childless women, aged 40 - 44	1980	6.0
Divorce rate (per woman)	...	...

[1] A sole male applicant is not permitted to adopt a girl, except under special circumstances.

[2] It was assumed that 60 per cent of adoptive children are under age five.

[3] Median age at first birth among women aged 25 to 29 years at the date of the survey.

Government policies

Type of adoption permitted	
Domestic adoption	Yes
Intercountry adoption..	Yes
Single male permitted to adopt	Yes
Single female permitted to adopt	Yes
Age requirements for adopting parents[1]	Aged 35 years or older and at least 19 years older than the child
Child's age of consent for adoption	...
Year of ratification of legal instruments on child adoption	
Convention on the Rights of the Child......................	1995
Hague Convention on Intercountry Adoption	Not ratified
National legislation governing adoption	Decree of 4 April 1974
Government body responsible for adoption approval	Judiciary; Ministry of Social Affairs

Adoption indicators	Year	Number	Percentage
Total children adopted	1994-1999	2 435	100
Of which:			
Domestic adoptions...	1994-1999	338	14
Intercountry adoptions[2]	1994-1999	2 097	86
Of which:			
Adoptions by step-parents or other relatives[3]	1994-1999	338	100.0
Adoptions per 100,000 births......................................	1994-1999	169.0	
Adoptions per 100,000 children under age 18	1994-1999	10.8	
Adoptions per 100,000 children under age 5[4]	1994-1999	22.7	

Demographic indicators	Year	Value
Female singulate mean age at marriage (years)	2000	22.3
Mean age at first birth (years)[5].....................................	2000	21.9
Total fertility (children per woman).............................	2000-2005	4.0
Percentage of childless women, aged 40 - 44	2000	8.2
Divorce rate (per woman)	...	...

[1] Step-parents must be at least 10 years older than the child.
[2] Based on data from selected receiving countries, the main receiving country in 2003: France.
[3] Data refer to domestic adoptions by relatives only. The percentage is calculated based on the total number of domestic adoptions.
[4] It was assumed that 60 per cent of adoptive children are under age five.
[5] Median age at first birth among women aged 25 to 29 years at the date of the survey.

Government policies

Type of adoption permitted
    Domestic adoption ....
    Intercountry adoption... ...

Single male permitted to adopt ....

Single female permitted to adopt ....

Age requirements for adopting parents ....

Child's age of consent for adoption ....

Year of ratification of legal instruments on child adoption
    Convention on the Rights of the Child...................... 1990
    Hague Convention on Intercountry Adoption .... Not ratified

National legislation governing adoption ....

Government body responsible for adoption approval ....

Adoption indicators	Year	Number	Percentage
Total children adopted	...	...	...
Of which:			
Domestic adoptions..	...	...	...
Intercountry adoptions	...	...	...
Of which:			
Adoptions by step-parents or other relatives..............	...	...	...
Adoptions per 100,000 births..	...	...	
Adoptions per 100,000 children under age 18	...	...	
Adoptions per 100,000 children under age 5	...	...	

Demographic indicators	Year	Value
Female singulate mean age at marriage (years)	...	...
Mean age at first birth (years)..	...	...
Total fertility (children per woman)................................	2000-2005	1.0
Percentage of childless women, aged 40 - 44	...	...
Divorce rate (per woman)	...	...

Government policies

Type of adoption permitted	
Domestic adoption	Yes
Intercountry adoption..	Yes
Single male permitted to adopt	Yes
Single female permitted to adopt	Yes
Age requirements for adopting parents	Aged 30 years or older and at least 15 years older than the child
Child's age of consent for adoption	...
Year of ratification of legal instruments on child adoption	
Convention on the Rights of the Child.......................	1990
Hague Convention on Intercountry Adoption	Not ratified
National legislation governing adoption	Constitution of the Republic of Honduras, Decree No. 131 of 11 January 1982; Family Code, Decree No. 76-84 of 31 May 1984; Code on Children and Adolescents, Decree No. 73-96 of 5 September 1996; Regulations on Adoption of the National Social Welfare Board
Government body responsible for adoption approval	Judiciary; National Social Welfare Board

Adoption indicators	Year	Number	Percentage
Total children adopted	2004	50	100
Of which:			
Domestic adoptions..	2004	20	40
Intercountry adoptions[1]	2004	30	60
Of which:			
Adoptions by step-parents or other relatives.............	...	...	...
Adoptions per 100,000 births..	2004	24.3	
Adoptions per 100,000 children under age 18	2004	1.5	
Adoptions per 100,000 children under age 5[2]	2004	3.1	

Demographic indicators	Year	Value
Female singulate mean age at marriage (years)	1996	20.4
Mean age at first birth (years).......................................	...	...
Total fertility (children per woman)..............................	2000-2005	3.7
Percentage of childless women, aged 40 - 44	2001	5.8
Divorce rate (per woman)	...	...

[1] Based on data from selected receiving countries, the main receiving country: Spain.
[2] It was assumed that 60 per cent of adoptive children are under age five.

Government policies

Type of adoption permitted
    Domestic adoption ....   Yes
    Intercountry adoption...   Yes

Single male permitted to adopt ....

Single female permitted to adopt ....

Age requirements for adopting parents ....   Aged 16 to 45 years older than the child

Child's age of consent for adoption[1] ....   Aged 14 years or older

Year of ratification of legal instruments on child adoption
    Convention on the Rights of the Child.......................   1991
    Hague Convention on Intercountry Adoption   2005

National legislation governing adoption ....   Family Law Act; Act XXXI of 1997 on the Protection of the Child and on the Management of Public Guardianship; Act IX of 2002 on the Amendment of the Child Protection Act

Government body responsible for adoption approval ......   Guardianship Authority; National Child and Youth Protection Institute; National Institute of Family and Social Policies

Adoption indicators	Year	Number	Percentage
Total children adopted	2004	750	100
Of which:			
Domestic adoptions...	2004	656	87
Intercountry adoptions[2]...	2004	94	13
Of which:			
Adoptions by step-parents or other relatives..............	...	...	...
Adoptions per 100,000 births...	2004	792.6	
Adoptions per 100,000 children under age 18	2004	37.6	
Adoptions per 100,000 children under age 5[3]	2004	93.6	

Demographic indicators	Year	Value
Female singulate mean age at marriage (years)	2000	26.3
Mean age at first birth (years)...	2001	25.3
Total fertility (children per woman).................................	2000-2005	1.3
Percentage of childless women, aged 40 - 44	1990	8.5
Divorce rate (per woman)	1997	0.33

[1] The maturity of the child is also considered.
[2] Data include 14 foreign children adopted by Hungarian citizens as well as 80 Hungarian children adopted abroad. Main receiving country: Italy.
[3] It was assumed that 60 per cent of adoptive children are under age five.

Government policies

Type of adoption permitted	
Domestic adoption	Yes
Intercountry adoption...	Yes
Single male permitted to adopt[1]	No
Single female permitted to adopt[1]	No
Age requirements for adopting parents	Aged 25 years or older
Child's age of consent for adoption[2]	Aged 12 years or older
Year of ratification of legal instruments on child adoption	
Convention on the Rights of the Child........................	1992
Hague Convention on Intercountry Adoption	2000
National legislation governing adoption	Adoption Act No. 130/1999
Government body responsible for adoption approval	Ministry of Justice; Adoption Board; Child Welfare Committee

Adoption indicators

	Year	Number	Percentage
Total children adopted	2003	44	100
Of which:			
Domestic adoptions...	2003	21	48
Intercountry adoptions[3]	2003	23	52
Of which:			
Adoptions by step-parents or other relatives[4]	2003	17	80.9
Adoptions per 100,000 births..	2003	1 066.4	
Adoptions per 100,000 children under age 18	2003	56.3	
Adoptions per 100,000 children under age 5[5]	2003	126.5	

Demographic indicators

	Year	Value
Female singulate mean age at marriage (years)	2000	30.5
Mean age at first birth (years).......................................	2000	25.5
Total fertility (children per woman)..............................	2000-2005	2.0
Percentage of childless women, aged 40 - 44	...	...
Divorce rate (per woman)	2000	0.40

---

[1] Permission for adoption may be granted to a single person under special circumstances.
[2] The maturity of the child is also considered.
[3] Main country of origin: China.
[4] Data refer to domestic adoptions by step-parents only. The percentage is calculated based on the total number of domestic adoptions.
[5] It was assumed that 60 per cent of adoptive children are under age five.

Government policies

Type of adoption permitted[1]
    Domestic adoption .... Yes
    Intercountry adoption... Yes

Single male permitted to adopt .... Yes

Single female permitted to adopt .... Yes

Age requirements for adopting parents ....

Child's age of consent for adoption ....

Year of ratification of legal instruments on child adoption
    Convention on the Rights of the Child...................... 1992
    Hague Convention on Intercountry Adoption 2003

National legislation governing adoption .... Guardians and Wards Act of 1890; Hindu Adoptions and Maintenance Act LXXVIII of 1956

Government body responsible for adoption approval ...... Judiciary; Central Adoption Resource Agency; Juvenile Welfare Board; Scrutiny Agencies

Adoption indicators	Year	Number	Percentage
Total children adopted	2003	3 047	100
Of which:			
Domestic adoptions..	2003	1 949	64
Intercountry adoptions[2]..	2003	1 098	36
Of which:			
Adoptions by step-parents or other relatives..............	...	...	...
Adoptions per 100,000 births..	2003	11.7	
Adoptions per 100,000 children under age 18	2003	0.7	
Adoptions per 100,000 children under age 5[3]	2003	1.5	

Demographic indicators	Year	Value
Female singulate mean age at marriage (years)	1999	19.9
Mean age at first birth (years)[4].......................................	1998-1999	19.5
Total fertility (children per woman)..............................	2000-2005	3.1
Percentage of childless women, aged 40 - 44	1998-1999	5.5
Divorce rate (per woman)	...	...

[1] Procedures differ according to the religion of the adoptive child or parent.
[2] Main receiving country: United States of America.
[3] It was assumed that 60 per cent of adoptive children are under age five.
[4] Median age at first birth among women aged 25 to 29 years at the date of the survey.

Government policies

Type of adoption permitted	
Domestic adoption	Yes
Intercountry adoption...	Yes
Single male permitted to adopt	No
Single female permitted to adopt	No
Age requirements for adopting parents	...
Child's age of consent for adoption	...
Year of ratification of legal instruments on child adoption	
Convention on the Rights of the Child......................	1990
Hague Convention on Intercountry Adoption	Not ratified
National legislation governing adoption	Staatsblad 1917 No. 129; Civil Code; Circular letters No. 6/1983 and No. 4/1989; Circular Letter KMA/III/II/1994; Decree of the Minister of Social Affairs No. 13/HUK/1993
Government body responsible for adoption approval	Judiciary; Department of Social Affairs

---

Adoption indicators

	Year	Number	Percentage
Total children adopted	1999	43	100
Of which:			
Domestic adoptions..	1999	33	77
Intercountry adoptions	1999	10	23
Of which:			
Adoptions by step-parents or other relatives..............	...	...	...
Adoptions per 100,000 births...	1999	1.0	
Adoptions per 100,000 children under age 18	1999	0.1	
Adoptions per 100,000 children under age 5[1]	1999	0.1	

Demographic indicators

	Year	Value
Female singulate mean age at marriage (years)	2000	22.5
Mean age at first birth (years)[2]......................................	1997	21.6
Total fertility (children per woman)...............................	2000-2005	2.4
Percentage of childless women, aged 40 - 44	2002-2003	7.2
Divorce rate (per woman)	...	...

---

[1] It was assumed that 60 per cent of adoptive children are under age five.

[2] Median age at first birth among women aged 25 to 29 years at the date of the survey.

Government policies

Type of adoption permitted
    Domestic adoption .... No
    Intercountry adoption... No

Single male permitted to adopt .... Not applicable

Single female permitted to adopt .... Not applicable

Age requirements for adopting parents .... Not applicable

Child's age of consent for adoption .... Not applicable

Year of ratification of legal instruments on child adoption
    Convention on the Rights of the Child....................... 1994
    Hague Convention on Intercountry Adoption .... Not ratified

National legislation governing adoption .... Not applicable

Government body responsible for adoption approval ...... Not applicable

Adoption indicators	Year	Number	Percentage
Total children adopted	...	..	..
Of which:			
Domestic adoptions...	...	..	..
Intercountry adoptions	...	..	..
Of which:			
Adoptions by step-parents or other relatives..............	...	..	..
Adoptions per 100,000 births...............................	...	..	
Adoptions per 100,000 children under age 18	...	..	
Adoptions per 100,000 children under age 5	...	..	

Demographic indicators	Year	Value
Female singulate mean age at marriage (years)	1996	22.1
Mean age at first birth (years).........................	...	...
Total fertility (children per woman).............................	2000-2005	2.1
Percentage of childless women, aged 40 - 44	...	...
Divorce rate (per woman)...............................	...	...

Government policies

Type of adoption permitted	
Domestic adoption	No
Intercountry adoption...	No
Single male permitted to adopt	Not applicable
Single female permitted to adopt	Not applicable
Age requirements for adopting parents............................	Not applicable
Child's age of consent for adoption	Not applicable
Year of ratification of legal instruments on child adoption	
Convention on the Rights of the Child........................	1994
Hague Convention on Intercountry Adoption	Not ratified
National legislation governing adoption	Not applicable
Government body responsible for adoption approval	Not applicable

Adoption indicators

	Year	Number	Percentage
Total children adopted	...	..	..
Of which:			
Domestic adoptions..	...	..	..
Intercountry adoptions	...	..	..
Of which:			
Adoptions by step-parents or other relatives..............	...	..	..
Adoptions per 100,000 births..	...	..	
Adoptions per 100,000 children under age 18	...	..	
Adoptions per 100,000 children under age 5	...	..	

Demographic indicators

	Year	Value
Female singulate mean age at marriage (years)	1987	22.3
Mean age at first birth (years)..	...	...
Total fertility (children per woman)...............................	2000-2005	4.8
Percentage of childless women, aged 40 - 44	1997	4.5
Divorce rate (per woman)	...	...

Government policies

Type of adoption permitted[1]
    Domestic adoption .... Yes
    Intercountry adoption... Yes

Single male permitted to adopt[2] .... No

Single female permitted to adopt[2] .... No

Age requirements for adopting parents .... Aged 21 years or older

Child's age of consent for adoption .... Aged 7 years or older

Year of ratification of legal instruments on child adoption
    Convention on the Rights of the Child........................ 1992
    Hague Convention on Intercountry Adoption[3] .... Not ratified

National legislation governing adoption .... Adoption Act of 1952; Adoption Act of 1991; Adoption Act of 1998

Government body responsible for adoption approval ...... Adoption Board; Health Board

Adoption indicators	Year	Number	Percentage
Total children adopted	2003	621	100
Of which:			
Domestic adoptions..	2003	263	42
Intercountry adoptions[4]......................................	2003	358	58
Of which:			
Adoptions by step-parents or other relatives[5]............	2003	171	65.0
Adoptions per 100,000 births.......................................	2003	1 010.4	
Adoptions per 100,000 children under age 18	2003	61.8	
Adoptions per 100,000 children under age 5[6]	2003	129.6	

Demographic indicators	Year	Value
Female singulate mean age at marriage (years)	2002	30.9
Mean age at first birth (years).....................................	2001	28.0
Total fertility (children per woman)...............................	2000-2005	1.9
Percentage of childless women, aged 40 - 44	2002	7.6
Divorce rate (per woman)	...	...

[1] Adopted children must be under 18 years of age.
[2] Widowed persons are permitted to adopt. Close relatives are permitted to adopt, regardless of their marital status.
[3] Year of signature: 1996.
[4] Data refer to number of adoptions overseas. Main country of origin: Russian Federation.
[5] Data refer to domestic adoptions only. The percentage is calculated based on the total number of domestic adoptions.
[6] It was assumed that 60 per cent of adoptive children are under age five.

Government policies

Type of adoption permitted[1]
    Domestic adoption .... Yes
    Intercountry adoption.. Yes

Single male permitted to adopt[2] .... No

Single female permitted to adopt[2] .... No

Age requirements for adopting parents[3] .... At least 18 years older than the child

Child's age of consent for adoption[4] .... Aged 9 years or older

Year of ratification of legal instruments on child adoption
    Convention on the Rights of the Child....................... 1991
    Hague Convention on Intercountry Adoption 1999

National legislation governing adoption .... Adoption of Children Law of 1981; Amendment to the Adoption of Children Law: International Adoption Agreement Permit for Adoption of Children of Parents of a Different Religion of 1997

Government body responsible for adoption approval ...... Judiciary; Ministry of Labor and Social Affairs; Central Authority for Intercountry Adoption

Adoption indicators	Year	Number	Percentage
Total children adopted	2003	382	100
Of which:			
Domestic adoptions...	2003	126	33
Intercountry adoptions[5]...	2003	256	67
Of which:			
Adoptions by step-parents or other relatives.............	...	...	...
Adoptions per 100,000 births..	2003	286.7	
Adoptions per 100,000 children under age 18	2003	17.9	
Adoptions per 100,000 children under age 5[6]	2003	35.1	

Demographic indicators	Year	Value
Female singulate mean age at marriage (years)	1999	25.0
Mean age at first birth (years)......................................	1997	21.7
Total fertility (children per woman)..............................	2000-2005	2.9
Percentage of childless women, aged 40 - 44	...	...
Divorce rate (per woman)	1996	0.15

[1] Adopted children must be under 18 years of age.
[2] A sole applicant is permitted to adopt in the case where one spouse adopts the child of the other. Close relatives are permitted to adopt, regardless of their marital status.
[3] In the case of intercountry adoption, at least one of the foreign prospective adoptive parents must be under age 48.
[4] The maturity of the child is also considered.
[5] Main country of origin: Ukraine.
[6] It was assumed that 60 per cent of adoptive children are under age five.

Government policies

Type of adoption permitted[1]	
Domestic adoption	Yes
Intercountry adoption..	Yes
Single male permitted to adopt[2]	No
Single female permitted to adopt[2]	No
Age requirements for adopting parents	Aged 18 years or older and less than 40 years older than the child
Child's age of consent for adoption[3]	Aged 12 years or older
Year of ratification of legal instruments on child adoption	
Convention on the Rights of the Child......................	1991
Hague Convention on Intercountry Adoption	2000
National legislation governing adoption	Act No. 431 of 5 June 1967; Act No. 184 of 4 May 1983; Law No. 476 of 31 December 1998; Law No. 149 of 28 March 2001
Government body responsible for adoption approval	Juvenile Court; Commission on Intercountry Adoptions

Adoption indicators	Year	Number	Percentage
Total children adopted	1999	3 197	100
Of which:			
Domestic adoptions...	1999	1 020	32
Intercountry adoptions[4]...	1999	2 177	68
Of which:			
Adoptions by step-parents or other relatives[5].............	1999	356	34.9
Adoptions per 100,000 births..	1999	601.9	
Adoptions per 100,000 children under age 18	1999	31.6	
Adoptions per 100,000 children under age 5[6]..................	1999	72.0	

Demographic indicators	Year	Value
Female singulate mean age at marriage (years)	1999	28.4
Mean age at first birth (years)...	1995	28.0
Total fertility (children per woman)..................................	2000-2005	1.3
Percentage of childless women, aged 40 - 44	1995-1996	13.0
Divorce rate (per woman)...	1994	0.05

[1] Prospective adoptive parents must have had the child in their care and custody for at least one year prior to the date of the adoption order.

[2] Prospective adoptive parents must have been married or lived in a stable union prior to marriage for at least three years. Close relatives are permitted to adopt, regardless of their marital status.

[3] The maturity of the child is also considered.

[4] Main country of origin: Russian Federation.

[5] Data refer to domestic adoptions only. The percentage is calculated based on the total number of domestic adoptions.

[6] It was assumed that 60 per cent of adoptive children are under age five.

Government policies

Type of adoption permitted
    Domestic adoption .... Yes
    Intercountry adoption... Yes

Single male permitted to adopt[1] .... Yes

Single female permitted to adopt .... Yes

Age requirements for adopting parents[2]......................... Aged 25 years or older

Child's age of consent for adoption .... Maturity of child considered

Year of ratification of legal instruments on child adoption
    Convention on the Rights of the Child...................... 1991
    Hague Convention on Intercountry Adoption .... Not ratified

National legislation governing adoption .... Children (Adoption of) Act of 2 January 1958

Government body responsible for adoption approval ...... Judiciary; Adoption Board, Ministry of Health

Adoption indicators	*Year*	*Number*	*Percentage*
Total children adopted	2002	255	100
Of which:			
Domestic adoptions...	2002	219	86
Intercountry adoptions[3]	2002	36	14
Of which:			
Adoptions by step-parents or other relatives.............	...	...	...
Adoptions per 100,000 births..	2002	474.6	
Adoptions per 100,000 children under age 18	2002	25.3	
Adoptions per 100,000 children under age 5[4]	2002	55.9	

Demographic indicators	*Year*	*Value*
Female singulate mean age at marriage (years)	1991	33.2
Mean age at first birth (years)[5].....................................	1975-1976	19.2
Total fertility (children per woman)..............................	2000-2005	2.4
Percentage of childless women, aged 40 - 44	1991	9.6
Divorce rate (per woman)	1995	0.06

[1] A sole male applicant is not permitted to adopt a girl, except under special circumstances.
[2] Prospective adoptive parents must be aged 18 years or older to adopt a relative.
[3] Main receiving country: United States of America.
[4] It was assumed that 60 per cent of adoptive children are under age five.
[5] Median age at first birth among women aged 25 to 29 years at the date of the survey.

Government policies

Type of adoption permitted[1]	
Domestic adoption	Yes
Intercountry adoption...	Yes
Single male permitted to adopt[2]	Yes
Single female permitted to adopt[2]	Yes
Age requirements for adopting parents	One adoptive parent must be aged 25 years or older and the other must be aged 20 years or older
Child's age of consent for adoption	...
Year of ratification of legal instruments on child adoption	
Convention on the Rights of the Child.......................	1994
Hague Convention on Intercountry Adoption	Not ratified
National legislation governing adoption	Civil Code
Government body responsible for adoption approval	Judiciary; Child Guidance Center

Adoption indicators	Year	Number	Percentage
Total children adopted	1995	1 931	100
Of which:			
Domestic adoptions[3]	1995	1 632	85
Intercountry adoptions	1995	299	15
Of which:			
Adoptions by step-parents or other relatives..............	...	...	...
Adoptions per 100,000 births..	1995	159.6	
Adoptions per 100,000 children under age 18	1995	7.7	
Adoptions per 100,000 children under age 5[4]	1995	19.3	

Demographic indicators	Year	Value	
Female singulate mean age at marriage (years)	2000	28.6	
Mean age at first birth (years)...	1998	27.9	
Total fertility (children per woman)................................	2000-2005	1.3	
Percentage of childless women, aged 40 - 44	...	...	
Divorce rate (per woman)...	1997	0.16	

[1] Prospective adoptive parents must have had the child in their care and custody for at least six months prior to the date of the adoption order.
[2] Prospective adoptive parents must be aged 25 years or older.
[3] Data include regular and special adoptions.
[4] It was assumed that 60 per cent of adoptive children are under age five.

Government policies

Type of adoption permitted
    Domestic adoption .... No
    Intercountry adoption .... No

Single male permitted to adopt .... Not applicable

Single female permitted to adopt .... Not applicable

Age requirements for adopting parents .... Not applicable

Child's age of consent for adoption .... Not applicable

Year of ratification of legal instruments on child adoption
    Convention on the Rights of the Child 1991
    Hague Convention on Intercountry Adoption .... Not ratified

National legislation governing adoption .... Not applicable

Government body responsible for adoption approval ...... Not applicable

Adoption indicators	Year	Number	Percentage
Total children adopted	...	..	..
Of which:			
Domestic adoptions	...	..	..
Intercountry adoptions	...	..	..
Of which:			
Adoptions by step-parents or other relatives	...	..	..
Adoptions per 100,000 births	...	..	
Adoptions per 100,000 children under age 18	...	..	
Adoptions per 100,000 children under age 5	...	..	

Demographic indicators	Year	Value
Female singulate mean age at marriage (years)	1994	25.3
Mean age at first birth (years)[1]	1997	24.7
Total fertility (children per woman)	2000-2005	3.5
Percentage of childless women, aged 40 - 44	2002	13.4
Divorce rate (per woman)	1997	0.17

[1] Median age at first birth among women aged 25 to 29 years at the date of the survey.

Government policies

Type of adoption permitted
    Domestic adoption .... Yes
    Intercountry adoption... Yes

Single male permitted to adopt[1] .... Yes

Single female permitted to adopt[1] .... Yes

Age requirements for adopting parents ....

Child's age of consent for adoption .... Aged 10 years or older

Year of ratification of legal instruments on child adoption
    Convention on the Rights of the Child....................... 1994
    Hague Convention on Intercountry Adoption .... Not ratified

National legislation governing adoption .... Marriage and Family Act of 17 December 1998; Civil Code

Government body responsible for adoption approval ...... Judiciary; Ministry of Education and Science

Adoption indicators	Year	Number	Percentage
Total children adopted	2002	3 600	100
Of which:			
Domestic adoptions...	2002	2 652	74
Intercountry adoptions[2]..	2002	948	26
Of which:			
Adoptions by step-parents or other relatives[3]............	2002	65	1.8
Adoptions per 100,000 births...	2002	1 500.9	
Adoptions per 100,000 children under age 18	2002	75.7	
Adoptions per 100,000 children under age 5[4]	2002	196.6	

Demographic indicators	Year	Value
Female singulate mean age at marriage (years)	1999	23.4
Mean age at first birth (years)..	1999	23.5
Total fertility (children per woman)................................	2000-2005	2.0
Percentage of childless women, aged 40 - 44	1999	7.1
Divorce rate (per woman)	1997	0.28

[1] Prospective adoptive parents must be at least 16 years older than the child.
[2] Based on data from selected receiving countries, the main receiving country: United States of America.
[3] Data refer to children adopted by relatives outside of Kazakhstan.
[4] It was assumed that 60 per cent of adoptive children are under age five.

Government policies

Type of adoption permitted
    Domestic adoption ....   Yes
    Intercountry adoption[1] ....   Yes

Single male permitted to adopt ....

Single female permitted to adopt[1] ....

Age requirements for adopting parents ....   Aged 25 years or older and at least 21 years older than the child

Child's age of consent for adoption ....   Aged 14 years or older

Year of ratification of legal instruments on child adoption
    Convention on the Rights of the Child......................   1990
    Hague Convention on Intercountry Adoption ....   Not ratified

National legislation governing adoption ....   Adoption Act; Guardianship of Infants Act; Children Bill; Children's Act of 2001

Government body responsible for adoption approval ......   Judiciary

Adoption indicators

	Year	Number	Percentage
Total children adopted[2]	1998	143	100
Of which:			
Domestic adoptions..	...	...	...
Intercountry adoptions	...	...	...
Of which:			
Adoptions by step-parents or other relatives..............	...	...	...
Adoptions per 100,000 births[2]	1998	13.0	
Adoptions per 100,000 children under age 18[2]	1998	0.9	
Adoptions per 100,000 children under age 5[3]	1998	1.8	

Demographic indicators

	Year	Value
Female singulate mean age at marriage (years)	1998	21.7
Mean age at first birth (years)[4]	1998	19.6
Total fertility (children per woman)...............................	2000-2005	5.0
Percentage of childless women, aged 40 - 44	2003	4.2
Divorce rate (per woman)	...	...

[1] Prospective adoptive parents must have resided in the country and had the child in their care and custody for at least three consecutive months prior to the date of the adoption application.

[1] A sole foreign female applicant is allowed to adopt under special circumstances.

[2] Data refer to the estimated number of adoption applications recorded by the Child Welfare Society of Kenya.

[3] Data refer to the estimated number of adoption applications recorded by the Child Welfare Society of Kenya. It was assumed that 60 per cent of adoptive children are under age five.

[4] Median age at first birth among women aged 25 to 29 years at the date of the survey.

Government policies

Type of adoption permitted
    Domestic adoption[1] .... Yes
    Intercountry adoption ....

Single male permitted to adopt ....

Single female permitted to adopt ....

Age requirements for adopting parents ....

Child's age of consent for adoption ....

Year of ratification of legal instruments on child adoption
    Convention on the Rights of the Child 1995
    Hague Convention on Intercountry Adoption .... Not ratified

National legislation governing adoption ....

Government body responsible for adoption approval ...... Magistrates court

Adoption indicators	Year	Number	Percentage
Total children adopted	...	...	...
Of which:			
Domestic adoptions..	...	...	...
Intercountry adoptions[2]	2004-2006	3	...
Of which:			
Adoptions by step-parents or other relatives	...	...	...
Adoptions per 100,000 births...	...	...	
Adoptions per 100,000 children under age 18	...	...	
Adoptions per 100,000 children under age 5	...	...	

Demographic indicators	Year	Value
Female singulate mean age at marriage (years)	...	...
Mean age at first birth (years)..	...	...
Total fertility (children per woman).................................	2000-2005	4.0
Percentage of childless women, aged 40 - 44	...	...
Divorce rate (per woman)	...	...

[1] Adoptions are recognized only within the country.
[2] Estimate.

Government policies

Type of adoption permitted	
Domestic adoption	No
Intercountry adoption..	No
Single male permitted to adopt	Not applicable
Single female permitted to adopt	Not applicable
Age requirements for adopting parents	Not applicable
Child's age of consent for adoption	Not applicable
Year of ratification of legal instruments on child adoption	
Convention on the Rights of the Child.......................	1991
Hague Convention on Intercountry Adoption	Not ratified
National legislation governing adoption	Not applicable
Government body responsible for adoption approval	Not applicable

Adoption indicators	Year	Number	Percentage
Total children adopted	...	..	..
Of which:			
Domestic adoptions...	...	..	..
Intercountry adoptions	...	..	..
Of which:			
Adoptions by step-parents or other relatives..............	...		
Adoptions per 100,000 births..	...		
Adoptions per 100,000 children under age 18	...		
Adoptions per 100,000 children under age 5	...		

Demographic indicators	Year	Value
Female singulate mean age at marriage (years)	1996	25.2
Mean age at first birth (years)..	1986	24.1
Total fertility (children per woman)..............................	2000-2005	2.4
Percentage of childless women, aged 40 - 44	1996	12.3
Divorce rate (per woman)...	1992	0.22

Government policies

Type of adoption permitted
    Domestic adoption .... Yes
    Intercountry adoption .... Yes

Single male permitted to adopt ....

Single female permitted to adopt ....

Age requirements for adopting parents .... Aged 18 years or older

Child's age of consent for adoption .... Aged 10 years or older

Year of ratification of legal instruments on child adoption
    Convention on the Rights of the Child 1994
    Hague Convention on Intercountry Adoption .... Not ratified

National legislation governing adoption .... Marriage and Family Code; Government Decision No. 825 of
13 November 1994

Government body responsible for adoption approval ...... Judiciary; Ministry of Education

Adoption indicators	Year	Number	Percentage
Total children adopted[1]	1999	1 683	100
Of which:			
Domestic adoptions	...	...	...
Intercountry adoptions	...	...	...
Of which:			
Adoptions by step-parents or other relatives	...	...	...
Adoptions per 100,000 births[1]	1999	1 468.8	
Adoptions per 100,000 children under age 18[1]	1999	82.3	
Adoptions per 100,000 children under age 5[2]	1999	184.7	

Demographic indicators	Year	Value
Female singulate mean age at marriage (years)	1999	21.9
Mean age at first birth (years)	1998	23.3
Total fertility (children per woman)	2000-2005	2.7
Percentage of childless women, aged 40 - 44	1997	4.8
Divorce rate (per woman)	1996	0.19

[1] Data include children that have been adopted and those placed with guardians.
[2] Data include children that have been adopted and those placed with guardians. It was assumed that 60 per cent of adoptive children are under age five.

Government policies

Type of adoption permitted	
Domestic adoption	Yes
Intercountry adoption..	Yes
Single male permitted to adopt	...
Single female permitted to adopt	...
Age requirements for adopting parents	...
Child's age of consent for adoption	Aged 10 years or older
Year of ratification of legal instruments on child adoption	
Convention on the Rights of the Child.......................	1991
Hague Convention on Intercountry Adoption	Not ratified
National legislation governing adoption	Family Law; Lao Nationality Law
Government body responsible for adoption approval	Judiciary

Adoption indicators

	Year	Number	Percentage
Total children adopted	...	...	...
Of which:			
Domestic adoptions...	...	...	...
Intercountry adoptions	...	...	...
Of which:			
Adoptions by step-parents or other relatives..............	...	...	...
Adoptions per 100,000 births..	...	...	
Adoptions per 100,000 children under age 18	...	...	
Adoptions per 100,000 children under age 5	...	...	

Demographic indicators

	Year	Value
Female singulate mean age at marriage (years)	2000	20.8
Mean age at first birth (years)	...	...
Total fertility (children per woman)...............................	2000-2005	4.8
Percentage of childless women, aged 40 - 44	2000	6.2
Divorce rate (per woman)...	...	...

Government policies

Type of adoption permitted
    Domestic adoption .... Yes
    Intercountry adoption .... Yes

Single male permitted to adopt .... Yes

Single female permitted to adopt .... Yes

Age requirements for adopting parents .... Aged 25 years or older and at least 18 years older than the child

Child's age of consent for adoption .... Aged 12 years or older

Year of ratification of legal instruments on child adoption
    Convention on the Rights of the Child 1992
    Hague Convention on Intercountry Adoption 2002

National legislation governing adoption .... Civil Law; Law on Orphan's Courts and Parish Courts; Law on Protection of the Rights of the Child; Civil Procedure Law

Government body responsible for adoption approval ...... Ministry of Justice; Ministry of Welfare; Ministry for Social Assignments for Children and Family Affairs

Adoption indicators	Year	Number	Percentage
Total children adopted	2003	106	100
Of which:			
Domestic adoptions..	2003	27	25
Intercountry adoptions[1]	2003	79	75
Of which:			
Adoptions by step-parents or other relatives.............	...	...	...
Adoptions per 100,000 births...	2003	522.1	
Adoptions per 100,000 children under age 18	2003	22.0	
Adoptions per 100,000 children under age 5[2]	2003	65.7	

Demographic indicators	Year	Value
Female singulate mean age at marriage (years)	2002	26.9
Mean age at first birth (years).......................................	2001	24.6
Total fertility (children per woman)...............................	2000-2005	1.3
Percentage of childless women, aged 40 - 44	1995	9.4
Divorce rate (per woman)	1997	0.32

[1] Main receiving country: France.

[2] It was assumed that 60 per cent of adoptive children are under age five.

Government policies

Type of adoption permitted[1]	
Domestic adoption	Yes
Intercountry adoption...................................	Yes
Single male permitted to adopt	Yes
Single female permitted to adopt	Yes
Age requirements for adopting parents	Aged 40 years or older and at least 18 years older than the child
Child's age of consent for adoption	...
Year of ratification of legal instruments on child adoption	
Convention on the Rights of the Child......................	1991
Hague Convention on Intercountry Adoption	Not ratified
National legislation governing adoption[2]	Varies depending on the religion of the adoptive child or parent
Government body responsible for adoption approval[3]	Judiciary

Adoption indicators	Year	Number	Percentage
Total children adopted	...	...	...
Of which:			
Domestic adoptions..	...	...	...
Intercountry adoptions	...	...	...
Of which:			
Adoptions by step-parents or other relatives.............	...	...	...
Adoptions per 100,000 births.......................................	...	...	
Adoptions per 100,000 children under age 18	...	...	
Adoptions per 100,000 children under age 5	...	...	

Demographic indicators	Year	Value
Female singulate mean age at marriage (years)	1970	23.2
Mean age at first birth (years)	...	...
Total fertility (children per woman).............................	2000-2005	2.3
Percentage of childless women, aged 40 - 44	...	...
Divorce rate (per woman)...	...	...

[1] Procedures differ according to the religion of the adoptive child or parent.
[2] The country does not have civil laws governing adoption, but under Christian personal laws, adoption is permitted.
[3] Civil courts oversee intercountry adoptions and adoptions of children of different religious affiliation than their prospective adoptive parents.

Government policies

Type of adoption permitted	
Domestic adoption	Yes
Intercountry adoption..	Yes
Single male permitted to adopt	Yes
Single female permitted to adopt	Yes
Age requirements for adopting parents	At least 25 years older than the child
Child's age of consent for adoption	Aged 10 years or older
Year of ratification of legal instruments on child adoption	
Convention on the Rights of the Child......................	1992
Hague Convention on Intercountry Adoption............	Not ratified
National legislation governing adoption	Adoption Proclamation No. 62 of 1952; Adoption Proclamation No. 690 of 1959
Government body responsible for adoption approval	Judiciary; Department of Social Welfare

Adoption indicators

	Year	Number	Percentage
Total children adopted	...	...	...
Of which:			
Domestic adoptions...	...	...	...
Intercountry adoptions	...	...	...
Of which:			
Adoptions by step-parents or other relatives..............	...	...	...
Adoptions per 100,000 births...	...	...	
Adoptions per 100,000 children under age 18	...	...	
Adoptions per 100,000 children under age 5	...	...	

Demographic indicators

	Year	Value
Female singulate mean age at marriage (years)	1986	21.3
Mean age at first birth (years)...	...	...
Total fertility (children per woman)................................	2000-2005	3.6
Percentage of childless women, aged 40 - 44	1977	7.6
Divorce rate (per woman)	...	...

Government policies

Type of adoption permitted
    Domestic adoption .... Yes
    Intercountry adoption.. Yes

Single male permitted to adopt ....

Single female permitted to adopt ....

Age requirements for adopting parents ....

Child's age of consent for adoption ....

Year of ratification of legal instruments on child adoption
    Convention on the Rights of the Child....................... 1993
    Hague Convention on Intercountry Adoption .... Not ratified

National legislation governing adoption .... Domestic Relation Law of Liberia

Government body responsible for adoption approval ...... Ministry of Justice

Adoption indicators	Year	Number	Percentage
Total children adopted	...	...	...
Of which:			
Domestic adoptions..	...	...	...
Intercountry adoptions	...	...	...
Of which:			
Adoptions by step-parents or other relatives..............	...	...	...
Adoptions per 100,000 births.......................................	...	...	
Adoptions per 100,000 children under age 18	...	...	
Adoptions per 100,000 children under age 5	...	...	

Demographic indicators	Year	Value
Female singulate mean age at marriage (years)	1986	20.2
Mean age at first birth (years)[1]	1986	19.0
Total fertility (children per woman)..............................	2000-2005	6.8
Percentage of childless women, aged 40 - 44	1986	5.7
Divorce rate (per woman)...	...	...

[1] Median age at first birth among women aged 25 to 29 years at the date of the survey.

Government policies

Type of adoption permitted
    Domestic adoption .... No
    Intercountry adoption.. No

Single male permitted to adopt .... Not applicable

Single female permitted to adopt .... Not applicable

Age requirements for adopting parents .... Not applicable

Child's age of consent for adoption .... Not applicable

Year of ratification of legal instruments on child adoption
    Convention on the Rights of the Child...................... 1993
    Hague Convention on Intercountry Adoption .... Not ratified

National legislation governing adoption .... Not applicable

Government body responsible for adoption approval ...... Not applicable

Adoption indicators	Year	Number	Percentage
Total children adopted	...	..	..
Of which:			
Domestic adoptions..	...	..	..
Intercountry adoptions	...	..	..
Of which:			
Adoptions by step-parents or other relatives..............	...	..	..
Adoptions per 100,000 births..	...	..	
Adoptions per 100,000 children under age 18	...	..	
Adoptions per 100,000 children under age 5	...	..	

Demographic indicators	Year	Value
Female singulate mean age at marriage (years)	1995	29.2
Mean age at first birth (years)...	...	...
Total fertility (children per woman)................................	2000-2005	3.0
Percentage of childless women, aged 40 - 44	1995	8.0
Divorce rate (per woman)	...	...

Government policies

Type of adoption permitted	
Domestic adoption	Yes
Intercountry adoption	Yes
Single male permitted to adopt	No
Single female permitted to adopt	No
Age requirements for adopting parents	At least 18 years older than the child, father must be aged 30 years or older and mother must be aged 28 years or older
Child's age of consent for adoption	Aged 5 years or older
Year of ratification of legal instruments on child adoption	
Convention on the Rights of the Child	1995
Hague Convention on Intercountry Adoption	Not ratified
National legislation governing adoption	General Civil Code
Government body responsible for adoption approval	Judiciary; Office of Social Affairs; Children's and Youth Services

Adoption indicators	Year	Number	Percentage
Total children adopted	2003-2004	6	100
Of which:			
Domestic adoptions	2003-2004	1	17
Intercountry adoptions	2003-2004	5	83
Of which:			
Adoptions by step-parents or other relatives	...	...	...
Adoptions per 100,000 births	2003-2004	821.9	
Adoptions per 100,000 children under age 18	2003-2004	41.0	
Adoptions per 100,000 children under age 5[1]	2003-2004	94.7	

Demographic indicators	Year	Value
Female singulate mean age at marriage (years)	...	...
Mean age at first birth (years)	...	...
Total fertility (children per woman)	2000-2005	1.4
Percentage of childless women, aged 40 - 44	...	...
Divorce rate (per woman)	...	...

[1] It was assumed that 60 per cent of adoptive children are under age five.

Government policies

Type of adoption permitted
    Domestic adoption .... Yes
    Intercountry adoption... Yes

Single male permitted to adopt[1] .... No

Single female permitted to adopt[1] .... No

Age requirements for adopting parents[2] .... Under age 50 and at least 18 years older than the child

Child's age of consent for adoption .... Aged 10 years or older

Year of ratification of legal instruments on child adoption
    Convention on the Rights of the Child...................... 1992
    Hague Convention on Intercountry Adoption 1998

National legislation governing adoption .... Civil Code; Code of Civil Procedure; Resolution No. 1422 of 10 September 2002; Resolution No. 1674 of 23 October 2002; Resolution No. 1983 of 17 December 2002

Government body responsible for adoption approval ...... Judiciary; Adoption Agency, Ministry of Social Security and Labor

Adoption indicators	Year	Number	Percentage
Total children adopted	2004	196	100
Of which:			
Domestic adoptions...	2004	93	47
Intercountry adoptions[3]	2004	103	53
Of which:			
Adoptions by step-parents or other relatives..............	...	...	...
Adoptions per 100,000 births...	2004	638.6	
Adoptions per 100,000 children under age 18	2004	25.5	
Adoptions per 100,000 children under age 5[4]	2004	76.2	

Demographic indicators	Year	Value
Female singulate mean age at marriage (years)	2001	24.8
Mean age at first birth (years)..	2001	24.1
Total fertility (children per woman)................................	2000-2005	1.3
Percentage of childless women, aged 40 - 44	1994-1995	14.7
Divorce rate (per woman)	1997	0.34

[1] Permission for adoption may be granted to a single person under special circumstances.
[2] Step-parents must be at least 15 years older than the child.
[3] Main receiving country: Italy.
[4] It was assumed that 60 per cent of adoptive children are under age five.

Government policies

Type of adoption permitted	
Domestic adoption	Yes
Intercountry adoption..	Yes
Single male permitted to adopt[1]	No
Single female permitted to adopt[1]	No
Age requirements for adopting parents[2]	At least 15 years older than the child, one spouse must be aged 25 years or older and the other must be aged 21 years or older
Child's age of consent for adoption	Aged 15 years or older
Year of ratification of legal instruments on child adoption	
Convention on the Rights of the Child......................	1994
Hague Convention on Intercountry Adoption	2002
National legislation governing adoption	Civil Code; Act of 31 January 1998 on the Accreditation of Adoption Services and the Definition of their Obligations
Government body responsible for adoption approval	Judiciary; Ministry of the Family, Social Solidarity and Youth

Adoption indicators	Year	Number	Percentage
Total children adopted	2003	54	100
Of which:			
Domestic adoptions...	2003	3	6
Intercountry adoptions[3]	2003	51	94
Of which:			
Adoptions by step-parents or other relatives..............	...	...	...
Adoptions per 100,000 births...	2003	946.7	
Adoptions per 100,000 children under age 18	2003	53.3	
Adoptions per 100,000 children under age 5[4]	2003	113.2	

Demographic indicators	Year	Value
Female singulate mean age at marriage (years)	1991	26.0
Mean age at first birth (years)	2001	28.3
Total fertility (children per woman)...............................	2000-2005	1.7
Percentage of childless women, aged 40 - 44	1991	18.8
Divorce rate (per woman)	1996	0.22

[1] Prospective adoptive parents aged 25 years or older may engage in simple adoptions.

[2] Different age requirements apply to single adoptive parents.

[3] Data refer to children in the process of undergoing adoption. Main country of origin: Republic of Korea.

[4] It was assumed that 60 per cent of adoptive children are under age five.

Government policies

Type of adoption permitted	
Domestic adoption	Yes
Intercountry adoption[1]	Yes
Single male permitted to adopt	Yes
Single female permitted to adopt	Yes
Age requirements for adopting parents	Aged 30 years or older
Child's age of consent for adoption	...
Year of ratification of legal instruments on child adoption	
Convention on the Rights of the Child......................	1991
Hague Convention on Intercountry Adoption	2004
National legislation governing adoption	Act No. 63-022 of 20 November 1963; Decree No. 94-272 of 19 April 1994
Government body responsible for adoption approval	Judiciary

Adoption indicators

Adoption indicators	Year	Number	Percentage
Total children adopted	...	...	...
Of which:			
Domestic adoptions..	...	...	...
Intercountry adoptions[2]..	2002	373	...
Of which:			
Adoptions by step-parents or other relatives.............	...	...	...
Adoptions per 100,000 births..	...	...	
Adoptions per 100,000 children under age 18	...	...	
Adoptions per 100,000 children under age 5	...	...	

Demographic indicators

Demographic indicators	Year	Value
Female singulate mean age at marriage (years)	1997	20.6
Mean age at first birth (years)[3]	1997	19.8
Total fertility (children per woman)..............................	2000-2005	5.4
Percentage of childless women, aged 40 - 44	2003-2004	5.6
Divorce rate (per woman)	...	...

[1] Adoptive parents must remain in the country for one month until the deadline for an appeal to the adoption order has passed.
[2] Based on data from selected receiving countries, the main receiving country in 2003: France.
[3] Median age at first birth among women aged 25 to 29 years at the date of the survey.

Government policies

Type of adoption permitted
    Domestic adoption .... Yes
    Intercountry adoption.. No

Single male permitted to adopt[1] .... Yes

Single female permitted to adopt[2] .... Yes

Age requirements for adopting parents .... Aged 25 years or older and at least 21 years older than the child

Child's age of consent for adoption ....

Year of ratification of legal instruments on child adoption
    Convention on the Rights of the Child...................... 1991
    Hague Convention on Intercountry Adoption .... Not ratified

National legislation governing adoption .... Adoption of Children Act

Government body responsible for adoption approval ...... Judiciary; Ministry of Gender, Youth and Community Services

Adoption indicators	Year	Number	Percentage
Total children adopted	2001	714	100
Of which:			
Domestic adoptions...	2001	714	100
Intercountry adoptions	...	..	..
Of which:			
Adoptions by step-parents or other relatives..............	...	...	...
Adoptions per 100,000 births..	2001	132.9	
Adoptions per 100,000 children under age 18	2001	11.4	
Adoptions per 100,000 children under age 5[3]	2001	19.1	

Demographic indicators	Year	Value
Female singulate mean age at marriage (years)	2000	18.9
Mean age at first birth (years)[4].....................................	2000	19.2
Total fertility (children per woman).............................	2000-2005	6.1
Percentage of childless women, aged 40 - 44	2000	4.1
Divorce rate (per woman)	...	...

[1] A sole male applicant is not permitted to adopt a girl.
[2] A sole female applicant is not permitted to adopt a boy.
[3] It was assumed that 60 per cent of adoptive children are under age five.
[4] Median age at first birth among women aged 25 to 29 years at the date of the survey.

Government policies

Type of adoption permitted[1]
  Domestic adoption .... Yes
  Intercountry adoption[2] .... Yes

Single male permitted to adopt ....

Single female permitted to adopt ....

Age requirements for adopting parents .... At least 21 years older than the child and one spouse must be aged 25 years or older

Child's age of consent for adoption ....

Year of ratification of legal instruments on child adoption
  Convention on the Rights of the Child 1995
  Hague Convention on Intercountry Adoption .... Not ratified

National legislation governing adoption .... Adoption Act of 1952 (Act 257) (Revised 1981); Registration of Adoptions Act of 1952 (Act 253) (Revised 1981)

Government body responsible for adoption approval ...... Judiciary; Ministry of National Unity and Social Development

Adoption indicators	Year	Number	Percentage
Total children adopted	...	...	...
Of which:			
Domestic adoptions..	...	...	...
Intercountry adoptions	...	...	...
Of which:			
Adoptions by step-parents or other relatives..............	...	...	...
Adoptions per 100,000 births...	...	...	
Adoptions per 100,000 children under age 18	...	...	
Adoptions per 100,000 children under age 5	...	...	

Demographic indicators	Year	Value
Female singulate mean age at marriage (years)	2000	25.1
Mean age at first birth (years)[3].....................................	1974	22.3
Total fertility (children per woman)................................	2000-2005	2.9
Percentage of childless women, aged 40 - 44[4]	1980	6.3
Divorce rate (per woman)	...	...

[1] Procedures differ according to the religion of the adoptive child or parent.
[2] Prospective adoptive parents must have had the child in their care and custody for two years prior to the date of the adoption.
[3] Median age at first birth among women aged 25 to 29 years at the date of the survey.
[4] Never married added.

Government policies

Type of adoption permitted
    Domestic adoption .... No
    Intercountry adoption... No

Single male permitted to adopt .... Not applicable

Single female permitted to adopt .... Not applicable

Age requirements for adopting parents .... Not applicable

Child's age of consent for adoption .... Not applicable

Year of ratification of legal instruments on child adoption
    Convention on the Rights of the Child....................... 1991
    Hague Convention on Intercountry Adoption .... Not ratified

National legislation governing adoption .... Not applicable

Government body responsible for adoption approval ...... Ministry of Justice and Islamic Affairs

Adoption indicators	Year	Number	Percentage
Total children adopted	...	..	..
Of which:			
Domestic adoptions...	...	..	..
Intercountry adoptions	...	..	..
Of which:			
Adoptions by step-parents or other relatives	...	..	..
Adoptions per 100,000 births.....................................	...	..	
Adoptions per 100,000 children under age 18	...	..	
Adoptions per 100,000 children under age 5	...	..	

Demographic indicators	Year	Value
Female singulate mean age at marriage (years)	2000	21.8
Mean age at first birth (years)	...	...
Total fertility (children per woman).............................	2000-2005	4.3
Percentage of childless women, aged 40 - 44	2000	4.1
Divorce rate (per woman)	...	...

Government policies

Type of adoption permitted	
Domestic adoption	Yes
Intercountry adoption....................................	Yes
Single male permitted to adopt	Yes
Single female permitted to adopt	Yes
Age requirements for adopting parents	...
Child's age of consent for adoption	...
Year of ratification of legal instruments on child adoption	
Convention on the Rights of the Child.......................	1990
Hague Convention on Intercountry Adoption	2006
National legislation governing adoption	Order No. 36/CMLN of 31 July 1973 (Family Relations Code)
Government body responsible for adoption approval	Judiciary; Adoption Committee, National Social Welfare Department

Adoption indicators

	Year	Number	Percentage
Total children adopted	2003	135	100
Of which:			
Domestic adoptions...	2003	1	1
Intercountry adoptions[1]..	2003	134	99
Of which:			
Adoptions by step-parents or other relatives..............	...	...	...
Adoptions per 100,000 births..	2003	21.3	
Adoptions per 100,000 children under age 18	2003	1.9	
Adoptions per 100,000 children under age 5[2]..................	2003	3.3	

Demographic indicators

	Year	Value
Female singulate mean age at marriage (years)	1996	18.4
Mean age at first birth (years)[3].....................................	2001	18.6
Total fertility (children per woman).................................	2000-2005	6.9
Percentage of childless women, aged 40 - 44	2001	4.9
Divorce rate (per woman)	...	...

[1] Based on data from selected receiving countries, the main receiving country: France.

[2] It was assumed that 60 per cent of adoptive children are under age five.

[3] Median age at first birth among women aged 25 to 29 years at the date of the survey.

Government policies

Type of adoption permitted
    Domestic adoption .... Yes
    Intercountry adoption... Yes

Single male permitted to adopt .... Yes

Single female permitted to adopt .... Yes

Age requirements for adopting parents .... Aged 30 to 60 years and at least 21 years older than the child

Child's age of consent for adoption .... Aged 14 years or older

Year of ratification of legal instruments on child adoption
    Convention on the Rights of the Child...................... 1990
    Hague Convention on Intercountry Adoption 2004

National legislation governing adoption .... Civil Code

Government body responsible for adoption approval ...... Judiciary; Adoption Unit, Ministry for the Family and Social Solidarity

Adoption indicators	Year	Number	Percentage
Total children adopted	1996	12	100
Of which:			
Domestic adoptions...	1996	7	58
Intercountry adoptions[1]...	1996	5	42
Of which:			
Adoptions by step-parents or other relatives..............	...	...	...
Adoptions per 100,000 births..	1996	245.9	
Adoptions per 100,000 children under age 18	1996	11.9	
Adoptions per 100,000 children under age 5[2]	1996	28.1	

Demographic indicators	Year	Value
Female singulate mean age at marriage (years)	1985	22.2
Mean age at first birth (years).......................................	...	...
Total fertility (children per woman)...............................	2000-2005	1.5
Percentage of childless women, aged 40 - 44	...	...
Divorce rate (per woman)	...	...

[1] Main country of origin: Romania.
[2] It was assumed that 60 per cent of adoptive children are under age five.

Government policies

Type of adoption permitted	
Domestic adoption	Yes
Intercountry adoption[1]	Yes
Single male permitted to adopt	Yes
Single female permitted to adopt	Yes
Age requirements for adopting parents	At least 15 years older than the child
Child's age of consent for adoption	Aged 12 years or older
Year of ratification of legal instruments on child adoption	
Convention on the Rights of the Child......................	1993
Hague Convention on Intercountry Adoption	Not ratified
National legislation governing adoption	Adoption Act of 2002 (Public Law 2002-64)
Government body responsible for adoption approval	Judiciary; Central Adoption Agency

Adoption indicators

	Year	Number	Percentage
Total children adopted	...	...	...
Of which:			
Domestic adoptions...	...	...	...
Intercountry adoptions	...	...	...
Of which:			
Adoptions by step-parents or other relatives..............	...	...	...
Adoptions per 100,000 births..	...	...	
Adoptions per 100,000 children under age 18	...	...	
Adoptions per 100,000 children under age 5	...	...	

Demographic indicators

	Year	Value
Female singulate mean age at marriage (years)	...	...
Mean age at first birth (years)...	...	...
Total fertility (children per woman).................................	2000-2005	5.3
Percentage of childless women, aged 40 - 44	...	...
Divorce rate (per woman)	...	...

[1] Parliament imposed a moratorium on all intercountry adoptions from September 1999 to December 2000.

Government policies

Type of adoption permitted	
Domestic adoption	No
Intercountry adoption	No
Single male permitted to adopt	Not applicable
Single female permitted to adopt	Not applicable
Age requirements for adopting parents	Not applicable
Child's age of consent for adoption	Not applicable
Year of ratification of legal instruments on child adoption	
Convention on the Rights of the Child	1991
Hague Convention on Intercountry Adoption	Not ratified
National legislation governing adoption	Not applicable
Government body responsible for adoption approval	Not applicable

Adoption indicators	Year	Number	Percentage
Total children adopted[1]	2000	7	100
Of which:			
Domestic adoptions	...	..	...
Intercountry adoptions	...	..	..
Of which:			
Adoptions by step-parents or other relatives	...	..	..
Adoptions per 100,000 births[1]	2000	6.2	
Adoptions per 100,000 children under age 18[1]	2000	0.5	
Adoptions per 100,000 children under age 5[2]	2000	0.9	

Demographic indicators	Year	Value
Female singulate mean age at marriage (years)	2001	22.1
Mean age at first birth (years)[3]	2000-2001	21.9
Total fertility (children per woman)	2000-2005	5.8
Percentage of childless women, aged 40 - 44	2003-2004	8.6
Divorce rate (per woman)	...	...

[1] Estimate. Data refer to children placed through kafalah.
[2] Estimate. Data refer to children placed through kafalah. It was assumed that 60 per cent of adoptive children are under age five.
[3] Median age at first birth among women aged 25 to 29 years at the date of the survey.

Government policies

Type of adoption permitted
    Domestic adoption .... Yes
    Intercountry adoption... Yes

Single male permitted to adopt[1] .... Yes

Single female permitted to adopt[1] .... Yes

Age requirements for adopting parents[2] .... At least 15 years older than the child

Child's age of consent for adoption .... Aged 15 years or older

Year of ratification of legal instruments on child adoption
    Convention on the Rights of the Child...................... 1990
    Hague Convention on Intercountry Adoption 1998

National legislation governing adoption .... Civil Code

Government body responsible for adoption approval[3] ..... Judiciary; National Adoption Council; Prime Minister's Office

Adoption indicators	Year	Number	Percentage
Total children adopted	2004	105	100
Of which:			
Domestic adoptions[4]	2004	92	88
Intercountry adoptions...	2004	13	12
Of which:			
Adoptions by step-parents or other relatives..............	...	...	...
Adoptions per 100,000 births......................................	2004	529.3	
Adoptions per 100,000 children under age 18	2004	28.9	
Adoptions per 100,000 children under age 5[5]	2004	64.1	

Demographic indicators	Year	Value
Female singulate mean age at marriage (years)	1990	23.8
Mean age at first birth (years)...	1997	24.5
Total fertility (children per woman)................................	2000-2005	2.0
Percentage of childless women, aged 40 - 44	2000	4.6
Divorce rate (per woman)	...	...

---

[1] Prospective adoptive parents must be aged 30 years or older to engage in simple adoptions.

[2] Step-parents must be at least 10 years older than the child. Different age requirements apply to single adoptive parents.

[3] The National Adoption Council oversees the adoption of national children by foreigners. The Prime Minister's Office oversees the adoption of foreign children by nationals.

[4] Data include both simple and full adoptions.

[5] It was assumed that 60 per cent of adoptive children are under age five.

Government policies

Type of adoption permitted	
Domestic adoption	Yes
Intercountry adoption...	Yes
Single male permitted to adopt	Yes
Single female permitted to adopt	Yes
Age requirements for adopting parents	Aged 25 years or older and at least 17 years older than the child
Child's age of consent for adoption[1]	Aged 12 years or older
Year of ratification of legal instruments on child adoption	
Convention on the Rights of the Child.......................	1990
Hague Convention on Intercountry Adoption	1994
National legislation governing adoption	Civil Code; Code of Civil Procedure
Government body responsible for adoption approval	Civil Registry Judges; State System for the Full Development of the Family

Adoption indicators	Year	Number	Percentage
Total children adopted	2004	973	100
Of which:			
Domestic adoptions..	2004	873	90
Intercountry adoptions[2]...	2004	100	10
Of which:			
Adoptions by step-parents or other relatives..............	...	...	...
Adoptions per 100,000 births.......................................	2004	44.2	
Adoptions per 100,000 children under age 18	2004	2.4	
Adoptions per 100,000 children under age 5[3]...............	2004	5.3	

Demographic indicators	Year	Value
Female singulate mean age at marriage (years)	2000	22.7
Mean age at first birth (years)[4]......................................	1997	23.8
Total fertility (children per woman)...............................	2000-2005	2.4
Percentage of childless women, aged 40 - 44	2000	7.3
Divorce rate (per woman)	1997	0.05

[1] The maturity of the child is also considered.

[2] Data refer to intercountry adoptions to States that are parties to the Convention on Protection of Children and Co-operation in Respect of Intercountry Adoption.

[3] It was assumed that 60 per cent of adoptive children are under age five.

[4] Median age at first birth among women aged 25 to 29 years at the date of the survey.

Government policies

Type of adoption permitted
    Domestic adoption .... Yes
    Intercountry adoption[1] .... No

Single male permitted to adopt .... Yes

Single female permitted to adopt .... Yes

Age requirements for adopting parents ....

Child's age of consent for adoption .... Aged 12 years or older

Year of ratification of legal instruments on child adoption
    Convention on the Rights of the Child..................... 1993
    Hague Convention on Intercountry Adoption .... Not ratified

National legislation governing adoption .... 6 Federated States of Micronesia Code, subchapter III, Adoption

Government body responsible for adoption approval ...... Judiciary

Adoption indicators	Year	Number	Percentage
Total children adopted	...	...	...
Of which:			
Domestic adoptions...................................	...	...	...
Intercountry adoptions	...	..	..
Of which:			
Adoptions by step-parents or other relatives	...	...	...
Adoptions per 100,000 births............................	...	...	
Adoptions per 100,000 children under age 18	...	...	
Adoptions per 100,000 children under age 5	...	...	

Demographic indicators	Year	Value
Female singulate mean age at marriage (years)	1994	...
Mean age at first birth (years).........................	...	...
Total fertility (children per woman)................................	2000-2005	4.4
Percentage of childless women, aged 40 - 44	...	...
Divorce rate (per woman)	...	...

---

[1] Non-citizens are not permitted to adopt.

Government policies

Type of adoption permitted	
Domestic adoption	Yes
Intercountry adoption...	Yes
Single male permitted to adopt	Yes
Single female permitted to adopt	Yes
Age requirements for adopting parents	Aged 28 years or older and at least 15 years older than the child
Child's age of consent for adoption	Aged 15 years or older
Year of ratification of legal instruments on child adoption	
Convention on the Rights of the Child.......................	1993
Hague Convention on Intercountry Adoption	1999
National legislation governing adoption	Civil Code
Government body responsible for adoption approval	Judiciary

Adoption indicators

	Year	Number	Percentage
Total children adopted[1]	2000	10	100
Of which:			
Domestic adoptions...	...	...	
Intercountry adoptions	...	...	...
Of which:			
Adoptions by step-parents or other relatives..............	...	...	...
Adoptions per 100,000 births[1]	2000	2 785.5	
Adoptions per 100,000 children under age 18[1]	2000	144.2	
Adoptions per 100,000 children under age 5[2]	2000	332.8	

Demographic indicators

	Year	Value
Female singulate mean age at marriage (years)	...	...
Mean age at first birth (years)...	...	...
Total fertility (children per woman)...............................	2000-2005	2.0
Percentage of childless women, aged 40 - 44	...	...
Divorce rate (per woman)	...	...

[1] Estimate.
[2] Estimate. It was assumed that 60 per cent of adoptive children are under age five.

Government policies

Type of adoption permitted
    Domestic adoption .... Yes
    Intercountry adoption..................................... Yes

Single male permitted to adopt ....

Single female permitted to adopt ....

Age requirements for adopting parents ....

Child's age of consent for adoption .... Aged 7 years or older

Year of ratification of legal instruments on child adoption
    Convention on the Rights of the Child....................... 1990
    Hague Convention on Intercountry Adoption 2000

National legislation governing adoption .... Family Law of 1999

Government body responsible for adoption approval ...... Judiciary; Ministry of Social Welfare and Labour; Board of Foreigners

Adoption indicators	Year	Number	Percentage
Total children adopted	2004	1 890	100
Of which:			
Domestic adoptions....................................	2004	1 861	98
Intercountry adoptions	2004	29	2
Of which:			
Adoptions by step-parents or other relatives..............	...	...	....
Adoptions per 100,000 births...........................	2004	3 247.6	
Adoptions per 100,000 children under age 18	2004	187.3	
Adoptions per 100,000 children under age 5[1]	2004	422.4	

Demographic indicators	Year	Value
Female singulate mean age at marriage (years)	2000	23.7
Mean age at first birth (years).......................	...	...
Total fertility (children per woman)............................	2000-2005	2.4
Percentage of childless women, aged 40 - 44	1998	2.5
Divorce rate (per woman).............................	...	...

---

[1] It was assumed that 60 per cent of adoptive children are under age five.

Government policies

Type of adoption permitted
    Domestic adoption ....
    Intercountry adoption... ...

Single male permitted to adopt ....

Single female permitted to adopt ....

Age requirements for adopting parents ....

Child's age of consent for adoption ....

Year of ratification of legal instruments on child adoption
    Convention on the Rights of the Child...................... 2006
    Hague Convention on Intercountry Adoption .... Not ratified

National legislation governing adoption ....

Government body responsible for adoption approval ....

Adoption indicators	Year	Number	Percentage
Total children adopted	...	...	...
Of which:			
Domestic adoptions..	...	...	...
Intercountry adoptions	...	...	...
Of which:			
Adoptions by step-parents or other relatives	...	...	...
Adoptions per 100,000 births.......................................	...	...	
Adoptions per 100,000 children under age 18	...	...	
Adoptions per 100,000 children under age 5	...	...	

Demographic indicators	Year	Value
Female singulate mean age at marriage (years)	...	...
Mean age at first birth (years).......................................	...	...
Total fertility (children per woman)..............................	...	...
Percentage of childless women, aged 40 - 44	...	...
Divorce rate (per woman)	...	...

Government policies

Type of adoption permitted
    Domestic adoption .... No
    Intercountry adoption... No

Single male permitted to adopt .... Not applicable

Single female permitted to adopt .... Not applicable

Age requirements for adopting parents .... Not applicable

Child's age of consent for adoption .... Not applicable

Year of ratification of legal instruments on child adoption
    Convention on the Rights of the Child...................... 1993
    Hague Convention on Intercountry Adoption .... Not ratified

National legislation governing adoption .... Not applicable

Government body responsible for adoption approval ...... Not applicable

Adoption indicators	*Year*	*Number*	*Percentage*
Total children adopted	...	..	..
Of which:			
Domestic adoptions..	...	..	..
Intercountry adoptions	...	..	..
Of which:			
Adoptions by step-parents or other relatives..............	...		..
Adoptions per 100,000 births....................................	...	..	
Adoptions per 100,000 children under age 18	...	..	
Adoptions per 100,000 children under age 5	...	..	

Demographic indicators	*Year*	*Value*
Female singulate mean age at marriage (years)	1994	25.3
Mean age at first birth (years)[1]	1995	23.3
Total fertility (children per woman)................................	2000-2005	2.8
Percentage of childless women, aged 40 - 44	2003-2004	17.6
Divorce rate (per woman)	...	...

[1]   Median age at first birth among women aged 25 to 29 years at the date of the survey.

Government policies

Type of adoption permitted
Domestic adoption .... Yes
Intercountry adoption[1] .... Yes

Single male permitted to adopt[2] .... No

Single female permitted to adopt[2] .... No

Age requirements for adopting parents ....

Child's age of consent for adoption .... Aged 14 years or older

Year of ratification of legal instruments on child adoption
Convention on the Rights of the Child....................... 1994
Hague Convention on Intercountry Adoption .... Not ratified

National legislation governing adoption .... Civil Code

Government body responsible for adoption approval ...... Judiciary; Provincial Directorate of Social Action

Adoption indicators	Year	Number	Percentage
Total children adopted	1990-1998	90	100
Of which:			
Domestic adoptions..	1990-1998	45	50
Intercountry adoptions	1990-1998	45	50
Of which:			
Adoptions by step-parents or other relatives..............	...	...	...
Adoptions per 100,000 births...	1990-1998	1.5	
Adoptions per 100,000 children under age 18	1990-1998	0.1	
Adoptions per 100,000 children under age 5[3]	1990-1998	0.2	

Demographic indicators	Year	Value
Female singulate mean age at marriage (years)	1997	18.0
Mean age at first birth (years)[4]..	1997	18.7
Total fertility (children per woman)................................	2000-2005	5.5
Percentage of childless women, aged 40 - 44	2003	5.6
Divorce rate (per woman)..	...	...

[1] Intercountry adoptions are granted only in exceptional cases.
[2] Prospective adoptive parents must have been married at least five years.
[3] It was assumed that 60 per cent of adoptive children are under age five.
[4] Median age at first birth among women aged 25 to 29 years at the date of the survey.

Government policies

Type of adoption permitted
    Domestic adoption .... Yes
    Intercountry adoption ....

Single male permitted to adopt .... Yes

Single female permitted to adopt .... Yes

Age requirements for adopting parents ....

Child's age of consent for adoption ....

Year of ratification of legal instruments on child adoption
    Convention on the Rights of the Child 1991
    Hague Convention on Intercountry Adoption .... Not ratified

National legislation governing adoption .... Registration of Kittima Adoption Act of 1941; Child Law of 1993

Government body responsible for adoption approval ...... Social Welfare Department

Adoption indicators

Adoption indicators	Year	Number	Percentage
Total children adopted[1]	1999-2000	9	100
Of which:			
Domestic adoptions	...	...	...
Intercountry adoptions	...	...	...
Of which:			
Adoptions by step-parents or other relatives	...	...	...
Adoptions per 100,000 births[1]	1999-2000	0.8	
Adoptions per 100,000 children under age 18[1]	1999-2000	0.0	
Adoptions per 100,000 children under age 5[2]	1999-2000	0.1	

Demographic indicators

Demographic indicators	Year	Value
Female singulate mean age at marriage (years)	1991	24.5
Mean age at first birth (years)	...	...
Total fertility (children per woman)	2000-2005	2.5
Percentage of childless women, aged 40 - 44[3]	1983	10.8
Divorce rate (per woman)	...	...

[1] Data refer to the fiscal year.
[2] Data refer to the fiscal year. It was assumed that 60 per cent of adoptive children are under age five.
[3] Never married added.

Government policies

Type of adoption permitted[1]
    Domestic adoption .... Yes
    Intercountry adoption[2] .... No

Single male permitted to adopt .... Yes

Single female permitted to adopt .... Yes

Age requirements for adopting parents .... Aged 25 years or older and at least 25 years older than the child

Child's age of consent for adoption .... Aged 10 years or older

Year of ratification of legal instruments on child adoption
    Convention on the Rights of the Child....................... 1990
    Hague Convention on Intercountry Adoption .... Not ratified

National legislation governing adoption .... Children's Act No. 33 of 1960

Government body responsible for adoption approval ...... Judiciary

Adoption indicators	Year	Number	Percentage
Total children adopted[3]	1990-1992	127	100
Of which:			
Domestic adoptions[3]	1990-1992	127	100
Intercountry adoptions	...	..	..
Of which:			
Adoptions by step-parents or other relatives..............	...	...	...
Adoptions per 100,000 births[3]	1990-1992	86.2	
Adoptions per 100,000 children under age 18[3]	1990-1992	7.1	
Adoptions per 100,000 children under age 5[4]	1990-1992	12.2	

Demographic indicators	Year	Value
Female singulate mean age at marriage (years)	1992	26.4
Mean age at first birth (years)[5]..	1992	21.2
Total fertility (children per woman)...............................	2000-2005	4.0
Percentage of childless women, aged 40 - 44	2000	4.8
Divorce rate (per woman)	...	...

[1] Adopted children must be under 16 years of age.

[2] Intercountry adoptions are granted only to nationals living abroad who are also relatives of the prospective adoptive child or to permanent residents who have applied and qualified for naturalization.

[3] Data refer to adoptions registered between March 1990 and August 1992.

[4] Data refer to adoptions registered between March 1990 and August 1992. It was assumed that 60 per cent of adoptive children are under age five.

[5] Median age at first birth among women aged 25 to 29 years at the date of the survey.

Government policies

Type of adoption permitted
    Domestic adoption ....
    Intercountry adoption ....

Single male permitted to adopt ....

Single female permitted to adopt ....

Age requirements for adopting parents ....

Child's age of consent for adoption ....

Year of ratification of legal instruments on child adoption
    Convention on the Rights of the Child 1994
    Hague Convention on Intercountry Adoption .... Not ratified

National legislation governing adoption ....

Government body responsible for adoption approval ....

Adoption indicators	Year	Number	Percentage
Total children adopted	...	...	...
Of which:			
Domestic adoptions	...	...	...
Intercountry adoptions	...	...	...
Of which:			
Adoptions by step-parents or other relatives	...	...	...
Adoptions per 100,000 births	...	...	
Adoptions per 100,000 children under age 18	...	...	
Adoptions per 100,000 children under age 5	...	...	

Demographic indicators	Year	Value
Female singulate mean age at marriage (years)	...	...
Mean age at first birth (years)	...	...
Total fertility (children per woman)	2000-2005	2.2
Percentage of childless women, aged 40 - 44	...	...
Divorce rate (per woman)	...	...

Government policies

Type of adoption permitted
  Domestic adoption .... Yes
  Intercountry adoption .... Yes

Single male permitted to adopt ....

Single female permitted to adopt ....

Age requirements for adopting parents .... The male adoptive parent must be at least 25 years older than the child when adopting a girl

Child's age of consent for adoption ....

Year of ratification of legal instruments on child adoption
  Convention on the Rights of the Child 1990
  Hague Convention on Intercountry Adoption .... Not ratified

National legislation governing adoption .... Civil Code of 1963; Children's Act of 1992

Government body responsible for adoption approval ...... Judiciary; Ministry of Women, Children and Social Welfare

Adoption indicators	Year	Number	Percentage
Total children adopted	...	...	...
Of which:			
Domestic adoptions	...	...	...
Intercountry adoptions[1]	2000	78	...
Of which:			
Adoptions by step-parents or other relatives	...	...	...
Adoptions per 100,000 births	...	...	
Adoptions per 100,000 children under age 18	...	...	
Adoptions per 100,000 children under age 5	...	...	

Demographic indicators	Year	Value
Female singulate mean age at marriage (years)	2001	19.0
Mean age at first birth (years)[2]	2001	19.7
Total fertility (children per woman)	2000-2005	3.7
Percentage of childless women, aged 40 - 44	2001	4.6
Divorce rate (per woman)	...	...

[1] Based on data from selected receiving countries, the main receiving country: Spain.
[2] Median age at first birth among women aged 25 to 29 years at the date of the survey.

Government policies

Type of adoption permitted	
Domestic adoption	Yes
Intercountry adoption...	Yes
Single male permitted to adopt	Yes
Single female permitted to adopt	Yes
Age requirements for adopting parents	Under age 46
Child's age of consent for adoption	...
Year of ratification of legal instruments on child adoption	
Convention on the Rights of the Child......................	1995
Hague Convention on Intercountry Adoption	1998
National legislation governing adoption	Civil Code; Netherlands Nationality Act; Placement of Foreign Foster Children Act of 15 July 1989
Government body responsible for adoption approval	Ministry of Justice

Adoption indicators

	Year	Number	Percentage
Total children adopted[1]	2004	1 368	100
Of which:			
Domestic adoptions[2]	2004	299	22
Intercountry adoptions[3]	2004	1 069	78
Of which:			
Adoptions by step-parents or other relatives[4]	2004	252	18.4
Adoptions per 100,000 births[1]	2004	721.6	
Adoptions per 100,000 children under age 18[1]	2004	38.5	
Adoptions per 100,000 children under age 5[5]	2004	83.9	

Demographic indicators

	Year	Value
Female singulate mean age at marriage (years)	2002	29.9
Mean age at first birth (years)	2001	28.6
Total fertility (children per woman).............................	2000-2005	1.7
Percentage of childless women, aged 40 - 44[6]	1993	17.5
Divorce rate (per woman)	1996	0.25

---

[1] Data refer to adoptions granted by Dutch courts.
[2] Estimate.
[3] Estimate. Main country of origin: China.
[4] Data refer to adoptions by step-parents only.
[5] Data refer to adoptions granted by Dutch courts. It was assumed that 60 per cent of adoptive children are under age five.
[6] Up to age 42.

Government policies

Type of adoption permitted
    Domestic adoption .... Yes
    Intercountry adoption.. Yes

Single male permitted to adopt .... Yes

Single female permitted to adopt .... Yes

Age requirements for adopting parents ....

Child's age of consent for adoption ....

Year of ratification of legal instruments on child adoption
    Convention on the Rights of the Child...................... 1993
    Hague Convention on Intercountry Adoption 1998

National legislation governing adoption .... Adoption Act of 1955; Adoption Regulations of 1959; Adult Adoption Information Act of 1985

Government body responsible for adoption approval ...... New Zealand Central Authority; Department of Justice

Adoption indicators	Year	Number	Percentage
Total children adopted[1]	2002-2003	631	100
Of which:			
Domestic adoptions[1]	2002-2003	295	47
Intercountry adoptions[1]	2002-2003	336	53
Of which:			
Adoptions by step-parents or other relatives[2]...........	2002-2003	198	67.1
Adoptions per 100,000 births[1]	2002-2003	1 154.1	
Adoptions per 100,000 children under age 18[1]	2002-2003	60.1	
Adoptions per 100,000 children under age 5[3]	2002-2003	136.5	

Demographic indicators	Year	Value
Female singulate mean age at marriage (years)	1996	25.4
Mean age at first birth (years).....................................	1998	29.6
Total fertility (children per woman).............................	2000-2005	2.0
Percentage of childless women, aged 40 - 44	...	...
Divorce rate (per woman)...	1997	0.30

[1] Data refer to the fiscal year.
[2] Data refer to domestic adoptions only. The percentage is calculated based on the total number of domestic adoptions. Data refer to the fiscal year.
[3] Data refer to the fiscal year. It was assumed that 60 per cent of adoptive children are under age five.

Government policies

Type of adoption permitted
    Domestic adoption .... Yes
    Intercountry adoption .... Yes

Single male permitted to adopt .... Yes

Single female permitted to adopt .... Yes

Age requirements for adopting parents[1] .... Aged 25 to 40 years and at least 15 years older than the child

Child's age of consent for adoption ....

Year of ratification of legal instruments on child adoption
    Convention on the Rights of the Child 1990
    Hague Convention on Intercountry Adoption .... Not ratified

National legislation governing adoption .... Adoption Act (Decree No. 862) of 12 October 1981; Code on Children and Adolescents (Act No. 287) of 24 March 1998

Government body responsible for adoption approval ...... Judiciary; National Adoption Council, Ministry of Social Welfare

Adoption indicators	Year	Number	Percentage
Total children adopted[2]	1994	86	100
Of which:			
Domestic adoptions[2]	1994	69	80
Intercountry adoptions[3]	1994	17	20
Of which:			
Adoptions by step-parents or other relatives	...	...	...
Adoptions per 100,000 births[2]	1994	56.3	
Adoptions per 100,000 children under age 18[2]	1994	3.8	
Adoptions per 100,000 children under age 5[4]	1994	7.2	

Demographic indicators	Year	Value
Female singulate mean age at marriage (years)	1998	20.6
Mean age at first birth (years)[5]	1997-1998	19.8
Total fertility (children per woman)	2000-2005	3.3
Percentage of childless women, aged 40 - 44	2001	6.0
Divorce rate (per woman)	...	...

[1] Requirements regarding age difference do not apply to adoptions by step-parents.
[2] Estimate.
[3] Estimate. Data refer to children adopted by foreign citizens residing in Nicaragua.
[4] Estimate. It was assumed that 60 per cent of adoptive children are under age five.
[5] Median age at first birth among women aged 25 to 29 years at the date of the survey.

Government policies

Type of adoption permitted
    Domestic adoption .... Yes
    Intercountry adoption... Yes

Single male permitted to adopt[1] .... No

Single female permitted to adopt[1] .... No

Age requirements for adopting parents .... Aged 35 years old or older

Child's age of consent for adoption ....

Year of ratification of legal instruments on child adoption
    Convention on the Rights of the Child....................... 1990
    Hague Convention on Intercountry Adoption .... Not ratified

National legislation governing adoption .... Civil Code

Government body responsible for adoption approval ...... Judiciary; Department of Child Protection, Ministry of Social Development

Adoption indicators	Year	Number	Percentage
Total children adopted[2]	1997-1998	12	100
Of which:			
Domestic adoptions[2]	1997-1998	4	33
Intercountry adoptions[2]......................................	1997-1998	8	67
Of which:			
Adoptions by step-parents or other relatives..............	...	...	...
Adoptions per 100,000 births[2]	1997-1998	1.0	
Adoptions per 100,000 children under age 18[2]	1997-1998	0.1	
Adoptions per 100,000 children under age 5[3]	1997-1998	0.2	

Demographic indicators	Year	Value
Female singulate mean age at marriage (years)	1998	17.6
Mean age at first birth (years)[4]...	1998	19.6
Total fertility (children per woman).................................	2000-2005	7.9
Percentage of childless women, aged 40 - 44	1998	5.2
Divorce rate (per woman)...	...	...

[1] Prospective adoptive parents must have been married at least ten years.
[2] Data refer to adoptions of abandoned children.
[3] Data refer to adoptions of abandoned children. It was assumed that 60 per cent of adoptive children are under age five.
[4] Median age at first birth among women aged 25 to 29 years at the date of the survey.

Government policies

Type of adoption permitted	
Domestic adoption	Yes
Intercountry adoption[1]	No
Single male permitted to adopt	Varies by state
Single female permitted to adopt	Varies by state
Age requirements for adopting parents	Varies by state
Child's age of consent for adoption	Maturity of child considered
Year of ratification of legal instruments on child adoption	
Convention on the Rights of the Child......................	1991
Hague Convention on Intercountry Adoption	Not ratified
National legislation governing adoption	Varies by state
Government body responsible for adoption approval	Varies by state

Adoption indicators	Year	Number	Percentage
Total children adopted	...	...	...
Of which:			
Domestic adoptions......................................	...	...	
Intercountry adoptions	...	..	
Of which:			
Adoptions by step-parents or other relatives.............	...	...	...
Adoptions per 100,000 births............................	...	...	
Adoptions per 100,000 children under age 18	...	...	
Adoptions per 100,000 children under age 5	...	...	

Demographic indicators	Year	Value
Female singulate mean age at marriage (years)	1999	21.4
Mean age at first birth (years)[2]...................................	1999	20.4
Total fertility (children per woman)...............................	2000-2005	5.8
Percentage of childless women, aged 40 - 44	2003	7.8
Divorce rate (per woman)	...	...

[1]　Non-citizens are not permitted to adopt.
[2]　Median age at first birth among women aged 25 to 29 years at the date of the survey.

Government policies

Type of adoption permitted
    Domestic adoption ....
    Intercountry adoption ....

Single male permitted to adopt ....

Single female permitted to adopt ....

Age requirements for adopting parents ....

Child's age of consent for adoption ....

Year of ratification of legal instruments on child adoption
    Convention on the Rights of the Child...................... 1995
    Hague Convention on Intercountry Adoption .... Not ratified

National legislation governing adoption ....

Government body responsible for adoption approval ....

Adoption indicators	Year	Number	Percentage
Total children adopted	...	...	...
Of which:			
Domestic adoptions..	...	...	
Intercountry adoptions	...	...	
Of which:			
Adoptions by step-parents or other relatives.............	...	...	...
Adoptions per 100,000 births..	...	...	
Adoptions per 100,000 children under age 18	...	...	
Adoptions per 100,000 children under age 5	...	...	

Demographic indicators	Year	Value
Female singulate mean age at marriage (years)	...	...
Mean age at first birth (years)..	...	...
Total fertility (children per woman)................................	2000-2005	2.3
Percentage of childless women, aged 40 - 44	...	...
Divorce rate (per woman)..	...	...

Government policies

Type of adoption permitted
    Domestic adoption .... Yes
    Intercountry adoption.................................... Yes

Single male permitted to adopt .... Yes

Single female permitted to adopt .... Yes

Age requirements for adopting parents[1] .... Aged 25 years or older

Child's age of consent for adoption .... Aged 12 years or older

Year of ratification of legal instruments on child adoption
    Convention on the Rights of the Child................... 1991
    Hague Convention on Intercountry Adoption 1997

National legislation governing adoption .... Act of 28 February 1986 No. 8 Relating to Adoption

Government body responsible for adoption approval ...... Government Adoption Office; National Office for Children, Youth and Family Affairs

Adoption indicators	Year	Number	Percentage
Total children adopted	2003	870	100
Of which:			
Domestic adoptions..	2003	206	24
Intercountry adoptions[2]...................................	2003	664	76
Of which:			
Adoptions by step-parents or other relatives[3]............	2003	158	18.2
Adoptions per 100,000 births...........................	2003	1 567.7	
Adoptions per 100,000 children under age 18	2003	80.6	
Adoptions per 100,000 children under age 5[4]...............	2003	180.3	

Demographic indicators	Year	Value
Female singulate mean age at marriage (years)	2002	31.4
Mean age at first birth (years)....................................	2001	27.0
Total fertility (children per woman)............................	2000-2005	1.8
Percentage of childless women, aged 40 - 44[5]	1988-1989	9.1
Divorce rate (per woman)..	1997	0.27

[1] Prospective adoptive parents aged 20 to 24 years are permitted to adopt under special circumstances.
[2] Main country of origin: China.
[3] Data refer to adoptions by step-parents only.
[4] It was assumed that 60 per cent of adoptive children are under age five.
[5] Exact age 43.

Government policies

Type of adoption permitted
    Domestic adoption .... No
    Intercountry adoption.. No

Single male permitted to adopt .... Not applicable

Single female permitted to adopt .... Not applicable

Age requirements for adopting parents........................... Not applicable

Child's age of consent for adoption .... Not applicable

Year of ratification of legal instruments on child adoption
    Convention on the Rights of the Child...................... 1996
    Hague Convention on Intercountry Adoption .... Not ratified

National legislation governing adoption .... Not applicable

Government body responsible for adoption approval ...... Not applicable

Adoption indicators

	Year	Number	Percentage
Total children adopted	...	..	..
Of which:			
Domestic adoptions...	...	..	..
Intercountry adoptions..	...	..	..
Of which:			
Adoptions by step-parents or other relatives..............	...	..	...
Adoptions per 100,000 births.............................	...	..	
Adoptions per 100,000 children under age 18	...	..	
Adoptions per 100,000 children under age 5	...	..	

Demographic indicators

	Year	Value
Female singulate mean age at marriage (years)	1995	21.7
Mean age at first birth (years)...	...	...
Total fertility (children per woman)...............................	2000-2005	3.8
Percentage of childless women, aged 40 - 44	1995	4.0
Divorce rate (per woman)..	...	...

Government policies

Type of adoption permitted
    Domestic adoption .... No
    Intercountry adoption.. No

Single male permitted to adopt .... Not applicable

Single female permitted to adopt .... Not applicable

Age requirements for adopting parents .... Not applicable

Child's age of consent for adoption .... Not applicable

Year of ratification of legal instruments on child adoption
    Convention on the Rights of the Child....................... 1990
    Hague Convention on Intercountry Adoption .... Not ratified

National legislation governing adoption .... Not applicable

Government body responsible for adoption approval ...... Not applicable

Adoption indicators	Year	Number	Percentage
Total children adopted	...	..	..
Of which:			
Domestic adoptions...	...	..	..
Intercountry adoptions	...	..	..
Of which:			
Adoptions by step-parents or other relatives.............	...	..	..
Adoptions per 100,000 births....................................	...	..	
Adoptions per 100,000 children under age 18	...	..	
Adoptions per 100,000 children under age 5	...	..	

Demographic indicators	Year	Value
Female singulate mean age at marriage (years)	1998	21.3
Mean age at first birth (years)[1]	1990-1991	22.0
Total fertility (children per woman).............................	2000-2005	4.3
Percentage of childless women, aged 40 - 44	1990-1991	7.2
Divorce rate (per woman)	...	...

[1] Median age at first birth among women aged 25 to 29 years at the date of the survey.

Government policies

Type of adoption permitted
    Domestic adoption .... Yes
    Intercountry adoption... Yes

Single male permitted to adopt ....

Single female permitted to adopt ....

Age requirements for adopting parents ....

Child's age of consent for adoption .... Aged 12 years or older

Year of ratification of legal instruments on child adoption
    Convention on the Rights of the Child...................... 1995
    Hague Convention on Intercountry Adoption .... Not ratified

National legislation governing adoption .... Palau National Code, Title 21.401-409

Government body responsible for adoption approval ...... Judiciary

Adoption indicators	Year	Number	Percentage
Total children adopted	1997	32	100
Of which:			
Domestic adoptions..	...	...	...
Intercountry adoptions	...	...	...
Of which:			
Adoptions by step-parents or other relatives..............	...	...	...
Adoptions per 100,000 births..	1997	11 111.1	
Adoptions per 100,000 children under age 18	1997	571.1	
Adoptions per 100,000 children under age 5[1]	1997	1 210.6	

Demographic indicators	Year	Value
Female singulate mean age at marriage (years)	...	...
Mean age at first birth (years)	...	...
Total fertility (children per woman).................................	2000-2005	1.9
Percentage of childless women, aged 40 - 44	...	...
Divorce rate (per woman)	...	...

[1] It was assumed that 60 per cent of adoptive children are under age five.

Government policies

Type of adoption permitted	
Domestic adoption	Yes
Intercountry adoption..................................	Yes
Single male permitted to adopt[1]	Yes
Single female permitted to adopt[2]	Yes
Age requirements for adopting parents	Aged 21 years or older and at least 15 years older than the child
Child's age of consent for adoption	Aged 7 years or older
Year of ratification of legal instruments on child adoption	
Convention on the Rights of the Child......................	1990
Hague Convention on Intercountry Adoption	1999
National legislation governing adoption	Civil Code; Family Code of 1994; Act No. 33 of 28 May 1998; Act No. 105 of 30 December 1998; Act No. 18 of 2 May 2001
Government body responsible for adoption approval	Judiciary; Ministry of Youth, Women, Children and the Family

Adoption indicators	Year	Number	Percentage
Total children adopted	2001-2003	40	100
Of which:			
Domestic adoptions...	2001-2003	38	95
Intercountry adoptions	2001-2003	2	5
Of which:			
Adoptions by step-parents or other relatives..............	...	...	...
Adoptions per 100,000 births...	2001-2003	19.1	
Adoptions per 100,000 children under age 18	2001-2003	1.2	
Adoptions per 100,000 children under age 5[3]	2001-2003	2.4	

Demographic indicators	Year	Value
Female singulate mean age at marriage (years)	2000	21.9
Mean age at first birth (years).......................................	1997	22.3
Total fertility (children per woman)..............................	2000-2005	2.7
Percentage of childless women, aged 40 - 44	1990	6.9
Divorce rate (per woman)	1997	0.01

[1] A sole male applicant is not permitted to adopt a girl.

[2] A sole female applicant is not permitted to adopt a boy.

[3] It was assumed that 60 per cent of adoptive children are under age five.

Government policies

Type of adoption permitted
    Domestic adoption .... Yes
    Intercountry adoption... Yes

Single male permitted to adopt ....

Single female permitted to adopt ....

Age requirements for adopting parents ....

Child's age of consent for adoption ....

Year of ratification of legal instruments on child adoption
    Convention on the Rights of the Child....................... 1993
    Hague Convention on Intercountry Adoption .... Not ratified

National legislation governing adoption .... Adoption Act

Government body responsible for adoption approval ...... Judiciary

Adoption indicators	Year	Number	Percentage
Total children adopted[1]	2000	300	100
Of which:			
Domestic adoptions...	...	...	...
Intercountry adoptions	...	...	...
Of which:			
Adoptions by step-parents or other relatives..............	...	...	...
Adoptions per 100,000 births[1]	2000	166.1	
Adoptions per 100,000 children under age 18[1]	2000	11.8	
Adoptions per 100,000 children under age 5[2]	2000	21.8	

Demographic indicators	Year	Value
Female singulate mean age at marriage (years)	1996	20.8
Mean age at first birth (years).....................................	...	...
Total fertility (children per woman)...............................	2000-2005	4.1
Percentage of childless women, aged 40 - 44	1996	9.5
Divorce rate (per woman)	...	...

[1] Estimate.
[2] Estimate. It was assumed that 60 per cent of adoptive children are under age five.

Government policies

Type of adoption permitted	
Domestic adoption	Yes
Intercountry adoption	Yes
Single male permitted to adopt	Yes
Single female permitted to adopt	Yes
Age requirements for adopting parents	Aged 25 to 50 years
Child's age of consent for adoption	Aged 12 years or older
Year of ratification of legal instruments on child adoption	
Convention on the Rights of the Child	1990
Hague Convention on Intercountry Adoption	1998
National legislation governing adoption	Juvenile Code; Adoption Act (No. 1116) of 22 October 1997
Government body responsible for adoption approval	Judiciary; Adoption and Family Placement Office; Adoption Centre

Adoption indicators	Year	Number	Percentage
Total children adopted[1]	1999-2001	30	100
Of which:			
Domestic adoptions	...	...	...
Intercountry adoptions	...	...	...
Of which:			
Adoptions by step-parents or other relatives	...	...	...
Adoptions per 100,000 births[1]	1999-2001	6.0	
Adoptions per 100,000 children under age 18[1]	1999-2001	0.4	
Adoptions per 100,000 children under age 5[2]	1999-2001	0.8	

Demographic indicators	Year	Value
Female singulate mean age at marriage (years)	1992	21.5
Mean age at first birth (years)[3]	1990	21.6
Total fertility (children per woman)	2000-2005	3.9
Percentage of childless women, aged 40 - 44	2004	8.0
Divorce rate (per woman)	...	...

[1] Estimate.
[2] Estimate. It was assumed that 60 per cent of adoptive children are under age five.
[3] Median age at first birth among women aged 25 to 29 years at the date of the survey.

Government policies

Type of adoption permitted
    Domestic adoption ....   Yes
    Intercountry adoption..   Yes

Single male permitted to adopt ....   Yes

Single female permitted to adopt ....   Yes

Age requirements for adopting parents[1] ....   At least 18 years older than the child

Child's age of consent for adoption ....   Aged 10 years or older

Year of ratification of legal instruments on child adoption
    Convention on the Rights of the Child......................   1990
    Hague Convention on Intercountry Adoption   1995

National legislation governing adoption ....   Civil Code (Decree Law No. 295 of 24 July 1984); General Adoption Law (Decree Law 25934 of 9 December 1992); Children's and Adolescents' Code (Decree Law No. 26102 of 28 December 1992); Children's and Adolescents' Code (Decree Law No. 27337 of 2 August 2000)

Government body responsible for adoption approval ......   Judiciary; National Secretariat for Adoptions

Adoption indicators	Year	Number	Percentage
Total children adopted	2004	187	100
Of which:			
Domestic adoptions...	2004	95	51
Intercountry adoptions[2]...	2004	92	49
Of which:			
Adoptions by step-parents or other relatives..............	...	...	...
Adoptions per 100,000 births...	2004	29.8	
Adoptions per 100,000 children under age 18	2004	1.7	
Adoptions per 100,000 children under age 5[3]	2004	3.7	

Demographic indicators	Year	Value
Female singulate mean age at marriage (years)	1996	23.1
Mean age at first birth (years)[4]..	2000	22.2
Total fertility (children per woman)...............................	2000-2005	2.9
Percentage of childless women, aged 40 - 44	2003	9.2
Divorce rate (per woman)...	...	...

[1] Different age requirements apply to single adoptive parents.
[2] Main receiving country: Spain.
[3] It was assumed that 60 per cent of adoptive children are under age five.
[4] Median age at first birth among women aged 25 to 29 years at the date of the survey.

Government policies

Type of adoption permitted
    Domestic adoption .... Yes
    Intercountry adoption... Yes

Single male permitted to adopt .... Yes

Single female permitted to adopt .... Yes

Age requirements for adopting parents[1] .... At least 16 years older than the child

Child's age of consent for adoption .... Aged 10 years or older

Year of ratification of legal instruments on child adoption
    Convention on the Rights of the Child....................... 1990
    Hague Convention on Intercountry Adoption 1996

National legislation governing adoption .... Family Code of 1987; Intercountry Adoption Act of 1995;
Domestic Adoption Act of 1998

Government body responsible for adoption approval ...... Judiciary; Department of Social Welfare and Development;
Intercountry Adoption Board

Adoption indicators	Year	Number	Percentage
Total children adopted	2003	1 902	100
Of which:			
Domestic adoptions...	...	...	...
Intercountry adoptions	...	...	...
Of which:			
Adoptions by step-parents or other relatives..............	...	...	...
Adoptions per 100,000 births....................................	2003	93.5	
Adoptions per 100,000 children under age 18	2003	5.6	
Adoptions per 100,000 children under age 5[2]...............	2003	11.6	

Demographic indicators	Year	Value
Female singulate mean age at marriage (years)	1995	24.1
Mean age at first birth (years)[3].....................................	1998	23.9
Total fertility (children per woman)..............................	2000-2005	3.2
Percentage of childless women, aged 40 - 44	2003	9.3
Divorce rate (per woman)	...	...

[1] In the case of intercountry adoption, prospective adoptive parents must be aged 27 years or older.
[2] It was assumed that 60 per cent of adoptive children are under age five.
[3] Median age at first birth among women aged 25 to 29 years at the date of the survey.

Government policies

Type of adoption permitted[1]	
Domestic adoption	Yes
Intercountry adoption..	Yes
Single male permitted to adopt	...
Single female permitted to adopt	...
Age requirements for adopting parents	...
Child's age of consent for adoption	Aged 13 years or older
Year of ratification of legal instruments on child adoption	
Convention on the Rights of the Child.......................	1991
Hague Convention on Intercountry Adoption	1995
National legislation governing adoption	Family and Guardianship Code
Government body responsible for adoption approval	Guardianship Court; Ministry of National Education

Adoption indicators

	Year	Number	Percentage
Total children adopted[2]	1997	2 441	100
Of which:			
Domestic adoptions[2]	1997	2 236	92
Intercountry adoptions[3]..	1997	205	8
Of which:			
Adoptions by step-parents or other relatives..............	...	...	...
Adoptions per 100,000 births[2]	1997	584.9	
Adoptions per 100,000 children under age 18[2]	1997	23.7	
Adoptions per 100,000 children under age 5[4]	1997	64.1	

Demographic indicators

	Year	Value
Female singulate mean age at marriage (years)	1999	25.2
Mean age at first birth (years)...	2001	24.8
Total fertility (children per woman).................................	2000-2005	1.3
Percentage of childless women, aged 40 - 44	1991	8.6
Divorce rate (per woman)	1997	0.14

[1] Adopted children must be under 18 years of age.
[2] Data refer to adoption rulings by the courts.
[3] Data refer to adoption rulings by the courts. Based on data from selected receiving countries, the main receiving country in 2004: Italy.
[4] Data refer to adoption rulings by the courts. It was assumed that 60 per cent of adoptive children are under age five.

Government policies

Type of adoption permitted
     Domestic adoption ....   Yes
     Intercountry adoption...   Yes
Single male permitted to adopt[1] ....   Yes
Single female permitted to adopt[1] ....   Yes
Age requirements for adopting parents[2] ....   Under age 50
Child's age of consent for adoption ....   Aged 12 years or older
Year of ratification of legal instruments on child adoption
     Convention on the Rights of the Child   1990
     Hague Convention on Intercountry Adoption   2004
National legislation governing adoption ....   Civil Code; Decree Law No. 185 of 22 May 1993; Decree Law No. 120 of 8 May 1998; Law No. 7 of 11 May 2001; Law No. 31 of 22 August 2003

Government body responsible for adoption approval ......   Ministry of Justice; Department of Social Action

Adoption indicators	Year	Number	Percentage
Total children adopted	2003	409	100
Of which:			
Domestic adoptions...	2003	403	99
Intercountry adoptions[3]	2003	6	1
Of which:			
Adoptions by step-parents or other relatives..............	...	...	...
Adoptions per 100,000 births..	2003	363.2	
Adoptions per 100,000 children under age 18	2003	20.3	
Adoptions per 100,000 children under age 5[4]	2003	43.7	

Demographic indicators	Year	Value
Female singulate mean age at marriage (years)	1991	23.9
Mean age at first birth (years).....................................	2001	26.7
Total fertility (children per woman)...............................	2000-2005	1.5
Percentage of childless women, aged 40 - 44	1991	10.0
Divorce rate (per woman)	1997	0.17

---

[1] Prospective adoptive parents must be aged 30 years or older.
[2] In the case of adoption by a couple, both prospective parents must be aged 25 years or older.
[3] Data include 1 foreign child adopted by Portuguese citizens as well as 5 Portuguese children adopted abroad.
[4] It was assumed that 60 per cent of adoptive children are under age five.

Government policies

Type of adoption permitted
    Domestic adoption .... No
    Intercountry adoption... No

Single male permitted to adopt .... Not applicable

Single female permitted to adopt .... Not applicable

Age requirements for adopting parents .... Not applicable

Child's age of consent for adoption .... Not applicable

Year of ratification of legal instruments on child adoption
    Convention on the Rights of the Child..................... 1995
    Hague Convention on Intercountry Adoption .... Not ratified

National legislation governing adoption .... Not applicable

Government body responsible for adoption approval ...... Not applicable

Adoption indicators	Year	Number	Percentage
Total children adopted	...	..	..
Of which:			
Domestic adoptions..	...	..	..
Intercountry adoptions	...	..	..
Of which:			
Adoptions by step-parents or other relatives.............	...	..	..
Adoptions per 100,000 births..	...	..	
Adoptions per 100,000 children under age 18	...	..	
Adoptions per 100,000 children under age 5	...	..	

Demographic indicators	Year	Value
Female singulate mean age at marriage (years)	1998	26.3
Mean age at first birth (years)......................................	1997	24.9
Total fertility (children per woman)...............................	2000-2005	3.0
Percentage of childless women, aged 40 - 44	1998	13.3
Divorce rate (per woman)	1993	0.20

Government policies

Type of adoption permitted	
Domestic adoption	Yes
Intercountry adoption..	Yes
Single male permitted to adopt	...
Single female permitted to adopt	...
Age requirements for adopting parents[1]	Aged 25 to 50 years
Child's age of consent for adoption	Aged 15 years or older
Year of ratification of legal instruments on child adoption	
Convention on the Rights of the Child.......................	1991
Hague Convention on Intercountry Adoption	Not ratified
National legislation governing adoption	Civil Code; Special Adoption Act of 1999
Government body responsible for adoption approval[2]	Judiciary; Ministry of Health and Welfare

Adoption indicators

	Year	Number	Percentage
Total children adopted	2004	3 899	100
Of which:			
Domestic adoptions...................................	2004	1 641	42
Intercountry adoptions[3].............................	2004	2 258	58
Of which:			
Adoptions by step-parents or other relatives..............	...	...	...
Adoptions per 100,000 births.......................................	2004	834.2	
Adoptions per 100,000 children under age 18	2004	35.3	
Adoptions per 100,000 children under age 5[4]	2004	92.8	

Demographic indicators

	Year	Value
Female singulate mean age at marriage (years)	1995	26.1
Mean age at first birth (years)	1998	27.1
Total fertility (children per woman)...............................	2000-2005	1.2
Percentage of childless women, aged 40 - 44	2000	2.8
Divorce rate (per woman)...	1997	0.18

[1] In the case of intercountry adoption, the foreign prospective adoptive parents must be under age 45.
[2] Adoptions can be arranged directly between the child's guardian and the potential adoptive parents.
[3] Based on data from selected receiving countries, the main receiving country: United States of America.
[4] It was assumed that 60 per cent of adoptive children are under age five.

Government policies

Type of adoption permitted
    Domestic adoption .... Yes
    Intercountry adoption .... Yes

Single male permitted to adopt .... Yes

Single female permitted to adopt .... Yes

Age requirements for adopting parents .... Aged 25 years or older and at least 15 years older than the child

Child's age of consent for adoption .... Aged 10 years or older

Year of ratification of legal instruments on child adoption
    Convention on the Rights of the Child...................... 1993
    Hague Convention on Intercountry Adoption 1998

National legislation governing adoption .... Marriage and Family Code

Government body responsible for adoption approval ...... Judiciary; Committee for Adoption

Adoption indicators	Year	Number	Percentage
Total children adopted	2004	219	100
Of which:			
Domestic adoptions..	2004	137	63
Intercountry adoptions[1]..	2004	82	37
Of which:			
Adoptions by step-parents or other relatives..............	...	...	...
Adoptions per 100,000 births.......................................	2004	513.5	
Adoptions per 100,000 children under age 18	2004	20.8	
Adoptions per 100,000 children under age 5[2]................	2004	62.3	

Demographic indicators	Year	Value
Female singulate mean age at marriage (years)	1989	21.1
Mean age at first birth (years).....................................	2001	22.8
Total fertility (children per woman)...............................	2000-2005	1.2
Percentage of childless women, aged 40 - 44	1997	8.2
Divorce rate (per woman)...	1991	0.39

[1] Main receiving country: United States of America.
[2] It was assumed that 60 per cent of adoptive children are under age five.

Government policies

Type of adoption permitted
    Domestic adoption .... Yes
    Intercountry adoption[1] .... Yes

Single male permitted to adopt ....

Single female permitted to adopt ....

Age requirements for adopting parents ....

Child's age of consent for adoption .... Aged 10 years or older

Year of ratification of legal instruments on child adoption
    Convention on the Rights of the Child..................... 1990
    Hague Convention on Intercountry Adoption 1994

National legislation governing adoption .... Law No. 87 of 1998; Law No. 273 of 2004; Government Decision No. 1435 of 2004; Government Decision No. 1442 of 2004; Government Decision No.1441 of 2004; Government Decision No. 1436 of 2004; Order No.45 of 2004 of the Secretary of State of the National Authority for Child Protection and Adoption

Government body responsible for adoption approval ...... Ministry of Justice; National Authority for Child Protection and Adoption

Adoption indicators	Year	Number	Percentage
Total children adopted	2004	1 673	100
Of which:			
Domestic adoptions......................................	2004	1 422	85
Intercountry adoptions[2]...............................	2004	251	15
Of which:			
Adoptions by step-parents or other relatives.............	...	...	...
Adoptions per 100,000 births.....................................	2004	786.2	
Adoptions per 100,000 children under age 18	2004	37.3	
Adoptions per 100,000 children under age 5[3]	2004	94.4	

Demographic indicators	Year	Value
Female singulate mean age at marriage (years)	2000	24.1
Mean age at first birth (years)...	2000	23.6
Total fertility (children per woman)...............................	2000-2005	1.3
Percentage of childless women, aged 40 - 44	1999	7.4
Divorce rate (per woman)..	1997	0.19

[1] Intercountry adoptions are granted only to adoptive parents who have either a blood or familial link to the adopted child.

[2] Data refer to children previously protected in public or private placement centers or in substitute families. Based on data from selected receiving countries, the main receiving country: Italy.

[3] It was assumed that 60 per cent of adoptive children are under age five.

Government policies

Type of adoption permitted
    Domestic adoption .... Yes
    Intercountry adoption.. Yes

Single male permitted to adopt[1] .... Yes

Single female permitted to adopt[1] .... Yes

Age requirements for adopting parents ....

Child's age of consent for adoption .... Aged 10 years or older

Year of ratification of legal instruments on child adoption
    Convention on the Rights of the Child...................... 1990
    Hague Convention on Intercountry Adoption[2]........... Not ratified

National legislation governing adoption .... Family Code; Code of Civil Procedure

Government body responsible for adoption approval ...... Judiciary

---

Adoption indicators	Year	Number	Percentage
Total children adopted[3]	2001	23 108	100
Of which:			
Domestic adoptions[3]	2001	17 331	75
Intercountry adoptions[4]..	2001	5 777	25
Of which:			
Adoptions by step-parents or other relatives..............	...	...	...
Adoptions per 100,000 births[3]	2001	1 656.0	
Adoptions per 100,000 children under age 18[3]	2001	69.6	
Adoptions per 100,000 children under age 5[5]	2001	209.6	

Demographic indicators	Year	Value
Female singulate mean age at marriage (years)	1989	21.8
Mean age at first birth (years).....................................	1998	23.1
Total fertility (children per woman)..............................	2000-2005	1.3
Percentage of childless women, aged 40 - 44	1994	7.0
Divorce rate (per woman)	1995	0.57

---

[1] Prospective adoptive parents must be at least 16 years older than the child.
[2] Year of signature: 2000.
[3] Estimate.
[4] Based on data from selected receiving countries, the main receiving country: United States of America.
[5] Estimate. It was assumed that 60 per cent of adoptive children are under age five.

Government policies

Type of adoption permitted	
Domestic adoption	Yes
Intercountry adoption..	Yes
Single male permitted to adopt	Yes
Single female permitted to adopt	Yes
Age requirements for adopting parents	At least 15 years older than the child
Child's age of consent for adoption	...
Year of ratification of legal instruments on child adoption	
Convention on the Rights of the Child......................	1991
Hague Convention on Intercountry Adoption	Not ratified
National legislation governing adoption	Civil Code; Law No. 42 of 27 October 1988
Government body responsible for adoption approval	Judiciary

Adoption indicators

	Year	Number	Percentage
Total children adopted	...	...	...
Of which:			
Domestic adoptions..	...	...	...
Intercountry adoptions	2001	9	...
Of which:			
Adoptions by step-parents or other relatives..............	...	...	...
Adoptions per 100,000 births.............................	...	...	
Adoptions per 100,000 children under age 18	...	...	
Adoptions per 100,000 children under age 5	...	...	

Demographic indicators

	Year	Value
Female singulate mean age at marriage (years)	2000	22.7
Mean age at first birth (years)[1]	2000	22.0
Total fertility (children per woman)...............................	2000-2005	5.7
Percentage of childless women, aged 40 - 44	2000	3.6
Divorce rate (per woman)	...	...

[1] Median age at first birth among women aged 25 to 29 years at the date of the survey.

Government policies

Type of adoption permitted
    Domestic adoption .... Yes
    Intercountry adoption.. Yes

Single male permitted to adopt ....

Single female permitted to adopt ....

Age requirements for adopting parents .... Aged 25 years or older and at least 21 years older than the child

Child's age of consent for adoption ....

Year of ratification of legal instruments on child adoption
    Convention on the Rights of the Child...................... 1990
    Hague Convention on Intercountry Adoption .... Not ratified

National legislation governing adoption .... Adoption Act; Guardianship of Infants Act

Government body responsible for adoption approval ...... Judiciary; Probation and Child Welfare Board

---

Adoption indicators	Year	Number	Percentage
Total children adopted	...	...	...
Of which:			
Domestic adoptions...	...	...	...
Intercountry adoptions	...	...	...
Of which:			
Adoptions by step-parents or other relatives	...	...	...
Adoptions per 100,000 births.......................................	...	...	...
Adoptions per 100,000 children under age 18	...	...	...
Adoptions per 100,000 children under age 5	...	...	...

Demographic indicators	Year	Value
Female singulate mean age at marriage (years)	...	...
Mean age at first birth (years)	...	...
Total fertility (children per woman)...............................	2000-2005	2.4
Percentage of childless women, aged 40 - 44	...	...
Divorce rate (per woman)	...	...

Government policies

Type of adoption permitted[1]	
Domestic adoption	Yes
Intercountry adoption..	Yes
Single male permitted to adopt[2]	Yes
Single female permitted to adopt	Yes
Age requirements for adopting parents[3]..........................	Aged 25 years or older and at least 21 years older than the child
Child's age of consent for adoption	Maturity of child considered
Year of ratification of legal instruments on child adoption	
Convention on the Rights of the Child.......................	1993
Hague Convention on Intercountry Adoption	Not ratified
National legislation governing adoption	Adoption Ordinance of 1954
Government body responsible for adoption approval	Judiciary; Division of Human Services and Family Affairs

Adoption indicators	Year	Number	Percentage
Total children adopted	...	...	...
Of which:			
Domestic adoptions....................................	...	...	...
Intercountry adoptions	...	...	...
Of which:			
Adoptions by step-parents or other relatives.............	...	...	...
Adoptions per 100,000 births...........................	...	...	
Adoptions per 100,000 children under age 18	...	...	
Adoptions per 100,000 children under age 5	...	...	

Demographic indicators	Year	Value
Female singulate mean age at marriage (years)	1991	33.7
Mean age at first birth (years).........................	1998	23.1
Total fertility (children per woman)................................	2000-2005	2.2
Percentage of childless women, aged 40 - 44	2001	9.8
Divorce rate (per woman)	...	...

---

[1] Prospective adoptive parents must have had the child in their care and custody for at least three months prior to the date of the adoption order.

[2] A sole male applicant is not permitted to adopt a girl, except under special circumstances.

[3] Prospective adoptive parents must be aged 21 years or older to adopt a relative.

Government policies

Type of adoption permitted	
Domestic adoption	Yes
Intercountry adoption..	Yes
Single male permitted to adopt	Yes
Single female permitted to adopt	Yes
Age requirements for adopting parents	...
Child's age of consent for adoption	...
Year of ratification of legal instruments on child adoption	
Convention on the Rights of the Child......................	1993
Hague Convention on Intercountry Adoption	Not ratified
National legislation governing adoption	Adoption Act
Government body responsible for adoption approval	Judiciary; Adoption Board

Adoption indicators

	Year	Number	Percentage
Total children adopted	...	...	...
Of which:			
Domestic adoptions...	...	...	...
Intercountry adoptions	...	...	...
Of which:			
Adoptions by step-parents or other relatives	...	...	...
Adoptions per 100,000 births..	...	...	
Adoptions per 100,000 children under age 18	...	...	
Adoptions per 100,000 children under age 5	...	...	

Demographic indicators

	Year	Value
Female singulate mean age at marriage (years)	1991	30.9
Mean age at first birth (years)..	1997	22.1
Total fertility (children per woman)................................	2000-2005	2.3
Percentage of childless women, aged 40 - 44	1991	6.4
Divorce rate (per woman)	...	...

Government policies

Type of adoption permitted
    Domestic adoption .... Yes
    Intercountry adoption[1] .... Yes

Single male permitted to adopt .... Yes

Single female permitted to adopt .... Yes

Age requirements for adopting parents ....

Child's age of consent for adoption .... Aged 12 years or older

Year of ratification of legal instruments on child adoption
    Convention on the Rights of the Child...................... 1994
    Hague Convention on Intercountry Adoption .... Not ratified

National legislation governing adoption .... Infants Ordinance of 1961; Infants (Adoption) Amendment Act of 2005

Government body responsible for adoption approval ...... Judiciary

Adoption indicators	Year	Number	Percentage
Total children adopted	2002	438	100
Of which:			
Domestic adoptions...	...	...	...
Intercountry adoptions	...	...	...
Of which:			
Adoptions by step-parents or other relatives	...	...	...
Adoptions per 100,000 births...	2002	8 084.2	
Adoptions per 100,000 children under age 18	2002	511.0	
Adoptions per 100,000 children under age 5[2]	2002	964.2	

Demographic indicators	Year	Value
Female singulate mean age at marriage (years)	1999	23.9
Mean age at first birth (years)......................................	1976	27.8
Total fertility (children per woman)................................	2000-2005	4.4
Percentage of childless women, aged 40 - 44	1981	3.8
Divorce rate (per woman)...	...	...

[1] Intercountry adoptions are granted only to adoptive parents who have either a blood or familial link to the adopted child or where the child has been abandoned or orphaned.
[2] It was assumed that 60 per cent of adoptive children are under age five.

Government policies

Type of adoption permitted
    Domestic adoption .... Yes
    Intercountry adoption... Yes

Single male permitted to adopt .... Yes

Single female permitted to adopt .... Yes

Age requirements for adopting parents .... Aged 25 years or older and 18 to 45 years older than the child

Child's age of consent for adoption ....

Year of ratification of legal instruments on child adoption
    Convention on the Rights of the Child....................... 1991
    Hague Convention on Intercountry Adoption 2004

National legislation governing adoption .... Law No. 49 of 26 April 1986; Law No. 83 of 20 July 1999

Government body responsible for adoption approval ...... Judiciary; Minor Service

---

Adoption indicators	Year	Number	Percentage
Total children adopted	...	...	...
Of which:			
Domestic adoptions...	...	...	...
Intercountry adoptions	...	...	...
Of which:			
Adoptions by step-parents or other relatives..............	...	...	...
Adoptions per 100,000 births..	...	...	
Adoptions per 100,000 children under age 18	...	...	
Adoptions per 100,000 children under age 5	...	...	

Demographic indicators	Year	Value
Female singulate mean age at marriage (years)	...	...
Mean age at first birth (years).......................................	...	...
Total fertility (children per woman)..............................	2000-2005	1.3
Percentage of childless women, aged 40 - 44	...	...
Divorce rate (per woman)	...	...

Government policies

Type of adoption permitted[1]
Domestic adoption .... Yes
Intercountry adoption... ...

Single male permitted to adopt ....

Single female permitted to adopt ....

Age requirements for adopting parents ....

Child's age of consent for adoption .... Aged 7 years or older

Year of ratification of legal instruments on child adoption
Convention on the Rights of the Child...................... 1991
Hague Convention on Intercountry Adoption .... Not ratified

National legislation governing adoption .... Act No. 2/77

Government body responsible for adoption approval ...... Judiciary

Adoption indicators	Year	Number	Percentage
Total children adopted	...	...	...
Of which:			
Domestic adoptions...	...	...	...
Intercountry adoptions	...	...	...
Of which:			
Adoptions by step-parents or other relatives..............	...	...	...
Adoptions per 100,000 births..	...	...	
Adoptions per 100,000 children under age 18	...	...	
Adoptions per 100,000 children under age 5	...	...	

Demographic indicators	Year	Value
Female singulate mean age at marriage (years)	1991	17.8
Mean age at first birth (years)...	...	...
Total fertility (children per woman)..................................	2000-2005	4.1
Percentage of childless women, aged 40 - 44	1991	5.2
Divorce rate (per woman)	...	...

[1] Adopted children must be under 16 years of age.

Government policies

Type of adoption permitted
    Domestic adoption .... No
    Intercountry adoption.. No

Single male permitted to adopt .... Not applicable

Single female permitted to adopt .... Not applicable

Age requirements for adopting parents........................... Not applicable

Child's age of consent for adoption .... Not applicable

Year of ratification of legal instruments on child adoption
    Convention on the Rights of the Child....................... 1996
    Hague Convention on Intercountry Adoption........... Not ratified

National legislation governing adoption .... Not applicable

Government body responsible for adoption approval ...... Not applicable

Adoption indicators	*Year*	*Number*	*Percentage*
Total children adopted	...	..	..
Of which:			
Domestic adoptions...	...	..	..
Intercountry adoptions	...	..	..
Of which:			
Adoptions by step-parents or other relatives..............	...	..	..
Adoptions per 100,000 births......................................	...	..	
Adoptions per 100,000 children under age 18	...	..	
Adoptions per 100,000 children under age 5	...	..	

Demographic indicators	*Year*	*Value*
Female singulate mean age at marriage (years)	1987	21.7
Mean age at first birth (years).......................................	...	...
Total fertility (children per woman)..............................	2000-2005	4.1
Percentage of childless women, aged 40 - 44	1996	5.0
Divorce rate (per woman)...	...	...

Government policies

Type of adoption permitted
    Domestic adoption .... Yes
    Intercountry adoption.. Yes

Single male permitted to adopt[1] .... Yes

Single female permitted to adopt[1] .... Yes

Age requirements for adopting parents[2] .... At least 15 years older than the child

Child's age of consent for adoption .... Aged 15 years or older

Year of ratification of legal instruments on child adoption
    Convention on the Rights of the Child....................... 1990
    Hague Convention on Intercountry Adoption .... Not ratified

National legislation governing adoption .... Family Code

Government body responsible for adoption approval ...... Judiciary

Adoption indicators	Year	Number	Percentage
Total children adopted	...	...	...
Of which:			
Domestic adoptions...	...	...	...
Intercountry adoptions	2005	14	...
Of which:			
Adoptions by step-parents or other relatives..............	...	...	
Adoptions per 100,000 births..	...	...	
Adoptions per 100,000 children under age 18	...	...	
Adoptions per 100,000 children under age 5	...	...	

Demographic indicators	Year	Value
Female singulate mean age at marriage (years)	1997	21.5
Mean age at first birth (years)[3]	1997	20.4
Total fertility (children per woman).................................	2000-2005	5.0
Percentage of childless women, aged 40 - 44	1997	4.7
Divorce rate (per woman)..	...	...

[1] Prospective adoptive parents must be aged 35 years or older.
[2] Step-parents must be at least 10 years older than the child. Different age requirements apply to single adoptive parents.
[3] Median age at first birth among women aged 25 to 29 years at the date of the survey.

Government policies

Type of adoption permitted
    Domestic adoption .... Yes
    Intercountry adoption... ...

Single male permitted to adopt ....

Single female permitted to adopt ....

Age requirements for adopting parents ....

Child's age of consent for adoption ....

Year of ratification of legal instruments on child adoption
    Convention on the Rights of the Child....................... 2001
    Hague Convention on Intercountry Adoption .... Not ratified

National legislation governing adoption ....

Government body responsible for adoption approval ....

Adoption indicators	Year	Number	Percentage
Total children adopted	2001	247	100
Of which:			
Domestic adoptions...	...	...	...
Intercountry adoptions	...	...	...
Of which:			
Adoptions by step-parents or other relatives..............	...	...	...
Adoptions per 100,000 births......................................	2001	198.0	
Adoptions per 100,000 children under age 18	2001	9.7	
Adoptions per 100,000 children under age 5[1]	2001	23.8	

Demographic indicators	Year	Value
Female singulate mean age at marriage (years)	1991	23.1
Mean age at first birth (years)	2000	25.0
Total fertility (children per woman)..............................	2000-2005	1.7
Percentage of childless women, aged 40 - 44	1991	8.4
Divorce rate (per woman)	1995	0.10

NOTE: Data refer to Serbia and Montenegro.
[1] It was assumed that 60 per cent of adoptive children are under age five.

Government policies

Type of adoption permitted
    Domestic adoption .... Yes
    Intercountry adoption[1] .... No

Single male permitted to adopt .... Yes

Single female permitted to adopt .... Yes

Age requirements for adopting parents .... Aged 21 years or older

Child's age of consent for adoption[2] .... Aged 14 years or older

Year of ratification of legal instruments on child adoption
    Convention on the Rights of the Child 1990
    Hague Convention on Intercountry Adoption .... Not ratified

National legislation governing adoption .... Children's Act

Government body responsible for adoption approval ...... Judiciary; Division of Social Affairs

Adoption indicators	Year	Number	Percentage
Total children adopted	2001	6	100
Of which:			
Domestic adoptions...	2001	6	100
Intercountry adoptions	...	..	..
Of which:			
Adoptions by step-parents or other relatives..............	...	...	...
Adoptions per 100,000 births...	2001	483.9	
Adoptions per 100,000 children under age 18	2001	23.5	
Adoptions per 100,000 children under age 5[3]	2001	58.6	

Demographic indicators	Year	Value
Female singulate mean age at marriage (years)	...	...
Mean age at first birth (years).......................................	...	...
Total fertility (children per woman)...............................	2000-2005	1.9
Percentage of childless women, aged 40 - 44	...	...
Divorce rate (per woman)	...	...

[1] Intercountry adoptions are granted only to nationals living abroad who are also relatives of the prospective adoptive child or to permanent residents who have applied and qualified for naturalization.
[2] The maturity of the child is also considered.
[3] It was assumed that 60 per cent of adoptive children are under age five.

Government policies

Type of adoption permitted
    Domestic adoption .... Yes
    Intercountry adoption[1] .... Yes

Single male permitted to adopt .... Yes

Single female permitted to adopt .... Yes

Age requirements for adopting parents .... Aged 30 years or older

Child's age of consent for adoption ....

Year of ratification of legal instruments on child adoption
    Convention on the Rights of the Child 1990
    Hague Convention on Intercountry Adoption .... Not ratified

National legislation governing adoption .... Adoption Act of 1989

Government body responsible for adoption approval ...... Judiciary; Ministry of Social Welfare, Gender and Children's Affairs

Adoption indicators	Year	Number	Percentage
Total children adopted	...	...	...
Of which:			
Domestic adoptions	...	...	...
Intercountry adoptions	...	...	...
Of which:			
Adoptions by step-parents or other relatives	...	...	...
Adoptions per 100,000 births	...	...	
Adoptions per 100,000 children under age 18	...	...	
Adoptions per 100,000 children under age 5	...	...	

Demographic indicators	Year	Value
Female singulate mean age at marriage (years)	1992	19.8
Mean age at first birth (years)	...	...
Total fertility (children per woman)	2000-2005	6.5
Percentage of childless women, aged 40 - 44	...	...
Divorce rate (per woman)	...	...

[1] Prospective adoptive parents must have resided in the country and had the child in their care and custody for at least 12 consecutive months prior to the date of the adoption.

Government policies

Type of adoption permitted

Domestic adoption	Yes
Intercountry adoption[1]	Yes

Single male permitted to adopt[2] ...... Yes

Single female permitted to adopt ...... Yes

Age requirements for adopting parents ...... Aged 25 years or older and at least 21 years older than the child

Child's age of consent for adoption ....

Year of ratification of legal instruments on child adoption

Convention on the Rights of the Child	1995
Hague Convention on Intercountry Adoption	Not ratified

National legislation governing adoption ...... Adoption of Children Act of 1972

Government body responsible for adoption approval ...... Judiciary

Adoption indicators

	Year	Number	Percentage
Total children adopted	2002	713	100
Of which:			
Domestic adoptions	2002	265	37
Intercountry adoptions[3]	2002	448	63
Of which:			
Adoptions by step-parents or other relatives	...	...	...
Adoptions per 100,000 births	2002	1 648.7	
Adoptions per 100,000 children under age 18	2002	68.5	
Adoptions per 100,000 children under age 5[4]	2002	170.4	

Demographic indicators

	Year	Value
Female singulate mean age at marriage (years)	2001	26.5
Mean age at first birth (years)	1998	28.1
Total fertility (children per woman)	2000-2005	1.4
Percentage of childless women, aged 40 - 44	2000	6.9
Divorce rate (per woman)	1997	0.15

[1] Prospective adoptive parents must be residents of the country at the time of applying for an adoption. This, however, does not preclude prospective adoptive parents residing in Singapore from adopting children from other countries.

[2] A sole male applicant is not permitted to adopt a child, except under special circumstances.

[3] Main country of origin: Malaysia.

[4] It was assumed that 60 per cent of adoptive children are under age five.

Government policies

Type of adoption permitted
  Domestic adoption .... Yes
  Intercountry adoption.. Yes

Single male permitted to adopt .... Yes

Single female permitted to adopt .... Yes

Age requirements for adopting parents ....

Child's age of consent for adoption .... Maturity of child considered

Year of ratification of legal instruments on child adoption
  Convention on the Rights of the Child....................... 1993
  Hague Convention on Intercountry Adoption 2001

National legislation governing adoption .... Family Act

Government body responsible for adoption approval ...... Judiciary

Adoption indicators	Year	Number	Percentage
Total children adopted	1999	465	100
Of which:			
Domestic adoptions...	...	...	...
Intercountry adoptions	...	...	...
Of which:			
Adoptions by step-parents or other relatives[1].............	1999	145	31.2
Adoptions per 100,000 births......................................	1999	838.7	
Adoptions per 100,000 children under age 18	1999	34.3	
Adoptions per 100,000 children under age 5[2]................	1999	92.6	

Demographic indicators	Year	Value
Female singulate mean age at marriage (years)	2001	25.4
Mean age at first birth (years).......................................	2001	24.3
Total fertility (children per woman)..............................	2000-2005	1.2
Percentage of childless women, aged 40 - 44	...	...
Divorce rate (per woman)	1995	0.58

[1] Data refer to adoptions by step-parents only.
[2] It was assumed that 60 per cent of adoptive children are under age five.

Government policies

Type of adoption permitted
 Domestic adoption .... Yes
 Intercountry adoption.. Yes

Single male permitted to adopt .... Yes

Single female permitted to adopt .... Yes

Age requirements for adopting parents .... At least 18 years older than the child

Child's age of consent for adoption .... Aged 10 years or older

Year of ratification of legal instruments on child adoption
 Convention on the Rights of the Child...................... 1992
 Hague Convention on Intercountry Adoption 2002

National legislation governing adoption .... Marriage and Family Relations Act

Government body responsible for adoption approval ...... Ministry of Labour, Family and Social Affairs

Adoption indicators	Year	Number	Percentage
Total children adopted	2002	46	100
Of which:			
Domestic adoptions...	2002	45	98
Intercountry adoptions	2002	1	2
Of which:			
Adoptions by step-parents or other relatives[1].............	2002	23	50.0
Adoptions per 100,000 births...	2002	265.4	
Adoptions per 100,000 children under age 18	2002	12.5	
Adoptions per 100,000 children under age 5[2]	2002	31.5	

Demographic indicators	Year	Value
Female singulate mean age at marriage (years)	2001	29.8
Mean age at first birth (years)...	2001	26.7
Total fertility (children per woman)...............................	2000-2005	1.2
Percentage of childless women, aged 40 - 44	1994	5.1
Divorce rate (per woman)	1996	0.12

[1] Data refer to adoptions by step-parents only.
[2] It was assumed that 60 per cent of adoptive children are under age five.

Government policies

Type of adoption permitted
    Domestic adoption .... Yes
    Intercountry adoption[1] .... No

Single male permitted to adopt ....

Single female permitted to adopt ....

Age requirements for adopting parents ....

Child's age of consent for adoption ....

Year of ratification of legal instruments on child adoption
    Convention on the Rights of the Child..................... 1995
    Hague Convention on Intercountry Adoption .... Not ratified

National legislation governing adoption .... Adoption Act of 1958

Government body responsible for adoption approval ...... Judiciary; Social Welfare Office

Adoption indicators	Year	Number	Percentage
Total children adopted	1995	2	100
Of which:			
Domestic adoptions...	1995	2	100
Intercountry adoptions	...	..	...
Of which:			
Adoptions by step-parents or other relatives..............	...	...	...
Adoptions per 100,000 births...............................	1995	15.3	
Adoptions per 100,000 children under age 18	1995	1.1	
Adoptions per 100,000 children under age 5[2]...............	1995	2.1	

Demographic indicators	Year	Value
Female singulate mean age at marriage (years)	1970	22.3
Mean age at first birth (years).......................................	...	...
Total fertility (children per woman).............................	2000-2005	4.3
Percentage of childless women, aged 40 - 44	1976	8.1
Divorce rate (per woman)...	...	...

---

[1] Prospective adoptive parents residing in the Solomon Islands may adopt children from other countries.
[2] It was assumed that 60 per cent of adoptive children are under age five.

Government policies

Type of adoption permitted	
Domestic adoption	...
Intercountry adoption...	...
Single male permitted to adopt	...
Single female permitted to adopt	...
Age requirements for adopting parents	...
Child's age of consent for adoption	...
Year of ratification of legal instruments on child adoption	
Convention on the Rights of the Child[1]	Not ratified
Hague Convention on Intercountry Adoption	Not ratified
National legislation governing adoption	...
Government body responsible for adoption approval	...

Adoption indicators	Year	Number	Percentage
Total children adopted	...	...	...
Of which:			
Domestic adoptions..	...	...	...
Intercountry adoptions	...	...	...
Of which:			
Adoptions by step-parents or other relatives..............	...	...	...
Adoptions per 100,000 births......................................	...	...	
Adoptions per 100,000 children under age 18	...	...	
Adoptions per 100,000 children under age 5	...	...	

Demographic indicators	Year	Value
Female singulate mean age at marriage (years)	...	...
Mean age at first birth (years).....................................	...	...
Total fertility (children per woman)...............................	2000-2005	6.4
Percentage of childless women, aged 40 - 44	...	...
Divorce rate (per woman)	...	...

---

[1] Year of signature: 2002.

Government policies

Type of adoption permitted	
Domestic adoption	Yes
Intercountry adoption.......................................	Yes
Single male permitted to adopt	Yes
Single female permitted to adopt	Yes
Age requirements for adopting parents	...
Child's age of consent for adoption	Aged 10 years or older
Year of ratification of legal instruments on child adoption	
Convention on the Rights of the Child................	1995
Hague Convention on Intercountry Adoption	2003
National legislation governing adoption	Child Care Amendment Act of 1996
Government body responsible for adoption approval	Judiciary

Adoption indicators

	Year	Number	Percentage
Total children adopted	2001	2 218	100
Of which:			
Domestic adoptions...	2001	1 906	86
Intercountry adoptions[1].................................	2001	312	14
Of which:			
Adoptions by step-parents or other relatives..............	...	...	...
Adoptions per 100,000 births............................	2001	199.2	
Adoptions per 100,000 children under age 18	2001	12.1	
Adoptions per 100,000 children under age 5[2]	2001	25.3	

Demographic indicators

	Year	Value
Female singulate mean age at marriage (years)	1996	27.9
Mean age at first birth (years)[3].......................	1998	20.9
Total fertility (children per woman).......................	2000-2005	2.8
Percentage of childless women, aged 40 - 44	1998	7.0
Divorce rate (per woman)	...	...

[1] Main receiving country: Sweden.

[2] It was assumed that 60 per cent of adoptive children are under age five.

[3] Median age at first birth among women aged 25 to 29 years at the date of the survey.

Government policies

Type of adoption permitted
    Domestic adoption .... Yes
    Intercountry adoption.................................. Yes

Single male permitted to adopt .... Yes

Single female permitted to adopt .... Yes

Age requirements for adopting parents[1] .... Aged 25 years or older and at least 14 years older than the child

Child's age of consent for adoption .... Aged 12 years or older

Year of ratification of legal instruments on child adoption
    Convention on the Rights of the Child...................... 1990
    Hague Convention on Intercountry Adoption 1995

National legislation governing adoption .... Civil Code; Civil Proceedings Act; Act 21/1987 of 11 November; Legal Protection of Minors (Organization) Act, 1/1996 of 15 January

Government body responsible for adoption approval ...... Varies by state

Adoption indicators	Year	Number	Percentage
Total children adopted	2003	4 847	100
Of which:			
Domestic adoptions.....................................	2003	896	18
Intercountry adoptions[2]............................	2003	3 951	82
Of which:			
Adoptions by step-parents or other relatives.............	...	...	...
Adoptions per 100,000 births...........................	2003	1 107.4	
Adoptions per 100,000 children under age 18	2003	65.8	
Adoptions per 100,000 children under age 5[3]	2003	139.0	

Demographic indicators	Year	Value
Female singulate mean age at marriage (years)	1991	26.0
Mean age at first birth (years)......................................	2000	29.1
Total fertility (children per woman)...............................	2000-2005	1.3
Percentage of childless women, aged 40 - 44	1995	13.0
Divorce rate (per woman)...	...	...

[1] In the case of adoption by a couple, only one of the parents must be aged 25 years or older.
[2] Main country of origin: Russian Federation.
[3] It was assumed that 60 per cent of adoptive children are under age five.

Government policies

Type of adoption permitted[1]	
Domestic adoption	Yes
Intercountry adoption...	Yes
Single male permitted to adopt	...
Single female permitted to adopt	...
Age requirements for adopting parents	...
Child's age of consent for adoption	Aged 10 years or older
Year of ratification of legal instruments on child adoption	
Convention on the Rights of the Child.......................	1991
Hague Convention on Intercountry Adoption	1995
National legislation governing adoption[2]	Adoption of Children Ordinance of 1941
Government body responsible for adoption approval	Judiciary; Department of Probation and Childcare Services

Adoption indicators	Year	Number	Percentage
Total children adopted	2001	932	100
Of which:			
Domestic adoptions..	2001	881	95
Intercountry adoptions[3]	2001	51	5
Of which:			
Adoptions by step-parents or other relatives..............	...	...	...
Adoptions per 100,000 births..	2001	279.8	
Adoptions per 100,000 children under age 18	2001	14.8	
Adoptions per 100,000 children under age 5[4]..............	2001	34.1	

Demographic indicators	Year	Value
Female singulate mean age at marriage (years)	1993	25.3
Mean age at first birth (years).......................................	1995	26.2
Total fertility (children per woman)...............................	2000-2005	2.0
Percentage of childless women, aged 40 - 44	1993	14.9
Divorce rate (per woman)...	...	...

[1] Adopted children must be under 14 years of age.

[2] Intercountry adoption is governed by the Adoption Ordinance as amended in 1992.

[3] Based on data from selected receiving countries, the main receiving country: Germany.

[4] It was assumed that 60 per cent of adoptive children are under age five.

Government policies

Type of adoption permitted[1]
    Domestic adoption .... Yes
    Intercountry adoption... Yes

Single male permitted to adopt .... No

Single female permitted to adopt ....

Age requirements for adopting parents .... Aged 30 to 50 years

Child's age of consent for adoption ....

Year of ratification of legal instruments on child adoption
    Convention on the Rights of the Child...................... 1990
    Hague Convention on Intercountry Adoption .... Not ratified

National legislation governing adoption[2]....................... Child Welfare Act of 1971

Government body responsible for adoption approval ...... Varies by state

Adoption indicators

	Year	Number	Percentage
Total children adopted[3]	2002	52	100
Of which:			
Domestic adoptions...	...	...	...
Intercountry adoptions	...	...	...
Of which:			
Adoptions by step-parents or other relatives..............	...	...	...
Adoptions per 100,000 births[3]	2002	4.5	
Adoptions per 100,000 children under age 18[3]	2002	0.3	
Adoptions per 100,000 children under age 5[4]	2002	0.6	

Demographic indicators

	Year	Value
Female singulate mean age at marriage (years)	1993	22.7
Mean age at first birth (years)[5]......................................	1990	22.8
Total fertility (children per woman)...............................	2000-2005	4.4
Percentage of childless women, aged 40 - 44	1993	4.3
Divorce rate (per woman)	...	...

[1] Procedures differ according to the religion of the adoptive child or parent.
[2] The Child Welfare Act only applies to non-Muslim children.
[3] Data refer only to the State of Khartoum.
[4] Data refer only to the State of Khartoum. It was assumed that 60 per cent of adoptive children are under age five.
[5] Median age at first birth among women aged 25 to 29 years at the date of the survey.

Government policies

Type of adoption permitted	
Domestic adoption	Yes
Intercountry adoption..	Yes
Single male permitted to adopt	No
Single female permitted to adopt	No
Age requirements for adopting parents	Under age 50 and mother must not be 40 years older than the child
Child's age of consent for adoption	Aged 12 years or older
Year of ratification of legal instruments on child adoption	
Convention on the Rights of the Child.......................	1993
Hague Convention on Intercountry Adoption	Not ratified
National legislation governing adoption	Code of Civil Procedure; Adoption Act of 1972
Government body responsible for adoption approval	Judiciary; Family Law Bureau

Adoption indicators

	Year	Number	Percentage
Total children adopted	...	...	...
Of which:			
Domestic adoptions..	...	...	...
Intercountry adoptions	...	...	...
Of which:			
Adoptions by step-parents or other relatives..............	...	...	...
Adoptions per 100,000 births..	...	...	
Adoptions per 100,000 children under age 18	...	...	
Adoptions per 100,000 children under age 5	...	...	

Demographic indicators

	Year	Value
Female singulate mean age at marriage (years)	1964	18.6
Mean age at first birth (years).......................................	1995	24.2
Total fertility (children per woman)..............................	2000-2005	2.6
Percentage of childless women, aged 40 - 44	...	...
Divorce rate (per woman)	1991	0.36

Government policies

Type of adoption permitted	
Domestic adoption	Yes
Intercountry adoption..	Yes
Single male permitted to adopt	Yes
Single female permitted to adopt	Yes
Age requirements for adopting parents	Aged 25 years or older and at least 25 years older than the child
Child's age of consent for adoption	Aged 10 years or older
Year of ratification of legal instruments on child adoption	
Convention on the Rights of the Child......................	1995
Hague Convention on Intercountry Adoption	Not ratified
National legislation governing adoption	Adoption of Children Act of 1952
Government body responsible for adoption approval	Judiciary

Adoption indicators	*Year*	*Number*	*Percentage*
Total children adopted	…	…	…
Of which:			
Domestic adoptions...	2005	24	..
Intercountry adoptions	…	…	…
Of which:			
Adoptions by step-parents or other relatives..............	…	…	…
Adoptions per 100,000 births................................	…	…	
Adoptions per 100,000 children under age 18	…	…	
Adoptions per 100,000 children under age 5	…	…	

Demographic indicators	*Year*	*Value*
Female singulate mean age at marriage (years)	1991	26.0
Mean age at first birth (years).........................	…	…
Total fertility (children per woman)...............................	2000-2005	4.0
Percentage of childless women, aged 40 - 44	1997	5.9
Divorce rate (per woman)	…	…

Government policies

Type of adoption permitted	
Domestic adoption	Yes
Intercountry adoption..	Yes
Single male permitted to adopt	Yes
Single female permitted to adopt	Yes
Age requirements for adopting parents[1]	Aged 25 years or older
Child's age of consent for adoption[2]	Aged 12 years or older
Year of ratification of legal instruments on child adoption	
Convention on the Rights of the Child.......................	1990
Hague Convention on Intercountry Adoption	1997
National legislation governing adoption	Act on International Legal Relations Concerning Adoption (1971:796); Foreign Adoption Orders (Approval) Ordinance (1976:834); Code of Parenthood and Guardianship; Intercountry Adoption Intermediation Act (1997:192); Social Services Act (2001:453)
Government body responsible for adoption approval	Judiciary; National Board for Intercountry Adoptions

Adoption indicators	Year	Number	Percentage
Total children adopted	2004	1 669	100
Of which:			
Domestic adoptions...	2004	576	35
Intercountry adoptions[3]	2004	1 093	65
Of which:			
Adoptions by step-parents or other relatives..............	...	...	...
Adoptions per 100,000 births...	2004	1 755.3	
Adoptions per 100,000 children under age 18	2004	85.6	
Adoptions per 100,000 children under age 5[4]	2004	208.9	

Demographic indicators	Year	Value
Female singulate mean age at marriage (years)	2001	32.3
Mean age at first birth (years)..	2001	28.2
Total fertility (children per woman)...............................	2000-2005	1.6
Percentage of childless women, aged 40 - 44[5]	1992	14.0
Divorce rate (per woman)	1996	0.29

[1] Prospective adoptive parents aged 18 to 24 years are permitted to adopt under special circumstances.
[2] The maturity of the child is also considered.
[3] Main country of origin: China.
[4] It was assumed that 60 per cent of adoptive children are under age five.
[5] Exact age 43.

Government policies

Type of adoption permitted
    Domestic adoption .... Yes
    Intercountry adoption.. Yes

Single male permitted to adopt .... Yes

Single female permitted to adopt .... Yes

Age requirements for adopting parents .... Aged 35 years or older and at least 16 years older than the child

Child's age of consent for adoption .... Maturity of child considered

Year of ratification of legal instruments on child adoption
    Convention on the Rights of the Child....................... 1997
    Hague Convention on Intercountry Adoption 2002

National legislation governing adoption .... Civil Code of 1907; Federal Ordinance Regulating the Placement of Children of 19 October 1977; Federal Act of 18 December 1987 on International Private Law

Government body responsible for adoption approval ...... Varies by canton

Adoption indicators	Year	Number	Percentage
Total children adopted	2002	702	100
Of which:			
Domestic adoptions..	2002	144	21
Intercountry adoptions[1]	2002	558	79
Of which:			
Adoptions by step-parents or other relatives[2]............	2002	180	25.6
Adoptions per 100,000 births..	2002	990.0	
Adoptions per 100,000 children under age 18	2002	46.9	
Adoptions per 100,000 children under age 5[3]	2002	111.3	

Demographic indicators	Year	Value
Female singulate mean age at marriage (years)	2001	29.1
Mean age at first birth (years)[4]..	2001	28.8
Total fertility (children per woman).................................	2000-2005	1.4
Percentage of childless women, aged 40 - 44	1994-1995	22.9
Divorce rate (per woman)	1996	0.26

[1] Main country of origin: Colombia.
[2] Data refer to adoptions by step-parents only.
[3] It was assumed that 60 per cent of adoptive children are under age five.
[4] Mean age at first birth within current marriage.

Government policies

Type of adoption permitted
    Domestic adoption .... No
    Intercountry adoption... No

Single male permitted to adopt .... Not applicable

Single female permitted to adopt .... Not applicable

Age requirements for adopting parents .... Not applicable

Child's age of consent for adoption .... Not applicable

Year of ratification of legal instruments on child adoption
    Convention on the Rights of the Child....................... 1993
    Hague Convention on Intercountry Adoption .... Not ratified

National legislation governing adoption .... Not applicable

Government body responsible for adoption approval ...... Not applicable

Adoption indicators	Year	Number	Percentage
Total children adopted	...	..	..
Of which:			
Domestic adoptions...	...	..	..
Intercountry adoptions	...	..	..
Of which:			
Adoptions by step-parents or other relatives..............	...	..	..
Adoptions per 100,000 births.......................................	...	..	
Adoptions per 100,000 children under age 18	...	..	
Adoptions per 100,000 children under age 5	...	..	

Demographic indicators	Year	Value
Female singulate mean age at marriage (years)	1970	20.7
Mean age at first birth (years).......................................	...	...
Total fertility (children per woman)..............................	2000-2005	3.5
Percentage of childless women, aged 40 - 44	1994	3.8
Divorce rate (per woman)	...	...

Government policies

Type of adoption permitted	
Domestic adoption	Yes
Intercountry adoption[1]	Yes
Single male permitted to adopt[2]	Yes
Single female permitted to adopt[2]	Yes
Age requirements for adopting parents	...
Child's age of consent for adoption	Aged 10 years or older
Year of ratification of legal instruments on child adoption	
Convention on the Rights of the Child......................	1993
Hague Convention on Intercountry Adoption	Not ratified
National legislation governing adoption[3]	Family Code of 1998
Government body responsible for adoption approval	Ministry of Education; Ministry of Justice

Adoption indicators

	Year	Number	Percentage
Total children adopted	...	...	...
Of which:			
Domestic adoptions..	...	...	...
Intercountry adoptions	...	...	...
Of which:			
Adoptions by step-parents or other relatives.............	...	...	...
Adoptions per 100,000 births..	...	...	
Adoptions per 100,000 children under age 18	...	...	
Adoptions per 100,000 children under age 5	...	...	

Demographic indicators

	Year	Value
Female singulate mean age at marriage (years)	1989	21.2
Mean age at first birth (years)...	...	...
Total fertility (children per woman).................................	2000-2005	3.8
Percentage of childless women, aged 40 - 44	1989	4.2
Divorce rate (per woman)	1994	0.10

[1] At least one prospective adoptive parent must be a citizen.

[2] Prospective adoptive parents must be at least 16 years older than the child.

[3] There is no legislation regarding international adoption.

Government policies

Type of adoption permitted	
Domestic adoption	Yes
Intercountry adoption..	Yes
Single male permitted to adopt	No
Single female permitted to adopt	No
Age requirements for adopting parents	Aged 25 years or older and at least 15 years older than the child
Child's age of consent for adoption	Aged 15 years or older
Year of ratification of legal instruments on child adoption	
Convention on the Rights of the Child.......................	1992
Hague Convention on Intercountry Adoption	2004
National legislation governing adoption	Civil and Commercial Code; Child Adoption Act of 1979; Adoption Act of 1990
Government body responsible for adoption approval	Judiciary; Department of Public Welfare; Child Adoption Board; Ministry of Foreign Affairs

---

Adoption indicators

	Year	Number	Percentage
Total children adopted	2005	51	100
Of which:			
Domestic adoptions..	2005	1	2
Intercountry adoptions	2005	50	98
Of which:			
Adoptions by step-parents or other relatives..............	…	…	…
Adoptions per 100,000 births.......................................	2005	5.1	
Adoptions per 100,000 children under age 18	2005	0.3	
Adoptions per 100,000 children under age 5[1]	2005	0.6	

Demographic indicators

	Year	Value
Female singulate mean age at marriage (years)	1990	23.5
Mean age at first birth (years)[2].....................................	1987	23.0
Total fertility (children per woman)..............................	2000-2005	1.9
Percentage of childless women, aged 40 - 44[3]	2000	10.3
Divorce rate (per woman)	…	…

---

[1] It was assumed that 60 per cent of adoptive children are under age five.

[2] Median age at first birth among women aged 25 to 29 years at the date of the survey.

[3] Never married added.

Government policies

Type of adoption permitted	
Domestic adoption	Yes
Intercountry adoption[1]	Yes
Single male permitted to adopt	Yes
Single female permitted to adopt	Yes
Age requirements for adopting parents	At least 18 years older than the child
Child's age of consent for adoption	Aged 10 years or older
Year of ratification of legal instruments on child adoption	
Convention on the Rights of the Child.......................	1993
Hague Convention on Intercountry Adoption	Not ratified
National legislation governing adoption	Family Act
Government body responsible for adoption approval	Center for Social Work; Ministry of Labor and Social Policy

Adoption indicators	Year	Number	Percentage
Total children adopted	...	...	...
Of which:			
Domestic adoptions...	...	...	...
Intercountry adoptions	...	...	...
Of which:			
Adoptions by step-parents or other relatives..............	...	...	...
Adoptions per 100,000 births..	...	...	
Adoptions per 100,000 children under age 18	...	...	
Adoptions per 100,000 children under age 5	...	...	

Demographic indicators	Year	Value
Female singulate mean age at marriage (years)	1994	22.9
Mean age at first birth (years)..	2001	24.3
Total fertility (children per woman)................................	2000-2005	1.5
Percentage of childless women, aged 40 - 44	2002	6.0
Divorce rate (per woman)..	1997	0.07

[1] Foreign nationals need a special permission from the Ministry of Labour and Social Policy to adopt.

Government policies

Type of adoption permitted
    Domestic adoption ....
    Intercountry adoption... ...

Single male permitted to adopt ....

Single female permitted to adopt ....

Age requirements for adopting parents ....

Child's age of consent for adoption ....

Year of ratification of legal instruments on child adoption
    Convention on the Rights of the Child...................... 2003
    Hague Convention on Intercountry Adoption .... Not ratified

National legislation governing adoption ....

Government body responsible for adoption approval ....

Adoption indicators	Year	Number	Percentage
Total children adopted	...	...	...
Of which:			
Domestic adoptions..	...	...	...
Intercountry adoptions...	...	...	...
Of which:			
Adoptions by step-parents or other relatives..............	...	...	...
Adoptions per 100,000 births....................................	...	...	
Adoptions per 100,000 children under age 18	...	...	
Adoptions per 100,000 children under age 5	...	...	

Demographic indicators	Year	Value
Female singulate mean age at marriage (years)	...	...
Mean age at first birth (years)......................................	...	...
Total fertility (children per woman).............................	2000-2005	7.8
Percentage of childless women, aged 40 - 44[1]	2003	4.8
Divorce rate (per woman)...	...	...

[1] Never married added.

Government policies

Type of adoption permitted
    Domestic adoption .... Yes
    Intercountry adoption.. Yes

Single male permitted to adopt ....

Single female permitted to adopt ....

Age requirements for adopting parents ....

Child's age of consent for adoption ....

Year of ratification of legal instruments on child adoption
    Convention on the Rights of the Child...................... 1990
    Hague Convention on Intercountry Adoption .... Not ratified

National legislation governing adoption .... Individuals and Family Code

Government body responsible for adoption approval ...... Judiciary; Ministry of Social Affairs

Adoption indicators	Year	Number	Percentage
Total children adopted	2003	34	100
Of which:			
Domestic adoptions...	2003	9	26
Intercountry adoptions	2003	25	74
Of which:			
Adoptions by step-parents or other relatives..............	...	...	...
Adoptions per 100,000 births..	2003	14.8	
Adoptions per 100,000 children under age 18	2003	1.1	
Adoptions per 100,000 children under age 5[1]	2003	2.1	

Demographic indicators	Year	Value
Female singulate mean age at marriage (years)	1998	21.3
Mean age at first birth (years)[2]	1998	18.9
Total fertility (children per woman).................................	2000-2005	5.4
Percentage of childless women, aged 40 - 44	1998	3.9
Divorce rate (per woman)...	...	...

[1] It was assumed that 60 per cent of adoptive children are under age five.
[2] Median age at first birth among women aged 25 to 29 years at the date of the survey.

Government policies

Type of adoption permitted
    Domestic adoption ....
    Intercountry adoption... ...

Single male permitted to adopt ....

Single female permitted to adopt ....

Age requirements for adopting parents ....

Child's age of consent for adoption ....

Year of ratification of legal instruments on child adoption
    Convention on the Rights of the Child....................... 1995
    Hague Convention on Intercountry Adoption .... Not ratified

National legislation governing adoption ....

Government body responsible for adoption approval ....

Adoption indicators	Year	Number	Percentage
Total children adopted	...	...	...
Of which:			
Domestic adoptions...	...	...	...
Intercountry adoptions	...	...	...
Of which:			
Adoptions by step-parents or other relatives..............	...	...	...
Adoptions per 100,000 births..	...	...	
Adoptions per 100,000 children under age 18	...	...	
Adoptions per 100,000 children under age 5	...	...	

Demographic indicators	Year	Value
Female singulate mean age at marriage (years)	1996	25.5
Mean age at first birth (years)	...	...
Total fertility (children per woman)...............................	2000-2005	3.5
Percentage of childless women, aged 40 - 44	1996	14.2
Divorce rate (per woman)	...	...

Government policies

Type of adoption permitted	
Domestic adoption	Yes
Intercountry adoption	Yes
Single male permitted to adopt[1]	No
Single female permitted to adopt	Yes
Age requirements for adopting parents	Aged 25 years or older and at least 21 years older than the child
Child's age of consent for adoption	Maturity of child considered
Year of ratification of legal instruments on child adoption	
Convention on the Rights of the Child.......................	1991
Hague Convention on Intercountry Adoption	Not ratified
National legislation governing adoption	Adoption of Children Regulations; Adoption of Children Act, No. 67 of 2000
Government body responsible for adoption approval	Judiciary; Adoption Board

Adoption indicators	Year	Number	Percentage
Total children adopted	2002	18	100
Of which:			
Domestic adoptions.....................................	...	...	...
Intercountry adoptions	...	...	...
Of which:			
Adoptions by step-parents or other relatives..............	...	...	...
Adoptions per 100,000 births...........................	2002	99.3	
Adoptions per 100,000 children under age 18	2002	4.6	
Adoptions per 100,000 children under age 5[2]	2002	12.4	

Demographic indicators	Year	Value
Female singulate mean age at marriage (years)	1990	26.8
Mean age at first birth (years).........................	1997	23.8
Total fertility (children per woman)...............................	2000-2005	1.6
Percentage of childless women, aged 40 - 44	1990	10.1
Divorce rate (per woman)	1995	0.10

[1] A sole male applicant is not permitted to adopt a child, except under special circumstances.

[2] It was assumed that 60 per cent of adoptive children are under age five.

Government policies

Type of adoption permitted	
Domestic adoption	Yes
Intercountry adoption..	Yes
Single male permitted to adopt[1]	No
Single female permitted to adopt[1]	No
Age requirements for adopting parents	...
Child's age of consent for adoption	...
Year of ratification of legal instruments on child adoption	
Convention on the Rights of the Child......................	1992
Hague Convention on Intercountry Adoption	Not ratified
National legislation governing adoption	Act No. 58-27 of 4 March 1958
Government body responsible for adoption approval	Judiciary; National Institute for the Protection of Children

Adoption indicators

	Year	Number	Percentage
Total children adopted	...	...	
Of which:			
Domestic adoptions...	...	...	...
Intercountry adoptions	...	...	...
Of which:			
Adoptions by step-parents or other relatives..............	...	...	...
Adoptions per 100,000 births.......................................	...	...	
Adoptions per 100,000 children under age 18	...	...	
Adoptions per 100,000 children under age 5	...	...	

Demographic indicators

	Year	Value
Female singulate mean age at marriage (years)	1994	26.6
Mean age at first birth (years)......................................	1997	26.9
Total fertility (children per woman)..............................	2000-2005	2.0
Percentage of childless women, aged 40 - 44	1988	9.5
Divorce rate (per woman)	1971	0.13

[1] A judge may waive the marriage requirement for a widowed or divorced individual.

Government policies

Type of adoption permitted
    Domestic adoption .... Yes
    Intercountry adoption...................................... Yes

Single male permitted to adopt .... Yes

Single female permitted to adopt .... Yes

Age requirements for adopting parents .... Aged 30 years or older and at least 18 years older than the child

Child's age of consent for adoption ....

Year of ratification of legal instruments on child adoption
    Convention on the Rights of the Child...................... 1995
    Hague Convention on Intercountry Adoption 2004

National legislation governing adoption .... Civil Code

Government body responsible for adoption approval ...... Judiciary; General Directorate of the Social Services and Child Protection Agency

Adoption indicators	Year	Number	Percentage
Total children adopted	1998-2000	1 329	100
Of which:			
Domestic adoptions......................................	1998-2000	1 299	98
Intercountry adoptions[1]	1998-2000	30	2
Of which:			
Adoptions by step-parents or other relatives..............	...	...	...
Adoptions per 100,000 births...........................	1998-2000	29.0	
Adoptions per 100,000 children under age 18	1998-2000	1.8	
Adoptions per 100,000 children under age 5[2]	1998-2000	3.7	

Demographic indicators	Year	Value
Female singulate mean age at marriage (years)	1998	22.0
Mean age at first birth (years)...........................	1985	21.7
Total fertility (children per woman)..............................	2000-2005	2.5
Percentage of childless women, aged 40 - 44	2000	4.1
Divorce rate (per woman)	1996	0.12

[1] Data include 27 adoptions by Turkish families residing abroad.
[2] It was assumed that 60 per cent of adoptive children are under age five.

Government policies

Type of adoption permitted
    Domestic adoption .... Yes
    Intercountry adoption.. Yes

Single male permitted to adopt .... Yes

Single female permitted to adopt .... Yes

Age requirements for adopting parents ....

Child's age of consent for adoption .... Aged 10 years or older

Year of ratification of legal instruments on child adoption
    Convention on the Rights of the Child...................... 1993
    Hague Convention on Intercountry Adoption .... Not ratified

National legislation governing adoption .... Marriage and Family Code

Government body responsible for adoption approval ...... Judiciary; Agencies of tutorship and guardianship of the regional, city and district authorities

Adoption indicators	Year	Number	Percentage
Total children adopted	...	...	...
Of which:			
Domestic adoptions..................................	...	...	...
Intercountry adoptions	...	...	...
Of which:			
Adoptions by step-parents or other relatives..............	...	...	...
Adoptions per 100,000 births......................	...	...	
Adoptions per 100,000 children under age 18	...	...	
Adoptions per 100,000 children under age 5	...	...	

Demographic indicators	Year	Value
Female singulate mean age at marriage (years)	2000	23.4
Mean age at first birth (years)[1]	2000	23.3
Total fertility (children per woman).............................	2000-2005	2.8
Percentage of childless women, aged 40 - 44	2000	4.3
Divorce rate (per woman)	...	...

[1] Median age at first birth among women aged 25 to 29 years at the date of the survey.

Government policies

Type of adoption permitted
    Domestic adoption ....
    Intercountry adoption...   ...

Single male permitted to adopt ....

Single female permitted to adopt ....

Age requirements for adopting parents ....

Child's age of consent for adoption ....

Year of ratification of legal instruments on child adoption
    Convention on the Rights of the Child......................   1995
    Hague Convention on Intercountry Adoption ....   Not ratified

National legislation governing adoption ....

Government body responsible for adoption approval ....

Adoption indicators	Year	Number	Percentage
Total children adopted	...	...	...
Of which:			
Domestic adoptions..	...	...	...
Intercountry adoptions	...	...	...
Of which:			
Adoptions by step-parents or other relatives..............	...	...	...
Adoptions per 100,000 births....................................	...	...	
Adoptions per 100,000 children under age 18	...	...	
Adoptions per 100,000 children under age 5	...	...	

Demographic indicators	Year	Value
Female singulate mean age at marriage (years)	...	...
Mean age at first birth (years)..	...	...
Total fertility (children per woman)...............................	2000-2005	3.7
Percentage of childless women, aged 40 - 44	...	...
Divorce rate (per woman)	...	...

Government policies

Type of adoption permitted
    Domestic adoption .... Yes
    Intercountry adoption[1] .... Yes

Single male permitted to adopt[2] .... Yes

Single female permitted to adopt[3] .... Yes

Age requirements for adopting parents .... Aged 25 years or older and at least 21 years older than the child

Child's age of consent for adoption .... Aged 14 years or older

Year of ratification of legal instruments on child adoption
    Convention on the Rights of the Child 1990
    Hague Convention on Intercountry Adoption .... Not ratified

National legislation governing adoption .... Children Statute

Government body responsible for adoption approval ...... Judiciary; Probation and Welfare Department

Adoption indicators	Year	Number	Percentage
Total children adopted[4]	2005	156	100
Of which:			
Domestic adoptions	...	...	...
Intercountry adoptions	...	...	...
Of which:			
Adoptions by step-parents or other relatives	...	...	...
Adoptions per 100,000 births[4]	2005	10.6	
Adoptions per 100,000 children under age 18[4]	2005	0.9	
Adoptions per 100,000 children under age 5[5]	2005	1.6	

Demographic indicators	Year	Value
Female singulate mean age at marriage (years)	2001	19.6
Mean age at first birth (years)[6]	2000-2001	18.9
Total fertility (children per woman)	2000-2005	7.1
Percentage of childless women, aged 40 - 44	2000-2001	7.0
Divorce rate (per woman)	...	...

---

[1] Prospective adoptive parents must have resided in the country for at least three years prior to the date of the adoption application.
[2] A sole male applicant is not permitted to adopt a girl, except under special circumstances.
[3] A sole female applicant is not permitted to adopt a boy, except under special circumstances.
[4] Estimate.
[5] Estimate. It was assumed that 60 per cent of adoptive children are under age five.
[6] Median age at first birth among women aged 25 to 29 years at the date of the survey.

Government policies

Type of adoption permitted
    Domestic adoption .... Yes
    Intercountry adoption .... Yes

Single male permitted to adopt .... Yes

Single female permitted to adopt .... Yes

Age requirements for adopting parents .... At least 15 years older than the child

Child's age of consent for adoption .... Aged 10 years or older

Year of ratification of legal instruments on child adoption
    Convention on the Rights of the Child 1991
    Hague Convention on Intercountry Adoption .... Not ratified

National legislation governing adoption .... Marriage and Family Code

Government body responsible for adoption approval ...... Judiciary; Adoptions Centre, Ministry of Education

Adoption indicators	Year	Number	Percentage
Total children adopted	2001	7 593	100
Of which:			
Domestic adoptions	2001	4 921	65
Intercountry adoptions[1]	2001	2 672	35
Of which:			
Adoptions by step-parents or other relatives	...	...	...
Adoptions per 100,000 births	2001	1 921.8	
Adoptions per 100,000 children under age 18	2001	71.2	
Adoptions per 100,000 children under age 5[2]	2001	225.0	

Demographic indicators	Year	Value
Female singulate mean age at marriage (years)	1999	21.7
Mean age at first birth (years)	...	...
Total fertility (children per woman)	2000-2005	1.1
Percentage of childless women, aged 40 - 44	1999	8.2
Divorce rate (per woman)	1995	0.48

[1] Based on data from selected receiving countries, the main receiving country: United States of America.
[2] It was assumed that 60 per cent of adoptive children are under age five.

Government policies

Type of adoption permitted	
Domestic adoption	No
Intercountry adoption..	No
Single male permitted to adopt	Not applicable
Single female permitted to adopt	Not applicable
Age requirements for adopting parents	Not applicable
Child's age of consent for adoption	Not applicable
Year of ratification of legal instruments on child adoption	
Convention on the Rights of the Child.......................	1997
Hague Convention on Intercountry Adoption	Not ratified
National legislation governing adoption	Not applicable
Government body responsible for adoption approval	Not applicable

Adoption indicators	Year	Number	Percentage
Total children adopted	...	..	..
Of which:			
Domestic adoptions..	...	..	..
Intercountry adoptions	...	..	..
Of which:			
Adoptions by step-parents or other relatives..............	...	..	..
Adoptions per 100,000 births...	...	..	
Adoptions per 100,000 children under age 18	...	..	
Adoptions per 100,000 children under age 5	...	..	

Demographic indicators	Year	Value
Female singulate mean age at marriage (years)	1987	23.1
Mean age at first birth (years).....................................	...	...
Total fertility (children per woman).............................	2000-2005	2.5
Percentage of childless women, aged 40 - 44	1995	4.5
Divorce rate (per woman)...	...	...

Government policies

Type of adoption permitted[1]	
Domestic adoption	Yes
Intercountry adoption..	Yes
Single male permitted to adopt	Yes
Single female permitted to adopt	Yes
Age requirements for adopting parents	Aged 21 years or older
Child's age of consent for adoption	Maturity of child considered
Year of ratification of legal instruments on child adoption	
Convention on the Rights of the Child......................	1991
Hague Convention on Intercountry Adoption	2003
National legislation governing adoption	Adoption Agencies Regulations of 1983; Adoption Rules of 1984; Magistrates Court Rules of 1984; Children Act of 1989; Adoption (Intercountry Aspects) Act of 1999; Adoption and Children Act of 2002
Government body responsible for adoption approval	Judiciary

Adoption indicators

	Year	Number	Percentage
Total children adopted	2002	6 239	100
Of which:			
Domestic adoptions[2]	2002	5 910	95
Intercountry adoptions[3]	2002	329	5
Of which:			
Adoptions by step-parents or other relatives	...	...	...
Adoptions per 100,000 births...	2002	923.6	
Adoptions per 100,000 children under age 18	2002	46.8	
Adoptions per 100,000 children under age 5[4]	2002	108.0	

Demographic indicators

	Year	Value
Female singulate mean age at marriage (years)	1991	26.4
Mean age at first birth (years)[5]......................................	2000	29.1
Total fertility (children per woman).................................	2000-2005	1.7
Percentage of childless women, aged 40 - 44	...	...
Divorce rate (per woman)	1996	0.33

[1] Prospective adoptive parents must have resided in the British Isles for at least one year.
[2] Estimate.
[3] Data refer to the number of applications for intercountry adoptions received by the Department of Health during the year ending 31 March. Main country of origin: China.
[4] It was assumed that 60 per cent of adoptive children are under age five.
[5] Mean age at first birth within current marriage.

Government policies

Type of adoption permitted
    Domestic adoption .... Yes
    Intercountry adoption[1] .... No

Single male permitted to adopt ....

Single female permitted to adopt ....

Age requirements for adopting parents ....

Child's age of consent for adoption ....

Year of ratification of legal instruments on child adoption
    Convention on the Rights of the Child...................... 1991
    Hague Convention on Intercountry Adoption .... Not ratified

National legislation governing adoption .... Adoption Ordinance

Government body responsible for adoption approval ...... Judiciary; Department of Social Welfare

Adoption indicators	Year	Number	Percentage
Total children adopted	1999	15	100
Of which:			
Domestic adoptions..	1999	15	100
Intercountry adoptions	...	..	..
Of which:			
Adoptions by step-parents or other relatives..............	...	...	...
Adoptions per 100,000 births......................................	1999	1.1	
Adoptions per 100,000 children under age 18	1999	0.1	
Adoptions per 100,000 children under age 5[2]	1999	0.2	

Demographic indicators	Year	Value
Female singulate mean age at marriage (years)	1996	20.5
Mean age at first birth (years)[3].....................................	1999	19.5
Total fertility (children per woman)...............................	2000-2005	5.0
Percentage of childless women, aged 40 - 44	1999	4.2
Divorce rate (per woman)	...	...

[1] Prospective adoptive parents must reside within the East African Territories.
[2] It was assumed that 60 per cent of adoptive children are under age five.
[3] Median age at first birth among women aged 25 to 29 years at the date of the survey.

Government policies

Type of adoption permitted	
Domestic adoption	Yes
Intercountry adoption...	Yes
Single male permitted to adopt	Varies by state
Single female permitted to adopt	Varies by state
Age requirements for adopting parents	Varies by state
Child's age of consent for adoption	Varies by state
Year of ratification of legal instruments on child adoption	
Convention on the Rights of the Child[1]	Not ratified
Hague Convention on Intercountry Adoption[2]..........	Not ratified
National legislation governing adoption	Varies by state
Government body responsible for adoption approval[3]	State Court; Indian Tribal Court

Adoption indicators

	Year	*Number*	*Percentage*
Total children adopted	2001	127 407	100
Of which:			
Domestic adoptions..	2001	108 351	85
Intercountry adoptions[4]...	2001	19 056	15
Of which:			
Adoptions by step-parents or other relatives..............	...	...	...
Adoptions per 100,000 births...	2001	3 156.4	
Adoptions per 100,000 children under age 18	2001	172.6	
Adoptions per 100,000 children under age 5[5]	2001	385.3	

Demographic indicators

	Year	*Value*
Female singulate mean age at marriage (years)	2000	26.3
Mean age at first birth (years)......................................	1998	25.0
Total fertility (children per woman)...............................	2000-2005	2.0
Percentage of childless women, aged 40 - 44	2000	21.5
Divorce rate (per woman)	1990	0.25

[1] Year of signature: 1995.
   Year of signature: 1994.
[3] Varies by state.
[4] Data refer to children who entered under an orphan visa for purposes of adoption. These include children with an IR-3 visa status who were adopted abroad and children with an IR-4 status who were to be adopted in the United States of America. Main country of origin: China.
[5] It was assumed that 60 per cent of adoptive children are under age five.

Government policies

Type of adoption permitted
    Domestic adoption .... Yes
    Intercountry adoption[1] .... Yes

Single male permitted to adopt[2] .... Yes

Single female permitted to adopt[2] .... Yes

Age requirements for adopting parents .... Aged 25 years or older and at least 15 years older than the child

Child's age of consent for adoption ....

Year of ratification of legal instruments on child adoption
    Convention on the Rights of the Child...................... 1990
    Hague Convention on Intercountry Adoption 2003

National legislation governing adoption .... Code of Children and Adolescents, Law No. 17,823 of 14 September 2004

Government body responsible for adoption approval ...... Judiciary; Institute of the Child and Adolescent

Adoption indicators	Year	Number	Percentage
Total children adopted	...	...	...
Of which:			
Domestic adoptions..	...	...	...
Intercountry adoptions	...	...	...
Of which:			
Adoptions by step-parents or other relatives..............	...	...	...
Adoptions per 100,000 births.....................................	...	...	
Adoptions per 100,000 children under age 18	...	...	
Adoptions per 100,000 children under age 5	...	...	

Demographic indicators	Year	Value
Female singulate mean age at marriage (years)	1996	23.3
Mean age at first birth (years)..	1996	23.8
Total fertility (children per woman)...............................	2000-2005	2.3
Percentage of childless women, aged 40 - 44	1996	10.6
Divorce rate (per woman)	...	...

[1] Prospective adoptive parents must have resided in the country and had the child in their care and custody for at least six months prior to the date of the adoption application.
[2] Unmarried foreign citizens are not permitted to adopt.

Government policies

Type of adoption permitted[1]
    Domestic adoption .... Yes
    Intercountry adoption... Yes

Single male permitted to adopt .... Yes

Single female permitted to adopt .... Yes

Age requirements for adopting parents .... At least 15 years older than the child

Child's age of consent for adoption .... Aged 10 years or older

Year of ratification of legal instruments on child adoption
    Convention on the Rights of the Child...................... 1994
    Hague Convention on Intercountry Adoption .... Not ratified

National legislation governing adoption .... Family Code

Government body responsible for adoption approval ...... Judiciary; Ministry of Education; Makhalla Committees

Adoption indicators	Year	Number	Percentage
Total children adopted	2005	2 836	100
Of which:			
Domestic adoptions..	2005	2 828	100
Intercountry adoptions	2005	8	0
Of which:			
Adoptions by step-parents or other relatives..............	...	...	...
Adoptions per 100,000 births..	2005	461.1	
Adoptions per 100,000 children under age 18	2005	26.4	
Adoptions per 100,000 children under age 5[2]	2005	59.9	

Demographic indicators	Year	Value
Female singulate mean age at marriage (years)	1996	20.6
Mean age at first birth (years)......................................	1999	23.4
Total fertility (children per woman)..............................	2000-2005	2.7
Percentage of childless women, aged 40 - 44	2002	5.1
Divorce rate (per woman)	...	...

[1] Adopted children must be under 18 years of age.
[2] It was assumed that 60 per cent of adoptive children are under age five.

Government policies

Type of adoption permitted
    Domestic adoption ....
    Intercountry adoption......................................   ...

Single male permitted to adopt ....

Single female permitted to adopt ....

Age requirements for adopting parents ....

Child's age of consent for adoption ....

Year of ratification of legal instruments on child adoption
    Convention on the Rights of the Child......................   1993
    Hague Convention on Intercountry Adoption ....   Not ratified

National legislation governing adoption[1] ....   Not applicable

Government body responsible for adoption approval ......   Not applicable

Adoption indicators	Year	Number	Percentage
Total children adopted	...	...	...
Of which:			
Domestic adoptions..	...	...	...
Intercountry adoptions....................................	...	...	...
Of which:			
Adoptions by step-parents or other relatives.............	...	...	...
Adoptions per 100,000 births....................................	...	...	
Adoptions per 100,000 children under age 18	...	...	
Adoptions per 100,000 children under age 5	...	...	

Demographic indicators	Year	Value
Female singulate mean age at marriage (years)	1989	22.6
Mean age at first birth (years).................................	...	...
Total fertility (children per woman)..............................	2000-2005	4.2
Percentage of childless women, aged 40 - 44	...	...
Divorce rate (per woman).................................	...	...

[1] Traditional adoptions are practiced. The country does not have legislation concerning adoption.

Government policies

Type of adoption permitted
    Domestic adoption .... Yes
    Intercountry adoption.. Yes

Single male permitted to adopt[1] .... Yes

Single female permitted to adopt[1] .... Yes

Age requirements for adopting parents .... Aged 30 years or older and at least 18 years older than the child

Child's age of consent for adoption .... Aged 12 years or older

Year of ratification of legal instruments on child adoption
    Convention on the Rights of the Child...................... 1990
    Hague Convention on Intercountry Adoption 1997

National legislation governing adoption .... Civil Code; Minors Protection Act of 1980; Adoption Act of 1983

Government body responsible for adoption approval ...... Judiciary; National Children's Institute

Adoption indicators	Year	Number	Percentage
Total children adopted	1995	1 992	100
Of which:			
Domestic adoptions..	...	...	...
Intercountry adoptions	...	...	...
Of which:			
Adoptions by step-parents or other relatives..............	...	...	...
Adoptions per 100,000 births...	1995	352.2	
Adoptions per 100,000 children under age 18	1995	21.3	
Adoptions per 100,000 children under age 5[2].................	1995	43.5	

Demographic indicators	Year	Value
Female singulate mean age at marriage (years)	1990	22.1
Mean age at first birth (years)...	1998	23.6
Total fertility (children per woman).................................	2000-2005	2.7
Percentage of childless women, aged 40 - 44	2001	8.0
Divorce rate (per woman)	1972	0.04

[1] Prospective adoptive parents must be aged 40 years or older.
[2] It was assumed that 60 per cent of adoptive children are under age five.

Government policies

Type of adoption permitted
    Domestic adoption .... Yes
    Intercountry adoption.. Yes

Single male permitted to adopt .... Yes

Single female permitted to adopt .... Yes

Age requirements for adopting parents .... At least 20 years older than the child

Child's age of consent for adoption .... Aged 9 years or older

Year of ratification of legal instruments on child adoption
    Convention on the Rights of the Child....................... 1990
    Hague Convention on Intercountry Adoption .... Not ratified

National legislation governing adoption .... Civil Code of 1995; Ordinance on Marriage and Family between Vietnamese and Foreign Citizens of 1993; Government Decree 184/CP of 1994; Law on Family and Marriage of 2000; Government Decree No. 32/2002/ND-CP of 2002; Government Decree No. 68/2002/ND-CP of 2002

Government body responsible for adoption approval ...... Local People's Committees; Ministry of Justice

Adoption indicators	Year	Number	Percentage
Total children adopted	2001	2 881	100
Of which:			
Domestic adoptions..	2001	1 462	51
Intercountry adoptions[1]...	2001	1 419	49
Of which:			
Adoptions by step-parents or other relatives..............	...	...	...
Adoptions per 100,000 births.....................................	2001	178.0	
Adoptions per 100,000 children under age 18	2001	9.2	
Adoptions per 100,000 children under age 5[2]...............	2001	22.4	

Demographic indicators	Year	Value
Female singulate mean age at marriage (years)	1997	22.1
Mean age at first birth (years)......................................	...	...
Total fertility (children per woman)...............................	2000-2005	2.3
Percentage of childless women, aged 40 - 44	2002	10.1
Divorce rate (per woman)	...	...

[1] Based on data from selected receiving countries, the main receiving country: United States of America.
[2] It was assumed that 60 per cent of adoptive children are under age five.

Government policies

Type of adoption permitted
    Domestic adoption .... No
    Intercountry adoption .... No

Single male permitted to adopt .... Not applicable

Single female permitted to adopt .... Not applicable

Age requirements for adopting parents .... Not applicable

Child's age of consent for adoption .... Not applicable

Year of ratification of legal instruments on child adoption
    Convention on the Rights of the Child...................... 1991
    Hague Convention on Intercountry Adoption .... Not ratified

National legislation governing adoption .... Not applicable

Government body responsible for adoption approval ...... Not applicable

Adoption indicators

	Year	Number	Percentage
Total children adopted	...	..	..
Of which:			
Domestic adoptions...	...	..	..
Intercountry adoptions	...	..	..
Of which:			
Adoptions by step-parents or other relatives..............	...	..	..
Adoptions per 100,000 births...............................	...	..	
Adoptions per 100,000 children under age 18	...	..	
Adoptions per 100,000 children under age 5	...	..	

Demographic indicators

	Year	Value
Female singulate mean age at marriage (years)	1997	20.7
Mean age at first birth (years)[1].....................................	1997	19.2
Total fertility (children per woman)...............................	2000-2005	6.2
Percentage of childless women, aged 40 - 44	1997	5.9
Divorce rate (per woman)	...	...

[1] Median age at first birth among women aged 25 to 29 years at the date of the survey.

Government policies

Type of adoption permitted
    Domestic adoption .... Yes
    Intercountry adoption[1] .... Yes

Single male permitted to adopt[2] .... Yes

Single female permitted to adopt .... Yes

Age requirements for adopting parents[3] .... Aged 25 years or older and at least 21 years older than the child

Child's age of consent for adoption .... Maturity of child considered

Year of ratification of legal instruments on child adoption
    Convention on the Rights of the Child...................... 1991
    Hague Convention on Intercountry Adoption .... Not ratified

National legislation governing adoption .... Adoption Act of 1958

Government body responsible for adoption approval ...... Judiciary; Commissioner for Juvenile Welfare

Adoption indicators	Year	Number	Percentage
Total children adopted	...	...	...
Of which:			
Domestic adoptions.....................................	...	...	...
Intercountry adoptions	...	...	...
Of which:			
Adoptions by step-parents or other relatives.............	...	...	...
Adoptions per 100,000 births....................................	...	...	
Adoptions per 100,000 children under age 18	...	...	
Adoptions per 100,000 children under age 5	...	...	

Demographic indicators	Year	Value
Female singulate mean age at marriage (years)	1999	21.1
Mean age at first birth (years)[4].................................	2001-2002	19.0
Total fertility (children per woman)..............................	2000-2005	5.7
Percentage of childless women, aged 40 - 44	2001-2002	4.0
Divorce rate (per woman)	...	...

[1] Prospective adoptive parents must have resided in the country and had the child in their care and custody for at least three consecutive months prior to the date of the adoption order.
[2] A sole male applicant is not permitted to adopt a girl, except under special circumstances.
[3] Prospective adoptive parents must be aged 21 years or older to adopt a relative.
[4] Median age at first birth among women aged 25 to 29 years at the date of the survey.

Government policies

Type of adoption permitted	
Domestic adoption	Yes
Intercountry adoption..	Yes
Single male permitted to adopt	No
Single female permitted to adopt[1]	Yes
Age requirements for adopting parents[2]...........................	Aged 25 years or older
Child's age of consent for adoption	...
Year of ratification of legal instruments on child adoption	
Convention on the Rights of the Child........................	1990
Hague Convention on Intercountry Adoption	Not ratified
National legislation governing adoption	Children's Protection and Adoption Act
Government body responsible for adoption approval	Judiciary; Ministry of Public Services, Labour and Social Welfare

Adoption indicators

	Year	Number	Percentage
Total children adopted	...	...	...
Of which:			
Domestic adoptions..	...	...	...
Intercountry adoptions	...	...	...
Of which:			
Adoptions by step-parents or other relatives..............	...	...	...
Adoptions per 100,000 births...............................	...	...	
Adoptions per 100,000 children under age 18	...	...	
Adoptions per 100,000 children under age 5	...	...	

Demographic indicators

	Year	Value
Female singulate mean age at marriage (years)	1999	21.1
Mean age at first birth (years)[3].......................................	1999	20.3
Total fertility (children per woman)................................	2000-2005	3.6
Percentage of childless women, aged 40 - 44	1999	5.0
Divorce rate (per woman)	...	...

[1] Permission for adoption may be granted to a single person only under special circumstances.

[2] Prospective adoptive parents must be aged 21 years or older to adopt a relative.

[3] Median age at first birth among women aged 25 to 29 years at the date of the survey.

ANNEXES

ANNEX I. DERIVATION OF GLOBAL ESTIMATES OF TOTAL, DOMESTIC AND INTERCOUNTRY ADOPTIONS

Estimating the global number of children adopted each year is not straightforward. Missing data, inconsistent definitions and underreporting are the major problems encountered in producing a global estimate. Nevertheless, it is important to establish a global benchmark, even if approximate.

Based on available data, two global estimates were derived. The first refers to the number of adoptions that took place in 2001, the latest year for which a substantial number of countries reported adoption statistics. According to this estimate, about 240,000 children were adopted in 2001 at the global level, including 205,000 adopted domestically and 35,000 adopted through intercountry procedures.

A second estimate was obtained by considering, for each country, the number of adoptions reported for the most recent year between 1990 and 2005. This approach yielded an estimated 260,000 children adopted per year, including 220,000 domestic adoptions and 40,000 intercountry adoptions.

Both estimates are approximate and have limitations and strengths. The first estimate is based on statistics that refer to the same point in time, the year 2001, but it incorporates the statistics of fewer countries than the second estimate does. The latter is based on the statistics reported by a larger number of countries but it does not actually represent the experience of a single year. Only by assuming that the number of adoptions remains fairly constant for every country over the period 1990 to 2005 can the second estimate be considered indicative of the annual number of adoptions occurring globally. However, that assumption is unlikely to be met in practice. Indeed, available data show that the number of adoptions at the national level often fluctuates from year to year, sometimes sharply. In the United States, the country registering the highest number of adoptions, their number increased from 118,138 in 1990 to 127,407 in

2001 (United States, Child Welfare Information Gateway, 2004c).

In deriving both estimates, the number of domestic adoptions reported nationally were added with the number of intercountry adoptions reported by countries that are net receivers of intercountry adoptions. To avoid double counting, the number of intercountry adoptions reported by countries that are net sources of children adopted abroad were not included in the sum. The following countries were considered to be net receivers of intercountry adoptions: Andorra, Australia, Austria, Belgium, Canada, Cyprus, Denmark, Finland, France, Germany, Greece, Iceland, Ireland, Israel, Italy, Japan, Liechtenstein, Luxembourg, Malta, the Netherlands, New Zealand, Norway, Portugal, Singapore, Spain, Sweden, Switzerland, the United Kingdom and the United States.

This strategy did not ensure that no double counting of adopted children took place. One reason for double counting is the existence of some children moving between the countries considered to be net receivers of intercountry adoptions for the purpose of adoption. Thus, in 2004, Canada received 79 children from the United States through intercountry adoptions (Canada, Adoption Council, 2005) and in 2002 Germany received 5 adopted children from Austria, 18 from Italy, 3 from Portugal and 5 from Spain through intercountry procedures (Germany, Federal Statistics Office, 2004). In producing the global estimates, no attempt was made to correct for these small numbers of children moving between the major receiving countries of intercountry adoptions, mainly because the data to do so systematically were generally lacking.

In this report, a global estimate of 260,000 adoptions has been used as indicative of the global number of adoptions occurring annually. That estimate does not make any allowance for the number of adoptions occurring in countries that do not release statistics on adoptions. To get a sense of the possible downward bias that ignoring those countries introduces in the global estimate, the number of adoptions in the 57 countries that lacked data was estimated by assuming that they had the same under-18 adoption rates as neighbouring countries. Hence, the average under-18 adoption rate of neighbouring countries was multiplied by the population under-18 in each country lacking adoption data and the results were added up. The result was an additional 10,000 adoptions, which would bring the global total to between 250,000 and 270,000 according to first and second estimates discussed above. Since there is no basis for deciding whether these additional 10,000 adoptions were entirely domestic or not, this adjustment was not made to the global estimates reported in the body of this report.

ANNEX II. REFERENCES FOR COUNTRY PROFILES

Afghanistan

United States of America, Bureau of Consular Affairs (2006). Intercountry adoption: Afghanistan. Washington, D.C.: Department of State. Available from http://travel.state.gov/family/adoption/country/country_362.html (accessed 27 October 2006).

Albania

United Nations (2004a). Initial periodic report of States parties due in 1994: Albania (CRC/C/11/Add.27).
_____ (2004b). Written replies by the Government of Albania (CRC/C/RESP/77) concerning the list of issues received by the Committee on the Rights of the Child (CRC/C/Q/ALB/1) relating to the consideration of the initial periodic report of Albania.
United States, Bureau of Consular Affairs (2006). Intercountry adoption: Albania. Washington, D.C.: Department of State. Available from http://travel.state.gov/family/adoption/country/country_373.html (accessed 27 October 2006).

Algeria

United Nations (2005). Second periodic reports of States parties due in 2000: Algeria (CRC/C/93/Add.7).

Andorra

Andorra, Ministry of Health, Social Welfare and the Family (2005). Response to the 2005 questionnaire on the practical operation of the Hague Convention of 29 May 1993 on Protection of Children and Co-operation in Respect of Intercountry Adoption. Available from http://www.hcch.net/index_en.php?act=publications.details&pid=3520&dtid=33 (accessed 10 October 2007).
United Nations (2001). Initial reports of States parties: Andorra (CRC/C/61/Add.3).
_____ (2001). Written replies by the Government of Andorra (CRC/C/RESP/AND/1) concerning the list of issues received by the Committee on the Rights of the Child (CRC/C/Q/AND/1) relating to the consideration of the initial periodic report of Andorra.

Angola

United Nations (2004). Initial reports of States parties due in 1993: Angola (CRC/C/3/Add.66).

Antigua and Barbuda

United Nations (2003). Initial reports of States parties due in 1995: Antigua and Barbuda (CRC/C/28/Add.22).

Argentina

Argentina (n.d.). Civil Code, book I, part II, title IV. Available from http://www.redetel.gov.ar/Normativa/Archivos%20de%20Normas/CodigoCivil.htm (accessed 12 February 2006).
United Nations (2002). Periodic reports of States parties due in 1998: Argentina (CRC/C/70/Add.10).
World Health Organization, Pan American Health Organization (1999). *Encuesta sobre Salud, Bienestar y Envejecimiento en América Latina y el Caribe.* Available from http://www.ssc.wisc.edu/sabe/question/Argentina.pdf (accessed 07 November 2006).

Armenia

United Nations (1997). Initial reports of States parties due in 1995: Armenia (CRC/C/28/Add.9).
_____ (2003a). Second periodic reports of States parties due in 2000: Armenia (CRC/C/93/Add.6).
_____ (2003b). Written replies by the Government of Armenia (CRC/C/RESP/46) concerning the list of issues received by the Committee on the Rights of the Child (CRC/C/Q/ARM/2) relating to the consideration of the second periodic report of Armenia.
United States, Bureau of Consular Affairs (2006). Intercountry adoption: Armenia. Washington, D.C.: Department of State. Available from http://travel.state.gov/family/adoption/country/country_394.html (accessed 27 October 2006).

Australia

Australia (2005). Response to the 2005 questionnaire on the practical operation of the Hague Convention of 29 May 1993 on Protection of Children and Co-operation in Respect of Intercountry Adoption (Prel.Doc. No. 1 of March 2005). Available from http://www.hcch.net/index_en.php?act=publications.details&pid=3521&dtid=33 (accessed 31 October 2006).
Australia, Australian Institute of Health and Welfare (2003). *Adoptions Australia 2002-2003.* Child Welfare Series, No. 33. Canberra. Available from http://www.aihw.gov.au/publications/cws/aa02-03/aa02-03.pdf (accessed 30 October 2006).

_____ (2004). *Adoptions Australia 2003-2004.* Child Welfare Series No. 35. Canberra. Available from http://www.aihw.gov.au/publications/cws/aa03-04/aa03-04.pdf (accessed 30 October 2006).

Australia, Department of Immigration and Citizenship (2006). *Child Migration.* Available from http://www.immi.gov.au/allforms/booklets/1128.pdf (accessed 12 February 2006).

_____ (2007). *Child Migration.* Available from http://www.immi.gov.au/allforms/booklets/books2.ht m (accessed 07 December 2007).

United Nations (1996). Initial reports of States parties due in 1993: Australia (CRC/C/8/Add.31).

_____ (2004). Second and third periodic reports of States parties due in 1998 and 2003: Australia (CRC/C/129/Add.4).

_____ (2005). Written replies by the Government of Australia (CRC/C/RESP/90) concerning the list of issues received by the Committee on the Rights of the Child (CRC/C/Q/AUS/3) relating to the consideration of the second and third periodic reports of Australia.

Western Australia, Department for Community Development (2003). *Policy for the Adoption of Children.* Available from http://www.aph.gov.au/house/committee/fhs/adoption/subs/sub183attch1.pdf (accessed 30 October 2006).

_____ (n.d.). *Models of Out of Home Placement.* Available from http://www.signposts.communitydeve loppment.wa.gov.au/type/view.aspx?TypeID=3#_ftn4 (accessed 28 September 2007).

_____ (n.d.). Parliamentary Counsel's Office of Western Australia. Adoption Regulations 1995. Available from http://www.hcch.net/upload/adoxtra1 _au.pdf (accessed 07 November 2006).

Western Australia, Law Reform Commission (2002). Succession rights of adopted children. In *Thirtieth Anniversary Reform Implementation Report*, p. 78.

Austria

Austria, Federal Ministry of Justice (2005). Response to the 2005 questionnaire on the practical operation of the Hague Convention of 29 May 1993 on Protection of Children and Co-operation in Respect of Intercountry Adoption. Available from http://www.hcch.net/upload/adop2005_at.pdf (accessed 10 October 2007).

Austria, Statistics Austria (1999). Youth Welfare Statistics. Vienna: Verlag Österreich GmbH.

United Nations (1997). Initial reports of States parties due in 1994: Austria (CRC/C/11/Add.14).

_____ (1999). Written replies by the Government of Austria (CRC/C/RESP/AUSTRIA.1) concerning the list of issues received by the Committee on the Rights of the Child (CRC/C/Q/AUSTRIA.1)

relating to the consideration of the initial periodic report of Austria.

_____ (2004a). Second periodic report of States parties due in 1999: Austria (CRC/C/83/Add.8).

_____ (2004b). Written replies by the Government of Austria (CRC/C/RESP/75) concerning the list of issues received by the Committee on the Rights of the Child (CRC/C/Q/AUT/2) relating to the consideration of the second periodic report of Austria.

United States, Embassy to Austria (2006). *Adopting a Child in Austria.* Available from http://vienna. usembassy.gov/en/embassy/cons/adoption.htm (accessed 12 February 2006).

Azerbaijan

United Nations (1996). Initial reports of States parties due in 1994: Azerbaijan (CRC/C/11/Add.8).

_____ (2005). Second period report of States parties due in 1999: Azerbaijan (CRC/C/83/Add.13).

United States, Bureau of Consular Affairs. (2006). Intercountry adoption: Azerbaijan. Washington, D.C.: Department of State.

Bahamas

United Nations (2004). Initial reports of States parties due in 1993: Bahamas (CRC/C/8/Add.50).

_____ (2005). Written replies by the Government of Bahamas (CRC/C/RESP/BHS/1) concerning the list of issues received by the Committee on the Rights of the Child (CRC/C/Q/BHS/1) relating to the consideration of the initial periodic report of Bahamas.

United States, Bureau of Consular Affairs (2001). Intercountry adoption: Bahamas. Washington, D.C.: Department of State. Available from http://travel. state.gov/family/adoption/country/country_436.html (accessed 27 October 2006).

Bahrain

United Nations (2001). Initial reports of States parties due in 1994: Bahrain (CRC/C/11/Add.24).

Bangladesh

United Nations (1995). Initial reports of States parties due in 1992: Bangladesh (CRC/C/3/Add.38).

_____ (2003a). Second periodic reports of States parties due in 1997: Bangladesh (CRC/C/65/Add.22).

_____ (2003b). Written replies by the Government of Bangladesh (CRC/C/RESP/41) concerning the list of issues received by the Committee on the Rights of the Child (CRC/C/Q/BGD/2) relating to the consideration of the second periodic report of Bangladesh.

Barbados

United Nations (1997). Initial reports of States parties due in 1992: Barbados (CRC/C/3/Add.45).

World Health Organization, Pan American Health Organization and University of the West Indies (1999). Study of Ageing and Health in Barbadian Elders Project SABE. Available from http://www.ssc.wisc.edu/sabe/question/BarbQuest.pdf (accessed 07 November 2006).

Belarus

United Nations (1993). Initial reports of States parties due in 1992: Belarus (CRC/C/3/Add.14).

_____ (2001). Second period report of States parties due in 1997: Belarus (CRC/C/65/Add.15).

_____ (2002). Written replies by the Government of Belarus (CRC/C/RESP/BEL/2) concerning the list of issues received by the Committee on the Rights of the Child (CRC/C/Q/BEL/2) relating to the consideration of the second periodic report of Belarus.

United States, Bureau of Consular Affairs. (2006). Intercountry adoption: Belarus. Washington, D.C.: Department of State. Available from http://travel.state.gov/family/adoption/country/country_354.html (accessed 27 October 2006).

Belgium

Belgium, Ministry of Justice (2005). *L'Adoption*. Available from http://www.just.fgov.be/img_justice/publications/pdf/199.pdf (accessed 12 February 2006).

Belgium, National Office of Family Benefits for Salaried Persons (2002). Statistiques démographiques par caisse d'allocations familiales année 2002. Bruxelles. Available from www.rkw.be/Fr/Documentation/Publication/Statistics/StatDemoCAF2002.pdf (accessed 21 October 2006).

_____ (2004). Rapport démographique 2003. *Séries statistiques 1993-2003*. Bruxelles. Available from http://www.rkw.be/Fr/Documentation/Publication/Statistics/seriesStatistiques2003.pdf (accessed 10 October 2007).

Belgium, Kind en Gezin, Flemish Minister of Welfare (1999). *The Child in Flanders*. Available from http://www.kindengezin.be/Images/Childinflande rs99_tcm149-229 77.pdf (accessed 10 October 2007).

_____ (2000). *The Child in Flanders*. Available from http://www.kindengezin.be/Images/Child_in_Flanders_2000_tcm149-23567.pdf (accessed 10 October 2007).

_____ (2003). *The Child in Flanders 2003*. Available from http://www.kindengezin.be/Images/Child_in_Flanders_2003_tcm149-37000.pdf (accessed 10 October 2007).

United Nations (1994). Initial reports of States parties due in 1994: Belgium (CRC/C/11/Add.4).

_____ (2000). Second periodic reports of States parties due in 1999: Belgium (CRC/C/83/Add.2).

Belize

Belize (2000). Families and Children Act, Chapter 173 (revised edition 2000).

United Nations (1997). Initial reports of States parties due in 1992: Belize (CRC/C/3/Add.46).

_____ (2004a). Second periodic report of States parties due in 1997: Belize (CRC/C/65/Add.29).

_____ (2004b). Written replies by the Government of Belize (CRC/C/RESP/76) concerning the list of issues received by the Committee on the Rights of the Child (CRC/C/Q/BLZ/2) relating to the consideration of the second periodic report of Belize.

Benin

United Nations (1997). Initial reports of States parties due in 1992: Benin (CRC/C/3/Add.52).

_____ (2005a). Second periodic reports of States parties due in 1997: Benin (CRC/C/BEN/2).

_____ (2005b). Written replies by the Government of Benin concerning the list of issues received by the Committee on the Rights of the Child (CRC/C/BEN/Q/2) relating to the consideration of the second periodic report of Benin.

Bolivia (Plurinational State of)

Bolivia, Ministry of Justice and Human Rights (1999). El Honorable Congreso Nacional, Decreta: Código del Niño, Niña y Adolescente Disposiciones Fundamentales Capítulo Único, October 1999. Available from http://www.cinterfor.org.uy/public/spanish/region/ampro/cinterfor/temas/youth/legisl/bol/iii/ (accessed 31 October 2006).

United Nations (1997). Periodic reports of States parties due in 1997: Bolivia (CRC/C/65/Add.1).

_____ (2004). Third reports of States parties due in 2002: Bolivia (CRC/C/125/Add.2).

Botswana

United Nations (2004a). Initial reports of States parties due in 1997: Botswana (CRC/C/51/Add.9).

_____ (2004b). Written replies by the Government of Botswana (CRC/C/RESP/66) concerning the list of issues received by the Committee on the Rights of the Child (CRC/C/Q/BWA/1) relating to the consideration of the third periodic report of Botswana.

Bosnia and Herzegovina

United Nations (2004). Initial report of States parties due in 1999: Bosnia and Herzegovina (CRC/C/11/Add.28).

_____ (2005). Written replies by the Government of Bosnia and Herzegovina (CRC/C/RESP/85) concerning the list of issues received by the Committee on the Rights of the Child (CRC/C/Q/BIH/1) relating to the consideration of the initial report of Bosnia and Herzegovina.

Brazil

Brazil (2005). Response to the 2005 questionnaire on the practical operation of the Hague Convention of 29 May 1993 on Protection of Children and Co-operation in Respect of Intercountry Adoption. Available from http://www.hcch.net/upload/adop2005_br.pdf (accessed 6 July 2006).

United Nations (2003). Initial reports of States parties due in 1992: Brazil (CRC/C/3/Add.65).

United States, Bureau of Consular Affairs (2006). International adoption: Brazil. Washington, D.C.: Department of State. Available from http://travel.state.gov/family/adoption/country/country_358.html (accessed 27 October 2006).

World Health Organization, Pan American Health Organization and University of São Paulo, Brazil (1999). Saúde, Bem-Estar e Envelhecimento na América Latina e Caribe. Available from http://www.ssc.wisc.edu/sabe/question/BrasQuest.pdf (accessed 07 November 2006).

Brunei Darussalam

United Nations (2003). Initial reports of States parties due in 1998: Brunei Darussalam (CRC/C/61/Add.5).

Bulgaria

Bulgaria, National Assembly (1992). Family Code No. 41/28.1985, Amended SG No. 11&15/1992.

Tzvetkova-Anguelova, J. (2001). Trends and Indicators on Child and Family Well-Being in Bulgaria. Background paper prepared for *A Decade of Transition. Regional Monitoring Report*, No. 8. Florence, Italy: UNICEF Innocenti Research Centre. Available from http://www.unicef-icdc.org/research/ESP/CountryReports2000_01/Bulgaria00.pdf (accessed 31 October 2006).

United Nations (1995). Initial reports of States parties due in 1993: Bulgaria (CRC/C/8/Add.29).

_____, Economic Commission for Europe (n.d.). Family and Fertility Survey of Bulgaria. Available from http://www.unece.org/pau/ffs/bg_englquest.pdf (accessed 07 November 2006).

Burkina Faso

United Nations (2002a). Initial reports of States parties due in 1997: Burkina Faso (CRC/C/65/Add.18).

_____ (2002b). Written replies by the Government of Burkina Faso (CRC/C/RESP/ BURK/2) concerning the list of issues received by the Committee on the Rights of the Child (CRC/C/Q/BURK/2) relating to the consideration of the initial report of Burkina Faso.

Burundi

Burundi (2005). Response to the 2005 questionnaire on the practical operation of the Hague Convention of 29 May 1993 on Protection of Children and Co-operation in Respect of Intercountry Adoption. Available from http://www.hcch.net/upload/adop2005_bu.pdf/ (accessed 6 July 2006).

United Nations (1998). Initial reports of States parties due in 1992: Burundi (CRC/C/3/Add.58).

United States, Bureau of Consular Affairs (2006). International adoption: Burundi. Washington, D.C.: Department of State. Available from http://travel.state.gov/family/adoption/country/country_360.html (accessed 27 October 2006).

Cambodia

United Nations (1998). Initial reports of States parties due in 1994: Cambodia (CRC/C/11/Add.16).

Cameroon

United Nations (2001). Initial reports of States parties due in 1995: Cameroon (CRC/C/28/Add.16).

Canada

Alberta, Children's Services (2005). Summary of Adoption in Alberta Statistics. Available from http://www.child.gov.ab.ca/whatwedo/adoption/page.cfm?pg=Adoption%20statistics (accessed 19 October 2005).

Canada (2005). Response to the 2005 questionnaire on the practical operation of the Hague Convention of 29 May 1993 on Protection of Children and Co-operation in Respect of Intercountry Adoption. Available from http://www.hcch.net/upload/adop2005_cae.pdf (accessed 6 July 2006).

Canada, Adoption Council of Canada (2003a). International adoptions steady: 1,891 in 2002. 06 May 2003. Available from http://www.adoption.ca/news/030506st ats02.htm (accessed 27 October 2006).

_____ (2003b). Canadians adopt almost 20,000 children from abroad. 12 December 2003. Available from http://www.adoption.ca/news/031212cicstats.htm (accessed 27 October 2006).

_____ (2004a). International adoptions up: 2,181 in 2003. 28 June 2004. Available from http://www.adoption.ca/news/040628stats03.htm (accessed 27 October 2006).

_____ (2004b). Survey of countries reveals closures, slowdowns in international adoption. Available from http://www.adoption.ca/news/040609cystatus.htm (accessed 5 May 2005).

_____ (2005a). China leads adoption statistics for 2004. 27 May 2005. Available from http://www.adoption.ca/news/050527stats04.htm (accessed 27 October 2006).

_____ (2005b). Country survey reveals status of international adoption. Available from http://www.adoption.ca/news/050730cystatus.htm (accessed 21 February 2006).

Canada, Citizenship and Immigration Canada (2003). International adoptions. *The Monitor* (Fall). Available from http://www.cic.gc.ca/english/monitor/issue03/ind ex.html (accessed 27 October 2006).

Canada, Human Resources and Social Development (2004). *Child and Family Services Statistical Report 1998-1999 to 2000-2001*. Available from http://www.sdc.gc.ca/en/cs/sp/sdc/socpol/publications/statistics/2004-002599/ page02.shtml (accessed 04 December 2007).

Canada, Statistics Canada (2007). General Social Survey, 2006, Cycle 20, Family Transitions Survey. Available from http://www.statistiquecanada.ca/english/sdds/instrument/4501_Q1_V4_E.pdf (accessed 07 November 2006).

United Nations (2003). Second periodic reports of States parties due in 1999: Canada (CRC/C/83/Add.6).

Cape Verde

United Nations (2001a). Initial Report from Cape Verde. Press release, 10 October 2001.

_____ (2001b). Periodic reports due in 1994: Cape Verde (CRC/C/11/Add.23).

_____ Written replies by the Government of Cape Verde (CRC/C/RESP/CAP/2) concerning the list of issues received by the Committee on the Rights of the Child (CRC/C/Q/CAP/1) relating to the consideration of the initial report of Cape Verde.

Central African Republic

United Nations (1998). Initial reports of States parties due in 1994: Central African Republic (CRC/C/11/Add.18).

_____ (2000). Written replies by the Government of the Central African Republic (CRC/C/RESP/CAR/1) concerning the list of issues received from the Committee on the Rights of the Child (CRC/C/Q/CAR/1) in connection with the initial report of the Central African Republic.

Chad

United Nations (1997). Initial reports of States parties due in 1992: Chad (CRC/C/3/Add.50).

Chile

Chile (n.d.). Act No. 19,620 of 1999. Available from http://www.sernam.gov.cl/admin/docdescargas/seccion/categorias/subcategorias/subcat_164.doc (accessed 12 May 2006).

Chile, National Service for Minors (2005). Response to the 2005 questionnaire on the practical operation of the Hague Convention of 29 May 1993 on Protection of Children and Co-operation in Respect of Intercountry Adoption. Available from http://www.hcch.net/upload/adop2005_cl.pdf (accessed 6 July 2006).

United Nations (2001a). Periodic reports of States parties due in 1997: Chile (CRC/C/65/Add.13).

_____ (2001b). Written replies by the Government of Chile (CRC/C/RESP/CHI/2) concerning the list of issues received by the Committee on the Rights of the Child (CRC/C/Q/CHI/2) relating to the consideration of the second periodic report of Chile.

_____ (2005). Third periodic reports of States parties due in 1997: Chile (CRC/C/CHL/3).

United States, Bureau of Consular Affairs (2006). International adoption: Chile. Washington, D.C.: Department of State. Available from http://travel.state.gov/family/adoption/country/country_364.html (accessed 27 October 2006).

World Health Organization, Pan American Health Organization and University of Chile, Institute of Nutrition and Food Technology (INTA) (1999). *Encuesta sobre Salud, Bienestar y Envejecimiento en América Latina y el Caribe*. Available from http://www.ssc.wisc.edu/sabe/question/chilea-c.pdf (accessed 07 November 2006).

China

China, (2005). Response to the 2005 questionnaire on the practical operation of the Hague Convention of 29 May 1993 on Protection of Children and Co-operation in Respect of Intercountry Adoption. Available from http://www.hcch.net/upload/adop 2005_cn.pdf (accessed 6 July 2006).

_____ (2006). New criteria spelt out for adoption by foreigners. Available from http://english.gov. cn/2006-12/25/content_477509.htm (accessed 21 February 2007).

China, The Legislative Affairs Commission of the Standing Committee of the National People's Congress of the People's Republic of China (1998). Adoption Law. Adopted at the 23rd Meeting of the Standing Committee of the Seventh National People's Congress on 29 December 1991 and revised in accordance with the Decision on Revising the Adoption Law of the People's Republic of China adopted at the 5th Meeting of the Standing Committee of the Ninth National People's Congress on 4 November 1998 and promulgated by Order No. 10 of the President of the People's Republic of China. Available from http://english.gov.cn/2005-08/31/ content_26770.htm (accessed 12 May 2006).

China, Ministry of Civil Affairs (2000). *Statistical Yearbook 2000*. Beijing: China Statistics Press.

_____ (2001). *Statistical Yearbook 2001*. Beijing: China Statistics Press.

_____ (2002). *Statistical Yearbook 2002*. Beijing: China Statistics Press.

_____ (2005). *Statistical Yearbook 2005*. Beijing: China Statistics Press.

China, National Bureau of Statistics of the People's Republic of China (2002). *China Statistical Yearbook 2002*. Beijing: China Statistics Press.

United Nations (1995). Initial reports of States parties due in 1994: China (CRC/C/11/Add.7).

_____ (2005a). Second periodic report of States parties due in 1997: China (CRC/C/83/Add.9).

_____ (2005b). Written replies by the Government of China (CRC/C/RESP/89) concerning the list of issues received by the Committee on the Rights of the Child (CRC/C/Q/CHN/2) relating to the consideration of the second periodic report of China.

Colombia

Colombia (2004). Adopción. 27 enero 2004.

Colombia, Colombian Family Welfare Institute (2004). *Adopción*. Available from http://www.icbf.gov.co/ espanol/tramites5c.htm (accessed 27 October 2006).

_____ (2005). Response to the 2005 questionnaire on the practical operation of the Hague Convention of 29 May 1993 on Protection of Children and Co-operation in Respect of Intercountry Adoption. Available from http://www.hcch.net/index_en.php? act=publications.details&pid=3586&dtid=33 (accessed 6 July 2006).

United Nations (1993). Initial reports of States parties due in 1993: Colombia (CRC/C/8/Add.3).

_____ (2000). Periodic reports of States parties due in 1998: Colombia (CRC/C/70/Add.5).

_____ (2004). Third periodic reports of States parties due in 2003: Colombia (CRC/C/129/Add.6).

Comoros

United Nations (1998). Initial reports of States parties due in 1995: Comoros (CRC/C/28/Add.13).

Congo

United Nations (2006a). Initial reports of States parties due in 1999: Congo (CRC/C/COG/1).

_____ (2006b). Written replies by the Government of Congo (CRC/C/Q/COG/1/Add.1) concerning the list of issues received by the Committee on the Rights of the Child (CRC/C/Q/COG/1) relating to the consideration of the initial report of Congo.

Costa Rica

Centro Centroamericano de Población (CCP), Universidad de Costa Rica (1999). *Encuesta Nacional De Salud Reproductiva, Costa Rica*. Available from http://encuest as.ccp.ucr.ac.cr/camerica/pdf/cimcr99.pdf#search=%22 Encuesta%20de%20Fecundidad%20cuestionario%20ni nos%20adoptados%22 (accessed 07 November 2006).

Costa Rica, National Adoption Council (2005). Response to the 2005 questionnaire on the practical operation of the Hague Convention of 29 May 1993 on Protection of Children and Co-operation in Respect of Intercountry Adoption. Available from http://www.hcch.net/upload/ adop2005_cr.pdf (accessed 6 July 2006)

United Nations (1993). Initial reports of States parties due in 1992: Costa Rica (CRC/C/3/Add.8).

_____ (1998). Periodic reports of States parties due in 1997: Costa Rica (CRC/C/65/Add.7).

_____ (2004). Third periodic reports of States Parties due in 2002: Costa Rica (CRC/C/125/Add.4).

_____ (2005). Written replies by the Government of Costa Rica (CRC/C/RESP/81) concerning the list of issues received by the Committee on the Rights of the Child (CRC/C/Q/CRI/3) relating to the consideration of the third periodic report of Costa Rica.

United States, Bureau of Consular Affairs (2006). International adoption: Costa Rica. Washington, D.C.: Department of State. Available from http://travel. state.gov/family/adoption/country/country_367.html (accessed 27 October 2006).

Côte d'Ivoire

United Nations (2000). Initial reports of States parties due in 1993: Côte d'Ivoire (CRC/C/8/Add.41).

Croatia

United Nations (1994). Initial report of States parties due in 1993: Croatia (CRC/C/8/Add.19).

_____ (2003). Second periodic reports of States parties due in 1998: Croatia (CRC/C/70/Add.23).

United States, Bureau of Consular Affairs (2006). International adoption: Croatia. Washington, D.C.: Department of State. Available from http://travel. state.gov/family/adoption/country/country_370.html (accessed 27 October 2006).

Cyprus

Cyprus, Ministry of Labour and Social Insurance (2005). Response to the 2005 questionnaire on the practical operation of the Hague Convention of 29 May 1993 on Protection of Children and Co-operation in Respect of Intercountry Adoption. Available from http://www.hcch.net/upload/adop2005_cy.pdf (accessed 6 July 2006).

United Nations (1995). Initial reports of States parties due in 1993: Cyprus (CRC/C/8/Add.24).

_____ Second periodic reports of States parties due in 1998: Cyprus (CRC/C/70/Add.16).

_____ (2003). Written replies by the Government of Cyprus (CRC/C/RESP/CYP/2) concerning the list of issues received by the Committee on the Rights of the Child (CRC/C/Q/CYP/2) relating to the consideration of the second periodic report of Cyprus.

Czech Republic

Bruthansová, D., and others (2005). Institutional health and social care aiming to children under three. Prague,

Research Centre Brno. Available from http://www.vup sv.cz/Fulltext/vz_177.pdf (accessed 6 July 2006).

Czech Republic (2002). Act of the Czech Republic No. 94/1963 Sb. on Family as amended by the Acts No. 132/1982 Sb., No. 234/1992 Sb., by the decision of the Constitutional Court No. 72/1995Sb., by the Acts No. 91/1998 Sb., by the Acts No. 360/1999 Sb., No. 301/2000 Sb. and No. 109/2002 Sb.

_____ (2005). Response to the 2005 questionnaire on the practical operation of the Hague Convention of 29 May 1993 on Protection of Children and Co-operation in Respect of Intercountry Adoption. Available from http://www.hcch.net/upload/adop 2005_cz.pdf (accessed 6 July 2006).

Czech Republic, Institute of Health Information and Statistics (2002). *Czech Health Statistics Yearbook 2001*. Prague.

_____ (2003). *Czech Health Statistics Yearbook 2002*. Prague.

_____ (2004). *Czech Health Statistics Yearbook 2003*. Prague.

_____ (2005). *Czech Health Statistics Yearbook 2004*. Prague.

Novak, J. (2001). Trends and indicators on child and family well-being in the Czech Republic. Background paper prepared for *A Decade of Transition. Regional Monitoring Report*, No. 8. Prague: Czech Statistical Office; and Florence, Italy: UNICEF Innocenti Research Centre. Available from http://www.unicef-irc.org/research/ESP/CountryReports2000_01/CzechR ep00.pdf (accessed 27 October 2006).

United Nations (1996). Initial reports of States parties due in 1994: Czech Republic (CRC/C/11/Add.11).

_____ (2002). Periodic reports of States parties due in 1999: Czech Republic (CRC/C/83/Add.4).

_____ (2003). Written replies by the Government of Czech Republic (CRC/C/RESP/CZE/2) concerning the list of issues received by the Committee on the Rights of the Child (CRC/C/Q/CZE/2) relating to the consideration of the periodic report of Czech Republic.

Democratic People's Republic of Korea

United Nations (1996). Initial reports of States parties due in 1992: Democratic People's Republic of Korea (CRC/C/3/Add.41).

_____ (2003). Second periodic reports of States parties due in 1997: Democratic People's Republic of Korea (CRC/C/65/Add.24).

_____ (2004). Written replies by the Government of the Democratic People's Republic of Korea (CRC/C/ RESP/61) concerning the list of issues received by the Committee on the Rights of the Child (CRC/C/ Q/PRK/2) relating to the second periodic report of the Democratic People's Republic of Korea.

Democratic Republic of the Congo

United Nations (2000). Initial reports of States parties due in 1992: Democratic Republic of Congo (CRC/C/3/Add.57).

_____ (2001). Written replies by the Government of the Democratic Republic of Congo (CRC/C/RESP/DRC/1) concerning the list of issues received by the Committee on the Rights of the Child (CRC/C/Q/DRC/1) relating to the initial report of the Democratic Republic of Congo.

Denmark

Denmark, Danish National Board of Adoption (2005). Statistical Information–some figures on foreign adoptions in Denmark. Available from http://www.adoptionsnae vnet.dk/info_english/default.htm (accessed 30 October 2006).

Denmark, Ministry of Family and Consumer Affairs (2004). The Danish Adoption (Consolidation) Act. Available from http://www.familiestyrelsen.dk/adop tion/lovgivning/love/the-danish-adoption-consolidati on-act/ (accessed 28 October 2006).

_____ (2005). Response to the 2005 questionnaire on the practical operation of the Hague Convention of 29 May 1993 on Protection of Children and Co-operation in Respect of Intercountry Adoption. Available from http://www.hcch.net/upload/adop 2005_dk.pdf (accessed 6 July 2006)

Denmark, Statistics Denmark (2003). *Statistical News. Population and Elections,* No. 3, Copenhagen, Denmark.

_____ (2004a). *Statistical News. Population and Elections,* No. 5, Copenhagen, Denmark.

_____ (2004b). Adoptioner af danske børn. Available from http://statistik.adoption.dk/danske_born/danskefoe d te_adopt_fra_1974.htm (accessed 27 October 2006).

_____ (2004c). Modtagne børn 2000-2004, fordelt på lande. Available from http://statistik.adoption.dk/udla nd/ fordelt_paa_lande_5aar.htm (accessed 27 October 2007).

_____ (2004d). *Statistical Yearbook 2004.* Copenhagen. Available from http://www.dst.dk/HomeUK/Statistics/ofs/ Publications/Yearbook/2004.aspx (accessed 27 October 2006).

_____ (2004e). Totalt antal adoptioner i Danmark siden 1938. Available from http://statistik.adoption. dk/generelt/totalantaladoptioner_fra_1938.htm (accessed 27 October 2006).

_____ (2005). The age of the female adoptant at adoption. *Statistical News.* Copenhagen, Denmark. Available from http://statistik.adoption.dk/generelt/adop tivmodresalder.htm (accessed 29 October 2006).

United Nations (1993). Initial reports of States parties due in 1993: Denmark (CRC/C/8/Add.8).

_____ (2005a). Third periodic reports of States parties due in 2003: Denmark (CRC/C/129/Add.3).

_____ (2005b). Written replies by the Government of Denmark (CRC/C/RESP/91) concerning the list of issues received by the Committee on the Rights of the Child (CRC/C/Q/DNK/3) relating to the consideration of the third periodic report of Denmark.

Dominica

United Nations (2003). Initial reports of States parties due in 1993: Dominica (CRC/C/8/Add.48).

_____ (2005b). Written replies by the Government of Dominica (CRC/C/RESP/DOM/1) concerning the list of issues received by the Committee on the Rights of the Child (CRC/C/Q/DMA/1) relating to the consideration of the initial periodic report of Dominica.

Dominican Republic

United Nations (1999). Initial reports of States parties due in 1993: Dominican Republic (CRC/C/8/Add.40).

United States, Bureau of Consular Affairs (2006). International adoption: Dominican. Washington, D.C.: Department of State. Available from http://travel.state.gov/family/adoption/country/ country_375.html (accessed 27 October 2006).

Ecuador

Ecuador, National Council for the Children and Adolescents (2005). Response to the 2005 questionnaire on the practical operation of the Hague Convention of 29 May 1993 on Protection of Children and Co-operation in Respect of Intercountry Adoption. Available from http://www. hcch.net/upload/adop2005_ec.pdf (accessed 6 July 2006).

United Nations (1996). Initial reports of States parties due in 1992: Ecuador (CRC/C/3/Add.44).

_____ (2004). Second and third periodic reports of States parties due in 1997 and 2002: Ecuador (CRC/C/ 65/Add.28).

_____ (2005). Written replies by the Government of Ecuador (CRC/C/RESP/86) concerning the list of issues received by the Committee on the Rights of the Child (CRC/C/Q/ECU/2) relating to the consideration of the second and third periodic reports of Ecuador.

United States, Bureau of Consular Affairs (2006). International adoption: Ecuador. Washington, D.C.: Department of State. Available from http://travel.state.gov/family/adoption/country/ country_376.html (accessed 27 October 2006).

El Salvador

United Nations (1993). Initial reports of States parties due in 1992: El Salvador (CRC/C/3/Add.9).

_____ (2003). Second periodic reports of States parties due in 1997: El Salvador (CRC/C/65/Add.25).

_____ (2004). Written replies by the Government of El Salvador (CRC/C/RESP/54) concerning the list of issues prepared by the Committee (CRC/C/Q/SLV/2) in connection with the consideration of the second periodic report of El Salvador.

Equatorial Guinea

United Nations (2004). Initial reports of States parties due in 1994: Equatorial Guinea (CRC/C/11/Add.26).

Eritrea

United Nations (2002). Initial reports of States parties due in 1996: Eritrea (CRC/C/41/Add.12).

United States, Bureau of Consular Affairs (2006). Intercountry adoption: Eritrea". Washington, D.C.: Department of State. Available from http://travel.state.gov/family/adoption/country/country_2975.html (accessed 20 February 2007).

Estonia

Estonia, Ministry of Social Affairs (2004). *Social Sector in Figures 2004*. Tallinn. Available from http://www.sm.ee/eng/HtmlPages/social_sector_2004/$file/social_sector_2004.pdf (accessed 27 October 2006).

_____ (2005). Response to the 2005 questionnaire on the practical operation of the Hague Convention of 29 May 1993 on Protection of Children and Co-operation in Respect of Intercountry Adoption. Available from http://www.hcch.net/upload/adop2005_ee.pdf (accessed 6 July 2006).

Estonia, Statistics Estonia (2006). Social welfare institutions for children, 31 December 2003. Available from http://pub.stat.ee/px-web.2001/dialog/statfileri.asp (accessed 27 October 2006).

United Nations (2002). Initial reports of States parties due in 1993: Estonia (CRC/C/8/Add.45).

_____, Economic Commission for Europe and Estonian Demographic Association (1993). Estonian Family and Fertility Survey. Available from http://www.unece.org/pau/ffs/est_engquest.pdf (accessed 07 November 2006).

United States, Bureau of Consular Affairs (2006). International adoption: Estonia. Washington, D.C.: Department of State. Available from http://travel.

state.gov/family/adoption/country/country_379.html (accessed 27 October 2006).

Ethiopia

Ethiopia (n.d.). The Revised Family Code of 2000, Proclamation No. 213/2000. Available from http://www.ethiopar.net/Archive/English/1stterm/5thyear/hopre/bills/1999_2000/pro213.html (accessed 12 May 2006).

United Nations (1995). Initial reports of States parties due in 1993: Ethiopia (CRC/C/8/Add.27).

_____ (2005). Third periodic report of States parties due in 2003: Ethiopia (CRC/C/129/Add.8).

United States, Bureau of Consular Affairs (2006). International adoption: Ethiopia. Washington, D.C.: Department of State. Available from http://travel.state.gov/family/adoption/country/country_380.html (accessed 27 October 2006).

Fiji

United Nations (1996). Initial reports of States parties due in 1995: Fiji (CRC/C/28/Add.7).

Finland

Finland (2005). Response to the 2005 questionnaire on the practical operation of the Hague Convention of 29 May 1993 on Protection of Children and Co-operation in Respect of Intercountry Adoption. Available from http://www.hcch.net/index_en.php?act=publications.details&pid=3536&dtid=33 (accessed 6 July 2006).

Finland, Finnish Adoption Board (2001). *Annual Report 2000*. Helsinki: Ministry of Social Affairs and Health. Available from http://pre20031103.stm.fi/english/pao/publicat/adopt01_7/report.htm (accessed 27 October 2006).

_____ (2004). *Annual Report 2003*. Helsinki: Ministry of Social Affairs and Health. Available from http://stm.fi/Resource.phx/publishing/store/2004/06/mk1087197406074/passthru.pdf (accessed 30 October 2006).

United Nations (1995). Initial reports of States parties due in 1993: Finland (CRC/C/8/Add.22).

_____ (1998). Second periodic reports of States parties due in 1998: Finland (CRC/C/70/Add.3).

_____ (2005a). Third periodic reports of States parties due in 2003: Finland (CRC/C/129/Add.5).

_____ (2005b). Written replies by the Government of Finland (CRC/C/RESP/95) concerning the list of issues received by the Committee on the Rights of the

Child (CRC/C/Q/FIN/3) relating to the consideration of the third periodic report of Finland.

France

Agence Française de l'Adoption (n.d.). Rapports de suivi. Available from http://www.agence-adoption.fr/home/spip.php?article19&bloc=1 (accessed 07 November 2006).

_____ (n.d.). Transmission de rapports de suivi des enfants adoptés. Available from http://agence-adoption.lnet.fr/home/IMG/pdf/Transmission_de_rapports_de_suivi_des_enfants_adoptes.pdf (accessed 07 November 2006).

France (2005). Response to the 2005 questionnaire on the practical operation of the Hague Convention of 29 May 1993 on Protection of Children and Co-operation in Respect of Intercountry Adoption. Available from http://www.hcch.net/upload/adop2005_fr.pdf (accessed 6 July 2006).

_____ (n.d.). Civil Code, book I, title VIII. Available http://195.83.177.9/code/liste.phtml?lang=uk&c=22&r=314 (accessed 29 October 2006).

_____ (n.d.). Law No. 2002-93 of 22 January 2002. Available from http://www.legifrance.gouv.fr/WAspad/UnTexteDeJorf?numjo=MESX0205318L (accessed 29 October 2006).

France, Ministry of Foreign Affairs (2005). *Adoption Internationale: Statistiques 2004*. Available from http://www.diplomatie.gouv.fr/fr/IMG/pdf/stat_adoption_2004.pdf (accessed 27 October 2006).

_____ (2006). *Adoption Internationale: Statistiques 2005*. Available from http://www.diplomatie.gouv.fr/fr/IMG/pdf/stat_adoption_2005.pdf (accessed 30 October 2006).

France, National Institute for Statistics and Economic Studies. *Questionnaires de l'Enquête Famille 1999*. Available from http://www-ehf.ined.fr/ (accessed 07 November 2006).

Halifax, J. (2001). *L'insertion Sociale des Enfants Adoptes. Résultats de L'enquête "Adoption Internationale et Insertion Sociale", 2000*. Available from http://www.ined.fr/fichier/t_publication/1069/publi_pdf1_98.pdf (accessed 04 December 2007).

_____, and C. Villeneuve-Gokalp (2005). L'adoption en France: qui sont les adoptés, qui sont les adoptants? *Population et Sociétés*, No. 417, pp. 1-4.

United Nations (2003). Second periodic reports of States due in 1997: France (CRC/C/65/Add.26).

_____ (2004). Written replies from the Government of France (CRC/C/RESP/60) to the list of issues to be taken up in connection with the consideration of the second periodic report of France by the Committee on the Rights of the Child (CRC/C/Q/FRA/2).

Gabon

United Nations (2001). Initial reports of States parties due in 1996: Gabon (CRC/C/41/Add.10).

Gambia

United Nations (2000). Initial reports of States parties due in 1992: Gambia (CRC/C/3/Add.61).

_____ (2001). Written replies by the Government of Gambia (CRC/C/RESP/GAM/1) concerning the list of issues received by the Committee on the Rights of the Child (CRC/C/Q/GAM/1) relating to the consideration of the initial report of Gambia.

Georgia

United Nations (1998). Initial reports of States parties due in 1996: Georgia (CRC/C/41/Add.4/Rev.1).

_____ (2003a). Second periodic reports of States parties due in 2001: Georgia (CRC/C/104/Add.1).

_____ (2003b). Written replies by the Government of Georgia (CRC/C/RESP/37) concerning the list of issues received by the Committee on the Rights of the Child (CRC/C/Q/GEO/2) relating to the consideration of the second periodic report of Georgia.

Germany

Germany (2005). Response to the 2005 questionnaire on the practical operation of the Hague Convention of 29 May 1993 on Protection of Children and Co-operation in Respect of Intercountry Adoption. Available from http://www.hcch.net/index_en.php?act=publications.details&pid=3557&dtid=33 (accessed 6 July 2006).

_____ (n.d.). Act on the adoption placement and the ban on the arrangement of surrogate mothers (Adoption Placement Act–AdVermiG). Available from http://www.bundeszentralregister.de/bzaa/bzaa_english/adop005engl.html (accessed 27 October 2006).

_____ (n.d.). Act on the Effects of Adoption According to Foreign Law. Available from http://www.bundeszentralregister.de/bzaa/bzaa_english/adop006engl.html (accessed 27 October 2006).

_____ (n.d.). Act on the Implementation of the Hague Convention of 29 May 1993 on the Protection of Children and Co-operation in the Field of International adoption (Adoption Convention Implementation Statute –AdÜbAG). Available from http://www.bundeszentralregister.de/bzaa/bzaa_english/adop004engl.html (accessed 27 October 2006).

_____ (n.d.). Civil Code (Bürgerliches Gesetzbuch) Seventh Title, adoption of a child. Available from http://www.bundeszentralregister.de/bzaa/bzaa_english/adop011engl.html (accessed 27 October 2006).

Germany, Federal Institute for Population Research (1992). German FFS questionnaire. Available from http://www.unece.org/pau/ffs/germany_eng.pdf (accessed 07 November 2006).

_____, and the Robert Bosch Foundation (2005). *The Demographic Future of Europe—Facts, Figures, Policies. Results of the Population Policy Acceptance Study (PPAS)*. Available from http://www.bosch-stiftung.de/content/language1/downloads/PPAS_en.pdf (accessed 30 October 2006).

Germany, Federal Statistical Office (1997). *Statistical Yearbook 1997*. Wiesbaden, Germany.

_____ (1998). *Statistical Yearbook 1998. Federal Statistical Office*. Wiesbaden, Germany.

_____ (1999). *Statistical Yearbook 1999. Federal Statistical Office*. Wiesbaden, Germany.

_____ (2000). *Statistical Yearbook 2000. Federal Statistical Office*. Wiesbaden, Germany.

_____ (2001). *Statistical Yearbook 2001. Federal Statistical Office*. Wiesbaden, Germany.

_____ (2002). *Statistical Yearbook 2002. Federal Statistical Office*. Wiesbaden, Germany.

_____ (2003). *Statistical Yearbook 2003. Federal Statistical Office*. Wiesbaden, Germany.

_____ (2004). *Statistical Yearbook 2004. Federal Statistical Office*. Wiesbaden, Germany.

United Nations (1994). Initial reports of States parties due in 1994: Germany (CRC/C/11/Add.5).

_____ (2003). Second periodic reports of States parties due in 1999: Germany (CRC/C/83/Add.7).

_____ (2004). Written replies by the Government of Germany (CRC/C/RESP/GER/2) concerning the list of issues received by the Committee on the Rights of the Child (CRC/C/Q/DEU/2) relating to the consideration of the second periodic report of Germany.

Ghana

United Nations (2005). Second periodic reports of States parties due in 1997: Ghana (CRC/C/65/Add.34).

Greece

United Nations (2001). Initial reports of States parties due in 1995: Greece (CRC/C/28/Add.17).

_____ (2002). Written replies by the Government of Greece (CRC/C/RESP/GRE/1) concerning the list of issues received by the Committee on the Rights of the Child (CRC/C/Q/GRE/1) relating to the consideration of the initial report of Greece.

United States, Bureau of Consular Affairs (2006). International adoption: Greece. Washington, D.C.: Department of State. Available from http://travel.state.gov/family/adoption/country/country_387.html (accessed 27 October 2006).

Grenada

United Nations (1997). Initial reports of States parties due in 1992: Grenada (CRC/C/3/Add.55).

United States, Bureau of Consular Affairs (2005). International adoption: Grenada. Washington, D.C.: Department of State. Available from http://travel.state.gov/family/adoption/country/country_388.html (accessed 27 October 2006).

Guatemala

Guatemala (n.d.). Civil Code, book I, title II, chapter VI. Available from http://www.mintrabajo.gob.gt/varios/compendio_leyes/codigo_civil (accessed 12 February 2006).

Guatemala, Office of the National Procurator-General (2005): Response to the 2005 questionnaire on the practical operation of the Hague Convention of 29 May 1993 on Protection of Children and Co-operation in Respect of Intercountry Adoption. Available from http://www.hcch.net/upload/adop2005_gt.pdf (accessed 6 July 2006).

United Nations (1995). Initial reports of States parties due in 1992: Guatemala (CRC/C/3/Add.33).

_____ (2000). Second periodic reports of States parties due in 1997: Guatemala (CRC/C/65/Add.10).

_____ (2001). Written replies by the Government of Guatemala (CRC/C/RESP/GUA2) concerning the list of issues received by the Committee on the Rights of the Child (CRC/C/Q/GUA/2) relating to the consideration of the second periodic report of Guatemala.

United States, Bureau of Consular Affairs (2007). International adoption: Guatemala. Washington, D.C.: Department of State. Available from http://travel.state.gov/family/adoption/country/country_389.html (accessed 14 June 2007).

Guinea

United Nations (1997). Initial reports awaited from the States parties for 1992: Guinea (CRC/C/3/Add.48).

United States, Bureau of Consular Affairs (2006). International adoption: Guinea. Washington, D.C.: Department of State. Available from http://travel.state.gov/family/adoption/country/country_390.html (accessed 27 October 2006).

Guinea-Bissau

United Nations (2001). Initial reports of States parties due in 1992: Guinea-Bissau (CRC/C/3/Add.63).

_____ (2002). Written replies by the Government of Guinea-Bissau (CRC/C/RESP/GUIB/1) concerning the list of issues received by the Committee on the Rights of the Child (CRC/C/Q/GUIB/1) relating to the consideration of the initial report of Guinea-Bissau.

Guyana

United Nations (2003a). Initial reports of States parties due in 1993: Guyana (CRC/C/8/Add.47).

_____ (2003b). Written replies by the Government of Guyana (CRC/C/RESP/47) concerning the list of issues received by the Committee on the Rights of the Child (CRC/C/Q/GUY/1) relating to the consideration of the initial report of Guyana.

Haiti

United Nations (2002a). Initial reports of States parties due in 1997: Haiti (CRC/C/51/Add.7).

_____ (2002b). Written replies by the Government of Haiti (CRC/C/RESP/21) concerning the list of issues received by the Committee on the Rights of the Child (CRC/C/Q/HAI/1) relating to the consideration of the initial report of Haiti.

Honduras

United Nations (1998). Periodic reports of States parties due in 1997: Honduras (CRC/C/65/Add.2).

Hungary

Hungary, Central Statistical Office (2000). *Statistical Yearbook 1999*. Budapest.

_____ (2001). *Statistical Yearbook 2000*. Budapest.

_____ (2002). *Statistical Yearbook 2001*. Budapest.

_____ (2003). *Statistical Yearbook 2002*. Budapest.

Hungary, Ministry of Youth, Family, Social Affaires and Equal Opportunities (2005). Response to the 2005 questionnaire on the practical operation of the Hague Convention of 29 May 1993 on Protection of Children and Co-operation in Respect of Intercountry Adoption. Available from http://www.hcch.net/upload/adop2005_hu.pdf (accessed 6 July 2006).

United Nations (2003). Report of the Government of the Republic of Hungary on its measures adopted for the implementation of the rights recognized in the Convention on the Rights of the Child, Periodic Report No. 2-3.

_____ (2005a). Second periodic reports of States parties due in 1998. Hungary (CRC/C/70/Add.25).

_____ (2005b). Written replies by the Government of Hungary (CRC/C/HUN/Q/2/Add.1) concerning the list of issues received by the Committee on the Rights of the Child (CRC/C/HUN/Q/2) relating to the consideration of the second periodic report of Hungary.

Iceland

Iceland, Ministry of Justice and Ecclesiastical Affairs (1999). Adoption Act, No. 130/1999. Available from http://eng.domsmalaraduneyti.is/laws-and-regulations/nr/90 (accessed 31 October 2006).

Iceland, Statistics Iceland (2003). *Statistical Yearbook 2003*. Reykjavík. Available from http://www.statice.is/?PageID=1342 (accessed 27 October 2006).

_____ (2004). *Statistical Yearbook 2004*. Reykjavík. Available from http://www.statice.is/ ?PageID=1342 (accessed 27 October 2006).

United Nations (2002). Periodic reports of States parties due in 1999: Iceland (CRC/C/83/Add.5).

India

India (2005). Response to the 2005 questionnaire on the practical operation of the Hague Convention of 29 May 1993 on Protection of Children and Co-operation in Respect of Intercountry Adoption. Available from http://www.hcch.net/upload/adop2005_in.pdf (accessed 6 July 2006).

_____ (n.d.). The Hindu Adoptions and Maintenance Act, No. 78 of 21 December 1956. Available from http://nrcw.nic.in/shared/sublinkimages/67.htm (accessed 30 October 2006).

India, Central Adoption Resource Agency (2006). Guidelines for adoption from India: 2006. Available from http://cara.nic.in/adoptionfromindia.htm (accessed 12 May 2006).

_____ (n.d.). Database. Available from http://www.cara.nic.in/carahome.html (accessed 27 October 2006).

India, Ministry of Women and Child Development. Quantitative Database. Available from http://wcd.nic.in/qdatabase.htm (accessed 07 November 2006).

United Nations (2003). Second periodic reports of States parties due in 2000: India (CRC/C/93/Add.5).

_____ (2004). Written replies by the Government of India (CRC/C/RESP/IND/2) concerning the list of issues received by the Committee on the Rights of the Child (CRC/C/Q/IND/2) relating to the consideration of the second periodic report of India.

Indonesia

United Nations (2003). Second periodic reports of States parties due in 1997: Indonesia (CRC/C/65/Add.23).

United States, Embassy to Indonesia (2006). Adopting Children in Indonesia. Available from http://jakarta.usembassy.gov/consular/ivadoptions.html (accessed 27 October 2006).

Ireland

Ireland (n.d.). Adoption Act, No. 25, 13 December 1952. Available from http://www.adoptionboard.ie/legislation/index.php (accessed 30 October 2006).

Ireland, The Adoption Board (2004). *Report of an Board Uchtála*. Dublin: The Stationery Office. Available from http://www.adoptionboard.ie/booklets/adoption_report_nov_25.pdf (accessed 27 October 2006).

_____ (n.d.). Domestic adoption in Ireland: an introduction to domestic adoption in Ireland. Available from http://www.adoptionboard.ie/domestic/index.php (accessed 12 February 2006).

Ireland, Department of Health and Children (2003). Minister Lenihan announces a bilateral adoption agreement between Ireland and Vietnam. Available from http://www.dohc.ie/press/releases/2003/20030716a.html (accessed 21 February 2006).

Ireland, International Adoption Association (n.d.). Bilateral agreements. Available from http://www.iaaireland.org/guide/bilateralagreements.htm (accessed 12 February 2006).

United Nations (1996). Initial reports of States parties due in 1994: Ireland (CRC/C/11/Add.12).

_____ (2005). Second periodic reports of States parties due in 1999: Ireland (CRC/C/IRL/2).

Israel

Israel (2005).Response to the 2005 questionnaire on the practical operation of the Hague Convention of 29 May 1993 on Protection of Children and Co-operation in Respect of Intercountry Adoption. Available from http://www.hcch.net/upload/adop2005_il.pdf (accessed 6 July 2006)

United Nations (2002). Periodic reports of States parties due in 1993: Israel (CRC/C/8/Add.44).

Italy

Italy, Commission on Intercountry Adoptions (2005). Response to the 2005 questionnaire on the practical operation of the Hague Convention of 29 May 1993 on Protection of Children and Co-operation in Respect of Intercountry Adoption. Available from http://www.hcch.net/upload/adop2005_it.pdf (accessed 6 July 2006)

Italy, Ministry of Justice (2001). Law No. 149 of 28 March 2001. Available from http://www.giustizia.it/cassazione/leggi/l149_01.html (accessed 30 October 2006).

_____ (2003). *Disciplina dell'Adozione e dell'Affidamento dei Minori negli Anni 1993-1999, Analisi Statistica*. Rome. Available from http://www.giustizia.it/statistiche/statistiche_dgm/analisi_statistiche/adoz1993_99.htm (accessed 27 October 2006).

_____ (n.d.). Model of an Adoption Register. Available from http://www.giustizia.it/documentazione/unico/modello30.pdf (accessed 07 November 2006).

_____ (n.d.). *Banca Dati dei Minori Adottabili*. Available from http://www.giustizia.it/minori/adozioni/banca_dati_min_adottabili.htm (accessed 07 November 2006).

Italy, Ministry of Labour and Social Policies (2003). Legge 24 novembre 2003, n. 326, "Conversione in legge, con modificazioni, del decreto-legge 30 settembre 2003, n. 269, recante disposizioni urgenti per favorire lo sviluppo e per la correzione dell'andamento dei conti pubblici".

Italy, National Statistical Institute (2005). Le coppie che chiedono l'adozione di un bambino. Anno 2003. Available from http://www.istat.it/salastampa/comunicati/non_calendario/20050201_01/testointegrale.pdf (accessed 26 October 2006).

Italy, Office of the Prime Minister, Commission for Intercountry Adoption (2004). Coppie e bambini nelle adozioni internazionali. Florence: UNICEF Innocenti Research Centre. Available from http://www.commissioneadozioni.it/FileServices/Download.aspx?id=83 (accessed 27 October 2006).

_____ (2005). Coppie e bambini nelle adozioni internazionali. Florence: UNICEF Innocenti Research Centre.

_____ (2006). Coppie e bambini nelle adozioni internazionali. Florence: UNICEF Innocenti Research

Centre. Available from http://www.commissioneado
zioni.it/FileServices/Download.aspx?ID=244
(accessed 02 October 2007).
United Nations (1995). Initial reports of States parties
due in 1993: Italy (CRC/C/8/Add.18).
_____ (2002). Periodic reports of States parties
due in 1998: Italy (CRC/C/70/Add.13).

Jamaica

United Nations (1994). Initial reports of States parties
due in 1993: Jamaica (CRC/C/8/Add.12).
_____ (2003). Periodic reports of States parties
due in 1998: Jamaica (CRC/C/70/Add.15).
_____ (2003). Written replies by the
Government of Jamaica (CRC/C/RESP/JAM/2)
concerning the list of issues received by the
Committee on the Rights of the Child
(CRC/C/Q/JAM/2) relating to the consideration of
the second periodic report of Jamaica.
United States, Bureau of Consular Affairs (2006).
International adoption: Jamaica. Washington,
D.C.: Department of State. Available from
http://travel.state.gov/family/adoption/country/cou
ntry_404.html (accessed 27 October 2006).

Japan

Japan (2005). Response to the 2005 questionnaire on
the practical operation of the Hague Convention of
29 May 1993 on Protection of Children and Co-
operation in Respect of Intercountry Adoption.
Available from http://www.hcch.net/upload/adop
2005_jp.pdf (accessed 6 July 2006)
United Nations (1996). Initial reports of States parties
due in 1996: Japan. (CRC/C/41/Add.1).
_____ (2003). Second periodic reports of States
parties due in 2001: Japan (CRC/C/104/Add.2).
_____ (2004). Written replies by the
Government of Japan (CRC/C/RESP/JAP/2)
concerning the list of issues received by the
Committee on the Rights of the - Child
(CRC/C/Q/JPN/2) relating to the consideration of
the second periodic report of Japan.

Jordan

United Nations (1993). Initial reports of States parties
due in 1993: Jordan (CRC/C/8/Add.4).
_____ (1999). Periodic reports of States parties
due in 1998: Jordan (CRC/C/70/Add.4).
_____ (2005). Third periodic report of States
parties due in 2003: Jordan (CRC/C/JOR/3).

Kazakhstan

United Nations (2002). Initial reports of States parties
due in 1996: Kazakhstan (CRC/C/41/Add.13).
_____ (2003). Written replies by the Government
of Kazakhstan (CRC/C/RESP/27) concerning the
list of issues received by the Committee on the
Rights of the Child (CRC/C/Q/KAZ/1) relating to
the consideration of the initial report of Kazakhstan.
United States, Bureau of Consular Affairs (2006).
International adoption: Kazakhstan. Washington,
D.C.: Department of State. Available from
http://travel.state.gov/family/adoption/country/count
ry_408.html (accessed 27 October 2006).

Kenya

United Nations (2001). Initial reports of States parties
due in 1992: Kenya (CRC/C/3/Add.62).
_____ (2006). Second periodic reports of States
parties due in 1997: Kenya (CRC/C/KEN/2).

Kiribati

United Nations (2005). Initial report of States parties
due in 1998: Kiribati (CRC/C/KIR/1).

Kyrgyzstan

United Nations (2004). Second periodic reports of
States parties due in 2001: Kyrgyzstan
(CRC/C/104/Add.4).

Lao People's Democratic Republic

United Nations (1996). Initial reports of States parties
due in 1993: Lao People's Democratic Republic
(CRC/C/8/Add.32).

Latvia

Latvia, Ministry for Children and Family Affairs
(2005). Response to the 2005 questionnaire on the
practical operation of the Hague Convention of
29 May 1993 on Protection of Children and Co-
operation in Respect of Intercountry Adoption.
Available from http://www.hc ch.net/upload/adop
2005_lv.pdf (accessed 6 July 2006)
_____ (2007). *Adoption to Foreign Countries
1st November, 2006.* Available from
http://www.bm.gov.lv/eng/adoption/statistics/?doc
=4998 (accessed 07 December 2007).

Latvia, Translation and Terminology Centre (2001). The Civil Law of Latvia. Riga. Available from http://www.ttc.lv/lv/publikacijas/civillikums.pdf (accessed 27 October 2006).

United Nations (2000). Initial reports of States parties due in 1994: Latvia (CRC/C/11/Add.22).

_____ (2005a). Second periodic reports of States parties due in 1999: Latvia (CRC/C/83/Add.16).

_____ (2005b). Written replies by the Government of Latvia (CRC/C/RESP/LVA/2) concerning the list of issues received by the Committee on the Rights of the Child (CRC/C/LVA/Q/2) relating to the consideration of the second periodic report of Latvia.

United Nations Children's Fund (UNICEF) (2003). Situation analysis of children and women in Latvia 2003. Republic of Latvia National Committee for UNICEF. Riga: Republic of Latvia National Committee for UNICEF.

Vaskis, E., co-ordinator (2000). Trends and indicators on child and family well-being in Latvia. Background paper prepared for *A Decade of Transition. Regional Monitoring Report*, No. 8. Riga, Latvia: Central Statistical Bureau of Latvia; and Florence, Italy: UNICEF Innocenti Research Centre.

_____ (2001). Poverty and welfare trends in Latvia over the 1990s. Background paper prepared for the *Innocenti Social Monitor, 2002*. Riga, Latvia: Central Statistical Bureau of Latvia and Florence, Italy: UNICEF Innocenti Research Centre.

Lebanon

United Nations (1995). Initial reports of States parties due in 1993: Lebanon (CRC/C/8/Add.23).

_____ (2002). Written replies by the Government of Lebanon (CRC/C/70/Add.8) concerning the list of issues received by the Committee on the Rights of the Child (CRC/C/Q/LEB/2) relating to the consideration of the second report of Lebanon.

_____ (2005). Third periodic reports of States parties due in 2003: Lebanon (CRC/C/129/Add.7).

United States, Bureau of Consular Affairs (2007). International adoption: Lebanon. Washington, D.C.: Department of State. Available from http://travel.state.gov/family/adoption/country/country_412.html (accessed 10 October 2007).

Lesotho

United Nations (1998). Initial reports of States parties due in 1994: Lesotho (CRC/C/11/Add.20).

Liberia

United Nations (2003). Initial reports of States parties due in 1995: Liberia (CRC/C/28/Add.21).

Liechtenstein

United Nations (1999). Initial report of States parties due in 1998: Liechtenstein (CRC/C/61/Add.1).

_____ (2005). Second periodic reports of States parties due in 2003: Liechtenstein (CRC/C/136/Add.2).

Lithuania

Lithuania, Ministry of Social Security and Labour (2005). Response to the 2005 questionnaire on the practical operation of the Hague Convention of 29 May 1993 on Protection of Children and Co-operation in Respect of Intercountry Adoption. Available from http://www.hcch.net/index_en.php?act=publications.details&pid=3540&dtid=33 (accessed 6 July 2006).

United Nations (1998). Initial reports of States parties due in 1994: Lithuania (CRC/C/11/Add.21).

_____ (2004). Second periodic reports of States parties due in 1999: Lithuania (CRC/C/83/Add.14).

Luxembourg

Luxembourg, Ministry of the Family, Social Solidarity and Youth (2005). Response to the 2005 questionnaire on the practical operation of the Hague Convention of 29 May 1993 on Protection of Children and Co-operation in Respect of Intercountry Adoption. Available from http://www.hcch.net/upload/adop2005_lu.pdf (accessed 6 July 2006).

Luxembourg, Central Service of Statistics and Economic Studies. (2006). *Statistiques des Adoptions 1997-2006*. Available from http://www.statistiques.public.lu/stat/TableViewer/tableView.aspx?ReportId=1162 (accessed 04 December 2007).

United Nations (1997). Initial reports of States parties due in 1996: Luxembourg (CRC/C/41/Add.2).

_____ (2004). Written replies by the Government of Luxembourg (CRC/C/RESP/79) concerning the list of issues received by the Committee on the Rights of the Child (CRC/C/Q/LUX/2) relating to the consideration of the initial report of Luxembourg.

Madagascar

United Nations (2003). Second periodic reports of States parties due in 1998: Madagascar (CRC/C/70/Add.18).

Malawi

United Nations (2001). Initial reports of States parties due in 1993: Malawi (CRC/C/8/Add.43).

_____ (2002). Written replies by the Government of Malawi (CRC/C/8/Add.43) concerning the list of issues received by the Committee on the Rights of the Child (CRC/C/Q/MALA/1) relating to the consideration of the initial report of Malawi.

Malaysia

Malaysia, Department of Social Welfare (1952). Adoption Act 1952 (Act 257).

_____ (n.d.). Registration of Adoption Act 1952 (Act 253). Department of Social Welfare.

United Nations (2006). Initial report of States parties due in 1997: Malaysia (CRC/C/MYS/1).

Maldives

United Nations (1996). Initial reports of States parties due in 1993: Maldives (CRC/C/8/Add.33).

_____ (2006). Second and third periodic reports of States parties due in 1998 and 2003: Maldives (CRC/C/MDV/3).

Mali

United Nations (1997). Initial reports of States parties due in 1992: Mali (CRC/C/3/Add.53).

_____ (2005). Second periodic reports of States parties due in 1997: Mali (CRC/C/MLI/2).

Malta

Malta (2005). Response to the 2005 questionnaire on the practical operation of the Hague Convention of 29 May 1993 on Protection of Children and Co-operation in Respect of Intercountry Adoption. Available from http://www.hcch.net/upload/adop20 05_mt.pdf (accessed 6 July 2006).

Malta, Ministry of Justice (n.d.) Chapter 16, Civil Code.

Malta, National Statistics Office (2003). Adoptions in Malta, 1995-2002. News release, No.19/2003: 18 February. Available from https://secure.gov.mt/nso/statdoc/docum ent_file.aspx?id=594 (accessed 27 October 2006).

United Nations (1998). Initial reports of States parties due in 1992: Malta (CRC/C/3/Add.56).

Marshall Islands

Marshall Islands (2002). Public Law 2002-64, Bill No. 92 N.D.2. 23rd Constitutional Regular Session, Nitijela of the Marshall Islands.

United Nations (1998). Initial reports of States parties due in 1995: Marshall Islands (CRC/C/28/Add.12).

_____ (2005). Second periodic reports of States parties due in 2000: Marshall Islands (CRC/C/93/Add.8).

Mauritania

United Nations (2001a). Initial reports of States parties due in 1993: Mauritania (CRC/C/8/Add.42).

_____ (2001b). Written replies by the Government of Mauritania (CRC/C/RESP/ MAU/1) concerning the list of issues received by the Committee on the Rights of the Child (CRC/C/Q/MAU/1) relating to the consideration of the initial report of Mauritania.

Mauritius

United Nations (1995). Initial report of States Parties due in 1992: Mauritius (CRC/C/3/Add.36).

_____ (2005). Second periodic report of States parties due in 1997: Mauritius (CRC/C/65/Add.35).

Mexico

Mexico (2005). Response to the 2005 questionnaire on the practical operation of the Hague Convention of 29 May 1993 on Protection of Children and Co-operation in Respect of Intercountry Adoption. Available from http://www.hcch.net/upload/adop2005_mx.pdf (accessed 6 July 2006)

_____ (n.d.). Civil Code, book I, title VII, chapter V. Available from http://www.diputados.gob.mx/Leyes Biblio/pdf/2.pdf (accessed 12 February 2006).

Mexico, State System for the Full Development of the Family (2003). 393 adopciones tramitadas en 2002, 55 de carácter internacional. *Reforma*, 29 junio.

United Nations (1993). Initial reports of States parties due in 1992: Mexico (CRC/C/3/Add.11).

_____ (1998). Periodic reports of States parties due in 1997: Mexico (CRC/C/65/Add.6).

_____ (2004). Third periodic reports of States parties due in 2002: Mexico (CRC/C/125/Add.7).

World Health Organization, Pan American Health Organization and Mexico, National Institute of Statistics, Geography and Informatics, and Ministry of Health (1999). *Encuesta sobre Salud,*

Bienestar y Envejecimiento en América Latina y el Caribe. Available from http://www.ssc.wisc.edu/sabe/question/mexQuest.pdf (accessed 07 November 2006).

Micronesia (Federated States of)

Federated States of Micronesia (n.d.). 2000 Census of Population and Housing. Available from http://unstats.un.org/unsd/demographic/sources/census/quest/FSM/Eng2000.pdf (accessed 07 November 2006).

United Nations (1996). Initial reports of States parties due in 1995: Federated States of Micronesia (CRC/C/28/Add.5).

Monaco

Monaco (2005). Response to the 2005 questionnaire on the practical operation of the Hague Convention of 29 May 1993 on Protection of Children and Co-operation in Respect of Intercountry Adoption. Available from http://www.hcch.net/upload/adop2005_mc.pdf (accessed 6 July 2006).

United Nations (2000). Initial reports of States parties due in 1995: Monaco (CRC/C/28/Add.15).

Mongolia

United Nations (1995). Initial reports of States parties due in 1992: Mongolia (CRC/C/3/Add.32).

_____ (2004). Second periodic reports of States parties due in 1997: Mongolia (CRC/C/65/Add.32).

_____ (2005). Written replies by the Government of Mongolia (CRC/C/RESP/87) concerning the list of issues) received by the Committee on the Rights of the Child (CRC/C/Q/MNG/2) relating to the consideration of the second periodic report of Mongolia.

Mozambique

United Nations (2001). Initial report of States parties due in 1996: Mozambique (CRC/C/41/Add.11).

Myanmar

United Nations (2003). Second periodic reports of States parties due in 1998: Myanmar (CRC/C/70/Add.21).

Namibia

United Nations (1993). Initial reports of States parties due in 1992: Namibia (CRC/C/3/Add.12).

Nepal

United Nations (1995). Initial reports of States parties due in 1992: Nepal (CRC/C/3/Add.34).

_____ (2004). Second periodic report of States parties due in 1997: Nepal (CRC/C/65/Add.30).

Netherlands

Netherlands (2005). Response to the 2005 questionnaire on the practical operation of the Hague Convention of 29 May 1993 on Protection of Children and Co-operation in Respect of Intercountry Adoption. Available from http://www.hcch.net/index_en.php?act=publications.details&pid=3544&dtid=33 (accessed 6 July 2006)

Netherlands, Statistics Netherlands (2005a). Adoptions from China continue to rise. Web Magazine. Available from http://www.cbs.nl/en-GB/menu/themas/bevolking/publicaties/artikelen/archief/2005/2005-1722-wm.htm (accessed 30 October 2006).

_____ (2005b). *Statistical Yearbook of the Netherlands 2005*.

_____ (2007). *Statistical Yearbook of the Netherlands 2007*.

United Nations (1997). Initial reports of States parties due in 1997: the Netherlands (CRC/C/51/Add.1).

_____ (2003a). Second periodic reports of States parties due in 2002: the Netherlands (CRC/C/117/Add.1).

_____ (2003b). Written replies by the Government of the Netherlands including Aruba (CRC/C/RESP/48) concerning the list of issues received by the Committee on the Rights of the Child (CRC/C/Q/NLD/2) relating to the consideration of the second periodic report of the Netherlands including the initial report of Aruba.

New Zealand

New Zealand, Department of Child, Youth and Family Services (2005). Response to the 2005 questionnaire on the practical operation of the Hague Convention of 29 May 1993 on Protection of Children and Co-operation in Respect of Intercountry Adoption. Available from http://www.hcch.net/index_en.php?act=publications.details&pid=3545&dtid=33 (accessed 23 October 2006s).

New Zealand, Law Commission (1999). Adoption: options for reform. *Preliminary Paper 38*. Wellington. Available from http://www.lawcom govt.nz/UploadFiles/Publications/Publication_72_143_PP38.pdf (accessed 23 October 2006).

_____ (2000). Adoption and its alternatives: a different approach and a new framework. *New Zealand Law Commission Report*, No. 65. Wellington. Available from http://www.lawcom.govt.nz/UploadFiles/Publications/Publication_72_144_R65.pdf?ProjectID=72 (accessed 23 October 2006).

_____ (2006). Access to court records–terms of reference. *New Zealand Law Commission Report*, No. 93. Wellington. Available from http://www.lawcom.govt.nz/UploadFiles/Publications/Publication_119_330_R93.pdf (accessed 04 December 2007).

New Zealand, Ministry of Justice (2005). Introduction to the Care of Children Act. Wellington. Available from http://www.justice.govt.nz/family/what-familycourt-does/children/introduction.asp (accessed 30 October 2006).

New Zealand, Ministry of Social Policy (2001). *Social Services Sector Statistical Report for the Year Ending 2000*. Wellington.

United Nations (1995). Initial reports of States parties due in 1995: New Zealand (CRC/C/28/Add.3).

_____ (2003). Second periodic reports of States parties due in 2000: New Zealand (CRC/C/93/Add.4).

Nicaragua

United Nations (1998). Periodic reports of States parties due in 1997: Nicaragua (CRC/C/65/Add.4).

_____ (2004). Third periodic reports of States parties due in 2002: Nicaragua (CRC/C/125/Add.3).

_____ (2005). Written replies by the Government of Nicaragua (CRC/C/RESP/83) concerning the list of issues) received by the Committee on the Rights of the Child (CRC/C/Q/NIC/3) relating to the consideration of the third periodic report of Nicaragua.

Niger

United Nations (2001). Initial reports of States parties due in 1992: Niger (CRC/C/3/Add.29/Rev.1).

United States, Bureau of Consular Affairs (2006). International adoption: Niger. Washington, D.C.: Department of State. Available from http://travel.state.gov/family/adoption/country/country_428.html (accessed 27 October 2006).

Nigeria

United Nations (1995). Initial reports of States parties due in 1993: Nigeria (CRC/C/8/Add.26).

_____ (2004a). Second periodic reports of States parties due in 1998: Nigeria (CRC/C/70/Add.24).

_____ (2004b). Written replies by the Government of Nigeria (CRC/C/RESP/72) concerning the list of issues received by the Committee on the Rights of the Child (CRC/C/Q/NGA/2) relating to the consideration of the second periodic report of Nigeria (CRC/C/70/Add.24).

Norway

Norway (2005). Response to the 2005 questionnaire on the practical operation of the Hague Convention of 29 May 1993 on Protection of Children and Co-operation in Respect of Intercountry Adoption. Available from http://www.hcch.net/upload/adop2005_no.pdf (accessed 6 July 2006).

Norway, Ministry of Children and Family Affairs (1986). Act of 28 February 1986 No. 8 relating to adoption. Available from http://www.dep.no/bld/english/doc/legislation/acts/004021-200002/dok-bn.html (accessed 27 October 2006).

Norway, Statistics Norway (2004a). Adoptions 2004, Population Statistics. http://www.ssb.no/vis/english/subjects/02/02/10/adopsjon_en/art-2005-06-16-01-en.html (accessed 18 January 2006).

_____ (2004b). Population statistics. Marriages and divorces. Available from http://www.ssb.no/skilsmisse_en/ arkiv/tab-2005-09-01-03-en.html (accessed 30 October 2006).

United Nations (1993). Initial reports of States parties due in 1992: Norway (CRC/C/8/Add.7).

_____ (1998). Periodic reports of States parties due in 1998: Norway (CRC/C/70/Add.2).

_____ (2004). Third periodic report of States parties due in 2003: Norway (CRC/C/129/Add.1).

Oman

United Nations (2000). Initial reports of States parties due in 1999: Oman (CRC/C/78/Add.1).

_____ (2006). Second periodic report of States parties due in 2004: Oman (CRC/C/OMN/2).

United States, Bureau of Consular Affairs (n.d.). International adoption: Oman. Washington, D.C.: Department of State. Available from http://travel.state.gov/family/adoption/country/country_430.html (accessed 27 October 2006).

Palau

United Nations (2000). Initial reports of States parties due in 1997: Palau (CRC/C/51/Add.3).

Panama

Panama, Ministry of Youth, Women, Children and the Family (2005). Response to the 2005 questionnaire on the practical operation of the Hague Convention of 29 May 1993 on Protection of Children and Co-operation in Respect of Intercountry Adoption. Available from http://www.hcch.net/index_en.php? act=publications.details&pid=3565&dtid=33 (accessed 6 July 2006).

United Nations (1995). Initial reports of States parties due in 1993: Panama (CRC/C/8/Add.28).

_____ (2003). Second periodic reports of States parties due in 1998: Panama (CRC/C/70/Add.20).

_____ (2004). Written replies by the Government of Panama (CRC/C/RESP/62) concerning the list of issues received by the Committee on the Rights of the Child (CRC/C/Q/PAN/2) relating to the consideration of the second periodic report of Panama.

Papua New Guinea

United Nations (2003). Initial reports of States parties due in 2000: Papua New Guinea (CRC/C/28/Add.20).

Paraguay

United Nations (1993). Initial reports of States parties due in 1992: Paraguay (CRC/C/3/Add.22).

_____ (2001a). Periodic reports of States parties due in 1997: Paraguay (CRC/C/65/Add.12).

_____ (2001b). Written replies by the Government of Paraguay (CRC/C/RESP/PAR/2) concerning the list of issues received by the Committee on the Rights of the Child (CRC/C/Q/PAR/2) relating to the consideration of the second periodic report of Paraguay.

United States, Bureau of Consular Affairs (2006). International adoption: Paraguay. Washington, D.C.: Department of State. Available from http://travel.state. gov/family/adoption/country/country_434.html (accessed 27 October 2006).

Peru

Peru, National Secretariat for Adoptions (2004). *Estadísticas sobre Adopciones*. Available from http://www.mim des.gob.pe/sna/estadistica.htm (accessed 27 October 2006).

_____ (2005). Response to the 2005 questionnaire on the practical operation of the Hague Convention of 29 May 1993 on Protection of Children and Co-operation in Respect of Intercountry Adoption. Available from http://www.hcch.net/upload/adop20 05_pe .pdf (accessed 6 July 2006)

United Nations (1998). Periodic reports of States parties due in 1997: Peru (CRC/C/65/Add.8).

_____ (2005). Third periodic reports of States parties due in 2004: Peru (CRC/C/125/Add.6).

United States, Bureau of Consular Affairs (2006). International adoption: Peru. Washington, D.C.: Department of State. Available from http://travel.state.g ov/family/adoption/country/country_435.html (accessed 27 October 2006).

Philippines

Flores-Oebanda, C. (2006). Addressing vulnerability and exploitation of child domestic workers: an open challenge to end a hidden shame. Paper presented at the Expert Group Meeting "Elimination of all forms of discrimination and violence against the girl child", UNICEF Innocenti Research Centre, Florence, Italy, 25-28 September 2006. Available from http://www.un. org/womenwatch/daw/egm/elim-disc-viol-girlchild/Ex pertPapers/EP.10%20%20Flores%20Oebanda.pdf (accessed 12 November 2006).

United Kingdom, Department for Children, Schools and Families (2006). "Intercountry adoption". Available from http://www.dfes.gov.uk/intercountryadoption/ (accessed 28 November 2006).

United Nations (1993). Initial reports of States parties due in 1992: Philippines (CRC/C/3/Add.23).

_____ (2004). Second periodic reports of States parties due in 1997: Philippines (CRC/C/65/Add.31).

_____ (2005). Written replies by the Government of Philippines (CRC/C/RESP/84) concerning the list of issues received by the Committee on the Rights of the Child (CRC/C/Q/PHL/2) relating to the consideration of the second periodic report of Philippines.

United States, Bureau of Consular Affairs (n.d.). International adoption: the Philippines. Washington, D.C.: Department of State. Available from http://travel. state.gov/family/adoption/country/country_437.html (accessed 27 October 2006).

Poland

Galazka, Z. (2001). Trends and Indicators on Child and Family Well-Being in Poland. Background paper prepared for *A Decade of Transition. Regional Monitoring Report*, No. 8. Florence, Italy: UNICEF Innocenti Research Centre. Available from http://www.unicef-icdc.org/research/ESP/Country

Reports2000_01/Poland00.pdf (accessed 27 October 2006).

Poland (2005). Response to the 2005 questionnaire on the practical operation of the Hague Convention of 29 May 1993 on Protection of Children and Co-operation in Respect of Intercountry Adoption. Available from http://www.hcch.net/upload/adop 2005_pl.pdf (accessed 6 July 2006)

United Nations (1994). Initial reports of States parties due in 1993: Poland (CRC/C/8/Add.11).

_____ (2002a). Periodic reports of States parties due in 1998: Poland (CRC/C/70/Add.12).

_____ (2002b). Written replies from the Government of Poland (CRC/C/RESP/POL/2) concerning the list of issues received by the Committee on the Rights of the Child (CRC/C/Q/POL/2) relating to the second periodic report of Poland.

_____, Economic Commission for Europe, Warsaw School of Economics and Central Statistical Office of Poland (1991). Family and Fertility in Poland. Available from http://www.unece.org/pau/ffs/pol_pquest.pdf (accessed 07 November 2006).

Portugal

Portugal (2005). Response to the 2005 questionnaire on the practical operation of the Hague Convention of 29 May 1993 on Protection of Children and Co-operation in Respect of Intercountry Adoption. Available from http://www.hcch.net/upload/adop2005_pt.pdf (accessed 6 July 2006).

_____ (2001). Law No. 7 of 11 May 2001. Available from http://www.dgci.min-financas.pt/NR/rdonlyres/6EAE2583-AE4D-4584-9783-8E F09A46B655/0/lei_7-2001_de_11_de_maio_i_seri e_a.pdf (accessed 12 February 2006).

_____ (n.d.). Civil Code, book IV, title IV. Available from http://www.confap.pt/docs/cod civil.PDF (accessed 2 February 2007).

United Nations (1994). Initial reports of States parties due in 1992: Portugal (CRC/C/3/Add.30).

_____ (2001). Periodic reports due in 1997: Portugal (CRC/C/65/Add.11).

Republic of Korea

Overseas Korean Foundation (n.d.). Guide to Korea for overseas adopted Koreans. Available from http://oaks. korean.net/download/pdf/guide-1.pdf (accessed 12 May 2006).

Republic of Korea, National Statistical Office (2004). *Yearbook of Health and Welfare Statistics*. Seoul: Ministry of Health and Welfare.

Republic of Korea, Ministry of Health and Welfare (2005). Domestic adoption of children increases 5% in 2004.

United Nations (2002). Periodic reports of States parties due in 1998: Republic of Korea (CRC/C/70/Add.14).

Republic of Moldova

Moldova (2005). Response to the 2005 questionnaire on the practical operation of the Hague Convention of 29 May 1993 on Protection of Children and Co-operation in Respect of Intercountry Adoption. Available from http://www.hcch.net/upload/adop2005_md.pdf (accessed 6 July 2006).

United Nations (2002a). Initial reports of States parties due in 1995: Republic of Moldova (CRC/C/28/Add.19).

_____ (2002b). Written replies by the Government of Moldova (CRC/C/RESP/14) concerning the list of issues received by the Committee on the Rights of the Child (CRC/C/Q/MOL/1) relating to the consideration of the initial report of Moldova.

Romania

Romania, Ministry of Labour, Social Solidarity and Family (2005). *Statistical Bulletin in the Field of Labour, Social Solidarity and Family*, No. 1 (49). Bucharest. Available from http://www.insse.ro/cms/files/pdf/ro/cap6.pdf (accessed 2 October 2007).

Romania, National Institute of Statistics (2001). *Analytical Report: Social Trends: Romania in the '90s*. Bucharest.

_____ (2004). *Romanian Statistical Yearbook 2004*. Bucharest.

Romania, Office for Adoption (2005). Response to the 2005 questionnaire on the practical operation of the Hague Convention of 29 May 1993 on Protection of Children and Co-operation in Respect of Intercountry Adoption. Available from http://www.hcch.net/index_en.php?act= publications.details&pid=3549&dtid=33 (accessed 6 July 2006).

Teodorescu, A.G. (2005). The Functioning of the new legislation on adoptions and provisions on defining the procedures in the moratorium. Paper presented at the Joint Parliamentary Committee European Union, Brussels, 22-23 November, 2005. Available from http://w ww.cdep.ro/docs_comisii/IE/CPM19_tema6_EN.pdf (accessed 12 May 2006).

United Nations (1993). Initial reports of States parties due in 1992: Romania (CRC/C/3/Add.16).

_____ (2002). Periodic reports of States parties due in 1997: Romania (CRC/C/65/Add.19).

_____ (2003). Written replies by the Government of Romania (CRC/C/RESP/ROM/1) concerning the list of issues received by the Committee on the Rights of the Child (CRC/C/Q/ROM/2) relating to the consideration of the second periodic report of Romania.

United States, Bureau of Consular Affairs (2004). Update on Romanian adoption moratorium, August 2004. Washington, D.C.: Department of State.

Russian Federation

United Nations (1998). Periodic reports of States parties due in 1997: Russian Federation (CRC/C/65/Add.5).

_____ (2003). Third periodic reports of States parties due in 2001: Russian Federation (CRC/C/125/Add.5).

_____ (2005). Written replies by the Government of the Russian Federation (CRC/C/RESP/92) concerning the list of issues received by the Committee on the Rights of the Child (CRC/C/Q/RUS/3) relating to the consideration of the third periodic report of the Russian Federation.

Rwanda

United Nations (2003). Second periodic reports of States Parties due in 1998: Rwanda (CRC/C/70/Add.22).

Saint Kitts and Nevis

United Nations (1997). Initial reports of States parties due in 1992: St. Kitts and Nevis (CRC/C/3/Add.51).

United States, Bureau of Consular Affairs (n. d.). International adoption: Saint Kitts and Nevis. Washington, D.C.: Department of State. Available from http://travel.state.gov/family/adoption/country/country_326.html (accessed 27 October 2006).

Saint Lucia

United Nations (2004). Initial reports of States parties due in 1995: Saint Lucia (CRC/C/28/Add.23).

Saint Vincent and the Grenadines

United Nations (2001). Initial reports of States parties due in 1995: Saint Vincent and the Grenadines (CRC/C/28/Add.18).

San Marino

United Nations (2003). Initial reports of States parties due in 1993: San Marino (CRC/C/8/Add.46).

Sao Tome and Principe

United Nations (2003). Initial reports of States parties due in 1993. Sao Tome and Principe: (CRC/C/8/Add.49).

Samoa

United Nations (2006). Initial report of States parties due in 1996: Samoa (CRC/C/WSM/1).

Saudi Arabia

United Nations (2005). Second periodic reports of States parties due in 2003: Saudi Arabia (CRC/C/136/Add.1).

Senegal

United Nations (1994). Initial reports of States parties due in 1992: Senegal (CRC/C/3/Add.31).

_____ (2006). Second periodic reports of States parties due in 1999: Senegal (CRC/C/SEN/2).

Serbia

Serbia and Montenegro (2005). Response to the 2005 questionnaire on the practical operation of the Hague Convention of 29 May 1993 on Protection of Children and Co-operation in Respect of Intercountry Adoption. Available from http://www.hcch.net/upload/adop2005_srp.pdf (accessed 6 July 2006).

Serbia and Montenegro, Statistical Office (2004). *Statistical Yearbook of Serbia and Montenegro*. Belgrade.

Seychelles

United Nations (2002). Initial reports of States parties due in 1995: Seychelles (CRC/C/3/Add.64).

_____ (2002). Written replies by the Government of Seychelles (CRC/C/RESP/17) concerning the list of issues received by the Committee on the Rights of the Child (CRC/C/Q/SEY/1) relating to the consideration of the initial report of Seychelles.

Sierra Leone

United Nations (1996). Initial reports of States parties due in 1992: Sierra Leone (CRC/C/3/Add.43).

United States, Bureau of Consular Affairs (2005). International adoption: Sierra Leone. Washington, D.C.: Department of State. Available from http://travel.state.gov/family/adoption/country/country_1475.html (accessed 23 September 2005).

Singapore

Singapore (1985). Adoption of Children Act (Chapter 4), 1985 revised edition. Available from http://statutes. agc.gov.sg/non_version/cgi-bin/cgi_getdata.pl?actno=1 939-REVED-4&doctitle=ADOPTION%20OF%20CH ILDREN%20ACT%0A&date=latest&method=whole (accessed 27 October 2006).

United Nations (2003a). Initial reports of States parties due in 1997: Singapore (CRC/C/51/Add.8).

_____ (2003b). Written replies by the Government of Singapore (CRC/C/RESP/43) concerning the list of issues received by the Committee on the Rights of the Child (CRC/C/Q/SGP/1) relating to the consideration of the initial report of Singapore.

Slovakia

Slovak Republic (2005). Response to the 2005 questionnaire on the practical operation of the Hague Convention of 29 May 1993 on Protection of Children and Co-operation in Respect of Intercountry Adoption. Available from http://www.hcch.net/index_ en.php?act =publications.details&pid=3550&dtid=33 (accessed 6 July 2006).

United Nations (1998). Initial reports of States parties due in 1994: Slovak Republic (CRC/C/11/Add.17).

_____ (2000). Written replies by the Government of Slovakia (CRC/C/RESP/SLO/1) concerning the list of issues received by the Committee on the Rights of the Child (CRC/C/Q/SLO/1) relating to the consideration of the initial report of Slovakia.

_____ (2006). Second periodic reports due in 1999: Slovakia (CRC/C/SVK/2).

Slovenia

Banovec, T. (2001). Trends and indicators on child and family well-being in Slovenia, 1989-1999. Background paper prepared for *A Decade of Transition. Regional Monitoring Report*, No. 8. Florence, Italy: UNICEF Innocenti Research Centre. Available from http://www.unicef-icdc.org/research/ESP/CountryRepor ts2000_01/Slovenia00.pdf (accessed 30 October 2006).

United Nations (1995). Initial report of States parties due in 1993: Slovenia (CRC/C/8/Add.25).

_____ (2003). Second periodic reports of States parties due in 1998: Slovenia (CRC/C/70/Add.19).

_____ (2004). Written replies by the Government of Slovenia (CRC/C/RESP/SVN/2) concerning the list of issues received by the Committee on the Rights of the Child (CRC/C/Q/SVN/2) relating to the consideration of the second periodic report of Slovenia.

Solomon Islands

United Nations (2002). Initial reports of States parties due in 1997: Solomon Islands (CRC/C/51/Add.6).

South Africa

South Africa (2005). Response to the 2005 questionnaire on the practical operation of the Hague Convention of 29 May 1993 on Protection of Children and Co-operation in Respect of Intercountry Adoption. Available from http://www.hcch.net/index_en.php? act=publications.details&pid=3558&dtid=33 (accessed 6 July 2006).

South Africa, Government Communication and Information System (2001). *South Africa Yearbook 2001/02*. Pretoria.

South Africa, Law Reform Commission (2002). Discussion Paper 103. Review of the Child Care Act. Available from http://web.uct.ac.za/depts/ci/plr/htm docs/bills/salr cdis.htm (accessed 30 October 2006).

South Africa, Statistics South Africa (n.d.). Census 2001. Household Questionnaire. Available from http://unstats.un.org/unsd/demographic/sources/ census/quest/ZAF/Orig2001_hh.pdf (accessed 07 November 2006).

United Nations (1999). Initial reports of States parties due in 1997: South Africa (CRC/C/51/Add.2).

Spain

Spain (2005). Response to the 2005 questionnaire on the practical operation of the Hague Convention of 29 May 1993 on Protection of Children and Co-operation in Respect of Intercountry Adoption. Available from http://www.hcch.net/upload/adop 2005_es.pdf (accessed 6 July 2006).

Spain, Ministry of Labour and Social Affairs (2001). *Estadísticas sobre Adopción Internacional*. Madrid. Available from http://www.mtas.es/ SGAS/FamiliaInfanc/infancia/Adopcion/Estadis AdopcionIntern.htm (accessed 30 October 2006).

_____ (2005). *Estadísticas sobre Adopción Internacional*. Madrid. Available from http://www. mtas.es/SGAS/FamiliaInfanc/infancia/Adopcion/ Adopcion.pdf (accessed 30 October 2006).

_____ (2002). *Anuario de Estadísticas Laborales y de Asuntos Sociales 2002*. Madrid.

_____ (2007). *Adopción Internacional*. Available from http://www.mae.es/es/MenuPpal/ Consulares/Servicios+Consulares/Espa%C3%B1ol es+en+el+extranjero/Adopcion+Internacional/ (accessed 07 November 2007).

Spain, National Institute of Statistics (2001). *Encuesta de Fecundidad 1999*. Available from http://www.in e.es/inebase/cgi/um?M=%2Ft20%2Fp317&O=inebas e&N=&L= (accessed 07 November 2006).

United Nations (1993). Initial reports of States parties due in 1993: Spain (CRC/C/8/Add.6).

_____ (2001). Periodic reports of States parties due in 1999: Spain (CRC/C/70/Add.9).

_____ (2002). Written replies by the Government of Spain (CRC/C/RESP/SPA/2) concerning the list of issues received by the Committee on the Rights of the Child (CRC/C/Q/SPA/2) relating to the consideration of the second periodic report of Spain.

Sri Lanka

Sri Lanka (2005). Response to the 2005 questionnaire on the practical operation of the Hague Convention of 29 May 1993 on Protection of Children and Co-operation in Respect of Intercountry Adoption. Available from http://www.hcch.net/upload/adop2005_lk.pdf (accessed 6 July 2006).

United Nations (1994). Initial reports of States parties due in 1993: Sri Lanka (CRC/C/8/Add.13).

_____ (2002). Second periodic reports of States parties due in 1998: Sri Lanka (CRC/C/70/Add.17).

_____ (2003). Written replies by the Government of Sri Lanka concerning (CRC/C/RESP/35) the list of issues received by the Committee on the Rights of Child (CRC/C/Q/LKA/2) relating to the consideration of the second periodic report of Sri Lanka.

Sudan

United Nations (2001). Periodic reports of States parties due in 1997: Sudan (CRC/C/65/Add.17).

_____ (2002). Written replies by the Government of Sudan (CRC/C/RESP/10) concerning the list of issues received by the Committee on the Rights of the Child (CRC/C/Q/SUD/2) relating to the consideration of the second periodic report of Sudan.

United States, Bureau of Consular Affairs (2006). International adoption: Sudan. Washington, D.C.: Department of State. Available from http://travel.state.gov/family/adoption/country/country_329.html (accessed 27 October 2006).

Suriname

United Nations (1998). Initial reports of States parties due in 1995: Suriname (CRC/C/28/Add.11).

_____ (2005). Second periodic reports of States parties due in 2000: Suriname (CRC/C/SUR/2).

Swaziland

United Nations (2006). Initial report of States parties due in 1997: Swaziland (CRC/C/SWZ/1).

Sweden

Sweden (1949). Code of Parenthood and Guardianship (Chapter 4).

Sweden, Ministry of Health and Social Affairs (2005). Response to the 2005 questionnaire on the practical operation of the Hague Convention of 29 May 1993 on Protection of Children and Co-operation in Respect of Intercountry Adoption. Available from http://www.hc ch.net/index_en.php?act=publications.details&pid=35 62&dtid=33 (accessed 6 July 2006).

Sweden, National Board for Intercountry Adoption (2005). Survey of the number of foreign adoptive children placed into Swedish families over the years 1969-2003 by countries of origin.

Sweden, Statistics Sweden (2004). *Statistical Yearbook of Sweden 2005*. Edita Norstedts Tryckeri AB: Stockholm. Available from http://www.scb.se/templates/Standard _155777.asp (accessed 27 October 2006).

_____ (2005). *Statistical Yearbook of Sweden 2006*. Edita Norstedts Tryckeri AB: Stockholm. Available from http://www.scb.se/templates/Standard_155777 .asp (accessed 26 October 2006).

United Nations (1992). Initial reports of States parties due in 1992: Sweden (CRC/C/3/Add.1).

_____ (1998). Second periodic reports of States parties due in 1997: Sweden (CRC/C/65/Add.3).

_____ (2004a). Third periodic report of States parties due in 2002: Sweden (CRC/C/125/Add.1).

_____ (2004b). Written replies by the Government of Sweden (CRC/C/RESP/74) concerning the list of issues received by the Committee on the Rights of the Child (CRC/C/Q/SWE/3) relating to the consideration of the third periodic report of Sweden.

Switzerland

Switzerland, (2005). Response to the 2005 questionnaire on the practical operation of the Hague Convention of 29 May 1993 on Protection of Children and Co-operation in Respect of Intercountry Adoption. Available from http://www.hcch.net/index_en.php?act=publications. details&pid=3552&dtid=33 (accessed 6 July 2006).

_____ (n.d.). Civil Code, book II, part II, title VII, chapter IV. Available from http://www.admin. ch/ch/f/rs/210/index2.html#id-2-2-7-4.html (accessed 12 February 2006).

Switzerland, Swiss Federal Statistical Office (2004). *Statistical Yearbook of Switzerland 2004.* Neuchâtel: Editions Verlag Neue Zürcher Zeitung.

United Nations (2001). Initial reports of States parties due in 1999: Switzerland (CRC/C/78/Add.3).

_____ (2002). Written replies by the Government of Switzerland concerning (CRC/C/RESP/SWI/1) the list of issues received by the Committee on the Rights of Child (CRC/C/Q/SWI/1) relating to the consideration of the initial report of Switzerland.

Syrian Arab Republic

United Nations (2002). Periodic reports of States parties due in 2000: Syrian Arab Republic (CRS/C/93/Add.2).

Tajikistan

United Nations (1998). Initial reports of States parties due in 1995: Tajikistan (CRC/C/28/Add.14).

United States, Bureau of Consular Affairs (2006). International adoption: Tajikistan. Washington, D.C.: Department of State. Available from http://travel.state.gov/family/adoption/country/cou ntry_336.html (accessed 27 October 2006).

Thailand

Thailand, Ministry of Information and Communication Technology, National Statistical Office (2002). *Statistical Yearbook Thailand*, Number 49. Available from http://unpan1.un.org/intradoc/ groups/public/documents/APCITY/UNPAN01529 1.pdf (accessed 27 October 2006).

United Nations (1996). Initial reports of States parties due in 1994: Thailand (CRC/C/11/Add.13).

_____ (2005). Second periodic report of States parties due in 1999: Thailand (CRC/C/83/Add.15).

United States, Bureau of Consular Affairs (n.d.). International adoption: Thailand. Washington, D.C.: Department of State. Available from http://travel.state.gov/family/adoption/country/cou ntry_337.html (accessed 27 October 2006).

The former Yugoslav Republic of Macedonia

United Nations (1997). Initial report of States parties due in 1993: The former Yugoslav Republic of Macedonia (CRC/C/8/Add.36).

Togo

United Nations (1996). Initial reports of States parties due in 1992: Togo (CRC/C/3/Add.42).

_____ (2004a). Second periodic reports of States Parties due in 1997: Togo (CRC/C/65/Add.27).

_____ (2004b). Written replies by the Government of Togo concerning (CRC/C/RESP/78) the list of issues received by the Committee on the Rights of Child (CR C/C/Q/TGO/2) relating to the consideration of the second periodic report of Togo.

Trinidad and Tobago

United Nations (2004). Second periodic reports of States parties due in 1999: Trinidad and Tobago (CRC/C/83/Add.12).

Tunisia

United Nations (2001). Periodic reports of States parties due in 1999: Tunisia (CRC/C/83/Add.1).

Turkey

Turkey, General Directorate of the Social Services and Child Protection Agency (2005). Response to the 2005 questionnaire on the practical operation of the Hague Convention of 29 May 1993 on Protection of Children and Co-operation in Respect of Intercountry Adoption. Available from http://www.hcch.net/index_en.php?act =publications.details&pid=3584&dtid=33 (accessed 6 July 2006).

United Nations (2000). Initial reports of States parties due in 1997: Turkey (CRC/C/51/Add.4).

_____ (2001). Written replies by the Government of Turkey (CRC/C/51/Add.4) concerning the list of issues received by the Committee on the Rights of the Child (CRC/C/Q/TUR/1) relating to the consideration of the initial report of Turkey.

Turkmenistan

United Nations (2005). Initial reports of States parties due in 1995: Turkmenistan (CRC/C/TKM/1).

United States, Bureau of Consular Affairs (2006). International adoption: Turkmenistan. Washington, D.C.: Department of State. Available from http://trav el.state.gov/family/adoption/country/country_341.html (accessed 27 October 2006).

Uganda

United Nations (1996). Initial reports of States parties due in 1992: Uganda (CRC/C/3/Add.40).
_____ (2004). Second periodic report of States parties due in 1997: Uganda (CRC/C/65/Add.33).

Ukraine

United Nations (1995). Initial reports of States parties due in 1993: Ukraine (CRC/C/8/Add.10/Rev.10).
_____ (2001). Second periodic reports of States parties due in 1998: Ukraine (CRC/C/70/Add.11).
_____ (2002). Written replies by the Government of Ukraine (CRC/C/RESP/11) concerning the list of issues received by the Committee on the Rights of the Child (CRC/C/UKR/2) relating to the consideration of the second report of Ukraine.
United States, Bureau of Consular Affairs (n.d.). International adoption: Ukraine. Washington, D.C.: Department of State. Available from http://travel.state.gov/family/adoption/country/country_343.html (accessed 27 October 2006).

United Kingdom

United Kingdom (2002). Adoption and Children Act 2002 Elizabeth II. Chapter 38. Available from http://www.opsi.gov.uk/acts/acts2002/20020038.htm (accessed 30 October 2006).
_____ (2000). *Adoption: a new approach. A white paper*. London: Department of Health. Available from http://www.dh.gov.uk/assetRoot/04/08/05/12/04080512.pdf (accessed 30 October 2006).
_____ (2006a). *Summary Statistics on Children in Care and Children Adopted from Care, and Searching for Birth Relatives in England*. Available from http://www.baaf.org.uk/info/stats/england .shtml (accessed 8 December 2006).
_____ (2006b). *Summary Statistics on Children in Care and Children Adopted from Care, and Searching for Birth Relatives in Wales*. Available from http://www.baaf.org.uk/info/stats/wales.shtml (accessed 8 December 2006).
_____ (2006c). *Summary Statistics on Children in Care and Children Adopted from Care in Northern Ireland*. Available from http://www.baaf.org.uk/info/stats/ni.shtml (accessed 8 December 2006).
_____ (2006d). *Summary Statistics on Children in Care and Children Adopted from Care in Scotland*. Available from http://www.baaf.org.uk/info/stats/scotland.shtml (accessed 8 December 2006).

United Kingdom, Department for Education and Skills (2005). *Adoption Statistics: Intercountry Adoptions in the United Kingdom*. London. Available from http://www.dfes.gov.uk/adoption/adoptionreforms/statistics.shtml (accessed 10 October 2005).
United Kingdom, Office for National Statistics (2002). *Marriage, Divorce and Adoption Statistics*. Review of the Registrar General on marriages, divorces and adoptions in England and Wales, 2000. Series FM 2 No. 28. London: The Stationery Office. Available from http://www.statistics.gov.uk/downloads/theme_population/FM2_2000/FM2_28_v2.pdf (accessed 3 October 2007).
_____ (2004). *Annual Abstract of Statistics, 2004 Edition*. London: The Stationery Office. Available from http://www.statistics.gov.uk/downloads/theme_compendia/Aa2004/AA2004.pdf (accessed 30 October 2006).
_____ (2007). *Marriage, Divorce and Adoption Statistics*. Review of the Registrar General on marriages and divorces in 2004, and adoptions in 2005, in England and Wales. Series FM2 No. 32. London: The Stationery Office. Available from http://www.statistics.gov.uk/downloads/theme_population/FM2no32/FM2_32.pdf (accessed 3 October 2007).
United Nations (1994). Initial reports of States parties due in 1994: United Kingdom of Great Britain and Northern Ireland. (CRC/C/11/Add.1).
_____ (2002a). Periodic reports of States parties due in 1998: United Kingdom of Great Britain and Northern Ireland (CRC/C/83/Add.3).
_____ (2002b). Written replies by the Government of the United Kingdom of Great Britain and Northern Ireland (CRC/C/RESP/12) concerning the list of issues received by the Committee on the Rights of the Child (CRC/C/Q/UK/2) relating to the consideration of the second periodic report of the United Kingdom of Great Britain and Northern Ireland.

United Republic of Tanzania

United Nations (2000). Initial reports of States parties due in 1993: United Republic of Tanzania (CRC/C/8/Add.14/Rev.1).
_____ (2001). Written replies by the Government of Tanzania (CRC/C/8/Add.14/Rev.1) concerning the list of issues received by the Committee on the Rights of the Child (CRC/C/Q/TAN/1) relating to the consideration of the initial report of Tanzania.
_____ (2005). Second periodic reports of States parties due in 2004: United Republic of Tanzania (CRC/C/70/Add.26).
_____ (2006). Written replies by the Government of the United Republic of Tanzania (CRC/C/RESP/

TZA/2) concerning the list of issues received by the Committee on the Rights of the Child (CRC/C/TZA/Q/2) relating to the consideration of the second periodic report of the United Republic of Tanzania.

United States of America

United States (2005). Response to the 2005 questionnaire on the practical operation of the Hague Convention of 29 May 1993 on Protection of Children and Co-operation in Respect of Intercountry Adoption. Available from http://www.hcch.net/index_en.php?act=publications.details&pid=3555&dtid=33 (accessed 6 July 2006)

_____ (n.d.). Adoption and Safe Families Act, Public Law 105-89 of 19 November 1997. Available from http://www.acf.dhhs.gov/programs/cb/laws_policies/cblaws/public_law/pl105_89/pl105_89.htm (accessed 27 October 2006).

United States, Administration for Children and Families (2005). How many children were in foster care on September 30, 2003? 520,000. *AFCARS Report*, No. 10. Washington, D.C.: Department of Health and Human Services. Available from http://www.acf.dhhs.gov/programs/cb/stats_research/afcars/tar/report10.htm (accessed 27 October 2006).

_____ (2006). How many children were in foster care on September 30, 2005? 513,000. *AFCARS Report*, No. 13. Washington, D.C.: Department of Health and Human Services. Available from http://www.acf.hhs.gov/programs/cb/stats_research/afcars/tar/report13.pdf (accessed 27 October 2006).

United States, Bureau of the Census (2003). Adopted Children and Stepchildren: 2000. *Census 2000 Special Reports*. Available from http://www.census.gov/prod/2003pubs/censr-6.pdf (accessed 30 October 2006).

_____ (n.d.). Current Population Survey (CPS) – Definitions and Explanations. Available from http://www.census.gov/population/www/cps/cpsdef.html (accessed 16 October 2006).

United States, Bureau of Consular Affairs (n.d.). What is the Office of Children's Issues? Washington, D.C.: Department of State. Available from http://travel.state.gov/family/about/faq/faq_602.html (accessed 21 February 2006).

_____ (2006). Immigrant visas issued to orphans coming to the U.S. Washington, D.C.: Department of State. Available from http://travel.state.gov/family/adoption/stats/stats_451.html (accessed 27 October 2006).

United States, Child Welfare Information Gateway (2004a). *Access to Family Information by Adopted Persons: Summary of State Laws*. Washington, D.C.: Department of Health and Human Services.

_____ (2004b). *Infant Safe Haven Laws: Summary of State Laws*. Washington, D.C.: Department of Health and Human Services. Available from http://www.childwelfare.gov/systemwide/laws_policies/statutes/safehaven.pdf (accessed 23 October 2006).

_____ (2004c). *How many children were adopted in 2000 and 2001?* Washington, D.C.: U.S. Department of Health and Human Services. Available from http://www.childwelfare.gov/pubs/s_adopted/Index.cfm (accessed 23 October 2006).

_____ (2005). *Voluntary Relinquishment for Adoption: Numbers and Trends*. Washington, D.C.: Department of Health and Human Services. Available from http://www.childwelfare.gov/pubs/s_place.pdf (accessed 23 October 2006).

United States, Department of Health and Human Services, Centers for Disease Control and Prevention (2003). NSFG Cycle 6 Main Study Female Questionnaire. Available from http://www.cdc.gov/nchs/data/nsfg/C6female_capiliteMar03final.pdf (accessed 07 November 2006).

_____ (2007). *International Travel with Infants and Young Children*. Available from http://www2.ncid.cdc.gov/travel/yb/utils/ybGet.asp?section=children&obj=adoption.htm (ace.ssed 07 November 2006).

United States, Department of Homeland Security, Citizenship and Immigration Services (n.d.). Information sheet regarding the Intercountry Adoption Act of 2000. Available from http://www.uscis.gov/portal/site/uscis/menuitem.5af9bb95919f35e66f614176543f6d1a/?vgnextoid=009a98751de7d010VgnVCM10000048f3d6a1RCRD&vgnextchannel=063807b03d92b010VgnVCM10000045f3d6a1RCRD (accessed 12 May 2006).

_____ (n.d.). U.S. citizenship for a foreign-born adopted child. Available from http://www.uscis.gov/portal/site/uscis/menuitem.5af9bb95919f35e66f614176543f6d1a/?vgnextoid=28dc6138f898d010VgnVCM10000048f3d6a1RCRD&vgnextchannel=063807b03d92b010VgnVCM10000045f3d6a1RCRD (accessed 2 March 2007).

United States, Department of State (2005). *Trafficking in Persons Report*. Washington, D.C.: Department of State. Available from http://www.state.gov/g/tip/rls/tiprpt/2005/ (accessed 27 October 2006).

_____ (2006). Immigrant visas issued to orphans coming to the U.S. Washington, D.C.: Department of State. Available from http://travel.state.gov/family/adoption/stats/stats_451.html (accessed 27 October 2006).

_____ (n.d.). *International Adoption*. Washington, D.C.: Department of State. Available from http://travel.state.gov/family/adoption/notices/notices_473.html (accessed 07 November 2006).

_____ (n.d.). Legal Permanent Residents and Intercountry Adoptions. Available from http://travel.state.gov/visa/immigrants/types/types_1311.html (accessed 07 November 2006).

United States, Government Accountability Office (2005). *Foreign affairs: agencies have improved the intercountry adoption process, but further enhancements are needed* (Report No. GAO-06-133). Available from http://www.gao.gov/htext/d06133.html (accessed 21 February 2006).

Uruguay

United Nations (1995). Initial reports of States parties due in 1992: Uruguay (CRC/C/3/Add.37).

World Health Organization, Pan American Health Organization. *Encuesta sobre Salud, Bienestar y Envejecimiento en América Latina y el Caribe.* Available from http://www.ssc.wisc.edu/sabe/question/Uruguay.pdf (accessed 07 November 2006).

Uzbekistan

United Nations (2001a). Initial reports of States parties due in 1996: Uzbekistan (CRC/C/41/Add.8).

_____ (2001b). Written replies by the Government of Uzbekistan (CRC/C/RESP/UZB/1) concerning the list of issues received by the Committee on the Rights of the Child (CRC/C/Q/UZB/1) relating to the consideration of the initial periodic report of Uzbekistan.

_____ (2005). Second periodic reports of States parties due in 2001: Uzbekistan (CRC/C/104/Add.6).

_____ (2006). Written replies by the Government of Uzbekistan (CRC/C/RESP/UZB/2) concerning the list of issues received by the Committee on the Rights of the Child (CRC/C/UZB/Q/2) relating to the consideration of the second periodic report of Uzbekistan.

United States of America Department of State, (2006). International adoption: Uzbekistan. Washington, D.C.: Department of State. Available from http://travel.state.gov/family/adoption/country/country_347.html (accessed 27 October 2006).

Vanuatu

United Nations (1997). Initial reports of States parties due in 1995: Vanuatu (CRC/C/28/Add.8).

Venezuela (Bolivarian Republic of)

United Nations (1997). Initial report of States parties due in 1992: Venezuela (CRC/C/3/Add.54).

_____ (1998). Initial reports of States parties due in 1992: Venezuela supplementary report (CRC/C/3/Add.59).

United States, Bureau of Consular Affairs (2006). International adoption: Venezuela. Washington, D.C.: Department of State. Available from http://travel.state.gov/family/adoption/country/country_348.html (accessed 27 October 2006).

Venezuela, Nacional Statistical Institute (2000). *Anuario Estadístico de Venezuela 2000.* Caracas, Venezuela.

Viet Nam

United Nations (1992). Initial reports of States parties due in 1992: Viet Nam (CRC/C/3/Add.4).

_____ (2002). Periodic reports of States parties due in 1997: Viet Nam (CRC/C/65/Add.20).

_____ (2003). Written replies by the Government of Viet Nam (CRC/C/RESP/VIE/2) concerning the list of issues received by the Committee on the Rights of the Child (CRC/C/Q/VIE/2) relating to the consideration of the second periodic report of Viet Nam.

United States, Bureau of Consular Affairs (2006). International adoption: Vietnam. Washington, D.C.: Department of State. Available from http://travel.state.gov/family/adoption/country/country_349.html (accessed 27 October 2006).

Zambia

United Nations (2002). Initial reports of States parties due in 1994: Zambia (CRC/C/11/Add.25).

Zimbabwe

United Nations (1995). Initial reports of States parties due in 1992: Zimbabwe (CRC/C/3/Add.35).

United States, Bureau of Consular Affairs (2006). International adoption: Zimbabwe. Washington, D.C.: Department of State. Available from http://travel.state.gov/family/adoption/country/country_351.html (accessed 27 October 2006).

ANNEX III

ANNEX TABLES

TABLE A.III.1. STATUS OF ADOPTION, NATIONAL LEGISLATION AND INSTITUTIONAL ARRANGEMENTS CONCERNING
ADOPTIONS BY MAJOR AREA AND COUNTRY

	Type of adoption permitted		*National legislation governing adoption*	*Government body involved in the adoption procedure*
	Domestic	*Intercountry*		
AFRICA				
Algeria..............................	No	No	Not applicable	Not applicable
Angola..............................	Yes	Yes	Angolan Adoption Act of 27 August 1980 (Act No. 7/80); Family Code	Judiciary; National Assembly
Benin..............................	Yes	Yes	French Civil Code (1958 version); Dahomy Code of Customary Law	Judiciary
Botswana..............................	Yes	Yes[1]	Adoption of Children Act	Judiciary
Burkina Faso	Yes	Yes	Code on the Individual and the Family	Judiciary; Ministry of Social Action and the Family
Burundi..............................	Yes	Yes	Code of Personal and Family Affairs	Judiciary; Ministry for the Advancement of Women and Social Action
Cameroon..............................	Yes	Yes[2]	Civil Code	Judiciary; Ministry of Social Affairs
Cape Verde..........................	Yes	Yes	Civil Code	Judiciary
Central African Republic............	Yes	Yes	French Civil Code	Judiciary; Adoption Committee[3]
Chad..............................	Yes	Yes	Civil Code	Judiciary; Child Protection Office
Comoros..............................	Yes	...	French Civil Code[4]	Judiciary
Congo..............................	Yes	Yes	Family Code	Judiciary
Côte d'Ivoire	Yes	Yes	Law No.83-802 of 2 August 1983 modifying Law No. 64-378 of 7 October 1964 on Adoption; *Code de la nationalité ivoirienne*	Judiciary; Ministry of Health and Social Welfare
Democratic Republic of the Congo	Yes	Yes	Family Code	Ministry of Justice; the *Tribunal de Paix*
Djibouti	No	No	Not applicable	Not applicable
Egypt..............................	No	No	Not applicable	Not applicable
Equatorial Guinea...................	Yes	...	Spanish Civil Code	Government Procurator's Office
Eritrea..............................	Yes	Yes[5]	Transitional Civil Code of Eritrea	Judiciary; Ministry of Labour and Human Welfare
Ethiopia..............................	Yes	Yes	Civil Code; Family Code	Judiciary; Ministry of Labor and Social Affairs

TABLE A.III.1 (*continued*)

	Type of adoption permitted		National legislation governing adoption	Government body involved in the adoption procedure
	Domestic	Intercountry		
Gabon	Yes	...	Civil Code; Code on Nationality of Gabon	Judiciary; Department of Social Affairs
Gambia	Yes	Yes[6]	Adoption Act (Act No. 15 of 1992)	Judiciary; Department of Social Welfare
Ghana	Yes	Yes[6]	Adoption Act of 1962 (Act 104); Children's Act of 1998	Judiciary; Department of Social Welfare
Guinea	Yes	Yes	Civil Code	Judiciary; Ministry for the Promotion of Women and Children
Guinea-Bissau	Yes	...	Civil Code	Judiciary; Ministry of Child Protection
Kenya	Yes	Yes[2]	Adoption Act; Guardianship of Infants Act; Children Bill; Children's Act of 2001	Judiciary
Lesotho	Yes	Yes	Adoption Proclamation No. 62 of 1952; Adoption Proclamation No. 690 of 1959	Judiciary; Department of Social Welfare
Liberia	Yes	Yes	Domestic Relation Law of Liberia	Ministry of Justice
Libyan Arab Jamahiriya	No	No	Not applicable	Not applicable
Madagascar................................	Yes	Yes[7]	Act No. 63-022 of 20 November 1963; Decree No. 94-272 of 19 April 1994	Judiciary
Malawi.......................................	Yes	No	Adoption of Children Act	Judiciary; Ministry of Gender, Youth and Community Services
Mali	Yes	Yes	Order No. 36/CMLN of 31 July 1973 (Family Relations Code)	Judiciary; Adoption Committee, National Social Welfare Department
Mauritania	No	No	Not applicable	Not applicable
Mauritius	Yes	Yes	Civil Code	Judiciary; National Adoption Council; Prime Minister's Office[8]
Morocco	No	No	Not applicable	Not applicable
Mozambique...............................	Yes	Yes[9]	Civil Code	Judiciary; Provincial Directorate of Social Action
Namibia......................................	Yes	No[10]	Children's Act No. 33 of 1960	Judiciary
Niger..	Yes	Yes	Civil Code	Judiciary; Department of Child Protection, Ministry of Social Development
Nigeria.......................................	Yes	No[11]	Varies by state	Varies by state

TABLE A.III.1 (*continued*)

	Type of adoption permitted		National legislation governing adoption	Government body involved in the adoption procedure
	Domestic	Intercountry		
Rwanda...	Yes	Yes	Civil Code; Law No. 42 of 27 October 1988	Judiciary
São Tome and Principe......................	Yes	...	Act No. 2/77	Judiciary
Senegal..	Yes	Yes	Family Code	Judiciary
Seychelles...	Yes	No[10]	Children's Act	Judiciary; Division of Social Affairs
Sierra Leone	Yes	Yes[12]	Adoption Act of 1989	Judiciary; Ministry of Social Welfare, Gender and Children's Affairs
South Africa	Yes	Yes	Child Care Amendment Act of 1996	Judiciary
Sudan[13]	Yes	Yes	Child Welfare Act of 1971[14]	Varies by state
Swaziland..	Yes	Yes	Adoption of Children Act of 1952	Judiciary
Togo	Yes	Yes	Individuals and Family Code	Judiciary; Ministry of Social Affairs
Tunisia...	Yes	Yes	Act No. 58-27 of 4 March 1958	Judiciary; National Institute for the Protection of Children
Uganda	Yes	Yes[15]	Children Statute	Judiciary; Probation and Welfare Department
United Republic of Tanzania..............	Yes	No[16]	Adoption Ordinance	Judiciary; Department of Social Welfare
Zambia...	Yes	Yes[2]	Adoption Act of 1958	Judiciary; Commissioner for Juvenile Welfare
Zimbabwe..	Yes	Yes	Children's Protection and Adoption Act	Judiciary; Ministry of Public Services, Labour and Social Welfare
ASIA				
Afghanistan	No	No	Not applicable	Not applicable
Armenia..	Yes	Yes	Marriage and Family Code; Civil Code; 1995 Citizenship Act of Armenia	Judiciary; Commission on Adoption Issues; Ministry of Social Welfare
Azerbaijan	Yes	Yes	Family Code of 28 December 1999	Judiciary; Commission on Adoption Affairs of the Cabinet of Ministers
Bahrain	No	No	Not applicable	Not applicable
Bangladesh[13]......................................	Yes	No[11]	Varies depending on the religion of the adoptive child or parent[17]	Judiciary

TABLE A.III.1 (*continued*)

	Type of adoption permitted		National legislation governing adoption	Government body involved in the adoption procedure
	Domestic	Intercountry		
Bhutan	Yes	Yes	Resolution 4 of the sixty-seventh session of the National Assembly of 1988	Judiciary
Brunei Darussalam	Yes	Yes	Varies depending on the religion of the adoptive child or parent[18]	*Sharia* Court; High Court; Social Affairs Services Unit[19]
Cambodia	Yes	Yes	Marriage and Family Act; Council of Ministers Letter No.549 of 25 March 1991; Council of Ministers Decision of 23 June 1991	Communal authorities
China..	Yes	Yes	Adoption Act; Marriage Act	Chinese Center for Adoption Affairs, Ministry of Civil Administration
Cyprus..	Yes	Yes	Adoption Law No. 19(I) of 1995	Judiciary; Ministry of Labour and Social Insurance
Democratic People's Republic of Korea	Yes	Yes	Family Law of October 1990	Local population administration authorities
Georgia..	Yes	Yes	Law on Adoption Regulations of 17 November 1997; Orphaned and Neglected Children (Adoption Procedure) Act of 1999	Judiciary; Ministry of Education
India[13]	Yes	Yes	Guardians and Wards Act of 1890; Hindu Adoptions and Maintenance Act LXXVIII of 1956	Judiciary; Central Adoption Resource Agency; Juvenile Welfare Board; Scrutiny Agencies; the Central Adoption Resource Agency (CARA)
Indonesia	Yes	Yes	*Staatsblad* 1917 No. 129; Civil Code; Circular letters No. 6/1983 and No. 4/1989; Circular Letter KMA/III/II/1994; Decree of the Minister of Social Affairs No. 13/HUK/1993	Judiciary; Department of Social Affairs
Iran (Islamic Republic of)	No	No	Not applicable	Not applicable
Iraq	No	No	Not applicable	Not applicable

TABLE A.III.1 (*continued*)

| | Type of adoption permitted | | *National legislation governing adoption* | *Government body involved in the adoption procedure* |
	Domestic	*Intercountry*		
Israel	Yes	Yes	Adoption of Children Law of 1981; Amendment to the Adoption of Children Law: International Adoption Agreement Permit for Adoption of Children of Parents of a Different Religion of 1997; Nationality Law of Israel	Judiciary; Ministry of Labor and Social Affairs; Central Authority for Intercountry Adoption
Japan[20]	Yes	Yes	Civil Code	Judiciary; Child Guidance Center
Jordan	No	No	Not applicable	Not applicable
Kazakhstan	Yes	Yes	Marriage and Family Act of 17 December 1998; Civil Code	Judiciary; Ministry of Education and Science
Kuwait	No	No	Not applicable	Not applicable
Kyrgyzstan	Yes	Yes	Marriage and Family Code; Government Decision No. 825 of 13 November 1994	Judiciary; Ministry of Education
Lao People's Democratic Republic	Yes	Yes	Family Law; Lao Nationality Law	Judiciary
Lebanon[13]	Yes	Yes	Varies depending on the religion of the adoptive child or parent[21]	Judiciary[22]
Malaysia[13]	Yes	Yes[23]	Adoption Act of 1952 (Act 257) (Revised 1981); Registration of Adoptions Act of 1952 (Act 253) (Revised 1981)	Judiciary; Ministry of National Unity and Social Development
Maldives	No	No	Not applicable	Ministry of Justice and Islamic Affairs
Mongolia	Yes	Yes	Family Law of 1999	Judiciary; Ministry of Social Welfare and Labour; Board of Foreigners
Myanmar	Yes	...	Registration of Kittima Adoption Act of 1941; Child Law of 1993	Social Welfare Department
Nepal	Yes	Yes	Civil Code of 1963; Children's Act of 1992	Judiciary; Ministry of Women, Children and Social Welfare
Oman	No	No	Not applicable	Not applicable
Pakistan	No	No	Not applicable	Not applicable

TABLE A.III.1 (*continued*)

	Type of adoption permitted		National legislation governing adoption	Government body involved in the adoption procedure
	Domestic	Intercountry		
Philippines..	Yes	Yes	Family Code of 1987; Intercountry Adoption Act of 1995; Domestic Adoption Act of 1998	Judiciary; Department of Social Welfare and Development; Intercountry Adoption Board
Qatar..	No	No	Not applicable	Not applicable
Republic of Korea	Yes	Yes	Civil Code; Special Adoption Act of 1999	Judiciary; Ministry of Health and Welfare[24]
Saudi Arabia.....................................	No	No	Not applicable	Not applicable
Singapore..	Yes	Yes[25]	Adoption of Children Act of 1972	Judiciary
Sri Lanka	Yes	Yes	Adoption of Children Ordinance of 1941[26]	Judiciary; Department of Probation and Childcare Services
Syrian Arab Republic	No	No	Not applicable	Not applicable
Tajikistan..	Yes	Yes[27]	Family Code of 1998[28]	Ministry of Education; Ministry of Justice
Thailand..	Yes	Yes	Civil and Commercial Code; Child Adoption Act of 1979; Adoption Act of 1990	Judiciary; Department of Public Welfare; Child Adoption Board; Ministry of Foreign Affairs
Turkey	Yes	Yes	Civil Code; Turkish Citizenship Law of 1964	Judiciary; General Directorate of the Social Services and Child Protection Agency
Turkmenistan.....................................	Yes	Yes	Marriage and Family Code	Judiciary; Agencies of tutorship and guardianship of the regional, city and district authorities
United Arab Emirates.........................	No	No	Not applicable	Not applicable
Uzbekistan...	Yes	Yes	Family Code	Judiciary; Ministry of Education; *Makhalla* Committees
Viet Nam	Yes	Yes	Civil Code of 1995; Ordinance on Marriage and Family between Vietnamese and Foreign Citizens of 1993; Government Decree 184/CP of 1994; Law on Family and Marriage of 2000; Government Decree No. 32/2002/ND-CP of 2002; Government Decree No. 68/2002/ND-CP of 2002	Local People's Committees; Ministry of Justice
Yemen	No	No	Not applicable	Not applicable

TABLE A.III.1 (*continued*)

	Type of adoption permitted		National legislation governing adoption	Government body involved in the adoption procedure
	Domestic	Intercountry		
EUROPE				
Albania	Yes	Yes	Family Code; Law No. 7650 of 17 December 1992; Law No. 8624 of 15 June 2000	Judiciary; Albanian Committee for Adoption
Andorra	Yes	Yes	Qualified Law on Adoption of 21 March 1996; Regulations for Adoption of 10 June 1998	Judiciary; Adoption Service; Ministry of Foreign Affairs
Austria	Yes	Yes	Civil Code	Varies by state
Belarus	Yes	Yes	Marriage and Family Code	Judiciary; National Adoption Center; Ministry of Education
Belgium	Yes	Yes	Civil Code; Law of 24 April 2003	Varies by community
Bosnia and Herzegovina	Yes	Yes	Family Law	Judiciary;[29] Ministry of Social Welfare; Ministry of the Interior
Bulgaria	Yes	Yes	Family Code No. 41/28.05.1985 Amended SG No. 11 & 15/1992; Regulation of the Ministry of Justice on the Manner and Procedure for Adoption of 1992	Judiciary
Croatia	Yes	Yes	Family Act of 1998	Judiciary; Ministry of Labor and Social Policy
Czech Republic	Yes	Yes	Act on the Family (Act No. 94/1963 Coll., as amended by Act No. 91/1998 Coll.)	Judiciary; Ministry of Labour and Social Affairs; Office for International Legal Protection of Children
Denmark	Yes	Yes	Danish Adoption Act, cf. Consolidated Act No. 1040 of 16 December 1999; Adoption (Consolidation) Act, Act. No. 928 of 14 September 2004	Judiciary; Ministry of Family and Consumer Affairs; Regional Government Department; Central Adoption Board
Estonia	Yes	Yes	Family Law Act; Child Protection Act; Social Welfare Act	Judiciary; Ministry of Social Affairs
Finland	Yes	Yes	Adoption Act (153/1985); Decree on the Finnish Board of Inter-Country Adoption Affairs (508/1997)	Judiciary; The Finnish Adoption Board, Ministry of Social Affairs and Health

TABLE A.III.1 (*continued*)

	Type of adoption permitted		*National legislation governing adoption*	*Government body involved in the adoption procedure*
	Domestic	*Intercountry*		
France...	Yes[30]	Yes	Civil Code; Family and Social Welfare Code of 1985; Adoption Act No. 96-604 of 5 July 1996; Act No. 2001-111 of 6 February 2001	Judiciary; Family Council of Children in Care; Higher Council for Adoption; Intercountry Adoption Office, Minister of Foreign Affairs
Germany.....................................	Yes	Yes	Civil Code; Adoption on the Protection of Children and the Co-operation in the Field of International Adoption; Act on the Effects of the Adoption According to Foreign Law; Act on Placement for Adoption and the Ban on the Arrangement of Surrogate Mothers; Act on the Implementation of the Hague Convention of 29 May 1993	Guardianship Court;[31] Federal Central Office for Intercountry Adoption
Greece	Yes	Yes	Civil Code; Adoption Code (Law 2447/1996); Law 1049/1980; Presidential Decree 193/1973	Judiciary; Ministry of Health and Welfare
Hungary.....................................	Yes	Yes	Family Law Act; Act XXXI of 1997 on the Protection of the Child and on the Management of Public Guardianship; Act IX of 2002 on the Amendment of the Child Protection Act	Guardianship Authority; National Child and Youth Protection Institute; National Institute of Family and Social Policies
Iceland.......................................	Yes	Yes	Adoption Act No. 130/1999	Ministry of Justice; Adoption Board; Child Welfare Committee
Ireland	Yes	Yes	Adoption Act of 1952; Adoption Act of 1991; Adoption Act of 1998; Irish Nationality and Citizenship Act of 2004	Adoption Board; Health Authority Board
Italy[32]	Yes	Yes	Act No. 431 of 5 June 1967; Act No. 184 of 4 May 1983; Law No. 476 of 31 December 1998; Law No. 149 of 28 March 2001	Juvenile Court; Commission on Intercountry Adoptions
Latvia...	Yes	Yes	Civil Law; Law on Orphan's Courts and Parish Courts; Law on Protection of the Rights of the Child; Civil Procedure Law	Ministry of Justice; Ministry of Welfare; Ministry for Social Assignments for Children and Family Affairs

TABLE A.III.1 (*continued*)

	Type of adoption permitted		National legislation governing adoption	Government body involved in the adoption procedure
	Domestic	*Intercountry*		
Liechtenstein	Yes	Yes	General Civil Code	Judiciary; Office of Social Affairs; Children's and Youth Services
Lithuania	Yes	Yes	Civil Code; Code of Civil Procedure; Resolution No. 1422 of 10 September 2002; Resolution No. 1674 of 23 October 2002; Resolution No. 1983 of 17 December 2002	Judiciary; Adoption Agency, Ministry of Social Security and Labor
Luxembourg	Yes	Yes	Civil Code; Act of 31 January 1998 on the Accreditation of Adoption Services and the Definition of their Obligations	Judiciary; Ministry of the Family, Social Solidarity and Youth
Malta	Yes	Yes	Civil Code	Judiciary; Adoption Unit, Ministry for the Family and Social Solidarity
Monaco	Yes	Yes	Civil Code	Judiciary
Netherlands	Yes	Yes	Civil Code; Netherlands Nationality Act; Placement of Foreign Foster Children Act of 15 July 1989	Ministry of Justice
Norway	Yes	Yes	Act of 28 February 1986 No. 8 Relating to Adoption	Government Adoption Office; National Office for Children, Youth and Family Affairs
Poland	Yes	Yes	Family and Guardianship Code	Guardianship Court; Ministry of National Education
Portugal	Yes	Yes	Civil Code; Decree Law No. 185 of 22 May 1993; Decree Law No. 120 of 8 May 1998; Law No. 7 of 11 May 2001; Law No. 31 of 22 August 2003	Ministry of Justice; Department of Social Action
Republic of Moldova	Yes	Yes	Marriage and Family Code	Judiciary; Committee for Adoption

TABLE A.III.1 (*continued*)

	Type of adoption permitted		National legislation governing adoption	Government body involved in the adoption procedure
	Domestic	Intercountry		
Romania	Yes	Yes[33]	Law No. 87 of 1998; Law No. 273 of 2004; Government Decision No. 1435 of 2004; Government Decision No. 1442 of 2004; Government Decision No.1441 of 2004; Government Decision No. 1436 of 2004; Order No.45 of 2004 of the Secretary of State of the National Authority for Child Protection and Adoption	Ministry of Justice; National Authority for Child Protection and Adoption
Russian Federation	Yes	Yes	Family Code; Code of Civil Procedure	Judiciary
San Marino...	Yes	Yes	Law No. 49 of 26 April 1986; Law No. 83 of 20 July 1999	Judiciary; Minor Service
Serbia..	Yes	...	...	...
Slovakia..	Yes	Yes	Family Act	Judiciary
Slovenia..	Yes	Yes	Marriage and Family Relations Act	Ministry of Labour, Family and Social Affairs
Spain..	Yes	Yes	Civil Code; Civil Proceedings Act; Act 21/1987 of 11 November; Legal Protection of Minors (Organization) Act, 1/1996 of 15 January	Varies by state
Sweden...	Yes	Yes	Act on International Legal Relations Concerning Adoption (1971:796); Foreign Adoption Orders (Approval) Ordinance (1976:834); Code of Parenthood and Guardianship; Intercountry Adoption Intermediation Act (1997:192); Social Services Act (2001:453)	Judiciary; National Board for Intercountry Adoptions
Switzerland...	Yes	Yes	Civil Code of 1907; Federal Ordinance Regulating the Placement of Children of 19 October 1977; Federal Act of 18 December 1987 on International Private Law	Varies by canton
The former Yugoslav Republic of Macedonia	Yes	Yes[34]	Family Act	Center for Social Work; Ministry of Labor and Social Policy

TABLE A.III.1 (*continued*)

	Type of adoption permitted		National legislation governing adoption	Government body involved in the adoption procedure
	Domestic	*Intercountry*		
Ukraine.................................	Yes	Yes	Marriage and Family Code; 1991 Act on Citizenship of Ukraine	Judiciary; Adoptions Centre, Ministry of Education
United Kingdom[35]	Yes	Yes	Adoption Agencies Regulations of 1983; Adoption Rules of 1984; Magistrates Court Rules of 1984; Children Act of 1989; Adoption (Intercountry Aspects) Act of 1999; Adoption and Children Act of 2002; British Nationality Act of 1981	Judiciary

LATIN AMERICA AND THE CARIBBEAN

Antigua and Barbuda...........................	Yes	No	Adoption of Children Act	Judiciary
Argentina[20]..	Yes[36]	No[37]	Civil Code; Act No. 24.779 of 28 February 1997	Judiciary; Ministry of Health and Social Welfare
Bahamas...	Yes	Yes	Adoption of Children Act of 1954	Judiciary; Department of Social Services
Barbados...	Yes	Yes	Adoption Act of 1955; Child Care Board Act of 1981; Adoption (Amendment) Act of 1981; Adoption Regulations of 1986	Judiciary; Child Care Board
Belize...	Yes	Yes	Families and Children Act (Revised 31 December 2000)	Judiciary; Department of Human Development
Bolivia (Plurinational State of)............	Yes	Yes	Family Code; Code for Children and Adolescents	Juvenile Court; Vice-Ministry of Gender, Generational and Family Affairs
Brazil...	Yes	Yes[38]	Statute of the Child and Adolescent, Law No. 8.069 of 13 July 1990; Decree 2,427 of 17 December 1997; Decree 3,087 of 21 June 1999	State Judiciary Commission on Adoption; Department for the Child and Adolescent, Secretary of State for Human Rights of the Ministry of Justice
Chile..	Yes	Yes	Act No. 7,613 of 1943; Act No. 18,703 of 1988; Act No. 19,620 of 1999; Act No. 19,670 of 2000; Act No. 19,910 of 2003	Judiciary; National Service for Minors
Colombia..	Yes	Yes	Juvenile Code, Decree No. 2737 of 27 November 1989; Resolution No. 1267 of 1994	Judiciary; Adoption Division, Colombian Family Welfare Institute

TABLE A.III.1 (*continued*)

	Type of adoption permitted		National legislation governing adoption	Government body involved in the adoption procedure
	Domestic	Intercountry		
Costa Rica	Yes	Yes[39]	Adoptions Act; Family Code Law No. 7538 of 22 August 1995; Law No. 7517 of 1995	Judiciary; National Adoption Council; National Children's Trust
Dominica	Yes	Yes[9]	Adoption of Infants Act; Guardianship of Infant Act	Judiciary; Welfare Division Foster Care Program
Dominican Republic	Yes	Yes	Act No. 14-94; Act No. 24-97; Code for the Protection and Fundamental Rights of Children and Adolescents, Law No. 136-03	Executive Technical Department of the Governing Body of the System for the Protection of Children and Adolescents
Ecuador	Yes	Yes	Children's and Youth Code, Codification No. 2002-100. R.O. 737 of 3 January 2003	Judiciary; Ministry of Social Welfare
El Salvador	Yes	Yes	Family Code, D.L. No. 677 of 11 October 1993; Family Court Procedure Act, D.L. No. 133 of 14 September 1994	Office of the Procurator-General of the Republic; Salvadoran Institute for the Protection of Children
Grenada[40]	Yes	Yes	Adoption (Amendment) Act No. 17 of 1994	Judiciary; Department of Social Security, Grenada Adoption Board
Guatemala	Yes	Yes	Civil Code; Children and Adolescents Code of 1996	Office of the National Procurator-General; Office of Child and Family Welfare; Consejo Nacional de Adopciones
Guyana	Yes	Yes	Adoption of Children Act; Adoption (Amendment) Act of 1997	Judiciary; Adoption Board
Haiti	Yes	Yes	Decree of 4 April 1974	Judiciary; Ministry of Social Affairs
Honduras	Yes	Yes	Constitution of the Republic of Honduras, Decree No. 131 of 11 January 1982; Family Code, Decree No. 76-84 of 31 May 1984; Code on Children and Adolescents, Decree No. 73-96 of 5 September 1996; Regulations on Adoption of the National Social Welfare Board	Judiciary; National Social Welfare Board
Jamaica	Yes	Yes	Children (Adoption of) Act of 2 January 1958	Judiciary; Adoption Board, Ministry of Health

TABLE A.III.1 (*continued*)

	Type of adoption permitted		National legislation governing adoption	Government body involved in the adoption procedure
	Domestic	*Intercountry*		
Mexico...............................	Yes	Yes	Civil Code; Code of Civil Procedure	Civil Registry Judges; State System for the Full Development of the Family
Nicaragua	Yes	Yes	Adoption Act (Decree No. 862) of 12 October 1981; Code on Children and Adolescents (Act No. 287) of 24 March 1998	Judiciary; National Adoption Council, Ministry of Social Welfare
Panama	Yes	Yes	Civil Code; Family Code of 1994; Act No. 33 of 28 May 1998; Act No. 105 of 30 December 1998; Act No. 18 of 2 May 2001	Judiciary; Ministry of Youth, Women, Children and the Family
Paraguay............................	Yes	Yes	Juvenile Code; Adoption Act (No. 1116) of 22 October 1997	Judiciary; Adoption and Family Placement Office; Adoption Centre
Peru	Yes	Yes	Civil Code (Decree Law No. 295 of 24 July 1984); General Adoption Law (Decree Law 25934 of 9 December 1992); Children's and Adolescents' Code (Decree Law No. 26102 of 28 December 1992); Children's and Adolescents' Code (Decree Law No. 27337 of 2 August 2000)	Judiciary; National Secretariat for Adoptions
Saint Kitts and Nevis	Yes	Yes	Adoption Act; Guardianship of Infants Act	Judiciary; Probation and Child Welfare Board
Saint Lucia[40]	Yes	Yes	Adoption Ordinance of 1954	Judiciary; Division of Human Services and Family Affairs
Saint Vincent and the Grenadines........	Yes	Yes	Adoption Act	Judiciary; Adoption Board
Suriname	Yes	Yes	Code of Civil Procedure; Adoption Act of 1972	Judiciary; Family Law Bureau
Trinidad and Tobago	Yes	Yes	Adoption of Children Regulations; Adoption of Children Act, No. 67 of 2000	Judiciary; Adoption Board
Uruguay...	Yes	Yes[41]	Code of Children and Adolescents, Law No. 17,823 of 14 September 2004	Judiciary; Institute of the Child and Adolescent
Venezuela (Bolivarian Republic of)	Yes	Yes	Civil Code; Minors Protection Act of 1980; Adoption Act of 1983	Judiciary; National Children's Institute

TABLE A.III.1 (*continued*)

	Type of adoption permitted		National legislation governing adoption	Government body involved in the adoption procedure
	Domestic	Intercountry		
NORTHERN AMERICA				
Canada..................................	Yes	Yes	Varies by province or territory	National Adoption Desk[42]
United States of America.....................	Yes	Yes	Varies by state	State Court; Indian Tribal Court[31]
OCEANIA				
Australia..............................	Yes	Yes	Varies by state	Varies by state
Fiji....................................	Yes	Yes	Juveniles Act; Adoption of Infants Act	Department of Social Welfare, Ministry of Heath and Social Welfare; Adoption Court
Kiribati...............................	Yes[43]	Yes	...	Magistrates court
Marshall Islands................................	Yes	Yes[44]	Adoption Act of 2002 (Public Law 2002-64)	Judiciary; Central Adoption Agency
Micronesia (Federated States of).........	Yes	No[11]	6 Federated States of Micronesia Code, subchapter III, Adoption	Judiciary
New Zealand......................................	Yes	Yes	Adoption Act of 1955; Adoption Regulations of 1959; Adult Adoption Information Act of 1985; Citizens Amendment Act of 1992	New Zealand Central Authority; Department of Justice
Palau..	Yes	Yes	Palau National Code, Title 21.401-409	Judiciary
Papua New Guinea..............................	Yes	Yes	Adoption Act	Judiciary
Samoa..	Yes	Yes[45]	Infants Ordinance of 1961; Infants (Adoption) Amendment Act of 2005	Judiciary
Solomon Islands................................	Yes	No[46]	Adoption Act of 1958	Judiciary; Social Welfare Office
Vanuatu...	...	...	Not applicable[47]	Not applicable

Source: For a complete list of country references, see annex II.

[1] The adopted person must remain in the country for at least 12 months following the adoption decree.

[2] Prospective adoptive parents must have resided in the country and had the child in their care and custody for at least three consecutive months prior to the date of the adoption application or the adoption order.

[3] The Adoption Committee was established by Decree No. 95/06 of 21 April 1995.

[4] Adoption is not permitted under *Sharia* law, but it is legitimised, if necessary, by resorting to French Civil Law.

[5] Prospective adoptive parents who are not citizens must have resided in the country for at least six months prior to the date of the adoption application.

[6] Prospective adoptive parents who are not citizens must have resided in the country for at least six months prior to the date of the adoption.

[7] Adoptive parents must remain in the country for one month until the deadline for an appeal to the adoption order has passed.

[8] The National Adoption Council oversees the adoption of national children by foreigners. The Prime Minister's Office oversees the adoption of foreign children by nationals.

[9] Intercountry adoptions are granted only in exceptional cases.

[10] Intercountry adoptions are granted only to nationals living abroad who are also relatives of the prospective adoptive child or to permanent residents who have applied and qualified for naturalization.

TABLE A.III.1 (*continued*)

[11] Non-citizens are not permitted to adopt.

[12] Prospective adoptive parents must have resided in the country and had the child in their care and custody for at least 12 consecutive months prior to the date of the adoption.

[13] Procedures differ according to the religion of the adoptive child or parent.

[14] The Child Welfare Act only applies to non-Muslim children.

[15] Prospective adoptive parents must have resided in the country for at least three years prior to the date of the adoption application.

[16] Prospective adoptive parents must reside within the East African Territories.

[17] The country does not have civil laws governing adoption, but under the Hindu, Christian and Buddhist personal laws, adoption is permitted.

[18] The Islamic Adoption of Children Order 2001 applies to Muslims, and the Adoption of Children Order 2001 applies to non-Muslims.

[19] Adoptions made under the Islamic Adoption of Children Order 2001 must be approved by the *Sharia* Courts, and adoptions made under the Adoption of Children Order 2001 must be approved by the High Court.

[20] Prospective adoptive parents must have had the child in their care and custody for at least six months prior to the date of the adoption order.

[21] The country does not have civil laws governing adoption, but under Christian personal laws, adoption is permitted.

[22] Civil courts oversee intercountry adoptions and adoptions of children of different religious affiliation than their prospective adoptive parents.

[23] Prospective adoptive parents must have had the child in their care and custody for two years prior to the date of the adoption.

[24] Adoptions can be arranged directly between the child's guardian and the potential adoptive parents.

[25] Prospective adoptive parents must be residents of the country at the time of applying for an adoption. This, however, does not preclude prospective adoptive parents residing in Singapore from adopting children from other countries.

[26] Intercountry adoption is governed by the Adoption Ordinance as amended in 1992.

[27] At least one prospective adoptive parent must be a citizen.

[28] There is no legislation regarding international adoption.

[29] Varies by municipality.

[30] Prospective adoptive parents must have had the child in their care and custody for at least six months to engage in a full adoption.

[31] Varies by state.

[32] Prospective adoptive parents must have had the child in their care and custody for at least one year prior to the date of the adoption order.

[33] Intercountry adoptions are granted only to adoptive parents who have either a blood or familial link to the adopted child.

[34] Foreign nationals need a special permission from the Ministry of Labour and Social Policy to adopt.

[35] Prospective adoptive parents must have resided in the British Isles for at least one year.

[36] Prospective adoptive parents must have resided in the country for at least five years.

[37] Argentina's legislation does not pronounce against intercountry adoptions granted under the law of another country.

[38] Prospective adoptive parents must remain in the country up to one month (and no less than 15 days) before the completion of the adoption procedure.

[39] Intercountry adoptions to countries that have not implemented the Convention on Protection of Children and Co-operation in Respect of Intercountry Adoption were suspended.

[40] Prospective adoptive parents must have had the child in their care and custody for at least three months prior to the date of the adoption order.

[41] Prospective adoptive parents must have resided in the country and had the child in their care and custody for at least six months prior to the date of the adoption application.

[42] The National Adoption Desk coordinates intercountry adoptions for all provinces, with the exception of Quebec.

[43] Adoptions are recognized only within the country.

[44] Parliament imposed a moratorium on all intercountry adoptions from September 1999 to December 2000.

[45] Intercountry adoptions are granted only to adoptive parents who have either a blood or familial link to the adopted child or where the child has been abandoned or orphaned.

[46] Prospective adoptive parents residing in the Solomon Islands may adopt children from other countries.

[47] Traditional adoptions are practiced. The country does not have legislation concerning adoption.

TABLE A.III.2. SELECTED REQUIREMENTS FOR PROSPECTIVE ADOPTIVE PARENTS AND ADOPTED CHILDREN BY MAJOR AREA AND COUNTRY

	Single adoption permitted		Age requirements for prospective adoptive parents	Child's age of consent for adoption
	Male	*Female*		
AFRICA				
Angola...	...	...	...	Aged 10 years or older
Botswana.....................................	Yes	Yes	Aged 25 years or older[1]	Aged 10 years or older
Burkina Faso................................	...	...	...	Aged 15 years or older
Burundi.......................................	Yes	Yes	Under age 30 and at least 15 years older than the child[2]	Aged 16 years or older
Cameroon.....................................	Yes[3]	Yes[3]	One adoptive parent must be aged 35 years or older and at least 15 years older than the child[4]	Aged 16 years or older
Cape Verde..................................	...	...	...	Aged 12 years or older
Congo..	...	...	...	Aged 15 years or older
Côte d'Ivoire...............................	...	...	Aged 30 years or older and at least 15 years older than the child	Aged 16 years or older
Equatorial Guinea	...	...	Aged 25 years or older and at least 14 years older than the child	Aged 12 years or older
Eritrea...	...	...	...	Aged 10 years or older
Ethiopia.......................................	Yes	Yes	Aged 25 years or older	...
Gabon..	Yes	Yes	Aged 35 years or older and at least 15 years older than the child	...
Ghana..	Yes[5]	Yes[5]	...	...
Guinea...	...	...	Aged 35 years or older and at least 15 years older than the child	Aged 16 years or older
Guinea-Bissau..............................	No[6]	No[6]	Aged 25 to 60 years	Aged 14 years or older
Kenya..	...	...[7]	Aged 25 years or older and at least 21 years older than the child	Aged 14 years or older
Lesotho..	Yes	Yes	At least 25 years older than the child	Aged 10 years or older
Madagascar..................................	Yes	Yes	Aged 30 years or older	...
Malawi...	Yes[8]	Yes[9]	Aged 25 years or older and at least 21 years older than the child	...
Mali...	Yes	Yes	...	...
Mauritius.....................................	Yes[10]	Yes[10]	At least 15 years older than the child[11]	Aged 15 years or older
Mozambique	No[6]	No[6]	...	Aged 14 years or older

TABLE A.III.2 (*continued*)

	Single adoption permitted		Age requirements for prospective adoptive parents	Child's age of consent for adoption
	Male	*Female*		
Namibia..............................	Yes	Yes	Aged 25 years or older and at least 25 years older than the child	Aged 10 years or older
Niger..................................	No[12]	No[12]	Aged 35 years old or older	...
Nigeria	Varies by state	Varies by state	Varies by state	Maturity of child considered
Rwanda...............................	Yes	Yes	At least 15 years older than the child	...
São Tome and Principe	...	...	...	Aged 7 years or older
Senegal...............................	Yes[13]	Yes[13]	At least 15 years older than the child[11]	Aged 15 years or older
Seychelles	Yes	Yes	Aged 21 years or older	Aged 14 years or older[14]
Sierra Leone........................	Yes	Yes	Aged 30 years or older	...
South Africa........................	Yes	Yes	...	Aged 10 years or older
Sudan	No	...	Aged 30 to 50 years	...
Swaziland............................	Yes	Yes	Aged 25 years or older and at least 25 years older than the child	Aged 10 years or older
Tunisia	No[15]	No[15]	...	...
Uganda................................	Yes[16]	Yes[17]	Aged 25 years or older and at least 21 years older than the child	Aged 14 years or older
Zambia................................	Yes[16]	Yes	Aged 25 years or older and at least 21 years older than the child[18]	Maturity of child considered
Zimbabwe	No	Yes[19]	Aged 25 years or older[18]	...
ASIA				
Armenia	Yes	Yes	...	Aged 10 years or older
Azerbaijan..........................	Yes[20]	Yes[20]	...	Aged 10 years or older
Bangladesh..........................	Yes[21]	...	Aged 15 years or older	...
Brunei Darussalam..............................	Yes[22]	Yes[23]	...	Maturity of child considered
Cambodia.............................	...	...	Aged 25 years or older and at least 20 years older than the child	...
China..................................	Yes[24]	Yes[24]	Aged 30 years or older[25]	Aged 10 years or older
Democratic People's Republic of Korea...................................	...	...	...	Maturity of child considered
Georgia................................	Yes	Yes	...	Aged 10 years or older
India...................................	Yes	Yes	...	...
Indonesia.............................	No	No	...	...

TABLE A.III.2 (*continued*)

	Single adoption permitted		Age requirements for prospective adoptive parents	Child's age of consent for adoption
	Male	*Female*		
Israel	No[26,27]	No[26,27]	At least 18 years older than the child[28]	Aged 9 years or older[14]
Japan	Yes[29]	Yes[29]	One adoptive parent must be aged 25 years or older and the other must be aged 20 years or older	...
Kazakhstan..	Yes[20]	Yes[20]	...	Aged 10 years or older
Kyrgyzstan..	...	...	Aged 18 years or older	Aged 10 years or older
Lao People's Democratic Republic	...	...	...	Aged 10 years or older
Lebanon	Yes	Yes	Aged 40 years or older and at least 18 years older than the child	...
Malaysia..	...	...	At least 21 years older than the child and one spouse must be aged 25 years or older	...
Mongolia..	...	...	...	Aged 7 years or older
Myanmar..	Yes	Yes	...	...
Nepal...	...	...	The male adoptive parent must be at least 25 years older than the child when adopting a girl	...
Philippines	Yes	Yes	At least 16 years older than the child[30]	Aged 10 years or older
Republic of Korea..............................	...	...	Aged 25 to 50 years[31]	Aged 15 years or older
Singapore	Yes[32]	Yes	Aged 25 years or older and at least 21 years older than the child	...
Sri Lanka..	...	...	...	Aged 10 years or older
Tajikistan	Yes[20]	Yes[20]	...	Aged 10 years or older
Thailand..	No	No	Aged 25 years or older and at least 15 years older than the child	Aged 15 years or older
Turkey...	Yes	Yes	Aged 30 years or older and at least 18 years older than the child	...
Turkmenistan	Yes	Yes	...	Aged 10 years or older
Uzbekistan	Yes	Yes	At least 15 years older than the child	Aged 10 years or older
Viet Nam...	Yes	Yes	At least 20 years older than the child	Aged 9 years or older

EUROPE

Albania..	Yes	Yes	At least 18 years older than the child	Aged 10 years or older

TABLE A.III.2 (*continued*)

	Single adoption permitted		Age requirements for prospective adoptive parents	Child's age of consent for adoption
	Male	*Female*		
Andorra..	Yes	Yes	...	Aged 12 years or older[33]
Austria...	...	...	The male adoptive parent must be aged 30 years or older and the female adoptive parent must be aged 28 years or older	Aged 5 years or older
Belarus..	Yes	Yes	At least 16 years older than the child	Aged 10 years or older
Belgium..	Yes	Yes	Aged 25 years or older and at least 15 years older than the child	Aged 12 years or older
Bosnia and Herzegovina	...	...	...	Aged 10 years or older
Bulgaria..	Yes	Yes	Aged 18 years or older and at least 15 years older than the child	Aged 14 years or older
Croatia...	Yes	Yes	Aged 21 to 35 years and less than 40 years older than the child[34]	Aged 12 years or older
Czech Republic	No[19]	No[19]	...	Maturity of child considered
Denmark..	Yes	Yes	Aged 25 years or older	Aged 12 years or older
Estonia	Yes	Yes	Aged 25 years or older	Aged 10 years or older[14]
Finland	Yes	Yes	Aged 25 years or older and less than 45 years older than the child	Aged 12 years or older
France	Yes	Yes	Aged 28 years or older and at least 15 years older than the child[35]	Aged 13 years or older
Germany..	Yes	Yes	Aged 21 years or older[36]	Aged 14 years or older
Greece	Yes	Yes	Aged 18 to 50 years older than the child[2]	Aged 12 years or older
Hungary	...	...	Aged 16 to 45 years older than the child	Aged 14 years or older[14]
Iceland..	No[19]	No[19]	Aged 25 years or older	Aged 12 years or older[14]
Ireland	No[27,37]	No[27,37]	Aged 21 years or older	Aged 7 years or older
Italy	No[27,38]	No[27,38]	Aged 18 years or older and less than 40 years older than the child	Aged 12 years or older[14]
Latvia	Yes	Yes	Aged 25 years or older and at least 18 years older than the child	Aged 12 years or older
Liechtenstein.....................................	No	No	At least 18 years older than the child, father must be aged 30 years or older and mother must be aged 28 years or older	Aged 5 years or older

TABLE A.III.2 (*continued*)

	Single adoption permitted		Age requirements for prospective adoptive parents	Child's age of consent for adoption
	Male	*Female*		
Lithuania	No[19]	No[19]	Under age 50 and at least 18 years older than the child[39]	Aged 10 years or older
Luxembourg	No[40]	No[40]	At least 15 years older than the child, one spouse must be aged 25 years or older and the other must be aged 21 years or older[41]	Aged 15 years or older
Malta	Yes	Yes	Aged 30 to 60 years and at least 21 years older than the child	Aged 14 years or older
Monaco	Yes	Yes	Aged 28 years or older and at least 15 years older than the child	Aged 15 years or older
Netherlands	Yes	Yes	Under age 46	...
Norway	Yes	Yes	Aged 25 years or older[42]	Aged 12 years or older
Poland	...	...	...	Aged 13 years or older
Portugal	Yes[43]	Yes[43]	Under age 50[44]	Aged 12 years or older
Republic of Moldova	Yes	Yes	Aged 25 years or older and at least 15 years older than the child	Aged 10 years or older
Romania	...	...	...	Aged 10 years or older
Russian Federation	Yes[20]	Yes[20]	...	Aged 10 years or older
San Marino	Yes	Yes	Aged 25 years or older and 18 to 45 years older than the child	...
Slovakia	Yes	Yes	...	Maturity of child considered
Slovenia	Yes	Yes	At least 18 years older than the child	Aged 10 years or older
Spain	Yes	Yes	Aged 25 years or older and at least 14 years older than the child[45]	Aged 12 years or older
Sweden	Yes	Yes	Aged 25 years or older[46]	Aged 12 years or older[14]
Switzerland	Yes	Yes	Aged 35 years or older and at least 16 years older than the child	Maturity of child considered
The former Yugoslav Republic of Macedonia	Yes	Yes	At least 18 years older than the child	Aged 10 years or older
Ukraine	Yes	Yes	At least 15 years older than the child	Aged 10 years or older
United Kingdom	Yes	Yes	Aged 21 years or older	Maturity of child considered

TABLE A.III.2 (*continued*)

	Single adoption permitted		Age requirements for prospective adoptive parents	Child's age of consent for adoption
	Male	*Female*		
LATIN AMERICA AND THE CARIBBEAN				
Antigua and Barbuda	Yes[16]	Yes	Aged 25 years or older and at least 21 years older than the child	Maturity of child considered
Argentina	Yes	Yes	Aged 30 years or older and at least 18 years older than the child[47]	...
Bahamas...	Yes	Yes	Aged 25 years or older and at least 21 years older than the child[48]	...
Barbados	...	...	...	Aged 16 years or older[14]
Belize	Yes[16]	Yes	Aged 25 years or older and at least 12 years older than the child	Maturity of child considered
Bolivia (Plurinational State of)	Yes	Yes	Aged 25 to 50 years and at least 15 years older than the child	...
Brazil..	Yes	Yes	Aged 21 years or older and at least 16 years older than the child	Aged 12 years or older
Chile..	Yes[49]	Yes[49]	Aged 26 to 59 years and at least 20 years older than the child	Aged 14 years or older[50]
Colombia...	Yes	Yes	Aged 25 years or older and at least 15 years older than the child	...
Costa Rica	Yes	Yes	...	...
Dominica..	Yes[16]	Yes	Aged 25 years or older and at least 21 years older than the child	Maturity of child considered
Dominican Republic	Yes	Yes	Aged 30 to 60 years	Aged 12 years or older
Ecuador...	Yes	Yes	Aged 25 years or older and 14 to 45 years older than the child[35]	...
El Salvador..	Yes[51]	Yes[51]	Aged 25 years or older and at least 15 years older than the child	Aged 12 years or older
Grenada...	...	...	Aged 25 years or older and at least 21 years older than the child	...
Guyana..	Yes[16]	Yes	Aged 25 years or older and at least 21 years older than the child	Maturity of child considered
Haiti	Yes	Yes	Aged 35 years or older and at least 19 years older than the child[35]	...

TABLE A.III.2 (*continued*)

	Single adoption permitted		Age requirements for prospective adoptive parents	Child's age of consent for adoption
	Male	*Female*		
Honduras...	Yes	Yes	Aged 30 years or older and at least 15 years older than the child	...
Jamaica..	Yes[16]	Yes	Aged 25 years or older[48]	Maturity of child considered
Mexico	Yes	Yes	Aged 25 years or older and at least 17 years older than the child	Aged 12 years or older[14]
Nicaragua..	Yes	Yes	Aged 25 to 40 years and at least 15 years older than the child[52]	...
Panama..	Yes[8]	Yes[9]	Aged 21 years or older and at least 15 years older than the child	Aged 7 years or older
Paraguay..	Yes	Yes	Aged 25 to 50 years	Aged 12 years or older
Peru...	Yes	Yes	At least 18 years older than the child[41]	Aged 10 years or older
Saint Kitts and Nevis..........................	...	...	Aged 25 years or older and at least 21 years older than the child	...
Saint Lucia..	Yes[16]	Yes	Aged 25 years or older and at least 21 years older than the child[18]	Maturity of child considered
Saint Vincent and the Grenadines	Yes	Yes	...	...
Suriname	No	No	Under age 50 and mother must not be 40 years older than the child	Aged 12 years or older
Trinidad and Tobago............................	No[32]	Yes	Aged 25 years or older and at least 21 years older than the child	Maturity of child considered
Uruguay	Yes[5]	Yes[5]	Aged 25 years or older and at least 15 years older than the child	...
Venezuela (Bolivarian Republic of)....	Yes[3]	Yes[3]	Aged 30 years or older and at least 18 years older than the child	Aged 12 years or older
NORTHERN AMERICA				
Canada	Varies by province	Varies by province	Varies by province	...
United States of America	Varies by state	Varies by state	Varies by state	Varies by state
OCEANIA				
Australia..	Yes	Yes	...	Maturity of child considered
Marshall Islands	Yes	Yes	At least 15 years older than the child	Aged 12 years or older

TABLE A.III.2 (*continued*)

	Single adoption permitted		Age requirements for prospective adoptive parents	Child's age of consent for adoption
	Male	Female		
Micronesia (Federated States of).........	Yes	Yes	...	Aged 12 years or older
New Zealand......................................	Yes	Yes	...	...
Palau	...	...	...	Aged 12 years or older
Samoa	Yes	Yes	...	Aged 12 years or older

Source: For a complete list of country references, see annex II.

[1] Prospective adoptive parents must be at least 25 years older than the child if the child is aged 16 years or older.
[2] Different age requirements apply to adoptions by step-parents.
[3] Prospective adoptive parents must be aged 40 years or older.
[4] Age requirements apply to prospective adoptive parents who have been married at least ten years. Different age requirements apply to single adoptive parents.
[5] Unmarried foreign citizens are not permitted to adopt.
[6] Prospective adoptive parents must have been married at least five years.
[7] A sole foreign female applicant is allowed to adopt under special circumstances.
[8] A sole male applicant is not permitted to adopt a girl.
[9] A sole female applicant is not permitted to adopt a boy.
[10] Prospective adoptive parents must be aged 30 years or older to engage in simple adoptions.
[11] Step-parents must be at least 10 years older than the child. Different age requirements apply to single adoptive parents.
[12] Prospective adoptive parents must have been married at least ten years.
[13] Prospective adoptive parents must be aged 35 years or older.
[14] The maturity of the child is also considered.
[15] A judge may waive the marriage requirement for a widowed or divorced individual.
[16] A sole male applicant is not permitted to adopt a girl, except under special circumstances.
[17] A sole female applicant is not permitted to adopt a boy, except under special circumstances.
[18] Prospective adoptive parents must be aged 21 years or older to adopt a relative.
[19] Permission for adoption may be granted to a single person under special circumstances.
[20] Prospective adoptive parents must be at least 16 years older than the child.
[21] Unmarried Hindu men are not permitted to adopt a girl.
[22] A sole male applicant is not permitted to adopt a girl, unless they are related by blood.
[23] A sole female applicant is not permitted to adopt a boy, unless they are related by blood.
[24] The Ministry of Civil Affairs has devised new guidelines that require foreign prospective adoptive parents to have been married at least two years.
[25] The Ministry of Civil Affairs has devised new guidelines that require foreign prospective adoptive parents to be aged 30 to 50 years.
[26] A sole applicant is permitted to adopt in the case where one spouse adopts the child of the other.
[27] Close relatives are permitted to adopt, regardless of their marital status.
[28] In the case of intercountry adoption, at least one of the foreign prospective adoptive parents must be under age 48.
[29] Prospective adoptive parents must be aged 25 years or older.
[30] In the case of intercountry adoption, prospective adoptive parents must be aged 27 years or older.
[31] In the case of intercountry adoption, the foreign prospective adoptive parents must be under age 45.
[32] A sole male applicant is not permitted to adopt a child, except under special circumstances.
[33] The views of the adoptive child may be sought from 10 years of age.
[34] Prospective adoptive parents aged 35 years or older are permitted to adopt under special circumstances.
[35] Step-parents must be at least 10 years older than the child.
[36] In the case of adoption by a couple, one adoptive parent must be aged 25 years or older and the other must be aged 21 years or older.
[37] Widowed persons are permitted to adopt.
[38] Prospective adoptive parents must have been married or lived in a stable union prior to marriage for at least three years.
[39] Step-parents must be at least 15 years older than the child.
[40] Prospective adoptive parents aged 25 years or older may engage in simple adoptions.
[41] Different age requirements apply to single adoptive parents.
[42] Prospective adoptive parents aged 20 to 24 years are permitted to adopt under special circumstances.
[43] Prospective adoptive parents must be aged 30 years or older.
[44] In the case of adoption by a couple, both prospective parents must be aged 25 years older.
[45] In the case of adoption by a couple, only one of the parents must be aged 25 years or older.
[46] Prospective adoptive parents aged 18 to 24 years are permitted to adopt under special circumstances.
[47] Prospective adoptive parents under age 30 are permitted to adopt if they have been married for at least three years.
[48] Prospective adoptive parents must be aged 18 years or older to adopt a relative.
[49] Prospective adoptive parents must be permanent residents in the country.
[50] A female child above the age of 12 must be heard.
[51] Unmarried foreign citizens residing outside of the country are not permitted to adopt.
[52] Requirements regarding age difference do not apply to adoptions by step-parents.

TABLE A.IV.1. COUNTRIES THAT HAVE RATIFIED VARIOUS CONVENTIONS RELEVANT TO INTERCOUNTRY ADOPTIONS

| Country | *Year of ratification* | | | |
	United Nations Convention on the Reduction of Statelessness (1961)	United Nations Convention on the Rights of the Child (1989)	Convention on the Protection of Children and Co-operation in Respect of Intercountry Adoption (1993)	United Nations Optional Protocol to the Convention on the Rights of the Child, on the Sale of Children, Child Prostitution and Child Pornography (2000)
Afghanistan	...	1994	...	2002
Albania	2003	1992	2000	...
Algeria	...	1993	...	2006
Andorra	...	1996	1997	2001
Angola	...	1990	...	2005
Antigua and Barbuda	...	1993	...	2002
Argentina	...	1990	...	2003
Armenia	1994	1993	...	2005
Australia	1973	1990	1998	2007
Austria	1972	1992	1999	2004
Azerbaijan	1996	1992	2004	2002
Bahamas	...	1991	...	...
Bahrain	...	1992	...	2004
Bangladesh	...	1990	...	2000
Barbados	...	1990	...	...
Belarus	...	1990	2003	2002
Belgium	...	1991	2005	2006
Belize	...	1990	2005	2003
Benin	...	1990	...	2005
Bhutan	...	1990	...	..
Bolivia (Plurinational State of)	1983	1990	2002	2003
Bosnia and Herzegovina	1996	1993	...	2002
Botswana	...	1995	...	2003
Brazil	...	1990	1999	2004
Brunei Darussalam	...	1995	...	2006
Bulgaria	...	1991	2002	2002
Burkina Faso	...	1990	1996	2006
Burundi	...	1990	1998	...
Cambodia	...	1992	...	2002
Cameroon	...	1993	...	..
Canada	1978	1991	1996	2005
Cape Verde	...	1992	...	2002
Central African Republic	...	1992	...	...
Chad	1999	1990	...	2002
Chile	...	1990	1999	2003
China	...	1992	2005	2002
Colombia	...	1991	1998	2003
Comoros	...	1993	...	...
Congo	...	1993	...	...
Cook Islands	...	1997	...	...
Costa Rica	1977	1990	1995	2002
Côte d'Ivoire	...	1991	...	...
Croatia	...	1992	...	2002
Cuba	...	1991	...	2001
Cyprus	...	1991	1995	2006

TABLE A.IV.1 (*continued*)

	Year of ratification			
Country	United Nations Convention on the Reduction of Statelessness (1961)	United Nations Convention on the Rights of the Child (1989)	Convention on the Protection of Children and Co-operation in Respect of Intercountry Adoption (1993)	United Nations Optional Protocol to the Convention on the Rights of the Child, on the Sale of Children, Child Prostitution and Child Pornography (2000)
Czech Republic	2001	1993	2000	..
Democratic People's Republic of Korea	...	1990	...	...
Democratic Republic of the Congo	...	1990	...	2001
Denmark	1977	1991	1997	2003
Djibouti	...	1990	...	..
Dominica	...	1991	...	2002
Dominican Republic	..	1991	2006	2006
Ecuador	...	1990	1995	2004
Egypt	...	1990	...	2002
El Salvador	...	1990	1998	2004
Equatorial Guinea	...	1992	...	2003
Eritrea	...	1994	...	2005
Estonia	...	1991	2002	2004
Ethiopia	...	1991	...	...
Fiji	...	1993	...	..
Finland	...	1991	1997	..
France	..	1990	1998	2003
Gabon	...	1994	...	..
Gambia	...	1990	...	..
Georgia	...	1994	1999	2005
Germany	1977	1992	2001	..
Ghana	...	1990	...	..
Greece	...	1993	...	..
Grenada	...	1990	...	...
Guatemala	2001	1990	2002	2002
Guinea	...	1990	2003	...
Guinea-Bissau	...	1990	...	..
Guyana	...	1991	...	...
Haiti	...	1995	...	..
Holy See	...	1990	...	2001
Honduras	...	1990	...	2002
Hungary	...	1991	2005	..
Iceland	...	1992	2000	2001
India	...	1992	2003	2005
Indonesia	...	1990	...	..
Iran (Islamic Republic of)	...	1994	...	...
Iraq	...	1994	...	...
Ireland	1973	1992	..	..
Israel	..	1991	1999	..
Italy	...	1991	2000	2002
Jamaica	...	1991	...	..
Japan	...	1994	...	2005
Jordan	...	1991	...	2006
Kazakhstan	...	1994	...	2001

TABLE A.IV.1 (*continued*)

Country	*United Nations Convention on the Reduction of Statelessness (1961)*	*United Nations Convention on the Rights of the Child (1989)*	*Convention on the Protection of Children and Co-operation in Respect of Intercountry Adoption (1993)*	*United Nations Optional Protocol to the Convention on the Rights of the Child, on the Sale of Children, Child Prostitution and Child Pornography (2000)*
Kenya	...	1990	...	..
Kiribati	1983	1995	...	...
Kuwait	...	1991	...	2004
Kyrgyzstan	...	1994	...	2003
Lao People's Democratic Republic	...	1991	...	2006
Latvia	1992	1992	2002	2006
Lebanon	...	1991	...	2004
Lesotho	2004	1992	...	2003
Liberia	2004	1993	...	..
Libyan Arab Jamahiriya	1989	1993	...	2004
Liechtenstein	...	1995	...	..
Lithuania	...	1992	1998	2004
Luxembourg	...	1994	2002	..
Madagascar	...	1991	2004	2004
Malawi	...	1991	...	..
Malaysia	...	1995	...	...
Maldives	...	1991	...	2002
Mali	...	1990	2006	2002
Malta	...	1990	2004	..
Marshall Islands	...	1993	...	...
Mauritania	...	1991	...	...
Mauritius	...	1990	1998	..
Mexico	...	1990	1994	2002
Micronesia (Federated States of)	...	1993	...	..
Monaco	...	1993	1999	..
Mongolia	...	1990	2000	2003
Montenegro	...	2006	...	2006
Morocco	...	1993	...	2001
Mozambique	...	1994	...	2003
Myanmar	...	1991	...	...
Namibia	...	1990	...	2002
Nauru	...	1994	...	..
Nepal	...	1990	...	2006
Netherlands	1985	1995	1998	2005
New Zealand	2006	1993	1998	..
Nicaragua	...	1990	...	2004
Niger	1985	1990	...	2004
Nigeria	...	1991	...	...
Niue	...	1995	...	...
Norway	1971	1991	1997	2001
Oman	...	1996	...	2004
Pakistan	...	1990	...	..
Palau	...	1995	...	...
Panama	...	1990	1999	2001
Papua New Guinea	...	1993	...	...
Paraguay	...	1990	1998	2003

TABLE A.IV.1 (*continued*)

	Year of ratification			
Country	United Nations Convention on the Reduction of Statelessness (1961)	United Nations Convention on the Rights of the Child (1989)	Convention on the Protection of Children and Co-operation in Respect of Intercountry Adoption (1993)	United Nations Optional Protocol to the Convention on the Rights of the Child, on the Sale of Children, Child Prostitution and Child Pornography (2000)
Peru	...	1990	1995	2002
Philippines	...	1990	1996	2002
Poland	...	1991	1995	2005
Portugal	...	1990	2004	2003
Qatar	...	1995	...	2001
Republic of Korea	...	1991	...	2004
Republic of Moldova	...	1993	1998	..
Romania	2006	1990	1994	2001
Russian Federation	...	1990	..	...
Rwanda	2006	1991	...	2002
Saint Kitts and Nevis	...	1990	...	...
Saint Lucia	...	1993	...	...
Saint Vincent and the Grenadines	...	1993	...	2005
Samoa	...	1994	...	...
San Marino	...	1991	2004	..
São Tome and Principe	...	1991	...	...
Saudi Arabia	...	1996	...	...
Senegal	2005	1990	...	2003
Serbia		2001	...	2002
Seychelles	...	1990	...	..
Sierra Leone	...	1990	...	2001
Singapore	...	1995	...	...
Slovakia	2000	1993	2001	2004
Slovenia	...	1992	2002	2004
Solomon Islands	...	1995	...	...
Somalia	...	..	...	...
South Africa	...	1995	2003	2003
Spain	...	1990	1995	2001
Sri Lanka	...	1991	1995	2006
Sudan	...	1990	...	2004
Suriname	...	1993	...	..
Swaziland	1999	1995	...	...
Sweden	1969	1990	1997	2007
Switzerland	...	1997	2002	2006
Syrian Arab Republic	...	1993	...	2003
Tajikistan	...	1993	...	2002
Thailand	...	1992	2004	2006
The former Yugoslav Republic of Macedonia	...	1993	...	2003
Timor-Leste	...	2003	...	2003
Togo	...	1990	...	2004
Tonga	...	1995	...	...
Trinidad and Tobago	...	1991	...	...
Tunisia	2000	1992	...	2002
Turkey	...	1995	2004	2002

TABLE A.IV.1 (*continued*)

Country	Year of ratification			
	United Nations Convention on the Reduction of Statelessness (1961)	United Nations Convention on the Rights of the Child (1989)	Convention on the Protection of Children and Co-operation in Respect of Intercountry Adoption (1993)	United Nations Optional Protocol to the Convention on the Rights of the Child, on the Sale of Children, Child Prostitution and Child Pornography (2000)
Turkmenistan..	...	1993	...	2005
Tuvalu	...	1995	...	...
Uganda	...	1990	...	2001
Ukraine	...	1991	...	2003
United Arab Emirates...........................	...	1997	...	...
United Kingdom...................................	1966	1991	2003	..
United Republic of Tanzania.................	...	1991	...	2003
United States	...	..	..	2002
Uruguay...	2001	1990	2003	2003
Uzbekistan...	...	1994	...	...
Vanuatu	...	1993	...	..
Venezuela (Bolivarian Republic of).....	...	1990	1997	2002
Viet Nam	...	1990	...	2001
Yemen	...	1991	...	2004
Zambia	...	1991	...	...
Zimbabwe..	...	1990	...	...
Total number of ratifications...................	33	193	70	117

Sources: United Nations 1975a, 1990, and 2002, and Hague Conference on Private International Law, 1996.

NOTES: As of January 2007. Ratification includes acceptance, approval, accession or succession. Two dots (..) indicate that the treaty was signed but not ratified. Three dots (...) indicate that the treaty has been neither ratified nor signed.

TABLE A.V.1. SELECTED ADOPTION RATES BY MAJOR AREA AND COUNTRY

	Year	Total number of adoptions	Adoptions per 100,000 births	Adoption rate (per 100,000 persons)	
				Under age 5	Under age 18
AFRICA					
Benin............................	2005	4	1.1	0.2	0.1
Central African Republic	1995-1998	24	4.2	0.6	0.3
Congo[1,2]	2000	103	67.9	9.6	5.6
Eritrea[1]	1993-2002	50	3.6	0.5	0.3
Ethiopia............................	2002-2003[3]	872	28.8	4.1	2.3
Gabon..............................	1980-1998	40	5.9	0.8	0.5
Gambia.............................	1998-2000	18	12.4	1.8	1.0
Ghana..............................	2004	534	78.6	10.4	5.3
Guinea-Bissau....................	1998-2000	13	6.5	1.0	0.6
Kenya[4]	1998	143	13.0	1.8	0.9
Malawi............................	2001	714	132.9	19.1	11.4
Mali...............................	2003	135	21.3	3.3	1.9
Mauritius..........................	2004	105	529.3	64.1	28.9
Mozambique.......................	1990-1998	90	1.5	0.2	0.1
Namibia	1990-1992[5]	127	86.2	12.2	7.1
Niger[6]	1997-1998	12	1.0	0.2	0.1
Seychelles	2001	6	483.9	58.6	23.5
South Africa.......................	2001	2 218	199.2	25.3	12.1
Sudan[7]	2002	52	4.5	0.6	0.3
Togo...............................	2003	34	14.8	2.1	1.1
Uganda[1]	2005	156	10.6	1.6	0.9
United Republic of Tanzania	1999	15	1.1	0.2	0.1
ASIA					
Armenia	2001-2003[8]	415	482.8	55.9	17.9
Azerbaijan.........................	2003-2005[9]	1 930	583.8	76.0	27.4
Bangladesh[1,10]	2001-2003	100	0.9	0.1	0.1
China..............................	2001	45 844	252.0	29.5	12.2
Cyprus.............................	2001	216	2 173.7	251.9	101.0
Democratic People's Republic of Korea	2003	267	74.6	8.9	3.9
Georgia	2002	154	301.2	36.6	13.0
India	2003	3 047	11.7	1.5	0.7
Indonesia..........................	1999	43	1.0	0.1	0.1
Israel	2003	382	286.7	35.1	17.9
Japan	1995	1 931	159.6	19.3	7.7
Kazakhstan........................	2002	3 600	1 500.9	196.6	75.7
Kyrgyzstan[11]	1999	1 683	1 468.8	184.7	82.3
Mongolia..........................	2004	1 890	3 247.6	422.4	187.3
Myanmar...........................	1999-2000[3]	9	0.8	0.1	0.0
Philippines	2003	1 902	93.5	11.6	5.6
Republic of Korea.................	2004	3 899	834.2	92.8	35.3
Singapore	2002	713	1 648.7	170.4	68.5
Sri Lanka..........................	2001	932	279.8	34.1	14.8
Thailand...........................	2005	51	5.1	0.6	0.3
Turkey.............................	1998-2000	1 329	29.0	3.7	1.8
Uzbekistan	2005	2 836	461.1	59.9	26.4
Viet Nam..........................	2001	2 881	178.0	22.4	9.2

TABLE A.V.1 (*continued*)

	Year	Total number of adoptions	Adoptions per 100,000 births	Adoption rate (per 100,000 persons)	
				Under age 5	Under age 18
EUROPE					
Albania.................................	2003	82	154.6	18.8	7.7
Andorra.................................	2001-2003	11	508.6	60.9	29.6
Austria.................................	1999	862	1 075.7	123.4	52.3
Belarus.................................	2001	868	974.3	120.2	37.7
Belgium	2003	451	402.7	47.8	21.1
Bosnia and Herzegovina..........	2002	71	186.7	19.9	8.2
Bulgaria.................................	1999	2 288	3 460.7	410.3	140.4
Croatia.................................	2003	151	365.2	42.1	16.8
Czech Republic[12]...................	2001	545	614.4	74.3	26.8
Denmark.................................	2003	1 249	1 956.7	225.8	104.7
Estonia.................................	2003	130	999.3	126.5	46.1
Finland.................................	2004	496	895.6	105.9	44.8
France.................................	2003	4 445	596.5	71.9	33.4
Germany.................................	2002	5 668	797.4	89.9	36.9
Greece[1].................................	2001	600	580.7	68.8	29.1
Hungary.................................	2004	750	792.6	93.6	37.6
Iceland.................................	2003	44	1 066.4	126.5	56.3
Ireland.................................	2003	621	1 010.4	129.6	61.8
Italy.................................	1999	3 197	601.9	72.0	31.6
Latvia.................................	2003	106	522.1	65.7	22.0
Liechtenstein.........................	2003-2004	6	821.9	94.7	41.0
Lithuania.................................	2004	196	638.6	76.2	25.5
Luxembourg.............................	2003	54	946.7	113.2	53.3
Malta.................................	1996	12	245.9	28.1	11.9
Monaco[1].................................	2000	10	2 785.5	332.8	144.2
Netherlands[13].........................	2004	1 368	721.6	83.9	38.5
Norway.................................	2003	870	1 567.7	180.3	80.6
Poland[14].................................	1997	2 441	584.9	64.1	23.7
Portugal.................................	2003	409	363.2	43.7	20.3
Republic of Moldova	2004	219	513.5	62.3	20.8
Romania.................................	2004	1 673	786.2	94.4	37.3
Russian Federation[1]	2001	23 108	1 656.0	209.6	69.6
Serbia[15].................................	2001	247	198.0	23.8	9.7
Slovakia.................................	1999	465	838.7	92.6	34.3
Slovenia.................................	2002	46	265.4	31.5	12.5
Spain.................................	2003	4 847	1 107.4	139.0	65.8
Sweden.................................	2004	1 669	1 755.3	208.9	85.6
Switzerland.............................	2002	702	990.0	111.3	46.9
Ukraine	2001	7 593	1 921.8	225.0	71.2
United Kingdom	2002	6 239	923.6	108.0	46.8
LATIN AMERICA AND THE CARIBBEAN					
Argentina	1998	80	11.4	1.4	0.7
Bahamas.................................	2001	22	356.1	43.4	20.5
Belize.................................	2003	79	1 128.7	141.0	68.5
Bolivia (Plurinational State of).................................	2003	348	131.6	17.1	8.7
Brazil[16].................................	2003	4 150	111.4	14.0	6.7
Chile	2003	536	215.0	25.5	10.7

TABLE A.V.1 (*continued*)

	Year	Total number of adoptions	Adoptions per 100,000 births	Adoption rate (per 100,000 persons)	
				Under age 5	Under age 18
Colombia	2004	1 409	145.2	17.9	8.4
Costa Rica	2003	64	80.9	9.8	4.3
Dominica[1]	2003	15	1 168.2	143.4	65.8
Ecuador	2004	118	39.9	4.9	2.3
El Salvador	2003	253	152.1	18.9	9.4
Grenada	1995	15	601.4	73.2	32.5
Guatemala	2004	3 834	885.8	115.7	62.1
Guyana	2002	123	745.1	93.7	45.5
Haiti	1994-1999	2 435	169.0	22.7	10.8
Honduras	2004	50	24.3	3.1	1.5
Jamaica	2002	255	474.6	55.9	25.3
Mexico	2004	973	44.2	5.3	2.4
Nicaragua[1]	1994	86	56.3	7.2	3.8
Panama	2001-2003	40	19.1	2.4	1.2
Paraguay[1]	1999-2001	30	6.0	0.8	0.4
Peru	2004	187	29.8	3.7	1.7
Trinidad and Tobago	2002	18	99.3	12.4	4.6
Venezuela (Bolivarian Republic of)	1995	1 992	352.2	43.5	21.3
NORTHERN AMERICA					
Canada[1]	2000-2001[3]	4 118	1 233.8	142.5	58.2
United States	2001	127 407	3 156.4	385.3	172.6
OCEANIA					
Australia	2003-2004[3]	502	201.8	23.8	10.4
Fiji	1994	89	434.0	56.3	27.4
New Zealand	2002-2003[3]	631	1 154.1	136.5	60.1
Palau	1997	32	11 111.1	1 210.6	571.1
Papua New Guinea[1]	2000	300	166.1	21.8	11.8
Samoa	2002	438	8 084.2	964.2	511.0
Solomon Islands	1995	2	15.3	2.1	1.1

Source: For a complete list of country references, see annex II. For the population under age five and under age 18 and number of births, see United Nations, 2005.

NOTES: Total adoptions refer to the sum of domestic and intercountry adoptions as reported by the country. For countries that are primarily destinations for intercountry adoptions (listed in annex I), data include foreign-born children adopted from abroad. For countries of origin of intercountry adoptions, data include nationals adopted abroad by non-citizens. Because intercountry adoptions are included in both the data of the country of origin and the country of destination, the total number of adoptions in the world cannot be computed by summing the number of total adoptions for each country as shown in this table. For a description of the estimation procedure used to obtain the total number of adoptions worldwide see annex I. The adoption ratio is calculated by dividing the total number of adoptions by the number of live births. The under-five adoption rate is calculated by dividing the total number of adoptions of children under age five by the number of children under age five. It is assumed that 60 per cent of the children adopted are under age five at the time of adoption. The under-18 adoption rate is calculated by dividing the total number of adoptions of persons under age 18 by the number of persons under age 18. It is assumed that all adopted persons are under age 18 at the time of adoption. Because the number of adoptions is very small in many of the countries considered, some of the percentages and rates may vary considerably over time.

[1] Estimate.
[2] Data refer to adoptions heard by the Brazzaville District Court.
[3] Data refer to the fiscal year.
[4] Data refer to the estimated number of adoption applications recorded by the Child Welfare Society of Kenya.
[5] Data refer to adoptions registered between March 1990 and August 1992.
[6] Data refer to adoptions of abandoned children.
[7] Data refer only to the State of Khartoum.
[8] Data for 2003 refer to the first six months only.
[9] Data for 2005 refer to the first six months only.

TABLE A.V.1 (*continued*)

[10] Data refer to children placed in families.
[11] Data include children that have been adopted as well as those placed with guardians.
[12] Data refer to children placed in pre-adoption care.
[13] Data refer to adoptions granted by Dutch courts.
[14] Data refer to adoption rulings by the courts.
[15] Data refer to Serbia and Montenegro.
[16] Data refer only to the State of São Paulo.

TABLE A.V.2. SELECTED ADOPTION INDICATORS BY MAJOR AREA AND COUNTRY

	Year	Number of adoptions			Percentage		
		Total	*Domestic*	*Intercountry*	*Total*	*Domestic*	*Intercountry*
AFRICA							
Benin..........................	2005	4	3	1	100	75	25
Burkina Faso....................	1996	...	...	48	...	...	...
Burundi[1]	1998	...	...	50	...	...	...
Cameroon......................	1996-1997	...	...	12[2]	...	...	...
Central African Republic	1995-1998	24	11	13	100	46	54
Chad[1]	1993-1996	...	...	4	..	...	...
Congo[1,3]	2000	103	51	52	100	50	50
Eritrea[1]	1993-2002	50	...	...	100	...	...
Ethiopia......................	2002-2003[4]	872	62	810	100	7	93
Gabon........................	1980-1998	40	...	...	100	...	...
Gambia.......................	1998-2000	18	8	10	100	44	56
Ghana........................	2004	534	529	5	100	99	1
Guinea-Bissau..................	1998-2000	13	...	...	100	...	...
Kenya........................	1998	143[5]	...	...	100	...	...
Madagascar....................	2002	...	...	373	..	...	...
Malawi.......................	2001	714	714	..	100	100	..
Mali.........................	2003	135	1	134	100	1	99
Mauritius.....................	2004	105	92[6]	13	100	88	12
Mozambique	1990-1998	90	45	45	100	50	50
Namibia	1990-1992[7]	127	127	..	100	100	..
Niger[8]	1997-1998	12	4	8	100	33	67
Rwanda	2001	...	...	9	...	...	...
Senegal.......................	2005	...	...	14	...	...	...
Seychelles	2001	6	6	..	100	100	..
South Africa...................	2001	2 218	1 906	312	100	86	14
Sudan[9]......................	2002	52	...	...	100	...	...
Swaziland.....................	2005	...	24	...	...	...	...
Togo.........................	2003	34	9	25	100	26	74
Uganda[1]	2005	156	...	...	100	...	...
United Republic of Tanzania	1999	15	15	..	100	100	..
ASIA							
Armenia	2001-2003[10]	415	272	143	100	66	34
Azerbaijan....................	2003-2005[11]	1 930	1 787	143	100	93	7
Bangladesh[1,12]...............	2001-2003	100	100	..	100	100	..
China........................	2001	45 844	37 200	8 644	100	81	19
Cyprus.......................	2001	216	51	165	100	24	76
Democratic People's Republic of Korea	2003	267	267	0	100	100	0
Georgia	2002	154	35	119	100	23	77
India........................	2003	3 047	1 949	1 098	100	64	36
Indonesia.....................	1999	43	33	10	100	77	23
Israel	2003	382	126	256	100	33	67
Japan........................	1995	1 931	1 632[13]	299	100	85	15
Kazakhstan....................	2002	3 600	2 652	948	100	74	26
Kyrgyzstan[14]	1999	1 683	...	...	100	...	...
Mongolia.....................	2004	1 890	1 861	29	100	98	2
Myanmar.....................	1999-2000[4]	9	...	...	100	...	...
Nepal........................	2000	...	...	78	...	...	...
Philippines	2003	1 902	...	...	100	...	...

TABLE A.V.2 (*continued*)

	Year	Number of adoptions			Percentage		
		Total	*Domestic*	*Intercountry*	*Total*	*Domestic*	*Intercountry*
Republic of Korea	2004	3 899	1 641	2 258	100	42	58
Singapore	2002	713	265	448	100	37	63
Sri Lanka	2001	932	881	51	100	95	5
Thailand	2005	51	1	50	100	2	98
Turkey	1998-2000	1 329	1 299	30[15]	100	98	2
Uzbekistan	2005	2 836	2 828	8	100	100	0
Viet Nam	2001	2 881	1 462	1 419	100	51	49
EUROPE							
Albania	2003	82	56	26	100	68	32
Andorra	2001-2003	11	4	7	100	36	64
Austria	1999	862	...	...	100	...	...
Belarus	2001	868	421	447	100	49	51
Belgium	2003	451	21[16]	430[17]	100	5	95
Bosnia and Herzegovina	2002	71	...	...	100	...	...
Bulgaria	1999	2 288	1 278	1 010	100	56	44
Croatia	2003	151	148	3	100	98	2
Czech Republic[18]	2001	545	519[1]	26	100	95	5
Denmark	2003	1 249	561	688	100	45	55
Estonia	2003	130	115	15	100	88	12
Finland	2004	496	207	289	100	42	58
France	2003	4 445	450	3 995	100	10	90
Germany	2002	5 668	3 749	1 919	100	66	34
Greece[1]	2001	600	...	...	100	...	...
Hungary	2004	750	656	94[19]	100	87	13
Iceland	2003	44	21	23	100	48	52
Ireland	2003	621	263	358[20]	100	42	58
Italy	1999	3 197	1 020	2 177	100	32	68
Latvia	2003	106	27	79	100	25	75
Liechtenstein	2003-2004	6	1	5	100	17	83
Lithuania	2004	196	93	103	100	47	53
Luxembourg	2003	54	3	51[21]	100	6	94
Malta	1996	12	7	5	100	58	42
Monaco[1]	2000	10	...	...	100	...	...
Netherlands[22]	2004	1 368	299[1]	1 069[1]	100	22	78
Norway	2003	870	206	664	100	24	76
Poland[23]	1997	2 441	2 236	205	100	92	8
Portugal	2003	409	403	6[24]	100	99	1
Republic of Moldova	2004	219	137	82	100	63	37
Romania	2004	1 673	1 422	251[25]	100	85	15
Russian Federation	2001	23 108[1]	17 331[1]	5 777	100	75	25
Serbia[26]	2001	247	...	...	100	...	...
Slovakia	1999	465	...	...	100	...	...
Slovenia	2002	46	45	1	100	98	2
Spain	2003	4 847	896	3 951	100	18	82
Sweden	2004	1 669	576	1 093	100	35	65
Switzerland	2002	702	144	558	100	21	79
Ukraine	2001	7 593	4 921	2 672	100	65	35
United Kingdom	2002	6 239	5 910[1]	329[27]	100	95	5

United Nations Department of Economic and Social Affairs/Population Division
Child Adoption: Trends and Policies

TABLE A.V.2 (*continued*)

	Year	Number of adoptions			Percentage		
		Total	Domestic	Intercountry	Total	Domestic	Intercountry
LATIN AMERICA AND THE CARIBBEAN							
Argentina	1998	80	80	..	100	100	..
Bahamas	2001	22	14	8	100	64	36
Belize	2003	79	74	5	100	94	6
Bolivia (Plurinational State of)	2003	348	145	203	100	42	58
Brazil[28]	2003	4 150	4 030	120	100	97	3
Chile	2003	536	445	91	100	83	17
Colombia	2004	1 409	563	846	100	40	60
Costa Rica	2003	64	32[29]	32[30]	100	50	50
Dominica[1]	2003	15	...	...	100	...	...
Ecuador	2004	118	75	43	100	64	36
El Salvador	2003	253	136	117	100	54	46
Grenada	1995	15	4	11	100	27	73
Guatemala	2004	3 834	108	3 726	100	3	97
Guyana	2002	123	...	...	100	...	...
Haiti	1994-1999	2 435	338	2 097	100	14	86
Honduras	2004	50	20	30	100	40	60
Jamaica	2002	255	219	36	100	86	14
Mexico	2004	973	873	100[31]	100	90	10
Nicaragua[1]	1994	86	69	17[32]	100	80	20
Panama	2001-2003	40	38	2	100	95	5
Paraguay[1]	1999-2001	30	...	...	100	...	...
Peru	2004	187	95	92	100	51	49
Trinidad and Tobago	2002	18	...	...	100	...	...
Venezuela (Bolivarian Republic of)	1995	1 992	...	...	100	...	...
NORTHERN AMERICA							
Canada[1]	2000-2001[4]	4 118	2 243	1 875	100	54	46
United States	2001	127 407	108 351	19 056[33]	100	85	15
OCEANIA							
Australia	2003-2004[4]	502	132	370	100	26	74
Fiji	1994	89	79[1]	10[1]	100	89	11
Kiribati[1]	2004-2006	...	...	3	...	...	...
New Zealand	2002-2003[4]	631	295	336	100	47	53
Palau	1997	32	...	...	100	...	...
Papua New Guinea[1]	2000	300	...	...	100	...	...
Samoa	2002	438	...	...	100	...	...
Solomon Islands	1995	2	2	..	100	100	..

Source: For a complete list of country references, see annex II.

NOTES: Total adoptions refer to the sum of domestic and intercountry adoptions as reported by the country. For countries that are primarily destinations for intercountry adoptions (listed in annex I), data include foreign-born children adopted from abroad. For countries of origin for intercountry adoptions, data include nationals adopted abroad. Percentage of domestic and intercountry adoptions is calculated based on the total number of adoptions. Because the number of adoptions is very small in many of the countries considered, some of the percentages and rates may vary considerably over time.

[1] Estimate.
[2] Data refer to intercountry adoption requests.
[3] Data refer to adoptions heard by the Brazzaville District Court.
[4] Data refer to the fiscal year.
[5] Data refer to the estimated number of adoption applications recorded by the Child Welfare Society of Kenya.
[6] Data include both simple and full adoptions.

TABLE A.V.2 (*continued*)

[7] Data refer to adoptions registered between March 1990 and August 1992.

[8] Data refer to adoptions of abandoned children.

[9] Data refer only to the State of Khartoum.

[10] Data for 2003 refer to the first six months only.

[11] Data for 2005 refer to the first six months only.

[12] Data refer to children placed in families.

[13] Data include regular and special adoptions.

[14] Data include children that have been adopted as well as those placed with guardians.

[15] Data include 27 adoptions by Turkish families residing abroad.

[16] Data refer to domestic adoptions in the region of Flanders.

[17] Data refer to intercountry adoptions in the regions of Flanders and Wallonia.

[18] Data refer to children placed in pre-adoption care.

[19] Data include 14 foreign children adopted by Hungarian citizens as well as 80 Hungarian children adopted abroad.

[20] Data refer to number of adoptions overseas.

[21] Data refer to children in the process of undergoing adoption.

[22] Data refer to adoptions granted by Dutch courts.

[23] Data refer to adoption rulings by the courts.

[24] Data include 1 foreign child adopted by Portuguese citizens as well as 5 Portuguese children adopted abroad.

[25] Data refer to children previously protected in public or private placement centres or in substitute families.

[26] Data refer to Serbia and Montenegro.

[27] Data refer to the number of applications for intercountry adoptions received by the Department of Health during the year ending 31 March.

[28] Data refer only to the State of São Paulo.

[29] Data refer to adoptions arranged by the National Children's Trust.

[30] Data refer to both adoptions arranged by the National Children's Trust as well as by direct contact between the parties concerned in the metropolitan area.

[31] Data refer to intercountry adoptions by citizens of States that are parties to the Convention on Protection of Children and Co-operation in Respect of Intercountry Adoption.

[32] Data refer to children adopted by foreign citizens residing in Nicaragua.

[33] Data refer to children who entered under an orphan visa for purposes of adoption. These include children with an IR-3 visa status who were adopted abroad and children with an IR-4 status who were to be adopted in the United States.

TABLE A.V.3. MAIN COUNTRIES OF DESTINATION OF INTERCOUNTRY ADOPTIONS
FOR SELECTED COUNTRIES OF ORIGIN

Country of origin	Year	Main receiving country				
		1st	2nd	3rd	4th	5th
Albania[1]	2003	United States	Italy	...	...	...
Belarus[1]	2001	Italy	United States	Sweden	Denmark	Ireland
Bolivia (Plurinational State of)[1]	2003	Spain	Italy	France	Denmark and United States	Sweden
Brazil[1]	2003	Italy	France	Switzerland	United States	Norway
Bulgaria[1]	1999	Italy	United States	Spain	Sweden	Denmark
Chile	2003	Italy	France	Germany	Spain and Norway	United States
China[1]	2001	United States	Spain	Canada	France[2]	Netherlands
Colombia	2004	France	Italy	Spain	Norway	Netherlands
Costa Rica	2003	Spain	United States	Italy	...	...
Czech Republic............	2001	Denmark	Italy	...	...	...
Ecuador	2004	United States	Italy	Spain	Belgium, Demark, Netherlands and Norway	Switzerland
Estonia..........................	2003	United States	Sweden	Finland	...	...
Ethiopia[1]	2002-2003[3]	France	United States	Spain	Switzerland	Netherlands
Georgia[1]	2002	United States	Canada	Italy	...	...
Guatemala.....................	2004	United States	France	United Kingdom	Belgium and Italy	Ireland
Haiti[1]	2003	France	United States	Canada	Netherlands	Spain
Honduras[1]	2004	Spain	United States	...	...	...
Hungary.......................	2004	Italy	Norway	Spain	France	United States
India...........................	2003	United States	Italy	Spain	Sweden	Denmark
Jamaica	2002	United States	Canada	...	...	...
Kazakhstan[1]	2002	United States	Ireland	Canada	...	...
Latvia..........................	2003	France	United States	Canada, Spain and Sweden	Russian Federation	...
Lithuania.....................	2004	Italy	France and United States	Sweden	Australia	Spain
Madagascar[1]	2003	France	Spain	Switzerland	Italy	...
Mali[1]	2003	France	Spain	...	...	...
Nepal[1]	2000	Spain	Denmark and Italy	...	...	...
Peru	2004	Spain	Italy	Norway	Belgium, Demark, Germany and Luxembourg	France, Netherlands and Sweden
Poland..........................	2004	Italy	United States	France	Netherlands	Sweden
Republic of Korea[1]	2004	United States	Sweden	Australia	Canada	Denmark
Republic of Moldova....	2004	United States	Italy	Israel	Spain	Canada
Romania[1]	2004	Italy	United States	Spain	France	Germany
Russian Federation[1]	2001	United States	Spain	France[2]	Germany	Canada

TABLE A.V.3 (*continued*)

| Country of origin | Year | Main receiving country | | | | |
		1st	2nd	3rd	4th	5th
Slovakia[4]	2004	Italy	France	Canada	...	...
South Africa	2003	Sweden	Netherlands	Finland	Denmark	United States
Sri Lanka[1]	2001	Germany	Italy	Netherlands	Australia	Switzerland
Ukraine[1]	2001	United States	Italy	Spain	France[2]	Germany
Viet Nam[1]	2001	United States	Germany	Canada	Sweden	Denmark

Source: For a complete list of country references, see annex II.

[1] Estimate based on data from selected receiving countries.
[2] Data refer to 2004.
[3] Data refer to the fiscal year.
[4] Data refer to intercountry adoptions by citizens of States that are parties to the Convention on Protection of Children and Co-operation in Respect of Intercountry Adoption.

TABLE A.V.4. MAIN COUNTRIES OF ORIGIN OF INTERCOUNTRY ADOPTIONS
FOR SELECTED COUNTRIES OF DESTINATION

Receiving country	Year	Main country of origin				
		1st	*2nd*	*3rd*	*4th*	*5th*
Andorra	2002	Romania	...	...	…	…
Australia	2003-2004[1]	China	Republic of Korea	Ethiopia	Thailand	Philippines
Belgium[2].................	2003	China	Ethiopia	Cambodia	Russian Federation	India
Canada......................	2003-2004[1]	China	Haiti	Russian Federation	Republic of Korea	United States
Denmark...................	2003	China	India	Colombia	Republic of Korea	Thailand
Finland......................	2004	China	Russian Federation	Thailand	South Africa	Colombia
France.......................	2004	Haiti	China	Russian Federation	Ethiopia	Viet Nam
Germany...................	2002	Russian Federation	Viet Nam	Ukraine	Romania	Poland
Iceland.....................	2003	China	India	…	…	…
Ireland	2003	Russian Federation	China	Belarus and Viet Nam	Kazakhstan	Thailand
Israel........................	2003	Ukraine	Russian Federation	Belarus	Georgia	Romania
Italy	2004	Russian Federation	Ukraine	Colombia	Belarus	Brazil
Luxembourg	2003	Republic of Korea	Guatemala	India and South Africa	Colombia, Peru and Romania	…
Malta	2002	Romania	Pakistan	Kenya and Morocco	…	…
Netherlands..............	2003	China	Colombia	Haiti	South Africa	Ethiopia
Norway.....................	2003	China	Colombia	Republic of Korea	Ethiopia	India
Singapore.................	2002	Malaysia	China	Indonesia	India	Thailand
Spain........................	2003	Russian Federation	China	Ukraine	Colombia	Bulgaria
Sweden	2004	China	Republic of Korea	Colombia	South Africa	Russian Federation
Switzerland..............	2002	Colombia	Russian Federation	Romania	India	Thailand
United Kingdom[3]......	2002	China	Guatemala	India	Thailand	United States
United States	2005	China	Russian Federation	Guatemala	Republic of Korea	Ukraine

Source: For a complete list of country references, see annex II.

[1] Data refer to the fiscal year.
[2] Main countries of origin for the region of Flanders only.
[3] Data refer to the number of applications for intercountry adoptions received by the Department of Health during the year ending 31 March.

TABLE A.VI.1. TOTAL NUMBER OF ADOPTIONS AND PERCENTAGE DISTRIBUTION OF ADOPTIONS
BY AGE OF THE CHILD AT THE TIME OF ADOPTION

| Country | Year | Total adoptions | | | | | | | Mean age at the time of adoption[1] |
| | | Number | Percentage of adopted children under age | | | | | | |
			1	2	3	4	5	6	
Albania	1994-1998[2]	298	14.4	...	...	...	...	89.6	4.3
Andorra	2001-2003	11	18.2	...	...	...	100.0	...	2.1
Armenia	2001-2003[3]	415	...	...	...	...	67.0	...	5.4
Australia	2003-2004[4]	502	43.0	...	...	...	83.5	...	3.2
Belgium[5]	2003	186	42.5	74.2	87.1	91.4	94.1	...	1.8
Chile	2003	536	32.3	...	...	...	77.2	...	3.4
Colombia	2004	1 409	17.3	...	...	...	68.3	...	4.4
Costa Rica	2003	64[6]	12.1	37.9	46.6	48.3	53.4	58.6	4.9
Croatia	2003	151	19.9	...	...	...	64.9	...	4.4
Denmark	2003	1 249	20.0	40.3	46.0	49.6	53.5	55.9	9.3
Ecuador	2004	118	2.5	...	...	...	72.9	...	5.0
France	2003	4 445	33.6[1]	...	...	...	...	...	3.4
Gambia	1998-2000	18	...	5.6	...	...	...	16.7	11.3
Germany	2002	5 668	2.0	...	24.5	...	...	41.0	8.2
Ireland	2003	621	26.7	50.2	58.8	66.0	68.3	71.2[1]	4.5
Lithuania	2004	196	...	...	...	49.5	...	...	4.7
New Zealand	2002-2003[4]	631	13.2	...	...	...	40.1	...	7.7
Norway	2003	870	29.3	...	68.3	...	...	...	4.6
Panama	2001-2003	40	...	...	...	...	52.5	...	5.6
Peru	2004	187	...	...	...	...	...	83.4	4.2
Philippines	2003	1 902[7]	...	...	24.5	...	...	46.4	7.7
Republic of Moldova	2004	219	22.8	...	...	...	57.1	...	5.4
Samoa	2002	438	6.4	10.3	12.8	14.6	16.9	19.9	11.2
Singapore	2002	713	...	...	75.0	...	...	85.7	3.2
Switzerland	2002	702	0.4	...	...	...	39.7	...	8.5
United Kingdom	2002	6 239	5.0	...	...	...	48.9	...	6.3
Median	..	..	18.2	39.1	46.6	49.6	64.9	57.3	4.8

Source: For a complete list of country references, see annex II.

NOTE: Because the number of adoptions is very small in many of the countries considered, some of the percentages may vary considerably over time.

[1] Estimate.
[2] Data refer to the period May 1994 to February 1998.
[3] Data for 2003 refer only to the first six months.
[4] Data refer to the fiscal year.
[5] Data refer to adoptions in the region of Flanders.
[6] Of these, six are of unknown age.
[7] Of these, nine are of unknown age.

United Nations Department of Economic and Social Affairs/Population Division
Child Adoption: Trends and Policies

TABLE A.VI.2. NUMBER OF DOMESTIC ADOPTIONS AND PERCENTAGE DISTRIBUTION OF DOMESTIC ADOPTIONS
BY AGE OF THE CHILD AT THE TIME OF ADOPTION

Country	Year	Number	Domestic adoptions Percentage of adopted children under age						Mean age at the time of adoption[1]
			1	2	3	4	5	6	
Andorra	2001-2003	4	50.0	...	...	...	100.0	...	1.5
Australia	2003-2004[2]	132	48.5	...	...	...	55.3	...	5.9
Chile	2003	445	38.9	...	...	...	89.0	...	2.6
Colombia	2004	563	22.0	...	...	...	59.7	...	5.2
Costa Rica	2003	32	21.9	65.6	78.1	81.3	87.5	90.6	2.6
Denmark[1]	2003	561	12.8	14.1	14.8	16.4	18.4	20.0	15.8
Ecuador	2004	75	0.0	...	...	...	73.3	...	5.4
France	2003	450	57.0	...	...	...	...	...	2.7
Gambia[3]	1998-2000	8	0.0	0.0	0.0	0.0	0.0	0.0	14.3
Germany	2002	3 749	...	...	23.6	...	...	40.4	7.9
Ireland	2003	263	2.3	20.2	24.3	28.1	31.6	...	8.2
Israel	1997	149	...	47.7	...	...	...	...	4.7
Lithuania	2004	93	...	...	...	74.2	...	...	3.2
Mongolia	2004	1 861	...	...	37.3	...	...	...	6.3
Netherlands[4]	2003	29	58.6	...	...	...	75.9	...	3.7
New Zealand	2002-2003[2]	295	18.0	...	...	...	49.5	...	6.7
Norway	2003	206	1.5	...	6.8	...	...	...	12.2
Portugal[5]	2003	403	19.1	...	...	...	56.3	...	5.1
Republic of Moldova	2004	137	35.0	...	...	...	61.3	...	4.8
Switzerland	2002	144	0.0	...	...	...	15.3	...	11.9
United States of America	1988	19 000[6]	6.2	...	...	...	...	52.7	6.8
Median	..	..	19.1	20.2	23.6	28.1	58.0	40.4	5.4

Source: For a complete list of country references, see annex II.

NOTE: Because the number of adoptions is very small in many of the countries considered, some of the percentages may vary considerably over time.

[1] Estimate.
[2] Data refer to the fiscal year.
[3] All domestic adoptions between 1998 and 2000 involved children above age six.
[4] Data refer to a sub-set of all domestic adoptions.
[5] Data refer to dual-national emigrants and non-resident aliens.
[6] Data refer to children adopted from public child welfare at the end of fiscal year 1988. Data by age collected for 22 states only.

TABLE A.VI.3. NUMBER OF INTERCOUNTRY ADOPTIONS AND PERCENTAGE DISTRIBUTION OF INTERCOUNTRY ADOPTIONS BY AGE OF THE CHILD AT THE TIME OF ADOPTION

| Country | Year | Number of adoptions | Intercountry adoptions | | | | | | Mean age at the time of adoption[1] |
| | | | Percentage of adopted children under age | | | | | | |
			1	2	3	4	5	6	
Andorra	2001-2003	7	0.0	...	...	...	100.0	...	2.5
Australia	2003-2004[2]	370	41.1	...	...	...	93.5	...	2.3
Belarus	2001	447	8.1	...	38.7	...	...	59.5	5.6
Canada	2001	1 875[3]	...	...	...	...	78.4	...	4.6
Chile	2003	91	0.0	...	...	...	19.8	...	7.5
Colombia	2004	846	14.2	...	...	...	74.1	...	3.9
Costa Rica	2003	32[4]	0.0	3.8	7.7	7.7	11.5	19.2	7.9
Denmark[1]	2003	688	25.9	61.6	71.5	76.7	82.1	85.2	4.0
Ecuador	2004	43	7.0	...	...	...	72.1	...	4.4
Finland	2004	289	33.2	65.7	81.7	86.5	92.4	94.8	2.2
France	2003	3 995	31.0	...	...	...	...	...	3.4
Gambia	1998-2000	10	...	10.0	...	...	...	30.0	9.0
Germany	2002	1 919	...	...	26.4	...	...	42.2	8.3
Ireland	2003	358	44.7	72.3	84.1	93.9	95.3	96.1	1.8
Israel	2003	256	31.3	...	...	...	99.6	...	2.2
Italy	2000-2004	10 538	6.5	...	...	...	55.1	...	5.6
Kazakhstan[5]	2002	948	...	...	63.0	...	...	86.6	3.5
Lithuania	2004	103	...	...	...	27.2	...	...	6.2
Netherlands	2003	1 154	...	65.3	...	...	95.3	...	2.2
New Zealand	2002-2003[2]	336	8.9	...	...	...	31.8	...	8.6
Norway	2003	664	38.0	...	87.3	...	...	...	2.2
Republic of Moldova	2004	82	2.4	...	...	...	50.0	...	6.5
Romania[6]	2003	332	0.3	...	...	...	70.8	...	4.7
Slovakia[6]	2004	125	1.6	...	...	...	58.4	...	4.9
Sweden	2004	1 109[7]	...	65.6	...	88.1	...	93.9	2.3
Switzerland	2002	558	0.5	...	...	...	46.1	...	6.8
United States of America	2001-2002[2]	21 368	44.2	...	...	...	87.2	...	2.8
Median	..	..	8.5	65.3	67.3	81.6	74.1	85.2	4.4

Source: For a complete list of country references, see annex II.

NOTE: Because the number of adoptions is very small in many of the countries considered, some of the percentages may vary considerably over time.

[1] Estimate.
[2] Data refer to the fiscal year.
[3] Of these, three are of unknown age.
[4] Of these, six are of unknown age.
[5] Of these, 65 are of unknown age. These children were adopted by relatives outside of Kazakhstan.
[6] Data refer to intercountry adoptions by citizens of States that are parties to the Convention on Protection of Children and Co-operation in Respect of Intercountry Adoption.
[7] Data based on a survey by the Swedish National Board of Intercountry Adoptions.

TABLE A.VI.4. SEX RATIO OF ADOPTED CHILDREN AND PERCENTAGE DISTRIBUTION BY SEX

Country	Year	Number of adoptions	Sex ratio of adopted children (boys per 100 girls)	Boys (1))	Girls (2)	Difference in percentages of boys and girls (1)-(2) (Percentage points)
				Total adoptions		
				Percentage distribution of adopted children by sex		
Albania	1994-1998[1]	298	97.4	49.3	50.7	-1.4
Andorra	2001-2003	11	83.3	45.5	54.5	-9.0
Armenia	2001-2003[2]	415	100.5	50.1	49.9	0.2
Australia	2003-2004[3]	502[4]	81.6	44.9	55.1	-10.2
Bahamas	2001-2003	53[5]	92.6	48.1	51.9	-3.8
Chile	2003	536	86.8	46.5	53.5	-7.0
Colombia	2004	1 409	101.0	50.2	49.8	0.4
Costa Rica	2003	64	77.8	43.8	56.3	-12.5
Denmark	2003	1 249	77.2	43.6	56.4	-12.8
Ecuador	2004	118	96.7	49.2	50.8	-1.6
Ethiopia	2002-2003[3]	872	92.5	48.1	51.9	-3.8
France	2003	4 445	98.8	49.7	50.3	-0.6
Gambia	1998-2000	18	80.0	44.4	55.6	-11.2
Georgia	2002	154	85.5	46.1	53.9	-7.8
Germany	2002	5 668	104.3	51.1	48.9	2.2
Grenada	1990-1995	172	43.3	30.2	69.8	-39.6
India	2003	3 047	58.5	36.9	63.1	-26.2
Ireland	2003	621	88.2	46.9	53.1	-6.2
Jamaica	2002	255	79.6	44.3	55.7	-11.4
New Zealand	2002-2003[3]	631[6]	85.8	46.2	53.8	-7.6
Norway	2003	870	54.5	35.3	64.7	-29.4
Panama	2001-2003	40	66.7	40.0	60.0	-20.0
Paraguay[7]	1999-2001	30[5]	45.0	31.0	69.0	-38.0
Peru	2004	187	92.8	48.1	51.9	-3.8
Philippines	2003	1 902	72.3	42.0	58.0	-16.0
Republic of Moldova	2004	219	72.4	42.0	58.0	-16.0
Samoa	2002	438	91.3	47.7	52.3	-4.6
Seychelles	1999-2001	17	54.5	35.3	64.7	-29.4
Singapore	2002	713	85.7	46.1	53.9	-7.8
Sudan[8]	2002	52	136.4	57.7	42.3	15.4
Sweden	2004	1 669	58.2	36.8	63.2	-26.4
Switzerland	2002	702	96.6	49.1	50.9	-1.8
Thailand	2002-2005	233	147.9	59.7	40.3	19.4
Togo	2003	34	142.9	58.8	41.2	17.6
Turkey	1998-2000	1 329	122.2	55.0	45.0	10.0
Uganda	2005	156[7]	85.7	46.2	53.8	-7.6
United Kingdom	2002	6 239	101.3	50.3	49.7	0.6
Venezuela (Bolivarian Republic of)[9]	2000	990	92.2	48.0	52.0	-4.0
Viet Nam	2001	2 881	129.9	56.5	43.5	13.0
Median	..	..	86.8	46.5	53.5	-7.0

Source: For a complete list of country references, see annex II.

NOTE: Because the number of adoptions is very small in many of the countries considered, some of the percentages may vary considerably over time.

[1] Data refer to the period May 1994 to February 1998.
[2] Data for 2003 refer only to the first six months.
[3] Data refer to the fiscal year.

TABLE A.VI.4 (*continued*)

[4] Of these, eight are of unknown sex.
[5] Of these, one is of unknown sex.
[6] Of these, 265 are of unknown sex.
[7] Estimate.
[8] Data refer only to the State of Khartoum.
[9] Data refer to persons in the process of being adopted.

TABLE A.VI.5. SEX RATIO OF CHILDREN ADOPTED DOMESTICALLY AND PERCENTAGE DISTRIBUTION BY SEX

Country	Year	Number of adoptions	Sex ratio of adopted children (boys per 100 girls)	Percentage distribution of adopted children by sex		Difference in percentages of boys and girls (1)-(2) (Percentage points)
				Boys (1)	Girls (2)	
Andorra................................	2001-2003	4	100.0	50.0	50.0	0.0
Australia	2003-2004[1]	132[2]	134.0	57.3	42.7	14.6
Chile	2003	445	84.6	45.8	54.2	-8.4
Colombia	2004	563	76.5	43.3	56.7	-13.4
Costa Rica	2003	32	100.0	50.0	50.0	0.0
Denmark	2003	561	82.1	45.1	54.9	-9.8
Ecuador................................	2004	75	82.9	45.3	54.7	-9.4
Ethiopia	2002-2003[1]	62	226.3	69.4	30.6	38.8
France	2003	450	116.3	53.8	46.2	7.6
Gambia	1998-2000	8	100.0	50.0	50.0	0.0
Georgia	2002	35	94.4	48.6	51.4	-2.8
Germany	2002	3 749	104.4	51.1	48.9	2.2
India	2003	1 949	67.7	40.4	59.6	-19.2
Ireland..................................	2003	263	115.6	53.6	46.4	7.2
Jamaica................................	2002	219	75.2	42.9	57.1	-14.2
Lithuania..............................	2004	93	69.1	40.9	59.1	-18.2
Malawi..................................	2001	714	84.5	45.8	54.2	-8.4
Myanmar	1991-2000[1]	94	49.2	33.0	67.0	-34.0
New Zealand..........................	2002-2003[1]	295	85.5	46.1	53.9	-7.8
Norway	2003	206	67.5	40.3	59.7	-19.4
Portugal	2003	403	113.2	53.1	46.9	6.2
Republic of Moldova...............	2004	137	63.1	38.7	61.3	-22.6
Singapore..............................	2002	265	119.0	54.3	45.7	8.6
Sri Lanka	2001	881	69.7	41.1	58.9	-17.8
Sweden	2004	576	77.8	43.8	56.3	-12.5
Switzerland...........................	2002	144	97.3	49.3	50.7	-1.4
Thailand...............................	2002-2005	5	150.0	60.0	40.0	20.0
Togo	2003	9	50.0	33.3	66.7	-33.4
United Republic of Tanzania	1997-1999	45	87.5	46.7	53.3	-6.6
Viet Nam	2001	1 462	163.9	62.1	37.9	24.2
Median..................................	..	..	86.5	46.4	53.6	-7.2

Source: For a complete list of country references, see annex II.

NOTE: Because the number of adoptions is very small in many of the countries considered, some of the percentages may vary considerably over time.

[1] Data refer to the fiscal year.
[2] Of these, eight are of unknown sex.

TABLE A.VI.6. SEX RATIO OF CHILDREN ADOPTED THROUGH AN INTERCOUNTRY PROCEDURE AND PERCENTAGE DISTRIBUTION BY SEX

Country	Year	Number of adoptions	Sex ratio of adopted children (boys per 100 girls)	Boys (1))	Girls (2))	Difference in percentages of boys and girls (1)-(2) (Percentage points)
				Percentage distribution of adopted children by sex		
Andorra	2001-2003	7	75.0	42.9	57.1	-14.2
Australia	2003-2004[1]	370	68.9	40.8	59.2	-18.4
Belarus	2001	447	92.7	48.1	51.9	-3.8
Canada	2001	1 875[2]	47.8	32.3	67.7	-35.4
Chile	2003	91	97.8	49.5	50.5	-1.0
Colombia	2004	846	121.5	54.8	45.2	9.6
Costa Rica	2003	32	60.0	37.5	62.5	-25.0
Denmark	2003	688	73.3	42.3	57.7	-15.4
Ecuador	2004	43	126.3	55.8	44.2	11.6
Ethiopia	2002-2003[1]	810	86.6	46.4	53.6	-7.2
Finland	2004	289	96.6	49.1	50.9	-1.8
France	2003	3 995	97.0	49.2	50.8	-1.6
Gambia	1998-2000	10	66.7	40.0	60.0	-20.0
Georgia	2002	119	83.1	45.4	54.6	-9.2
Germany	2002	1 919	104.1	51.0	49.0	2.0
India	2003	1 098	44.3	30.7	69.3	-38.6
Ireland	2003	358	72.1	41.9	58.1	-16.2
Italy	2000-2004	10 538	132.6	57.0	43.0	14.0
Jamaica	2002	36	111.8	52.8	47.2	5.6
Kazakhstan[3]	2002	948	77.7	43.7	56.3	-12.6
Lithuania[4]	2003	104	116.7	53.8	46.2	7.6
Malta	1995-2002	300	81.8	45.0	55.0	-10.0
Mauritius	2002-2004	31	93.8	48.4	51.6	-3.2
Mongolia	2004	29	107.1	51.7	48.3	3.4
Netherlands	2003	1 154	53.5	34.8	65.2	-30.4
New Zealand	2002-2003[1]	336[5]	86.8	46.5	53.5	-7.0
Norway	2003	664	50.9	33.7	66.3	-32.6
Republic of Moldova	2004	82	90.7	47.6	52.4	-4.8
Singapore	2002	448	70.3	41.3	58.7	-17.4
Slovakia[4]	2004	125	220.5	68.8	31.2	37.6
Sweden	2004	1 093	49.5	33.1	66.9	-33.8
Switzerland	2002	558	96.5	49.1	50.9	-1.8
Thailand	2002-2005	228	147.8	59.6	40.4	19.2
Togo	2003	25	212.5	68.0	32.0	36.0
United States	2001-2002[1]	21 368	54.9	35.5	64.5	-29.0
Viet Nam	2001	1 419	103.0	50.7	49.3	1.4
Median	..	..	88.8	47.0	53.0	-5.9

Source: For a complete list of country references, see annex II.

NOTE: Because the number of adoptions is very small in many of the countries considered, some of the percentages may vary considerably over time.

[1] Data refer to the fiscal year.

[2] Of these, three are of unknown sex.

[3] Of these, 65 are of unknown sex. These children were adopted by relatives outside of Kazakhstan.

[4] Data refer to intercountry adoptions by citizens of States that are parties to the Convention on Protection of Children and Co-operation in Respect of Intercountry Adoption.

[5] Of these, 265 are of unknown sex.

United Nations Department of Economic and Social Affairs/Population Division
Child Adoption: Trends and Policies

TABLE A.VII.1. TOTAL, DOMESTIC AND INTERCOUNTRY UNDER-FIVE ADOPTION RATES AND SELECTED INDICATORS OF DESIRED FAMILY SIZE IN COUNTRIES THAT ARE NOT MAJOR DESTINATIONS FOR INTERCOUNTRY ADOPTIONS

| | Under-five adoption rate | | | Desired family size among married women aged 15-49 | | | |
Country	Total	Domestic	Intercountry	Desired family size	Wanted fertility	Total fertility	Total unwanted fertility[1]
Armenia	55.9	36.6	19.3	2.8	1.5	1.7	0.2
Bangladesh	0.1[2,3]	0.1[2,3]	..	2.5[4]	2.2[4]	3.3[4]	1.1[4]
Benin	0.2	0.2	0.1	5.2	4.6	5.6	1.0
Bolivia (Plurinational State of)	17.1	7.1	10.0	2.8	2.5	4.2	1.7
Brazil	14.0[5]	13.6[5]	0.4[5]	2.5	1.8	2.5	0.7
Burkina Faso	...	...	1.5	5.9	5.7	6.4	0.7
Cameroon	...	...	0.3[6]	6.5	4.3	4.8	0.5
Central African Republic	0.6	0.3	0.3	6.7	4.7	5.1	0.4
Chad	...	...	0.0[2]	8.5	6.1	6.4	0.3
Colombia	17.9	7.1	10.7	2.5	1.8	2.6	0.8
Eritrea	0.5[2]	...	...	6.6	5.7	6.1	0.4
Ethiopia	4.1	0.3	3.8	5.8	4.7	5.5	0.8
Gabon	0.8	...	...	5.4	3.5	4.2	0.7
Ghana	10.4	10.3	0.1	4.6	3.6	4.4	0.8
Guatemala	115.7	3.3	112.4	3.7	4.1	5.0	0.9
Haiti	22.7	3.2	19.5	3.3	2.8	4.7	1.9
India	1.5	1.0	0.5	2.7	2.1	2.8	0.7
Indonesia	0.1	0.1	0.0	2.9	2.4	2.8	0.4
Kazakhstan	196.6	144.8	51.8	3.0	1.9	2.0	0.1
Kenya	1.8[7]	...	...	4.1	3.5	4.7	1.2
Kyrgyzstan	184.7[8]	...	...	3.9	3.1	3.4	0.3
Madagascar	...	...	7.5	5.7	5.2	6.0	0.8
Malawi	19.1	19.1	..	5.3	5.2	6.3	1.1
Mali	3.3	0.0	3.3	6.5	6.1	6.8	0.7
Mozambique	0.2	0.1	0.1	6.2	4.7	5.2	0.5
Namibia	12.2	12.2	..	5.7	4.8	5.4	0.6
Nepal	...	...	1.3	2.6	2.5	4.1	1.6
Nicaragua	7.2[2]	5.8[2]	1.4[2,9]	3.2	2.3	3.2	0.9
Niger	0.2[10]	0.1[10]	0.1[10]	8.5	7.0	7.2	0.2
Paraguay	0.8[2]	...	...	4.4	4.0	4.7	0.7
Peru	3.7	1.9	1.8	2.6	1.8	2.8	1.0
Philippines	11.6	...	...	3.5	2.7	3.7	1.0
Rwanda	...	...	0.4	5.0	4.7	5.8	1.1
Senegal	...	...	0.5	5.7	4.6	5.7	1.1
South Africa	25.3	21.7	3.6	3.3	2.3	2.9	0.6
Togo	2.1	0.6	1.5	4.9	4.2	5.2	1.0
Turkey	3.7	3.6	0.1[11]	2.5	1.9	2.6	0.7
Uganda	1.6[2]	...	...	5.1	5.3	6.9	1.6
United Republic of Tanzania	0.2	0.2	..	5.7	4.8	5.6	0.8
Uzbekistan	59.9	59.7	0.2	3.8	3.1	3.3	0.2
Viet Nam	22.4	11.4	11.0	2.5	1.9	2.3	0.4
Median	3.9	3.3	1.4	4.4	3.6	4.7	0.7

Sources: For a complete list of country references, see annex II. The population under age five was obtained from United Nations, 2005; the desired family size among married women aged 15-49 was obtained from Zlidar and others, 2003.

NOTES: The under-five adoption rate is calculated by dividing the number of adoptions of children under age five by the number of children under age five with the result expressed per 100,000 children. If no data are available on the age distribution of adopted children, it is assumed that 60 per cent of adopted children were under age five at the time of adoption. Data on the desired family size among married women aged 15-49 refer to the latest available year in the period 1990-2001; the data on desired family size and adoptions do not necessarily refer to the same year.

TABLE A.VII.1 (*continued*)

[1] Refers to the difference between the total and wanted fertility.
[2] Estimate.
[3] Data refer to children placed with families.
[4] Data refer to women aged 10-49.
[5] Data refer only to the State of São Paulo.
[6] Data refer to intercountry adoption requests.
[7] Data refer to the estimated number of adoption applications recorded by the Child Welfare Society of Kenya.
[8] Data include children that have been adopted as well as those placed with guardians.
[9] Data refer to children adopted by foreign citizens residing in Nicaragua.
[10] Data refer to adoptions of abandoned children.
[11] Data include 27 adoptions by Turkish families residing abroad.

TABLE A.VII.2. TOTAL, DOMESTIC AND INTERCOUNTRY UNDER-FIVE ADOPTION RATES AND SELECTED INDICATORS OF THE DESIRE FOR MORE CHILDREN IN COUNTRIES THAT ARE NOT MAJOR DESTINATIONS OF INTERCOUNTRY ADOPTIONS

| | Under-five adoption rate | | | Percentage of married women aged 15-49 who | | | | | |
| | | | | Want to have another child | | | Want no more children | Are sterilized | Want to end childbearing[1] |
Country	Total	Domestic	Intercountry	within 2 years	in more than 2 years	Are undecided			
Armenia	55.9	36.6	19.3	7.8	8.6	6.4	71.7	2.7	74.4
Azerbaijan	76.0	70.3	5.6	13.9[2]	8.5[2]	1.7[2]	68.0[2]	1.0[2]	69.4[2]
Bangladesh	0.1[3,4]	0.1[3,4]	..	11.8[5]	23.6[5]	3.2[5]	51.7[5]	7.2[5]	58.9[5]
Benin	0.2	0.2	0.1	23.8	36.7	10.1	25.6	0.3	25.9
Bolivia (Plurinational State of)	17.1	7.1	10.0	8.6	13.2	2.7	64.8	6.5	71.3
Brazil	14.0[6]	13.6[6]	0.4[6]	7.0	11.5	3.4	31.6	42.7	74.3
Burkina Faso	...	...	1.5	19.9	44.4	12.0	19.6	0.1	19.7
Cameroon	...	...	0.3[7]	34.1	31.2	9.9	18.1	1.5	19.6
Central African Republic	0.6	0.3	0.3	35.9	26.9	17.4	11.9	0.4	12.3
Chad	...	...	0.0[3]	32.5	39.0	11.9	9.8	0.2	10.0
Colombia	17.9	7.1	10.7	11.3	15.1	1.6	41.5	28.1	69.6
Costa Rica	9.8	4.9[8]	4.9[9]	8.0	29.0	3.0	39.0	21.0	60.0
Czech Republic	74.3[10]	70.8[3,10]	3.5[10]	13.0[2]	8.0[2]	8.0[2]	68.0[2]	3.0[2]	71.0[2]
Ecuador	4.9	3.1	1.8	11.0	17.0	3.0	46.0	23.0	69.0
El Salvador	18.9	10.2	8.7	8.0	24.0	3.0	33.0	32.0	65.0
Eritrea	0.5[3]	...	...	20.6	51.0	5.6	17.9	0.3	18.2
Ethiopia	4.1	0.3	3.8	22.3	36.4	6.3	31.7	0.3	32.0
Gabon	0.8	...	...	26.2	28.5	17.5	22.1	1.0	23.1
Georgia	36.6	8.3	28.3	21.0	7.0	7.0	63.0	2.0	65.0
Ghana	10.4	10.3	0.1	18.4	34.6	8.3	33.7	1.3	35.0
Guatemala	115.7	3.3	112.4	11.0	22.1	6.4	40.9	17.5	58.4
Haiti	22.7	3.2	19.5	13.4	21.0	5.6	53.8	3.1	56.9
Honduras	3.1	1.2	1.9	7.0	35.0	1.0	39.0	18.0	57.0
India	1.5	1.0	0.5	14.8	13.3	3.1	27.5	36.1	63.6
Indonesia	0.1	0.1	0.0	15.5	25.3	8.6	46.3	3.3	49.6
Jamaica	55.9	48.0	7.9	10.0	28.0	11.0	39.0	12.0	51.0
Kazakhstan	196.6	144.8	51.8	12.2	12.9	12.3	55.4	2.8	58.2
Kenya	1.8[11]	...	...	13.8	25.0	5.3	47.1	6.2	53.3
Kyrgyzstan	184.7[12]	...	...	12.4	25.5	9.5	45.1	1.8	46.9
Madagascar	...	...	7.5	21.1	31.5	6.1	37.1	1.0	38.1
Malawi	19.1	19.1	..	15.7	37.1	2.1	37.5	4.8	42.3
Mali	3.3	0.0	3.3	26.4	37.7	11.6	21.2	0.3	21.5
Mauritius	64.1	56.2[13]	7.9	3.0	3.0	2.0	85.0	7.0	92.0
Mozambique	0.2	0.1	0.1	34.5	28.7	14.2	16.2	0.7	16.9
Namibia	12.2	12.2	..	26.0	29.6	7.2	25.8	7.7	33.5
Nepal	...	...	1.3	11.5	16.6	2.7	44.3	21.3	65.6
Nicaragua	7.2[3]	5.8[3]	1.4[3,14]	10.2	22.1	1.3	38.9	25.8	64.7
Niger	0.2[15]	0.1[15]	0.1[15]	33.0	45.6	8.4	9.5	0.1	9.6
Paraguay	0.8[3]	...	...	12.0[2]	37.0[2]	4.0[2]	40.0[2]	8.0[2]	48.0[2]
Peru	3.7	1.9	1.8	8.9	19.4	1.6	54.5	12.8	67.3
Philippines	11.6	...	...	12.0	18.7	5.4	51.4	10.4	61.8
Republic of Moldova	62.3	39.0	23.3	22.0[2]	13.0[2]	4.0[2]	58.0[2]	3.0[2]	61.0[2]
Romania	94.4	80.2	14.2[16]	18.0[2]	9.0[2]	4.0[2]	66.0[2]	3.0[2]	69.0[2]
Rwanda	...	...	0.4	15.2	45.4	5.0	33.0	0.8	33.8

TABLE A.VII:2 (*continued*)

| Country | Under-five adoption rate | | | Percentage of married women aged 15-49 who | | | | | |
| | | | | Want to have another child | | | Want no more children | Are sterilized | Want to end childbearing[1] |
	Total	Domestic	Intercountry	within 2 years	in more than 2 years	Are undecided			
Senegal	...	...	0.5	23.7	39.1	9.9	22.5	0.5	23.0
South Africa.......	25.3	21.7	3.6	15.8	12.4	6.6	43.6	17.9	61.5
Togo...................	2.1	0.6	1.5	18.9	35.3	13.7	28.2	0.4	28.6
Turkey................	3.7	3.6	0.1[17]	10.6	13.6	4.5	62.1	4.3	66.4
Uganda..............	1.6[3]	...	...	18.5	34.7	5.0	36.4	2.0	38.4
Ukraine	225.0	145.9	79.2	6.0[2]	8.0[2]	11.0[2]	74.0[2]	1.0[2]	75.0[2]
United Republic of Tanzania...........	0.2	0.2	..	28.0	35.6	3.7	26.7	2.0	28.7
Uzbekistan	59.9	59.7	0.2	12.9	24.2	9.8	50.9	0.7	51.6
Viet Nam............	22.4	11.4	11.0	4.8	16.0	4.6	65.9	6.9	72.8
Median	11.0	7.1	2.6	13.9	25.0	5.6	39.0	3.0	56.9

Sources: For a complete list of country references, see annex II. The population under age five was obtained from United Nations, 2005; the desired family size among married women aged 15-49 was obtained from Zlidar and others, 2003.

NOTES: The under-five adoption rate is calculated by dividing the number of adoptions of children under age five by the number of children under age five, with the result expressed per 100,000 children. If no data are available on the age distribution of adopted children, it is assumed that 60 per cent of adopted children were under age five at the time of adoption. Data on the percentage of married women aged 15-49 who desire more children refer to the latest available year in the period 1990-2001; the data on desired family size and adoptions do not necessarily refer to the same year.

[1] Data refer to women who want no more and those who are sterilized.
[2] Data refer to women aged 15-44.
[3] Estimate.
[4] Data refer to children placed with families.
[5] Data refer to women aged 10-49.
[6] Data refer only to the State of São Paulo.
[7] Data refer to intercountry adoption requests.
[8] Data refer to adoptions arranged by the National Children's Trusts.
[9] Data refer to both adoptions arranged by the National Children's Trusts and by direct contact between the parties concerned in the metropolitan area.
[10] Data refer to children placed in pre-adoption care.
[11] Data refer to the estimated number of adoption applications recorded by the Child Welfare Society of Kenya.
[12] Data include children that have been adopted as those well as placed with guardians.
[13] Data include both simple and full adoptions.
[14] Data refer to children adopted by foreign citizens residing in Nicaragua.
[15] Data refer to adoptions of abandoned children.
[16] Data refer to children previously protected in public or private placement centres or in substitute families.
[17] Data include 27 adoptions by Turkish families residing abroad.

TABLE A.VII.3. TOTAL, DOMESTIC AND INTERCOUNTRY UNDER-FIVE ADOPTION RATES AND SELECTED INDICATORS OF FERTILITY IN COUNTRIES THAT ARE MAJOR DESTINATIONS OF INTERCOUNTRY ADOPTIONS

Country	Under-five adoption rate			Female singulate mean age at marriage (SMAM)	Mean age at first birth	Percentage childless among women aged		Total fertility (per woman)
	Total	Domestic	Intercountry			35-39	40-44	
Andorra	60.9	22.1	38.8	...	...	...	...	1.3
Australia	23.8	6.3	17.5	28.7	27.7	11.9	9.7	1.7
Austria	123.4	...	...	26.1	23.0	16.1	10.1	1.4
Belgium	47.8	2.2[1]	45.6[2]	27.9	26.4	12.4[3]	...	1.7
Canada	142.5[4]	77.6[4]	64.9	26.8	26.7	19.8	15.9	1.5
Cyprus	251.9	59.5	192.4	23.1	28.6	12.4[5]	11.5[5]	1.6
Denmark	225.8	101.4	124.4	30.7	27.4	...	...	1.8
Finland	105.9	44.2	61.7	30.2	27.5	21.1	16.8	1.7
France	71.9	7.3	64.6	30.2	28.7[6]	13.5	10.2	1.9
Germany	89.9	59.5	30.5	...	28.2	...	...	1.3
Greece	68.8[4]	...	...	24.5	27.3	...	...	1.3
Iceland	126.5	60.4	66.1	30.5	25.5	...	...	2.0
Ireland	129.6	54.9	74.7[7]	30.9	28.0	13.9	7.6	1.9
Israel	35.1	11.6	23.5	25.0	21.7	2.7[8]	2.7[8]	2.9
Italy	72.0	23.0	49.0	28.4	28.0	18.8	13.0	1.3
Japan	19.3	16.3[9]	3.0	28.6	27.9	4.2[10]	3.2[10]	1.3
Liechtenstein	94.7	15.8	78.9	...	...	...	...	1.4
Luxembourg	113.2	6.3	106.9[11]	26.0	28.3	22.9	18.8	1.7
Malta	28.1	16.4	11.7	22.2	...	...	...	1.5
Monaco	332.8[4]	...	...	...	...	...	...	2.0
Netherlands	83.9	18.3	65.6	29.9	28.6	19.2	17.5[12]	1.7
New Zealand	136.5	63.8	72.7	25.4	29.6	9.6[8]	8.7[8]	2.0
Norway	180.3	42.7	137.6	31.4	27.0	11.6[13]	9.1[14]	1.8
Portugal	43.7	43.0	0.6[15]	23.9	26.7	10.6	10.0	1.5
Singapore	170.4	63.3	107.1	26.5	28.1	9.5	6.9	1.4
Spain	139.0	25.7	113.3	26.0	29.1	11.4	13.0	1.3
Sweden	208.9	72.1	136.8	32.3	28.2	13.7[13]	14.0[14]	1.6
Switzerland	111.3	22.8	88.4	29.1	28.8[6]	24.7	22.9	1.4
United Kingdom	108.0	102.3	5.7[16]	26.4	29.1[6]	...	...	1.7
United States	385.3	327.6	57.6[17]	26.3	25.0	22.3	21.5	2.0
Median	109.6	42.7	64.9	27.4	28.0	13.5	10.9	1.7

Sources: For a complete list of country references, see annex II. The population under age five and total fertility per woman was obtained from United Nations, 2005; the estimates of childlessness were obtained from United Nations, 2004a and forthcoming; the female singulate mean age at marriage and mean age at first birth were obtained from United Nations, 2004a.

NOTES: The under-five adoption rate is calculated by dividing the number of adoptions of children under age five by the number of children under age five, with the result expressed per 100,000 children. If no data are available on the age distribution of adopted children, it is assumed that 60 per cent of adopted children were under age five at the time of adoption. Data on the selected fertility indicators refer to the latest available year in the period 1985-2004; the data on selected fertility indicators and adoptions do not necessarily refer to the same year.

[1] Data refer to domestic adoptions in the region of Flanders.
[2] Data refer to intercountry adoptions in the regions of Flanders and Wallonia.
[3] Data refer only to the Dutch-speaking community of the Flemish Region of Belgium.
[4] Estimate.
[5] Never married added.
[6] Mean age at first birth within current marriage.
[7] Data refer to number of adoptions overseas.
[8] Data refer to ever married women.
[9] Data include regular and special adoptions.
[10] Data refer to currently married women.
[11] Data refer to children in the process of undergoing adoption.
[12] Data refer to women aged 40-42.
[13] Data refer to women aged 38 years.
[14] Data refer to women aged 43 years.

TABLE A.VII.3 (*continued*)

[15] Data include one foreign child adopted by Portuguese citizens as well as five Portuguese children adopted abroad.

[16] Data refer to the number of applications for intercountry adoptions received by the Department of Health during the year ending 31 March.

[17] Data refer to children who entered under an orphan visa for purposes of adoption. These include children with an IR-3 visa status who were adopted abroad and children with an IR-4 status who were to be adopted in the United States.

TABLE A.VII.4. TOTAL, DOMESTIC AND INTERCOUNTRY UNDER-FIVE ADOPTION RATES AND SELECTED INDICATORS OF FERTILITY IN COUNTRIES THAT ARE NOT MAJOR DESTINATIONS OF INTERCOUNTRY ADOPTIONS

| Country | Under-five adoption rate | | | Female singulate mean age at marriage (SMAM) | Mean age at first birth | Percentage childless among women aged | | Total fertility (per woman) |
	Total	Domestic	Intercountry			35-39	40-44	
Albania	18.8	12.9	6.0	22.9	24.7	8.8	6.6	2.3
Argentina	1.4	1.4	..	23.3	23.7	14.1	12.9	2.4
Armenia	55.9	36.6	19.3	23.0	23.0	9.9	10.5	1.3
Azerbaijan	76.0	70.3	5.6	23.9	24.7	15.1	13.5	1.9
Bahamas	43.4	27.6	15.8	27.2	23.5	10.9	8.3	2.3
Bangladesh	0.1[1,2]	0.1[1,2]	..	18.7	18.2	5.4	4.7	3.2
Belarus	120.2	58.3	61.9	22.8	23.4	6.8	6.0	1.2
Belize	141.0	132.0	8.9	26.2	...	7.6	6.0	3.2
Benin	0.2	0.2	0.1	19.9	20.2	3.7	3.3	5.9
Bolivia (Plurinational State of)	17.1	7.1	10.0	22.8	21.0	7.3	6.5	4.0
Bosnia and Herzegovina	19.9	...	...	...	23.6	...	...	1.3
Brazil	14.0[3]	13.6[3]	0.4[3]	23.4	22.1	12.9	11.1	2.3
Bulgaria	410.3	229.2	181.1	21.1	23.1	10.5	10.7	1.2
Burkina Faso	...	...	1.5	18.9	19.0	3.2	4.1	6.7
Burundi	...	...	2.6[1]	22.5	20.9	5.6	5.7	6.8
Cameroon	...	...	0.3[4]	20.2	20.3	6.1	6.1	4.6
Central African Republic	0.6	0.3	0.3	19.7	19.4	9.9	10.2	5.0
Chad	...	...	0.0[1]	18.1	18.2	5.1	6.3	6.7
Chile	25.5	21.2	4.3	23.4	23.4	8.7	7.9	2.0
China	29.5	23.9	5.6	23.1	...	1.2	1.1	1.7
Colombia	17.9	7.1	10.7	23.1	21.8	11.0	11.0	2.6
Congo	9.6[1,5]	4.8[1,5]	4.8[1,5]	22.6	...	...	...	6.3
Costa Rica	9.8	4.9[6]	4.9[7]	20.9	22.6	9.7	8.9	2.3
Croatia	42.1	41.2	0.8	26.2	25.5	10.7	9.3	1.3
Czech Republic	74.3[8]	70.8[1,8]	3.5[8]	25.3	25.3	6.7	5.5	1.2
Democratic People's Republic of Korea	8.9	8.9	0.0	...	...	...	...	2.0
Dominica	143.4[1]	...	...	...	...	...	...	2.0
Ecuador	4.9	3.1	1.8	21.5	23.0	9.1	7.9	2.8
El Salvador	18.9	10.2	8.7	22.3	23.0	9.8	7.2	2.9
Eritrea	0.5[1]	...	...	19.6	20.6	7.7	5.4	5.5
Estonia	126.5	111.9	14.6	22.1	24.2	9.7[9]	9.1[9]	1.4
Ethiopia	4.1	0.3	3.8	20.5	20.1	5.9	4.1	5.9
Fiji	56.3	50.0[1]	6.3[1]	22.9	22.3	8.6	7.2	2.9
Gabon	0.8	...	...	22.1	18.7	6.9	5.4	4.0
Gambia	1.8	0.8	1.0	19.6	...	...	...	4.7
Georgia	36.6	8.3	28.3	24.3	24.2	15.7	13.1	1.5
Ghana	10.4	10.3	0.1	21.2	20.9	7.5	5.1	4.4
Grenada	73.2	19.5	53.6	...	...	...	...	2.4
Guatemala	115.7	3.3	112.4	20.5	22.7	7.2	8.7	4.6
Guinea-Bissau	1.0	...	...	...	...	...	...	7.1
Guyana	93.7	...	...	27.8	20.4	6.8	6.0	2.3
Haiti	22.7	3.2	19.5	22.3	21.9	6.2	8.2	4.0
Honduras	3.1	1.2	1.9	20.4	...	7.3	5.8	3.7
Hungary	93.6	81.9	11.7[10]	26.3	25.3	8.9	8.5	1.3
India	1.5	1.0	0.5	19.9	19.5	7.2	5.5	3.1
Indonesia	0.1	0.1	0.0	22.5	21.6	9.3	7.2	2.4
Jamaica	55.9	48.0	7.9	33.2	19.2	10.6	9.6	2.4
Kazakhstan	196.6	144.8	51.8	23.4	23.5	7.4	7.1	2.0

TABLE A.VII.4 (*continued*)

Country	Under-five adoption rate			Female singulate mean age at marriage (SMAM)	Mean age at first birth	Percentage childless among women aged		Total fertility (per woman)
	Total	Domestic	Intercountry			35-39	40-44	
Kenya	1.8[11]	...	...	21.7	19.6	5.2	4.2	5.0
Kiribati	...	...	4.5[1]	...	...	...	...	4.0
Kyrgyzstan	184.7[12]	...	...	21.9	23.3	5.8	4.8	2.7
Latvia	65.7	16.7	49.0	26.9	24.6	7.5	9.4	1.3
Lithuania	76.2	36.2	40.0	24.8	24.1	11.6	14.7	1.3
Madagascar	...	...	7.5	20.6	19.8	8.7	5.6	5.4
Malawi	19.1	19.1	..	18.9	19.2	4.6	4.1	6.1
Mali	3.3	0.0	3.3	18.4	18.6	5.4	4.9	6.9
Mauritius	64.1	56.2[13]	7.9	23.8	24.5	5.0	4.6	2.0
Mexico	5.3	4.8	0.5[14]	22.7	23.8	9.2	7.3	2.4
Mongolia	422.4	415.9	6.5	23.7	...	3.9	2.5	2.4
Mozambique	0.2	0.1	0.1	18.0	18.7	6.6	5.6	5.5
Myanmar	0.1	...	...	24.5	...	11.5[15]	10.8[15]	2.5
Namibia	12.2	12.2	..	26.4	21.2	7.1	4.8	4.0
Nepal	...	...	1.3	19.0	19.7	6.9	4.6	3.7
Nicaragua	7.2[1]	5.8[1]	1.4[1,16]	20.6	19.8	7.2	6.0	3.3
Niger	0.2[17]	0.1[17]	0.1[17]	17.6	19.6	4.0	5.2	7.9
Palau	1 210.6	...	...	...	...	...	...	1.9
Panama	2.4	2.3	0.1	21.9	22.3	7.9	6.9	2.7
Papua New Guinea	21.8[1]	...	...	20.8	...	11.0	9.5	4.1
Paraguay	0.8[1]	...	...	21.5	21.6	9.4	8.0	3.9
Peru	3.7	1.9	1.8	23.1	22.2	10.3	9.2	2.9
Philippines	11.6	...	...	24.1	23.9	12.9	9.3	3.2
Poland	64.1[18]	58.7[18]	5.4[18]	25.2	24.8	11.7	8.6	1.3
Republic of Korea	92.8	39.1	53.7	26.1	27.1	3.4	2.8	1.2
Republic of Moldova	62.3	39.0	23.3	21.1	22.8	7.8	8.2	1.2
Romania	94.4	80.2	14.2[19]	24.1	23.6	9.9	7.4	1.3
Russian Federation	209.6[1]	157.2[1]	52.4	21.8	23.1	7.5	7.0	1.3
Rwanda	...	...	0.4	22.7	22.0	4.8	3.6	5.7
Samoa	964.2	...	...	23.9	27.8	6.5	3.8	4.4
Senegal	...	...	0.5	21.5	20.4	5.3	4.7	5.0
Serbia[20]	23.8	...	...	23.1	25.0	9.6	8.4	1.7
Seychelles	58.6	58.6	..	...	...	...	...	1.9
Slovakia	92.6	...	...	25.4	24.3	...	...	1.2
Slovenia	31.5	30.8	0.7	29.8	26.7	5.7	5.1	1.2
Solomon Islands	2.1	2.1	..	22.3	...	...	...	4.3
South Africa	25.3	21.7	3.6	27.9	20.9	7.3	7.0	2.8
Sri Lanka	34.1	32.3	1.9	25.3	26.2	18.1	14.9	2.0
Sudan	0.6[21]	...	...	22.7	22.8	3.7	4.3	4.4
Swaziland	...	10.6	...	26.0	...	6.7	5.9	4.0
Thailand	0.6	0.0	0.6	23.5	23.0	11.7[15]	10.3[15]	1.9
Togo	2.1	0.6	1.5	21.3	18.9	5.1	3.9	5.4
Trinidad and Tobago	12.4	...	...	26.8	23.8	12.4	10.1	1.6
Turkey	3.7	3.6	0.1[22]	22.0	21.7	4.7	4.1	2.5
Uganda	1.6[1]	...	...	19.6	18.9	6.0	7.0	7.1
Ukraine	225.0	145.9	79.2	21.7	...	9.1	8.2	1.1
United Republic of Tanzania	0.2	0.2	..	20.5	19.5	5.7	4.2	5.0
Uzbekistan	59.9	59.7	0.2	20.6	23.4	6.9	5.1	2.7
Venezuela (Bolivarian Republic of)	43.5	...	...	22.1	23.6	10.2	8.0	2.7

United Nations Department of Economic and Social Affairs/Population Division
Child Adoption: Trends and Policies

TABLE A.VII.4 (*continued*)

Country	Under-five adoption rate			Female singulate mean age at marriage (SMAM)	Mean age at first birth	Percentage childless among women aged		Total fertility (per woman)
	Total	Domestic	Intercountry			35-39	40-44	
Viet Nam............................	22.4	11.4	11.0	22.1	...	9.3	10.1	2.3
Median.................................	20.8	12.2	4.4	22.5	22.6	7.5	7.0	2.7

Sources: For a complete list of country references, see annex II. The population under age five and total fertility per woman were obtained from United Nations, 2005; estimates of childlessness were obtained from United Nations, 2004a and forthcoming; the female singulate mean age at marriage and mean age at first birth were obtained from United Nations, 2004a.

NOTES: The under-five adoption rate is calculated by dividing the number of adoptions of children under age five by the number of children under age five, with the result expressed per 100,000 children. If no data are available on the age distribution of adopted children, it is assumed that 60 per cent of adopted children were under age five at the time of adoption. Data on the selected fertility indicators refer to the latest available year in the period 1985-2004; the data on selected fertility indicators and adoptions do not necessarily refer to the same year.

[1] Estimate.
[2] Data refer to children placed with families.
[3] Data refer only to the State of São Paulo.
[4] Data refer to intercountry adoption requests.
[5] Data refer to adoptions heard in the Brazzaville District Court.
[6] Data refer to adoptions arranged by the National Children's Trusts.
[7] Data refer to both adoptions arranged by the National Children's Trusts and by direct contact between the parties concerned in the metropolitan area.
[8] Data refer to children placed in pre-adoption care.
[9] Data refer to native and foreign born.
[10] Data include 14 foreign children adopted by Hungarian citizens as well as 80 Hungarian children adopted abroad.
[11] Data refer to the estimated number of adoption applications recorded by the Child Welfare Society of Kenya.
[12] Data include children that have been adopted as well as those placed with guardians.
[13] Data include both simple and full adoptions.
[14] Data refer to intercountry adoptions by citizens of States that are parties to the Convention on Protection of Children and Co-operation in Respect of Intercountry Adoption.
[15] Never married added.
[16] Data refer to children adopted by foreign citizens residing in Nicaragua.
[17] Data refer to adoptions of abandoned children.
[18] Data refer to adoption rulings by the courts.
[19] Data refer to children previously protected in public or private placement centres or in substitute families.
[20] Data refer to Serbia and Montenegro.
[21] Data refer only to the State of Khartoum.
[22] Data include 27 adoptions by Turkish families residing abroad.

TABLE A.VII.5. TOTAL, DOMESTIC AND INTERCOUNTRY UNDER-FIVE ADOPTION RATES
AND PERCENTAGE OF EXTRAMARITAL BIRTHS IN COUNTRIES THAT ARE MAJOR
DESTINATIONS OF INTERCOUNTRY ADOPTIONS

Country	Under-five adoption rate			Percentage of extra-marital births
	Total	Domestic	Intercountry	
Australia	23.8	6.3	17.5	27.4
Austria	123.4	…	…	33.1
Belgium	47.8	2.2[1]	45.6[2]	17.3
Canada	142.5[3]	77.6[3]	64.9	38.4
Cyprus	251.9	59.5	192.4	2.3
Denmark	225.8	101.4	124.4	45.1
Finland	105.9	44.2	61.7	39.5
France	71.9	7.3	64.6	42.6
Germany	89.9	59.5	30.5	23.4
Greece	68.8[3]	…	…	3.9
Iceland	126.5	60.4	66.1	65.2
Ireland	129.6	54.9	74.7[4]	31.2
Israel	35.1	11.6	23.5	3.1
Italy	72.0	23.0	49.0	9.7
Japan	19.3	16.3[5]	3.0	1.4
Luxembourg	113.2	6.3	106.9[6]	17.5
Malta	28.1	16.4	11.7	12.9
Netherlands	83.9	18.3	65.6	27.2
New Zealand	136.5	63.8	72.7	42.5
Norway	180.3	42.7	137.6	49.7
Portugal	43.7	43.0	0.6[7]	23.8
Spain	139.0	25.7	113.3	17.7
Sweden	208.9	72.1	136.8	55.5
Switzerland	111.3	22.8	88.4	11.4
United Kingdom	108.0	102.3	5.7[8]	40.1
United States	385.3	327.6	57.6[9]	33.0
Median	109.7	42.9	64.8	27.3

Sources: For a complete list of country references, see annex II. The population under age five was obtained from United Nations, 2005; the percentage of extra-marital births was obtained from United Nations, 2004a.

NOTES: The under-five adoption rate is calculated by dividing the number of adoptions of children under age five by the number of children under age five, with the result expressed per 100,000 children. If no data are available on the age distribution of adopted children, it is assumed that 60 per cent of adopted children were under age five at the time of adoption. Data on extra-marital births refer to the latest available year in the period 1995-2001; the data on extra-marital births and adoptions do not necessarily refer to the same year.

[1] Data refer to domestic adoptions in the region of Flanders.
[2] Data refer to intercountry adoptions in the regions of Flanders and Wallonia.
[3] Estimate.
[4] Data refer to number of adoptions overseas.
[5] Data include regular and special adoptions.
[6] Data refer to children in the process of undergoing adoption.
[7] Data include one foreign child adopted by Portuguese citizens as well as five Portuguese children adopted abroad.
[8] Data refer to the number of applications for intercountry adoptions received by the Department of Health during the year ending 31 March.
[9] Data refer to children who entered under an orphan visa for purposes of adoption. These include children with an IR-3 visa status who were adopted abroad and children with an IR-4 status who were to be adopted in the United States.

TABLE A.VII.6. TOTAL, DOMESTIC AND INTERCOUNTRY UNDER-FIVE ADOPTION
RATES AND PERCENTAGE OF EXTRAMARITAL BIRTHS IN COUNTRIES THAT ARE NOT
MAJOR DESTINATIONS OF INTERCOUNTRY ADOPTIONS

| Country | Under-five adoption rate | | | *Percentage of extra-marital births* |
	Total	*Domestic*	*Intercountry*	
Argentina	1.4	1.4	..	53.0
Armenia	55.9	36.6	19.3	15.3
Azerbaijan	76.0	70.3	5.6	6.6
Bahamas	43.4	27.6	15.8	56.2
Belarus	120.2	58.3	61.9	20.5
Belize	141.0	132.0	8.9	58.1
Bosnia and Herzegovina	19.9	...	...	7.4
Bulgaria	410.3	229.2	181.1	42.0
Chile	25.5	21.2	4.3	45.8
Costa Rica	9.8	4.9[1]	4.9[2]	48.2
Croatia	42.1	41.2	0.8	9.4
Czech Republic	74.3[3]	70.8[3,4]	3.5[3]	23.5
El Salvador	18.9	10.2	8.7	72.8
Estonia	126.5	111.9	14.6	56.2
Georgia	36.6	8.3	28.3	44.4
Hungary	93.6	81.9	11.7[5]	30.3
Jamaica	55.9	48.0	7.9	86.2
Kazakhstan	196.6	144.8	51.8	21.8
Kyrgyzstan	184.7[6]	...	...	27.4
Latvia	65.7	16.7	49.0	42.1
Lithuania	76.2	36.2	40.0	25.4
Mauritius	64.1	56.2[7]	7.9	18.2
Mexico	5.3	4.8	0.5[8]	37.8
Mongolia	422.4	415.9	6.5	19.4
Panama	2.4	2.3	0.1	79.9
Poland	64.1[9]	58.7[9]	5.4[9]	13.1
Republic of Moldova	62.3	39.0	23.3	17.5
Romania	94.4	80.2	14.2[10]	26.7
Russian Federation	209.6[4]	157.2[4]	52.4	28.8
Slovakia	92.6	...	...	19.8
Slovenia	31.5	30.8	0.7	39.4
Sri Lanka	34.1	32.3	1.9	1.4
Turkey	3.7	3.6	0.1[11]	4.5
Ukraine	225.0	145.9	79.2	18.0
Uzbekistan	59.9	59.7	0.2	8.4
Median	64.1	44.6	8.7	26.7

Sources: For a complete list of country references, see annex II. The population under age five was obtained from United Nations, 2005; the percentage of extra-marital births was obtained from United Nations, 2004a.

NOTES: The under-five adoption rate is calculated by dividing the number of adoptions of children under age five by the number of children under age five, with the result expressed per 100,000 children. If no data are available on the age distribution of adopted children, it is assumed that 60 per cent of adopted children were under age five at the time of adoption. Data on extra-marital births refer to the latest available year in the period 1989-2001; the data on extra-marital births and adoptions do not necessarily refer to the same year.

[1] Data refer to adoptions arranged by the National Children's Trusts.
[2] Data refer to both adoptions arranged by the National Children's Trusts and by direct contact between the parties concerned in the metropolitan area.
[3] Data refer to children placed in pre-adoption care.
[4] Estimate.
[5] Data include 14 foreign children adopted by Hungarian citizens as well as 80 Hungarian children adopted abroad.

TABLE A.VII.6 (*continued*)

[6] Data include children that have been adopted as well as those placed with guardians.

[7] Data include both simple and full adoptions.

[8] Data refer to intercountry adoptions by citizens of States that are parties to the Convention on Protection of Children and Co-operation in Respect of Intercountry Adoption.

[9] Data refer to adoption rulings by the courts.

[10] Data refer to children previously protected in public or private placement centres or in substitute families.

[11] Data include 27 adoptions by Turkish families residing abroad.

TABLE A.VII.7. TOTAL, DOMESTIC AND INTERCOUNTRY UNDER-FIVE ADOPTION RATES AND SELECTED INDICATORS
OF ABORTION AND CONTRACEPTIVE USE IN COUNTRIES THAT ARE MAJOR DESTINATIONS
OF INTERCOUNTRY ADOPTIONS

Country	Under-five adoption rate			Abortion rate	Percentage of married women using contraception	
	Total	Domestic	Intercountry		Any method	Modern method
Andorra	60.9	22.1	38.8	...	...	...
Australia	23.8	6.3	17.5	19.7	76.1	72.2
Austria	123.4	...	...	1.3	50.8	46.8
Belgium	47.8	2.2[1]	45.6[2]	7.5	78.4[3]	74.3[3]
Canada	142.5[4]	77.6[4]	64.9	15.2	74.7	73.3
Cyprus	251.9	59.5	192.4	...	...	...
Denmark	225.8	101.4	124.4	14.3	78.0[5]	72.0[5]
Finland	105.9	44.2	61.7	11.1	77.4	75.4
France	71.9	7.3	64.6	16.9	74.6	69.3
Germany	89.9	59.5	30.5	7.8	74.7	71.8
Greece	68.8[4]	...	...	5.0	...	...
Iceland	126.5	60.4	66.1	14.1	...	...
Ireland	129.6	54.9	74.7[6]	...	...	...
Israel	35.1	11.6	23.5	13.9	68.0[7]	51.9[7]
Italy	72.0	23.0	49.0	10.6	60.2	38.9
Japan	19.3	16.3[8]	3.0	12.3[9]	55.9	51.0
Liechtenstein	94.7	15.8	78.9	...	...	...
Luxembourg	113.2	6.3	106.9[10]	...	...	...
Malta	28.1	16.4	11.7	...	...	...
Monaco	332.8[4]	...	...	...	...	...
Netherlands	83.9	18.3	65.6	10.4	78.5	75.6
New Zealand	136.5	63.8	72.7	19.7	74.9	72.0
Norway	180.3	42.7	137.6	15.2	73.8[11]	69.2[11]
Portugal	43.7	43.0	0.6[12]	0.2	...	...
Singapore	170.4	63.3	107.1	12.6	62.0	53.0
Spain	139.0	25.7	113.3	8.3	80.9	67.4
Sweden	208.9	72.1	136.8	20.2	...	...
Switzerland	111.3	22.8	88.4	7.3	82.0	77.5
United Kingdom	108.0	102.3[4]	5.7[13]	17.0[14]	84.0[15]	81.0[15]
United States	385.3	327.6	57.6[16]	20.8	76.4	70.5
Median	109.7	42.7	64.9	12.6	74.9	71.8

Sources: For a complete list of country references, see annex II. The population under age five was obtained from United Nations, 2005; the percentage of married women using contraception was obtained from United Nations, 2006a; the abortion rate was obtained from United Nations, 2007.

NOTES: The under-five adoption rate is calculated by dividing the number of adoptions of children under age five by the number of children under age five, with the result expressed per 100,000 children. If no data are available on the age distribution of adopted children, it is assumed that 60 per cent of adopted children were under age five at the time of adoption. The latest contraceptive prevalence data refer to the most recent available data as of 1 October 2005. The most recent data were collected using representative surveys carried out since 1985. Regional aggregates were estimated by the United Nations Population Division based on the survey data shown and using as weights the estimated number of women aged 15-49 who were married or in a consensual union in 2005. Estimates of the abortion rate, measured as the number of abortions per 1,000 women aged 15-49, are the latest available within the period 1986-2005. The estimates of contraceptive prevalence, abortion rates and adoptions do not necessarily refer to the same year.

[1] Data refer to domestic adoptions in the region of Flanders.
[2] Data refer to intercountry adoptions in the regions of Flanders and Wallonia.
[3] Data refer to the region of Flanders only.
[4] Estimate.
[5] Data refer to sexually active women, irrespective of marital status.
[6] Data refer to number of adoptions overseas.
[7] Data refer to the Jewish population only.
[8] Data include regular and special adoptions.
[9] Data refer to Japanese nationals residing in Japan only.

TABLE A.VII.7 (*continued*)

[10] Data refer to children in the process of undergoing adoption.

[11] Data refer to women in union born in 1945, 1950, 1955, 1960, 1965 or 1968.

[12] Data include one foreign child adopted by Portuguese citizens as well as five Portuguese children adopted abroad.

[13] Data refer to the number of applications for intercountry adoptions received by the Department of Health during the year ending 31 March.

[14] Data refer to residents of England and Wales only.

[15] Data do not include Northern Ireland.

[16] Data refer to children who entered under an orphan visa for purposes of adoption. These include children with an IR-3 visa status who were adopted abroad and children with an IR-4 status who were to be adopted in the United States.

TABLE A.VII.8. TOTAL, DOMESTIC AND INTERCOUNTRY UNDER-FIVE ADOPTION RATES AND SELECTED INDICATORS OF ABORTION AND CONTRACEPTIVE USE IN COUNTRIES THAT ARE NOT MAJOR DESTINATIONS OF INTERCOUNTRY ADOPTIONS

	Under-five adoption rate			Abortion rate	Percentage of married women using contraception	
Country	*Total*	*Domestic*	*Intercountry*		*Any method*	*Modern method*
Albania	18.8	12.9	6.0	9.6	75.1	7.9
Argentina	1.4	1.4	..	...	...	...
Armenia	55.9	36.6	19.3	13.9	60.5	22.3
Azerbaijan	76.0	70.3	5.6	9.0	55.4	11.9
Bahamas	43.4	27.6	15.8	...	61.7[1]	60.1[1]
Bangladesh	0.1[2,3]	0.1[2,3]	..	...	58.1	47.3
Belarus	120.2	58.3	61.9	31.7	50.4	42.1
Belize	141.0	132.0	8.9	...	46.7[1]	41.8[1]
Benin	0.2	0.2	0.1	...	18.6	7.2
Bolivia (Plurinational State of)	17.1	7.1	10.0	...	58.4	34.9
Bosnia and Herzegovina	19.9	...	...	...	47.5	15.7
Brazil	14.0[4]	13.6[4]	0.4[4]	...	76.7	70.3
Bulgaria	410.3	229.2	181.1	21.3	41.5	25.6
Burkina Faso	...	...	1.5	...	13.8	8.6
Burundi	...	...	2.6[2]	...	15.7	10.0
Cameroon	...	...	0.3[5]	...	26.0	12.5
Central African Republic	0.6	0.3	0.3	...	27.9	6.9
Chad	...	...	0.0[2]	...	7.9	2.1
Chile	25.5	21.2	4.3	...	...	...
China	29.5	23.9	5.6	24.2	90.2	90.0
Colombia	17.9	7.1	10.7	...	76.9	64.0
Congo	9.6[2,6]	4.8[2,6]	4.8[2,6]	...	44.1	13.5
Costa Rica	9.8	4.9[7]	4.9[8]	...	80.0	70.7
Croatia	42.1	41.2	0.8	5.7	...	...
Czech Republic	74.3[9]	70.8[2,9]	3.5[9]	12.2	72.0	62.6
Democratic People's Republic of Korea	8.9	8.9	0.0	...	61.8	53.0
Dominica	143.4[2]	...	...	...	49.8[1]	48.2[1]
Ecuador	4.9	3.1	1.8	...	65.8	50.1
El Salvador	18.9	10.2	8.7	...	67.3	61.0
Eritrea	0.5[2]	...	...	...	8.0	5.1
Estonia	126.5	111.9	14.6	33.3	70.3[10]	56.4[10]
Ethiopia	4.1	0.3	3.8	...	14.7	13.9
Fiji	56.3	50.0[2]	6.3[2]	...	...	...
Gabon	0.8	...	...	...	32.7	11.8
Gambia	1.8	0.8	1.0	...	9.6	8.9
Georgia	36.6	8.3	28.3	19.1	47.2	26.5
Ghana	10.4	10.3	0.1	...	25.2	18.7
Grenada	73.2	19.5	53.6	...	54.3[1]	...
Guatemala	115.7	3.3	112.4	...	43.3	34.4
Guinea-Bissau	1.0	...	...	...	7.6	3.6
Guyana	93.7	...	...	...	37.3	36.0
Haiti	22.7	3.2	19.5	...	28.1	22.3
Honduras	3.1	1.2	1.9	...	61.8	50.8
Hungary	93.6	81.9	11.7[11]	23.4	77.4	68.4
India	1.5	1.0	0.5	3.1	48.2[12]	42.8[12]
Indonesia	0.1	0.1	0.0	...	60.3	56.7
Jamaica	55.9	48.0	7.9	...	65.9[1]	62.6[1]

TABLE A.VII.8 (*continued*)

| Country | Under-five adoption rate | | | Abortion rate | Percentage of married women using contraception | |
	Total	Domestic	Intercountry		Any method	Modern method
Kazakhstan	196.6	144.8	51.8	35.0	66.1	52.7
Kenya	1.8[13]	...	...	...	39.3	31.5
Kiribati	...	...	4.5[2]	...	...	...
Kyrgyzstan	184.7[14]	...	...	15.8	59.5	48.9
Latvia	65.7	16.7	49.0	27.3	48.0	39.3
Lithuania	76.2	36.2	40.0	13.9	46.6	30.5
Madagascar	...	...	7.5	...	27.1	16.7
Malawi	19.1	19.1	..	...	32.5	28.1
Mali	3.3	0.0	3.3	...	8.1	5.7
Mauritius	64.1	56.2[15]	7.9	...	74.7	48.9
Mexico	5.3	4.8	0.5[16]	0.1	68.4	59.5
Mongolia	422.4	415.9	6.5	21.7	67.4	54.3
Mozambique	0.2	0.1	0.1	...	16.5	11.8
Myanmar	0.1	...	...	...	37.0	32.8
Namibia	12.2	12.2	..	...	43.7	42.6
Nepal	...	...	1.3	...	39.3	35.4
Nicaragua	7.2[2]	5.8[2]	1.4[2,17]	...	68.6	66.1
Niger	0.2[18]	0.1[18]	0.1[18]	...	14.0	4.3
Palau	1 210.6	...	...	...	...	...
Panama	2.4	2.3	0.1	0.0	...	...
Papua New Guinea	21.8[2]	...	...	...	25.9	19.6
Paraguay	0.8[2]	...	...	...	72.8	60.5
Peru	3.7	1.9	1.8	...	70.5	46.7
Philippines	11.6	...	...	...	48.9	33.4
Poland	64.1[19]	58.7[19]	5.4[19]	0.0	49.4	19.0
Republic of Korea	92.8	39.1	53.7	...	80.5	66.9
Republic of Moldova	62.3	39.0	23.3	17.6	62.4	42.8
Romania	94.4	80.2	14.2[20]	27.8	63.8	29.5
Russian Federation	209.6[2]	157.2[2]	52.4	53.7	65.3	47.1
Rwanda	...	...	0.4	...	13.2	4.3
Samoa	964.2	...	...	...	...	...
Senegal	...	...	0.5	...	11.8	10.3
Serbia[21]	23.8	...	...	...	...	...
Seychelles	58.6	58.6	..	21.6	...	...
Slovakia	92.6	...	...	11.7	74.0[22]	41.0[22]
Slovenia	31.5	30.8	0.7	15.2	73.8	59.1
Solomon Islands	2.1	2.1	..	...	...	...
South Africa	25.3	21.7	3.6	4.5	56.3	55.1
Sri Lanka	34.1	32.3	1.9	...	70.0	49.6
Sudan	0.6[23]	...	...	...	9.9[24]	6.9[24]
Swaziland	...	10.6	...	...	27.7	26.0
Thailand	0.6	0.0	0.6	...	72.2	69.8
Togo	2.1	0.6	1.5	...	25.7	9.3
Trinidad and Tobago	12.4	...	...	...	38.2[1]	33.2[1]
Turkey	3.7	3.6	0.1[25]	...	63.9	37.7
Uganda	1.6[2]	...	...	...	22.8	18.2
Ukraine	225.0	145.9	79.2	27.5	67.5	37.6
United Republic of Tanzania	0.2	0.2	..	...	26.4	20.0
Uzbekistan	59.9	59.7	0.2	7.8	67.7	62.8

TABLE A.VII.8 (*continued*)

Country	Under-five adoption rate			Abortion rate	Percentage of married women using contraception	
	Total	Domestic	Intercountry		Any method	Modern method
Venezuela (Bolivarian Republic of)	43.5	...	...	...	...	...
Viet Nam..............................	22.4	11.4	11.0	35.2[26]	78.5	56.7
Median....................................	20.9	12.2	4.4	16.7	49.6	35.4

Sources: For a complete list of country references, see annex II. The population under age five was obtained from United Nations, 2005; the percentage of married women using contraception was obtained from United Nations, 2006a; the abortion rate was obtained from United Nations, 2007.

NOTES: The under-five adoption rate is calculated by dividing the number of adoptions of children under age five by the number of children under age five, with the result expressed per 100,000 children. If no data are available on the age distribution of adopted children, it is assumed that 60 per cent of adopted children were under age five at the time of adoption. The latest contraceptive prevalence data refer to the most recent available data as of 1 October 2005. The most recent data were collected using representative surveys carried out since 1985. Regional aggregates were estimated by the United Nations Population Division based on the survey data shown and using as weights the estimated number of women aged 15-49 who were married or in a consensual union in 2005. Estimates of the abortion rate, measured as the number of abortions per 1,000 women aged 15-49, are the latest available within the period 1986-2005. The estimates of contraceptive prevalence, abortion rates and adoptions do not necessarily refer to the same year.

[1] The data include women living in visiting unions, that is, in non-cohabiting but regular relationships.
[2] Estimate.
[3] Data refer to children placed with families.
[4] Data refer only to the State of São Paulo.
[5] Data refer to intercountry adoption requests.
[6] Data refer to adoptions heard in the Brazzaville District Court.
[7] Data refer to adoptions arranged by the National Children's Trusts.
[8] Data refer to both adoptions arranged by the National Children's Trusts and by direct contact between the parties concerned in the metropolitan area.
[9] Data refer to children placed in pre-adoption care.
[10] Data refer to women who were sexually active during the previous month.
[11] Data include 14 foreign children adopted by Hungarian citizens as well as 80 Hungarian children adopted abroad.
[12] Data do not cover the state of Tripura.
[13] Data refer to the estimated number of adoption applications recorded by the Child Welfare Society of Kenya.
[14] Data include children that have been adopted as well as those placed with guardians.
[15] Data include both simple and full adoptions.
[16] Data refer to intercountry adoptions by citizens of States that are parties to the Convention on Protection of Children and Co-operation in Respect of Intercountry Adoption.
[17] Data refer to children adopted by foreign citizens residing in Nicaragua.
[18] Data refer to adoptions of abandoned children.
[19] Data refer to adoption rulings by the courts.
[20] Data refer to children previously protected in public or private placement centres or in substitute families.
[21] Data refer to Serbia and Montenegro.
[22] Data refer to sexually active women, irrespective of marital status.
[23] Data refer only to the State of Khartoum.
[24] Data refer only to Northern Sudan.
[25] Data include 27 adoptions by Turkish families residing abroad.
[26] Data do not include abortions in private-sector clinics.

TABLE A.VII.9. TOTAL, DOMESTIC AND INTERCOUNTRY UNDER-FIVE ADOPTION RATES AND SELECTED INDICATORS OF ORPHANHOOD IN COUNTRIES THAT ARE NOT MAJOR DESTINATIONS OF INTERCOUNTRY ADOPTIONS

	Under-five adoption rate			Double orphans		
Country	*Total*	*Domestic*	*Intercountry*	*Total*	*Due to AIDS*	*As a percentage of all children under age 18*
Argentina	1.4	1.4	..	25 000	...	0.2
Bahamas	43.4	27.6	15.8	500	...	0.5
Bangladesh	0.1[1,2]	0.1[1,2]	..	650 000	...	1.1
Belize	141.0	132.0	8.9	200	...	0.2
Benin	0.2	0.2	0.1	43 000	11 000	1.1
Bolivia (Plurinational State of)	17.1	7.1	10.0	23 000	...	0.6
Brazil	14.0[3]	13.6[3]	0.4[3]	210 000	...	0.4
Burkina Faso	...	...	1.5	160 000	100 000	2.0
Burundi	...	...	2.6[1]	140 000	90 000	3.5
Cameroon	...	...	0.3[4]	150 000	83 000	1.9
Central African Republic	0.6	0.3	0.3	65 000	48 000	3.3
Chad	...	...	0.0[1]	76 000	35 000	1.9
Chile	25.5	21.2	4.3	5 000	...	0.1
China	29.5	23.9	5.6	1 000 000	...	0.3
Colombia	17.9	7.1	10.7	31 000	...	0.2
Congo	9.6[1,5]	4.8[1,5]	4.8[1,5]	47 000	33 000	2.4
Costa Rica	9.8	4.9[6]	4.9[7]	1 000	...	0.1
Democratic People's Republic of Korea	8.9	8.9	0.0	52 000	...	0.7
Ecuador	4.9	3.1	1.8	12 000	...	0.2
El Salvador	18.9	10.2	8.7	7 000	...	0.2
Eritrea	0.5[1]	...	...	23 000	9 000	1.2
Ethiopia	4.1	0.3	3.8	460 000	190 000	1.3
Fiji	56.3	50.0[1]	6.3[1]	2 000	...	0.5
Gabon	0.8	...	...	7 000	4 000	1.4
Gambia	1.8	0.8	1.0	4 000	500	0.8
Ghana	10.4	10.3	0.1	120 000	49 000	1.2
Guatemala	115.7	3.3	112.4	29 000	...	0.4
Guinea-Bissau	1.0	...	...	11 000	...	1.4
Guyana	93.7	...	...	2 000	...	0.5
Haiti	22.7	3.2	19.5	99 000	...	2.5
Honduras	3.1	1.2	1.9	15 000	...	0.5
India	1.5	1.0	0.5	4 000 000	...	1.0
Indonesia	0.1	0.1	0.0	560 000	...	0.7
Jamaica	55.9	48.0	7.9	1 000	...	0.1
Kenya	1.8[8]	...	...	450 000	330 000	3.0
Madagascar	...	...	7.5	130 000	7 000	1.4
Malawi	19.1	19.1	..	240 000	190 000	3.4
Mali	3.3	0.0	3.3	80 000	21 000	1.0
Mexico	5.3	4.8	0.5[9]	57 000	...	0.1
Mongolia	422.4	415.9	6.5	6 000	...	0.6
Mozambique	0.2	0.1	0.1	290 000	190 000	2.9
Myanmar	0.1	...	...	200 000	...	1.0
Namibia	12.2	12.2	..	24 000	19 000	2.4
Nepal	...	...	1.3	140 000	...	1.3
Nicaragua	7.2[1]	5.8[1]	1.4[1,10]	6 000	...	0.2
Niger	0.2[11]	0.1[11]	0.1[11]	71 000	5 000	1.2
Panama	2.4	2.3	0.1	1 000	...	0.1
Papua New Guinea	21.8[1]	...	...	21 000	...	1.1

TABLE A.VII.9 (*continued*)

Country	Under-five adoption rate			Double orphans		
	Total	*Domestic*	*Intercountry*	*Total*	*Due to AIDS*	*As a percentage of all children under age 18*
Paraguay	0.8[1]	...	...	6 000	...	0.2
Peru	3.7	1.9	1.8	34 000	...	0.3
Philippines	11.6	...	...	130 000	...	0.4
Republic of Korea	92.8	39.1	53.7	22 000	...	0.2
Rwanda	...	...	0.4	240 000	120 000	4.8
Senegal	...	...	0.5	54 000	4 000	1.1
South Africa	25.3	21.7	3.6	360 000	290 000	2.1
Sri Lanka	34.1	32.3	1.9	15 000	...	0.3
Sudan	0.6[12]	...	...	120 000	18 000	0.8
Swaziland	...	10.6	...	32 000	29 000	5.3
Thailand	0.6	0.0	0.6	97 000	...	0.5
Togo	2.1	0.6	1.5	34 000	18 000	1.7
Trinidad and Tobago	12.4	...	...	1 000	...	0.3
Uganda	1.6[1]	...	...	470 000	380 000	2.6
United Republic of Tanzania	0.2	0.2	..	500 000	370 000	3.6
Venezuela (Bolivarian Republic of)	43.5	...	...	14 000	...	0.1
Viet Nam	22.4	11.4	11.0	160 000	...	0.5
Median	8.1	4.9	1.9	47 000	35 000	0.8

Sources: For a complete list of country references, see annex II. The population under five was obtained from United Nations, 2005; the number of double orphans, number of double orphans due to AIDS and percentage of double orphans out of the population under 18 were obtained from UNAIDS, UNICEF and USAID, 2004.

NOTES: The under-five adoption rate is calculated by dividing the number of adoptions of children under age five by the number of children under age five, with the result expressed per 100,000 children. If no data are available on the age distribution of adopted children, it is assumed that 60 per cent of adopted children were under age five at the time of adoption. Data on the percentage of double orphans refer to 2003. The data on orphanhood and on adoptions do not necessarily refer to the same year.

[1] Estimate.
[2] Data refer to children placed with families.
[3] Data refer only to the State of São Paulo.
[4] Data refer to intercountry adoption requests.
[5] Data refer to adoptions heard in the Brazzaville District Court.
[6] Data refer to adoptions arranged by the National Children's Trusts.
[7] Data refer to both adoptions arranged by the National Children's Trusts and by direct contact between the parties concerned in the metropolitan area.
[8] Data refer to the estimated number of adoption applications recorded by the Child Welfare Society of Kenya.
[9] Data refer to intercountry adoptions by citizens of States that are parties to the Convention on Protection of Children and Co-operation in Respect of Intercountry Adoption.
[10] Data refer to children adopted by foreign citizens residing in Nicaragua.
[11] Data refer to adoptions of abandoned children.
[12] Data refer only to the State of Khartoum.